FRANCE IN THE AGE OF
LOUIS XIII AND RICHELIEU

FRANCE IN THE AGE OF LOUIS XIII AND RICHELIEU

VICTOR-L. TAPIÉ

translated and edited by
D. McN. Lockie

with a Foreword by
Professor A. G. Dickens

PRAEGER PUBLISHERS
New York

Published in the United States of America in 1975
by Praeger Publishers, Inc.
111 Fourth Avenue, New York, N.Y. 10003

First published in Great Britain
by The Macmillan Press 1974

First published in French as *La France de Louis XIII et de Richelieu*
by Flammarion 1952, second edition © Flammarion 1967
Translation and additional editorial matter
© The Macmillan Press Ltd 1974

Library of Congress Cataloging in Publication Data

Tapié, Victor Lucien, 1900–
France in the age of Louis XIII and Richelieu.

Translation of La France de Louis XIII et de
Richelieu.
Bibliography: p.
1. France—History—Louis XIII, 1610–1643.
I. Title.
DC123.T313   944'.032   74–8919
ISBN 0-275-52530-9

Printed in the United States of America

Author's dedication:
A ma femme
Translator's dedication:
To my wife

Contents

List of Maps

List of Plates

The above are reproduced by kind permission of the following: The Mansell Collection (nos. 1, 3, 4, 6, 7, 8); Collection Viollet (2); Photographie Giraudon (5).

Foreword

In reality this book needs no help I can give it: it brings its own commendation. Yet duly flattered by the invitation to contribute my mite, I can at least do something for the translator which he cannot overtly do for himself. I can draw attention to the vast but unappreciated difficulties of his art, to his success in overcoming an exceptional challenge, even to certain desirable additions he has appended on his own account.

The original book by Professor Tapié has long presented a persuasive case for an English translation. Though based upon weighty scholarship, it is no mere collection of specialised, technical researches: it is a synthesis beautifully organised and written. By no means of inordinate length for its theme, it has nevertheless been conceived upon a large scale and under the influence of generous ideas. While it must have excited the emulation of many other historians, it remains primarily concerned to introduce the educated yet non-specialist reader to one of the most fascinating periods of French history. This it does with verve and readability, yet without flamboyant gesticulation. It is rich in human personality and in a sense its hero appears in Cardinal Richelieu, one of the three or four giant figures in the annals of French politics. All the same, Tapié has written one of those books which should help to convince the biography-crazed reading public that the history of a nation can be more fascinating, more rewarding than the history of a man!

Many foreign historical works remain untranslated into our language, even though long recognised as classics and covering fields of profound interest to British and American readers. For these omissions we sometimes blame unadventurous publishers, yet we should appreciate the obstacles, both real and apparent. One has even heard it argued—both untruly and irrelevantly—that most readers interested in a period of French history would as easily be able to read French. More often and more legitimately the lack of a translation may arise from the fact that a capable and devoted translator had failed to swim into the ken of a sympathetic publisher. Such a task is indeed far better accomplished by a volunteer than by a conscript or a mercenary. In the case of a major work it

xi

demands drive and patience throughout years of drafting and multiple revisions, an expenditure of man-hours which the market can seldom reward *pro rata*.

Moreover the first-rate version calls for specialist knowledge almost matching that of the original author, and there are few scholars of this calibre prepared to submerge their personal ambitions in such a task. The effective translator of history needs not merely a general sense for the nuances of both tongues, but also a historian's knowledge of accepted usages and technical terms within the field of the work. But whatever else historiography may be, it certainly remains a branch of literature. He who translates in its service must suffer something like schizophrenia. On the one hand he seeks to convey exactly the sense of every passage; on the other to transmute it by his alchemy into the quite different metal of another language. French is not difficult to paraphrase loosely, yet it remains very hard to translate with the right blend of precision and freedom. To render a master of French, one cannot be less than a master of English. In the last resort the sin of paraphrase is perhaps a shade more venial than the sin of over-literalism, since the English-speaking reader hates above all to be jolted back into the realisation that he is acquiring the product in a second-hand market.

By dint of his historical training and experience, his long residence in France, his natural gifts, David Lockie has here attained in unusual measure these exacting ideals. Now the long task is finished he can rest assured that he has performed a creative and not merely an imitative act. It is perhaps too much to expect that any translator should gain the applause he has earned, but I know Mr Lockie will feel rewarded in the knowledge that he has produced a version worthy of Professor Tapié and has rendered a major service to all lovers of seventeenth-century history. And even this short foreword must draw attention to a contribution over and beyond the main task. This is the wide-ranging critical bibliography of books and articles in the English language which the translator has added to the bibliography of the original work. If anything were needed to complete the usefulness of the book for English-speaking readers, here it is in truth. In sum, any British, Commonwealth or American library with a tolerable section on European history cannot neglect to acquire a copy of this book. And with equal confidence one may prophesy that every serious reader in the field of 'early modern' Europe will want one for his private shelves.

May 1974   A. G. DICKENS

Editorial Note and Acknowledgements

This is a complete and unabridged translation of the second edition of Victor L. Tapié's *La France de Louis XIII et de Richelieu*, as published in 1967. All passages in the text of this translation which have been placed in round brackets occur in the French original also. Square brackets have been used to indicate my own occasional interpolations or when quoting the original words of which a translation has just been given. If the passage which is cited in this way consists of more than a few words or calls for explanation or comment, it is either printed at the bottom of the page or relegated to the numbered notes at the end of the book. Professor Tapié's notes (which are of course given in translation) are followed by his initials, any additions to them being placed in square brackets. I have occasionally expanded his references for the benefit of English and American readers, but the system by which sources are cited in the French edition of his book has otherwise been left unchanged. My own notes are printed without my initials but contain references to a number of works whose titles are given in the form of initials. A table explaining these and other abbreviations which I have used when referring to certain books precedes the notes.

Throughout this translation French ranks and titles are sometimes given in French and sometimes in English. For example, Schomberg is entitled the maréchal de Schomberg in one place and Marshal Schomberg in another, and I refer to the duke of Rohan but to the duc de Vendôme: I have simply used whichever form seemed to me the more euphonious or the more natural. With the exception of the Spanish title marqués (which has been used instead of marquis to emphasise the fact that the marqués de Mirabel for example was a Spaniard and not a Frenchman), the ranks and titles belonging to countries other than France are given in English or in their Anglicised form—e.g. margrave.

Unless a generally recognised English form of a place-name exists, I have used the form and spelling now given to it in the country where it is at present situated. Thus as far as French place-names are concerned I have retained the English spelling Rheims since it is still in general use, but rejected Rhé in favour of Ré when referring to the island of that name. Similarly the modern French spelling Alès has been preferred to the old form Alais (which continues to feature in most English textbooks on seventeenth-century French or European history but is not to be found on a modern map) and Clérac appears as Clairac. On the same principle I have used the French forms of Alsatian place-names as given by Professor Tapié rather than the German forms current at the time and reintroduced during the German occupation of Alsace—e.g. Saverne rather than Zabern.

In the case of places that are now in Czechoslovakia both the old German and the current Czech names have often been supplied by Professor Tapié himself, and only a few additions have been necessary. On the other hand in dealing with Italian, German and Spanish place-names it has been necessary to effect a number of substitutions to ensure that the places concerned are identifiable by an English reader. It may be helpful to give some examples:

Avigliana *for* Veillane	Breisach *for* Brisach
Bruzòlo *for* Brussol	Jülich *for* Juliers
Pinerolo *for* Pignerol	Regensburg *for* Ratisbon (ne)
Susa *for* Suze	Monzón *for* Monçon
Vercelli *for* Verceil	Fuenterrabía *for* Fontarabie

The island of St Christopher has been referred to as St Kitts.

As the Russian historian Porshnev is mentioned several times in the bibliographical guide to works in English relating to this period of European history, which is printed after Professor Tapié's own bibliography, the English spelling of his name has been used throughout in preference to the French form Porchnev except when specific reference is made to the French edition of his book.

The translation and editing of this important work by Professor Tapié and the compilation of the bibliographical guide have taken several years, during which I have incurred a large number of obligations. My first obligation must be to Professor A. G. Dickens for his sympathetic interest and encouragement and for his kindness in writing the Foreword.

I am also grateful to Professor Charles K. Warner for his kindly interest and to Professor Tapié himself for answering my queries courteously and promptly on two occasions.

This book is not, however, intended solely for those who would have difficulty in reading the French original and I owe a considerable debt to a number of scholars (and in some cases to their translators also), whose researches have made it possible for me to edit as well as translate it. Some of them are listed on pages 457–61. Full details of other works that I have consulted and the names of various historians who have kindly supplied me with particular items of information are given in the notes themselves. My obligations to John Cooper and Keith Thomas are indicated in the prefatory note to the bibliographical guide.

I am sorry that I have not been able to refer in my notes to four recent books in particular, all of which unfortunately appeared too late for me to be able to consult them for editorial purposes: W. F. Church, *Richelieu and Reason of State*; H. M. Solomon, *Public Welfare, Science and Propaganda in Seventeenth Century France: the innovations of Théophraste Renaudot*; Martin Wolfe, *The Fiscal System of Renaissance France*; Julian Dent, *Crisis in Finance: Crown, financiers and society in Seventeenth Century France*. Details of these important and scholarly works will, however, be found in the bibliographical guide.

On the other hand I have been fortunate to be able to enlist the help of my friend, the Rev. J. R. Fox, M.C., M.A. (Oxon.), Canon Regular of the Abbey of St Maurice, Valais, Switzerland, who has kindly supplied me with further information about the different congregations of Augustinians mentioned by Professor Tapié as well as about other matters connected with religious history.

Among a number of other friends to whom I am particularly indebted for their sustained encouragement over the years I should mention M. le doyen Marcel A. Ruff, of the University of Nice, and Mlle Odette Bornand, formerly Lecturer in English at the University of Aix-en-Provence.

As far as the bibliographical guide is concerned, I am deeply grateful to Oliver and Phoebe Scott, without whose generous hospitality much of the preliminary research could not have been undertaken; also to my good neighbour, M. Jean Dalmas, for allowing me the use of a room where I could work undisturbed on this material and which I could leave for weeks on end in a state of (scholarly) disorder. In so far as my guide is both comprehensive and comprehensible, this is largely due to the promptness and efficiency of the Librarian and staff of the London Library in keeping me supplied with a stream of books and answering my bibliographical queries, as well as to the skill of Mme Pascale Jouando in deciphering and typing my manuscript.

I would also like to convey my thanks to M. Paul Forestier, Conservateur de la Bibliothèque et des Archives Municipales de la ville de Grasse and to his staff; to the Librarian and staff of the Institute of Historical Research, University of London; and to the Librarians and staff of the Universities of Nice, Geneva and Strasbourg. I am grateful to Signora Marconcini for her kind hospitality to two travellers who arrived unexpectedly at the *castello* of Bruzòlo and for presenting one of them with a copy of her husband's article on the treaties which were signed there in April 1610.

The manuscript of this translation has greatly benefited from the patience and excellent typing of Betty Pearson, Sheila Bryant and Frances Coulson, and from the copy-editing of Naomi Bowen. I would also like to thank Harry Bawden for his valuable assistance. My debt to Rex Allen for his help and kindness in countless ways has grown like a snowball over the years and has now reached monstrous proportions. I hope that he has not suffered too much from the vagaries of a translator who, like J. Alfred Prufrock, was only too apt to feel that there was

. . . time yet for a hundred indecisions
And for a hundred visions and revisions. . . .

'Traduttore—traditore.' 'Les traductions sont comme les femmes; lorsqu'elles sont belles, elles ne sont pas fidèles, et lorsq'uelles sont fidèles, elles ne sont pas belles.' In short there is really no end to the problems that can beset the wretched translator. On the human plane, therefore, my deepest debt of gratitude is to my wife who has not only continued to live with me whilst this translation has been in progress but has also come to my rescue with the *mot juste* on innumerable occasions when I was floundering in a linguistic morass. On the supernatural plane I would like to express my thanks to St Jerome, the patron of translators, for a number of very helpful suggestions. The mistakes that remain are, of course, mine not his.

Sainte-Anne-de-Grasse   D. McN. Lockie
7 May 1974

Author's Preface

Today historians no longer think of a reign as a rational division of the past, for a society its behaviour and techniques do not automatically change when one king dies and another comes to the throne. The fact remains, however, that in the days when systems of government were monarchical, policy used to vary with the ruler; and policy in its turn can control and modify the life of an entire country, the development of society and the material conditions that give it support. On these grounds the reign of Louis XIII can be justifiably regarded as a complete entity with a definite unity of its own.

With the name of the king the name of Richelieu will always be associated: Louis XIII and Richelieu—the two are inseparable. As a man the minister was superior to his master. He was more intelligent and more cultivated; he had a broader outlook and a deeper insight into Europe, the world, and the times in which they lived. However the king was no cipher. There was an element of greatness in him too. In addition he was endowed with common sense, that invaluable quality which enables a person of moderate intelligence to enlist the services and assistance that he needs in order to carry out his task. Moreover since a sovereign ruler was then held to be the source of all power and initiative, everything that the cardinal did was necessarily dependent on the king's approval. Hence the strange but indissoluble alliance between the two men: indeed it is no exaggeration to say that they reigned jointly.

For a long time political history used to be confined to great events such as battles and treaties which were embellished with anecdotes that related primarily to the great men of the day. The real factors upon which any policy must depend—the economic conditions prevalent in the country concerned and the attitude of public opinion towards the policy in question, whether hostile, passive, or favourable and co-operative—these were generally neglected. Considered in this light, the history of France amounted for the most part to an incomplete record of the policy of her governments.

Every effort has been made in this survey of Louis XIII's reign to devote ample space to the French people, to link France as she then was with the France that Louis XIII and Richelieu tried to make her. This is all the more necessary because the reign constitutes a period of transition in French history. Between the years 1610 and 1643 many features from the preceding era are obliterated while newly acquired characteristics become more marked; France has also unquestionably a far more important role to play in world affairs than she had in the past and this to a large extent because her rulers willed that it should be so. These are the years when she is preparing herself for her glorious future.

But it is a mistake to suppose that results such as these could be achieved without effort in a simple straightforward way. The historian who sets out to enumerate its more gratifying successes can easily give the impression that the reign of Louis XIII was a glorious age whose glory gave the contemporary Frenchman cause for rejoicing. In reality it was a very difficult time in which to live; the outlook was uncertain, conflicting and, very often, disheartening. The appalling sufferings of the people caused the king endless remorse. To us after a lapse of three centuries they seem to represent the agonising price that France had to pay for a policy that was bold in its general conception and fruitful in its results.

I should add that this book does not claim to be more than a sketch, a tentative interpretation. A far larger one would be needed to cover every aspect of France's immensely varied history during these thirty-four years. The series to which it belongs makes no provision for the insertion of detailed notes and references such as would have enabled me to specify the various sources that I have used and to acknowledge my obligations to other historians; but I must at least place on record how much this work owes to the learned studies of my former masters Georges Pagès and Josef Pekař, to the researches of my colleague M. Roland Mousnier, and to Boris Porshnev's stimulating book. They have all thrown light upon a number of vital points. The advice of my friend Jean Meuvret has been of very great value to me and I extend to him my most grateful thanks.

It is my hope that this book will augment the interest that many people continue to show in the seventeenth century. It was an illustrious age, of that there can be no doubt, but even so it remains inadequately understood. Too many people who think that they know the seventeenth century allow the picture that they form of it to be coloured by their present-day preferences or antipathies.

It is unwise to project our current preoccupations into the past or to search there for arguments to guide our course of action. On the other hand it is well to remember that we are inseparably bound up with our country's history and may find therein the explanations that enable us to understand what we are, for this is no more than the truth.

VICTOR-L. TAPIÉ

GENEALOGICAL TREE

SHORT GENEALOGICAL TREE OF THE HOUSE OF BOURBON
IN THE SIXTEENTH AND SEVENTEENTH CENTURIES
(The irrelevant branches have been pruned)

Charles, Duke of Vendôme (1489–1537)

Antoine de Bourbon,   =   Jeanne d'Albret,
Duke of Vendôme   Queen of Navarre
(1518–62)   (d. 1572)
(King of Navarre
1555–62)

Charles, Cardinal de Bourbon
(1523–90)
(recognised as 'Charles X'
by the League, 1588–90)

Henry of Navarre   =   (1) Marguerite de Valois
(1553–1610)   (divorced, no issue)
(Henry IV of France   (2) Marie de Medici (1573–1642),
1589–1610)   younger daughter
                       of Francesco I,
                       Grand Duke of Tuscany
                       (d. 1587)

Louis XIII = Anne of Austria,   Elizabeth = Philip IV of Spain   Chrestienne (Christina)
(1601–43)   Infanta of Spain   (1602–44)   (d. 1665)   (1606–63)
            (1601–66)

Louis XIV   =   Maria Theresa,   Philippe   =   Henrietta, youngest daughter
(1638–1715)   daughter of Philip IV   (1640–1701)   of Charles I of England
                  of Spain and Elizabeth,   and Henrietta Maria,
                  sister of Louis XIII   sister of Louis XIII

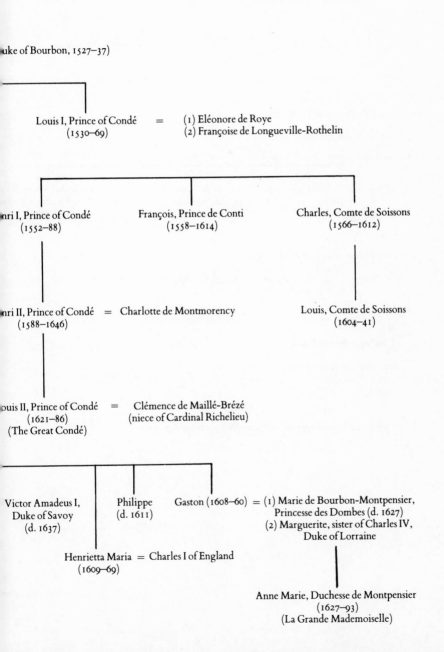

uke of Bourbon, 1527–37)

Louis I, Prince of Condé = (1) Eléonore de Roye
(1530–69) (2) Françoise de Longueville-Rothelin

nri I, Prince of Condé   François, Prince de Conti   Charles, Comte de Soissons
(1552–88)   (1558–1614)   (1566–1612)

nri II, Prince of Condé = Charlotte de Montmorency   Louis, Comte de Soissons
(1588–1646)   (1604–41)

ouis II, Prince of Condé = Clémence de Maillé-Brézé
(1621–86)   (niece of Cardinal Richelieu)
(The Great Condé)

Victor Amadeus I,   Philippe   Gaston (1608–60) = (1) Marie de Bourbon-Montpensier,
Duke of Savoy   (d. 1611)   Princesse des Dombes (d. 1627)
(d. 1637)   (2) Marguerite, sister of Charles IV,
Duke of Lorraine

Henrietta Maria = Charles I of England
(1609–69)

Anne Marie, Duchesse de Montpensier
(1627–93)
(La Grande Mademoiselle)

Henry IV's male illegitimate children

(1) by Gabrielle d'Estrées

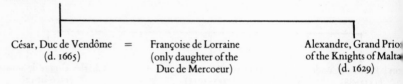

César, Duc de Vendôme   =   Françoise de Lorraine   Alexandre, Grand Prior
(d. 1665)   (only daughter of the   of the Knights of Malta
                             Duc de Mercoeur)   (d. 1629)

(2) by Henriette de Balsac d'Entragues*

Henri, Comte de Verneuil   =   Charlotte Séguier
(1600–1682)

(3) by Jacqueline de Bueil*

Antoine, Comte de Moret
(d. 1632)

* Professor Tapié refers to these ladies by their titles on p. 49.

Part One

France in Decline and a
Prey to Factions
(1610–24)

1 Boulonnais	11 Saumurois	21 Limousin
2 Picardy	12 Touraine	22 Auvergne
3 Normandy	13 Berry	23 Lyonnais
4 Ile de France	14 Nivernais	24 Dauphiné
5 Champagne	15 Burgundy	25 Languedoc
6 Orléanais	16 Bourbonnais	26 Guyenne & Gascony
7 Maine	17 Marche	27 Foix
8 Brittany	18 Angoumois	28 Provence
9 Anjou	19 Aunis	29 Comtat-Venaissin
10 Poitou	20 Saintonge	30 Béarn and Lower Navarre

Map 1 France in 1620

CHAPTER ONE

The France that Awaited Louis XIII
(1610)

ON THE MORNING of 14 May 1610 the people of Paris had resumed their usual occupations still dazzled by the joyful events of the previous day: the coronation of the queen at Saint-Denis,[1] the processions which they had watched first leaving and later returning to the Louvre. If they spoke of the days ahead it was of the king's imminent departure to join the army. Their attitudes varied according to each man's humour. Some expressed the opinion that the forthcoming campaign would be no more than a long promenade, the news of which would break the monotony of their daily lives; others declared that a serious war was about to begin —a war with no definite object that boded ill for everyone. The man in the street was capable of imagining anything except the news that suddenly began to circulate towards the middle of the afternoon. People could scarcely bring themselves to believe it; but the rumours seemed to be confirmed by the sight of troops moving along the narrow streets, of a horseman riding hurriedly past, of the dismayed faces of persons of consequence as they passed by in litters or coaches. Men were shouting, women were crying, while shopkeepers had begun to fold back their awnings and shut up their shops. The king was dead!

Because their astonishment and grief was so overwhelming contemporaries have left us a detailed record, so that we can follow hour by hour the latter part of this spring day which had promised to be so uneventful and commonplace compared to its resplendent predecessor and to the great developments that the morrow might bring.

The murder was committed a little before four o'clock.[2] The king had hesitated about leaving the palace. Was he tired or did he have some vague feeling of foreboding? He spoke as if he only wanted to 'go and come back', as if he meant to be back 'almost as soon as he had gone'. He did not get as far as the Arsenal:[3] Ravaillac stabbed him in the rue de la Ferronnerie. The royal coach was immediately driven back to the Louvre with its curtains drawn and the king's body was carried upstairs to his closet. In the confusion produced by a catastrophe of this magnitude, while everyone wondered whether one solitary wretch had been

3

responsible for the deed or whether it signalled the outbreak of a conspiracy, the king's entourage took steps to maintain order in the city before revealing the full extent of the disaster.

The duke of Épernon, the colonel general of the infantry, was in the carriage by the king's side when he collapsed. He immediately had the alert given to the French guards and to the Swiss guards stationed at the Louvre and sent five hundred men to surround the Hôtel de Ville⁴. When Sillery, the chancellor, entered the palace courtyard he found it already occupied by an armed troop. On seeing him, the officer, M. de Montferrand, promptly blurted out the news. Sillery ordered him to be silent as if he had uttered a blasphemy; but when he reached the first floor of the palace the queen in tears ran to meet him crying 'Alas! the king is dead.' The little dauphin, pale and deeply shaken, was passing them as she spoke. He and his brothers and sisters were being taken to a room where they would be out of harm's way. Sillery was sufficiently master of himself to reply as he pointed to the child who was now Louis XIII: 'Forgive me your Majesty, the king is alive. There he is, Madame!'

Such was the principle of monarchical perpetuity whereby the reigning sovereign was no more than a trustee for life. But however securely this principle was established, what was to happen to the realm? Who would really control power during the king's minority? Who was to act as regent?

There was no guiding rule for such an eventuality. Henry IV had never made his intentions known during his lifetime, although he was no longer young and had reason to fear that his heir might inherit the throne whilst still a minor. Possibly his motive in entrusting the realm during his absence to Marie de Medici, assisted by a Council, and in arranging for her authority as queen to be formally consecrated by coronation had been to give her the opportunity of acting as regent for a probationary period. Perhaps he had thought that such an experiment would help to guide him as to the arrangements that should be made for the future. But the king's relations, the princes of the blood, could claim the right to govern the kingdom quite as much as a queen of foreign birth. As a present-day historian has observed, government was a family affair and the nation had divested itself permanently of its sovereignty in favour of the royal family.⁵ Nonetheless Henry IV had kept his close relatives removed from the conduct of affairs; moreover the prince of Condé, who was openly on bad terms with him, had taken refuge with the hostile power of Spain and the comte de Soissons was not in Paris.*

* Henri II of Condé was the son of the king's first cousin, Henri I of Condé [d. 1588],

In the opinion of some of the late king's closest associates, it was advisable to proclaim the queen's assumption of the regency without delay; this would safeguard the realm from any sudden resurgence of rivalries and dissensions and also ensure the continuity of Henry IV's policy and reign.

In order to take this step it was necessary to have recourse to the Parlement. As will be seen later when we come to discuss France's political institutions, the Parlement was not a political body but a court of justice where the king's edicts, ordinances and declarations were registered. The Parlement did not make the law but it gave it sanction and in its capacity as chief sovereign court or supreme court of appeal it still claimed the right to intervene in matters of general policy.[6] The Parlement's ratification of a decision made by the king regarding the regency would give it legal justification and settle the matter once and for all.

On this afternoon of 14 May the Parlement was in fact holding a session at the monastery of the Grands Augustins,[7] for its usual court-rooms were being prepared for a banquet which had been arranged in honour of the queen's coronation. It was announced to the magistrates that an attempt had been made on the king's life without specifying whether it had proved fatal or had merely left him wounded, and they were requested not to disperse until there was further news.

The first president, Achille de Harlay, had remained at his house owing to an attack of gout. Immediately he was notified of what had occurred, he was helped to dress and had himself conveyed to the Grands Augustins. At the same time he convoked all the presidents and counsellors who happened to be at their homes so that the session in progress should take the form of an assembly of all the chambers of the Parlement.[8] The messengers whom he dispatched to the Louvre returned with the definite news that the king was dead. Soon the duke of Épernon appeared. As a peer of France he could participate in the Parlement's sessions;[9] he bowed to the president and apologised for not having had the time to attire himself more suitably. Then, taking the place to which his rank entitled him, he expressed his opinion: the question of the regency must be discussed without delay and there could be no better hands to which to entrust it than those of the queen.

Épernon represented the military strength of the realm while the magistrates of the Parlement stood for its traditions and laws. They

and as such his nearest kinsman after the king's own sons. Charles, comte de Soissons [d. 1612] was the younger brother of Henri I of Condé and thus King Henry IV's first cousin. [See genealogical tree.] (V.L.T.)

understood what was expected of them; and as they always welcomed an opportunity to regulate the workings of the monarchy as an institution, they declared, after a short debate which was purely a matter of form and courtesy, that the regency should be entrusted to the queen mother.

It was about half past six in the evening. It is astonishing not to find Sully playing any part in these events—Sully, whose name is so closely associated with that of Henry IV in history and legend alike. As soon as he had an inkling as to what had happened he had made for the Louvre accompanied by an escort; but on the way he met the troops commanded by Bassompierre and the latter advised him against proceeding any further. Deeply disturbed as to the possible outcome, and aware that others for whom he had no liking were in process of acting in his stead, Sully turned back towards the Bastille followed by his henchmen. He was the governor of the fortress and once there he shut himself up within it.

At the Hôtel de Ville the *lieutenant-civil* Le Jay, and Sanguin, the *prévôt des marchands*, had had time to take all necessary steps to maintain order.[10] When night fell on the dismayed city nothing occurred to disturb its mournful meditations.

For those about the king and the queen the first formal act that was called for on the following day was the completion and confirmation of the Parlement's pronouncement. The magistrates had been summoned early that morning to a royal session or *lit de justice*[11] at which the declaration of regency was to be registered in the presence of the young king. 124 counsellors belonging to the various chambers arrived to take their seats at the Grands Augustins from seven o'clock onwards, as did those cardinals, bishops, dukes and peers who were present in the capital. Among the latter was the duke of Mayenne, a survivor from the days of the League* and already an old man at the age of fifty-six. In those days life ran its course quickly and already the duke's great deeds belonged to a distant past.[12] In his person he symbolised the victories of the late king over the factions that had rent France for half a century. His infirmities would not allow him to take the seat to which his rank entitled him; he had to sit apart so that he could stretch out his rheumatic leg, but since this meant that he sat in front of everyone, it seemed to imply that he was being treated with greater respect than anyone else. Except for

---

* To avoid any possible confusion between this League and the Catholic League in Germany which was later to play such a prominent part in the Thirty Years War, I should make it clear that the former is referred to as "the League" and the latter is called "the Catholic League" throughout this book.

Mayenne, everyone rose when the queen mother and her son entered the room at about ten o'clock. Accompanied by the little king, and dressed in her widow's weeds, Marie de Medici advanced towards the throne like a tower of black crepe. Mother and son climbed the steps to the throne around which were grouped two princes of the blood (Conti and his nephew Enghien, the six-year-old son of the comte de Soissons),* the duke of Guise, the Constable Montmorency, the dukes of Montbazon and Sully, and the marshals of France. Sully had ventured to put in an appearance at the Louvre early the same morning and Marie de Medici had presented him to the king: 'This is Monsieur de Sully,' she said, 'you must love him well for he is one of the best and most loyal servants of the king your father.'

When all had taken their places the queen began to read aloud a short and carefully worded speech. But tears took possession of her at the outset and she had to stop several times.

'My lords', she said, 'it having pleased God to take unto Himself through a fell mishap my lord our good king, I have brought to you the king my son to beseech you all to have such care of him as is enjoined upon you by your duty to his father's memory, to yourselves, and to your country. It is my wish that in the conduct of his affairs he may follow your good advice and counsels; I beg you to proffer these to him in such manner as your consciences dictate.'

Then it was the turn of Louis XIII. His weak voice, already afflicted with a stammer, did not carry far and surprisingly his audience paid no attention to what he said. The murmur of general conversation drowned his words. The seventeenth century had no love of children, and despite their respect for the monarchy all these exalted personages treated the melancholy ceremony that was being performed by a little boy as if it was merely an interlude. This is what Louis XIII had been told to say: 'My lords, God having taken to Himself my lord and father, I have come to this place by the advice and counsel of the queen my mother to say to you all that I wish to follow your good counsels in the conduct of my affairs. I hope that God will give me the grace to profit by the good example and precepts of my lord and father. I pray you therefore to give me your good advice and to deliberate presently on those matters which I have commanded my lord chancellor to expound to you.'

---

*[François prince de Conti [d. 1614] was the older brother of the comte de Soissons see genealogical tree]. Louis duc d'Enghien, the comte de Soissons's son, subsequently inherited his father's title and his own title passed to the son of the prince of Condé who was born in 1621.(V.L.T.)

Silence was restored when the chancellor began his speech. He set forth the reasons that justified the investiture of Marie de Medici with the regency. He stressed the confidence that Henry IV had shown in his wife on the eve of his death; he declared that in this way the late king's intentions would undoubtedly be fulfilled. The first president was the next to speak, and after a fulsome eulogy of Henry IV and the queen, he expressed the same opinion as the chancellor. Then Servin, the advocate general, reminded his audience of the formal pronouncement which the Parlement had made on the previous evening and proposed that it should be published in all the *bailliages* and *sénéchaussées* of the kingdom.[13] Thereupon the chancellor rose and by way of conclusion announced that votes would now be taken.

He respectfully approached the little king to ask for his vote, then he asked for the queen mother's and then, in order of precedence, he requested the votes of all those present. The motion was unanimously carried that 'the king being seated on his *lit de justice* did commit the realm to his mother's keeping that she might have the care of his education and sustenance, and of the administration of the affairs of his kingdom during his tender years'. Her investiture as regent being now legalised, Marie de Medici immediately withdrew and returned to the Louvre, where the body of Henry IV lay in state whilst the people of Paris paid their last respects. In the meantime Louis XIII was escorted to Notre Dame. All the way to the cathedral stood the common people shouting 'Long live the king', for they were more susceptible to a simple human emotion than the great men of the land. In acclaiming the orphaned child, they were paying tribute not merely to his father's memory but also to the permanent nature of the monarchy. For the time being its living embodiment was only a frail little boy: even so he was their master, the protector in whom they placed their trust and perhaps their benefactor too.

This little boy was king of France. Close though it is to the France of our day through the permanent nature of certain of its features, it requires an effort to imagine the France of 1610, for in other respects it is so dissimilar as to appear an entirely different world with which the French people of today have nothing in common except the ties formed by history.

Let us first consider its territorial extent. The France of 1610 was noticeably smaller than the France of today. The difference between them is most striking in the north, where the approximate boundary of the realm was formed by the river Somme. The capital was thus located far too close to the frontier and exposed to armies which could assail it from the Spanish Netherlands without encountering any natural obstacle. To the north-east and east (where the frontier was formed by two more rivers, the Meuse and the Saône) lay the bishoprics of Metz and Verdun —both garrisoned by French troops, which had however no positive right to remain there. These two bishoprics thus represented French encroachments on German territory while the bishopric of Toul, which was occupied in the same way, constituted a French enclave within the duchy of Lorraine. The latter was only in part a vassal of France; since it was also a semi-independent state whose rulers were feudatories of the emperor it formed a bone of contention between two rival political systems and as such was a dangerous neighbour. Burgundy was split into two: the western part, the duchy proper, was firmly attached to the realm, but the eastern part, Franche-Comté, as a result of inheritances of comparatively recent date had fallen into the hands of the king of Spain. It was only a short time since Henry IV had relieved the dangerously ex- posed position of Lyons by recovering Bresse and Bugey from the duke of Savoy.* Even so it was still not possible to travel from Lyons to the mouth of the Rhône without encountering enclaves of foreign territory. Avignon and the Comtat-Venaissin belonged to the pope, the princi- pality of Orange to the family of Nassau. On the western section of France's Mediterranean coast the present department of Pyrénées- Orientales, then known as Roussillon, was a dependency of Catalonia and thus of Spain. In consequence the Pyrenees did not form a barrier be- tween the two countries along their entire length.

The mere description of France's frontiers is enough to conjure up those problems of foreign policy that were to weigh heavily on Louis XIII's entire reign; but this is not the place to dwell upon them, for our concern at present is with the general features of the land.

The geographical changes that take place in the course of three hundred years are normally so slow as to be barely perceptible: in this smaller France of Louis XIII's day the same geographical structure and conditions existed as prevail today. The climate was similar to the cli- mate we know, with the same fluctuations between years of heavy rain- fall, long periods of drought, and periods of cold. These fluctuations can give human beings the false impression that they have witnessed great changes since their childhood, whereas in fact such changes as have oc-

---

* It must be remembered that Bresse and Bugey had been occupied by the French for more than twenty years in the middle of the sixteenth century only to be relinquished by the Treaty of Cateau-Cambrésis in 1559.

curred do not imply any marked alteration. Nevertheless in a few areas and in certain specific cases chance developments have led to a number of marked local differences in the course of the past three centuries.

The Loire, for example, was far more navigable than it is today. It carried more water and was in active use as a waterway. No traces of this river traffic remain in our day. The country between the Seine and the Garonne was more wooded and the marshes in those parts were more numerous. People did not know how to drain them or render them innocuous and the health of the inhabitants suffered in consequence. They were liable to attacks of malaria—those well-known tertian and quartan agues to which the literature of the time refers so repeatedly.

On the Atlantic coast the area of the Landes was poor, marshy, and, by present-day standards, treeless. Further north, from the mouth of the Garonne to the mouth of the Loire, the coast was far more broken and fringed with a larger number of islands which have since become merged in the network of salt marshes reclaimed from the sea and joined to the mainland of Poitou and the Vendée.

The general appearance of the landscape was thus essentially the same, but this cannot be said of its detailed characteristics, so great have been the changes brought about by different methods of cultivation and better use of the soil. If any of Louis XIII's subjects could be brought back to the window of some house that has been standing since their time, not one of them would believe that he had come back to the same spot. More changes have taken place through human agency between their age and ours than occurred between the early Middle Ages and their day. Perhaps the essential point to bear in mind is this, in that it corresponds most closely to the truth: the physical aspect of the land of France and of its cultivated areas in Louis XIII's day was still that of the Middle Ages. Probably this is also true of the physical appearance of the people in so far as we are able to form an accurate picture of mediaeval France from its illustrated records and to reconstruct it in our imaginations by a process of careful deduction. To be sure, the way people dressed was quite different, and we will revert to this subject later. But what of the physical man beneath?

The material conditions to which he was subject in Louis XIII's day had not varied for centuries. The same recipes for hygiene and the same absence of hygiene were to be found in town and country alike. For the majority of the population, which lived on the land, there was the same inexorable obligation to rely on the produce of the area, the same strict dependence upon the harvests. If the harvests were bad, there was a serious dearth of food, followed by famine, with an immediate impact on the natural increase of population. The number of deaths rose sharply, the survival rate of the fittest was reduced, conception and birth temporarily ceased. As in the Middle Ages there were sudden outbreaks of epidemics which nothing could restrain and which finally died out, as they had begun, of their own volition—epidemics that were left to follow Nature's course despite the efforts of physicians, the spells of sorcerers and the prayers of priests. Hence a population undoubtedly less handsome than ours but perhaps possessed of greater stamina—although this is by no means certain. People were shorter and physical deformities were more common: goitre, swellings of the neck and limbs, lameness, humped backs. The infirmities of old age made their appearance much sooner. Infections of the teeth which were neither foreseen nor remedied soon played havoc with many a face, ruining its appearance, leaving it sunken, or swollen with abscesses. The span of human life was shorter: seventy years was the extreme limit. Henry IV, who had not even reached the age of sixty, was regarded as an 'old king' at the time of his death. We read of eminent people—mentioned here because we are better informed of their health—who, whilst only middle-aged, were crippled by gout, with their limbs twisted and disabled. Because of the shortness of human life there was a general tendency to hasten its successive stages—hence girls were married off as soon as they were nubile. In his admirable study of Beauvais and the region of Beauvaisis between the years 1600 and 1730 Pierre Goubert observes that in rural areas at least 'the paucity of illegitimate births and of obvious cases of conception before marriage suggests that very considerable respect was paid to the Church's ruling forbidding conception outside the context of matrimony'.[14] However, the wills left by many of the nobility and bourgeoisie admit to the existence of bastard offspring and provide for their inheritance of a portion of the testator's property. Frequent and ill-supervised confinements caused the premature death of many women. Notarial deeds and inventories bear witness to a sequence of two or three marriages in most families—the mother having died in childbirth and the father immediately casting around for a stepmother to bring up the orphaned children and to give them more brothers. Moreover, although births were numerous, or, as the statisticians would say, the birth rate was high, so too was the rate of infant mortality. All this is thoroughly mediaeval. It is in no way peculiar to France but common to all Europe.

France had about fifteen million inhabitants and was therefore relatively densely populated although capable of supporting a larger population. The country's temperate and healthy climate and natural amenities enabled the French people to brave all their hardships under conditions that could have been worse.

Can one think of these fifteen million people as a united and coherent nation such as exists today? The contemporary Frenchman could not even conceive of such a thing. The growth of France had been a gradual process resulting from the proximity to each other of provinces acquired by conquest or by peaceful means. Some of these, such as Brittany, had only been recently annexed; an even more recent acquisition was Béarn, which Henry IV, in his capacity as king of Navarre, had bestowed upon France as a gift to mark his joyful entry into the possession of his new kingdom.

Customs, behaviour and even language differentiated northern from southern France. Brittany was Celtic, and its way of life archaic; the seaports, which had already been thrown open to international commerce, formed a marked contrast to the half-barbaric hinterland. It had little in common with the neighbouring provinces of Normandy and Poitou. Normandy bristled with little towns whose civilised and sharp-witted people were permeated with a legalistic outlook that made them quick to resort to law-suits and pettifogging litigation. Poitou was essentially the preserve of the gentry and had been the scene of continual battles between Catholics and Protestants. Thus the differences between one region and another, local peculiarities and local feeling easily outweighed influences for reconciliation and unity.

The population of France, we have said, possibly numbered fifteen million. In the present state of our knowledge it is impossible to be categorical about figures, but it seems clear that the period from 1580 to 1645 can be described as 'a period of rapid population increase, a sort of demographic ceiling, although these years are punctuated by brief and violent fluctuations' (P. Goubert). In France and elsewhere in Europe the relative prosperity of the sixteenth century and of the first thirty years of the seventeenth century were to form a contrast with the second half of the seventeenth century, a dazzling period in many respects but apparently far less vigorous in its biological impetus.

There remain other aspects of the matter that we should consider. What proportion of these fifteen million people can have been sufficiently well educated to attain to such abstract ideas as the superiority of the realm over the individual province, the general good, the subordination of privileges and local liberties to the law of the land, the meaning of kingship and the significance of the State? The masses were uneducated—today we would say illiterate. To borrow Villon's words, as true as ever after the lapse of two centuries: 'Ne rien ne sçay: oncques lettre ne leuz.' And in this connection we must bear in mind the varied forms of patois which were more frequently used than French in daily conversation, and created yet further barriers between one district and another.

Those who lived out their lives in these lowly and parochial conditions constituted the majority of the French population, and there was a bigger gulf between them and the élite than is to be found in our day. How many people could claim to belong to this élite? It would probably be impossible to calculate the total. The nobility and clergy present no great difficulty, for although there are some doubtful cases we could estimate the approximate number of fiefs and benefices (many of them accumulated in the same hands); the main problem arises when we come to deal with that active and vitally important class of society which after making money through trade and speculation had then begun to penetrate into the ranks of the nobility by dint of obtaining admission to public office.

Seventeenth-century French society was very far from being rigid. Not only could the king's favour lead to social preferment by means of letters patent bestowing noble rank, or to the grant of a more exalted title in the aristocratic hierarchy such as marquis or duke, but all over the country, through hard work, thrift and shrewd investment, families were in the process of improving their status within a few generations. The greatest capitalists in the land, with whom the king, his ministers and the nobility strove in turn to ingratiate themselves, had originally sprung from the humblest ranks of the bourgeoisie.

Bénigne Saulnier, who took over the farm of the *droit annuel* and of the *parties casuelles* in 1605, had begun life modestly.* His ancestors were vine growers in the Paris area. His aunts had married master market gardeners, master masons, tailors, racket makers or shopkeepers. One of his successors, Claude Marcel, was descended, through one or two generations of petty lawyers, from butchers, drapers and goldsmiths.[15]

The social élite of France, those who were above the common herd, are those whom we may call the French nation of that time because they were capable of realising that it was they who went to make up the

---

* See Professor Tapié's account of the system of tax-farming on p. 59. The *droit annuel* was an annual tax paid voluntarily by holders of offices and popularly known as the *paulette*, which is the name that will be given to it in this translation. The *parties casuelles* represented the revenues which the Crown derived from sales of offices and from forced loans made by office-holders.

realm; because of their awareness, too, that they were on certain occasions concerned in great events and in the broad objectives of policy.
Despite the virulent caste prejudices of the time, it was undoubtedly a
vast and shifting world, comprising an aristocracy that was essentially
military and landowning, a clergy consisting of bishops and parish
priests, seculars and regulars, clerics of every order and every grade, and
a bourgeoisie composed of officials, lawyers, merchants [*gens de robe et de
négoce*] and shopkeepers or itinerant traders. It also included the most industrious and prosperous of the peasants—vine-growers, farmers [*laboureurs*] and millers.

Louis XIII's true realm was composed of people such as these who
were above the amorphous mass of the population which was incapable
of seeing beyond the daily horizon. They already had some conception
of a mother country—the term is used by certain legal writers of the day
—but far more emphatically they accepted the idea of their common
subjection to one and the same ruler and the belief that their dependence
upon the king was both legitimate and necessary.

That this concept of the king as master, father and justiciary of his
people was widely held there can be no doubt, for neither the rebels
against royal authority (and Heaven knows there had been plenty of
them, and would be more while Louis XIII was king) nor the 'libertines'
or free-thinkers put forward ideas that could strictly be called republican—although some of the latter slyly introduced into their works
sceptical references to the power of princes.

Even when in conflict not merely with the king's policy but with his
armies in the field, men did not dispute the fact that the king in the last
resort was always the master. Whether he negotiated with them or constrained them to sue for pardon he remained as he had been, an image of
God.

In his conclusion to a memorable book, Marc Bloch pointed out that
before the power of the Crown came to be adopted by a limited number
of people as a political concept—a concept that was to be analysed and
justified during Louis XIII's reign by Le Bret in his treatise *De la
Souveraineté du Roi*, and by Richelieu in his *Testament politique*—it already
constituted for the country as a whole a kind of collective representation
and a source of prestige and religious emotion. In his *Histoire de la Réforme
française* the Protestant pastor Viénot assembled quotations from contemporary writers in order to defend his brethren against the charge of
having been disloyal Frenchmen, and the passages cited by him prove
that the Huguenots were monarchists like everyone else. The king was

the supreme embodiment of France; but this conviction did not mean that the same opinion was expressed everywhere as to the necessity for obeying him or doing exactly what he asked.

This was inevitable because so much remained that was feudal and mediaeval, especially among the nobility; it was also inevitable because the religious conflicts of the sixteenth century had not led to the triumph of one doctrine over the other but to a necessary compromise—the Edict of Nantes. The French people of 1610 lacked the ability to think of the State as abstract and unquestioned; they were not convinced that the king was absolute as well as supreme, nor were they converted to the idea that their primary duty was to serve and obey him. The order that the king might issue on one day was everywhere liable to be countered by reminders of the immunity which he had allowed to survive up to the day before—an immunity which he had guaranteed himself. For these reasons the extension of the king's government, the subordination of the whole realm to his service were to be the essential tasks of Louis XIII's reign. To understand this reign more fully we must now try to form a clearer picture of the different social classes.

The framework of society was still the traditional one. A very simple hierarchy existed consisting of three orders. The first, the clergy, that is to say the Catholic clergy, the only clergy who were recognised as such, occupied the highest place, for nothing was superior in dignity to God's service. The second was represented by the nobility; and at a lower remove were all those who were neither nobles nor clerics: the Third Estate, in other words the majority of the French people.

These distinctions were based upon the quality of the services rendered: they reflected a religious and military conception of society and, one might add, a primitive economy, since to outward appearance none of this was in any way connected with money, wealth or labour. How far removed such a society seems from ours, in which economic differences assume such great importance, despite the principle of equality for all, with capitalists and wage-earners constantly at variance!

But this hierarchical façade concealed other factors that were no less real, factors which owed their existence to economic developments not only in France but in the world. The great discoveries of the sixteenth century had cracked the mediaeval framework. Although these discoveries had less impact on daily life than the economic revolutions of the eighteenth and nineteenth centuries, brought about by steam, electricity and the internal combustion engine, they nevertheless constituted an event of equal importance. The sources of wealth had shifted. It no longer came from the land and products of Europe, nor from the spices brought by caravans as in the Middle Ages. Now it was to be found in commerce on the high seas and on the trade routes to the Indies. Most significant of all, the monetary system had been transformed—a major phenomenon to which present-day historians rightly attach supreme importance. The discovery of the silver mines of Potosi in South America in 1545—sixty-five years before Henry IV's death and thus a comparatively recent event—had led to a considerable influx of bullion first to Spain and thence to the whole of Europe. There resulted from it a kind of inflation and a general rise in the price of goods.

We are tempted nowadays to treat this as the explanation for everything, to see in the price revolution the main reason for the subsequent course of history, to believe that it was the underlying influence on all policy. This is undoubtedly an exaggeration. Even so, the fact that prices increased fivefold in a century on the great European markets, the fact that in France, as E. Levasseur has shown, a *livre tournois*[16] could buy only a fifth as much wheat in 1600 as in 1500 are both indicative of an economic revolution, even if we admit that the rise in the price of corn was steeper than the increase in the price of other produce.

From then onwards there existed a deep discrepancy—a contradiction, as Marxist historians would say—between the structure of French society, which still retained the social framework of the preceding centuries, and its economy, which had been profoundly altered. The handling of money in all its forms, the creation of capital, or quite simply the possession of ready money were henceforth indispensable and constituted the real driving force. Those who still calculated on the basis of the old figures, those whose revenues remained stationary with the same nominal value as in days gone by no longer had the same purchasing and spending power as their predecessors had had in the same circumstances. Among the victims of this economic revolution (of whom only a few, like Jean Bodin,[17] had recognised the causes) the nobility were the hardest hit. They took no part in commerce and their incomes had in many cases remained at the same level as before. However, it would be absurd to think of the nobility as ruined and degraded. A peasant would have been very surprised if anyone had told him that his lord was in straitened circumstances and that his power was on the wane: he could see for himself that his master's power was as formidable as ever.

For a number of reasons the nobility still controlled various sources of power which counteracted the effects of economic change and safe-guarded their authority in the land. It was to their birth that the nobles owed their distinctive features as a class. And although a great deal of exaggerated emphasis was given to the historic prestige and remote ancestry of the nobility, it was still true that a noble was someone who was born into a predetermined caste.

The king himself was no more than the first gentleman of the land. Henry IV prided himself on having no title that he valued more highly. Assembled about the king's person, the nobility constituted the military class *par excellence*. It was the nobility who were called upon to form the army or summoned to join the *ban* or the *arrière-ban*,* in which every man of noble birth might be called upon to serve in time of war. But ser-vice to the king was interpreted more widely than this. It was from the nobility that the king recruited those who were to be in personal attend-ance on him, those to whom he gave appointments at court, those whom he chose to govern his provinces, and, in theory, even those whom he charged with their administration. In theory of course; we will see later what happened in practice.

Because he served personally in time of war, the noble was exempt from payment of the *taille*—a general tax, but implicitly intended for commoners since it represented the contribution paid by those who did not fight towards the upkeep of the king's army.

As this exemption was a sign of noble rank a number of wily people, whose right to call themselves noble was open to question, made use of the fact that neither they nor their fathers nor grandfathers had paid the *taille* to claim that they belonged to the privileged class.

To reserve their time and energies for the king's service, nobles were forbidden to engage in trade as a profession on pain of losing their social privileges and being reduced to the status of commoners.[18] Thus the noble found himself a prisoner of the old economic system: he owned the land and lived on the income derived therefrom—either by exploiting it directly himself or by granting it, in accordance with the complicated forms of mediaeval law, to a copyholder (who would pay him quitrent) or alternatively to a tenant-farmer or a share-cropper who paid him either a money rent supplemented by dues or rent in kind.[19]

No land without a lord, says the proverb. In addition to these links be-

---

* This was the name given to the mustering of the King's vassals together with their retainers for military purposes. It was thus composed of holders of fiefs who owed mili-tary service directly or indirectly to the Crown. In future the whole expression will be translated as 'feudal levies'.

tween the landowner and his land there were innumerable feudal rights, rights that had once formed part of the king's prerogative [*anciens droits régaliens*], which the Crown had relinquished to private persons during the Middle Ages and had then resumed one after the other. The seigneur remained in many cases a justiciary in lower jurisdictions,[20] and certain of the greatest members of the nobility (the Montpensiers) used to mint their own money—a privilege whose economic consequences for the realm were more far-reaching than is generally realised. Throughout the length and breadth of the seigneurie, although by no means all the land belonged to him in terms of custom or usage, the seigneur exacted his feudal rights in the shape of dues for the use of his bakehouse or wine-press, tolls, marketing dues, dues for the use of his mills.[21] He levied fees when his peasants received an inheritance, on legal transactions, on the sale and purchase of real estate (*lods et ventes*); he drew a regular income from the interest on loans and from grants of land of long standing.

At the church, where the curé had often been nominated by him in virtue of his right as patron, the seigneur was treated with especial honour. The priest came to cense him as he stood in his pew opposite the funerary slab with its arched niche which would one day be raised to lower his coffin into the vault occupied by his forbears. On all sides there were indications that he was a person of more than common rank.

These outward and visible signs of his greatness explain the halo of glory with which the noble was invested. We may say that in the seventeenth century the nobility were not so much loved (fear rather than affection was the emotion that men sought to inspire) as generally envied. Public opinion was unanimous in upholding their prestige. The entire nation aspired to join the ranks of the nobility, and such preferment was possible, as we shall see. The king could raise a noble still higher in the aristocratic hierarchy by issuing letters patent making him a duke or a peer. Entering the king's service as one of his officials could lead to ennoblement. Moreover membership of a noble family, without in itself conferring a direct right to certain functions, operated as it were in the candidate's favour: thus it facilitated the admission of a younger son to a church benefice and made it easier for a daughter who had taken the veil at an early age to be appointed as abbess in succession to an aunt.

This attitude of public opinion from below and the firm conviction of the king and his entourage from above that it was not fitting for the second order of the realm to be allowed to sink into degradation were essential to maintain the nobility's position. The second order of the realm, in Richelieu's words,[22] ought to be regarded 'as one of the principal

sinews [*nerfs*] of the State capable of contributing greatly to its preservation and rehabilitation'; but the nobility, the class which embodied the
past, were turning their backs on the economic trends of the time by the
very nature of their activities. They felt themselves to be threatened: on
all sides they could be heard crying that they were being oppressed and
ruined, that the passage of years and the natural evolution of things
within the realm were reducing them to a dishonourable condition.
Except in time of war—and these are again the words of Richelieu himself, a noble through and through—the nobility were 'useless and burdensome to the State'.

Except in time of war: and warfare continued as an unavoidable necessity throughout the whole of Louis XIII's reign. It was this that saved the
nobility. But in 1610 there was no clear distinction in their minds between a definite war undertaken in the king's service solely to defend the
realm against the foreigner, and taking up arms for the furtherance of
private interests against the king if need be, whilst continuing to declare
that their only ultimate aim was to do him good service.

His precarious economic position is sufficient to explain the average
noble's need of a patron. We must distinguish, said Richelieu, between
the nobility at court and the nobility who live in the country. This traditional distinction is both true and necessary. But the country nobility
did not resign themselves to their lot: they too tended to come to court
since it was there that honours were distributed. The Richelieu family,
good country gentry from Poitou, owed to their court connections alone
the favours [*prébendes*] that were to enable their younger son to become a
bishop—until such time as his own enterprise opened up a career for
him. In consequence the average noble felt the need for backing: he
obtained it from relatives who were in a better position than himself and
for whom provision had already been made. He used to attach himself to
them at an early age and from then onwards his honour was bound up
with this personal connection. He belonged to the man to whom he had
committed himself and the latter could do what he chose with him.
Hence those situations that seem paradoxical to us but which explain, if
they do not excuse, incidents such as the following. The commander of
the fortified town of Saint-Antonin, when called upon to admit the
king's representatives, replied in the most natural manner in the world,
and without a trace of irony, that he was the duke of Rohan's man before
he was the king's and since his loyalty was to the duke he was taking his
orders from him.

It must have been a moving, not to say most stirring sight, when the governor of Poitou led fifteen hundred gentlemen in arms to Louis XIII and announced: 'Sire, there is not one of them who is not my kinsman.'[23] A fine following indeed, but to what use might it be put if not brought directly into the king's service? Dependence—that is the word which sums up the main feature of the situation. The French nobility were a class that was threatened, and those who belonged to it could only extricate themselves from their precarious situation by becoming or acquiring followers or dependants. Dependence offered the only escape from obscurity and poverty; likewise the more dependants a man had, the stronger he was.

This attitude of mind was commonly found among those great nobles in the king's entourage who are known to history as *les Grands*. No doubt their greatness was partly due to the king's favour but, to a far larger extent, it was due to the means at their disposal for obtaining his favour: they were favoured because they were feared.

The names of some of them have already been mentioned: the duke of Épernon and all those great personages who were seated on the steps of the throne at the monastery of the Grands Augustins on 15 May; Mayenne and his son, with his nephew the duke of Guise. There were also the princes of the house of Rohan who claimed to be descended from the ancient dukes of Brittany: Montbazon, Rohan and Soubise.[24] A powerful nobleman from Auvergne, Henri de la Tour, had become by his first marriage sovereign prince of Sedan and duke of Bouillon. As one who now held territories which straddled France and the Holy Roman Empire, and who had become by his second marriage the brother-in-law of the princes of Nassau in Holland and of the elector palatine, he treated on equal terms with foreign kings. Although essentially a vassal of the French Crown who looked to France for his most substantial benefits, he felt himself powerful and formidable in his own right. The duke of Nevers, whose power was based on immense domains in the centre of France and who was immediate chief of all the nobility in that region, was also the lord of Mézières on the frontiers of the realm. As a descendant of the Gonzaga family, he was related to the princely house of Mantua in Italy.

Among the members of the royal family there were three princes of the blood,* all of whom could lay claim to the throne in the event of the death of the little king and his brothers. All three were closely linked together by their common interests as a group: the prince of Condé (Louis

* i.e. those who were directly and legitimately descended from a king of France in the male line. (V.L.T.)

XIII's second cousin) and his uncles, Conti and Soissons. There were others also who, although excluded from the succession by irregularity of birth, nonetheless derived considerable prestige from being the sons of kings and from having in their following many former friends and servants of their fathers. Such was Charles de Valois, count of Auvergne and duke of Angoulême (the Valois had been unlucky, for Elizabeth, the wife of Charles IX, only bore him a daughter while it was his mistress Marie Touchet who gave him a son). Of the sons of Henry IV and Gabrielle d'Estrées, the oldest, the duke of Vendôme, had contracted an alliance with the ruling house of Lorraine and the family of the former dukes of Brittany by marrying the daughter of the duke of Mercoeur, whose wife was the last of the Penthièvres. Henry IV's other illegitimate sons, the comte de Verneuil (the son of Henriette d'Entragues and thus Marie Touchet's grandson—for there were traditions in certain lines of descent if not in families) and the comte de Moret, were both too young as yet to cut such a figure, though the opportunity awaited them if they chose.

Other great families included the Montmorencies, premier barons of Christendom, the Uzès, the Bellegardes and the Longuevilles; another powerful figure was Lesdiguières, the governor of Dauphiné, of whom Henry IV used to say jokingly that he was the *roi-dauphin*.[25]

It is easy to understand Henry IV's advice to Marie de Medici that she must reckon with the great nobles and keep them contented to prevent them from becoming dangerous. An immense social network centred on the court stretched out via these exalted personages to the nobility of the provinces, enveloping in its meshes castles that were still equipped to withstand a siege and roads along which passed both the money destined for the king's treasury and the nation's merchandise, its corn, its meat, its fabrics—in short the economic life-blood of the land. Thus the second order of the realm could either ensure its peace by remaining loyal or plunge it into upheaval by rising in rebellion.

The clergy of France, likewise a traditional order, occupied a very important place in the life of the country. At the peak of the hierarchy the bishops, several of whom were cardinals, were persons of considerable consequence whose influence made itself felt even on the king's policy. The clergy, whether secular or regular, were regarded as wealthy. In Burgundy in particular as well as throughout the other provinces of France, the Benedictines and the Cistercians possessed immense estates, both forested and under cultivation, which stretched for miles around their abbeys or priories. The *curé* too was a seigneur, for he imposed upon his parishioners a special tax of his own—the tithe.

How difficult it is to make a valid appraisal of the material wealth and moral worth of the clergy in about 1610! For during the previous fifty years the Church in France had passed through the most formidable crisis she had ever known. Abuses and scandals and the ignorance and mediocrity of the priesthood had combined to bring her into such disrepute that a very large number of the faithful had deserted her in favour of the reform movements first of Luther and then of Calvin. The religious crisis had led to a series of civil wars, horrible in their unbridled passion, wars in which both sides committed such appalling atrocities that historians who consider them a subject for polemics are merely wasting their time in trying to throw the responsibility on to one side in order to whitewash the other. Equally pointless are the attempts that have been made to draw up a balance sheet of the atrocities or crimes committed with the object of castigating one particular group and justifying its opponents.

There can be no doubt that the France of Gothic cathedrals and Romanesque churches suffered terribly from the struggle. To those who belonged to the Reformed religion, ritualistic worship, statues of the Virgin and the saints, representations of Christ and of scenes from the Bible were all tantamount to idolatry. To sack everything was accounted a righteous act. It is almost impossible to trace on a map the areas that were predominantly Calvinist since positions were continually shifting; but to represent the countryside as faithful to Catholicism and the towns as converted to the reform movement would be a serious over-simplification. Admittedly, Protestantism originated in the towns, the urban element of the population being inevitably more receptive to new ideas. But the country gentry also took a hand in the struggle. By example, persuasion or downright violence, they imposed the new religion on those around them. In towns where heresy had flourished Catholicism found centres of resistance—and of these towns Paris was the first —whereas there were some parts of the countryside such as Poitou and Saintonge where almost all the population forsook the old religion. Any attempt to determine whether the greater part of France was Protestant at certain dates or was tending imperceptibly in that direction would be quite futile. One thing is certain however: the government of France remained Catholic. Henry IV could only make sure of the throne by abjuring Protestantism. This alliance between the monarchy and the Catholic religion is to be attributed in no small measure to an agreement concluded between the king of France and the pope early in the sixteenth century—the Concordat of Bologna (1516). It gave the king such power over the Church in France that he could scarcely have wished for more.

Since it was a political transaction the Concordat in no way altered the religious crisis that was to follow, for the latter was the inevitable consequence of a state of mind and moral outlook on which a diplomatic treaty could have no effect. But although the Concordat did not prevent the Wars of Religion, at least it helped to limit their scope.

By the terms of the Concordat the king nominated to all bishoprics, archbishoprics and major benefices, and the pope confirmed the appointment within six months. Thus the king recruited his own clergy and the pope only opposed his choice if the candidate chosen did not fulfil the requirements of age or doctrine. The bishop-designate took an oath of fealty to the king and promised to advise him of any conspiracy against his person or against the safety of the State.

The bishops, or the most important holders of benefices (or those whom the latter in their turn appointed and controlled) were responsible for a certain number of public services—such as education, public charity and, from 1539 onwards, the maintenance of registers of births, deaths, etc. In the form of *décimes* or *dons gratuits*, that is to say 'voluntary' subsidies, the Assembly of Clergy contributed to royal finances. Consequently, there had been no need for the king of France to secularise the Church within his realm so as to ensure the loyalty of its priesthood and avail himself of the material resources of its clergy as many other European rulers had been tempted to do.

However the Concordat was not the only factor. The Wars of Religion had broken out relatively late in France—after the Catholic Church had committed itself to the great programme of reform elaborated by the Council of Trent between 1545 and 1563 and after the foundation and rapid emergence of a new religious order, the Jesuits, bent on fighting heresy at its source by restoring to Catholicism its intellectual qualities and its moral and spiritual values. From the time of the Council of Trent the Church in France was to have at its head bishops such as the cardinal of Lorraine, followed in due course by Cardinals La Rochefoucauld and du Perron—men who were fully endowed with the strength of mind that was needed if reform of the Church was to be undertaken.

What a task! It called for continual exertions over a very long period of time. Nevertheless there can be no doubt that there was an improvement in the moral standards of the French Church during the course of Henry IV's reign. The king, whose attitude had evolved in a rather curious way from that of a convert inspired by self-interest to that of a

believer who derived great emotional and spiritual satisfaction from his
new faith, was able to promise as early as 1598 'that with God's help the
Church in his realm would be as well graced as she had been a hundred
years past'. He had good reason in 1605 for boasting of his pride at perceiving that 'the bishops whom he had established differed greatly from
those of the past'. This does not alter the fact that the picture of the
French Church painted at this period was distinctly sombre.

'Through the practice of confidential simony* sundry of the nobility
and other lay persons then held the majority not only of the priories and
abbeys but also of the livings and bishoprics. So great was the laxity in
monasteries and convents in those days that naught was to be found but
scandalous behaviour and bad example among most of those to whom
one should look for edification.' This description of the state of the
Church in the time of Henry IV is given by Richelieu in his *Testament
politique*. What is the explanation for this severe judgement? The answer
is that since it was her decadence which had given rise to Protestantism
and since the wars that followed had reduced countless religious buildings to ruins, the reform of the Church was inevitably an extremely slow
process and its initial results took a very long time to appear. It could
only succeed through an improvement in intellectual and moral standards among the clergy and religious orders.

But the terms of the Concordat, while they favoured the Church's
revival in many respects, also contributed to her weakness. Only a king
deeply conscious of the Church's spiritual role could resist the temptations or advantages that they offered him. They enabled him for example to distribute ecclesiastical appointments to men who were loyal
rather than of high moral character, and to gratify the noble families
which came begging for a bishopric, priory or abbey for a younger son
or a daughter. Again, he could yield to the temptation of authorising the
accumulation of a large number of benefices in the same hands as tokens
of royal favour, after paying the persons concerned to serve him well or
ensuring that they did so, when one benefice alone would have been
enough to keep an incumbent fully occupied if it was to be efficiently administered and devoted to its proper religious purposes. It is an edifying
thought that the see of Luçon passed into the hands of the Richelieu
family simply as a vested interest and that it was granted in the first place
to the second son Alphonse and then to the third, Armand, when he was
canonically too young to occupy it. Henry IV could congratulate him-

---

* A kind of simony whereby the holder of a benefice handed it over to a layman together with its revenues. (V.L.T.)

self on having appointed some excellent bishops such as Dinet, Frémyot and Pierre du Vair, the bishops of Mâcon, Bourges and Vence; as for Jean-Pierre Camus, the bishop of Belley, he was both a friend of François de Sales and a model churchman, active in his priestly duties. However it was also Henry IV who requested the pope to authorise the enthrone-ment of a child of four (whose age he misrepresented) as bishop of Lodève.

The Council of Trent had laid down that the principal duty of bishops was to reside in their dioceses, but they did not do so. It had issued in-structions that seminaries were to be established to train the clergy of the future, but there was an absence of priests sufficiently well educated to teach at such institutions. It had called for a general reform of monastic life, but a worldly attitude persisted in monasteries and convents alike, sometimes taking the form of childish frivolity, sometimes finding ex-pression in scandalous licentiousness. Among the laity there were noble families such as the Gondi de Retz and bourgeois families such as the Acaries, the Séguiers and the Marillacs, in Paris, which included fervent Catholics well versed in their faith. Such people were eager to win souls for Christ; but they realised full well that it would be impossible to carry out religious reform without assistance from outside the realm, from those countries untouched by heresy where the progress made by the spiritual revival within the Church was becoming increasingly marked. Hence the appearance in France at the end of the sixteenth century of two new religious orders which came from Spain and Italy and which soon began to spread throughout the realm—the Jesuits and the Capu-chins. The former had suffered many hardships during the Wars of Re-ligion and owed their permanent establishment in France (which was formally authorised by the edict of 1603) to Henry IV's protection. Jesuit colleges, the most famous of which were at La Flèche and Paris, were attended by boys who came from wealthy families. Even so the new movement met with many obstacles even among Catholics. In legal and official circles (of which more later) it was regarded as a foreign invasion and aroused feelings of patriotic resentment and alarm. The pope pressed for the decrees of the Council of Trent to be recognised as the law of the land. His request was refused by the king's advisers. In the Council's decisions they scented a tendency to allow the pope supremacy over the whole Church as well as over Church councils, and—although it was not yet clearly defined—a sort of right of control over temporal rulers.

However much they believed in reform, many bishops disliked the re-ligious orders because they were subject to superiors who did not belong to the diocese—a state of affairs which involved a corresponding reduction in the rights of a bishop or his subordinates as ordinaries.[26] The forces of tradition in France countered the growing trend towards ultramontanism by emphasising the autonomy and particular customs of the Gallican Church, using them as a brake to arrest a movement which favoured converting Catholics the world over to the same practices and the same religious zeal. With even more justification the Protestants were also beginning to grow uneasy.

All through the reign of Henry IV the Huguenots had watched the advantages which they had obtained steadily shrinking in inverse proportion to the headway made by the Catholic Church and to the favours that those in authority lavished upon their opponents to spur them on. The Edict of Nantes had given some guarantees to the Huguenots which were in theory irrevocable, and a certain number of temporary privileges. The guarantees protected their liberty of conscience and imposed certain limitations on their freedom of worship. Protestant services were only authorised on the outskirts of towns or in the houses of nobles who were high justiciaries[27] in rural areas, on condition that not more than thirty persons were present. The letters patent appended to the Edict of Nantes provided the Huguenots temporarily (for eight years) with 'places of security', or fortified towns, where garrisons under Protestant command were maintained at the king's expense.[28] Their presence helped to reassure the Huguenots since it shielded them from possible Catholic violence. The political organisation which the Protestants had built up during the course of the Wars of Religion was also preserved. Provided the king gave his consent, they were allowed to summon their general assemblies, which were to all intents and purposes the Estates-General of the Huguenot party. There the position of the various Protestant Churches would be reviewed and complaints of any infringements of the Edict of Nantes were collected. The general assemblies also chose the deputies general, who were charged with the task of defending the interests of the Reformed religion at court where they resided.

It was to a large extent the Protestants who suffered from the progress of Catholicism, and they lived in a state of constant apprehension. The most trifling legal dispute was enough to arouse their alarm, so that they were always ready to complain and demand redress. Yet a number of very important people belonged to the Reformed Church and continued to protect it. Sully was a tenacious Protestant who had clung obstinately to his religion despite the promises made to lure him into changing his faith.[29] His son-in-law, the duke of Rohan, and the latter's brother Soubise were also Protestants; so too were the duc de Bouillon and Marshal Lesdiguières.

But among the Catholic clergy and laity the Edict of Nantes was denounced as an exorbitant concession which served to delay France's return to the ancient faith, created a State within a State and provided the Church's enemies with the military and legal resources that enabled them to assail her continually. Moreover, since the monarchy is Catholic, it was said, is not an attack on the Church an attack on the monarchy and a threat to its security?

In several respects the legal position of the clergy resembled that of the nobility. The clergy needed the king's protection and in return, as the spiritual leaders of the people, were expected to ensure that the king's subjects remained loyal to him. The nobility were quite incapable of giving him the financial support that came from the clergy; but as a power in the land the clergy, like the nobility, were neither docile nor contented. Rejuvenated, but a prey to conflicting influences, they found themselves face to face with another Church—a Church which, although it had suffered defeat in that it had failed to supplant the Catholic Church, was nevertheless still full of vigour thanks to the number and eminence of its adherents, and to the privileges that continued to protect its existence.

To sum up: the ardour of the Wars of Religion had cooled and was now perhaps a thing of the past; but it was not yet quenched and the sparks beneath the ashes might rekindle at any moment.

Whereas it is possible to give a relatively straightforward account of the condition of the nobility and clergy, the condition of the Third Estate of the realm was infinitely complex. It must be borne in mind that a rich tax farmer [*traitant*] like Saulnier or Paulet on whom the king depended for financial assistance[30] belonged to the same social order as a yokel eking out a miserable existence in grinding poverty in Auvergne or Rouergue. We have to remember that the Third Estate included not only the vast peasant population but also the bourgeoisie in the towns, comprising merchants and royal officials as well as lawyers and magistrates, the latter being a social category that bordered upon the hereditary nobility. The spokesmen for the Third Estate were office-holders and lawyers; although it formed a single order it was far from being composed of a single class.

Let us begin with the peasantry. For a long time they have been largely overlooked, yet it is the history of the peasantry which constitutes the real history of the realm. It was their labour as cultivators that provided France with her resources, for even her industries—as in the case of textiles and shoe-making—merely involved the conversion of raw materials derived from the soil and from the raising of stock; and the peasant's lot depended quite as much upon the market value of commodities as upon the vagaries of the weather. He was implicated without realising it in the fluctuation of prices—fluctuations that are analysed by the historians of today.

It is a mistake to think of the French peasantry as complete serfs with no property of their own. Hereditary tenure was far more common in the seventeenth century than has been supposed, and peasants who held land on this basis had some justification for thinking of it as their own property, since they could both sell it and pass it on to their children. In fact it was not fully theirs, for it was subject to various forms of feudal rent together with a considerable number of other charges. In addition their holding commonly consisted of bits and pieces and was often too small to support a whole family. In that event the peasant could round off his plot of ground by taking a lease on other fields; alternatively, if he had no land, or too little, available for his use, he could set himself up as a tenant on someone else's land. He thus became, on terms that were laid down by the actual agreement, by local custom, and by the period in which he lived, a tenant-farmer, that is to say a tenant who paid a money rent, or a share-cropper [*métayer*] who entered into partnership with the landlord, the latter providing some of the livestock and taking a share of the harvest. G. Roupnel has shown how during the sixteenth century a large number of estates in Burgundy were bought up by lawyers and office-holders belonging to the bourgeoisie. The peasants, however, were too poor to make payments in money for their lands and consequently the system of *métayage* came to be widely adopted, as being the most advantageous to both sides. The same phenomenon could be observed with considerable local variations in other provinces such as Brittany, Maine, Berry and Poitou.

Whether he was a copyholder, a tenant-farmer or a *métayer*, the peasant who ran a small farm and owned some livestock, carts and agricultural implements was relatively fortunate. Prosperity or the hope of it was not beyond the reach of the *laboureur*, who possessed his own team and plough. How wretched by comparison was the lot of the *brassiers*, whose only assets consisted of their own two arms—wage-workers whose uncertain salary, which varied according to the season or to the work for which they were hired, was paid partly in cash and partly in kind.[31]

Conditions of work were the more difficult because it was impossible to improve the traditional methods of cultivation owing to lack of technical knowledge or the ability to make use of it. Land was tilled with inadequate implements—the swing plough or the hoe, which did not dig deeply enough into the ground and turn over the layers of arable. Modern methods of improving the soil were unknown. The only fertiliser available consisted of the droppings of flocks and herds, or what could be obtained by such primitive expedients as *écobuage*, which involved burning weeds and using the ashes to fertilise the soil. It followed that the land was quickly impoverished and it was impossible to keep the same plots under continual cultivation. It was therefore necessary to give them a rest and let them lie fallow—in other words to abandon them to their natural flora for several years before ploughing and sowing them again. At first sight there was no difference between land that lay fallow and land that was never cultivated at all: stretches of waste covered with clumps of gorse, broom and heather, which were cut for use as fodder or as bedding for livestock. Animals were not well cared for. Only rough grazing was available, such as damp patches of ground at the bottom of a valley or beside a river. Consequently it was often necessary to go outside the domain and make use of the common land. 'Right of common' [*vaine pâture*] was also recognised, that is to say the right to drive one's flock or herd on to the adjacent domain when the harvest was done.

The French countryside was given over to two differing systems of agriculture. Especially to the north of the Massif Central, and to a lesser extent in the south of France, there was the open field system. In these parts of the country, where the growing of crops in two- or three-yearly rotations and common grazing were regular features of agrarian life, village communities were strong and well organised. In contrast there were the enclosed fields and copses of the west, where agrarian individualism was more widespread, though not universal. As a jurist of Louis XIV's time was to say: 'Once the fruits of the earth are removed the land becomes, by a kind of universal law, common to all.' Forests were a great asset. As in the Middle Ages the peasants would drive their cattle and horses there, and their pigs too when the acorns fell. But in the seventeenth century forests were diminishing: rather in the same way as a mine is worked out they were exploited wholesale for their timber, and also additional arable land could be gained by clearing areas of forest.

Already owners of large estates, whether noble or bourgeois, were tending to limit customary rights; they were apt to enclose their fields in order to terminate rights of common and to claim common lands for themselves. This was not a development that was encouraged by the government. An edict issued by Henry IV authorised parishes to redeem common lands of which they had been deprived and whose loss entailed severe hardship.

However as has been demonstrated by that leading authority on agrarian history Pierre de Saint-Jacob, whose work on the subject greatly redounds to the credit of French historiography,* the absorption of land, both by landlords who were noble or bourgeois, and by wealthy peasants, was a process which continued throughout Louis XIII's reign and far beyond it. This process is not only a most remarkable phenomenon; it also constitutes one of the major facts of French history.

It must be clearly realised that changes in the ownership of property upset the ancient feudal structure of the land. It was the agricultural unit, namely the *métairie* or the barn, which became the vital element in the agrarian landscape, featuring regularly in redistributions of land brought about by the partial or total sale of an estate or its inheritance. But this is not to say that the seigneurie had disappeared. On the contrary it continued to exist, in fact it was reconstituted. The same concern as before was shown over determining its territorial limits, and within them the seigneur (whether noble or bourgeois) continued as before to dispense justice and to levy a variety of dues.

In this way the seigneurial system, the distinctive features of which were economic, superseded the purely feudal system with its military connotations. But many of the affinities between the two were preserved —in particular the belief in a social hierarchy and in a paternal relationship which gave the seigneur the demeanour of a petty prince throughout his domain and made the peasants who were dependent on him seem like his subjects. But of course none of this impinged upon the increasing authority of the king and his officers—an authority whose presence everywhere proclaimed the superiority of the order of monarchy over all others.

Although France was far from being fully cultivated and the standard of such cultivation as there was left much to be desired, the variety of her resources assured her of a high reputation in Europe. Her chalky plateaux produced wheat, a cereal of high quality that was consumed in the Paris area and in the towns generally, as well as being exported, while in

* See Professor Tapié's bibliography, p. 512.

districts where the ground consisted largely of shale or where the soil was poor crops were confined to rye and buckwheat. Plants that produced textile fibres were widely cultivated—in particular hemp and flax were in great demand from the weavers, for the finished products of their workshops were destined for export as well as for the home market. Big pieces of canvas made in Brittany, Anjou and Normandy were to be seen regularly at fairs abroad and it was well known that it was French sail-cloth that the Spanish fleet needed for its sails. French fruits were likewise held in high repute far and wide—especially chestnuts from the Limousin, and walnuts. Cherries, plums, pears and apples appeared in succession upon the tables of the rich with the changing seasons of the year. Nor did they disdain fruits of an altogether humbler kind, such as are nowadays despised but were then a source of joy to the villagers when autumn descended on the countryside: bitter-tasting sorb-apples, which were knocked down from their sturdy trees by means of poles, and soft medlars, which would be left till they grew overripe in the first frosts that heralded the approach of winter.

A plant which flourished with particular abundance on French soil was the vine. It was cultivated everywhere; indeed the cultivation of vines was considered a noble occupation, encouraged by the Church, the monarchy and the landowning aristocracy alike. Sometimes these vines would be as carefully pruned as our present-day vine stocks; sometimes they were left to run riot and could be found climbing the nearby trees and twining their tendrils around the branches. But there was a marked distinction between vines that produced wine for local consumption (not all of it of good quality) and the vineyards which produced vintage wines that were highly esteemed by rich customers and foreign buyers. Wine was an important item in France's external trade. French wines were drunk not only in every country throughout northern Europe but also by the Spaniards. Their choice quality was the result of time-honoured methods patiently evolved over the years which regulated the conditions under which the grapes were to be gathered and their juice fermented and even brought about changes in the nature of the soil where the vines grew. Man's industry seemed to have exempted the vine, which had originally come from the Mediterranean, from the inevitable effects of climate and soil. The location of the main wine-producing areas has not been determined, as was for a long time wrongly believed, by physical conditions alone. It is far more the result of man's ability to carry out a complete conquest of the soil in these areas, as well as of the dictates of commerce. The best wines were produced in regions that were easily accessible and enjoyed good communications by river, road or sea ensuring their widespread sale. As Roger Dion has pointed out, Champagne 'in the vicinity of the Marne and around Rheims', the valley of the Loire, the slopes of the Saône and the Jura, the Atlantic seaboard (especially the district around Bordeaux) and the Mediterranean littoral in the Frontignan area—these were the regions that had become renowned for expert viticulture. The people who lived in these thickly populated districts were drawn away from the pursuit of agriculture or the production of textiles into occupations which, although highly exacting, required such expertise as to be a source of pride to any who engaged in them.[32] They were proud rather than rich—like many of the skilled craftsmen of the France of days gone by who had a feeling of satisfaction in a job well done and a sense of the dignity of their way of life. But even if the best vine-growing districts were not overflowing with money, life there was to a large extent both comfortable and prosperous.

There was already evidence of a tendency towards specialisation. Normandy, for example, was in the process of giving up vines in favour of the large-scale planting of apple trees which was to lead to the almost exclusive use of cider throughout the province.

Wine and corn. People still think that these two words conjure up a true picture of France. But noble though it is, the picture is oversimplified. Wine and corn have often confronted each other like adversaries on French soil. The good vine-growing districts abandoned agriculture, even when there was a chance of its being profitable. On the other hand the peasant who owned a team and plough, was bent on sowing as much land as possible, and if there was an irregular piece of ground which was unsuited for ordinary cultivation though suitable for vines, he would not attempt to make use of it. Indeed it would have required a revolution in local agricultural customs for him to have done so. Vine-grower and husbandman: two types of men engaged in two activities which were in fact mutually exclusive.

There is more justification for linking wine with salt. The salt from the salt marshes which lay to the south of Brittany, in areas where there was plenty of sun for at least part of the year, was highly valued by fishermen from the north, being of better quality than rock-salt and more suitable for salting fish. They used to come frequently to buy salt but were glad to take on a cargo of wine as well. Vines were cultivated only a short distance away from some seaports, and for that reason. In certain parts of France the areas where viticulture was practised as a skilled occupation can be seen on a map to correspond with the contours of the salt marshes.

To sum up: it was the certainty of a commercial outlet which in many cases had first dictated and still continued to determine the type of cultivation. It was for this reason that seventeenth-century France, so many of whose provinces were ill-served in this respect, remained a land of forest and moorland and scanty crops with which the greater part of the rural population had to be content. Later the network of roads that were to traverse the countryside also served to transform it by bringing to light its potential and undetected riches. Until this miraculous transformation or revolution came to pass, the few great highways which did exist might serve the turn of ponderous vehicles drawn by a team of horses and moving so slowly that they could be overtaken by a trotting horseman; but the sight most frequently to be observed in the French countryside was that of a solitary man stumbling along some muddy or stony footpath, bent double beneath his sack or leading his donkey to the mill or fair.

The French peasant thus pursued an occupation which brought him very little profit. During the winter months many of the peasantry tried to make something on the side by working at home. In Normandy, Maine and Anjou even the men used to spin and weave for manufacturers in the neighbouring towns. In particular the heavy financial exactions of the State and of the landlords, both lay and ecclesiastical, swallowed up a large part of the peasant's earnings; if a slump occurred in any shape or form these fiscal burdens reduced the countryside to a state of extreme poverty, soon followed in desperation by revolt.

Although a few pages back it was necessary to paint a gloomy picture of the physical condition of the French population owing to the prevalence of too many illusions on the subject, we must not forget that this population remained very numerous: too numerous for the country's resources such as they were, given the continual ravages of war and the poor state of the economy in general. Many hands were idle for lack of available employment. Some peasants could only obtain work by hiring themselves out as labourers when extra hands were needed in areas some distance away. Thus there existed, side by side with the permanently settled peasantry, a floating and nomadic population proportionately larger than in our day and with a correspondingly greater impact on the imagination. Often such people were practically vagabonds, and their existence added to the insecurity of rural life. This does not alter the fact that there were also peasants who were prosperous, and, indeed, careful not to reveal the extent of their prosperity, however inadequate it may seem by our standards. Inventories drawn up after death are both valuable and suspect as evidence, for it is always impossible to know to what extent they give a true picture despite their worth as an approximate estimate of a person's belongings. However, such documents tell us that well-to-do peasants possessed their own furniture, linen, crockery, and sometimes a hoard of silver coins—not to mention other items which they chose to conceal. The coins must often have been foreign: in the west, for instance, Spanish coins that had originally come from the seaports sometimes found their way far inland.

The daily life of the peasant was a harsh one. His hours of work were dictated by the duration of daylight. With little money at their disposal and little ability to regulate their expenditure, the peasantry were unable to provide themselves with adequate food or clothing. They only ate what they could not sell. As a general rule they never ate meat, although occasionally there might be poultry or game obtained by poaching, while the most prosperous peasants used to kill a pig on feast days which would then be salted. The peasant's usual diet, however, consisted of coarse vegetables, such as turnips or broad beans, and fruit; he drank only local wine of poor quality.

Everyone knows the paintings of Le Nain and Georges de la Tour. Their value as social documents is high, and the conditions that they illustrate held good for much of the seventeenth century. Not so long ago it used to be the fashion to be moved to pity by the poverty displayed in these pictures of peasant life; yet, in reality the peasants are not represented as desperately poor. It may be said that they are ill-clad and that their faces are grave, but in point of fact the painter has depicted them in old and shabby working clothes after their day's work is done. One of them is cutting a slice off a cottage loaf, another has a glass of wine in his hand, the women wear respectable headdresses, and healthy-looking children smile at us from the hay-laden cart. We can be sure that these admirable works of art portray peasants of a certain degree of affluence —peasants who are not so very different from those one could still meet until quite recently. Far more harrowing sights than these were to be seen often enough in seventeenth-century France.

It is extremely difficult to gauge the intellectual level of the French peasant at the beginning of the seventeenth century, to discover what he thought about, and whether he had any spiritual life. Contemporary texts are silent on this point. The peasant is scarcely mentioned except as an object of mockery; only rarely does anyone defend him or show pity for him.

The contrast between the intellectual élite, who belonged to the bourgeoisie or aristocracy and were endowed with the refinements of culture, and the peasant population, wallowing in ignorance, makes us more acutely aware of the absence of any intermediate class of society such as exists nowadays—people with a limited but practical outlook, whose views are basically sound. The educated man of the seventeenth century must have found it difficult to establish any contact with the man who tilled the soil. The former used his reason and could think in abstract terms; the latter could only argue from the evidence of his senses, his prejudices and his dreams. Consequently the average peasant must have seemed a small-minded, sly, ill-natured creature. But we must not be too categorical about this, for cultivated people of the seventeenth century, being far less rational and far more superstitious or imaginative than ourselves, to some extent shared the peasant's outlook. In addition they were far more rustic, spending as they did many months in close contact with country life. They were surely conscious of the bond of common tastes and interests that linked them with the peasantry more often than we with our urban ways can possibly realise.

The impoverishment of the nobility must have led to many sales of land, and the bourgeois who had taken advantage of this became nobles in their turn. When a noble had made a fortune at court he used to invest his capital in a country estate. Indeed the seventeenth-century Frenchman loved land firstly because an estate was generally a noble fief, which satisfied his vanity, and secondly because it represented a sound, if not highly profitable, investment. Until the Revolution this devotion to land remained a marked feature of the race; but too much concern was shown with the immediate income, however modest this might be, and not enough attention was paid to improving the estate. This was another reason why the French countryside as a whole continued to vegetate, following the same unvarying routines and sunk in poverty.

Those who were capable of educating the rural population were few in number. The high-ranking clergy—like Richelieu in his bishopric of Luçon—could hardly fail to note the crass ignorance of the mass of the priesthood. To the latter the theological ideas which had been so earnestly debated at the Council of Trent were generally incomprehensible —hence the prevalence of superstitions and confused beliefs, and the mechanical and inaudible performance of the sacramental rites of the Church. But here again we must be careful not to exaggerate, for in the year 1610 Vincent de Paul, a man of peasant stock with years of study, missionary activity and adventure behind him, wrote to his mother advising her to arrange for one of his nephews to study.[33] Was he an exception, or were there not many other cases like his when a group of peasants was afforded a glimpse into another world?—for we must emphasise that it would be most unfair to depict the peasantry as so engulfed in the darkness of brutish superstition that the light of a higher spiritual life could never reach them. Among the French peasantry of the time the Church has discovered some, like Ste Germaine Cousin, who were endowed with the virtues and piety of true saints.[34]

Although we are relatively well informed about the life of the French peasantry on the eve of the Revolution, we know less about their early seventeenth-century forbears. However, we do know that the improvements in the peasant's lot noted in about 1780 were the first to be brought about for a very long time. There is therefore good reason for thinking that although the French peasant did experience a little peace and security again under Henry IV's rule after France had emerged from the Wars of Religion, this merely meant that he reverted to the same conditions as had existed before these wars, conditions which had endured for centuries. In short his case remained wretched, but even so it was tolerable when compared to the abominations that were inflicted upon him in time of war or civil disorder. Neither Sully's attempts to regulate and interfere, nor the legend of the fowl in the cooking pot,[35] nor the treatises of Olivier de Serres (which are highly instructive for the Mediterranean area with its vines, olive-trees and mulberries, but reveal a blissful ignorance of northern France) made much difference to the peasant's lot. The hour had not yet come for the introduction of those techniques that were alone to alter it.

Was it possible for a man to rise from the peasantry and climb to a higher social rank? The case of St Vincent de Paul proves that it was and shows that study and a vocation for the priesthood could open the way for him. But outside the Church, although it was possible for a peasant who was already reasonably prosperous to gain admission to the ranks of the bourgeoisie, it used to take him a long time and was not a frequent occurrence. Further research in this field would probably bring to light occasions when the sons of peasants by entering their lord's service paved the way for the rise of an entire family. However, despite such changes, and although social conditions were more fluid than is often realised, seventeenth-century French society as a whole remained enclosed within class barriers which were certainly more rigid than ours.

There was no workers' proletariat because industry in the sense in which we understand it today was unknown.[36] Conditions of manufacture were entirely different from those that exist nowadays. No factories, no concentration of capital, or of labour—this is enough to point the contrast between the early seventeenth century and our own age. Instead of the factory there was the craft workshop with a very small number of workers; large-scale production could only be achieved by creating a large number of similar workshops. There were, however, manufactories where teams of salaried employees used to work in the same building on behalf of a contractor who provided the raw material. These manufactories, which produced luxury goods, had been founded by the king, or by private persons licensed by him to whom he might quite possibly have advanced the money, and they were primarily intended to meet one of the Crown's financial preoccupations: the need to guard against the export of gold and silver coin which the rich had to send abroad to pay for the luxury goods which they purchased outside the realm. Such manufactories were too few in number to achieve the hoped-for result or to be other than exceptional features of the country as a whole. There were forty-eight of them in 1610. It was thus the workshop which predominated, and it was there that the crafts were carried on. These crafts might be 'free' or they might be organised in guilds. In the latter event conditions of work and manufacture were strictly defined by the statutes of the guild.

Henry IV had encouraged the development of guilds for fiscal reasons, since the diploma which conferred the status of master in a craft guild was subject to a tax; and during his reign the number of crafts and trades that were regulated had increased to the detriment of those that were 'free'. The ostensible reason for this was creditable enough: to guarantee the quality of the article and the competence of the craftsman, who was only admitted as a master after he had served for a probationary period as an apprentice and had completed the 'masterpiece' required of him.[37] The real motives for the extension of the guild system lay deeper, however, and were less readily admitted; it suppressed competition and guarded against the possibility of any revolutionary change being introduced into the craft by some inventive or resourceful newcomer. In this way the dynasties of locksmiths, carpenters, masons, blacksmiths, weavers, lace makers, butchers, bakers and tripe sellers preserved their stability, as did the families engaged in any of the crafts connected with building, weaving and the sale of provisions [*alimentation*]. They were assured of their position and knew that they would be able to pass on their premises to their sons or sons-in-law. Shopkeepers engaged in the same craft or trade, far from avoiding each other, with each man seeking to cater for a different quarter of the town, used to have their shops jostled together in the same street, which would often bear the name of their guild: Tanners Street, Butchers Street.

Whereas in the towns the crafts were being increasingly controlled, in the countryside at all events they maintained their liberty. No doubt there were people all over France who championed the crafts that were 'free' as a matter of principle, but as Gaston Zeller has observed, their freedom in rural areas was primarily due to the conditions under which such work was carried on there. Many of the goods which are now manufactured by great industrial undertakings were then produced by small concerns scattered here and there in the villages. For example, metalwork was produced at a large number of forges in Normandy, Brittany and Anjou, and spinning, weaving and lace-making were occupations which used to be carried on at home; again, manufactured goods were produced by the seasonal labour of worker peasants—villagers who divided the year between the practice of some craft and work in the fields. All these rural activities were free from supervision and regulation and consequently also free from royal taxation. For fiscal reasons, therefore, the Crown tried to bring them under control and to subject them to the guild system.

The guilds were complemented by fraternities of a religious nature, which also played the part of mutual aid societies. *Compagnonnage* was not, as is sometimes thought, an intermediate stage between apprenticeship and mastership. Many *compagnons* or journeymen remained such all their lives, forming quite a distinctive social category. They loved their independence and liked to live from day to day; and as a whole they did not suffer unduly from their lack of security.

In the large towns certain crafts tended to separate themselves from the others and to form a kind of aristocracy. This aristocracy consisted of the crafts which provided the easiest and safest opportunities for making money or required extra knowledge or good taste and led to contacts with a higher class of customer. To the first category belonged the purveyors of foodstuffs [*métiers d'alimentation*]; amongst the second were the goldsmiths, the apothecaries, the tapestry makers (who welcomed the prospect of their sons becoming painters and architects), the wig makers and barbers (some of them surgeon barbers), the printers and booksellers. The latter were usually well educated and would often encourage their employees or relations to study in order to gain entry to the legal profession. Once a man was in contact with certain professions, the possible employments open to him increased in variety. A member of the rising generation was then in a position to choose between remaining loyal to his father's occupation, with the near-certainty of slowly growing richer and of enjoying the security which this implied, and the alternative of moving into a higher social category—an alternative which was more flattering to his vanity but involved accepting a few risks.

The place which industry with its large profits now occupies in our midst belonged in the early seventeenth century to commerce. Henry IV's peaceful reign had promoted its expansion by the creation or reconstruction of a system of roads and waterways. Journeys were certainly interminable. It took two days to travel from Paris to Orleans, three to reach Amiens, eleven to get to Lyons. However it was in fact at the fairs —such as the Foire Saint-Germain or the Foire Saint-Laurent in Paris, and the fairs held at Lyons, Bordeaux and Beaucaire—that the most important transactions took place.[38] The merchant whose turnover was on the increase made far larger profits than the manufacturer, if only because of the number of varying types of goods that he handled; he was clever and resourceful by virtue of the very nature of his different activities. Since he had capital at his disposal he was bound to make investments; as for the money which he had put by, he advanced it to financiers and shipowners.

In the course of the sixteenth century France had produced some really remarkable navigators and colonisers, whose exploits were memorable even if no means invariably successful. They had established temporary footholds at several points on the coastline of the American continent—in Canada, Florida, the West Indies and Brazil. France had arrived too late in the field to carve out a vast empire as Spain had done; but she had taken her place in international commerce.

In certain towns the wealth of the merchants put them in the forefront of urban life. In Burgundy, according to G. Roupnel, it was the mercers and drapers rather than members of the liberal professions who formed the real bridge between the nobility or privileged class and the craftsmen. In Paris the six merchant corporations known as the *Six Corps* (namely the drapers, grocers, mercers, furriers, hosiers and goldsmiths) saw their social importance continually increasing, while the position which they occupied in official ceremonies gave formal approval to their claim to be regarded as a kind of senate, presiding over the city's commerce.

It was undoubtedly among the trading community that the quickest fortunes were made, but there were other occupations open to the bourgeoisie which enjoyed greater prestige—occupations that repudiated the mechanical arts, shopkeeping or the workshop, that called for higher intellectual attainments and further study, and which went to make up the world of the law. In a society which was well versed in the technicalities of legal procedure and much addicted to litigation, it was more usual for a matter to give rise to a law-suit than for it to be settled in accordance with custom; similarly the claims of the various parties were apt to be more intricate and involved. Hence those who enforced the law and took part in the administration of justice were invested with a certain aura. It was necessary to have recourse to their services in connection with marriage contracts, conveyances, wills, questions of inheritance; and the respect with which they were treated corresponded to the extent that the family patrimony and the family honour seemed to depend upon their good offices.

Lawyers and office-holders: the two categories overlapped and were closely interconnected. The term *officiers* did not then signify officers in the armed forces but was applied to the officials whom we now call civil servants. It requires a certain effort on our part to understand the position that they occupied in the realm, which constitutes one of the most original features of seventeenth-century France.

It was natural for the king to entrust public duties or, to use the contemporary phrase, 'offices and charges' to people who deserved his confidence. These consisted firstly of officials concerned with fiscal matters, who administered the royal domain and its revenues and collected and allocated the *taille* and the *gabelle*—functions which were carried out by the *trésoriers de France* (styled *généraux des finances*), together with the *élus* and the administrators of the salt depots[39]: secondly there were the officers of justice—the *baillis* and *sénéchaux*, the *lieutenants de bailliage*, the judges of the higher courts known as *présidiaux* or *Cours présidiales*, and, above them, the counsellors of the Parlements, of the *Cour des Aides* and the *Chambre des Comptes*.[40]

Here we must emphasise an important point: under the ancien régime justice and administration were bracketed together. A *bailli*, for example, was in modern terminology both president of a court and subprefect at one and the same time. Such officials received a salary from the Treasury—*gages*, in contemporary parlance.*

It was still natural enough in theory for officials to be chosen from the privileged class, in other words from the nobles whose duty it was to

* In England this salary was called a 'fee'.

serve the king. In the middle of the sixteenth century the nobility demanded that half the presidents and a third of the counsellors in a Parlement should be men of gentle birth [*gentilhommes*]. The Ordinance of
Moulins (1586) reaffirmed that the office of *bailli* was to be reserved for
those who were gently born. For the fact is that the logical scheme of
things mentioned above had ceased to apply some time ago; in practice
the whole system had been revolutionised. From the sixteenth century
onwards it had become so much the custom for an office-hunter to bribe
some member of the royal entourage to ensure his nomination that an official who was about to take up an appointment was not even obliged to
swear that he had not obtained it by intrigue or peculation. But this was
not the most serious aspect of the matter.

Whereas the king at one time used only to levy chancellery dues
(which were paid into the *bureau des parties casuelles*)[41] when an official
was installed in his office, he had been impelled by financial necessity to
adopt the practice of borrowing from the new incumbent a certain sum
of money which varied according to the importance of the office. To all
intents and purposes, from the fifteenth and sixteenth centuries onwards,
a man was no longer nominated to an office; in reality he bought it.
Indeed matters had got beyond this stage. The king used to create new
offices, not to ensure the more efficient discharge of some function
which was too heavy a load for one man, but simply in order to provide
himself with fresh sources of revenue by doubling, tripling or quadru-
pling the number of people entitled to hold the same post. Thus venality
of office came to be established as a system[42]—not, however, without
vociferous complaints from the clergy, the nobility and the Parlement, as
well as from all those who had an interest in checking the increase in the
number of offices and in preventing wealth from becoming accepted as
an alternative criterion of appointment to birth or talent.

But the officials who had paid to take up their appointments were sufficiently conscious of their strength to demand the right to dispose of
their office freely in the same way as their family property. They wished
to be able to transfer it to a kinsman or son or to whomever they chose.
They claimed the right to include its value in the dowry which they settled on their daughters. By various tricks and subterfuges (the details of
which are of no consequence here, interesting though they may be) the
Crown had more or less concealed the traffic in offices between private
persons. But it was only by stages that it came to admit their hereditary
transmission. It was laid down that any official resigning his office must
survive his resignation by forty days, failing which its disposal reverted

unconditionally to the king. This proviso is to be explained by the fact that many office-holders used only to resign their appointments when on the point of death; it had been devised by the Treasury as a means of enabling the Crown to regain control over a quite considerable number of offices. The families that were affected by this ruling defended themselves as best they could, even going so far as to conceal the death or to postpone the funeral of the relative concerned so as to avoid its application.

This was how matters had stood until the comparatively recent date of 1604 when Henry IV had agreed to abandon the forty-day rule in return for the payment by office-holders of an annual tax which was in fact a kind of insurance premium. A financier named Paulet had taken the lease of this annual tax—which meant that he had paid into the Treasury an agreed sum of money and had himself assumed the responsibility for levying it; as a result it became known as the *paulette*. Provided that he made this annual payment, an office-holder could live and die in peace. It was not strictly speaking his office, but rather the value of his office, which was guaranteed to his heirs. The Crown did not nominate anyone to the appointment until the parties concerned had come to an agreement regarding the terms on which it was to be sold.[43]

Now most offices endowed their holder, at least as far as he personally was concerned, with noble rank. In addition he could be sure of an income from the capital spent on purchasing his office—an income derived both from his official emoluments and from the gifts, fees and many other supplementary perquisites which he received from the public. In consequence offices were in great demand and their value steadily increased. Later we shall see the effect of this traffic in offices on the monarchy. Socially, its main result was gradually to open to the trading interest among the bourgeoisie, or simply to anyone who was rich (usually a bourgeois), a roundabout means of access to the ranks of the nobility. 'In the sixteenth century,' writes Roland Mousnier, 'the preferments and profits derived from their offices tended to convert the most important office-holders into a new class occupying an intermediate position between the bourgeoisie of the business world and the *noblesse d'épée*.'[44]* It seems to be well established that an office seldom constituted

---

* These were the nobility (traditionally of ancient lineage) who derived their rank and privileges from military service to the Crown, whereas the *noblesse de robe* had acquired theirs as a result of holding some appointment of an official nature. Note that as stated at the beginning of this paragraph noble status could be personal only, not hereditary. It was not until 1644 that all the magistrates of the Parlement of Paris for example were granted hereditary noble status. (see Shennan, *Government*, pp. 42, 43, 67.)

its holder's sole source of wealth. A man would buy an office, or at least an important office, only when he already owned landed property or a noble fief. The Eyquiems, merchants of Bordeaux, possessed such an estate at Montaigne—a name that was to be immortalised when their son and grandson, the counsellor of the Parlement of Bordeaux assumed it as his own.

At the beginning of the seventeenth century the magistrates of the Parlement of Dijon, despite their plebeian origins, had joined the ranks of the nobility—partly because of their offices and status no doubt, but principally because of the fiefs which they held and of their style of living. Mme de Sévigné's ancestors, the Frémyots, are a case in point; President Jeannin had the same background. That the sons of old-established noble families [*gentilhommes d'épée*] should be eager suitors for the well-dowered daughters of these lawyers and that they should ally themselves to families which owed their wealth in the first place to a father or grandfather engaged in trade was regarded as normal. Nevertheless notarial instruments bear witness to the persistence with which offices used to be handed on from one member to another of the same social circle, creating, particularly in the provinces, a kind of middle class of petty office-holders firmly entrenched in their dignities and buttressed by their country estates.

And so we see that whilst the peasantry, its lowliest members, were enduring the full rigours of the seigneurial system and continuing to toil in subjection to the nobility, the upper strata of the Third Estate were infiltrating into the aristocracy, and seeking to merge themselves with the nobility, as if only noble connections and noble status could sanctify and recompense their labours.

The French nation had just passed through half a century of economic, religious and political upheaval, followed by a brief period of recovery—the reign of Henry IV. The passage of time has led historians to paint a rosy picture of his reign, but its benefits were not unanimously recognised by contemporaries, caught up as they were in the many difficulties of daily life. Royal authority had emerged strengthened from the crisis because the élite of the country—especially the lawyers and office-holders—had realised that France's salvation was to be found in an undisputed monarchy. The monarchy was above the religious divisions and the particularist interests that looked for support from foreign powers and jeopardised the unity and independence of the realm; it both stood for tradition and offered leadership towards the future.

It so happened that Henry IV was personally the kind of man who was needed. Whether one admits it or not, there are times when the destiny of a nation depends on a few men established in the seat of government; it is this fact that gives political history its justification. The great mistake is to believe that these few men accomplish everything, that the key to every mystery is to be found in their behaviour. Far more than is some-times allowed, those in authority are subject to the social and economic conditions of their time, to contemporary opinion formed by inherited attitudes of mind and everyday interests, and to the abilities of their col-leagues. The forces with which they have to compromise are far more numerous than those that they control. Their merit lies in their response to some general aspiration, and their readiness to lead their country, willy-nilly, towards something that it vaguely desires and which is es-sentially to its advantage.

For seventeen years, beginning with his conversion and coronation at Chartres, Henry IV had fulfilled this necessary role. Although he lacked creative imagination, he was endowed with a lively intelligence. He had an abundant experience and a profound knowledge of human nature, and it was this that was his supreme quality, allied with the gift for choosing the right men to serve him and a flair for delegating work. If Henry IV had no outstanding virtues, he was also devoid of serious vices; if he was far too flippant to be a fanatic, he was also too sensible not to be in earnest. His character was such as to provoke much criticism at close quarters but to appear at its best at a distance, endowing him with the qualities of a noble and legendary figure. He had protected France from foreign wars between 1598 and 1610 and he had allowed the French people to devote themselves peacefully to their own affairs. He had been a good king; indeed we may go further and call him a good master, for the France of his day, a land of social hierarchies largely inhabited by peasants, felt reassured by good leadership.

It was greatly to the credit of the last of the Valois kings that for all their obvious political weakness they gave encouragement to letters and the arts throughout their troubled reigns, and favoured the development of French literature. Ideas and tastes are vital factors in a nation's history. Through those who read, literature exercises an influence on those who do not. It produces a gradual alteration over an entire country in the way that people think and feel, indeed one might say in their reactions to daily events. It did not occur to Henry IV to make use of literature as an instrument for the service of his reign or for the promotion of his glory. But although neither artistic nor intellectual, he was not lacking in culture or taste.[45] He not only appreciated the need to effect some improvement in standards at his court, but also attached importance to the embellishment of his palaces and of Paris itself.

Du Perron had often spoken to Henry IV in praise of Malherbe, and in 1605 the poet was received by the king. He was introduced by the dauphin's tutor, des Yveteaux. Henry made him an official poet while attaching him to the person of the duc de Bellegarde, the most cultivated of his courtiers.

Around the king, both in Paris and throughout the realm, a transformation was taking place in the world of letters. Desportes, Bertaut and du Perron devoted themselves to religious poetry. Although Ronsard and the *Pléiade* still had admirers in legal and official circles, in the university world, and among the Jesuits, their tenets were no longer in accordance with the taste of the day. True, they were still accepted by the group of poets whom Queen Marguerite, Henry IV's first wife, used to receive at her residence in the quai Malaquais;* but even in this coterie new literary trends were in evidence. Its members had a partiality for platonic philosophy and for pastoral poetry in the style of Tasso's *Aminta.*† By this time the marquise de Rambouillet, an Italian lady who had married a great French nobleman, had opened the doors of her salon. Its influence is invariably attributed to a later date, but it was already a centre of courtesy, taste and good manners greatly influenced by Italy.

In sophisticated and aristocratic circles there was a reaction against the uncouth standards of behaviour which had been encouraged by the Wars of Religion and had even gained acceptance at court, producing a state of 'confusion' there.[46] In these circles the cult of honour and a code of chivalrous behaviour that derived from Spain were highly valued, while tribute was paid to the idealised concept of platonic love and pastoral life which permeated Italian literature at this time. Contemporary devotional writings by French Catholics, which took the form of sermons, canticles and works of edification, were likewise marked by Spanish and Italian influences. This stream of devotional literature represented a movement that rejected the pagan and hellenising aspects of the Renaissance, but its effect was also to delay the emergence of a formal school of literature governed by the rules of reason alone.

---

* The position of Marguerite de Valois calls to mind that of the Empress Josephine after she had been divorced by Napoleon, but the Renaissance princess was far more at ease in her invidious situation. (V.L.T.)

† This pastoral drama was published in 1573.

A zestful, ribald, truculent strain that was typically French was still active in the world of letters. It was then called Gaulish or Gothic and catered for a very large public. It bursts out of the works of Régnier, Malherbe's antagonist and an opponent of classicism who was in many respects the literary heir of Rabelais; and it was this same racy vigour that ensured the popularity of the farces performed by touring actors or the king's players at the Hôtel de Bourgogne.[47] These farces, with their smutty jokes and situations, catered admirably for the extremely spicy tastes of the average French bourgeois of 1610, who was very careful not to take his wife with him to see them performed. They gave far more pleasure to far more people than the tragi-comedies, pastoral pieces or tragedies which represented the new fashion in the theatre and had more intellectual content. It should be added that as far as both literary circles and theatres were concerned, the provinces, or at least certain provincial capitals such as Lyons, Tours and Bordeaux, were in no way behind Paris.

It is to be hoped that this brief outline will enable the reader to form a picture of the France that awaited Louis XIII and his government in those dark days of May 1610. Behind the façade of monarchical continuity and fixed social hierarchies the French nation was in full process of evolution. The Middle Ages still survived, largely owing to the stagnation of rural life; but the economic revolutions of the sixteenth century had brought about a shift in wealth, and altered the conditions upon which prosperity was based. The bourgeoisie showed their recent peasant origins by their caution and their thrift. They represented a powerful force in the realm; but they were so dazzled by the prestige that surrounded the nobility that their one idea was to win access to the ranks of the aristocracy. The noble thought of nothing save his privileges and his king, for it was the latter who upheld or increased them. The religious passions of the sixteenth century were only tempered, and although the combatants had laid down their arms (without, however, jettisoning them), the struggle still went on between Catholics and Protestants in all spheres and at all levels. In the meantime ideas and tastes were changing. All these different classes and creeds which together made up a great nation of fifteen million people had to be satisfied, guided, disciplined and educated; but the new king was only a child.

But child though he was, in October this little boy was to be consecrated in the cathedral at Rheims.[48] He would become a personage who was unique, he would be exalted above all his people. Even his mother the regent would be no more than the foremost of his subjects.

It was his royal blood, not his anointing and coronation, that was the hallmark of a king. But the ceremony of consecration, by providing him with the spiritual aids which he needed to accomplish his task, brought about a personal alliance between God and His Most Christian Majesty. It was more than an ordinary coronation. Amid the blessings of the priests the monarch was invested with the attributes of kingship—the sceptre, the crown, the ivory hand of justice, and the sword, symbolising political, legislative, judicial and military power.[49] The rite had less value than the six sacraments bestowed by the Church upon all the faithful, or the sacrament of orders reserved for clerics.* But it was an observance analogous to the sacraments and inferior to them alone—an observance of exceptional religious significance, which, although it did not confer upon the sovereign the spiritual status of a priest or bishop, nevertheless separated him from the rest of the laity. The archbishop used to anoint the king's forehead and limbs with oil from the Holy Phial mingled with chrism;[50] whereupon, as an outward visible sign of this supernatural favour, the king of France was invested with the prerogative of touching and healing those who suffered from scrofula—'the king's evil'. Thus the king became a worker of miracles.[51] On several days in the year he would exercise this mysterious power of healing in the midst of hapless victims who had flocked from far and wide to meet him on his progress.

But this was not the most important consequence of the ceremony. It had been as a result of their consecration that first Charles VII and later Henry IV had regained the allegiance of a torn and divided France. By general consent the ceremony performed at Rheims in accordance with the ancient rites, while the high vaulted roof resounded to the shouts of 'Noel' uttered by the throng,[52] rendered the king's person sacred and august as an image and reflection of God, as the representative of God's power charged by Him with the temporal leadership of the people.

---

* Namely Baptism, Confirmation, the Eucharist, Penance, Matrimony, Extreme Unction, and, in the case of clergy, Ordination.

CHAPTER TWO

The Regency of Marie de Medici
(1610–17)

THE MOTHER of the boy king was to govern in his name. Marie de Medici was thirty-seven years old. Her appearance is familiar to us from the paintings of Rubens, which make it hard to believe that this massive fair-haired woman was Italian; her ample curves, conforming to the painter's ideal of female beauty, make her look like a Flemish goddess. She was in fact partly of Germanic extraction, the noble blood of her mother, an Austrian archduchess, compensating for the recent and plebeian social origins of the grand dukes of Tuscany. Only marriage to a Spanish, Austrian or English princess was normally considered fitting for a king of France, but none of these possibilities had been open to Henry IV even after his conversion and the conclusion of peace between France and Spain. Moreover he was not only an ex-Huguenot; he had also a very bad reputation as a philanderer who was notorious for his free and easy private life. And yet it was the pope who had taken a hand in arrangements for his marriage to Marie de Medici. By the standards of the time she was no longer very young and she was only the niece, not the daughter, of the reigning grand duke. However, although it was a relatively poor match on personal grounds, it was made acceptable by the bride's princely birth and the size of her dowry. The royal pair presented as dignified a front to the outside world as was incumbent upon them in the light of such circumstances. Henry IV was fond of the queen even if she did not inspire his love: taken all in all, we may venture to say that he found her quite a good companion. Quarrels between them were frequent but were always followed by reconciliation. In addition, unlike the three previous queens of France, Marie de Medici proved to be fruitful.* The royal family at last began to increase its numbers. A son, Louis, was born in the first year of the marriage, followed by two daughters, Elisabeth and Chrestienne; after them came two sons, Philippe and

---

* No children were born of the marriage of Francis II and Mary, Queen of Scots; Elisabeth of Austria the wife of Charles IX failed to produce an heir to the throne since her only child was a daughter; Henry III's wife Louise de Lorraine was childless. (V.L.T.)

Gaston (the latter being given the Christian name that had belonged to the counts of Foix), and finally a daughter, Henriette, born in 1609—making six children in ten years, equally divided between boys and girls.* One could not ask for a better balanced family.

Henry IV lived like a sultan, and it is not very surprising that he should have chosen to bring up at court the children whom Gabrielle d'Estrées had borne him. After all, they had been legitimised, and the poor woman was dead; indeed, had she lived he might have made her his queen. But the way he paraded his affairs with the marquise de Verneuil and the comtesse de Moret, both of whom also bore him children, was a rather different matter. The dauphin used to be informed of the birth of these adulterine brothers and sisters by his faithful governess Mme de Montglat—'Mamanga' as he called her; and soon he was quite capable of pointing out that they were not altogether his brothers since they 'had not come out of mamma's belly'. Even so he would generally call them *féfé*†—although when he lost his temper he was apt to say that they were no better than his own shit, for the little prince used down-to-earth language as soon as he learnt to talk.

Marie de Medici used to put up with her husband's promiscuity, for she had witnessed equally tiresome goings-on in Italy. More surprisingly, bearing in mind the relative refinement of Italian society, she was also prepared to tolerate the use of coarse language and behaviour in her presence. We know little of her youth and her past, but after her arrival in France she certainly emerges as a woman devoid of distinction who was very apt to lapse into vulgarity. In his memoirs Sully gives us to understand that she and the king used to come to blows, and tells how on one occasion he intervened and shook the queen by the arm more roughly than he had intended. Those of Marie de Medici's letters which have come down to us prove, by their fantastic spelling and half-French, half-Italian style, that she never succeeded in learning the language of her adopted country or in acquiring its culture. She appreciated the arts, or at least, as a result of her Italian upbringing, she knew that this was expected of a ruler. The mediocrity of her intelligence made her easy to influence. She was incapable of a broad view of things, but she had some sense of vocation as a ruler, and aspirations towards greatness (although she failed to discover the means of securing it), allied with a certain aptitude for business. Thoroughly double-faced and jealous for her auth-

*Chrestienne and Henriette are generally referred to hereafter as Christina and Henrietta Maria. Philippe died in 1611—see p. 72 below.

†A childish form of *frère*.

ority, she loved to occupy the chief place and was prepared to fight fiercely to retain her position; nor was she lacking in physical or moral courage. Her greatest passion was undoubtedly for the power that she held, and she believed in it wholeheartedly. In the last resort she is to be pitied, for no one loved her. She had occasion to weep at the ingratitude of her sons and daughters; yet it is impossible to say for certain whether her tears were a sign of a mother's grief or of an ambitious woman's disappointment. She was Catholic primarily by habit and does not seem to have been aware of the great resources implicit in her Faith. All her qualities as a woman were subordinated to her role as queen.

From the very day that she became regent Marie de Medici could see for herself how much prestige her position gave her. Anyone who wished to exercise any authority would have to apply to her and adapt his own interests to the degree of furtherance that she was prepared to vouchsafe them. As sole regent, exempt from the control of both relations and political supporters, she wielded complete power. The late king's ministers who had placed her at the head of the realm now became her direct partners, but she was free to dissociate herself from them whenever she chose. She had undoubtedly taken over her husband's position.

In order to grasp fully how Marie de Medici was to exercise the sovereignty in her husband's stead, it is necessary to know how the realm was governed and administered. Here we must put forward a few basic ideas which, although perhaps rather uninteresting, are indispensable to a proper comprehension of all the ensuing period of history.

Admittedly France had no written constitution, but she did possess certain political traditions which had slowly evolved over the years, and a whole corpus of political or administrative institutions. These the king had to accept, and it was necessary to treat them with consideration. It was for him to enlist their services in every possible way while at the same time taking steps to secure their obedience.

True, the monarchy was absolute. The king's will—or the queen regent's—was law. *Lex Rex*. In theory it was a matter of the king's good pleasure; but this term should not be interpreted as signifying arbitrary decision or caprice, which is the meaning commonly ascribed to it. It bore a far closer resemblance to the way in which the father of a family is responsible for the decisions necessary for the good management of his household and affairs. We must never lose sight of the paternal character of the monarchy in the seventeenth century, nor must we forget the slowness of its evolution from the feudal monarchy of the Middle Ages, some traces of which still survived.

The king therefore, though absolute, was not a despot. He governed with the advice of his subjects although nothing in the letter of the law obliged him to do so; and in certain institutions which had been formally established or had evolved with the passage of time the king found at his disposal organs that could collaborate with him in the task of governing the country or that could be used to carry out his orders. To the first category belonged the Estates-General—assemblies of considerable importance which were attended by deputies representing the three orders or estates of the realm. They were summoned by the king when he chose, generally on serious occasions, in order to acquaint him with the grievances of all his subjects and to settle with him the broad outlines of future policy.

The King's Council or Councils and the Parlements belonged to the second category. It would appear that their origins are remote. Both the Parlement of Paris (whose main features were reproduced in the Parlements subsequently established in the provinces)[1] and the King's Council were offshoots of the old *Curia regis* or *Cour-le-Roi* of the first Capetians.* They had come into being as a result of what we would now call progressive specialisation, each becoming responsible for a specific portion of the functions of the *Curia regis*. The Parlement fulfilled the role of supreme court of justice and was thus a kind of court of appeal, while the King's Council assumed responsibility for the policy and administration of the realm.

The Council was thus concerned with a wide variety of different questions: general policy, relations with foreign countries, royal finances. These involved the administration of Crown lands, the allocation of direct and indirect taxes, military and religious matters, the government of the provinces and their administration by the king's agents, the execution of justice and conflicts between different jurisdictions, commerce, traffic on waterways and the high seas—in short, everything. As the territory ruled over by the French monarchy had expanded and its interests had become more numerous and more complicated the Council's role had become progressively more and more onerous.

Who belonged to this Council? In theory all those whose advice could be useful to the king, beginning with the chancellor, who, because of the

---

* The first of the Capetians was Hugh Capet who became king in 987. The direct line came to an end with the death of Charles IV in 1328, his successor being Philippe de Valois (Philip VI).

essentially judicial function of the monarchy, was the king's most important servant and a kind of viceroy. Then there were the members of the royal family who were associated with the king's duties as a ruler by virtue of their royal blood followed by the dukes and peers, the cardinals, the great captains and the great officers of the realm.* But in practice the Council was composed of persons who were quite familiar with the various questions that were to be discussed, having already been initiated into such matters through their legal studies or administrative and political experience. In consequence those who belonged to the Council were either 'councillors born', to use a contemporary expression—men whose membership was derived from high office or high birth—or councillors who were specialists. The *conseillers d'État* of modern France form quite a good parallel with the latter, for in many respects they are their heirs and successors.

This King's Council used to assume different forms according to the questions with which it had to deal. It was divided into sections, but each of them bore the title of *Conseil du Roi* and sometimes, indeed frequently, consisted of the same people.

Thus the *Conseil d'État des finances* was concerned with matters of administration, with financial affairs and with disputes arising therefrom; the *Conseil des finances*, also known as *la grande direction*, specialised increasingly in the task of initiating and controlling revenue and expenditure. The *Conseil d'État privé et des parties* exercised supreme adjudication in matters of justice and regulated the workings of the administration, a role which falls to the lot of the present-day *Conseil d'État*. Finally came the most important Council of all, at which the king would take necessary decisions in respect of general policy and which corresponded to the *Conseil des ministres* of modern times. It was given, and during Louis XIII's reign continued to be given, a variety of different names, thereby adding to the confusion: *Conseil des affaires, Conseil des affaires et des dépêches, Conseil des dépêches, Conseil direct, Conseil secret, Conseil de cabinet, Conseil des ministres* or *Conseil d'en haut*.

Under Henry IV this Council's membership was reduced to a very small number of people, who corresponded to the ministers of our day: the chancellor, or in other words the minister of justice (first Bellièvre, then Brûlart de Sillery), President Jeannin,[2] Sully, the superintendent of finance, and Villeroy, the secretary of state for foreign affairs, the latter being assisted by his son-in-law Brûlart de Puysieulx, the son of Chancellor Sillery. But its membership could be increased, and during the re-

* For a list of some of these, see chapter 4, n. 26.

gency of Marie de Medici such a large number of people were
summoned to its meetings that there were periods when it became more
like a senate, in which effective work was no longer possible.

Thanks to the works of Georges Pagès, and to Roland Mousnier's
more recent studies, we are now quite well-informed about the organisation of the King's Council and its complicated history. The important
point to remember is that the term *Conseil du Roi* was in fact applied to a
series of Councils—namely a Council of government, in which policy
was decided, and several other Councils which were concerned with the
administration of the realm.

In the administrative sections of the Council ability inevitably counted
for more than favouritism. Unlike many of the important appointments
under the ancien régime, the office of *Conseiller d'État* could not be
bought or sold. The king used to commission members of the legal profession to hold such posts, selecting for example the masters of requests of
the household,[3] or certain counsellors from the Parlement whom he
knew to be men of parts, although naturally the value of their talents had
been enhanced by the exercise of influence in the right quarters, as has
always been the case throughout the history of mankind. Often *Conseillers d'État* were recruited from the same families, but this handing on of
methods and traditions from father to son, this continued existence of
something approaching hereditary aptitudes, helped rather than hin-
dered the efficient working of the system. It was the administrative sections of the King's Council which saved the government from becoming
the exclusive preserve of the nobility. It was these sections which prepared the Council's decrees and submitted them for the king's approval
—decrees that promulgated order and justice and regulated public and
commercial law throughout the land. The part they played was therefore of vital importance and they do not deserve the neglect with which
historians have often treated them. It was the King's Council in its administrative aspect which ensured that the French monarchy in its civil
capacity was no less important than in its military or religious capacity. It
enabled the Crown to keep step with the economic realities of the time,
to remain a living force and to adapt itself to contemporary conditions.
And lastly it both gave the monarchy a sort of bourgeois foundation and
provided the monarch himself with a reserve of competent servants
which amply justified its existence by the high standard of service that its
members could offer.

The Parlement of Paris did not, strictly speaking, have a political role.
It acted as a court of appeal in the king's name. But since a law had to be

transcribed onto the registers of the Parlement of Paris or of the Parlements in the provinces in order to become operative, it had become a recognised practice for these courts, if they saw fit, to present the king with their observations or 'remonstrances' before the transcript was made—pointing out the inadvisability of the measure in question or its incompatibility with previous legislation. The king could overrule them and compel the magistrates to submit to his will at a royal session or *lit de justice*. The Parlement had therefore a certain potential as a check to the authority of the Crown, but it did not amount to much; however, it was enough to inflate the magistrates' sense of their own importance and to make them claim that the Parlement was a political institution. We have already seen how much weight its decision carried when the regency was established, and how Marie de Medici and the little king were made to request its advice in their speeches. As a sovereign court the Parlement refused to recognise any higher authority than the king and his chancellor. It affected to regard the King's Council as a collection of clerks and domestics in the king's service—men who held no real position in the State hierarchy.

From the central government we must now turn to the provinces, and see how royal authority was exercised there.

The provinces corresponded with the various segments of which France had consisted in the early Middle Ages. Although they had since been annexed to the realm, some of them still kept their own local Estates, which used to vote their own taxes. These provinces were certainly French, but they were French with just a dash of independence and they were proud to be deemed foreign or virtually foreign. The military governorship of such provinces was regarded as a perquisite of the princes of the blood or of persons of high rank who used to be vested with the command of the armed forces that were stationed there. In addition the governor of a province enjoyed the right to appoint to a certain number of offices and thus possessed some political power. But he was neither an administrator nor a judge. These functions were fulfilled by the *baillis*, the *sénéchaux* and the *présidiaux*—the latter being tribunals which occupied an intermediate place between the *bailliages* and the Parlements. Similarly the administration of the royal domain and the assessment and collection of the *taille* were the concern of the *trésoriers de France* and *généraux des finances*, (their circumscriptions being known as *généralités*) and of their subordinates the *élus*.[4]

We have seen that such appointments were bought and sold, and the effect of this traffic in offices on a section of the bourgeoisie has already been noted. The Crown was also affected by it in a variety of different ways. The Wars of Religion had offered boundless prospects to the ambitious and adventurous nobility; but the office-holders had needed the king's authority to shield them against the overbearing tyranny of the great nobles if they were to be sure of peacefully enjoying the fruits of office. Once Henry IV became converted to Catholicism, both their own interests and their concern for the future tenure of their appointments played a large part in inducing them to rally to the king. Thus the traffic in offices had proved advantageous to the monarchy in a way that those who had initiated it for purely fiscal reasons could not have anticipated, and the bourgeoisie, by welcoming and participating in this traffic, had formed an alliance with the Crown. It was sometimes lamented that the king by authorising the *paulette* had forfeited the power to choose his officials himself. In essence the king had given up recruiting his officers and left it to the office-holders themselves; but he had not greatly weakened his own power, for the hierarchical structure of French society and the influence exercised by the chief members of the aristocracy meant that it would otherwise have been the great nobles who would have installed their followers in most appointments. Indeed it would have been impossible to resist their incessant importunities. It was better therefore that officials should only have to deal with the king, the *trésorier des parties casuelles** and the tax farmers before taking up their appointments.

In other respects, however, venality of office presented more serious drawbacks. It was prejudicial to royal authority. It made the tenure of an official post a private matter in which the king had now practically no right to interfere. It made it difficult for him to alter the way in which the duties attaching to an appointment were carried out, for incumbents of offices proved to be opposed to any change, even when it was inspired by the most praiseworthy motives. Moreover those who held these appointments, being recruited on the spot and from the same families, quite soon came to form a sort of caste, almost a new species of feudal system. In their eyes their private interests were more important than the needs of the king's service. They became addicted to routine and increasingly self-satisfied. Certainly they were loyal; but their administrative standards were mediocre and they had no interest in the public welfare.

Henceforth the king could no longer rectify the shortcomings of his officials except by placing them under the supervision of men over whom he had better control. Such were the royal commissioners who

* See chapter 1, n. 41.

used to be sent into the provinces on a specific mission and for a limited period of time. As they were not 'officers', or in other words had not paid for their appointments, they could at one moment replace a *bailli* or an *élu* who had failed to carry out his duties and at another goad others in such posts into displaying more energy. Elsewhere they might dispense justice in the king's name in a given situation: for example they might institute an official inquiry or ensure that an edict was enforced.

Only by temporarily delegating his authority in this way could the king reassert his slackening grip on the administration and re-establish direct contact with his subjects in the provinces. No other solution was open to him. The only alternative would have been for him to abolish the traffic in offices, and resume effective control over the distribution of public appointments. Such a step was contemplated in the time of Henry IV and repeatedly discussed throughout the reign of Louis XIII. One compelling reason put a stop to every attempt to reform the system. For the King's Treasury the sale of offices represented the quickest and safest means of acquiring ready money, and financially the monarchy was for the most part in desperate straits.

We have already seen that official appointments were not necessarily created in answer to some administrative need: two or three *lieutenants de bailliage* might be appointed when only one was required. The government even went further and created ridiculous little posts, such as the controllers of titles and the visiting controllers and markers of hides who made their appearance in Henry IV's reign. In consequence there used to be complaints about the excessive number of officials, just as people complain today about the size of the civil service. These complaints were the more justified because, once an office had been created, a salary had to be paid to its holder and the sums of money that were spent in this way represented a severe drain on the Treasury.

Despite this the king would often issue a decree authorising an increase in such salaries. But this step was in no way concerned with the interests of the officials themselves. It was simply yet another ingenious and roundabout method of obtaining money. If the king arbitrarily increased the value of an office, the official who held it had to make up the difference between the price he had originally paid for his post and its new valuation; in other words, the increase in salary which he eventually received represented the interest on a forced loan.

Why, we must now ask ourselves, did the finances of the Crown continually show a deficit? Even Sully in Henry IV's day had done no more than introduce a little order into the system and mitigate its most glaring defects. To remedy its abuses was beyond him, as it was beyond the power of any one man. As with many other European governments, it was a virtual impossibility for the French monarchy to count on fixed or foreseeable income upon which to base its future expenditure.

Despite the relative richness of the country the resources of the Treasury were slender. They comprised revenues derived from Crown lands and from taxes. The former consisted of forests, woods, châteaux, châtellenies,[5] mills, tolls, feudal dues and rural estates directly owned by the king through inheritance, default of heirs, reversion to the Crown, mortmain or confiscation. But the administration of the royal domain was extremely complicated since a large part of it had been mortgaged—that is to say sold to private persons, with the option of redemption.

Of direct taxes the most important was the *taille*. The Council used to determine the total amount every year, calculating roughly on the basis of the figures for previous years and estimates of anticipated expenditure. The *trésoriers de France* and the *élus* were responsible for the process of assessment and for seeing that the money was collected; but when this had been done they did not at once dispatch the amount received to the Central Treasury [*Épargne*]. They would begin by settling on the spot a large number of ordinary expenses to which their particular province was liable, and in addition to these they might also be called upon to meet unforeseen commitments which had been foisted on them by the king. The latter in fact was apt to guarantee the payment by a provincial tax-receiving office of expenses that he was not in a position to meet himself and the local treasurer would not send in his accounts until he had dealt with all these items. This sort of transaction used to take him some time. If the Central Treasury began to press him for money the treasurer simply advanced it in the form of a loan, for one of the strangest features of the French fiscal system at this time was the perpetual confusion that the contemporary official used to maintain between public funds and his own personal fortune. If necessary therefore the treasurer would lend money to the king from his own coffers, but in fact it often happened that the sum which he advanced consisted of moneys received by him as due to the king, the accounts for which had not yet been verified.

These revoltingly dishonest practices were rendered yet more frequent by the difficulty involved in actually collecting the *taille*. Throughout the whole realm there was little short of an organised attempt to evade the hated tax. Since the *taille* was a plebeian tax by nature, anyone who paid it admitted that he was a commoner. Once a man rose a little in the social hierarchy he would contrive to join the ranks of the nobility or to pass himself off as a noble (which was not beyond the bounds of possibility) in order to escape from a humiliating obligation. Failing this there were other ways of being quit of it. Some urban communities, including even small towns, had secured exemption from the *taille* by paying it in instalments; they had obtained permission to pay a specified sum annually, the amount being fixed at quite a low rate. The king had agreed to this because at all events the actual business of collection went more quickly and provoked less argument. Exemptions were numerous even among the lower orders: for instance domestic servants and tenant farmers [*laboureurs*] who exploited an estate on behalf of a lay or ecclesiastical landlord used to escape payment of the tax.* In the last resort, the only people who still paid the *taille* were those who were very poor and those who lacked sufficient ingenuity to find some method of dodging it, and even in these cases we must remember that the money would be paid over as slowly as possible, very often in the form of clipped coins and devalued currency. This used to complicate the task of those who were responsible for the book-keeping entries on the spot and reduced the returns from the tax shown in the accounts.

This was not the end of the story. There was no lack of control on the part of the central authorities. The treasurer at the Central Treasury, the *Cour des comptes*[6] and the *Conseil des Finances* all used to examine the figures submitted to them. But no one could produce strictly kept accounts and money leaked away on all sides.

There remains one problem which has never been properly investigated, although many historians have drawn attention to it and pointed out that it could become the subject of a valuable work of scholarship. The men generally held to be the most honest of the monarchy's servants —that is to say Sully, Richelieu and later Colbert, who brought about Fouquet's fall by accusing him of embezzlement—all made considerable fortunes for themselves whilst managing State finances. How did they manage to do this?

Their enemies always attributed it partly to their corrupt administration of public money. From their enemies this was only to be expected. But even their friends did not dare to maintain the contrary. When Sully was disgraced in 1611 his son-in-law the duke of Rohan wanted to

---

* For the status of *laboureurs* see the references given in chapter 1, n. 31. Loyseau writing early in the seventeenth century defined them as 'those whose normal occupation is ploughing the land for others as tenant-farmers'. In addition they often used to collect seigneurial dues on behalf of their lords (Mousnier-Pearce pp. 9, 26).

object. The duc de Bouillon decided to make him listen to reason and reduced him to silence by the following observation: 'No matter how loyal or scrupulously exact a Superintendent of Finances may be, if his conduct be straitly examined, 'twere difficult indeed not to find somewhat that he hath done amiss wherewith to reproach him withal. If M. de Sully had been indicted by the Court a way would soon have been found to make him relinquish all his charges, relying solely on methods that were fully legal and in accordance with judical procedure.' Rohan protested and replied with threats. But he did not really press the point because there was nothing more that he could say. And it was Sully of all people!

It is impossible to believe that there was much more honesty or clarity in the system of indirect taxation. Indirect taxes, which were many in number, included impositions on alcoholic liquors, known as *aides*, and the *gabelle*—a tax on salt which compelled the inhabitants of inland provinces to buy a certain quantity of salt at royal warehouses. The latter was greatly hated, and led to continual smuggling across provincial frontiers. In addition there were the customs dues [*droits d'octroi*] known as the *cinq grosses fermes*,[7] tolls which were imposed on traffic on the Seine, taxes on various commodities, and a number of special duties. It would take a long time to give a complete list. These taxes used to be levied not by royal officials but by tax farmers who had made a contract with the King.* They had paid him a lump sum representing approximately the amount which the Treasury expected an indirect tax to yield and had then assumed the responsibility for levying the tax in question by means of their own agents. They calculated that this arrangement should result in a reasonable profit for themselves.

The agreement could be good business for the Treasury and the tax farmer alike; but sometimes it turned out badly for both, for we know of a number of tax farmers who declined to renew their lease or even surrendered it before it ran out because they were being ruined. However it was generally the Treasury which got the worst of the bargain, either because it had to agree to a lower figure than that originally asked owing to a lack of bidders, or because thanks to the powerful influence of some person at court who moved in high circles and obviously had an eye to his own interests, the terms of the contract had been quickly settled in favour of a wealthy financier [*traitant*].

Such were the financial resources of the State—inadequate in scope

* I have here translated *traitants ou fermiers* as 'tax farmers' because in English it is impossible to draw a distinction between them—see chapter 1, n. 30.

and even less adequately secured; and there were many expenses to be set off against them, expenses that were both very heavy and extremely varied.

By no means all of these commitments were unnecessary. Some were concerned with the army and the external defence of the realm. We should not form too flattering an idea of the king's army at this date. Like those in other fields, appointments in the army were venal and regiments were consequently staffed by officers who belonged to the well-to-do nobility. They were undisciplined and unacquainted with military strategy. Sometimes their primary loyalty was not even to the king. The rank and file were recruited by a system of voluntary enlistment and by levying soldiers abroad. The result was an army that was neither of a high standard nor truly royal and solely devoted to the king. Such as it was, however, it had a considerable reputation on account of its size and gallantry and made France respected abroad. It would be fair to say that without her army France counted for nothing in Europe.

The decline in her military reputation, even if this reputation was exaggerated, could easily lead to France's security being exposed to the most deadly dangers within the space of a few years. But her military expenses were heavy even in time of peace when they were confined to essentials. Once they were swollen by the outbreak of civil war or war abroad they became a crushing burden on the entire country.

The court represented yet another financial burden. In the days of the Valois it had glittered in glorious splendour and later, after years of poverty and thrift, it had been reinstated by Henry IV. Here again it would be a mistake to describe the outlay that was involved as a complete waste of money. The argument advanced nowadays that the court promoted trade in luxury goods was also occasionally put forward at the time; but it still carried little weight compared with the widespread importance attached to prestige—an idea which was fully in accordance with the general outlook. In the Middle Ages the cult of the king's person used to find expression in elaborate ceremonies which had much in common with religious ritual. It was unthinkable that the king should live like a bourgeois or even like a rich noble. On the contrary he should be surrounded by exceptional splendour and magnificence. Over the years this tradition had been reinforced by the opulent and sensual luxury of the Renaissance. Under Henry IV the court very soon became sumptuous once more, although it did not as yet adopt Spanish etiquette. The numerous embellishments to the Louvre, the many fine gardens with playing fountains, the Grand Gallery that extended to the Tuileries,[8] the mirrors and pictures that decorated the palace, the brilliant costumes with their shimmering silk, the coaches, the superb horses, the tournaments, the costumed ballets,* the various pastimes—all these provided innumerable occasions for expenditure on a scale which grew heavier every year.

Both Henry IV and the queen had had their separate households, calling for a large staff of gentlemen of the bedchamber, majordomos and servants together with a military guard composed of crack regiments. The king's household cost the Treasury 400,000 livres per annum, a very high figure by contemporary standards.

As a means of strengthening the authority of the Crown, and assuming that this authority was exercised to good purpose, it was not necessarily a bad thing for the nobility to take to frequenting the court and attaching themselves to the king's person. In an age when it was the custom to maintain a following of dependants and retainers, this meant that they became members of the ruler's personal household. But regular attendance at court also encouraged an itching palm. The nobility acquired the habit of claiming as their due pensions or high offices endowed with substantial revenues, for it was these alone that enabled a noble to live in grand style and do justice to his rank. Pensions and 'charges' reached a total of two million livres during the last years of Henry IV's reign. In the year 1610 alone they rose to three million. Appetites at court were evidently insatiable.

Finally it was necessary to allow for expenses incurred in connection with foreign policy. These too served a useful purpose. Quite apart from the smaller fry, the secret informers who were practically spies, it was customary for a ruler to maintain adherents in foreign countries and to retain the services of the most influential subjects of other rulers by paying them pensions. Such practices had been converted into a positive system by Spain and constituted an element of her power in Europe. France's position would have been gravely weakened if she had not followed suit.

For the Treasury the worst problem was not so much the high price of all these commitments as the impossibility of estimating the total cost beforehand and of taking steps to meet it. The king was continually signing *acquits au comptant*—that is to say orders instructing the Central Treasury to pay out a sum of money without any explanation of the reason. As a result the practice arose of constantly resorting to uncontrollable and unpredictable withdrawals from public funds. The important point was not

* There was a close resemblance between *ballet de cour* and the English masque.

whether such sums were well or ill employed, but that the realm's finances were in consequence reduced to a state of permanent disorder—a disorder which may be described as having been legally perpetuated.

Such was the governmental and administrative machine that was now to be entrusted to the hands of Marie de Medici. Its workings were in many ways complicated and inconsistent with each other. This was the price that had to be paid for the slowness with which it had evolved over the years. It had evolved in the light of circumstances and with the passage of time, for its institutions had not been created as a result of any clear-cut ideas. A mediaeval cast of mind still prevailed. The time had not yet come for those rational and Cartesian ways of thinking which nowadays condition the attitude of the French people towards everything. It was therefore imperative for the person who controlled the system to have a will of iron. By dint of co-ordinating the workings of the machine which so often functioned in opposition to each other, by reconciling natural divergences so that its various components worked in conjunction, the imperfections of the governmental system could be reduced and made to cancel each other out. But one is left with the impression that the whole apparatus could very quickly fall apart if this control were relaxed for lack of a central unifying force; and that in that event everything—general policy, good order and the efficiency of each man's contribution to the general welfare—would slither into chaos not as a result of any malice aforethought, but (and this was surely more serious) simply because of the sheer weakness of the actual structure.

We have already given an account of the circumstances under which Marie de Medici became regent. It remained to be seen whether she would confirm the arguments put forward in her favour by continuing Henry IV's policy.

For the first few weeks nothing seemed to be changed. The same ministers remained in office. The trial of Ravaillac was quickly carried out in accordance with the horrible judicial usages of the time. He was put to the torture to compel him to give the names of his accomplices. He declared that there had been none, and stuck to his story even when Harlay, the first president, threatened to have his father and mother brought from Angoulême and burnt alive in his presence—for they too could suffer punishment for his crime.

He was condemned to be tortured with red-hot pincers on his four limbs and on each breast. His wounds were to be sprinkled with molten lead and boiling oil and his body was then to be torn in pieces by four horses, the remains being subsequently burnt. The house in which he had been born was to be razed to the ground and it was forbidden to build upon the site. His parents were ordered to quit the realm within a fortnight on pain of death while his uncles, brothers and sisters were henceforth forbidden to use the name Ravaillac. But even during the agonies of his execution on 27 May, thirteen days after the king had been assassinated and two days before his funeral, the murderer still continued to cry out that he had had no accomplices.

A few months later a woman of easy virtue named d'Escouman, who had been a prisoner at the Conciergerie[9] at the same time as Ravaillac, went to see Queen Marguerite* and offered to reveal the names of his fellow-conspirators. She claimed that the plot could be traced back to the king's former mistress, the marquise de Verneuil, and to the duke of Épernon. Marie de Medici was informed and entrusted the examination of the matter to the Parlement. Nothing serious emerged from this investigation, and to make sure that d'Escouman did not continue with her incoherent ramblings she was sentenced to prison for the rest of her life.

Although the whole episode leaves one feeling vaguely uneasy, we can hardly linger over it here; for after all, like Ravaillac's trial and execution, the d'Escouman affair did not alter the disastrous fact that the king was dead. Some historians have elected to examine her story seriously and have taken the view that there was a plot which could well have originated at the Spanish court. Sensible people are so emphatic in refusing to give credence to tittle-tattle that whenever they see signs of an unhealthy addiction to melodrama or romantic atmosphere they tend to react in the opposite direction; but to get at the truth one must not be guided by prejudices deriving from one's intellectual make-up. If we consider the matter dispassionately, what should our verdict be?

Chiefs of State have always been exposed to the risk of assassination by some fanatic simply because they are eminent figures. The man who murdered the innocent and charming empress of Austria on the quayside at Geneva in 1898 was certainly not a Russian agent. But how can we overlook the fact that political crimes were frequent in the seventeenth century? There is no denying that the death of Henry IV, in that it dealt a disastrous blow to the power of France, was for that very reason advantageous to France's enemies. Whilst we incline to the view that the murder of Henry IV was the wanton act of an isolated individual, we cannot say categorically that there was no more to it than that; but it is

* Marguerite de Valois lived until 1615.

extremely unlikely that the full circumstances will ever be brought to light.

The effect of the king's violent death and of the misgivings which it aroused in people's minds was to make those who exercised some control over public opinion pay greater heed to their duties and responsibilities. Too much publicity was still being given to theories which made the obedience owed by the king's subjects depend upon their personal opinion of his policy—especially in matters of religion. Carried to extremes, such theories almost justified regicide; with a greater degree of certainty they can be said to have encouraged inflammatory sermons by fanatical preachers, whether Catholic or Protestant. Once these preachers came down from the pulpit their feelings would subside and they failed to realise the turmoil that their words had aroused in the minds of a few scatterbrained members of the congregation. The Sorbonne and the Parlement now took action against any writings which did not lay sufficient stress on the king's independence of any other power, whether spiritual or temporal, or did not plainly assert that he was subject to no other judge save God alone. This line of attack served to bring ultramontane doctrines under suspicion in their turn, on the grounds that they seemed to allow the pope too much authority. Thus the excessively Roman views put forward in Father Santarelli's thesis were to be followed by legal proceedings[10] whereas the nuncio and the Assembly of Clergy had some difficulty in securing the condemnation of the Gallican ideas championed by Richer, the syndic of the faculty [of theology] of Paris,[11] since his claim that bishops and parish priests were the main authorities in the Church limited the authority of the Pope.*

The attitude of two of the king's relatives, Soissons and Condé, both of whom had been absent from Paris at the time of the assassination and proclamation of the regency, showed how much headway had been made by royal authority. The comte de Soissons arrived back in Paris a week later. If he fretted and fumed a little against the Parlement's ruling, it was only to alarm the queen's ministers and to give himself airs. The prince of Condé hastened to leave Milan so as to return to Paris and regain royal favour. It has been suggested—and it would have been surprising had it not been suggested—that tempting proposals were made to him at this time by the Spaniards: since Henry IV's first marriage had

---

* Edmond Richer (1559–1631). Richer's insistence that the Church ought to be ruled by the whole company of its priesthood later gave rise to the school of Gallican thought known as *richérisme*. See for example John McManners *French ecclesiastical society under the ancien régime* (Manchester University Press 1960)

been dissolved in deference to the king's own wishes,* was it not possible to question the legitimacy of his second marriage to Marie de Medici, and might not the papacy be induced to declare it null and void?—in which event Condé would be able to claim the throne. But the prince paid no attention to such idle talk. Its only historical interest lies in the fact that it serves to point the contrast between the attitude of enlightened people which expressed itself in loyalty to the Crown—a trend which had been reinforced by Henry IV's reign and was growing steadily stronger—and all the relics of the disorders of the previous century which still survived in the popular imagination.

Religious passions were still simmering, and there was a risk of their boiling over at the most trivial incident, which could easily awaken the wildest apprehensions. Marie de Medici was wise to make the confirmation of the Edict of Nantes one of the first acts of her regency, for it was precisely because public opinion had believed religion to be involved that Henry IV's foreign policy had provoked such agitation during the last months of his reign.

Let us see how this came about. We can take it as certain that Henry IV never entertained thoughts of a *grand dessein* or grandiose scheme for Europe such as Sully described in his memoirs,[12] but on various occasions he may well have spoken of the desirability of effecting certain modifications, especially in those countries where the monarchy was elective; for although he had made peace with Spain, Henry realised that the peace was only a truce, that at any moment war might break out again between two rivals whose rivalry was only in abeyance. There is no such thing as an unavoidable or hereditary conflict between two nations; but there are long periods of insoluble rivalry during which the slightest weakening of the one constitutes a dangerous temptation to the other. Faced with these unstable conditions, Henry IV was determined not to allow the king of Spain or the emperor, Philip III's kinsman and associate, to embark on any new venture. France's alliances counterbalanced those of Spain, and Henry IV could not allow them to be threatened. In particular she was the protectress of the Protestant princes of the Empire, for the latter, although the emperor's vassals, were also his enemies.

In 1609 the duke of Jülich, a rich prince whose territories lay in the Rhineland, had died without issue. His only heirs were his cousins the

---

* Henry IV's marriage to Marguerite de Valois had been childless. However the grounds on which the divorce was obtained were that no Papal dispensation had been received for their marriage despite the blood relationship between them, and that Marguerite had been forced to marry Henry against her will by her brother (Charles IX) and her mother (Catherine de Medici).

elector of Brandenburg and the duke of Neuburg, both of whom were Protestants. Henry IV was bent on supporting the claims of these princes; the emperor, asserting his right as suzerain, had sent an army to occupy Jülich under the command of his nephew the Archduke Leopold. Meanwhile the prince of Condé, displeased by Henry IV's marked attentions to his young wife, formerly Charlotte de Montmorency, abruptly left the French court and took refuge in Milan—a Spanish possession.

In reply Henry IV strengthened his alliances with Spain's enemies, the United Provinces and the duke of Savoy, and announced his intention of putting himself at the head of an army to expel the emperor's troops from Jülich. These preparations to accept the twofold challenge from the enemy represented a more forceful policy than that which he had hitherto adopted.

Public opinion in France was aroused. Some inveighed against the danger of a general war. The Huguenots, who despite the Edict of Nantes had suffered from Henry IV's accommodating attitude towards the Catholics, were delighted to see him more firmly wedded to his Protestant alliances and at loggerheads with the Habsburgs and the pope. The Catholics, who for religious reasons were once more developing a feeling of sympathy towards Spain, began to grow alarmed at the prospect of war between the two countries. How are we to interpret the situation? Even nowadays there are some historians who think that Europe really was on the verge of a general war in May 1610. They believe that Henry IV committed himself to a course of action that was to revive the traditional struggle between France and the house of Austria —a struggle that was well nigh a conflict between two different systems, one of which almost sanctioned liberty of worship and the independence of petty princes, while the other aimed at imposing despotism and unity on Europe. In short, they claim that the so-called Thirty Years War instead of beginning in 1618, really broke out eight years previously.

At the beginning of this century a Czech historian named Kybal published a work on Henry IV's policy which is nowadays largely forgotten. His book was written in Czech and therefore attracted little attention, but it was based on documentary evidence of monumental proportions drawn from most of the archives of Europe. The conclusions that Kybal reached regarding Henry IV's foreign policy were very different from those which have been summarised above. Despite his preparations for a large-scale expedition and the arrangements he made for his own protracted absence (witness the coronation of Marie de Medici), the king constantly tried to procure the pope's arbitration and sought to prevent the conflict from spreading by every means in his power. If we grant that Henry IV's intentions were far less bellicose than he allowed them to appear, this was yet another reason for his successors to find themselves in an embarrassing position as a result of his death.

Two armies had been mobilised: the first, in Champagne, was to join the various German princes outside Jülich, while the second, in Dauphiné, was to support the duke of Savoy in attacking the Milanese.[13] In the present writer's opinion it was here that the greatest danger of war lay. In the history of the seventeenth century as a whole, insufficient attention is paid to Italy, to the strategic importance of Milan and to the rivalry between France and Spain in the Italian peninsula. This rivalry was more than a tradition inspired by the wars of the sixteenth century; it was primarily due to powerful influences which still remained alive in Italy, not all of them political, for Italy provided the key to the Mediterranean and to trade with the Levant. In Germany France was confronted only by the Empire, but in Italy she was directly up against the Spaniards.

However, neither of the royal armies had actually completed their preparations and it therefore remained for Marie de Medici and her ministers to consider what was the best course to adopt. After some discussion they decided to extricate themselves, at least in part, from the promises made by Henry IV. They gave up the idea of attempting anything in Italy and confined themselves to putting Marshal de la Châtre at the head of the army in Champagne with instructions to carry out the conquest of Jülich and terminate the emperor's sequestration of the duchy. After quite considerable casualties this operation was brought to an end in August.

France's German allies had no serious grounds for complaint. But the duke of Savoy, to whom more explicit undertakings had been given by the Treaties of Bruzòlo, was well and truly left in the lurch.[14] It was tantamount to handing him over to Spain. As he himself was too tired to undertake a journey like that to Canossa,[15] he sent to Madrid in his stead his eldest son, the prince of Piedmont. The young prince had to humble himself before Philip III and implore him to protect Savoy. The king answered harshly that he was willing to vouchsafe his protection because of his regard for France and his respect for His Holiness who had begged him to do so. There is no need here to dilate on the painful role of young Prince Victor Amadeus; the fact remains that France's cruel betrayal of her ally in defiance of the recent treaties compelled Savoy to exchange

her French alliance for Spanish tutelage. A small state is not in a position
to dispense with external support: if left in the lurch by its allies it has to
submit to the strongest Power.

The queen's policy (and in the event Villeroy's policy as well) was not
simply evasive; it represented more than a volte-face, and there was no
lack of arguments in its favour. How could France possibly run the risk
of war during a regency? A royal minority was an interim period, when
the wisest course was to protect the king's freedom of action in the future
by endeavouring to ensure that his realm remained obedient and peaceful. A war would have offered Spain a pretext for stirring up trouble in
France. That would have been a fine start!

All this was true enough, but at this particular moment there was no
halfway-house where relations with Spain were concerned. She was
either a friend or an enemy. France, like Savoy, was therefore reduced to
seeking Spanish friendship. A convenient method of doing so lay to
hand. Henry IV had been the first to envisage a marriage between the
dauphin and the elder infanta, who were of about the same age. The idea
was taken up with greater interest and extended to include a prospective
marriage between the prince of the Asturias and Louis XIII's eldest sister,
'Madame Elisabeth', who had hitherto been promised to the prince of
Piedmont.*

This rapprochement with Spain, in which Pope Paul V and the nuncio
Ubaldini were said to be particularly implicated, threw the French Protestants into a state of alarm. After only a few months they lost their chief
supporter at court. Sully was driven out of the government by his colleagues, and although the queen kept up appearances by sending him a
courteous letter of regret, she did nothing to keep him in office. Then, as
he was promptly and violently attacked by his enemies, she declared that
none of these attacks affected her attitude, for she was quite capable of
distinguishing between truth and falsehood.

The Protestants asked for permission to hold a General Assembly,
which according to the regulations was supposed to consist of seventy
deputies, thirty of them members of the nobility. Permission was granted
and the Assembly met at Saumur. Its ostensible task was to draw up a list
of six candidates for the two offices of deputy general of the Reformed

* The eldest son of the king of Spain was styled prince of the Asturias. In France the
king's sisters automatically bore the title of Madame, while in the seventeenth century
the brother next to the king in age became known as Monsieur. In this book Louis XIII's
brother Gaston is variously referred to by his Christian name, as Monsieur, as duke of
Anjou, and (from 1626) as duke of Orleans.

Church; from this list the king would select the two Protestants who were to reside permanently at court to ensure that the Edicts were observed. However, the Assembly's sessions proved to be distinctly animated. They were presided over by Duplessis-Mornay, assisted by pastor Chamier,[16] and the Assembly itself was more like a council of great nobles—men such as La Trémoille, Bouillon, Rohan, Soubise, La Force, Châtillon. To cajole Sully into a better humour, the court had recently granted him a further pension of 24,000 livres. The Assembly now examined the circumstances of his fall from power and urgently requested him not to give up those appointments which he still held, namely the grand mastership of the artillery and the governorship of Poitou.[17]

It was also decided to create new circumscriptions within the Reformed Church, known as circles. The assemblies of these circles were to be responsible for presenting grievances to the court when the General Assembly itself was not in session. Voluminous and detailed memorials were drawn up protesting against infringements of the Edict of Nantes, and some at least of the Huguenot leaders would have been glad to see its provisions extended to Béarn. Jeanne d'Albret had forbidden Catholic worship in Béarn,* but it was well known that Henry IV had promised the pope to restore Catholicism there despite his mother's earlier prohibition and some thought that the papal nuncio would now venture to demand that this promise be fulfilled. By recommending caution on every occasion Bouillon aroused the suspicions of his fellow-Protestants. Indeed, rumour had it that he had been bribed by the court.

The queen's commissioners arrived to urge the General Assembly to terminate its proceedings. The chancellor accepted the memorial of grievances, promising also to renew the articles of 1605 and to allow the Protestants their places of refuge or fortified towns for five more years; but he refused to comply with the other demands that were put forward—demands which the Huguenot leaders eventually abandoned when they realised that if they clung to them they would only make themselves unpopular. They therefore submitted the names of the six candidates for the king's choice, and the Assembly of Saumur broke up apparently without having achieved anything; but at least Rohan had been designated as virtual military commander of the Protestant party, and a skeleton organisation had been formed ready for use in the event of a rebellion if a deterioration in their position made it necessary for the Huguenots to resort to such an extreme step.

The fortunes of an obscure Italian couple, the Concinis, were now

* Further details about the situation in Béarn are given in the following chapter.

rapidly entering the ascendant at court amidst a growing chorus of disapproval. The wife, Léonora Galigaï, who was Marie de Medici's foster-sister, had accompanied her to France at the time of her marriage to Henry IV. Her dandified husband Concini showed astonishing effrontery. The Concinis were amongst the first to benefit from the multitude of pensions and offices which the queen lavished upon the nobility and upon her entourage. Their meteoric rise took place within the space of a few months. They managed to purchase the marquisate of Ancre from the Humières, and Concini himself obtained the governorship of Péronne, Roye and Montdidier. Indeed, he treated with the greatest families of the land. The duc de Créqui sold him the lieutenant-generalship of Picardy;[18] Bouillon sold him the post of first gentleman of the bed-chamber. In return the customs houses at the approaches to Sedan were suppressed and the principality waxed prosperous.

But many of those who later denounced Concini as the most discreditable of all court favourites would only have had to exert themselves slightly at the outset to prevent his outrageous promotion or put a stop to it. The queen's weakness was accentuated by the tacit approval of great nobles and ministers who, although they detested each other, were jointly and severally responsible for the very same abuses.

During Marie de Medici's regency governmental methods and procedures remained as they had been under the late king. With a few exceptions the personnel and the entire administration were the same. It was the absence of a controlling authority to regulate the workings of the administration that proved disastrous, and very quickly too. Officials may have thought that they were carrying out their duties in just the same way as two or three years previously; but although their actions were the same they had lost a great deal of their efficacy. The difference was that whereas during Henry IV's lifetime the king had prevailed to a greater or lesser extent over personal interests, within a few months the reverse had become the general rule. All of them were catering for their own interests or feathering their own nests but were highly indignant when their fellows did the same without regard for the public weal.

Pensions reached a total of 4,000,000 livres in 1611; they had almost doubled in two years. But it is difficult to check the accuracy of this proportion, for many gratuities went unrecorded, and those of which we do know probably add up to less than the actual amount involved. The government did not merely try to satisfy the great nobles: it strove to content the poorer nobility also by putting a stop to the creation of new offices and by abolishing a certain number of earlier creations. In 1611 the lease regulating the collection of the *paulette* was drawn up on terms which were more favourable to the monarchy, the right to succeed to an office being restricted to the sons and sons-in-law of office-holders. By these means it was hoped to revalue certain of the important offices and to prevent an increase in the value of others. But in the following year these provisions were withdrawn because those whose interests suffered from them protested violently.

Then the great nobles placed themselves at the head of the opposition. Mayenne had died in 1611, followed by Soissons at the end of 1612. The latter had died whilst still in the prime of life—'esteemed by each and every man and beloved by all those who love good and virtue in a prince', wrote the bishop of Luçon courteously to the dead man's widow.[19] In fact the only proofs of this virtue that had been forthcoming during Soissons's lifetime had been the disputes over precedence between himself and the house of Guise, with which he had inconvenienced the regency for months on end. However there remained Condé, Conti, Bouillon, Longueville, Nevers and Vendôme, all of whom plunged into intrigues against the government despite the fact that they were gorged with favours [*prébendes*] and pensions. They left the court and withdrew to their provincial governorships. This was a serious matter; in Paris they were restless, but in the provinces they became dangerous. They re-established contact with officers in command of fortresses, with nobles bound to themselves by oaths of personal fealty and even with the king's own officials. Not a day dawned but all these different groups found something fresh to complain about. They listened with ready sympathy to the great nobles who promised them the earth and taught them to detest a government that was both unknown and elusive, a government which could no longer be identified with the familiar and venerable figure of the late king.

We must picture to ourselves provinces that were normally steeped in somnolence being roused from their torpor by the coming and going of small groups of armed men or by secret gatherings endowed with an inflated importance. There was a widespread feeling of uneasiness. The government, which was increasingly falling under the influence of the marquis d'Ancre, managed to deal with day-to-day business and struggled to contend with conflicting difficulties.

The princes, while protesting their loyalty to the king, formed a powerful party within a few months—as is shown for instance by the action of the duc de Retz and the Breton nobility in hastening to Ancenis to meet the duke of Vendôme when the latter, escaping from Marie de

Medici's clutches, returned to Brittany to resume his governorship. Condé the noblest of them all whom the queen used to call 'nephew' was pushed to the fore by the others.

One of the king's two brothers, the duke of Orleans, had died at the end of 1611 at the age of four. This meant that apart from the duke of Anjou, who had been born in 1608, the prince of Condé was now Louis XIII's nearest male relative. He thus became the second in line to the throne, his position being reminiscent of that of Louis-Philippe during the Restoration—the Bourbon of the opposition and the rallying point for malcontents. Épernon advised raising a powerful army to compel the princes to return to their obedience, being under the impression that he would in this way enter into favour once more; but Ancre, though now a marshal of France (a scandalous act of preferment), was averse to resorting to arms, perhaps because he considered that a policy based on force would serve to revive Épernon's prestige. The queen's ministers for their part advised coming to terms. In the spring of 1614 discussions were opened at Soissons; they were transferred to Sainte-Menehould, which had been seized by Condé and the duke of Nevers. The queen mother underwent the humiliating experience of negotiating with the rebels. She promised them considerable sums of money (450,000 livres) to compensate them and their party for the expense they had incurred in arming themselves against her. She consented to disband her own troops to offset the disbandment of theirs. She agreed that the marriages arranged with the Spanish royal house should not take place immediately although the marriage contracts had been signed nearly two years previously. Finally she promised to summon the Estates-General to meet at Sens within three months. This was tantamount to submitting her regency to examination and scrutiny by the nation, for to convoke the Estates-General was to initiate a large-scale consultation of the realm.

However at this point the queen was sufficiently adroit to win a short period of respite. She took the young king to Nantes, which lay within the governorship of Vendôme, one of the most recalcitrant of the princes, who was not satisfied by the Treaty of Sainte-Menehould. The Estates of the province of Brittany proved to be more amenable than anyone could have dared to hope. Of the two sons of Henry IV, they openly preferred the one who was legitimate to the one who was a bastard. Their loyalty was to their king rather than to their governor. It was like a renewal of the agreement of 1532 between France and the independent duchy of Brittany.[20]

Encouraged by this response, the queen was able to obtain a breathing space until the end of September, when Louis XIII, having completed his thirteenth year, attained his majority—which was proclaimed at a *lit de justice* in Paris on 2 October 1614.

The chancellor made a speech extolling the queen's rule, and Louis XIII, like a dutiful child, thanked his mother and begged her to retain control of the government. In effect the regency continued as before. This was followed by a fresh demonstration of the Crown's prestige, for the elections to the Estates-General resulted in a defeat for the 'princes' party'.

The three Estates which assembled at Paris at the end of October were far less exacting than might have been feared. They comprised 140 deputies of the clergy, including five cardinals, seven archbishops, forty-seven bishops and two heads of religious houses (Clairvaux and Cîteaux);[21] 132 deputies representing the nobility; and 192 representatives of the Commons or Third Estate. But behind the apparently watertight compartments into which the three orders were divided social fluidity had already made such headway that some of the deputies of the Third Estate belonged to the nobility, while of those who were bourgeois or were among the 131 office-holders who counted as such, many possessed seigneuries. By adopting the names of these seigneuries as their own they were able to appear nobles whilst still remaining commoners.

Much time was lost by disputes over precedence which not only prevented the three orders meeting together but barred the way to any common action at all. It was the clergy who reaped the advantage. Being an aristocratic order, they did not try to humble the nobility, but it was not with the second order of the realm that their sympathies lay. The clergy consisted of the most highly educated of the prominent figures at the Estates-General, of the men who were most capable of responding to abstract ideas; they knew enough about the nobility not to follow them blindly. Only one thing mattered for them—the advancement of Catholicism. They would have liked to see the decrees of the Council of Trent recognised as the law of the land, but on this point they were unable to overcome the resistance of the Third Estate. They had their revenge by making their own arbitration necessary on several occasions, and by refusing to subscribe to a motion proposed by the Third Estate asserting that 'no power on earth, whatever it be, can deprive the king's sacred person of his realm'.[22]

The French clergy acknowledged that the king held his crown of God alone and that he was supreme within his realm; but, they asked, was this a reason for denying that his subjects could be absolved from their oath of allegiance by the pope or a General Council in the event of his committing a felony or of his avowed subscription to heresy? The Council of Trent had made no pronouncement at all on this point, which had remained one of the matters on which freedom of opinion was admitted (such opinions were described as 'probable', as opposed to 'certain'). It did not behove the Estates-General therefore to lay down the law on the subject in the way that the Protestant king of England was in the habit of doing. In short, whereas the Third Estate rejected the Council of Trent because it suspected that it was too ultramontane, the deputies of the clergy refused to sanction a declaration that was Gallican because they considered it tinged with latent hostility to the Holy See.

The result was that neither view was officially adopted. The realm agreed, so to speak, to do without doctrine. This meant that whichever view ultimately prevailed would do so because it was the more effectively supported.

The unanimity with which the Estates-General called for the abolition of venality of office and of the *paulette* indicates that there was quite a strong current of opinion on the subject. But did the 131 office-holders among the Commons or Third Estate really and truly desire these changes? We may be permitted to doubt it. The Commons agreed to ask for the abolition of the *paulette*, but in addition they called for the suppression of pensions to the nobility and for the reduction of the *taille* by a quarter—an insensate demand, for it threatened to deprive the monarchy of all its sources of revenue. In the end the three orders were only united in calling for judicial proceedings against the financiers who had within the past few years signed contracts with the State. But that committed no one.

The princes had expected the Estates-General to erupt in an outburst of nationalism against the rule of a foreign queen and her Italian favourite, with the deputies demanding that they should be readmitted to participation in the conduct of affairs as the representatives of the old political traditions. It was far too simple an answer. The Third Estate suspected that it represented an attempt to revert to a feudal form of government. When the nobles went so far as to reject the reassuring picture of the three orders as three children belonging to the same family in favour of the dictum of Senecey their own president that there was as big a distance between a noble and a member of the Third Estate as there was between a master and his servant, they naïvely displayed an outlook that was both odious and out of date.

The clergy and the Commons preferred the monarchy (which they thought they would be able to influence) to the nobility, and ended by testifying to their complete confidence in the government. At the closing session on 23 February the spokesman for the clergy, Armand-Jean de Richelieu, the young bishop of Luçon, made a brilliant speech. He expressed the hope that a member of the clergy would be admitted to the King's Councils emphasising the various ways in which a cleric's personal independence was safeguarded by his calling. He praised the queen mother highly, expressed approval of the marriages concluded with the Spanish royal house and called for the restoration of the Catholic religion in Béarn.

No further formal session of the Estates-General was permitted; however the deputies carried on negotiations with royal commissioners, and on 24 March 1615 they were summoned to the Louvre. The chancellor announced that the king undertook to abolish the purchase and sale of offices, to reduce the number of pensions and to have the financiers tried by a high court of justice. But the other articles were so numerous that the king could not yet come to a decision regarding them.

It has been said that the Estates-General broke up without achieving anything. This is incorrect. The Estates-General had been summoned at the behest of the princes, who counted on its bringing the monarchy under control, but instead it had strengthened royal authority. It is to be noted that the period during which the absolutism of the French Crown was most effective begins and ends with the meeting of an Estates-General. In 1614 absolute monarchy was sanctioned by the approval that it obtained from clergy and Commons. In 1789 it was condemned because the clergy wavered and the Commons rejected it.

With circumstances so much in her favour the queen's great mistake was not to part company with the maréchal d'Ancre and Leonora Galigaï. It was essential to sacrifice somebody.

For as long as she did not dispose of an army that was ready to obey her without question, Marie de Medici was not in a position to subdue the nobility. This is made plain by the intrigues which the great nobles fomented for the next two years—intrigues which were to culminate with the ruin of Marie de Medici herself.

For the time being, however, she was sufficiently well advised to prevent the formation of too close an alliance between princes and office-holders. The magistrates of the Parlement of Paris, whose interests had suffered severely from the abolition of venality of office but who did not dare to declare themselves openly opposed to a step which was both just and generally desired, tried to assert some control over the monarchy. They invited the princes to join them in examining the memorials submitted by the Estates-General and in supervising the enforcement of the measures promised by the Crown.

The ministers induced the queen to take a firm line, but warned her at the same time that earlier edicts had provided for the continuance of the *paulette* until the end of 1618 and that to withdraw this concession was impossible. Venality of office and the *paulette* were therefore restored on 13 May 1615 for at least three years; whereupon the magistrates became more docile. They pretended to be more indignant than they really were when the queen informed them haughtily that no regency in France had been happier than hers and that she willed them to take note of it. They registered the royal decree of 27 May which annulled their previous deliberations and forbade them or their fellows to take cognisance of matters of State.

Thus the alliance between the sovereign courts and the princes was broken—an alliance which, although basically flimsy, had been dangerous at the time. The only recourse now open to the princes was civil war, and this they had some difficulty in spreading. Lesdiguières told his fellow-Huguenots that the princes were only trying to secure the expulsion of certain ministers from the Council and that this was not a matter that affected the Protestant party. Even so the duke of Rohan mustered troops in the south-west, and it was with some anxiety that the court made its way to Bordeaux, where the royal marriages with Spain were to be concluded and the exchange of princesses was to take place. Louis XIII married the little Infanta Anne of Austria while his sister, 'Madame Elisabeth', set off on her journey to the Bidassoa to take up her position as future queen of Spain.[23]

Even so, the conflict with the princes had to be brought to an end and a treaty was negotiated at Loudun (3 May 1616). Condé agreed to disband his troops if he was admitted to the King's Council. As Marie de Medici said, 'It was the dish that crowned the whole meal: M. le Prince wanted to be regent and wield the pen.'* The aged Villeroy advised acceptance, thinking that the prince would be less dangerous inside the Council than outside. This would have been sound policy in Henry IV's day, for the king would have overawed Condé; indeed even without the king the old ministers could have kept the newcomer within bounds by virtue of their solidarity. But far from showing any such feeling, their only

---

* 'C'était le dernier plat pour le dessert. M. le Prince voulait être régent et avoir la plume.'

thought was of getting rid of each other. In their view submission to Concini or alliance with Condé were simply the means of achieving this end. Villeroy had Sillery, the chancellor, driven out of the government, but proved unable to control the way the wind was blowing. Whether he wanted it or not, others were also to be disgraced. Puysieulx, his former son-in-law and the chancellor's son, soon lost his appointment as secretary of state for foreign affairs. Concini replaced him by a master of requests named Mangot. When Condé moved to Paris in the middle of the summer of 1616 his arrival was greeted with popular enthusiasm, for the queen's favourite was hated in the capital. Within a few weeks the Louvre became 'a solitude', as Richelieu puts it in his memoirs, and Condé's house became what the Louvre had been.

Sully and Bassompierre advised Marie de Medici not to allow someone who was plainly her rival to thrive on his popularity, and on 1 September 1616 she had Condé arrested. Then she was seized with suspicion of the old ministers whom she knew to be unfavourably disposed to Concini and whom she thought had been secretly won over to Condé's side. In consequence Villeroy was dismissed, together with President Jeannin and du Vair, the keeper of the seals, whom Villeroy had himself installed a few months earlier in Sillery's place.* Immediately a little 'Concini ministry' came into being which consisted solely of d'Ancre's protégés. Mangot took over the seals, Barbin, the queen's intendant, assumed responsibility for finances, and Armand-Jean de Richelieu the bishop of Luçon took charge of foreign affairs and war.[24] During the winter the duke of Nevers levied troops in Champagne and revived the princes' party. He endeavoured to recruit mercenaries even from the Holy Roman Empire. Would there never be an end to civil disorder?

Later we shall see how the young bishop who had been appointed minister for war and foreign affairs laboured, with considerable skill and energy, to restore French prestige abroad and to renew the alliances forged by the late king. But at this date no one attached any importance to what the bishop of Luçon said or caused to be said. Feeling abroad was still sympathetic to the old ministers who had been removed from power; no such sympathy was extended to Concini's creatures.

Suddenly, when no one was giving him a thought, a new character appeared upon the stage—the king. Incited by a few gentlemen in his entourage to emerge from his obscurity, he gave the order for Concini's arrest, just as his mother had ordered Condé's arrest at the end of the pre-

---

* It should be noted that Sillery could be replaced but not dismissed. See p. 156n. below.

vious summer. Marie de Medici had not noticed Louis XIII's tears when Sillery had called to pay him his respects before leaving the court in disgrace. Throughout the ill-advised struggle of the past few months between a queen increasingly dominated by her Italian favourites and the old ministers of Henry IV's day, Louis XIII had sided with the former servants of his father. Marie de Medici's regency had lasted seven years. It had been established in the first place by men who had been Henry IV's associates in order to uphold at least some aspects of his policy against the ambitions of the princes. After a few creditable achievements it had foundered during its final months in a morass of intrigue—only to give way unexpectedly to the personal rule of the young king. Even so the regency did have this point in its favour—it had safeguarded the concept of kingship. Louis XIII was already of age and a consecrated king; as soon as he made his voice heard every head was bowed.

If we have given only a brief description of political disputes which past historians used to recount at some length, it is because these dissensions were essentially the outcome of the agitation carried on by a few prominent individuals and do not represent events of major historical importance. Not one of these men had the country behind him or managed to lay hands on the complex machinery of government that has been described above. France continued to live her own life and the transformations that were taking place were outside their scope or control. The regency witnessed many such changes which, even though they formed part of daily life, made such an impact that subsequent events were to be markedly affected by them.

Economic changes were probably not especially noticeable during this period. We are still ill informed about price trends during these years, but so far as we can judge the cost of living did not fall; neither did it soar abruptly, however, as it had done in the previous century. Even so the *livre tournois*, the nominal money of the kingdom, did lose some of its purchasing power, and this probably tended to accentuate (slowly but inevitably and without unduly alarming contemporary opinion) the distances separating the various strata of society. The value of the *livre tournois*, based on the prevailing price of gold at Amsterdam, was diminishing, although there had been no official devaluation. Its value in weight of fine silver dropped from 10·98 grammes in 1602 to 10·64 grammes in 1615. Apparently this decrease in the value of the livre and consequent rise in the price of cereals and certain goods gathered momentum between 1611 and 1617.

The rise in salaries, which necessarily took place in stages, is only noticeable when comparisons are made over quite a long period. For example the average salary of a journeyman builder [*compagnon du bâtiment*] rose in Normandy from 16 sols a day in about 1597 to 20 sols a day in about 1617,[25] and that of a hired labourer provided with board [*journalier nourri*] in the *sénéchaussée* of Château-Gontier in Anjou remained stationary between 1610 and 1615. Moreover such increase in wages as did occur in certain cases was not so much a feature of the period as a belated result of the general rise in prices during the previous century. There was thus no economic revolution at this time in France as a whole.

A far more considerable change occurred in ideas and behaviour during these years. Catholicism was everywhere regaining ground; but it was a rejuvenated Catholicism, different from that which had existed sixty years earlier at the beginning of the Wars of Religion, a Catholicism at once coherent in its doctrine and multiform in its operation, capable of reaching widely different sections of society and of altering outlooks and ways of life everywhere.

Admittedly, the men of the seventeenth century were for the most part liable to religious qualms. They were neither hardened atheists nor sunk in materialism. They might wallow in superstition and be tempted by magic and witchcraft or they might respond to the true word of God as contained in the Gospel or to the mysticism of Catholic worship; they might give full rein to their vices and heap crime upon crime: but the divine spark, the sense of the mystery of death remained alive in them and it is impossible to understand the Catholic revival in human terms unless this general attitude of mind is taken into account.

The clergy knew how to make the most of it. The Council of Trent had provided them with a better defined body of doctrine: seven sacraments, Christ's real presence in the Eucharist and transubstantiation, leading to adoration of the Host; purgatory and the intercession of the saints, leading to veneration of the Virgin Mary and the saints. They were equipped with a comprehensive body of regulations relating to discipline which dealt with the pastoral duties of bishops and parish priests, the reform of religious orders, the opening of schools to train deacons. It is a serious mistake to ascribe to the Council of Trent's teaching a narrow and formalist attitude of mind as if it were a collection of short harsh directives, as if in contrast to the freedom of individual inquiry sponsored by the Protestant Reformation or to the marvellous flowering of the Renaissance which set man free in body and soul it forcibly imposed obedience on a whole generation with the help of the secular arm.

Such a misconception reveals grave ignorance of two facts. The first is that though the Council of Trent provided a definite answer to a large number of questions, there were also a great many which were left undecided and allowed to remain open to varying individual interpretations. The second is that very wide freedom of action was given in order to achieve the object in view. Only this can explain how the most diverse, not to say antagonistic, temperaments and the most numerous and varied religious groups were able to establish themselves and find satisfaction within the same Church. Admittedly, the supreme authority within this Church intervened to condemn the errors which ensued from certain proceedings on several occasions with brutal, vexatious or disconcerting effect. This did not, however, prevent the Catholic reform movement from retaining considerable flexibility. So widespread and deep a transformation would never have been witnessed if the only catalysts had been the anathema and the stake.

It was the Council of Trent that was the point of departure for everything, and without it no order could have been introduced into the Church. It was Rome that provided the impulse—the Rome of Paul V, echoing to the tapping of masons and plasterers who were nearing the end of their work on St Peter's and embellishing Santa Maria Maggiore —the Rome of the Church of the Gesù and of the Palazzo della Sapienza.[26]

The city where the supreme authority resided was the source of every stream of spiritual activity—a source to which all of them ultimately returned. French bishops no longer thought it enough for Rome merely to issue the decretals for their enthronement. Now they extended a welcome to its teaching in order to propagate it themselves. A fact of major importance was the acceptance by the Assembly of Clergy of 1615 of the Tridentine decrees, which the Estates-General had refused to make the law of the land a year previously. The Assembly declared that these decrees laid down the doctrines which were henceforth to be accepted by the Church in France and taught in French seminaries, and it ordained that all preaching was to be based upon them. This declaration has been interpreted as a first attempt at separating Church from State on the doctrinal and spiritual plane and as an act of self-emancipation on the part of the Church. However it most certainly did not mean that all the bishops in France had turned into apostles of the reform movement; still less could they be described as saints. The same defects were still to be found within the episcopate—defects which were bound up with the material interests of the monarchy as an institution. It was at about this time that Leonora Galigaï's worthless brother was made archbishop of Tours.

What mattered far more, however, was the presence at the head of the reform movement of cardinals like du Perron and La Rochefoucauld and of men like Gondi de Retz. In the provinces there were Camus at Belley, Frémyot at Bourges, La Rocheposay at Poitiers and Cardinal Sourdis at Bordeaux, not to mention Richelieu installed in that 'muck heap', the bishop's palace at Luçon. Already in 1611 we find the latter telling the royal commissioner that his churches must be restored to him. Although his diocese lay in a strongly Protestant area we see him fighting hard for 'the reform of the clergy and the restoration of discipline and ecclesiastical authority in those places which have been most infected by heresy'.[27]

The revival of Catholicism was an undertaking requiring priests who were educated and devout, but parish clergy were for the most part ignorant and uncouth. Bérulle, who was later to be made a cardinal, had become acquainted whilst in Italy with the congregation of St Philip Neri, that company of fervent and zealous men who devoted themselves to the organisation and arrangement of divine service with rejoicing and song, *in hymnis et canticis*. In 1611 he too founded a confraternity 'to instruct priests in matters pertaining to their ministry, which is an inexpressible benefit in France where there are so many priests who are ignorant'. These priests followed no particular rule: they placed themselves at the disposal of the bishops who were to make use of them within their dioceses.

A few weeks previously Bérulle had sent to the peasants of Clichy in the vicinity of Paris an exceptionally zealous parish priest named Vincent de Paul, who developed such a liking for pastoral work in consequence that a few years later he decided to repeat the experiment and went off to live among the poverty-stricken peasantry of Châtillon in Dombes.[28] In another parish near Paris (Saint-Nicolas-du-Chardonnet) a priest named Bourdoise persuaded Froger, the parish priest, to live in common with his curates, to welcome young ordinands or clergy passing through, to teach them the catechism and the conduct of divine worship and to provide them with instruction and edification in the form of retreats devoted to teaching and prayer.[29]

In this way there was gradually built up a body of clergy that was capable of reorganising parishes and encouraging the people to develop religious habits, a body of priests who were able to instil into their parishioners the doctrine suited to their needs which theologians had defined at Trent. Its range, its application were world-wide; throughout Europe and indeed throughout Christendom monks and missionaries were spreading it far and wide by the same methods.

The regular clergy too were beginning to participate in the religious revival. Gregory XV had entrusted the task of reforming monasteries in France to Cardinal La Rochefoucauld—not only a devout priest with a strong character, but also a man of wide experience who had been bishop first of Clermont, then of Senlis, and who from 1619 onwards was abbot of Sainte-Geneviève.[30] It was a formidable undertaking, not so much because of the prevalence of scandal and vice as because of the need to wage war against a feudal and particularist frame of mind which made each order (whether Benedictine, Cistercian or Augustinian) and indeed each abbey a sort of miniature aristocratic republic, jealous of its privileges and more attached to them than to the Church as a whole. Everywhere one met with an abhorrence for all that was new, a complacent or accommodating attitude towards traditional practices, a fear that a monastery would suffer humiliation and the loss of its independence through being subjected to episcopal control. Each case was complicated by external intrigues carried on by noble families with a vested interest in the election of heads of religious houses—an interest based on their claim that their younger sons should benefit thereby.

However, by means of very modest expedients, by reforming a monastery or by transferring a few monks from one that had been reformed to another where the monks were refractory, some successful results were achieved. But there were so many factors which encouraged resistance to reform or a reversion to the convenient arrangements permitted earlier that these results remained precarious.

It was sometimes easier to win over the abbesses, for women were temperamentally readier to extend an enthusiastic welcome to the ideal that was set before them. It was now that there arose those great Benedictine abbesses portrayed in the Abbé Brémond's *Invasion mystique*, which is based on the writings of Mother Marie-Jacqueline de Blémur[31]: Marie de Beauvillier, abbess of Montmartre, Marguerite d'Angennes, abbess of Saint-Sulpice, Charlotte Flandrine de Nassau, abbess of Sainte-Croix de Poitiers, Claude de Choiseul-Praslin, abbess of Notre-Dame de Troyes, women of noble blood who, to reduce their flocks to order, were ready to wield the crozier as if it were a sword. This is only just a figure of speech. In their case the influence of nepotism (I had almost said of heredity) led to unusual consequences. They used to take their nieces to live with them whilst still very young; in this way a niece would be brought up in her aunt's convent to become first her coadjutrix and then her successor, appointed as guardian of her handiwork.

But how can one forget their rivals, who came from the bourgeoisie—in particular that admirable woman Angélique Arnauld, the Cistercian of Port-Royal, the heroine of the *Journée du Guichet* who reformed her abbey?[32] At Port-Royal, as in every convent, Mère Angélique's victory represented the triumph of monarchical authority over feudal codes of behaviour, of the rule of the order over privilege, and of the spirit of faith over free and easy ways. There were plenty of amiable canonesses who had converted their cells into small private parlours, and there was not one of them but was perfectly happy to sing psalms, while her thoughts ran on stroking her cat or on sampling her jam. They prided themselves on their beautiful rosaries and starched linen surplices. They gave and received presents, and inherited property which they administered themselves. It was women such as these who had to be turned into cloistered nuns.

The sign that a community was undergoing reform was very often its transfer from countryside to town. There it would be closer to churches, to preachers and to spiritual directors. For the religious community the country no longer represented a solitude or a wilderness or a colony of ascetics like the hermits of the Thebaid.[33] On the contrary, it meant a manorial estate and an agreeable stay in rural surroundings. In contrast the iron gates and cloister walls that enclosed an urban nunnery also safeguarded the spiritual regeneration of those within.

Through the reform of the old religious orders France rediscovered the spirit of mediaeval Christianity. Through the new religious orders she entered into contact with the spirit of the Counter-Reformation.

New centres of prayer and penitence came into being. Mme Acarie, a Parisian lady of bourgeois extraction with legal connections, was responsible for installing some Spanish Carmelites in the capital.[34] The strict rule recently espoused by St Teresa of Avila was passionately adopted by a number of Frenchwomen in a spirit of infectious fervour and self-sacrifice.

The Capuchins, with their rough serge cowls and bare feet, with their lives devoted to penitence and their essentially practical preaching intended for the poor and lowly, seemed to offer a striking contrast to the nobility, with their dash and swagger, and to the humanists, with their intellectual subtleties. However it was often noblemen and humanists who flocked to swell their numbers. Thus Ange de Joyeuse,

Épernon's brother-in-law and brother of an admiral and a cardinal, became a Capuchin after he was widowed and after many years of worldly and political success. The pious Benet of Canfield,[35] who was known to be endowed with a spiritual fervour that sometimes transported him into an ecstasy, introduced into the order a young humanist named François le Clerc du Tremblay, later to become the celebrated Father Joseph. The simple way in which the Capuchins sang the office and the care which they lavished on their churches, whose altars they decorated with flowers (a custom hitherto unknown in France), attracted the faithful. Moreover the Capuchins did not confine themselves to prayer; they were men of action too. Their mobility, their contact with their fellow-friars in other lands, both neighbouring and distant, meant that they were often employed far from their own monasteries on difficult and ambitious missions to the great men of the day, as if the lowly habit that they wore, by enabling them to come and go unnoticed, would be all the more effective a cover to their secrets.

But no religious order surpassed the Society of Jesus in the abundance and diversity of its activities or the variety of means at its disposal. It was omnipresent, and was at once loved and hated, praised and criticised. Like the emperor and the king of Spain, the king of France used to choose his confessor from among the Society's priests. Father Cotton fulfilled the same functions in respect of Louis XIII as had been entrusted to him by Henry IV. Jesuit colleges brought about a revolution in the type of education favoured by noble and upper-middle-class families. Hitherto young men of good family had been handed over to private tutors and had been taught a scattered selection of subjects, of which the most important were riding and dancing. Now the Jesuit Fathers gave them a complete education, extending over several years spent as boarders in Jesuit colleges. Young men were prepared for the role they would have to play in society: the culture of the humanists was instilled into them, they were nurtured on Latin and literary studies, they were trained to speak elegantly, their characters were moulded, they were inculcated with a sense of the spiritual life, and the regular observance of devotional practices was encouraged. The strongest argument in favour of the Jesuits was the affection that they inspired in their pupils. It was the underlying cause of their success, and of the favour with which it was the fashion to view them.

Establishments for educating girls drew their inspiration from the example set by the Jesuits. Mme de Saint-Beuve (a devout friend of Bérulle and Mme Acarie who was charmingly nicknamed 'la Sainte

Veuve') established the first Ursuline convent in Paris in 1604. The Ursulines were an Italian order founded by St Angela Merici in the previous century, and Ursuline houses attached to a number of different provincial congregations were soon to flourish all over France. It was these convents which prepared the brides-to-be for the pupils of the Jesuits—girls brought up in the same spirit and trained in the same religious observances.

The consequences of all this religious activity became very noticeable around 1615. There were many converts to Catholicism from among the Protestants. It may be argued that these converts included people with an eye to the main chance. Thus it is easy to draw a contrast between the obstinate tenacity of Sully or Duplessis-Mornay and the very advantageous change of religion soon to be made by Lesdiguières, while so far as contemporary writers are concerned one can say that the conversions of Théophile de Viaud, Saint-Amant and Boisrobert, all three Protestant by birth, were in each case inspired by opportunism. But this very opportunism reveals the existence of a general trend which it was impossible to check. Was it not said of Saint-Amant 'that it is exceedingly probable that in course of time he will end by adhering to the religion of the realm in the depths of his soul'?[36] Had not Father Joseph's mother been brought up as a Calvinist? Undoubtedly Protestantism still was, and would long remain, very powerful, while the free-thinkers, who often concealed their beliefs from the outside world, could still attract willing initiates to the small groups in which they used to meet in order to promote their views. But neither of these factors detracts from the progress made by Catholicism during the first decades of the seventeenth century. Unquestionably each generation had its own spiritual complexion, and there can be no doubt that, to a far greater extent than their elders, the men born around 1600 (Louis XIII was born in 1601) were not only Catholics but very apt to become Catholic devotees or *dévots*.

However, it was not only a question of the Catholic Church winning converts from among heretics or enemies. No less significant was the improvement in behaviour and in the observance of Christian ethics in circles where there was a Catholic tradition.

One day the general of the galleys, Gondi de Retz, who was a nephew of the bishop of Paris, planned to fight a duel. Vincent de Paul spoke to him confidentially after saying Mass: 'Allow me to tell you something in all humility, Monseigneur. I know on good authority that you intend to fight a duel. But I tell you solemnly in the name of my Saviour whom I have just shown you and whom you have just adored, that if you do not abandon your wicked intent He will execute His justice upon you and upon all your seed.'[37] The general of the galleys gave way and renounced his plan.

By bringing their influence to bear, by daily acts of intervention of this nature the enlightened members of the Catholic clergy were effecting a change in codes of behaviour; indeed it could be said that they were shaping a new society.

Two books in particular contained the practical teaching which was to give French society spiritual sustenance—the *Spiritual Exercises* of St Ignatius Loyola and *The Introduction to the Devout Life*.[38] The general principle was that love of God and the spiritual life should not be confined to church and cloister. All stations of life and every action committed within the course of a human life should be imbued with the Christian ideal and tend towards salvation. A Christian had to be devout; hence the important place allotted to prayer and meditation, a place far larger than in the past, and—for such comparisons can help us to understand the situation—probably larger than in our day.

This was not the same thing as mysticism, for mysticism is a state which some souls cannot attain. The emphasis was rather on loving God, on sustaining religious fervour by spiritual exercises, by meditation, by the use of rosaries, by regular reception of the sacraments and by adoration of the Host. These zealous Catholics or *dévots* were people with an inner spiritual life which they were encouraged to develop. They were also enjoined to show concern for their fellow-creatures, assisting them in their sufferings and seeing in them the suffering members of Christ. They were bidden to alleviate bodily pain in order to bring about the liberation of the soul. This attitude of mind could inspire an outpouring of truly brotherly love from one social group to another. It also explains the existence, in a world where distinctions between classes bulked large, of a powerful impulse to give help capable of overriding all social barriers.

Later, as trends of thought tended to harden, a division arose between those who belonged to circles that were zealously Catholic and those who declined to follow suit. But at the time of which we are writing, the *dévot* was inevitably brought into daily contact with relations or friends who were not, or were not yet *dévots* themselves and had to be won over by persuasion. In consequence these new religious trends were steeped in the general atmosphere of the age. It is tempting to apply the term 'baroque' to different aspects of Louis XIII's reign, and it is certainly necessary to use some specific epithet to describe an outlook which is no longer that of the pagan Renaissance, with its love of antiquity, but has not yet attained the equilibrium of classicism, poised between the forces of reason and emotion. The spirit of the age of Louis XIII was generous and still richly imaginative. Nothing human shocked its sensibilities. Readiness to make use of violent or exaggerated language was a common feature of secular and religious literature alike. Spanish and Italian ideas and tastes were mingled with the old Gaulish or Gothic substratum. The decoration and iconography of the new churches of the day illustrate this twofold influence. The old national themes and traditional saints of mediaeval France (Radegonde,[39] St Louis, St John the Baptist and the Virgin Mary) were supplemented by new themes which served to propagate devotional practices derived from southern Europe—the cult of the Infant Jesus and the Holy Family, devotion to St Augustine and the Doctors of the Church.[40]

Henceforth it was impossible for the Protestants not to feel alarmed. They could not but realise that the Catholic revival was gaining ground at their expense, that the extirpation of heresy was one of its avowed aims, and that their privileges, which were at the best of times ill defined, were going to be subjected to criticism or whittled away; nor were there enough ways available to them for countering this threat to their position. They felt themselves to be overwhelmed, the more so because it was among influential circles that the Catholic revival was making most headway. The best that the Protestants could do was firstly to maintain their positions obdurately in those areas where they were most firmly established and where Catholicism remained forbidden—in their fortified towns, in La Rochelle and in Béarn; and secondly to gather round some great noble who would be able to defend them by force of arms. This great noble was first and foremost Henri de Rohan, who may be said to have occupied the position of a kind of constable of the Protestant armed forces.

There is no denying the fact that during these years the government was subjected to a large number of pressing representations, all of them marked by hostility to the Protestants. Henry IV had postponed the settlement of various burning questions such as the restoration to the bishops of Béarn of property that had formerly belonged to the Church. The nuncio Ubaldini was sorely tempted to demand that promises made earlier should now be put into effect—promises which the queen and the young king would find it all the more difficult to evade because, in the troubled state of their realm, they were fully aware of the value of the

Church as an ally. La Rocheposay, the bishop of Poitiers, had refused to open the gates of his city to the prince of Condé in 1615, thus giving striking proof of a feeling of loyalty to the Crown of which the nobility were apparently incapable. As an outstanding reformer Cardinal La Rochefoucauld was one of those to whom the court was particularly ready to give ear, and we must add that his views were always those of a man of sound judgement and fine character. Bérulle also enjoyed great authority, and although he avoided accepting the bishopric that was offered him it was not long before he was to receive a cardinal's hat. In addition, had not the bishop of Luçon, at the Estates-General of 1614, gone so far as to call for the admission of a churchman into the King's Councils?

Now that he had assumed power himself, would the young king try to obstruct the movement in favour of Catholics and Catholicism, or would he, on the contrary, enlarge its field of action?

CHAPTER THREE

Louis XIII and the Catholic Cause
(1617–24)

WE KNOW a good deal nowadays about the childhood of Louis XIII and about his appearance and character at the time of his coup d'état when he was sixteen and a half. The diary kept by Héroard, his physician, provides us with a day-to-day record of his health, and Louis Batiffol's painstaking and elegantly written studies of the king at the age of twenty make him seem close and familiar to us as a person.

At a time when the idea of monarchy had gained increased acceptance in the realm, but when obedience to it was far from being generally admitted, the French throne was occupied by a youth who held a surprisingly strong belief in his mission. He was proud of being king and impatient to exercise his authority.

His mind gave no evidence of any outstanding qualities, nor did his thin body and bony face with its projecting jaw exercise any attraction. Yet one cannot but have a high regard for his admirable strength of will despite what seems to have been naturally poor health. In the last century liberal historians almost invariably held it as a grievance against kings for being what they were; they even blamed them for the shortcomings in their upbringing. One wonders whether had he lived in our own day, medical science and a more enlightened education might not have made a different man of Louis XIII. Nothing is more moving than a complaint which he uttered during the very last hours of his life, perhaps the only complaint he made during an agony endured with a resignation that set an example to everyone. 'I have had the unhappy lot of all great men —which is to be committed to the charge of physicians.'

In spite of, or rather because of, the attentions with which he was surrounded—for he was continually being supervised, dosed, purged and bled—Louis XIII trailed his shattered health about with him all his life, his most frequent ailments being attacks of enteritis which left him exhausted in body and dejected in spirit. His miseries increased and worsened with the years, until they no longer allowed him to support the difficulties and crushing burdens of his calling and at the same time to remain fully balanced. He was by nature suspicious, and he became neurotic. But it would be a great mistake to think of him as a dreamy or

Map 2 South-west France

weak creature easily subjected to another's will who was fortunate enough at a certain point in time to meet Richelieu and fall under his domination. The ensuing pages of this book will abundantly prove the contrary.

The fundamental point about Louis XIII is that he was very highly strung and in his case, as in the case of all such people, it is extremely difficult to distinguish between traits which were due to his physical make-up and traits that derived in the first place from his innate disposition. No one has expressed it better than Richelieu in his *Testament politique*: 'Your Majesty's mind rules your body so completely that the slightest access of emotion affects your heart and reacts upon your whole organism.'*

This is followed by a remark which is less valid in that it falls into the common error of underrating the physical infirmities of those who suffer from their nerves, and of ascribing them instead to imagination or to insufficient will-power. 'As a result of my experience on a number of occasions I am so sure of the truth of this observation that I can safely say that I have never seen your Majesty ill for any other reason.'[1]

However impeccable the motives of those who were responsible for his upbringing, and however much they wished him well, the fact remains that instead of guiding the evolution of the young king's character they resorted to coercion and never helped him to turn his natural propensities to account. He had a violent temper and was both wilful and apt to be moody. On the one hand he was encouraged to be conscious of his intrinsically privileged status, which had the effect of fostering his pride; on the other hand he was treated in a way that was humiliating and frightening. Henry IV used to tell Mme de Montglat to beat the dauphin as often as possible, being convinced that it was the best way to make a man of him and to strengthen a king's will. This treatment did not mean that Louis XIII was unhappier than other children, nor did he think himself a martyr, for such were the customs of the time; but it did lead to innumerable scenes which had the effect of stretching his nerves to breaking point instead of bringing them under control as his nature required. His extreme sensitiveness, which was basically feminine, meant that he needed affection and tenderness. It made him receptive to religious emotion and to all forms of beauty. He showed considerable aptitude for the arts. He was a musician—that is to say he was not only fond of music but also composed it.[2] He drew with elegance and good taste.

---

* *'L'esprit de V.M. dompte si absolument son corps que la moindre de ses passions saisit son coeur et trouble toute l'économie de sa personne.'*

He was from his early days extremely devout, with a real love of God, the Virgin and the saints, and ready to resort to prayer, which gave him calm, consolation and strength. But his suspicious nature, as well as making him distrustful of others, also caused him to be overscrupulous. He hated sin like all believers, but his dread of it was altogether excessive. His religious beliefs both sustained him and disturbed his peace of mind. He had been taught to be on his guard against the sins of the flesh. An unfortunate attempt at carnal relations with the young queen which he was allowed to make at the time of their first meeting in Bordeaux, when he was only fourteen, aroused in Louis XIII such a repugnance for physical love that it took him several years to overcome it. Not until 1619 was their marriage consummated.

Thereafter Louis XIII was the husband but never the lover, either of his wife or of any other woman. His need for love and tenderness remained unsatisfied all his life. Marie de Medici was only his mother in official declarations; he only knew her in her capacity as regent or as a person of very high rank towards whom he had certain religious and State obligations. He never knew what it was to be deeply loved—hence his attempts to find emotional satisfaction in relationships that were filled with tenderness and affection. Yet he knew that too fond a relationship was forbidden him, and was the first to deny himself such an indulgence —as in the case of his love-affairs with innocent girls like Mlle de la Fayette and Mlle de Hautefort, whom he made his sweethearts but not his mistresses. Her whom he loved most he conducted to a nunnery, and this with the full approval, indeed with the connivance, of contemporary society, for in Louis XIII's day it was held that anything which ended at the steps of an altar ended well. He also went through phases of ardent devotion to others of his own sex. In his youth he was attracted to men older than himself, of whose distinction and glamour he formed an exaggerated opinion; later he turned to younger men, and for a time he would fancy that he loved them as if they were his sons. There were moments when he felt a deep affection for Richelieu. But it was never long before Louis XIII developed suspicions about those whom he loved.

'If two people have a conversation His Majesty takes umbrage,' observed the cardinal,[3] particularly if he was passionately attached to one of them. Such traits were the combined result of an education which had repressed his sensitive instincts from his early youth and of his own unfortunate destiny as a person never to meet with the affection that might have made him completely happy.

If ever the expression 'happy as a king' really seems preposterous it is when it is applied to Louis XIII. Had he been an ordinary country gentleman happiness would not have been beyond his reach; but his position as king caused him to grow into a man who throughout the thirty-three years of his reign was never content, but was always too proud to complain. When the time had come for him to leave the affectionate custody of his guardian Mme de Montglat, the young king's education had been directed toward the profession of arms. He was trained in different forms of physical exercise. At Pluvinel's academy he learnt to become an excellent horseman.[4] He had early shown a fondness for the chase, which in turn developed his liking for warfare and inured him to fatigue and bad weather. All his life he was a king on horseback, a king who was used to commanding troops and ready to risk his own skin without hesitation, a king whose long rides across country brought him into direct contact with his realm. He thus came to know the country people, whom he saw with his own eyes as his father had done; he came to know the towns in the provinces, where he used to put up for the night with one of the inhabitants and sleep in a room which would be comfortably or only barely furnished as the case might be. Undoubtedly this represents the most successful part of Louis XIII's upbringing. He might have become a sham king, a king who appeared only in religious ceremonies or among his courtiers. His contact with the broad mass of Frenchmen brought him close to his contemporaries; it was this, the most endearing feature of his complex and tortured personality, which more than anything else gave strength to his rule.

The man responsible for the young king's decision to seize power was Charles d'Albert de Luynes. It was a step that was both the most natural and the most surprising thing imaginable. It was natural because the king had attained his majority; it was surprising because no one had anticipated it.

Luynes was considerably older than the king, having been born in 1578. He was thus thirty-nine years old in 1617. He was a very handsome man and a good horseman. He had induced his master to take an interest in small things as well as great, for at the outset he had helped to make Louis XIII's daily life less empty and monotonous by training hawks for the chase and by accompanying him on such expeditions, which constituted the young king's favourite occupation. His devoutness encouraged Louis XIII to trust him. Moreover Luynes was a good conversationalist, and contrived to say things which allayed his master's misgivings and flattered his pride. Within a few months he had come to occupy a very important place in the life of the young king, who was amazed to find how much their tastes coincided and thought that he saw in his friend the model gentleman that he himself wished to become. There was nothing remarkable about Luynes's social background; he came of a good Provençal family, nothing more. He had introduced his brothers, Cadenet and Brantes, and his cousin, Modène, to the king's close acquaintance. Out of a small group of 'persons of no consequence', consisting of Marsillac, an outcast from the prince of Condé's household; Tronson, 'a man meanly accounted at court'; Déageant, formerly one of Barbin's clerks; Deplan, a mere soldier of the guard; and a gardener at the Tuileries, Luynes had built up around the king a clique of people with such obscure antecedents that it was almost humiliating. They formed a camarilla which gave offence to no-one.

Luynes was the only person who counted. He has been so vilified that it is still difficult to make up one's mind about him. Even if he was the coward his enemies have made him out to be, he was certainly no fool. The queen mother knew that the king was devoted to him, and had had occasion to negotiate with him several times, especially during the last troubled months of her rule, when her need for allies, however humble, was becoming imperative. Richelieu, who was then trying to draw away from Concini (and who later stated in one of those apologies which people used to enjoy writing in the seventeenth century that he had intended to retire from office), made one or two gracious overtures in the same direction; but these were merely standard examples of a contemporary courtier's politeness, for Richelieu had no inkling of what might happen. Now Concini was dead, and the king for all his taste for power felt himself incapable of ruling without help.

Luynes, his saviour, was the only person whom he trusted, and he meant to have him always by his side. To deal with the actual business of government, about which Luynes knew little—although he had no intention of ignoring it—the old ministers were recalled to office. 'Father, do not forsake me,' the king exclaimed on receiving Villeroy, who had hastened to offer his congratulations. At a pinch Richelieu should have been able to worm his way into the new ministry thanks to Luynes's favour; but Villeroy could not abide him, and so the young bishop of Luçon was also involved in the downfall of Concini's party.

Within a few days everything was altered. The Paris mob, wildly excited by the sudden turn of events, dug up Concini's corpse, which they proceeded to mutilate and drag through the mire. Leonora Galigaï was imprisoned, pending her trial for witchcraft, and then condemned to be beheaded. Such was the courage with which she faced her end that the hatred which the people of Paris bore her turned to pity.[5] For a few days the queen mother seemed to fear for her own life. She was requested to remove herself to Moulins, where she held the governorship. Separated from all her children she took up her residence in the château at Blois until such time as a palace could be made ready for her. Richelieu returned to his bishopric of Luçon, where he set about composing polemics against the Protestants; but as it became known that he was corresponding with the queen mother, he was shortly afterwards ordered to quit the realm and go to Avignon, which was papal territory. Pope Gregory XV, who was anxious to implement the reforms laid down by the Council of Trent, protested against a measure which forcibly inhibited a bishop from carrying out the duty of residing in his diocese. Cardinal Borghese declared to the French ambassador that his government had set an example pregnant with dangerous consequences, and that 'if a king as pious as His Most Christian Majesty Louis XIII used bishops in such wise, albeit with some cause, other princes and potentates would in the event enter upon all manner of violent proceedings and oppressions against persons ecclesiastical, both wrongfully and without cause'.

As pious as Louis XIII! Indeed, the young king had demonstrated his zeal for the Catholic faith by the very first actions of his personal rule. Exactly two months had elapsed when on 25 June he signed an edict ordering the pastors of the Reformed Church in Béarn to hand back to the Catholic Church property which had been in their hands since the time of Jeanne d'Albret.[6] This was not a new departure. We have already seen that Henry IV had undertaken to re-establish Catholicism in Béarn, but realising the difficulties involved both he and the queen mother had avoided taking any action. Unlike them Louis XIII did not hesitate.

This step, apparently of only minor importance, was soon to rekindle the wars of religion. And perhaps it was yet another religious scruple which made the king decide to convoke an Assembly of Notables at Rouen in October of the same year. The promises made to the Estates-General had not yet been kept, especially in the matter of the purchase and sale of offices. The king desired to submit several plans for reform to representatives of the nobility and clergy and of the sovereign courts. This Assembly of Notables was to some extent an enlarged Council. The choice of Rouen was no doubt dictated by the fact that Luynes had just been appointed lieutenant-general of Normandy, the governorship of which was held by the queen mother.

The Assembly did not meet until December 1617. To it were summoned eleven deputies for the clergy, thirteen nobles (nine Catholics
and four Protestants, including Duplessis-Mornay, the governor of
Saumur) and twenty-seven members of the office-holding class
—presidents or attorneys-general[7] from the Parlement of Paris and from
the *Cours des Aides* and the *Chambres des Comptes* of Paris and Rouen.
Nobles and magistrates claimed precedence over each other: the former
maintained that the latter belonged to the Third Estate, to which the
magistrates retorted that the Assembly was not an Estates-General, and
that since magistrates could try nobles they should in consequence have
precedence over them.

The king submitted twenty proposals to the Assembly. Those of its
members who were office-holders had given up any hope of preventing
the abolition of the *paulette*, but petitioned that they be granted exemption from the forty-day rule. The king and his councillors listened to
their remonstrances, but nevertheless the *paulette* was abolished without compensation. An edict published during the course of 1618 also
put a stop to the purchase and sale of certain offices in the king's household.

The king even promised to abolish venality of office throughout the
whole realm, but admitted that he had not the financial resources to do so
under present conditions: a few more years of peace and tranquillity
would be needed before such a step could be taken. He was far from realising that his policy had already begun to endanger his prospects of
achieving the hoped-for result.

First let us look at the situation within the realm. The weakness of
Louis XIII's government leaps to the eye precisely because of its resemblance to his mother's regency. Although it benefited from the young
king's prestige, for he was more popular than the queen mother, the new
régime had the same characteristics as its predecessor: a weak ruler
unable to overcome the inertia and addiction to routine of his ministers,
and beside him a favourite who was busy accumulating in his own hands
every token of royal favour, whose privileged position caused widespread jealousy and who in the eyes of the public bore the responsibility
for every source of grievance.

Luynes had unwisely accepted a number of high offices, several of
which had been stripped from the two Concinis. He had allowed it to be
noised abroad that he was to marry the king's half-sister, Mlle de Verneuil, an illegitimate daughter of Henry IV. The match that he did in fact
make at the end of 1617, although not with a member of the royal family,

was certainly a splendid one; indeed it was almost provocative, for it united him, a mere squireen, to one of the most illustrious houses of France. His bride was Marie, daughter of the duc de Rohan-Montbazon, a dazzling fair-haired beauty in the prime of youth, who was both intelligent and ambitious. Under the name of her second husband, the duke of Chevreuse, she was to show herself a queen of intrigue throughout the entire reign of Louis XIII and during the Fronde, assuming the attributes of a legendary heroine in history and literature alike.

At first Luynes had pretended not to take part in meetings of the Council, but the king, with his stammer and timidity, was incapable of controlling its deliberations. The duke of Épernon was trying to pick a quarrel with du Vair, the keeper of the seals, who used to exchange insults with Chancellor Sillery in open Council in the king's own presence. The latter's authority suffered from such scandalous behaviour. The discontent of the great nobles, their mutual jealousies, the impression of mediocrity given by the king's ministers were all reminiscent of Concini's day and justified the comment of the duc de Bouillon, a contemptuous spectator of this sorry state of affairs: 'The tavern's the same; 'tis but the sign that's changed.'

But still more serious was the fact that French foreign policy had stagnated since Henry IV's death and this at a time when events of great importance were taking place in Europe.

Throughout the regency of Marie de Medici a steady decline in French prestige had been observed in Europe. France no longer took the initiative. Her ambassadors, who continued to receive their instructions from Villeroy and Puysieulx, the late king's ministers, derived a certain satisfaction from being able to pursue their habitual routine undisturbed. But this was precisely where the trouble lay: the habitual procedures, the routine approach were gaining a foothold everywhere. Moreover France's allies—the United Provinces, the German Protestant princes and the Venetian Republic—had learnt from the unhappy fate of the duke of Savoy. They had realised that henceforth they would be left to fend for themselves.

Opposite France loomed the house of Austria with its ambitions for dominating Europe, or at least the whole of the European mainland. Across the slow-moving centuries of the Middle Ages memories of the Roman Empire had been handed down from generation to generation. Feudalism had broken Europe into such small fragments that it was as if she had crumbled into particles of dust; and more recently she had been torn asunder by religious struggles. But divided though she was, she yet cherished a kind of nostalgia for her past unity. The formation of the great nation-states of England, France and Spain represented no more than a stage on the road towards its recovery. The Catholic Church, even if there was no longer any question of her establishing a temporal theocracy, did stand for a spiritual unity that transcended national distinctions, for all those who adhered to her were at least united by a common faith. Thus there was everywhere a kind of yearning for a common order of things, one might almost say a spiritual acquiescence in the idea. But no less strong was the tenacity with which rulers and subjects clung to their special privileges, without which they would not have felt themselves free. In short, Europe oscillated between the idea that she was intended to exist as an entity and a dread that any such consolidation would be brought about forcibly at the cost of each state's independence and of each man's personal right to order his daily life, his thoughts and his own affairs as he chose.

The power of the house of Austria was still considerable. There had been a time when the Emperor Charles V had been the equal of Charlemagne. A stained glass window in Ghent Cathedral illustrates this apparent achievement. He is represented as the supreme sovereign, surrounded by the great monarchs of Europe as if they were so many vassals. There is his brother Ferdinand, king of the Romans and master of the Alpine lands of Austria—Ferdinand, who by marrying the last of the Jagellons had established himself in Bohemia and Hungary.[8] There is his son Philip, who by his marriage with the queen of England had brought two great monarchies together. There are his two brothers-in-law Francis I, king of France (his antagonist for many years, but with intervals of reconciliation and friendship) and the king of Portugal, also both his enemy and his near kinsman.

Charles V had never succeeded in reducing Europe to lasting or definite submission. His destiny had been tragic rather than glorious, with war raging everywhere, even within the Empire.* But even so, what greatness was his! Above all, the unprecedented, fabulous achievement of founding a vast Empire beyond the seas, thus converting the Atlantic Ocean into little more than a wide Spanish canal, traversed by a succession of fleets laden with spices and ingots of gold and silver. Power of this magnitude, whatever its inherent defects, could only weaken very gradually.

---

* In addition he had to contend with one particular handicap that is insufficiently recognised: continual financial difficulties which interfered with his projects. (V.L.T.)

At the beginning of the seventeenth century the Habsburgs found themselves confronted with two bastions both of which had hitherto proved impregnable: England, whose sea power was expanding at their expense, and France, whom they had failed either to conquer or to reduce to a state of vassalage. They had been obliged to let her keep Burgundy and had barely succeeded in driving her out of Italy. Moreover the house of Habsburg had by this date split into several branches. From Madrid King Philip III, the son of Philip II and grandson of Charles V, ruled over Spain, Portugal and America. He also possessed the duchy of Milan and the kingdom of Naples in Italy, and in addition he was supreme sovereign of the Spanish Netherlands. In central Europe Philip III's cousin, the Emperor Matthias, was king of Bohemia and Hungary, archduke of Austria and suzerain of Alsace, while yet another kinsman, the Archduke Ferdinand, held Styria and certain territories bordering on the Alpine and Adriatic frontiers of the Venetian Republic.

With considerable skill Spanish policy had succeeded in maintaining a close alliance between these various princes. The imperial crown was elective, but had to remain within the house of Habsburg. There was thus no need for the king of Spain to claim it for himself. Matthias, who was childless, was already an old man: in 1617 he had reached the age of sixty. It was therefore necessary to come to an understanding about the succession to his inheritance.

The Spanish ambassador at the imperial court was the count of Oñate, a diplomat of great ability. In 1617 he entered into an agreement with the archduke of Styria at Graz whereby Ferdinand was to be nominated king of Bohemia and Hungary and, if possible, king of the Romans (that is to say future emperor) during Matthias's lifetime. Thus as soon as the latter died, Ferdinand would take possession of his entire heritage. In return, he was to hand over Alsace and the Tyrol to Spain.

For the Spaniards these represented two extremely valuable acquisitions. Although Philip III's chief possessions could be reached by sea (the maritime link between Spain and the Spanish Netherlands is a case in point), the overland routes were also vital, and it was essential for communications between the Milanese, Franche-Comté and the Low Countries to be made secure, especially for the passage of troops. From the Po valley to the North Sea, Spanish possessions stretched like an immense rampart sealing off western Europe; but there were a number of breaches in this rampart which it was advisable to fill in. The new acquisitions in Alsace were not only adjacent to Franche-Comté; in addition they gave Spain access to the road through the Rhineland and enabled her to establish close contact with her satellites the Catholic bishoprics on the Rhine. The Tyrol, on the other hand, gave the Spaniards possession of the Brenner Pass, the route to Italy.

At this period in history governments were not particularly interested in rounding off the territories under their control so as to make them more compact; they were mainly concerned with the holding of key points on the great trade routes—key points which were also strategic bases that safeguarded the levy or passage of troops and served to impede the movements of an actual or potential enemy. It was for this reason that Henry IV had been determined to keep the emperor's forces out of Jülich. It was for this reason also that the principality of Montferrat, situated between the duchy of Savoy-Piedmont and the Milanese but subject to the duke of Mantua, was the cause of repeated armed conflicts between the Spanish government in Milan and the duke of Savoy until it was eventually agreed that it should remain a Mantuan possession, since this would ensure that it did not pass into the hands of either of the contending powers. Similarly the Valtelline, a Swiss valley leading to the Engadine along which the river Adda flows, owed its importance to its control of communications between Italy and the Empire. The inhabitants of the valley, who were Catholics, were subject to the neighbouring 'Grey Leagues' or Grisons, which were allied to France. Later we shall see how at certain moments the question of the Valtelline became a matter that concerned all Europe.

Neither the silver of the Indies nor the woollen manufactures of the Low Countries, neither the ability of Habsburg diplomats nor the sagacious policy of Habsburg councillors had been sufficient of themselves to bring about this expansion in the power of the house of Austria throughout Europe.

When the Catholic Church had been tottering on the brink of collapse in the course of the sixteenth century, the house of Austria had remained unshakeably loyal. Only one of its princely members had apparently been tempted by heretical doctrines—Maximilian II, the son of Ferdinand I. Even in his case the effect of his vacillation had been counteracted by arranging for his children to be brought up in Spain where there was no taint of heresy. Thus Rudolf II and Matthias I, who became in succession kings of Bohemia and Hungary and emperors of the Holy Roman Empire, had both returned from Spain as ardent Catholics. Under Philip II in particular Spain had become the universal champion of the Catholic cause.

Germany was divided between three different religious creeds—Catholic, Lutheran and Calvinist. The peace of Augsburg (1555) had established a kind of balance between the first and the second. Calvinism was not officially recognised by the laws of the Empire, but this did not prevent it from thriving in certain parts of Germany. For the Catholic Church to maintain its position or recover the ground that it had lost, it required the assistance of the German princes and of their overlord, the emperor. The emperor did not wield direct power over the Empire comparable to that enjoyed by other European rulers in their own states, but even so he still possessed considerable authority since it was he who conferred fiefs and designated the holders of the highest offices.

The emperor was chosen by a college of seven electors, three of whom were ecclesiastics while the remaining four were laymen, and this electoral college generally used to nominate his successor, the king of the Romans, during his lifetime. As soon as the emperor died the king of the Romans would then take his place without further formalities. This custom of electing a ruler's successor during his lifetime was also observed in elective monarchies such as Bohemia and Hungary. It seemed the safest means of avoiding the complications of an interregnum. At this time three of the lay electors within the imperial electoral college belonged to the reformed religion—the duke of Saxony and the margrave of Brandenburg being Lutherans, while the count palatine was a Calvinist.[9] The only lay elector who was still a Catholic was the king of Bohemia. In consequence it was he who had the casting vote that ensured a Catholic majority of four to three. It had long been the practice for the king of Bohemia to be chosen as future emperor at an election in which he used to vote in his own favour. Whoever was elected as king of Bohemia could therefore be almost sure of subsequently becoming king of the Romans and emperor.

Anxious as he was to strengthen Catholicism in Germany, the Pope attached very great importance to the person who occupied the throne of Bohemia. As a Catholic elector, only he could ensure that the emperor would not be an adherent of the reformed religion; as emperor, he could favour Catholics by his distribution of imperial appointments, protect the Church against the Protestants in a wide variety of circumstances and lend support to the Jesuits and Capuchins in their task of reconquering lost ground. The election of Ferdinand of Styria, therefore, was not only in accordance with the wishes of Spain. No other choice could have given greater satisfaction to the pope, for to a much greater extent than

Rudolf or Matthias the archduke was a ruler deeply imbued with the spirit of the Counter-Reformation. He was a pupil of the Jesuits and an ardent proselytiser within his own dominions.

This necessary alliance between the papacy and the house of Austria had the effect of making Catholics throughout Europe very sympathetic towards Spanish policy. Wherever Spain prevailed, one could be certain that Catholicism would prevail also.

As opposed to Spain, France was also a Catholic power but less uncompromisingly so, for in France the Protestants were both numerous and influential. Provided she was strong, France could still resist Spain without prejudice to the Catholic cause; but if she was weak there was a danger of her allowing overmuch latitude to allies who were identified with the Protestant cause and active supporters of the Reformation.

The pope was well aware that the predominant position occupied by the house of Austria in Europe entailed considerable dangers as well as advantages. However strong his wish for the whole continent to return to the old faith—a wish which he realised could not be fulfilled within the near future—he could hardly desire its temporal submission to a single master, for this would have reduced his own position to that of an imperial chaplain. Furthermore as a temporal power in Italy the papacy welcomed the presence of several independent Catholic states in the peninsula such as Savoy, the duchy of Mantua and the grand duchy of Tuscany which acted as a counterweight to the Spaniards, firmly entrenched in Naples and Milan.

Quite apart from this the pope realised full well that Spanish imperialism was bound to encounter resistance and that there was a real danger of a general war in Europe. This was a prospect which was dreaded by the Holy See, not only because the eventual outcome of a general war was always uncertain, but also because of the possibility of its leading to the outbreak of hostilities between the two great Catholic Powers, France and Spain. In the pope's eyes the great danger was that the former would consequently be compelled to support Protestant rulers, thus providing Protestantism, temporarily at least, with opportunities for staging a comeback. The pope was therefore distinctly well disposed towards Spain, especially when it was a matter of helping her to obtain certain advantages which were beneficial to himself; but he took care to restrain her from the moment that the danger of a general war became more apparent. Served as he was by nuncios who were astute diplomats, and with a large number of Jesuits, Capuchins and Carmelites at his beck and call whom he could bring into action from one end of Europe to the other or distribute amongst the most varied sections of society, he had at his disposal means of temporal action which no king could match.

It was always necessary to reckon with the possibility of papal intervention, inspired by some broad yet complex view of the situation. Since the time of the Spanish marriages the French government had been attempting to preserve peace everywhere. Whenever it seemed to be threatened, France offered her services as mediator. In 1614, by the Treaty of Xanten, she had succeeded in arranging for a division of the Jülich succession between the two competitors. The elector of Brandenburg obtained Cleves, Mark and Ravensberg while Jülich and Berg were awarded to the palatine of Neuburg, who had assured himself of the emperor's favour by the happy stroke of becoming a Catholic convert.

In 1615 the French ambassador, the marquis de Rambouillet (the husband of Arthénice*) had helped to bring about an agreement between the Spanish governor of Milan and the duke of Savoy on the subject of Montferrat. But the Spaniard had proved recalcitrant, and it had taken three years to bring about complete disarmament and the restitution of the fortress of Vercelli to the duke of Savoy.

Richelieu's short-lived tenure of the ministries of war and foreign affairs during the winter of 1616–17 had certainly been marked by a brief revival in French foreign policy; but it had also made it possible to gauge the extent to which French influence had declined. Some seventy years ago Gabriel Hanotaux wrote a brilliant commentary on Richelieu's instructions to Schomberg, his emissary to the princes of Germany. He saw in these instructions a declaration of French independence from Spain which almost amounted to a breach of relations with her. This was to credit Richelieu with a more forceful attitude than he can have intended to adopt at the time. Schomberg's task was merely to give an explanation for Condé's arrest and to reassure the German princes as to the king's goodwill towards them. Richelieu's attention was primarily concentrated on Italy. He not only hoped to restore peace between the duke of Savoy and the king of Spain in the Milanese, but even contemplated acting as arbitrator in another armed conflict involving the Venetian Republic and the archduke of Styria.

But the Venetians, who had observed the dissensions in France, attached no credit to the bishop of Luçon's proposals; they preferred to treat directly with Madrid. This being the case, the only point worth

---

* Arthénice is an anagram of Cathérine, Mme de Rambouillet's Christian name. It was coined by Malherbe and became the name by which she was generally known in her circle.

remembering about the part played by Richelieu is the high standard of his dispatches, now preserved in the French archives. Although they only amount to a small bundle they are so alert, so lucid, so full of energy that they are sufficient to bear witness to a mind of rare quality, a mind quick to grasp the underlying significance of events, apt at evaluating principles and the means of applying them.

Henceforth Richelieu began to resort to a method of conducting diplomacy which he did not invent himself but in which he displayed more flexibility and energy than other men. He tended to ignore the ordinary run of intelligencers with their sluggish reactions, and had recourse to newcomers. He not only had memorials drawn up for his own use which he could study carefully but also commissioned 'discourses' and newsletters [*nouvelles à la main*] which he subsequently disseminated to enlighten public opinion and make it favourable to his policy. He enlisted the services of a Capuchin whom he had known for some years and whose religious fervour, knowledge of Europe and breadth of vision he valued highly: Father Joseph. During the nineteenth century Father Joseph was to find in Canon Dedouvres a biographer who came forward as his avowed champion and ascribed to him every important publication on these lines that appeared at the time. This is an obvious exaggeration; but the fact remains that Father Joseph knew a great many things and a great many people. He was undoubtedly the author of a very large number of 'discourses' and memorials concerned with European politics that circulated between 1617 and 1620. One of the topics canvassed in this way was the question of the imperial election.

In order to check the headway that the house of Austria was making in Europe, was it possible to prevent the imperial crown from passing to a member of the Habsburg family?

Could Louis XIII himself lay claim to the Empire, like his predecessor Francis I? In the event of his not becoming a candidate himself, should he put up a candidate of his own who was Catholic without being Spanish in his sympathies? If so, the duke of Bavaria seemed to be the only possibility; but the duke recoiled from taking such a hazardous step. However, in the last resort only one thing really mattered from the French point of view: the king of Spain must not be allowed to become emperor himself. It followed that the least dangerous candidate appeared to be Archduke Ferdinand of Styria: he would do as well as anyone. Richelieu and Puysieulx resigned themselves to the situation and gave instructions accordingly to Baugy, the resident French ambassador at Prague.

However, in order to become emperor the archduke had first to secure his nomination to the throne of Bohemia—a kingdom whose strongly knit political organisation and long-standing wealth (the silver mines of Joachimsthal*) made it the most important of the Habsburg dominions. In the interior of Bohemia and Moravia the population was Czech; on the periphery and in Silesia and Lusatia it was German. Though the people were predominantly Protestant there was an active Catholic minority, which controlled the most important offices of state. In Bohemia itself a charter issued by King Rudolf in 1609 and known as the Letter of Majesty had guaranteed important privileges to the Protestants.[10]

Ferdinand was nominated as king by the Bohemian diet without much difficulty in 1617, but he was not to exercise power until Matthias was dead and the Protestant nobles soon came to the conclusion that they still had time to change their minds. They aggravated an old dispute with the government and on 23 May 1618, taking advantage of the absence of King Matthias, they hurled two high dignitaries of the realm out of a window of Prague Castle. After carrying out the defenestration of these two Czech Catholics, they then organised themselves for open rebellion against their sovereign.[11]

The news was welcomed with enthusiasm by Protestants in the Empire, in particular by the Evangelical Union, a political and military league under the leadership of France's ally the elector palatine. At the same time a pamphleteering campaign was unleashed throughout Germany which even percolated into France. According to this propaganda a tremendous offensive was about to be launched against the Protestants at the instigation of the Jesuits; Matthias's government, which had fallen under the influence of Spain and the papacy, had violated the Letter of Majesty; Ferdinand's election as king of Bohemia had been irregular and was a preparatory step towards the subjection first of Bohemia and then of all the Empire to the Spanish yoke.

The Catholics—and especially the Jesuits—were no less active. They too disseminated tracts in defence of their co-religionists, in which they proclaimed the existence of a widespread Protestant conspiracy intended to overthrow legitimate Catholic rulers and where possible to suppress the exercise of the Catholic religion. Both the Bohemian rebels and the Emperor Matthias wrote to inform Louis XIII of what had occurred. Each side defended its own cause and begged the king not to give help to the enemy. But whereas the message from Matthias deftly appealed for solidarity between princes in the face of rebels who openly threatened

* Now Jáchymov. It was from these mines that the thaler or dollar derived its name.

their power, the letter from the Bohemian insurgents attacked the Jesuits violently. Did they not realise that Louis XIII's confessor Father Arnoux, was a Jesuit? Had they not heard that the king had recently re-established the College of Clermont against the advice of the Faculty of the University of Paris and authorised the teaching of theology in schools run by the Jesuits?

There was no reason for France to intervene immediately in this distant conflict. The best policy was for her to see how the situation developed and, since the outbreak of a new war in Europe was in no way to her advantage, to urge both sides to make peace. But it was not long before events in Bohemia became entangled with affairs in France in a singular way. For several months the pastors of the Reformed Church in Béarn had been refusing to carry out the king's orders to restore church property there to the Catholic clergy. They were promised compensation in the form of pensions derived from Crown lands [*rentes sur le domaine royal*] and assured that they would not be a penny the worse off.

It was all in vain. They had no wish to change their status from that of usufructuaries to that of pensioners, which to them implied a state of subjection. In the spring of 1618 Louis XIII sent a commissioner to Pau to enforce the execution of his edict, a certain sieur Renard de Bonchamps. The young men of Pau greeted him with jibes. They paraded the town wearing foxes' tails fastened to their doublets and shouting *au renard*! They came and delivered a battery of tremendous kicks at the door of the house where the commissioner was staying, and it was thought that they would knock the whole place down.

News of the turn of events in Prague and of the disturbances in Pau reached Louis XIII at almost the same time (June 1618). He could hardly help feeling that Protestants were everywhere showing themselves to be dangerous, refractory and unruly subjects: in venturing to lay violent hands on the representatives of their appointed rulers, they were clearly guilty of an affront to the majesty of sovereign princes. Not only this but apologies had been published justifying the resistance of the Béarnese pastors and excusing the muddle-headed behaviour of a few young men; and these apologies repeated almost word for word the arguments put forward in the Protestant pamphlets which had come from Bohemia. They quoted recent events in Prague as evidence that the Jesuits were plotting against the adherents of the Reformed religion in every country in Europe, and caused considerable alarm in England and Protestant Germany where they were widely circulated.

In a sense these were clever tactics. Protestants in conflict with their own king were bound to look for support abroad and to press foreign rulers of the same religion as themselves to intercede on their behalf. There can be no doubt that events in Béarn were of as much concern to the German princes, the Dutch and the English as those in Bohemia.

Certainly it was not in Louis XIII's interest for the Habsburgs to strengthen their grip on their own dominions, but neither was it to his advantage for the Protestants to meet with widespread success in Europe, since the effect would be to stiffen the obstinacy of the Béarnese and of the Huguenots in France proper. The king was becoming increasingly jealous of his power but realised that it was tottering everywhere.

Early in 1619 the duke of Épernon left Metz, of which he was governor, without permission and established himself in Angoulême, another of his cities. At Blois the queen mother had a hundred and one different things to complain about: she had been separated from her best servants, Barbin and the bishop of Luçon; the governor of her favourite son Gaston, the ten-year-old duke of Anjou, had been replaced without consulting her; the marriage of her daughter Christina to the prince of Piedmont had been arranged without reference to her. A strange Italian priest named Rucellaï, whose presence in her entourage had been over-looked, was busy intriguing and casting around for allies on her behalf. One winter's evening, although her corpulence made her clumsy at such escapades, Marie de Medici climbed out of one of the windows of the château and, descending a ladder, reached the moat beneath. She made good her escape from the precincts, was met by a coach and set off to join Épernon. As both the queen and the duke were governors of provinces they had both troops and strongholds at their disposal. They were in a position to start a civil war, and to Luynes it seemed that only Richelieu could avert this alarming possibility. The latter was accordingly told to leave Avignon and rejoin the queen mother. Negotiations began. Marie de Medici was awarded the governorship of Anjou, for it was thought inadvisable to grant her Brittany and Nantes, since they lay on the periphery of the kingdom: if she held the governorship of Brittany it would be dangerously easy for her to intrigue with foreign Powers. The queen mother was also promised large sums of money to wipe out the arrears of her debts, and Épernon was restored to favour. So nothing much had happened after all. Contemporary historians called this episode the first War between Mother and Son. In fact it had been a call to arms rather than a real war; but for the king and his authority it was a painful and humiliating experience.

Meanwhile the situation in Bohemia was growing progressively worse. Matthias had died in Vienna in the spring of 1619. The Bohemian rebels had continued to recognise him as king and all the bells in Prague were tolled in sign of mourning. However, it was not merely the emperor's knell that they sounded but that of his dynasty too, for the rebels would no longer allow that Ferdinand succeed him. The Bohemian throne was declared vacant. Although the province of Moravia formed an integral part of the kingdom of Bohemia, it was still relatively independent. Hitherto its loyalty to the Habsburgs had been assured by a Protestant nobleman named Karel of Žerotín, a personage overmuch neglected by historians for he had earlier played a part of some importance in European affairs. Karel of Žerotín was a humanist as well as an earnest Calvinist. He could write elegantly in German, Italian, French and Czech. He had lent large sums of money to Henry of Navarre and in 1592 had joined his army at the siege of Rouen. Thereafter he had remained in touch with Duplessis-Mornay.

Far from approving of the Bohemian insurrection, Žerotín had intervened in the hope of pacifying it, but without success. Early in May 1619 it spread to Moravia: the Jesuits were expelled from their colleges at Brno and Olomouc, and Žerotín himself was imprisoned.[12]

All over Protestant Europe the extremists were gaining the upper hand over the moderates. In the United Provinces the rigorist party [*la faction intransigeante*] the Gomarists, built up a case against Oldenbarneveldt. The venerable advocate of Holland, who had been loaded with honours in return for his services to his country, was accused of being an Arminian and of having deviated from strict Calvinist doctrine.[13] He was condemned to death. In vain did the French ambassador, Aubery du Maurier, intervene on his behalf on Louis XIII's orders; he was unable to prevent the odious sentence from being carried out. At about the same time suspicions arose that letters were passing between the Protestant Assembly at Loudun (which had met with Louis XIII's permission) and the English Court where the rigorists were temporarily popular. Admittedly James I disowned the correspondence; but he also told Tillières, the French ambassador, that Louis XIII should never have spoken in Oldenbarneveldt's favour, referring to the latter as a man who was both evil and mischievous.

Meanwhile a series of battles took place between the Bohemian army led by Mansfeld, a German Protestant subsidised by the Evangelical Union, and mercenary troops commanded in Ferdinand's name by Bucquoy, a Belgian noble. Both sides scored some successes, but in the course

Map 3 Bohemia and its neighbours

of the summer Bohemia and Moravia were virtually cleared of Catholic troops. The rebels were in touch with several European rulers, for they were anxious to find a new king. At one time they had in mind the duke of Savoy, who was sufficiently proud to be tempted by the offer despite the difference of religion; but they reached agreement more quickly with the young Elector Palatine Frederick V. The latter whose possessions lay in the area of Heidelberg and Mannheim, ruled over one of the largest states in western Germany, together with another principality on the Bohemian frontier, the Upper Palatinate centred on Amberg. More important still he was a Calvinist, the leader of the Evangelical Union and a prince with highly distinguished connections. Through his wife Elizabeth who was both more intelligent and more ambitious than himself, he was the son-in-law of James I of England, while through his mother, Louisa Juliana of Nassau, he was the nephew of the princes of Orange. He seemed therefore to guarantee the goodwill of the two great Protestant Powers towards Bohemia, and at the end of August 1619 he was elected king by the Bohemian Diet.

Curiously enough, in July, only a few weeks previously, the electoral Diet of the Empire had met at Frankfurt for the election of the new emperor, and Ferdinand of Styria, upon whom the choice fell, was chosen in his capacity as king of Bohemia. He was elected unanimously, the votes cast in his favour including not only his own but even more paradoxically that of his rival the elector palatine. The latter did not attend the Diet in person, but even so his ambassadors had been instructed to express doubts about Ferdinand as a condidate; however, they had been told to accept him if there was no other claimant. (28 August).

Clearly the existing political structure of Europe had already been upset. The house of Austria still retained the imperial title but its power in central Europe had been gravely impaired. The Habsburgs were progressively losing control of the entire kingdom of Bohemia. Hungary, which was for the most part Protestant, was preparing to break away and to choose as its king Gabriel Bethlen, prince of Transylvania.[14] It was not even certain that Ferdinand would retain control of Austria, where there were many Protestants among the nobility who were planning to ally themselves with the rebels in nearby Bohemia and Hungary. In the autumn he was besieged in Vienna and only saved by the timely arrival of some Polish dragoons.

In short, Spain was in the process of losing her indispensable ally in the east. It looked as if the threat of Spanish hegemony could be warded off for a long time to come. Nor did there seem to be any other great power in Eastern Europe which was in a position to profit from the house of Austria's weakness and become an immediate danger as a result of its aggrandisement. Poland, despite her vast territories, had only limited resources at her disposal, and the same could be said of the grand duchy of Moscow. Not only was far-off Archangel her only outlet to the sea,* but her lack of political efficiency made Muscovy still seem alien to Europe.

The position of Turkey was very different. The Ottoman Empire stretched far into Europe, overlapping the whole Balkan peninsula. With the exception of Pressburg,† it dominated the Hungarian plain up to the mountains of Slovakia and its authority extended over the whole of Transylvania. The sultan had a fleet and a powerful army. There was no guarantee that he would not resume the policy of Suleiman the Magnificent, and no reason for assuming that he lacked the strength to do so. With Christian Europe in the throes of a crisis, there was nothing to stop him from taking the opportunity of avenging the memorable defeat inflicted on the Turks at Lepanto.

The question of Turkey was of grave concern to many people all over Europe. The accounts given by travellers who had managed to penetrate into the Ottoman Empire aroused great interest, because they provided valuable information about a wide variety of topics connected with both trade and missions. In Rome, and among Catholics everywhere, Turkish affairs were discussed with real passion. A new order of chivalry was being formed—the Christian Militia. Its object was to assume the custody of the holy places, and its recruits were to be drawn from the most illustrious families in Europe. The new order was intended to revive the crusading spirit. Bérulle and Father Joseph took an active part in its organisation, and its command had been entrusted to the duke of Nevers.

The king of France was confronted with the most serious problem to face him since the beginning of his reign—indeed since even earlier for Henry IV had never been placed in such a predicament. It was Louis XIII's duty to ensure that his policy was guided by the interests of his realm; but how could he be sure where those interests lay? Spain now found herself deprived of her Austrian ally, an ally to whom, strangely enough, she had apparently given only half-hearted support. Was not this unexpected humiliation of her Spanish rival in France's interests? But what if the penalty for Spain's decline turned out to be not only the

* The economic importance of Archangel was however considerable as we shall see later. (V.L.T.)

† Now Bratislava.

revival of the Turkish menace but, more immediately, the sudden emergence of a Protestant threat encouraging the outbreak of insurrections within France herself? Would not this be a very heavy price to pay —too heavy in fact?

Father Joseph had examined this question at the beginning of the year in his 'Discourse on the affairs of Bohemia'. He had ended by advising the French king to impose his arbitration with a view to establishing a reasonable agreement between the house of Austria and its Bohemian subjects as soon as possible. If need be the traditional liberties of the latter should be guaranteed, thus preventing the elected ruler of a state hitherto dominated by its aristocracy from becoming too absolute.

Father Joseph's ideas coincided with those of Puysieulx; but the latter, although endowed with far more insight and experience than Luynes or the king in matters of foreign policy, was little more than a competent subordinate and thus incapable of taking the initiative.

Almost the whole of the year 1619 went by without France making any move. In the last weeks of December Ferdinand sent the prince of Fürstenberg to Paris as his ambassador extraordinary. His mission was to ask Louis XIII for effective help with men and arms. Puysieulx and Jeannin, the king's ministers, still favoured diplomatic intervention; but Louis XIII was very susceptible to arguments based on religious considerations. He was growing increasingly devout. Harassed as he was by difficulties and trials within his own realm and in his private life, he felt that God would never bestow his heavenly grace upon him if he contributed to the triumph of heresy in Europe. Against the wishes of his ministers he promised armed assistance.

The emperor was immediately informed of this offer, but very soon afterwards the French government had to go back on the king's ill-advised decision. It was postponed on the plea that the first step should be to send ambassadors, the better to assess the situation. An important diplomatic mission was organised led by the duke of Angoulême, the son of Charles IX, a half-kinsman to the king and almost a prince of the blood.

But by acting in this way France had exasperated everyone: she had displeased the Protestants by openly siding with the emperor and antagonised the emperor by undertaking to come to his rescue and then failing to fulfil her promise. In the spring the embassy crossed into Germany. The whole Empire was in arms. The two great German leagues were mobilising to go to the help of their respective co-religionists. On the one side was the Evangelical Union, now led by a man of determination the margrave of Ansbach. On the other was the Catholic League, under its equally forceful leader, the duke of Bavaria. In the Netherlands a Spanish army commanded by Spinola was preparing to invade the Rhenish or Lower Palatinate in order to chastise the anti-king of Bohemia on his own territory.

Towards the end of June 1620 the French embassy reached Ulm, at the very moment when the respective armies of the two leagues were approaching the town. It seemed as if once they were face to face nothing could prevent them from opening fire on each other. But the duke of Angoulême, turning to good account the more accommodating attitude of the member of the Evangelical Union from Württemberg, succeeded in arranging for the signature of an agreement which neutralised Germany. As he watched the two armies marching away in opposite directions (the Protestants to the north to defend the Palatinate, the Catholics following the Danube downstream towards Austria), the duke thought that he had preserved peace. But he had not foreseen the consequences of his intervention. The army of the Catholic League set off to join the troops in Ferdinand's service. The latter had now sufficient forces at his disposal to launch an offensive against Bohemia. On Saturday, 7 November the emperor's troops under Bucquoy and those of the Catholic League under the command of Tilly (also a Belgian) reached the heights overlooking the river Vltava a short distance from Prague. They then saw Frederick's army, which had been looking for them further south and was now returning in the direction of Prague. It was commanded by Anhalt, a prince of the Empire.

At dawn on the following day fighting began on the hillock known as the White Mountain. It looked as if the Catholics, who were occupying positions closer to Prague, were defending the capital while the Protestant forces seemed to be attacking it. Within a few hours the latter were driven back. Panic broke out in their ranks and horsemen gave rein in full flight up to the very outskirts of Prague. King Frederick was simultaneously informed that a battle was raging and that his army had ceased to exist. He just had time to cross the stone bridge with his train of carriages and reach the road to Germany, abandoning the realm over which he had reigned for but a single winter.

The French embassy had not long arrived at Vienna when tidings of these events reached the city. So incredible did they seem that it took several couriers to confirm the news. From then onwards it only remained for the French to listen to courteous expressions of thanks for good offices which no longer served any useful purpose. But although they had not realised it at the time, it had been their intervention at Ulm that had decided the outcome of the struggle.

Ferdinand soon re-established his authority over Bohemia. Like Frederick, he too was a foreigner, and he had very bitter memories of the trials that his kingdom had caused him over the past two years. He allowed cruel reprisals to be carried out in his name. In the following spring twenty-seven people perished on the scaffold in Prague for high treason. Far more serious were the confiscations of property, the prohibition of Protestant worship and the abolition of the Letter of Majesty (the original document, slashed twice with a dagger, is still preserved in the archives of Prague).[15] A few years later the monarchy in Bohemia, which had hitherto been elective, was declared to be hereditary, and German, the language of the Habsburgs, was given the same official status as Czech, the language of the ancient liberties of Bohemia.

Nor was Ferdinand slow in making the effects of his new power felt in Germany. He had the princes who had borne arms against him put under the ban of the Empire, which entailed the confiscation of the territories over which they ruled and the loss of their rights and dignities. In this way Frederick V was stripped of his hereditary possessions, the Upper Palatinate being occupied by the duke of Bavaria while Spinola's Spanish army took over the Rhenish or Lower Palatinate. A similar punishment was meted out to Frederick's principal allies, the prince of Anhalt, the margrave of Jägerndorf[16] (a Hohenzollern) and the count of Hohenlohe* (1621). The emperor, now absolute master of Bohemia, seemed to be on the verge of establishing a like supremacy within the Empire.

It was the weakness and incompetence of the French government which had enabled the house of Austria to re-establish its power and —what was worse in the long run—had indirectly facilitated the triumph of Spain. Neither the one nor the other felt under any debt of gratitude to France, and forty years of ceaseless struggle from 1620 to 1659 were to be necessary to avert the dangers with which she was faced as a result of Spain's success.

Whose fault was it? Was it the king who was to blame? Or did the responsibility lie with Luynes or Puysieulx? In fact it is futile to look for a culprit. The reason for this disastrous blunder was the lack of a strong-minded, far-sighted statesman at the head of the government. France required a man who, even if unable to find the ideal solution (for no such thing exists in this world of ours) was at least capable of preventing the worst from happening. But it would be childish to deny that the victory

---

* Together with Matthias von Thurn, Georg von Hohenlohe had been elected supreme commander of the rebel army by the Bohemian Diet in 1618.

of the house of Austria, disastrous though it was for France's political interests, was nevertheless a great victory for Catholicism.

The armies which confronted each other on the White Mountain were not national armies. They were composed of mercenaries from all over Europe: Flemings, Walloons, Italians, Germans, Hungarians, as well as French (there is a tradition that Descartes served as a soldier in Ferdinand's army). But the Catholic forces were fired with a missionary zeal by their leaders. On the morning of 8 November priests administered Communion to the troops as they were drawn up for battle. A Carmelite, Father Domenico di Gesù Maria, preached that the cause for which they fought was holy and drew inspiration from the Gospel for the day: *Reddite Caesari quae sunt Caesaris et Deo quae sunt Dei*: 'render unto Caesar the things which are Caesar's and unto God the things that are God's'. The army commanders sang the Salve Regina* and the duke of Bavaria had given *Sancta Maria* as watchword for the day. In the spiritual conflict between the forces of the Reformation and the Catholic Church the Virgin Mary was a permanent symbol. For the Protestants she symbolised the idolatry that had taken the place of worship of God alone; for the Catholics she was the gentle intermediary who personified the chain of graces linking Heaven to the Church Militant.

A Lutheran church in Prague, dedicated to the Holy Trinity, was taken over for Catholic worship and rededicated to Our Lady of Victories in memory of the day: Panna Maria Vitežná. It was entrusted to some Carmelite friars and the Emperor Ferdinand arranged for a wax figure of the Infant Jesus, the gift of a noble lady, to be conveyed there as a kind of votive offering. Popular devotion led to the growth of a cult around this figure and made it famous. It became known as the Infant Jesus of Prague.[17] In Rome itself another church, one of the most charming examples of the baroque style that was then fashionable, was dedicated with the same intention of thanksgiving, and soon the architect Soria provided it with a magnificent main entrance like a triumphal arch. This was the Church of Santa Maria della Vittoria, where Bernini was later to set his astounding 'Ecstasy of St Teresa'.[18] To the Catholic world the battle of the White Mountain seemed like another Lepanto.

It is essential to see events in this perspective if we are to understand the feelings of Louis XIII and of those close to him, and if we are to appreciate how it was that they could underestimate the European significance

---

* Hail, Holy Queen, Mother of Mercy . . .'—one of the oldest anthems to the Virgin Mary.

of what had just occurred. Under the erroneous impression that he had disposed of his problems outside the realm by giving contradictory answers to Ferdinand II, the king turned to deal with fresh difficulties caused by his mother, as his ambassadors proceeded on their way through Germany. Marie de Medici was advised by Richelieu, by her confessor, Father Suffren, and by Cardinal La Rochefoucauld not to dally at Angers but to resume her place at court by her son's side. However, she listened to the advice given by others and, being jealous of Luynes, allowed herself to be persuaded that she would obtain more power for herself by making further demands. She joined in a conspiracy which was more far-reaching than that of the previous year. A combination which included such great nobles as the dukes of Épernon, Mayenne and Longueville, the comte de Soissons, the two Vendômes and the dukes of Nemours, Retz, la Trémoille, Roannes and Rohan provided her with the military and financial resources of a large party—a party that was quite capable of stirring up rebellion from Normandy to Bordeaux and of establishing contact by road with the Spanish Netherlands and the archbishoprics on the Rhine. However, its power was more apparent than real. Neither Parlements nor office-holders were disposed to support the princes, and their refusal to take part in the war doomed it to become no more than a surface agitation, a prolonged progress through provinces which failed to prove responsive.

Louis XIII and his councillors realised this. The king reintroduced the *paulette* for office-holders, skilfully sweetening the pill according to the grade of official concerned and exalting the prestige of the Parlements in the eyes of the other institutions. He appeared in Normandy with a military escort, held a *lit de justice* at Rouen and occupied the château at Caen. The local nobility and representatives of the towns came obsequiously to pay their respects and assure him of their loyalty. On the insistence of Richelieu, Bérulle and the archbishop of Sens, Marie de Medici at once agreed to negotiate. But a force of three thousand infantry and four hundred cavalry, armed with three cannons and bearing colours decorated with her monogram, was guarding Ponts de Cé on the Loire. Two dukes—the duc de Vendôme and the duc de Retz—were in command of this little army. It was dispersed by the king's troops on 8 August, and on the next day the château of Angers surrendered. On 10 August the king concluded a peace treaty with Marie de Medici. After meeting her again at Brissac he ordered an official declaration of her innocence to be registered by the Parlement.

This second War between Mother and Son was to have unexpected consequences. There were some who thought that since there were troops ready to hand, they should be put to use. In other words, they held that the time had come to break the resistance of the Béarnese Protestants once and for all. Whether he resorted to outright war or simply deployed his forces as a threat to intimidate them, the king should not disband his army but should lead it into Béarn. Father Lerat, the Oratorian and biographer of Cardinal Bérulle, tells us that Louis XIII, who knew from personal experience 'the wisdom of this man of God', was very willing to give ear to his counsels. Bérulle himself was encouraged to offer his advice to the king by the nuncio Bentivoglio, who later declared that if he had done anything of value during his nunciature it had been through Bérulle's agency. In addition, the latter was a friend of la Salette, the bishop of Lescar.* Finally there were a number of signs and portents that pointed in the same direction. Mother Magdeleine de Saint Joseph, the superior of the Order of Carmelite Sisters, had announced to Bérulle that he would shortly see heresy extirpated. Another Carmelite nun, the Archduchess Margaret, gave inspired advice to the Spanish government from the seclusion of her convent. Oratorians, Capuchins, Carmelite friars, Carmelite nuns: all of them spoke in similar terms. In this we should undoubtedly see the effect of the Catholic revival, mentioned earlier in this book as the outstanding feature of the previous ten years. Now it was developing into a kind of fever.

Some historians have made out that it was Luynes alone who was responsible for the new direction taken by the king's policy, whereas in fact his role was merely that of a puppet. But du Perron, the archbishop of Sens, and Father Arnoux, the king's confessor, told Richelieu of the great plan that was now afoot and kept him informed of its progress. He listened quietly to what they told him. We must not lose sight of the fact that Béarn was only linked to France by the personal union of a common ruler. The Edict of Nantes was not applicable in Béarn and consequently Louis XIII's sovereignty there was subject to no restrictions.

The king advanced at the head of an army across largely Protestant territory as far as Poitiers. In September he was at Bordeaux, perhaps still uncertain as to his next move. But the maréchal de la Force, the governor, and Casaux, the president of the Supreme Council of Béarn, only brought him dilatory answers. Evidently the precious edict of restitution had still not been promulgated, and even if royal threats ensured its publication what reason was there to suppose that it would be put into effect? Despite the misgivings of some who pointed out that the roads

* Lescar is located about ten miles from Pau, the capital of Béarn.

were inadequate, that autumn rains represented a real danger and that if there were a general rising he might well find his army unequal to the task, Louis XIII decided to march on Pau. To La Force he remarked, rather cruelly: 'You are such a weak governor that it is in your interest for me to go there to prop up your authority.' Attempts to scare him only had the effect of tempting him to action. An expedition, a long march at the head of his troops—never before had he experienced such an adventure. The spirit of Henry IV seemed to live again in his son.

On 14 October the king made his entry into Pau. He refused the honours due to a sovereign, because Catholic worship was not allowed there. 'It would ill become me to receive them,' he explained, 'until I have rendered thanks to God from whom I hold all my states and my regal authority.' Three days later he entered the stronghold of Navarreins. Its military governor had for many years been M. de Salles, now an octogenarian; indeed he had already been established there in the time of Queen Jeanne. But Louis XIII was left unmoved by these memories and brutally removed the old Huguenot from his charge. Then on 19 October he returned to Pau and proclaimed the annexation of Béarn and Lower Navarre to the French Crown.[19] Catholic worship was re-established and the principal church in Pau was set aside for this purpose. Church property was restored to the Catholics, the pastors of the Reformed Church being awarded pensions. Bishops were reinstated in their dioceses and resumed their places on the Supreme Council of Pau, with the right to vote and to take part in its deliberations.

Cardinal du Perron and Father Arnoux had accompanied the king. They wrote to Richelieu so that he could inform the queen mother, and their letters sang a song of triumph. 'The world must be restored to its first condition; the righteous must band together to fight the evil that can be wrought by the wicked,' declared the archbishop of Sens—meaning by this that Catholics should no longer quarrel amongst themselves but should join forces to overwhelm the Protestants. The Jesuit confessor was in a state of exultation. 'It is a jubilee,' he exclaimed, and continued: 'it was fifty years ago upon the very self-same day as this eighteenth day of October that the sieur de Montgomery entered this town by commandment of Queen Jeanne and proscribed the Mass.[20] The whole army makes merry, the whole court is filled with admiration. The Huguenots are for the most part disposed to become Catholics once more, having only forsaken the Church because of coercion and downright tyranny. Tomorrow two of our Fathers go to Navarreins, where no priest has been for fifty years. Soon we shall say Mass in churches where heretics preached their sermons. In short, once God is enthroned there the king will be master of the place.'

At the beginning of November Louis XIII returned with all speed to Paris, feeling that he had achieved a minor triumph. It had given him no pleasure to humiliate the Huguenots, for although he sometimes had cruel impulses he was basically a good man. He was, moreover, deeply convinced that since mercy was one of the attributes of his kingship, nothing enhanced his royal prestige more than its exercise; but he also believed that a king is only obeyed if he knows how to show his strength.

A happy combination of circumstances made the first weeks of winter particularly pleasant for the king. The party which supported Luynes and the queen mother's faction had apparently merged with each other. Épernon's son, la Valette, received a cardinal's hat and Richelieu, who had been encouraged to expect a like honour, arranged for the marriage of his favourite niece, Mlle de Pont Courlay, to Luynes's nephew, the marquis de Combalet. The queen mother awarded a dowry to the bride-to-be and loaded her with jewellery. Cadenet, Luynes's brother, was made a peer of France and duc de Chaulnes.

But the Protestants in the realm were in a state of consternation 'at the fearsome storm which had smitten their brethren of Béarn and which seemed to threaten them also most nearly'. They summoned an assembly at La Rochelle without asking for the king's permission. Having learnt their lesson from the turn of events in central Europe, they looked for help abroad, addressing themselves to England. The Protestants in the south rose in revolt. The governors of the provinces concerned had to muster their troops, recapture Privas and Villeneuve de Berg and reinforce the garrisons left in Béarn. On all sides the fire was kindling; Louis XIII's wars of religion had begun.

Wars of religion: such is the name given to Louis XIII's struggle with the Huguenots, by Charles Bernard, the king's official historiographer. Unfortunately it is justified. Separated by quite long intervals of peace, these wars continued until the Grace of Alès in 1629, in other words for nine years out of a reign that lasted for thirty-three. Richelieu took part in them, therefore, but it is generally admitted that he did so primarily for political reasons. For the fact is that these wars never lost their political complexion. They differed markedly from the religious wars of the previous century in that the king never failed to declare that he would respect past edicts and would not deprive the Protestants of their liberties, but that he wished them to behave like dutiful subjects and therefore would not permit his orders to be discussed or their execution evaded. No assembly was to be held without his permission and no movement of troops was to take place without his knowledge and control. Louis XIII loved his authority and could not allow it to be threatened. The clergy and the *dévot* faction in the king's following desired more than this. They hoped to see Catholicism triumph and wanted to restore the old religion throughout the length and breadth of France. Father Griffet, who wrote a history of Louis XIII's reign, reflected their opinions a hundred years later when he gave an account of the capture of various towns and noted with satisfaction: 'On the following day Mass was said there for the first time for sixty years.' Indeed the comment runs like a refrain throughout his narrative. But for the king this was not the main objective: first and foremost he wanted obedient subjects. When he set out on his first campaign in 1621 Louis XIII issued a declaration which was registered by the Parlement of Paris on 27 April, placing under his personal protection all those Protestants who remained within his obedience. It is certain that there was as yet no question of restricting the practical application of the Edict of Nantes, as was done in the time of Louis XIV during the twenty years prior to the Revocation. The government was not declaring war on heresy as such. It did not intend to repudiate the guarantees previously given to the Huguenots.

Louis XIII is alleged to have said 'I do not like the Protestants.' Quite possibly he did say this; yet after they had rebelled and been defeated, he showed no hatred for them. His attitude was coloured by the fact that he had been in personal contact with them. When the king surveyed his rebellious subjects assembled before his very eyes and at his mercy, when he saw them kneeling in the dust before the still-smoking walls of some town, he was moved to pity. In August 1621 the people of Clairac came before him and said, in the elegant phraseology of their time: 'May it please your Majesty to earn the distinction of being called "the Merciful" as deservedly as you are now styled "the Just". If your Majesty grants us (our lives) . . . our mouths shall open only to bless Your Majesty's name and glorious reign. Our hearts desire naught but the greatness and maintenance of your sceptre, and just as we have been the most rebel of your subjects and least deserving of your mercy, so shall we from this time forth be the most loyal and obedient.' Louis XIII's heart was softened. He really felt the emotion of a father brought face to face with his prodigal sons. 'He very nearly pardoned every one of them without exception', comments Father Griffet.

This affection for the French people constitutes an essential feature of the monarchy under Louis XIII. It forms a contrast with Louis XIV's concept of kingship. The latter loved his people too, but in a more abstract way as a general principle, because he lived too far removed from the mass of the population. Like Henry IV, Louis XIII mixed with the French people. He knew how a Norman, a Poitevin or a Gascon lived and how he spoke. He knew the nobility, the soldiers, the priests, the lawyers and the cast of mind of each social category. He may have had serious defects of character, and he was inclined to make mistakes like anyone else. He was certainly only an ordinary man, but it is impossible to understand him or his reign or his age unless we remember that not only in his policy but also in his inmost feelings, indeed, one might say, to the very marrow of his bones, Louis XIII was the father of his subjects and king of France.

This does not alter the fact that these wars included some frightful episodes. Towns were sacked—like Nègrepelisse in 1622. In this particular case the king agreed to make an example of the town in the full knowledge that there would be no stopping the excesses of his soldiers once they were let loose. But only a few weeks previously the people of Nègrepelisse had treacherously wiped out Vaillac's regiment which was quartered there, the women showing themselves no less rabid than the men. It is always a waste of time for historians to engage in polemics regarding the responsibility for such atrocities. All wars are horrible and are marked by the type of atrocity that belongs to their particular epoch. There were occasions when both sides gave rein to their bestial instincts. The real horror of these fratricidal struggles lies in the fact that they resulted in the same hideous, bloodcurdling atrocities being perpetrated by Frenchmen against Frenchmen and on French soil as one reads about in narratives of the Thirty Years War. At least in the case of the latter they were inflicted on each other by mutual foes and foreigners—a fact which to some extent helps to extenuate them.

In the spring of 1621 the king re-established the office of constable, thereby showing his intention of giving more strength and cohesion to his army. He conferred it upon Luynes—a ludicrous choice. Lesdiguières, who should have been appointed to the office but had not yet made up his mind to pay the necessary price by abjuring Protestantism, was appointed marshal general of the king's camps and armies. Louis XIII was now determined to reduce the Huguenot provinces to obedience—namely Poitou, Guyenne, Saintonge and Languedoc.

The Assembly at La Rochelle, foreseeing the outbreak of war, had made plans during its long winter sessions for a division of the realm into military circles, which were to be presided over by the great nobles of the Huguenot party—Bouillon, Soubise, Rohan, la Trémoille, Lesdiguières and la Force. There were some grounds for thinking that this represented a Protestant plot to remodel France as a federation on lines similar to the United Provinces, and that the unity of the realm as well as the king's authority were in imminent danger; this at least was what the *dévots* asserted—no doubt in good faith. But they failed to appreciate the position correctly. Several of these commanders-designate had no taste for such a role—certainly not Lesdiguières, who was far too attached to the court, and to his riches. Bouillon who was one of the best informed of the Huguenot leaders on Protestant affairs generally thanks to his connections with Holland and Germany was playing a waiting game.[21] This left hardly anyone who was prepared to implement the scheme except the two Rohans (Henri de Rohan and his younger brother, Benjamin de Soubise) and la Force. Moreover, of the provinces which were allocated to these Huguenot leaders by the Assembly, some had a Catholic population while in others where the Protestants were in a majority it was necessary to reckon with the office-holders whose interests bade them remain loyal to the king or rally to his side. Only in two areas, therefore, was the danger a real one. The first extended from the Loire to the Garonne and followed the contours of the Massif Central. Its long seaboard, inadequately defended by the king's navy, was controlled by the coastal population and its ports lay ready to receive aid from overseas. The second danger zone consisted of the Cévennes and Languedoc.

In 1621 the Twelve Years Truce, which had suspended hostilities between the United Provinces and the Spanish Netherlands, came to an end. In Germany the war went on, as we shall see later. There was thus an additional risk of a link being established between all these different movements—but this possibility was rendered less likely by the fact that James I of England favoured peace and detested rebellions, because for one reason or another they threatened royal authority. His attitude towards his son-in-law the elector palatine was only lukewarm for he disapproved of his policy; indeed he was more inclined to favour Spain, with whom he desired a rapprochement. The pamphlets put out by the two sides sometimes bore witness to the existence of two currents of opinion within each party—the one uncompromising and the other more conciliatory. Those who asserted that the Protestants would be unable to hold out against Louis XIII's forces indefinitely were right; but so too were those who reckoned that the king was not in a position to root out heresy completely and felt that he was impairing his prestige by acting as the head of a party.

Louis XIII was to spend the next two years fighting his Protestant subjects. He moved from one province to another, often accompanied by the queen mother, Luynes and the prince of Condé. The latter, who had been restored to favour in 1619, exhorted him to adopt severe measures. Anne of Austria remained at Paris together with part of the Council. The king enjoyed being constantly on the move. He was brave, in fact positively rash, in the way that he exposed himself to danger, and showed admiration for courage whenever he saw it. He liked the company of officers and noblemen, and he himself behaved far more like a knight than a statesman. He believed that he was carrying out his duty as king by imposing obedience on his subjects by force of arms and by acting sternly or mercifully when victory was won. He even felt that this task exonerated him from another aspect of his calling—affairs of state. Although he did not totally neglect them, he felt that the active life he was leading justified his paying less attention to them and letting the Council deal with them. The importunities of his elderly ministers used to exasperate him: 'Lord, how wearisome these people are! When I think to pass my time pleasantly they come and pester me, and for the most part they have nothing to tell me.'

In 1621, after removing old Duplessis-Mornay from the governorship of Saumur as he passed through the town, Louis XIII proceeded to besiege Saint-Jean-d'Angély, which Soubise was forced to surrender. Next the king and Lesdiguières captured Clairac, which also submitted after a gallant resistance.

Henri de Rohan now prepared to make a stand at Montauban. 'Were there but two men left who adhered to the true religion, I would be one of them', he declared. All available forces were deployed against the town—the king, the constable, Mayenne, Lesdiguières, the duke of Angoulême, Bassompierre with his Swiss troops and Schomberg with his artillery. Rohan stood his ground, rejected all negotiations and encouraged the citizens in their resistance. He declared that Luynes was the cause of all the trouble and that those who fought for the true religion were also fighting for a better France. The king's army was eventually forced to raise the siege. It returned homewards via Toulouse, where Louis XIII was well received. Monheurt was invested and capitulated, only to be needlessly burnt by the soldiery after its surrender.

At this point Luynes fell a victim to the purple fever. Owing to ignorance of the treatment required, it carried him off within a few days. Thus a career attended by belated but nevertheless dazzling good fortune came to an abrupt end. In addition to holding the office of constable, Luynes had also had the custody of the seals for the past few months.* His promotion had aroused feelings of passionate jealousy everywhere. The saddest thing of all was that even Louis XIII had begun to grow jealous of him. Latterly he had ceased to feel any affection for Luynes. He begrudged his erstwhile favourite the honours he had showered upon him, referring to him as 'King Luynes' and complaining about him to Bassompierre, whom he was beginning to regard with increasing favour. The ardent devotion of earlier days had died out; so cold had Louis XIII's attitude to Luynes become that, far from feeling grief at his death, he felt liberated by it. He returned to Paris full of regrets that the advent of winter had forced him to break off hostilities. Richelieu had succeeded in convincing the ministers that the queen mother must be readmitted to the Council. Through her he could make his opinions heard. He wished for negotiations to be opened with the Huguenots; but Louis XIII was waiting impatiently for the spring and the prospect of further operations. Since the war was bound to be an expensive business, the government had recourse to the usual sources of financial aid—an extraordinary donation from the clergy and fresh sales of offices.

At the end of March 1622 the king left the capital. The journey from Orleans to Blois was made by river. At Saumur he gave orders for the fortifications built by Duplessis-Mornay to be demolished. Then he crossed the Loire at Nantes and entered Poitou.

His first halting place was Challans, which lay almost at the end of terra firma. Soubise was entrenched on the island of Rié.† Around him extended a strange, wild stretch of country where sea and land merged in a mesh of inlets studded with islands. The king advanced towards him at the head of his men-at-arms,[22] accompanied by Bassompierre and a group of young nobles who were his comrades and belonged to the most illustrious families in France—Courtanvaux, Humières, Nesle, Mortemart and Liancourt. He was filled with excitement at the inviting prospect opened up by this fresh campaign. It was April and the weather was magnificent.

* This did not prevent Sillery from remaining Chancellor until 1624—see p. 156n. below.

† Rié or Riez. All this region is now at some distance from the sea from which it is separated by land that used to consist of polders forming part of the *Marais breton*. (V.L.T.)

Soubise did not attempt to defend Rié. He tried to evacuate his army on flat-bottomed craft, but low water and an insufficient ebb tide on the sands prevented his troops from making their getaway. The king's forces made a clean sweep of the Huguenots.

This victory was followed by the capture of the fort of la Chaume, near Sables d'Olonne. Next came the siege of Royan. From Royan the war shifted to Guyenne, assuming a different, and grimmer, character. Sainte-Foy, Moissac and Agen submitted and at Agen the king was met by Sully, who had come to surrender four fortified towns in Quercy of which he was the governor. The army then set off to lay siege to Nègrepelisse, which led to the worst atrocity of the whole war. Saint-Antonin was taken, and the king's troops continued their advance via Toulouse, Carcassonne and Béziers towards Montpellier, which they reached in July. Despite the extreme heat they began to besiege the town; but bad news arrived. Mercenaries under the nobly born bastard Count Ernst von Mansfeld who now commanded the German Protestant forces, had entered Champagne to create a diversion and ease the pressure on their co-religionists in the south of France. However the duke of Nevers, the governor of Champagne, entered into negotiations with Mansfeld and succeeded in diverting him and his soldiers away from the realm.

By now Louis XIII had come to realise that there was every danger of a serious war on a large scale. He saw that it would be far more sensible to revert to the bishop of Luçon's earlier suggestion. Peace must be restored in France by means of a general treaty with the Huguenots. Rohan asked for nothing better. He was to find a treaty very much to his personal advantage. Like the agreements made earlier with the queen mother, the terms of the new treaty were remarkably favourable to the rebels. The Edict of Nantes was confirmed, together with all the declarations, grants by letters patent and secret articles that supplemented it. Article 27, which guaranteed the admission of Protestants to offices and appointments, was therefore covered by the new treaty. The two religions were re-established everywhere where they had been practised before the outbreak of hostilities. Huguenot assemblies remained forbidden without permission from the king, and new fortifications were to be demolished, but those at La Rochelle and Montauban, the two Protestant cities of refuge officially recognised as such, remained intact.

Had it really been necessary to spend two years fighting in order to make peace on terms such as these? The *dévots* regarded the Treaty of Montpellier as a preposterous settlement; to their way of thinking the king had capitulated to the Protestants. Rohan and his brother were granted pensions to mark their return to the king's obedience, and Huguenot officials resumed their appointments. But the Protestants were left with appalling memories of their prolonged call to arms and a dreadful mistrust of their enemies. There were many, too, whose thoughts were to turn to the poor people of Monheurt and Nègrepelisse, just as we cannot avoid thinking of them when we call these years of France's history to mind. Poor victims of passions which had now been stilled enabling others to savour life's sweetness once more—what use were amnesties or offices to them?

The most alarming thing of all was the absence of a guiding hand to direct the affairs of the realm as a whole. When not taken up with his campaigns against the Huguenots, Louis XIII was conscious of this deficiency and felt it keenly. Around him he saw only men who were mediocre, men with limited ideas. Everyone's first thought was to protect himself against his enemies; personal quarrels were rife everywhere. After the peace of Montpellier the prince of Condé had gone to Italy on a pilgrimage. By doing so he simply showed that he was quite unfit to play a leading part in affairs. Lesdiguières, who had at last been converted to Catholicism, had been appointed constable. He was seventy-nine years old and remarkably spry for his age, but he lacked breadth of vision. The two chief ministers, Chancellor Sillery, and his son Puysieulx, the first very old and the second far from young, were known as 'the greybeards' and found themselves exposed to the envy of the great nobles. The king was beginning to grow suspicious not only of the young queen's entourage but of the queen herself. Now that she had been freed from the rigours of Spanish etiquette, Anne of Austria was becoming over-ready to indulge in the more free and easy ways of her adopted country. She was simultaneously flirtatious and devout. She had begun to fall under the bad influence of Marie de Rohan, who shortly after the death of Luynes had married the duke of Chevreuse, a younger member of the house of Lorraine. Marie loved intrigues, whether amorous or political, and was emerging as a pushing, ambitious woman. There was only one person who seemed cautious and sensible—someone who had not always been so. The queen mother had lost none of her ambition or desire for power, but now she strove to avoid any upheaval. She confined herself to telling Louis XIII that his realm was badly governed, that his ministers were no longer achieving anything notable, that they were especially negligent in their conduct of foreign policy, and that in consequence French prestige was on the wane all over Europe. She would not have had the insight to make such apposite remarks of her own volition. In reality she was obediently reciting something that she had been taught, in just the same way as she had been accustomed to repeat whatever words the Concinis and the Abbé Rucellaï had put into her mouth in days gone by. But this time what she had learnt was sensible, for it was the bishop of Luçon who told her what to say.

Louis XIII was beginning to feel slightly less prejudiced against Richelieu. On his way from Languedoc he bestowed upon him a cardinal's biretta which had been obtained from the pope at the instance of Marie de Medici. The king, who received Richelieu at Lyons in the presence of the two queens, took some pleasure in reminding him that Luynes, the late constable, had been responsible for the delay; to which Richelieu deftly replied that the cardinal's purple would have lost much of its lustre if it had passed through the hands of the king's former favourite. He resorted to particularly glowing epithets to assure the queen mother of his gratitude: 'Madam, this purple for which I am beholden to your Majesty will ever call to my remembrance the solemn vow that I have made to shed my blood in your service.' He was soon to resign his bishopric in Poitou, where he no longer thought it possible to carry out his apostolic duties. Henceforth he would be Cardinal Richelieu. Even so he held a number of abbeys and priories in consequence of his post as chaplain to the queen mother.

Anyone who spoke to Louis XIII about the decline of French power in Europe touched a particularly sensitive spot. He had been fully aware for some time, but especially during the last few months, of the extent to which Spain was regaining her ascendancy in Europe, despite the fact that the Spanish treasury was continually rumoured to be involved in financial difficulties.

Since 1598 the Spanish Netherlands (present-day Belgium) had formed a sort of self-governing kingdom which, although still subject to Spain, was under the personal rule of Philip II's daughter and son-in-law Isabella Clara Eugenia and the Archduke Albert, who were jointly known as 'the archdukes'. In 1621 Archduke Albert died. The archduchess, who was already advanced in years, devoted herself increasingly to works of piety. Henceforth she invariably wore the habit of a Franciscan tertiary such as she is shown wearing in a celebrated portrait by Van Dyck.[23] Although she continued to concern herself with affairs of state—an occupation which she enjoyed and in which she showed sound judgement—the archduchess was now readier to fall into line with the opinions held in Madrid. As we have already seen, the war against the United Provinces had been resumed. Spinola was in charge of operations against the stadtholder of Holland, Prince Maurice of Nassau. In short, Spain was consolidating her strength in Belgium with a view to reconquering the United Provinces.

In the area of the Rhine, Mansfeld and Christian of Brunswick, the Lutheran bishop of Halberstadt, were jointly attempting to recover the Palatinate, which had been confiscated from Frederick and occupied by Spanish forces. Meeting with no success, their armies embarked on a series of raids into Alsace, where they proceeded to sack the monasteries. Catholics living in these threatened areas placed all their hopes in Spanish protection.

On the Italian border the crisis in the Valtelline affected French interests even more directly. In 1620 the Catholic inhabitants of the valley, who had suffered terrible ill-treatment from their Protestant overlords, the Grisons, had appealed to Spain for protection. The troops sent to their assistance from the Milanese had not only entered the valley but had erected forts there. In this way, on grounds that were ostensibly to her credit, Spain had managed to obtain control of a route through the mountains to which she had no right, but which offered her better communications with the Tyrol. Spanish soldiers had bolted a door between Italy and the Swiss cantons simultaneously isolating both Piedmont and Venice.

Louis XIII fully realised the importance of the Valtelline, which had been explained to him by Puysieulx, an old hand at European affairs and far from ill informed whatever his shortcomings in other respects. The French government had appealed to the pope, who approved of Spanish policy but was particularly anxious in view of the difficult situation prevailing in Europe generally, that there should be no quarrel between the two Catholic Powers. Only a few days before his death, Philip III of Spain, feeling some qualms of conscience on the subject enjoined his successor to come to an understanding with France about the Valtelline. A treaty was accordingly signed at Madrid providing for the restoration of the status quo in its entirety (25 April 1621).[24] However, this treaty remained a dead letter, not least because du Fargis, the French ambassador in Spain, was a zealous Catholic over-ready to oblige the Spaniards.

Furthermore the Archduke Leopold, the governor of the Tyrol, claiming that the Treaty of Madrid did not concern him, proceeded to carry out a series of raids into the Valtelline on behalf of the Austrians. Louis XIII had an interview with the duke of Savoy and the Venetian ambassador whilst passing through Avignon in 1622 at which it was decided to send armed forces to expel both Spaniards and Austrians from the valley. The Spaniards thereupon hit upon the expedient of arranging for their garrisons in the Valtelline to be relieved by papal troops. Gregory XV agreed to be a party to this manoeuvre, and Sillery and Puysieulx, their courage failing them in the face of the pope's intervention, advised Louis XIII to leave it at that. The question of the Valtelline was thus provisionally settled, but definitely not in a way that was satisfactory for France.

While this was happening, Sillery and his son, who were detested by La Vieuville, the new superintendent of finance, lost all their appointments. The chancellor, who was now eighty-one, was worn out. He relinquished the seals, which were given to Aligre, whilst Puysieulx had to resign from his post as secretary for foreign affairs. La Vieuville arranged for this last appointment to be divided between three different people, namely Phelippeaux d'Herbaut, Potier d'Oguerre and La Ville-aux-Clercs. The new ministers were not men of any distinction although none of them were bad underlings.[25]

Marie de Medici was thus given the chance to tell her son that he must invite a man of greater eminence to join his Council—a man who would invest the government and its conduct of affairs with fresh lustre; and so it was that a figure dressed in the red robe of a cardinal could now be seen proceeding along the road to power.

There was already one cardinal in the Council—La Rochefaucauld. La Vieuville thought that the two cardinals would neutralise each other, leaving him with the real authority. Louis XIII raised some objections. He feared Richelieu, being aware of his boundless ambition, but in view of how things stood he gave way.

Thus on 29 April 1624, Cardinal Richelieu once more made his appearance in the king's Council, which he had left seven years previously. At first he behaved with great discretion, taking care to remain on good terms with his fellow-cardinal (his senior in years and a cardinal of much longer standing than himself) as well as with old Constable Lesdiguières. He kept a careful eye on La Vieuville, whose conduct of affairs was marked by vigour and determination for he was anxious to give his ministry prestige. Within a few weeks negotiations were opened with the English court for the marriage of the king's youngest sister, Henrietta Maria, with the prince of Wales. A treaty of alliance was signed with the United Provinces, and subsidies were granted to Mansfeld to assist him against the Spaniards.

But La Vieuville committed some blunders in his dealings with financial circles. A pamphleteering campaign was launched against him, and he proved unable to fight back. The disgrace which he sensed approaching descended upon him suddenly and more brutally than he had anticipated. In the middle of August, as he was preparing to retire from office, he was arrested on the king's orders and taken to the château of Amboise.[26]

And so, four months after he had joined the Council, Richelieu found himself without a rival.

Part Two

Recovery (1624–30)

CHAPTER FOUR

Richelieu in the Service of King and Nation (1624–27)

RICHELIEU WAS henceforth principal minister and head of the King's Council.* Even though he did not assume these titles immediately, for they were only bestowed on him in the course of time, he was to occupy the chief position continuously until his death eighteen years later. From it he was to dominate France and allow no change to take place in Europe over which he did not exercise some measure of control. After his life had come to an end he was to remain one of the greatest figures in French history, to which he belongs as inseparably as St Louis belongs to its earlier stages or as Napoleon is associated with a later era. Almost as much as Louis XIV he was to incarnate absolute monarchy, but in a way which somehow made it more national and less of a cult. Philippe de Champaigne's portrait of the cardinal has served to impress his profile and his haughty expression on the popular memory. His moustaches and short pointed beard seem to form a contrast with his priestly robes and to give to his face a military look which dissociates him from the Church and transposes him to the temporal world.

Since his own day he has been portrayed in a number of different ways. Poets and novelists have vied with historians in creating a legend around the cardinal which has both made him widely known and shrouded him in mystery. Historical textbooks (whose opinions, having been thrust upon people in their youth, are sometimes accepted by them as authoritative for the rest of their lives) praise Richelieu's achievements highly and give the impression that he was always right. His opponents or enemies consequently appear as men whose intentions were evil, men who were perverse or culpable. Yet since the hatred which Richelieu aroused has become a literary theme and still echoes in our ears, the present-day Frenchman reveres him while realising that he was a formidable master and that it was none too pleasant to live under his rule. To Richelieu belongs the credit for great victories in the field and for the terms of

---

* The title 'principal minister' was generally conferred upon everyone who was admitted to the inner or privy Council. (V.L.T.)

the Treaties of Westphalia, which, although concluded after his death, bear the imprint of his ideas. A united France with her eyes turned towards the future; the foundation of a colonial empire; and a period of astounding literary and intellectual activity symbolised by Descartes and Corneille: these, too, form part and parcel of Richelieu's glory.

Richelieu exalted the power of the French monarchy beyond compare: yet certain aspects of his work have been invoked by governments ill disposed towards absolute monarchy. Some have credited this champion of authority with ideas which would have been appropriate to the nineteenth century with its liberal outlook. For example, as the ally of Protestant princes fighting against the hegemony of a single power, was not Richelieu the harbinger of a federal Europe? However, during the present century voices have been raised in dissent outside France: on the contrary, did not Richelieu's imperialism give rise to interminable struggles between France and her neighbours? Did he not prevent the union of all Christian peoples and substitute a passionate nationalism for the brotherhood of man advocated by the Christian religion? By relying overmuch on authority, did he not create a malaise in French society which was eventually to find expression in the Revolution? By ruining the house of Austria did he not prepare the way for the rise of Prussia and of a united and conquering Germany? But there is no need to press such questions further, for the existence of so many contradictions around the cardinal's memory only goes to prove his essential greatness. There is no denying that like all great men (indeed like all men, but especially those who are great) he will always remain partly an enigma. Even so he meant to hand down his secret to posterity. He drew up a 'political testament' for Louis XIII. The authenticity of the *Testament politique* has long been a matter for argument, but it remains one of the essential books of all time. In addition he left some memoirs, and a large part of his correspondence has been collected and published. But is all this sufficient? Was Richelieu always sincere in what he wrote? Did he reveal everything? Is a man ever capable of revealing everything?

No one can be sure of understanding Richelieu completely. But the risk of misjudging him is far greater if one attempts to explain him by reference to subsequent events and epochs later than his own instead of placing him in the social context to which he belonged and the age that was his—an age which he certainly observed very closely and which he understood very well.

Armand Jean du Plessis de Richelieu belonged to a noble family which derived from both the *noblesse d'épée* and the *noblesse de robe*, a family subject to a mixture of influences both provincial and Parisian. He was born in 1585, the son of François du Plessis and Suzanne de la Porte. He did not enter the Church of his own choice but so as to keep the gift of the bishopric of Luçon within the family when his brother Alphonse renounced it in order to become a Carthusian. This lack of a sense of vocation, or rather his previous inclination which pointed unmistakably to a military career, endowed Richelieu with a capacity for feeling at home in secular life [*une aisance dans le siècle*] and a taste for acting like a layman which to a large extent explain his career. As a noble belonging to that intermediate section of the nobility which looked to the court for its welfare, he always kept his eyes turned towards the seat of government. First he sought the protection of the great personages of the day such as Concini and the queen mother: then he made himself one of their clientele; and finally, by attaching himself directly to the king, he became a dependant of the most exalted personage of them all.

As we shall see, Richelieu extended the operation of this system of patronage to a marked degree. Whilst proclaiming political principles in which he also believed, he sought in practice, and as far as the means at his disposal allowed, to place all France at the king's service and to admit no other clientele than the king's.

Although Richelieu was a churchman without a vocation, it would be a serious error to imagine that he was lukewarm in his religious convictions and that he only valued his position as bishop or cardinal as a means of achieving his ambitions or as a cover for his policy. The seventeenth century was an age that was fervently religious and to seventeenth-century eyes Richelieu was neither an apostle nor a saint. Occasionally he shocked Louis XIII himself, who on days when he was in a bad temper used to accuse the cardinal of believing in nothing. He is reputed to have indulged in relations which were not merely amorous but incestuous; of this, however, there is no proof. He was answerable only to his own conscience or to his confessor for his thoughts and weaknesses, but he never caused a scandal and never gave the appearance of being a bad priest. Indeed for fifteen years, from 1608 to 1623, he was a very good bishop, attentive to the needs of his flock and active in nurturing it on the Church's teaching.

Not only had Richelieu himself made a considerable study of theology, but in addition his entourage included theologians whom he used to consult frequently. Moreover he appreciated the services which the Church and its clergy could render the monarchy—an attitude that was based on his own experience as priest and bishop. These three factors combined to keep him indissolubly wedded to the Church. He lived in an age and a society that were deeply impregnated by religion, in which there were a variety of ways by which the Church's interests could be upheld. He was far from being the only Catholic priest or bishop in Europe to concern himself with politics. Precisely because the papacy was anxious to implement the Tridentine programme of reform by a number of different methods, it was held to be no bad thing at Rome for a churchman to be at the head of a government. As general practice it would not have been welcome, but some exceptions seemed extremely useful. One has only to note the place occupied by chapter 2 ('Concerning the Church') in the *Testament politique* to appreciate the services that could be rendered to the Catholic Church by a statesman who was well informed about its doctrine and fully qualified to draw a dividing line between the City of God and the City of Man.* As was his duty as a statesman, Richelieu the king's minister subordinated everything to 'the conservation of the Crown'; but he never sacrificed Catholic doctrine or the Catholic faith.

But what of Richelieu as a person? In the first place he possessed a high level of intelligence which undoubtedly set him apart from the majority of men; with it he had the gift of perceiving what was essential in the different aspects of a situation and an equally marked aptitude for distinguishing between the general and the particular. He possessed both a creative imagination which enabled him to plan major ventures, and a common sense which kept him clear of wild schemes. The broad sweep of his ideas was to a degree rarely found in great men equalled by his interest in detail. His capacity for work was astounding. Louis XIII, a man of very meagre parts compared to Richelieu but far from being a fool, for he was endowed with plenty of common sense, undoubtedly appreciated the power of the cardinal's intellect compared to that of others with whom he had dealings. It was for this reason that he came to regard Richelieu as the man who served him best.

The paramount traits in Richelieu's character were his ambition and his will-power, which inevitably carried him on towards greatness and made him fanatically determined in anything he undertook. These attributes prevailed over his excessively highly strung disposition and indifferent health. Unlike Louis XIII, who is believed in the light of present-day medical knowledge to have been tuberculous, Richelieu had a basically sound constitution which he wore out through overwork and the

---

* In his great work *The City of God* St Augustine divided mankind into two 'cities' whose inhabitants intermingled—the heavenly city and the earthly city.

effects of a moral strain which was too much for his nerves. He was very often ill, apparently as a result of driving himself too hard. He suffered from intermittent disorders of the kidneys and bladder, and his nervous exhaustion frequently betrayed itself not in violent scenes but in sudden fits of weeping. His tendency to give way to tears was stigmatised as play-acting by those who disliked him, but Richelieu himself found it humiliating. The pliancy, not to say toadying, of which this arrogant man was capable may well cause surprise. It was derived from contemporary behaviour and the customs of the court, confirmed perhaps by those current in the Church—an Italianate tendency towards exaggerated humility accompanied by an abundance of flattering gestures and turns of phrase. The cardinal indulged in these to such an extent that he inevitably acquired a reputation for duplicity and double-dealing.

It is difficult to speak of the inner man. Richelieu spent his life in a continual battle with his enemies. He knew that he was hated and, being far too clear-sighted to entertain any illusions, could see how his own duplicity was matched by other men's hypocrisy. Did he allow any place in his life for private affections and those tender emotions which Louis XIII was for ever seeking? Richelieu was certainly not inhuman. He was sometimes implacable but not pitiless.

After sacrificing some guilty person to the overriding needs of the State, he would display, by his tactful choice of words, delicacy of feeling and respect for the sorrow of those whom his severity had plunged into mourning. He showed solicitude for his close relations, but this was a trait which was characteristic of his class and his age rather than a symptom of his own soft-heartedness. He was sensitive to beauty and grace. Many people have made fun of his fondness for cats, which is to be explained by his need for light relief and relaxation, and may also have reflected a certain disenchantment with the company of human beings. He undoubtedly felt affection for the king, 'the best master that ever was'; although he found Louis XIII's uneasy and moody temper disquieting, it also aroused his pity, and he was touched by his acts of kindness. He was fond of Father Joseph with his unwearying self-sacrifice, and of his graceful and devoted niece, Mme de Combalet, the duchess of Aiguillon.[1] The sculptor Girardon was to portray her weeping figure on the cardinal's tomb. But none of these attachments claimed Richelieu entirely. Perhaps his lot as a priest explains his rejection of the pleasures of private life in favour of his mission and the pursuit of his ideals. He had renounced the quest for happiness in this world. His will to participate in great deeds overrode everything.

Richelieu brought with him on his accession to power an extremely wide range of experience. There was scarcely a problem which he had not already examined. As Henri Hauser has pointed out in a book that we will have occasion to mention again,[2] the difficulties of an impecunious existence during his youth and his modest beginnings at Luçon had given Richelieu a sense of reality and a first-hand acquaintance with the economics of everyday life which stood him in good stead when he became the king's minister; but the period that he spent in provincial seclusion had added to his store of knowledge in other ways also. His muddy province of Poitou was a good school. There he got to know the poor peasants of the countryside, the sailors who lived on the sea coast, the small-town officials and the Protestant country gentry so numerous in those parts. It is always said that Richelieu knew nothing of, and despised, the peasantry. This is incorrect; it would be more accurate to say that more important affairs diverted his attention elsewhere. But in the earlier part of his career he saw the peasantry for himself and observed them at close hand. At the other end of the social scale, he knew the court better than anyone. He had fathomed both its pettiness and its grandeur.

Richelieu had had some experience of ministerial office during the six months in 1616–17 when he had been secretary of state for war and foreign affairs. He knew the men who formed what we would nowadays call the personnel of the diplomatic service. To take a case in point: the fact that Nicolas de Baugy, the resident French ambassador in Brussels, now came under Richelieu's orders once more was not without importance, for he was an experienced diplomat who seven years previously had held the difficult post of ambassador at Prague. In addition Richelieu was fully acquainted with what went on in the Council and in the various administrative departments. Neither their methods nor their staff held any mystery for him. He had had dealings with, or had met, most of the chief army officers, and during the armed demonstrations of 1620 and the wars of 1621 and 1622 he had followed the course of events with the keen interest of a man who still felt the attraction of a military career. Nothing escaped his notice therefore, neither the levying of troops nor the changes of fortune that had marked the various sieges. He weighed up the arguments for and against each operation.

Richelieu never left France, apart from a journey to Rome in 1608, for his period of exile at Avignon can hardly be considered as residence abroad. But this did not prevent him from being highly knowledgeable about Europe and the world in general. Travellers from afar, monks and missionaries were all welcomed into the intimacy of his household and used to tell him about all sorts of different things to which his contemporaries paid little attention.

He owed a great deal to Father Joseph, a shrewd observer who had formed a clear idea of the frame of mind peculiar to each nation. Like the Capuchin, Richelieu saw Europe as varied, indeed variegated: its peoples differed from each other not only in their aptitudes and tastes but also in their outlook. He attached great importance to foreign opinion and believed that France's external policy should take it into account.

The number of his acquaintances enabled Richelieu to gauge the extent to which the last few years (which he possibly thought of as beginning with the death of Henry IV) had been disastrous for France. The realm was 'a sick body' to which remedies must be applied. These are his own words. A sick body but basically robust. He saw no reason for despair or for simply accepting the situation.

But the disease had made inroads everywhere. It had undoubtedly gained a hold within the government, owing to the incompetence of some of the ministers and to the way that the others had allowed routine to blunt their initiative.* Indeed, was there a single section of society that was not affected? The nobility were unruly, idle, quarrelsome, and always cadging for favours. They were of vital importance to the State in that it was they who went to make up the army and formed its 'sinews'; but they were always ready to embark on some mischief. Duels had been becoming increasingly frequent for some time. It is difficult for us to realise the full gravity of the situation except by thinking of those waves of crime which occasionally sweep through certain districts or particular cities. 'The blood of the nobility flowed in streams,' said Richelieu. In vain did the Church take alarm and hurl anathemas. A false sense of honour, or rather a cruel fashion which engulfed an entire class, plunging it into anarchy, prevailed over all other considerations. Shameless pillaging of the Treasury by persons who had obtained orders for sums to be paid them without given reason [*acquits au comptant*]; court favourites and great nobles who gorged themselves on offices and pensions; officials who throve on graft and jobbery: these were among the other alarming features that went to make up the general picture.

This picture is painted by Richelieu himself as a sort of introduction to the *Testament politique* in the section entitled 'Succincte narration des grandes actions du Roi'. One word in particular recurs over and over

* *la routine où s'étaient rouillés les autres.*

again—"disorder" [*dérèglement*]—and one sentence sums up everything: 'Each man used his effrontery as a yardstick to measure his deserts.'*

'The conduct of those to whom Your Majesty had entrusted the helm of your State could not be continued without utter ruin', Richelieu goes on to say, 'yet their course of action could not be straightway changed without violating the dictates of prudence, which do not suffer a man to pass from one extreme to the other without first attempting the middle course.' With these words, probably written in 1638, Richelieu defines the guiding principle which had inspired his conduct of affairs for nearly fifteen years: strength of purpose tempered by caution. And in a subsequent passage he indicates the programme which he had set himself: 'I promised Your Majesty to employ all my industry and all the authority which it pleased you to grant me to ruin the Huguenot party, to abase the pride of the great nobles, to reduce all your subjects to the obedience that they owe you and to restore your name among foreign nations to the position which it should rightly hold.'3

This celebrated passage has been the starting-point for a disastrous tradition in the scholastic world according to which Richelieu's work as a statesman amounted to the realisation of a three-point programme which he carried out in successive stages: the ruin of the Huguenot party (up to the capture of La Rochelle); the subjection of the great nobles (apparently completed after the Day of Dupes in 1630, or at least after the execution of Montmorency in 1632); and then from 1635 to 1642 war with the house of Austria. For a long time it was even believed that Richelieu intended to restore to France her natural frontiers, the boundaries of ancient Gaul—an error which must be unsparingly condemned, for it still finds acceptance in recent publications. It must therefore be emphasised that this theory was refuted many years ago in more than one important historical work.† Further proof of its falsity is provided by the recent edition of Richelieu's *Testament politique* published by Louis André.

The references to the boundaries of ancient Gaul which have been attributed to Richelieu are not in fact his. They do not appear in the authentic version of the *Testament politique*, they have the effect of distorting certain of its statements and completely altering their meaning, and are taken from a pseudo-testament in Latin entitled *Testamentum christianum, testamentum politicum* written by Father Labbé, a Jesuit (1596–1678). Later

* '*Chacun mesurait son mérite sur son audace.*'

† Those of Gaston Zeller. (V.L.T.)

we will see by what motives the cardinal was inspired in his contest with the house of Austria.

In the year 1624, when he proclaimed the need to 'restore the king's name among foreign nations', Richelieu was thinking in terms of an unmistakable decline in France's position in the world, which represented more than a decline in her diplomatic prestige. He was greatly concerned to observe that France's maritime commerce was everywhere rapidly on the wane, that most commodities destined for internal trade were brought to French ports by foreign seamen, and that French manufactured and agricultural products were likewise transported from French ports in foreign ships.

He knew that French shipping in the Mediterranean was harassed by Barbary corsairs from north Africa who used to sail up to the coast of Provence with complete impunity. A large number of Frenchmen had been carried off as captives 'to Algiers' and enslaved or condemned to serve in the crews of their captors.* In planning the formation of his Christian Militia Father Joseph envisaged a crusade against the Turks which would have rescued a large number of these Christian captives.

But there was more to Richelieu's concern with France's weakness at sea than this. Although he may not have been acquainted with all the secrets of the court at Madrid, he knew that the Spain of Philip IV, now governed by an extremely able minister, the count-duke of Olivares, was giving renewed attention to maritime affairs. Since the resumption of the war against the Dutch, Olivares had formed the opinion that it was not enough to use land forces only to conquer them. The Dutch must be fought with their own weapons: their sea-borne commerce must be made to suffer so that Dutch trade was everywhere superseded by Spanish.

In this same year, 1624, Spain created a privileged trading company, the Almirantazgo, composed of Spanish, Flemish and Hanseatic merchants; it was to be responsible for trade with ports located in Spanish possessions or with foreign ports requiring Spanish goods. In addition a royal ordinance, or *pragmàtica*† issued in 1623, had imposed severe controls on commerce and forbidden the import into Spain of foreign manu-

---

* This had happened to Saint Vincent de Paul in the course of only a short trip on business. The ship on which he was travelling was boarded by corsairs off Marseilles. (V.L.T.)

† 'An ordinance made by the King outside the Cortes and having the force of law in so far as it did not conflict with the statutes made jointly by King and Cortes.' (Elliott, p. 577).

factured goods which were not strictly required for domestic
consumption or for trade within the Spanish Empire. Thus the French
saw outlets for their overseas trade being closed to them on all sides,
while on the other hand foreigners, whether Dutch, Spanish or English
(but especially the Dutch), had access to French ports, where they were
establishing a commercial monopoly.

The French merchant fleet was not large enough to cope with France's
maritime trade and was in no position to take risks in the absence of protection from the King's navy. Indeed there was no longer any question of
such protection being available. 'The navy was at that time so neglected
that Your Majesty had not a single ship left.' The decadent condition of
the navy, positively frightening in the case of a country which was bordered by the sea on three sides, was undoubtedly one of Richelieu's main
anxieties when he assumed power.

To the cardinal's mind two threats to France's security were rendered
yet more acute by her weakness at sea. Of these the first, a threat from
within, came from the Protestants. It was not the question of religion
that was at issue but simply that of royal authority. How could the king
agree to the control of France's western seaboard being exercised by
unruly subjects who were ready to engage in war against him and to seek
alliance with foreign powers? It was no longer a question of determining
which side had been the first offender. It was impossible to allow
France's maritime interests, vital as they were to her welfare, to be endangered by private interests any longer.

The second threat stemmed from recent events in the Valtelline, where
the clash of religious principles and interests had also been detrimental to
France. To please the pope the Valtelline had been virtually handed over
to the Spaniards. There were now no communications by land between
France and the Venetian Republic or the petty Italian princes. The only
route into Italy lay through the territory of the duke of Savoy, an ally of
France admittedly, but not an ally whose loyalty could be relied upon in
all circumstances. And after entering Savoy, what next? The French
would find astride their path the Milanese—one of the provinces where
Spanish garrisons were strongest and most numerous. It followed that
the occupation of the Valtelline made the sea route from France to Italy
via the Mediterranean more vital than ever. But France was no better
supplied with galleys than she was with ocean-going ships, and thus
found herself equally handicapped in the Mediterranean: there too she
derived no advantage from her geographical position or from the sea-
coast of Provence.

This capacity to take a broad view of the situation enabled Richelieu to rise above the interests of factions and groups and to prepare himself for the pursuit of a policy that would serve both the nation and the monarchy.

The Protestants were well aware that the cardinal was not leniently disposed towards them. He had attacked their political views in a little book entitled *Les Principaux points de la Foi*,[4] in which he took them to task 'for conceding to the people an authority greatly exceeding that which they themselves denied to the pope' and for allowing that a people could judge its kings and, if need be, depose them too. In short, to Richelieu's mind Protestant opinions smacked of republicanism. His own political convictions, based as they were, in M. Deloche's words, 'on an unalterable, superior and universal system of belief',[5] were opposed to a doctrine which attributed both the source and the control of power 'to human forces allowed to follow separately their own devices'; this was a view which *a priori* justified 'particularism'. The complete incompatability of Richelieu's ideas with those of the Protestants did not, however, mean that once he was in power he would embark on hostilities against the Huguenots. His actions were to be governed by prudence alone.

The Protestants therefore placed no hope in Richelieu. As for the Catholics, each of the two factions had some grounds for believing that the cardinal was on its side.

Those who were known as the *dévots* desired the king and his Council, no matter what the circumstances, to adopt a policy both at home and abroad which was in conformity with the interests of the Catholic Church. In advocating this policy they had no intention of sacrificing French interests; they simply refused to admit that there could be any incompatibility between the interests of France and the admonitions of the papacy. The *dévot* party often drew its inspiration from the Jesuits; and it was the Jesuits moreover who were blamed by their opponents for everything that the *dévots* said or did.

The Catholics who belonged to the other group called themselves *les bons Français*. They too were faithful to the Church of Rome but they had been indoctrinated with Gallican traditions. Descended as they were from the *Politiques* of the sixteenth century, they tended to form a sort of 'third force' occupying an intermediate position between Huguenot individualism and the universal claims of Rome. They wanted royal policy to be first and foremost independent and French, and they wished it to be exclusively concerned with furthering the interests of the realm. A number of magistrates in the Parlements, lawyers and merchants belonged to this party.

The *dévots* thought that a churchman who had originally been a

member of the queen mother's coterie and who was also a friend of
Bérulle and Father Joseph (himself closely associated with the duke of
Nevers, a very militant Catholic), could not fail to belong to their party.
But the *bons Français* counted on the cardinal's support quite as fully as the
dévots because he condemned the policy pursued by his predecessors—a
policy which had been very markedly tinged by *dévot* influence.

The two parties were not organised like the parties of our own day,
but were a reflection of two trends of opinion. Representatives of both
schools of thought could be found within one and the same family. The
influence of a single person (especially in the shape of a confessor or of a
priest who was also a friend) could be enough to bring about a change in
opinion or a shift in attitude.

Although they had hitherto been at loggerheads with each other,
Richelieu met at the outset with an equally friendly reception from both
sides. It was therefore incumbent on him to guide and instruct this unstable trend of opinion thus prolonging the strange and precarious
alliance between the two parties for his own benefit. He had to take care
that it did not disintegrate and maintain as broad a measure of support
behind him as possible.

Despite the absence of a national press like ours, there was no lack of
means for influencing public opinion. Little printed pamphlets used to be
circulated, consisting of four or five pages or sometimes more. By these
means a man could keep himself informed and read arguments in
favour of such and such a cause. Sometimes these pamphlets were
newsletters which described what was happening, sometimes they were
lampoons attacking some great person or his coterie or policy. At other
times they would take the form of 'discourses' or memorials, which
would be written in a more detached manner and devoted to the examination of some topic, but ended by adopting a certain point of
view.

In short, these pamphlets resembled present-day 'leaders' published
separately. They might be anonymous or semi-anonymous, they might
give a true or presumptive indication of their origin: 'a letter from a
gentleman', 'the opinion of an impartial theologian', 'the answer of a
true (or of a good) Frenchman', and so on. Sometimes they would give
one another the cue for a come-back, like controversial writers of our
own day. A certain number of these pamphlets were republished every
year in *Le Mercure François*, a kind of annual review; or again after a
few months they might be incorporated in a collection of items or 'dis-

courses' which comprised everything that had been written about a person or event.

In legal and official circles and amongst the bourgeoisie in towns all over France—for it would be an exaggeration to think too exclusively in terms of Paris, although Paris was certainly the place where public opinion counted most—these publications were greatly relished. A man would discuss them with his neighbours. They would be passed from hand to hand. They did not represent the press as we know it, but they had at least a comparable influence. They played a considerable part during the regency of Marie de Medici, and an even more important role during the first years of Louis XIII's government.

The cardinal, who had been connected with the pamphleteering campaign that had hastened the fall of La Vieuville, was now about to resort to the same means in order to publicise and justify his policy. One of the most ardent of the propagandists on behalf of the *bons Français* was a cleric named François Langeais Fancan, a canon of Saint-Germain-l'Auxerrois.[6] Fancan was one of the most brilliant controversialists who ever lived. He had entered Richelieu's service early —in about 1617 or 1618. In 1623, in an allegory entitled *La France mourante ou Discours du chancelier de l'Hôpital au chevalier Bayard, dit sans reproche*, he had painted a picture of the disastrous plight into which France had fallen.[7] After attacking the Brûlarts and the prince of Condé, he ended with a pathetic appeal to the king in which he implicitly advised him to call upon Richelieu. Fancan was not only a wholehearted *bon Français* and a passionate enemy of Spain, but also had a certain secret leaning towards the 'libertines' or free-thinkers. Even so, he was, together with Father Joseph, one of Richelieu's ablest propagandists until in 1627 he was mysteriously disgraced and sent to the Bastille, where he remained a prisoner for the rest of his life.

Father Joseph himself composed a large number of discourses on European affairs, and although his biographer, Canon Dedouvres, has been overgenerous in attributing to him the authorship of every contemporary pamphlet which happened to be well informed, he certainly showed himself to be a leading expert on European affairs. Despite his fervent Catholicism and unqualified devotion to Rome, Father Joseph had no liking for Spain and used to defend his master's forceful yet cautious policy with arguments that were highly effective. He was Richelieu's constant adviser, and there were times when it was he who provided the inspiration for Richelieu's policy.

We must also mention Mathieu de Morgues or de Mourgues who quarrelled with Richelieu as early as 1626 and who after the Day of Dupes harnessed his career to the queen mother's chariot wheels. He was to become one of the cardinal's bitterest and most dangerous enemies. Other propagandists in Richelieu's service included Paul Hay du Chastelet, Jean Sirmond, Jean de Silhon and du Ferrier, a former pastor of the Reformed Church who, after being converted to Catholicism, became a *Conseiller d'État*.* The list could be extended even further.

Richelieu did not have to make any changes during the first months of his ministry. All outstanding business had been initiated in La Vieuville's day. The cardinal simply took over where the latter had left off, but gave to his conduct of affairs the imprint of his own personality.

La Vieuville had sent an ambassador extraordinary to Switzerland charged with the task of settling matters in the Valtelline. The envoy chosen was the marquis de Coeuvres—Annibal d'Estrées, the brother of the fair Gabrielle. He was not to confine himself to diplomatic negotiations but was to levy troops, appear in force before the fortresses occupied by the pope's soldiers and demand that they be handed over to him. This he proceeded to do during the winter of 1624–5—to the great alarm of the *dévots*, who denounced his behaviour as scandalous and tantamount to war against the pope. The sovereign pontiff, Urban VIII, who had succeeded Gregory XV in 1623, soon dispatched a legate to Paris in the shape of his nephew, the young Cardinal Francesco Barberini. It was the latter's mission to secure an undertaking that at least the Catholic inhabitants of the Valtelline should not be transferred back to the brutal rule of the Grisons. But Richelieu replied that the Grisons had rights over the valleys in question and were, in addition, allies of France: for the sake of his reputation and security the king could not allow his allies to suffer prejudice.

It was also La Vieuville who a few weeks before his disgrace had concluded the Treaty of Compiègne with the Estates-General of the United Provinces, whereby Louis XIII paid the Dutch a subsidy of 2,200,000 livres to enable them to continue the war against Spain. In return the Dutch placed twenty warships at the king's disposal and undertook to make no truce or peace without France's consent. They also guaranteed the free exercise of the Catholic religion to all Frenchmen who entered their service.

* For the role of a *Conseiller d'État*, see p. 53 above. Jérémie du Ferrier (*c.* 1570–1626) had been a pastor at Nîmes. (Léonard, pp. 368–9)

It was yet again La Vieuville who had opened negotiations for the marriage of the prince of Wales with Louis XIII's sister, Henrietta Maria —negotiations which dashed the hopes of the young princess. She had been brought up in the expectation that she would marry her cousin, the comte de Soissons, and the two children had indulged in an innocent love affair. But there were strong political arguments in favour of an alliance with England. It was essential to bar the way to a rapprochement between England and Spain, which had been mooted all too often in recent years; in addition it was necessary to bind the English King firmly to the interests of the French monarchy so as to prevent any collusion between him and the Huguenots.

The *dévots* welcomed the English marriage. They hoped that the French government would induce the king of England to adopt a more liberal policy towards his Catholic subjects—possibly in the shape of a declaration authorising them to worship freely [*une déclaration de liberté*].* At this time Catholic clergy were working secretly for the conversion of England—one of the papacy's major preoccupations. However, there were no grounds for being unduly optimistic. In Richelieu's opinion the main point had been won when James I gave a private undertaking not to enforce the penal laws and to tolerate the celebration of Mass by English Catholics in their own homes. Bérulle had gone to Rome to obtain the necessary dispensations for the marriage. It was understood that Henrietta Maria was to remain a Catholic, that her children were to be brought up as Catholics until they reached the age of twelve and that she was to have her own chapel in London at which French priests were to officiate. While negotiations were still in progress James I died. It was not the prince of Wales therefore, but the new king of England, Charles I, represented by the duke of Chevreuse, to whom 'Madame Henriette' was married by proxy on 11 May 1625 outside the west door of Notre-Dame Cathedral.[8]

Charles I sent the duke of Buckingham to meet his bride. The duke, who was both young and adventurous, was the new king's favourite just as he had been his father's, but the English thought him the devil incarnate. His standing meant that he was as powerful as he was hated. His mission was to propose secretly to Louis XIII an alliance between the two countries and an immediate declaration of war on Spain. But Riche-

---

* If this concession had been obtained it would no doubt have taken the form of a royal proclamation suspending the operation of the penal laws against Roman Catholics such as had been demanded by the Spaniards during the Anglo-Spanish marriage negotiations of 1623: *cf.* Charles II's Declaration of Indulgence of 1672.

lieu did not yet want to break with Spain completely. It suited him better to confine himself to clearing the Valtelline, and he preferred to injure the Spaniards indirectly by means of an expedition against their ally Genoa under the command of Lesdiguières and the duke of Savoy, or by subsidising Mansfeld to enable him to come to the rescue of the Dutch forces besieged in Breda. More than this the cardinal could not, for the moment, undertake.

Buckingham was displeased to find Richelieu so guarded in his attitude, and meanwhile his arrival at the French court provided other causes for anxiety. The duke was good-looking and well aware of his charm. He went so far as to pay court to Anne of Austria. Mme de Chevreuse took a delight in playing on the young queen's romantic imagination. Buckingham was pressing in his attentions, and the queen became disturbed and unhappy. By the time the court had taken up residence at Amiens on the eve of Henrietta's departure for England, the affair had almost become an open scandal.

The situation with regard to the Protestants was also deteriorating. The terms of the Peace of Montpellier remained a dead letter. The king delayed demolishing Fort-Louis, which enabled him to keep an eye on La Rochelle, and at several points the Huguenots continued to build fortifications.

Soubise had seized a small fleet in the Gulf of Morbihan which Father Joseph and the duke of Nevers had fitted out for the use of their Christian Militia on the proposed expedition to rescue Christians held captive by the Infidel. He also occupied Ré and Oléron,[9] but was driven out of these islands in September by Toiras, the king's *maréchal de camp*.[10]

Lacking ships himself, Louis XIII had been obliged to call upon the United Provinces to provide them in accordance with the recent treaty, and the Dutch had sent a small fleet to fight their own co-religionists on the French king's behalf. It had been a dangerous experiment, however, and to repeat it was out of the question. Did not this state of affairs justify what Richelieu had written in a memorandum to the king in the previous May: 'So long as the Huguenots have a foothold in France, the king will never be master in his own house and will be unable to carry out any notable exploit abroad.'[11]

Indeed, it looked as if 'notable exploits' were the exclusive prerogative of the king of Spain. Mansfeld's relieving forces failed to maintain their positions before Breda and the Dutch garrison there was compelled to surrender to Spinola. This event, which created a profound impression throughout Europe and is still regarded as one of the great military feats of the Thirty Years War, has been immortalised by Veláquez in his wonderful painting 'Las Lanzas'.

Even so, the *dévots* refused to be alarmed by Spanish victories. They denounced the inconsistency of royal policy in supporting heresy abroad despite the fact that the king was forced to fight the Protestants within his own dominions. Marie de Medici allowed herself to be won over by these arguments. It was surely of her that Richelieu was thinking when he mentioned to the king in a further memorandum dated 3 September 'evil bruits spread abroad daily by sundry well-known persons: that Your Majesty and his Council openly protect heretics'.[12]

The cardinal did not yet feel himself in a strong enough position to impose single-handed a policy which was patently disconcerting. It seemed to him essential for it to be approved by an extraordinary Council. This would invest his conduct of affairs with some measure of national approval: 'Moreover, Sire, all your subjects will have had the honour of giving their opinions, inasmuch as they will be represented by those principal personages who are to be summoned to the said Council. On being acquainted by them with Your Majesty's devout meaning and noble resolutions, your subjects will feel all the more eager and obliged to do their part for Your Majesty's service.'[13]

This Council met at Fontainebleau on 29 September. It included the queen mother, the cardinals, and the dukes and peers of the realm, together with some high-ranking army officers and magistrates from the Parlement.

The Council's main concern was with the Valtelline. A few days previously the pope's legate had asked for his farewell audience, and had left without any understanding being reached. Aligre, the chancellor, gave an exposé of the situation and expressed the opinion that hostilities should be continued both in the Valtelline and against Genoa. But he reminded those present that the king wanted to hear their views—views which they could all express freely. Marshal Schomberg spoke of the legate's ill will. Marie de Medici then intervened to say tartly that she had not noticed anything of the sort, that on the contrary the legate had seemed to her very well disposed towards France. Everyone looked at his neighbour and then lowered his eyes, duly noting this first sign of a change in the queen mother's accommodating attitude towards Richelieu's opinions. Cardinal Sourdis, the archbishop of Bordeaux, recommended an armistice. Richelieu became slightly agitated. He explained that he, too, preferred peace to war but that under present circumstances the king would bring dishonour on himself by breaking off hostilities. Cardinal La Valette made a very adroit speech. He reported what he had heard during his recent stay in Rome. The pope had consulted some theologians as to whether he was not committing a sin in allowing the Valtelline to revert to the power of the Grisons. The theologians had answered categorically that according to the Church's teaching it was the duty of all subjects to obey their rulers. It followed, therefore, that the Spaniards were making use of religion as a cover for their evil schemes and that it was right and proper for the king to stand firm. Bassompierre gave his approval, and then the first president of the Parlement of Paris assured the king of the whole-hearted support of his [judicial] officers and of their devoted loyalty to him in all his undertakings. As no one else asked to speak, the session apparently ended with unanimous approval of Richelieu's policy.

But his opponents did not consider themselves beaten. Within a few weeks pamphlets written in Latin, the international language of the time, were circulating in large numbers within the realm. They asserted that there was a diabolical conspiracy afoot in Europe to help the Huguenots, and begged the king of France to counter it by coming to terms with Spain and with the pope. The most noteworthy of these pamphlets were the 'Political Mysteries' (*Mysteria politica*) and the 'Admonition to King Louis XIII' (*Admonitio ad regem Ludovicum*). They were extremely disquieting, in that they seemed to vest the Church and the Holy See with the right to control the temporal policy of kings. Richelieu submitted them to an assembly of the French clergy which condemned them, explaining however in a preamble that the pope's spiritual rights were not in dispute.

Richelieu's propagandists retorted very sharply to these pamphlets. Fancan, Ferrier, Sirmond and Father Joseph all entered the lists. One of the best of these rejoinders was *Le Catholique d'État*. The identity of its author or authors remains unknown, but it justified alliances between two nations belong to different religious creeds, and in respect of France herself declared that 'the enemies of our kings are the enemies of God'.

Meanwhile, Richelieu was looking far ahead into the future. Amidst all these difficulties he was engaged in working out far-reaching plans for reform of which he only spoke to those in whom he could safely confide but which have been preserved for us amongst his archives. We are too much aware of his anxiety about France's weakness at sea to be surprised at finding that the first memorandum is concerned with maritime affairs. As the *Testament politique* was to put it later: 'It is a prerequisite of our armed strength that the king should not only be strong by land but also powerful at sea.' Richelieu's attempt to put this policy into effect thus dates from as early as 1625: to secure the safety of those of his subjects who trade with the Levant and in order to uphold his reputation and dignity in the eyes of foreigners, the king is to have forty galleys available in French ports which are to be ready for action in summer and winter alike.

The cardinal also envisaged a series of regulations applicable to all the affairs of the realm[14] which are almost revolutionary in their implications for there was not an abuse that he shrank from attacking and no innovation, however daring, that he was not determined to introduce. If it had been practicable to put his plans for general reform into effect, there would have been a radical change in the character of the realm. It would have become a well-governed and honestly administered country, religious in its outlook and sensible in its behaviour. Political reform was to be secured by arranging for the king to be assisted by four Councils—a Supreme Council composed of four high-ranking members of the clergy and two laymen, a Military and Judicial Council with powers for dealing with the most important cases, a Council of Finance, and a Council of State. Religious and moral reform were to be promoted by acceptance of the decrees of the Council of Trent (except where incompatible with Gallican liberties), by the establishment of a seminary in each diocese (to be financed by the abbeys), and by an increase in the authority of bishops over priests so that only persons fit for the task were appointed to parishes. There were to be severe punishments for atheists (the word is written in Richelieu's own hand) and blasphemers. In addition, duels were to be suppressed and the death penalty was to be imposed on those who sought to break their marriage ties on fictitious grounds, alleging compulsion, consanguinity or impotence. The administrative reforms advocated by the cardinal included a reduction in the expenses of the king's household, the suppression of *acquits au comptant* and finally, to crown everything, abolition of the traffic in offices, or in his own words, 'the prohibition to sell or buy an office either through the disbursement of moneys or through other such means, forasmuch as venality of office spoils virtue of its reward and deprives us (he is speaking in the king's name) of the means of rewarding, choosing or employing those of our subjects who have rendered us the most services and are best qualified to do so'. All the defects of the system would thus be eliminated.

It is very important to realise that Richelieu had thought of all this as early as the first year of his ministry, and that it represented the realm that he wished to erect in place of the disorderly realm of which he had taken charge. This was no far-fetched figment of the imagination thought up by a visionary or philosopher for his own amusement. It provided Richelieu with a goal which he meant to keep in sight, although he fully realised that he would only attain it after a long period of patient perseverance.

For the moment the cardinal was bent on restoring peace as soon as possible. He sensed that the *dévots* wanted to involve him in a serious war with the Protestants in order to bring about the complete reduction of La Rochelle, that semi-republic on France's western seaboard. He did not believe that the government was yet in a position to run such a risk. He also knew that the English wanted to make use of localised clashes between French and Spanish interests to force France into a definite war with Spain.

The cardinal certainly realised that the time would come when he would find it hard to avoid embarking on both these wars. But that time had not yet come, and what he wanted now was peace. He would have liked to allay some minor disturbances which had recently occurred in Languedoc, and in this way drive a wedge between the Protestants in the south of France and those in La Rochelle. He therefore tried to come to an understanding with the former, but when he saw that the Huguenots of the south were unwilling to leave their brethren in the lurch and would only agree to a general peace treaty, he accepted the situation. He told Spada, the Pope's nuncio, that he was going to outrage world opinion for a second time, and on 5 February 1626 he made peace with the Huguenots.

As in the case of the previous treaties with the Protestants, the terms were moderate. Indeed they could almost be described as favourable to the Huguenots. Rohan and Soubise were restored to the king's favour, and La Rochelle kept its privileges, the only proviso being that a few of the town's defence works should be demolished. It should be noted, however, that no such proviso applied to Fort-Louis, which remained in the king's hands, although he undertook in return not to interfere with La Rochelle's freedom of trade with the islands of Ré and Oléron.

This new treaty infuriated the *dévots* and led to a breach between them and Richelieu. The cardinal was reviled as the patriarch of atheists; he was styled the supreme pontiff of the Calvinists and the cardinal of La Rochelle. But he endured these insults with composure, although they made his second task more difficult—a deal with Spain.

To France's allies, Venice and Savoy, such an agreement was far from welcome, but Richelieu was absolutely determined to achieve it. Even so the terms would have to be satisfactory from the French point of view. However, the ambassador at Madrid, the comte du Fargis, belonged to the *dévot* party, and his wife was a friend of the queen mother. In the King's Council it was no longer possible to count on Aligre, the chancellor, while of those with whom the cardinal used to try to maintain good relations Bérulle, for one, favoured making considerable concessions. Indeed, in their heart of hearts all Catholics felt that the Grisons had been the first offenders, and no one ascribed to France's indirect rights in the Valtelline the importance which they really possessed.

The cardinal was staggered by the terms of the original treaty signed by du Fargis and Olivares at Monzón. Admittedly the Valtelline was restored to the Grisons, but the Spaniards were given such extensive rights that the practical value of this concession was almost nullified. Richelieu would have liked to break off negotiations completely, but this he was unable to do, for he did not feel in a position to disavow or recall du Fargis. The most that he could do was to persuade the king that it was impossible to ratify the treaty in its existing form. The French demanded some minor alterations, and stood firm when those first suggested by the Spanish government seemed to fall short of what was required. Eventually a form of words was agreed upon which was obscure and none too satisfactory. The treaty was intended to settle all disputes between France and Spain, some of which were trading disputes that had arisen recently in the course of the year 1625. The Spanish government had ordered the seizure of goods belonging to French merchants and declined to offer adequate compensation for the losses incurred. But by now time was pressing. Contarini, the Venetian ambassador, was growing worried by the reports reaching him from his colleague in Spain. The prince of Piedmont had begun to ask for explanations and the pope's legate, Barberini, reappeared in Paris with fresh demands to make. The time had come to put a stop to it all, to cut short these conflicting recriminations by confronting these people with a *fait accompli*. Reluctantly Richelieu decided to be satisfied with what he had got, and arranged for the treaty to be approved by Louis XIII.[15]

A new character now appeared upon the stage. During the summer of 1626 the fortunes of Richelieu were to pass through an extremely critical period.

Of the five surviving children of Henry IV and Marie de Medici only 'Monsieur'—namely Gaston, duke of Anjou—still remained at the French court. Their three daughters now adorned foreign courts: Elisabeth, queen of Spain, was at Madrid; Christina was at the court of Turin; and Henrietta was queen of England, though unhappy in her lot, for her entire suite of French attendants, including even her chaplains, had been removed from her on the grounds that she was intriguing on behalf of the English Catholics.

The duke of Anjou gave no sign of possessing any remarkable qualities. It was said that his mother had always preferred him to her other children and that she invariably forgave him all his pranks. He did, in fact, lead the rather dissipated existence of a frivolous and extravagant young nobleman, but this did not give rise to scandal for there were many such at court. If Gaston was becoming a person of some importance it was because he was now eighteen and the childlessness of the royal couple made him the heir to the throne.

That the king and queen were on bad terms was a secret to no one. As we would say nowadays, they were temperamentally incompatible to the last degree. Nevertheless, since the day in January 1619 when Luynes had grabbed hold of the young king, dragged him into the queen's bedchamber, and compelled them to consummate their marriage, Louis XIII and Anne of Austria had continued to live as man and wife. On several occasions it had been announced that the queen was expecting a child. At the end of Lent in 1622 an accident had occurred in preposterous circumstances. One evening, the queen being then pregnant, Mme de Chevreuse and Mlle de Verneuil took it into their heads to persuade her to join in a race that involved sliding along the gallery of the Louvre. The queen fell heavily and had a miscarriage.

It was by no means certain that the royal couple would never have a son, as was their duty; but ill-disposed persons enjoyed saying as much and spreading rumours of a breach in relations between the king and queen such as made it impossible that the succession to the throne would ever be assured in the direct line.*

Monsieur was thus the heir, and he was now approaching the age at which his own marriage could be celebrated. Would this be to Louis XIII's advantage or not? If the duke of Anjou had children before his brother, would not his position at court be strengthened, and would there not be cause for fearing that he might become dangerous owing to the strength of his following and his inordinate demands? For as long as

* The falsity of these rumours became evident shortly afterwards for the queen had another accident in the autumn of 1626. (V.L.T.)

the queen had not given birth to a dauphin, was it not better to ensure that Monsieur remained a bachelor, so that 'Monsieur le prince' (Condé) retained the position of heir in reversion? In this way the two cousins would counterbalance each other.

However, there was an alternative view. If Monsieur had one or several sons, thereby increasing the number of the king's possible heirs, Louis XIII would be placed in a stronger position vis-à-vis all the princes of the house of Bourbon. He would be able to build up more of a following among them and play off the moderates against the intriguers.

In that case who was to marry Monsieur? Henry IV had been in the habit of making plans for the marriages of all his children as and when they were born. He had intended that his little son Gaston (who was only two years old when Henry himself was murdered) should marry a princess of about the same age and belonging to his own family—Mlle de Bourbon-Montpensier, princesse des Dombes. The little princess, who had lost her father at an early age and whose mother had subsequently married the duke of Guise, had already entered into possession of her inheritance, which was one of the largest in France; so to put Henry IV's plans into practice was reasonable enough, if only to make sure that the princess's fortune passed to the royal family and prevent its acquisition by strangers. Since he had been forced to give up the idea of marrying Henrietta Maria, the comte de Soissons had taken to demanding to marry Mlle de Montpensier by way of compensation so that her large fortune should be secured for him.

In the spring of 1626, when it became known that Richelieu, after considerable hesitation, had begun to urge the king to hasten Monsieur's betrothal, a whole faction came into being at court with the object of fighting the plan. It was known as the 'party adverse to the marriage'. It comprised Soissons, Condé and his family (who wished to remain close to the succession to the throne for as long as possible), Mme de Chevreuse (who was only too willing to court the limelight) and Queen Anne (because she had been told that she would in this way injure the cardinal). In short, this party included all Richelieu's enemies. It was also supported by Monsieur, who was flattered at becoming an object of general attention and at having a leading part to play after having been no more than a figurehead.

A party which was both numerous and strong enough to bring about a change of government attracted the notice of foreign powers. The English, whose attitude to Richelieu had become extremely chilly, and the Dutch, who had not forgiven him for the Treaty of Monzón, were both in touch with this group at court.

The duke of Anjou's governor was the maréchal d'Ornano.* Feeling that his own future was linked to that of his young master, he began to give himself airs. When the question arose of admitting the duke to the Council's sessions, as was indeed his due, the marshal claimed the right to follow him there even if he had to remain standing like the secretaries of state. Such questions of etiquette and precedence were of considerable importance in the seventeenth century, and many people would rather have lost half their fortune than renounce a rank or place to which they claimed to be entitled.

Richelieu was soon convinced that the marshal was exercising a most dangerous influence on the duke of Anjou, and he obtained from Louis XIII an order for his arrest. He was taken to the Bastille on 6 May, at the same time as Déageant and Modène, both of whom had formerly been friends of Luynes, the late constable. The latter's brother was in charge of the fortress at the time, but on the next day the king withdrew the command from him and entrusted it to the sieur du Tremblay, Father Joseph's brother. The queen mother did not appear to be surprised by the marshal's arrest, and even tried to calm Monsieur when he filled the court with his recriminations and threats against ministers. When he cross-examined Aligre, the chancellor, the latter lost countenance and protested that he had had no part in the affair. Richelieu, who had for long mistrusted Aligre, realised that it was impossible to allow such a spiritless creature to hold this important appointment any longer, and shortly afterwards Louis XIII called upon the chancellor to give up the seals, which were bestowed upon Michel de Marillac.† When the duke of Anjou addressed himself to the cardinal, the latter replied that he had indeed urged the king to have the marshal arrested as being not merely advisable but absolutely essential for the safety of his person, for the tranquillity of the State, and also for the good of His Highness the Prince.

Henceforth Richelieu's power was strikingly apparent, and the most resolute of the plotters came to the conclusion that the time for half-measures had passed: the cardinal must be assassinated. It was decided that the duke of Anjou should go in company with several gentlemen to

---

* The sons of a king of France were generally handed over to a governor for him to supervise their general education when they reached the age of seven. A governor was not however a tutor in the modern sense of the word, and the person chosen to occupy this much-coveted past was invariably a high-ranking army officer or noble.

† As a chancellor of France could not be removed from office the king could not dismiss Aligre; but he could suspend him from exercising a chancellor's duties by entrusting the custody and use of the seals to someone else. (V.L.T.)

ask him without prior warning if he would offer them hospitality at a country house where he was staying at Fleury, not far from Fontainebleau. During dinner the conspirators were to simulate a quarrel and come to blows, and in the tumult the cardinal was to be given a mortal wound.

The duchess of Chevreuse had inveigled one of her many suitors into taking part in the conspiracy. He was Henri de Talleyrand-Périgord, comte de Chalais, a young noble of high birth who held the appointment of master of the king's wardrobe. He was of the same age as Louis XIII and had been brought up at court close to the king. Possibly he resented the fact that he enjoyed no influence with the king, who had suddenly become infatuated with a M. de Barradas, a sturdy loutish youth from an insignificant family of the petty nobility. Richelieu was wary in his dealings with the king's new favourite but did not appear to take exception to him. Chalais was scatterbrained and talkative. He confided in his uncle the seigneur de Valençay, a commander of the Knights of Malta;[16] the latter declared that it was an appalling plot and that the only thing to do was to warn the cardinal.

Richelieu listened calmly to this shocking revelation. On the appointed day he was visited long after nightfall by the duke of Anjou's officers, who came to inform him of the prince's impending arrival. But instead of waiting for him, the cardinal set out at once for Fontainebleau. He arrived there at dawn whilst the duke was still asleep. As soon as he awoke Richelieu presented himself and expressed his regret at not having been informed sooner of the duke's desire to stay at Fleury: he was vacating the house and removing himself to another country property at Maison-rouge.[17] Monsieur was very sheepish, but what could he say? As a precaution the king provided the cardinal with an armed guard.

For some time Richelieu remained at Limours on the plea of ill health. He received a visit from the duke of Anjou, spoke to him kindly but firmly, and dissuaded him from following the bad advice that he had been given which only tended to introduce discord into the royal family. Monsieur seemed shaken and promised to inform Richelieu of any plots hatched against him. Next day, in Paris, the king, the queen mother and Monsieur signed an agreement whereby all three undertook to live in the closest unity with each other. Louis XIII promised to treat Monsieur as if he were his son and Marie de Medici stood surety for a good understanding between the two brothers (31 May 1626).

However, the cardinal, who had alerted his spies, was fully aware that the conspirators were still active. We cannot say for certain whether he knew all the details or whether he believed (or forced himself to believe) that Monsieur was ignorant of all the secret plans which were being made in his name. It was impossible to fight against the natural order of things—Gaston was the heir to the throne and it was vital for the welfare of the monarchy that there should be no breach between the king and his brother. This meant that Monsieur was almost bound to escape punishment. Was he capable of perceiving the gravity of the issues involved or did he only see that there was a cabal engaged in intrigues in his favour? Here again we find a code of conduct that belonged to the Middle Ages or characterised the Italianate intrigues of the court of the Valois.

At all events, the ramifications of the plot extended beyond France. There was serious talk of arranging for the duke of Anjou to flee the country and of instigating a revolt within the realm. The conspirators also considered the possibility of seizing the king's person and declaring him incapable of ruling; this was, perhaps, to be followed by the annulment of his marriage on the grounds of his impotence and the marriage of the queen to Monsieur. Such was the mania for intrigue which prevailed among the small group of plotters that it is impossible to know where they would have stopped.

Early in June, Louis XIII left Paris for Nantes, where a session of the provincial Estates of Brittany was due to be held. Richelieu behaved as if he did not mean to accompany the court, and wrote to the king begging him to accept his resignation. On 9 June the king replied from Blois with a letter which was as laudatory as it was affectionate. It enabled the cardinal to gauge the extent to which he had risen in his master's confidence and esteem in the past two years. 'Thanks be to God, everything has gone well with my affairs since you entered my service. I have every trust in you, and truly I never met any man who served me so much to my liking. Wherefore I do will and require you not to leave my service, for my affairs would go ill. . . . Monsieur, my brother, and many others bear a grudge against you on my account, but rest assured that I shall protect you against whomsoever it be and shall never forsake you. Madame my mother makes the same promise. I told you long since that my Council must be strengthened, but you have always been reluctant to do so from fear of making alterations. But now the time has passed for paying heed to what others may say. It is enough that it is I who will it so. . . . I shall dispel all slanders that may be uttered against you and let it be known that I wish members of my Council to cooperate with you [*aient l'habitude avec vous*]. Rest assured that I shall never change and that no matter who attacks you I will be your second. At Blois, this 9 June 1626, Louis.'

Louis XIII had never spoken like this before. As in 1617, he wished to reassert his power, but this time it was in order to install Richelieu close beside him. Indeed the king now filled his Council with men who were the cardinal's loyal supporters. Now that Marillac had become keeper of the seals the post of superintendent of finance was vacant. It was given to the marquis d'Effiat, a man on whom Richelieu could rely. He could also count on Schomberg, another member of the Council, and Claude Bouthillier, the secretary of the queen mother's commandments, was greatly attached to him.[18]

Lastly, the king bade his half-brother, the grand prior,[19] go to Nantes and fetch the duc de Vendôme, the other son of Gabrielle d'Estrées, who was governor of Brittany. He was instructed to bring the latter back with him without delay.

When Henry IV's two bastard sons were both in his power at the château of Blois, Louis XIII made much of them for the next two days. But he was only very skilfully masking his intentions. On the morning of 13 June his most loyal officers, the captains of the King's Guards, entered the room where the two brothers were sleeping and arrested them both on their master's orders. Vendôme was stripped of his governorship of Brittany, there being no doubt at all that he had been involved in the conspiracy, and the two princes were taken by river to the château of Amboise. When Richelieu himself arrived at Blois a few days later he found the court apparently restored to calm, the king and Monsieur reconciled and a Council that was at his devotion. It seemed as if everything was in readiness for him to exercise his authority.

However, one evening the comte de Chalais was surprised leaving Monsieur's room, and through the disclosures of one of Chalais's companions, the comte de Louvigny, Richelieu learnt that the plot had not been abandoned. He realised that from now onwards there could be no security without a terrible eruption.

The court reached Nantes. The Estates of Brittany proved to be as amenable as could be wished. They begged the king not to entrust the government of the province in future to anyone who could claim to be related to the former dukes of Brittany, as Vendôme had been able to do through his mother-in-law, the last of the Penthièvres. Richelieu advised Louis XIII to appoint the maréchal de Thémines, and took care to emphasise that in making a recommendation which was in the interests of the State, he was setting aside all feelings of personal animosity. The marshal's son had killed the cardinal's brother, the marquis de Richelieu, in a duel and it was one of the bitterest memories of his private life.

It remained to complete arrangements for Monsieur's marriage as quickly as possible and to destroy the cabal by making an example of one of them.

The court had taken up residence in the old Breton city of Nantes on the banks of the Loire. At this time it was only a very small town, clustered around the château and the cathedral. The queen mother was lodged in the outskirts close by, at the Hôtel Miron.[20] Every day the king used to call on her, stopping on the way to say his devotions in the humble chapel belonging to the Minims, at the bottom of a narrow street.[21] On 9 July, the comte de Chalais was arrested and put under solitary confinement in the château. An extraordinary commission composed of magistrates belonging to the province was set up to examine the prisoner and pass sentence on him. French history abounds in curious cross-currents, for these judges included the fathers of Fouquet and Descartes.

Monsieur knew that Chalais's trial would reveal his own part in the conspiracy and that he had no alternative but to submit. He tried to lull his feelings of remorse by interceding with his mother on Chalais's behalf. Then he announced to the cardinal that he was prepared to marry. The king had summoned the duchess of Guise and Mlle de Montpensier to Nantes. They had been accompanied by a strong escort, for it was feared that the comte de Soissons would try to abduct his intended bride now that she was slipping from his grasp. But Monsieur had laid down certain conditions. He was given a splendid apanage, the title of duke of Orleans and a large pension. After obtaining leave of absence for five days of relaxation in the country, he returned to Nantes on 5 August in an amenable frame of mind.

The marriage ceremonies were quickly expedited. The contract was signed in the morning, the betrothal celebrated in the afternoon in the king's chamber at the château, and the forms of consent were exchanged in the evening—all within the space of a single day. On the following morning, 6 August, the Nuptial Mass was celebrated at the chapel of the Minims in the presence of king and cardinal. When the news reached him in his prison Chalais exclaimed: 'Oh great king, triply fortunate in having so great a minister!' Under the impact of the catastrophe that had befallen him he had acquired an experience of the world which he had lacked as a young courtier. His prediction as to the attitude that the princes of the blood would adopt was perfectly correct: the prince of Condé would tell everyone that the cardinal was a clever man and the comte de Soissons would merely go and cry in his mother's arms. No-one would lift a finger to help him, Chalais. After all was he not the perfect victim? He was well enough born for his punishment to have a resounding effect but, at the same time, as he was not of the blood royal like the others, he could be sacrificed without his death causing too much outcry.

Chalais's mother had hastened to Nantes to try to save him. The poor woman strove to soften the hearts of the king and cardinal by recalling the services rendered to the monarchy by her own kindred. She was the daughter of the maréchal de Montluc, one of the greatest and most celebrated French soldiers of the previous century.[22] As for her son, he was a godson of the late king, who had given him his own Christian name, and in addition he was the grandson by marriage of President Jeannin. With so many illustrious connections, did he not deserve a little pity?

She wrangled with the judges, attempting to challenge one of them, President Cussé, on the grounds that he was related by marriage to Marshal Schomberg, one of the king's ministers. She tried to obtain permission for her son to have a defending counsel. Her demands were considered, only to be rejected.

Meanwhile the duke of Orleans had been cross-examined by the king, the queen mother, the cardinal and the keeper of the seals. He had revealed Chalais's intrigues, and these exalted personages could judge for themselves how widespread the conspiracy had been. It was evident that first and foremost the duchesse de Chevreuse was implicated, followed by the dukes of Épernon and La Valette, the comte de Soissons, the duc de Vendôme and many others of lesser importance. The royal commissioners were also well briefed [*en savaient aussi long*], for the documents which had been submitted to them included a large number of letters. Marillac informed them that the king himself meant to decide the fate of the duchesse de Chevreuse and the comte de Soissons in view of their rank. The duchess was exiled to her château at Dampierre, but as she was none too sure what might befall her she preferred to flee. She took refuge at the court of Charles IV, duke of Lorraine, who was delighted to receive her and joined the ranks of her ardent admirers.

In addition, to use Richelieu's terminology, 'a personage of the highest consideration' was found to be 'appreciably engaged' in the conspiracy—the queen. Had Anne of Austria really agreed to abandon the king to his fate and to marry Monsieur?—that was the question. A painful domestic scene ensued between the king and the two queens. Anne's reply to the accusation was that she would have gained too little for the exchange of husbands to have been worth her while. But Louis XIII, cut to the quick by the wound dealt to his masculine dignity both as husband and as king, could never rid himself of the suspicion that she might very well have welcomed this dreadful scheme. As for the queen, she could never forget the king's suspicion of her—the more understandably if she was in fact innocent. Both of them bore the marks of this wound until the end, sixteen years later.

Chalais was cross-examined for several weeks. The cardinal visited him three times in his prison. There were some facts that were undeniable—in particular Chalais's participation in the plot for at least seventeen days and his intended role as one of the organisers of Monsieur's flight. This was enough to secure his condemnation, but efforts were made to induce him to disclose as much as possible and to reveal the worst. He was pressed to state whether or not the assassination of Louis XIII had been contemplated. Louvigny maintained that Chalais had spoken to him about it, but the latter denied that this was the case.

The young man was fully conscious that he was lost and resigned himself to his fate. He sent a message to his mother that he meant to die as a good Christian and that if he had died in his bed he would have been damned. His punishment, he declared, was necessary as an expiation for his sin.

The judges condemned him to be beheaded. His corpse was to be dismembered, his head exposed to view on the bridge of Sauvetout on the road out of Nantes, and his limbs were to be strung up on the gallows; his descendants were to be deprived of noble rank and proclaimed low-born commoners. But the king reduced this sentence to the usual form of punishment. Chalais was to be beheaded on the Place du Bouffay and his body handed over to his mother to be buried in consecrated ground. The court thereupon left Nantes so as to avoid being there on the day fixed for the execution.

But when the day came, the headsman could not be found, for Chalais's friends had spirited him away. As it would have taken too long to fetch another executioner from Rennes, a shoemaker from Touraine who was due to be hanged in three days' time was offered a pardon if he would take the executioner's place. He accepted the offer; but the axe, too, had disappeared. The makeshift executioner accordingly made use of a Swiss sword which he did not know how to handle. He only gashed the neck of his unfortunate victim, who collapsed beside the headsman's block covered with blood. The condemned man's body had to be moved back into position but the shoemaker now decided in favour of a different weapon. He was given a cooper's adze and resumed his task. After twenty-nine blows the head was at last severed from its trunk. What remained of the corpse after this butchery was placed in a coffin and transported by carriage to the monastery of the Cordeliers.[23] Mme de Chalais, who had spent the dreadful period of waiting in prayer with the monks, met the carriage at the threshold of the church. Everything was in readiness for the Vespers of the Dead, and the body was buried in a corner of the nave.

The king was as fully responsible as the cardinal for this demonstration of his strength. He had asserted his power in the face of the great nobles and his will to be obeyed and feared. The following year he was to give fresh proof of his determination—this time in connection with duels.

Early in 1626 a very severe edict had renewed the ban on duelling. The comte de Bouteville, a particularly inveterate swordsman who belonged to the Montmorency family and who had left the realm to escape the penalties he had incurred in this respect as early as 1624, had the effrontery to return to France and fight a duel with the marquis de Beuvron on the Place Royale right in the middle of Paris (14 May 1627).* Custom prescribed that seconds to a duel should also fight each other. So overpowering was the passion for this terrible pastime that Bussy d'Amboise, who had the reputation of being a fanatical duellist, left his sick-bed and rushed to the rendezvous with the object of assisting Beuvron. His opponent was the comte de Rosmadec des Chapelles, one of Bouteville's seconds; perhaps because his strength was failing him, Bussy failed to parry a thrust from his adversary and fell mortally wounded. He barely showed a glimmer of consciousness when a Minim hastened to the scene to give him absolution, and a few hours later he expired.

Soldiers of the Guard were instantly dispatched on the heels of Montmorency-Bouteville and Chapelles. They were overtaken in Champagne, brought back to the Bastille, and tried by the Parlement. A wave of feeling swept through the entire nobility. Bouteville was the duke of Montmorency's cousin, the nephew of the princesse de Condé (who had formerly been Charlotte de Montmorency) and the husband of Elisabeth de Vienne. In the opposite camp Mme la Présidente de Mesmes and the comtesse de Vignory, the mother and aunt of Bussy d'Amboise, called for the punishment of the guilty parties.†

* The Place Royale is now called the Place des Vosges. For further particulars see chapter 7.   † The mother of Bussy d'Amboise was styled Madame la Présidente because she had married the president of a sovereign court.

The comtesse de Bouteville went to waylay the king as he was leaving Mass after receiving Communion, and entreated him in Christ's name to be merciful to her husband. Louis XIII passed her by without answer, but to those who were with him he said: 'I am sorry for the woman but I must and will maintain my authority.'

The bishop of Nantes, who visited the prisoners in the Bastille, brought letters from them addressed to the cardinal. 'How did they come to procure pen, ink, and paper?' asked Richelieu in astonishment. 'It was I, my lord, who gave them these things', the bishop answered courageously. The cardinal had to remind him that he could not in all conscience speak on their behalf since he had himself helped to draw up the latest edict against duelling.[24] Thus religion, charity, justice and duty towards the law contended for mastery in men's minds.

The two prisoners were condemned to be beheaded on the Place de Grève. A last effort was made to save them. The princesse de Condé and the three duchesses of Montmorency, Angoulême and Ventadour conducted the comtesse de Bouteville to the queen's chamber. The five great ladies then fell on their knees before the king. The countess was pregnant; the child she bore in her womb was one day to be a famous man. He was the future Marshal Luxembourg of Louis XIV's reign who was to be nicknamed 'le tapissier de Notre-Dame'.* Through the services that he and the loyal nobility of his day were to render all France, he was to repair the damage done by the undisciplined nobility whom his father had come to epitomise.

Louis XIII refused to weaken: 'I am no less affected than you by their ruin,' he informed the princesse de Condé, 'but my conscience forbids me to pardon them.'

The cardinal wrote later in the *Testament politique*: 'I confess that I was never more torn by conflicting emotions than on this occasion, when I could scarcely prevent myself from succumbing to the compassion that was felt for them everywhere. . . . The tears of his wife (Mme de Bouteville) moved me very deeply . . . but the rivers of your nobility's blood (which could only be stemmed by the shedding of theirs) gave me the strength to withstand my weaker self, and harden your Majesty's resolve to enforce the sentence for the good of the State, although it was well nigh contrary to the feelings of everyone as well as to my own personal inclinations.'

* After Luxembourg had inflicted a severe defeat on William III at the battle of Landen or Neerwinden in 1693, the numerous colours which he had captured were hung up in Notre-Dame Cathedral.

The king himself arranged the details of the execution and chose the regiments which were to take up position on the Place de Grève. He gave orders that anyone in the crowd who called out 'Mercy' was to be arrested; but he agreed that the bodies should be decently buried and that no one should be allowed to despoil them.

The two noblemen made a brave and Christian end at five o'clock on the evening of 22 June. Bouteville was the first to die. As Chapelles reached the scaffold he passed his friend's body: he stopped and knelt to pray for him before delivering himself to the executioner.

It must be borne in mind that Louis XIII and Richelieu were themselves men of noble blood. Both in their social background and in their upbringing they felt themselves closely akin to the men whom they were sacrificing. Unquestionably it was only by doing violence to their innermost feelings that they were able to take such a step. And here we must stress yet again that the reign of Louis XIII was a period of transition from the Middle Ages to the modern social system, and that royal authority was the instrument which effected this far-reaching change. Here lies the explanation of Louis XIII's and Richelieu's policy towards duelling. Warm-hearted, fearless, Christian, such were the nobility in the time of Louis XIII. The spirit that belonged to the crusades, inspiring men to commit their youth, their lives, their enjoyment of life's pleasures and their thirst for greatness to the service of an ideal—this spirit was still alive in them. But the ideal had to be redefined and purified. It was no longer enough for a noble to be recklessly brave or to display all the Christian virtues when he came to die after behaving in a way that was far from virtuous. He must serve the king, and live and die in his service alone. Such was the terrifying but salutary lesson taught to those unruly children, the nobility, by the scaffolds on the Place du Bouffay and the Place de Grève where—to resort once more to Richelieu's well-chosen words—'those two young noblemen' had paid the price 'for their ill fortune and their valour'.

We have already seen that in 1625 Richelieu had drawn up in broad outline a plan for the reformation of the realm. At the end of 1626 he seems to have thought that the time had come to put it into effect. He urged Louis XIII to summon an Assembly of Notables at Paris on a larger scale than the extraordinary Council meeting of the previous year. It met early in December. It included the duke of Orleans, the princes of the blood and the cardinals, together with certain great nobles, ministers and members of the sovereign courts. It was noticed that the young queen was absent—no doubt because she had not been restored to the king's favour. 'My lords,' said Louis XIII as he opened the first session, 'my purpose is summoning you here is to cure the State's disorders with the help of your counsels.'

Important steps had already been taken in this direction. Everywhere there was evidence of the king's determination to reassert his authority generally, to make it effective and to break with practices that had weakened it.

At the beginning of the year Louis XIII had created for Richelieu the post of grand master and superintendent general of commerce and navigation. The significance of this new appointment was shown by the enforced resignation of two 'admirals of France'—the admiral of the western seaboard [*Ponant*]—in other words the admiral of Guyenne and Brittany—and the admiral of the eastern approaches [*Levant*]—namely Provence. Richelieu had bought out the holders of these two offices, the dukes of Montmorency and Guise, who strictly speaking did not command French naval forces, but had been charged with the administration of the entire sea coast and the fiscal jurisdiction that belonged to it. By edicts issued at Nantes, the king had announced that the ordinances, rights and privileges which formed part of Admiralty jurisdiction would remain in force 'in order that he who shall, under our authority, have the direction of the commerce of this realm, may the more easily promote, establish or continue the same'.

In short the king, who was conducting a campaign against the perpetuation of routine caused by the fact that high offices had become the preserve of great nobles on a purely hereditary basis, [*la féodalité des hautes charges*], took into his own hands, or entrusted to a minister entirely dependent upon him, the control of French coasts, navigation and shipping, whether merchant ships or ships of war.

Another great office of state had disappeared in September. When Lesdiguières, the constable, died, loaded with honours and burdened with years, the king declared that he would definitely abolish the appointment, which would never again be conferred on anyone else. And later Louis XIV, who observed the same inflexible rule, was to express his regret that he could not break it in favour of Marshal Villars after the latter had saved the realm on more than one frontier during the War of the Spanish Succession. The army, like the navy, was henceforth to depend on the king alone.

And now another bridge had to be crossed: corrupt practices and abuses within the realm must be eliminated so as to provide the king with better and more reliable sources of revenue; his subjects must be taught to develop an outlook which was most in accordance with the interests of the State and with the employment of private interests to good ends. It was thus a general reform of the realm that was to be considered; or at the very least an attempt ought to be made to define and lay down its basic principles.

At this same opening session of the Assembly of Notables the cardinal, who had presumably weighed each word, announced: 'The duration of this Assembly must be brief but the fruit of its deliberations must last for ever.' Perhaps Richelieu believed at the time that peace at home and abroad was sufficiently assured to allow him a breathing-space; only a breathing-space, however. One of his greatest intellectual attributes was his capacity never to lose sight of the whole, never to let himself be submerged by today's events. One cannot but be struck by the fact that of the above-mentioned edicts dealing with shipping and maritime affairs, to which he attached such exceptional importance, the first was published in March (in other words, immediately after the conclusion of peace with the Huguenots and during the negotiations for the Treaty of Monzón) and the others in the month of August at the time of Chalais's trial.

Nor did foreign affairs escape Richelieu's attention. He gauged the extent to which the Austro-Spanish party had profited from the march of events in Germany:* the elector palatine had been stripped of his dignities, the king of Denmark had been defeated by Tilly at the battle of Lutter, Mansfeld and Halberstadt had been utterly broken. Moreover, the emperor had found a highly talented army commander in the shape of Wallenstein, a Czech by birth, who was now conquering eastern Germany and cutting his way through to the Baltic. How could anyone imagine that some day France would not be compelled to intervene in the struggle? For the moment the cardinal sought to obtain a firm alliance with Bavaria with a view to making use of a Catholic state as a counter to Spain. He also noted the growing dissension between France and her Protestant allies, England and the United Provinces, which ruled out any possibility of their acting jointly for the time being. He wished

---

* This was a faction at the Imperial Court which favoured the closest political and military co-operation between Madrid and Vienna and disliked the Emperor's dependence on the army of the Catholic League. As a result of this co-operation it hoped to bring about not only the restoration of Imperial power and the triumph of the Counter-Reformation in Germany but also the commercial ruin and destruction of the United Provinces.

therefore, by means of internal reforms, to place France in a position where she could adopt an independent policy, whose timing could then perhaps be decided by herself according to her strength. This is clearly what is meant by another passage in his speech to the Notables: 'If we succeed in carrying out this project [*dessein*], we shall not fail to meet the challenge for lack of money when we have to withstand an invasion from abroad or a rebellion from within—if God allows these things to recur because of our sins—or when the time comes to put into effect some project that will be useful to the State and redound to its glory.'

What could it be, this 'project' which would be 'useful to the State and redound to its glory', other than war against Spain?—not an immediate war, of course, but one that would later become unavoidable.

Such a policy would cost money. It was advisable for the realm's finances to be put on a sound basis, and the Assembly's first task was to give its approval to the principle of large-scale fiscal reform.

In one of the best books that he wrote, the historian Henri Hauser stressed another aspect of Richelieu's plans—namely the economic aspect.[25] But in fact it is impossible to consider any part of his programme of reform in isolation from the rest. Financial reform involved both the elimination of old abuses and the organisation of a new economic system which would make France independent of the foreigner and ensure that her natural resources were put to better use. This new economic system in turn presupposed a change in the ideas and customs of the French people. Since such a change could not be effected amongst the adult population, it must be fostered amongst the rising generation by an appropriate system of training. This implied the introduction of a programme of education.

It is scarcely going too far to compare the cardinal's plans for total reform with the efforts made in the same direction by the Constituent Assembly, the Convention and the Consulate. It represented an attempt to found a new France which was to be entirely different from the France of the past. The effect of the reforms would be revolutionary, but great caution would be shown in putting them into operation. Richelieu's consciousness of France's past glory, and his respect for tradition (to which he alludes repeatedly) ensured that his proposals would entail no violent changes or breach with the past. 'Since an excess of medicines can be as fatal to a sick man as no medicine at all, what is required to restore a State to its original grandeur is not a multitude of regulations but the serious enforcement of existing laws.'

Rarely has such an ambitious programme been presented in such an unobtrusive way. Here we see a particular facet of Richelieu's genius —remarkable daring tempered by exceptional discretion and restraint. The age of Louis XIII abounds in characters who link it with the extravagances and exuberant fancies of baroque art, but Richelieu's statecraft has something essentially classical about it.

Richelieu's advance preparations for the Assembly of Notables have been laboriously pieced together by Henri Hauser. The cardinal had questioned his agents abroad about trading conditions—Fargis in Madrid, Baugy in Brussels, Blainville in London. He had collected a mass of information about the vexations to which French maritime trade was exposed, about the exorbitant duties imposed by foreigners on imported French products and about the flood of foreign goods entering France. Furthermore, in a memorandum concerning the navy 'dispatched to my lord keeper of the seals this 18 November 1626' he had emphasised 'this great reproach to our nation—that the king, who is the eldest son of the Church [*l'aîné de tous les rois chrétiens*], is inferior to the pettiest prince in Christendom in his maritime power. His Majesty, seeing the harm that his realm and subjects have suffered therefrom, is resolved to remedy the same by making himself as powerful at sea as he is by land. Had it not been for this His Majesty's resolve, our trade would have disappeared altogether [*il ne fallait plus faire état d'aucun trafic*] but now these trials and tribulations will cease. . . .'

At the Assembly of Notables Louis XIII called upon Michel de Marillac to speak, and the latter gave an account of the defects that urgently required correction. He pointed out that the recent civil wars had been a crushing financial burden. Since 1620 expenditure had risen to forty million livres, while receipts only amounted to sixteen million. The first step that had to be taken was to cut down expenditure wherever possible. The king was setting an example by abolishing certain great offices;[26] he would also effect economies by demolishing fortresses where rebels could take refuge, thus forcing him to maintain garrisons or levy troops solely to restore order within the realm. In other words, the king wished his military expenditure to be confined to France's frontiers. It was also advisable to strengthen the financial reserves by reviewing the Crown's debts and by redeeming Crown lands which had been alienated.

Next there followed a long passage devoted to commerce and the navy. 'He [Marillac] expatiated at some length on this article,' comments Father Griffet, 'and he assured the Assembly that his Majesty would be glad to give ear to its counsels.'[27]

Even so, when speaking of the navy, Marillac did not repeat everything suggested in the memorandum of 18 November.[28] There has been
some argument among historians as to whether he deliberately toned
down or misrepresented the cardinal's ideas on the subject, or whether
both men, for reasons unknown to us, had agreed to put forward their
views at rather less length than they had originally intended.

In any event, after Schomberg had given an account of the realm's
military requirements it was Richelieu's turn to address the Notables,
and in the course of his speech he returned to the need for general
reform: 'We have to choose between leaving the realm exposed to the
assaults and machinations [*mauvais desseins*] of those who daily meditate
its decline and ruin, and finding some positive means of ensuring its
safety.'[29] The lofty aim of restoring France's greatness is admirably conveyed in the following sentence: 'The king means to organise and regulate this realm to such good purpose that his reign will not only be as
great as, or greater than, that of any of his forbears, but will also serve as a
model and example for his successors.'

Richelieu did not give a detailed account of the reforms that he had in
mind. If he and his colleagues had not needed the advice of the Notables
and had announced at the outset that they had already decided what they
were going to do, it would have looked as if there had been no point in
summoning the Assembly. He confined himself therefore to broad issues.
Speaking of the redemption of Crown lands, he laid down the principle
that the State must show honesty in all its dealings: the trust that any private person reposed in the State was based upon its honesty and integrity:
'There is no question of the power of the State being used to take from
private persons that which they rightfully hold. The greatest success that
rulers and states can achieve is to retain public confidence, which forms
an inexhaustible well for it is always found to contain further resources.'

The Assembly's sessions continued until 24 February. On 11 January
Richelieu presented a memorandum of thirteen articles, which summed
up the salient features of the plan of 1625, and suggested the reforms
which should be carried out. One cannot but be struck by a remarkable
omission: nothing is said about venality of office or the *paulette*, although
if ever a reform seemed vital for the future of the realm, it was this.

Richelieu had recognised as much in 1625. Why did he not mention
the subject in 1627? Because war was imminent, says Roland Mousnier.
No doubt this was a contributory factor, but the main reason was that he
saw that the kingdom's finances were in no condition to meet the cost of
a wholesale redemption of offices, and that public opinion seemed far

from ready to accept such an idea. He was relying upon an indirect method of making this reform both possible and effective in the near future: that is to say, he was relying upon the effect of a change in out-look and behaviour among the population. Richelieu's silence on a matter of such importance should be regarded as one of those concessions to temporarily prevailing circumstances that used to determine the timing of his actions. He was ready to postpone anything which he con-sidered impracticable for the time being, but he did not give up the idea of carrying it out some day.

The Assembly gave its approval to Richelieu's programme as a whole and displayed particular enthusiasm over his proposals regarding mari-time affairs and commerce. The royal declaration of 1 March 1627 prom-ised 'to restore commerce in merchandise, renewing and extending its privileges so that those engaged in such traffic are held in appropriate honour and highly accounted among our subjects, in order that each one of them may continue to participate gladly therein without jealousy of those of other degree'.

It is important not to overlook the proposals which the nobility pre-sented separately on 10 February. The abolition of the purchase and sale of a large number of offices was precisely what these nobles called for, together with a reduction in the number of colleges,* the creation of ex-hibitions or bursaries [*bourses*] for the sons of poorer gentry, and the es-tablishment of a new order of knighthood under the patronage of St Louis to reward services rendered in time of war.

It would be the worst possible mistake to interpret Richelieu's contest with the great nobles as evidence of his basic hostility towards the nobi-lity as a whole. He never forgot that they constituted the sinews of the State. He had no belief whatever in equality (which, like government by the people, seemed to him an unthinkable heresy), and he considered the nobility an essential part of the social structure. However, they must not be idle or unruly. If there was a class for which Richelieu had little liking —perhaps because of his own prejudices as a noble—it was the magis-tracy and the lawyers. He thought them vain and stupid, and in an age which had a passion for litigation blamed them for encouraging people to become mean-spirited and self-centred. He would have liked to divert their interests and energies towards commerce and towards work that was useful to the State. What is more, he thought that this would be to their advantage.

* A *collège* was a boarding-school. It was situated in a town and invariably run by clergy.

The desire expressed by the nobility for a limitation in the traffic in offices and for new arrangements in respect of schooling corresponded in both cases with Richelieu's own wishes. Something must be said here about his views on education. They are mentioned in the plan of 1625, and he returns to them and comments on them in considerably greater detail in the *Testament politique*.

Richelieu had no desire for education in general and higher education in particular to be made available to all without discrimination. He deplored the fact that young people were educated with a view to facilitating their tenure of some office. 'Even the poorest of the people put their children to school,' he said in 1626, 'diverting them from the profession of arms and from trade, which is what nourishes a State.' He was in favour of maintaining small schools where the rudiments would be taught, 'to retrieve the young from gross ignorance, which is prejudicial to those who intend to devote themselves to arms, or desire to engage in commerce'. He wanted 'more masters in mechanical arts than masters in liberal arts to teach letters'. For the latter, it was enough to ensure that there were colleges in a certain number of towns within the realm, the proportion being two colleges per town with four colleges in Paris itself.[30] Hauser sums up the cardinal's intentions very well: 'A system of selection would enable the most talented children to rise above the rank and file. In short he envisaged a technical and commercial education with a few classical touches. The training of soldiers and merchants—that was always the cardinal's objective.'[31]

This is true enough, but it does not cover all Richelieu's ideas about education. He did not expect schools and colleges merely to act as recruiting agencies for two social categories. He wanted more than this. He wanted children who had been nurtured on doctrines which he believed to be true and beneficial: he wanted good Catholics and obedient subjects.

He regarded a multiplication in the number of colleges or the uncontrolled proliferation of all sorts of ideas as a source of spiritual danger: 'If learning were profaned by being made available to all and sundry, it would be found that there were more people capable of creating doubts than of resolving them, and many would show themselves more apt in opposing truth than in defending it,' he observed in 1625. Richelieu wanted fewer teachers but better teaching—a point of view expressed with even greater force in the *Testament politique*: 'Experience enables us to appreciate how important it is to have people everywhere who are able to teach the masses where their salvation lies and to resist heresy.'

This pointed remark is obviously aimed partly at the Protestants, but primarily at the 'libertines' or free-thinkers, who were responsible for purveying a number of different heresies.

The cardinal therefore opted for the teaching of a preselected doctrine. We might almost have expected him to create a monopoly, to reserve, for example, the giving of all such instruction for the universities or for a particular religious order such as the Jesuits; but this would be to misunderstand his attitude profoundly. He would not have a monopoly at any price. In deciding that there should be two colleges in each town where he proposed to establish them Richelieu was guided by a most enlightened purpose—surprising though it may at first seem. He feared the possibility of education falling under the control of a single organisation, and preferred to think of it as stimulated by competition between different institutions which might sometimes be rivals. He favoured maintaining a balance between secular masters (whether laymen or priests) and masters who were monks. For although Richelieu respected the Jesuits, his appreciation of them was not uncritical. He felt misgivings about their close dependence on their general, who lived outside France, and about their sympathetic attitude towards Spain. He would have hated to see them spreading on ostensibly religious grounds opinions that were suspect or contrary to French interests. Submissive though he was to the doctrines laid down by the Council of Trent, the cardinal did not forget that there were, even in religious questions, certain points on which 'the Faith allowed every man the liberty of his own opinion'.

A similar danger would arise if the universities were given the right to teach the young, 'separately and to the exclusion of all others'. Thus competition represented the only way of making sure that religious instruction avoided any extremes: 'Since the frailty of our human condition requires a counter-weight in all things, and since this is also the foundation of all justice,' declares the *Testament politique*, 'it is more fitting that the universities and the Jesuits should teach in emulation of each other so that the rivalry between them stimulates their good qualities, and learning [*les sciences*] is more securely established because it has been committed to the care of two guardians; thus if one of them loses awareness of his sacred trust, he can regain it from the other.' In this way, with the two principles of loyalty to the Church and obedience to the king effectively safeguarded, there would be opportunities for men's minds to range freely; research, if not a questioning attitude, would also be safeguarded.[32]

In approving the cardinal's programme, therefore, the Notables were preparing the way for a general renovation of the realm. In his first speech Richelieu had ventured to say in the king's presence that 'it might be possible to find ways and means of completing this programme within six years'.[33] It is impossible to read this statement without a feeling of surprise. To bring such a large-scale undertaking to a conclusion within the space of a few years was obviously quite out of the question. Why did the cardinal speak in terms of six years? Long afterwards, at an equally critical moment in French history, the time limit chosen was seven years, because it represented a long enough period in the life of a human being to appeal to everyone's sense of optimism but did not extend so far into the future that those who set it did not seem reasonably likely to achieve their aim. If some such thought as this was in Richelieu's mind, we should interpret his remark as an orator's trick cleverly designed to encourage his audience. Or did he sincerely believe that by preventing the outbreak of any fresh war at home and abroad, and by confining himself to covert, indirect methods of protecting French interests, he would be able to ensure that the realm enjoyed six years of peace which could be devoted to internal reform? If so, he was to be cruelly deceived by events.[34] His attention was to be diverted by more urgent tasks which compelled him first to postpone his plan for several months, and then to abandon it without ever deciding on a date for its resumption. But in a spirit such as his the hope that he would one day be free to carry out the full task he had set himself could never die.

CHAPTER FIVE

The Western Seaboard, La Rochelle and Italy

THE PROGRAMME of 1626 was to be abandoned, therefore, and the years of peace which the cardinal had declared to be so necessary were to be transformed into years of war—war within the realm against the king's own subjects. Should we ascribe this change to the pressure of circumstances that Richelieu was unable to avert, or should we see it as a deliberate reversal of his policy? True, the cardinal was determined not to tolerate any disobedience or any obstacle to the reforms that he proposed to carry out, but for a man with his abilities persuasion was a weapon that could be used as effectively as war.

To speak of 'the Protestant party' is an oversimplification, for the Protestants were very far from being unanimous in their political aims. Religious interests were never the only consideration. Amongst the Protestants there were nobles whose social condition was indistinguishable from that of nobles who were Catholics, and there were office-holders whose preoccupation with their offices gave them the same outlook as all the other officials in royal service. The government was scarcely able to conceive of a general Protestant insurrection against the king, let alone feel alarmed by the prospect.

This being the case, a Protestant historian has argued that the war resulted from a campaign launched by the *dévot* party.[1] He believes that in the course of the spring of 1627 the cardinal had to effect a rapprochement with powerful members of the party at court and take steps to live down his earlier record for moderation towards the Huguenots. He thinks that, once embarked upon this course, Richelieu fell increasingly under the influence of his Catholic advisers—the Capuchin Father Joseph and the Oratorian Bérulle. Neither of these men had given up the hopes which they had always cherished of a crusade against heresy. Now that Béarn was reduced to submission their target was La Rochelle, a sort of Protestant capital, a kind of privileged mercantile republic in league with foreign Powers. By campaigning against the edicts by which the king had made peace with the Huguenots, they hoped to drive its people to desperation, goad them into revolt and bring about the

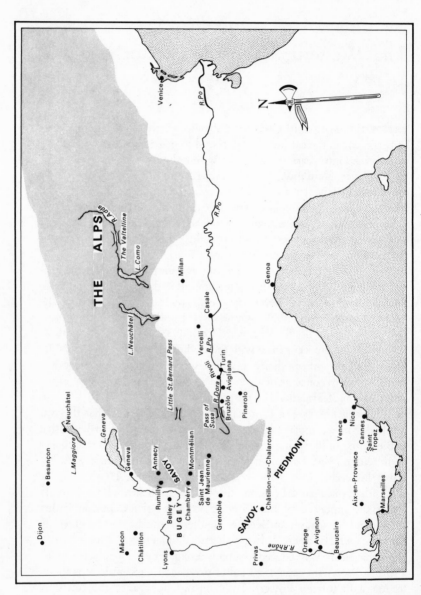

Map 4 South-east France and Savoy

city's downfall. Richelieu's willingness to allow Fancan first to be falsely attacked and then to be imprisoned in June 1627 was an indication that he had abandoned the sensible and prudent policy which he had hitherto preferred to follow, for Fancan had been one of his ablest apologists among the *bons Français*. In short, having formed an alliance with the *dévot* party, the cardinal proceeded to adopt its uncompromising aims.

Thus while the traditional theory credits Richelieu with the intention of destroying the Huguenot party as a state within the state, and as such a formidable threat to the king's authority, the interpretation put forward by Protestant historians reflects their conviction that no such danger existed—in support of which they adduce numerous proofs of loyal feelings among the Huguenots. However neither theory provides the key to the mystery: why this revolution in the cardinal's policy? Perhaps his attitude was uncertain or inconsistent and was in fact far more subject to events than responsible for them. Why not indeed?

Let us try to see from his correspondence what Richelieu's main preoccupations were during the winter of 1626–7. The news which reached him from England convinced him that despite Charles I's marriage to a French princess the alliance that had been envisaged was patently unattainable. England gave evidence of her hostility to France in all kinds of ways, and the dissension between her king and queen only served to reflect the political differences between the two countries. When Bassompierre visited London in the autumn of 1626 with the object of settling the disputes between the two courts in a courteous manner, Charles I went so far as to ask him if he had been sent to declare war. Ships were being armed on Buckingham's orders. The duke's personal reasons for hostility towards France—his grudge against Richelieu or his lover's spite after his abortive attempt to pay court to the French queen —were supplemented by a loftier motive based on general policy: the determination not to allow France, whose power at sea had dwindled away, to carry out her declared objective of reviving her naval strength. He was seeking promises of help from other Powers and preparing for war—a preventive war. The aim was to strike at France while she was still weak and before Richelieu's programme, the details of which had been widely publicised, had had time to bear fruit.

The support which the Huguenots gave England was of great value. Soubise, now a refugee in London, tried to incite the English government against Louis XIII and called upon Charles I to come to the rescue of the Protestants of France claiming that they were threatened by the *dévots*, and that the French king no longer meant to abide by the promises he had made. Charles I, who had intervened in the last treaty between Louis XIII and the Huguenots and would scarcely have been guilty of exaggeration in proclaiming himself its guarantor, became the natural patron of the Reformed Churches in France. Even so, this appeal from a French Protestant to a foreign Power did not mean that Soubise was the official spokesman for all the Huguenots, nor did he compromise their loyalty to Louis XIII by setting himself up as their advocate. Nevertheless there were reasons other than religious for the people of La Rochelle to feel alarmed, and unfortunately they coincided with those of England. As mariners and Frenchmen they had no reason to be afraid of French sea power as such; but they had good cause for fearing that the new form which it was assuming would entail the destruction of their privileges. They dreaded the creation of large chartered companies which would swallow up their trade. Moreover, as masters of their own fate, owing their fortune to no man, they were disturbed by the general authority that the cardinal claimed to exercise over French coasts and seaports. Richelieu urged that efforts be made to allay their anxieties (see his letters to Guron, the royal governor at Marans, 12 February 1627, and to Le Doux, his agent at La Rochelle, on 16 February); but basically the alarm felt by the people of La Rochelle was the same as that shown by the Catholic inhabitants of St Malo, to whom he himself had to offer similar assurances: 'So far am I from wishing to reduce your privileges that I shall on the contrary strive to increase them in every way that lies in my power.' On the cardinal's instructions this assurance was repeated by the governor of St Malo, the marquis de Coëtquen, comte de Combourg (20 February).

Nevertheless Richelieu remained deeply worried by the prospect of a war with England in which the latter would be necessarily hand in glove with the Huguenots. In his letters to Guron he summarises the information passed on to him by his agents: before long the English are likely to land on Oléron or on Ré or at Marans.[2] Arrangements must therefore be set in train to guard the coasts and for troops to be sent to the Isle of Oléron, and every effort should be made to convince the people of La Rochelle that far from intending to do them any mischief, the government's aim is to protect them from harm.

This was all very well, but did the Rochelais really expect that they would come to any harm at the hands of the English? In March Richelieu was inclined to think that there was less cause for anxiety than in February, but early in April his fears revived. All the time he continued with his preparations. He gave the order for all ports to be alerted and for cutters and pinnaces, in fact boats of all kinds, to be repaired and refitted. Nor was this all; he knew that English agents were active abroad, and later we will turn to consider the general situation in Europe during these months. However, Richelieu had no alternative but to let European affairs follow their own course. His only concern for the moment was the possibility that England might be directly aided at sea by Spain, Holland or Venice. This made it imperative for France to do her utmost not to lose Dutch friendship and to prevent any rapprochement between England and Spain. One cannot choose one's allies. Buckingham was engaged in some strange negotiations with Philip IV's chief minister, the count-duke of Olivares, in which the painter Rubens was involved, and Richelieu was convinced that if he did not himself form an alliance with the Spaniards the latter would come to an understanding with England. So it was that a year after the Treaty of Monzón, Fargis signed a second treaty with Spain—this time a treaty of alliance. The *dévots* were in ecstasies at the news: henceforth the two great Catholic Powers were both in the same camp. However, the revival of French sea power was as detrimental to Spain's maritime interests as to England's, and Richelieu had no illusions as to the sincerity of the agreement. In the words of the *Testament politique*, the only concern of the Spaniards was with outward appearances;[3] but it certainly counted for something that this semblance of friendship was in France's favour.

A letter dated 28 May brought the news that the English fleet was increasing in strength daily and awaiting a suitable moment to make its departure. In addition small ships were being loaded with corn to be conveyed to La Rochelle. Two days later Navailles was therefore sent to urge the citizens to arrest and punish everyone who came to the town to foment disobedience: 'They will gain as much by this manner of proceeding as they will lose if they follow the course which the sieur de Soubise would fain have them embrace.'

Admittedly Richelieu's correspondence may not reveal his innermost thoughts, but it does not appear that he contemplated taking any action against La Rochelle during these months of alert, nor did the inhabitants themselves provide him with an excuse for punitive measures. However the sea coast and its fortifications had to be manned with troops, and despite previous undertakings there could be no question of demolishing even the smallest outwork. It was from the sea that the threat would come. Whether it was to be war or peace between the king and the merchant city of La Rochelle would only be decided when the sails of an English fleet came into view.

The English preparations were completed towards the middle of June. The fleet consisted of more than sixty ships* of a variety of different sizes and carried an expeditionary force of between eight and ten thousand men. On 27 June it set sail from Portsmouth.

Buckingham was in command of the expedition in his capacity as lord high admiral. In point of fact, although the general opinion was that it was undoubtedly intended for use against France, the purpose of the expedition had not been officially stated, the more so as there was no open war between the two countries. There was nothing to preclude the assumption that Spain was the objective. However, as de Vaux de Folletier has made clear in his book *Le Siège de La Rochelle*,[4] the instructions given to Buckingham by Charles I explicitly declared that 'the chief design both of our enemies and [of our] ill-affected friends is to dispossess us of that sovereignty in those seas to which the kingdoms of Great Britain have given denomination and which all our ancestors have enjoyed time out of mind;' and these instructions then went on to denounce the French king's plan 'to extend his monarchy into the Ocean—to the prejudice of free trade and especially of our merchants'.[5] As we know, this plan did exist. Admittedly Richelieu held the position of grand master and superintendent of commerce and navigation while Buckingham himself was lord high admiral; but behind the conflict between two monarchies, each controlled by a minister who was also a favourite, can be seen a more fundamental rivalry between two maritime Powers, a rivalry primarily inspired by commercial motives—the only object of naval supremacy being to protect commerce on the high seas. There is plenty of supporting evidence. Henri Hauser has stressed the cardinal's repeated requests for information about French commercial activity in remote parts of the world and in countries that could be reached by sea. Father Joseph had supplied him with a mass of data obtained from fellow-Capuchins, missionaries and agents. He had also put the cardinal in touch with the brothers Razilly, two gentlemen from Touraine who were to render their country outstanding services both in naval engagements and in France's new colonies. After exploring the mouths of the Amazon near the island of Marajó and sailing along the coast of Morocco, Isaac de Razilly submitted a memorandum on French trade to Richelieu in 1626. It includes the following passage, which seems to Hauser to echo the jeers of seamen in some port of call: 'It wrings my heart when I think of the

---

* According to Father Griffet the English fleet consisted of ninety ships excluding small craft and longboats. (V.L.T.).

remarks that foreigners make about us when speaking of France: for they would say "What sort of a king is yours who has not even the power to defeat one of his own nobles (Rohan) without the help of England, Holland and Malta? He would cut an even sorrier figure if he were fighting the king of England!" [6]

The expansion of French sea power was no longer attainable without the risk of a clash with England. Richelieu was certainly not blind to something which seemed obvious enough to any old sea dog. Repeated incidents—that is to say the seizure of ships by both sides whether for good reasons or for bad—gave ample proof of the uncompromising antagonism between the two countries. For a time he may have imagined that he would be able to avoid a collision and that the marriage of Charles I and Henrietta Maria would ensure that peace was preserved. In the event, however, both governments made the situation worse by interfering in each other's religious affairs. France protected the English Catholics just as England supported the French Protestants. And now the latter were to be more directly wooed and implicated in the struggle by the appearance of an English fleet in their waters.

The French were scarcely prepared for a landing on the Isle of Ré, the objective chosen for Buckingham's expedition. There was only a small garrison on the island, although it was commanded by one of the ablest officers in the king's army—Toiras, who held the rank of *maréchal de camp* and was governor of Aunis. The only defences consisted of two forts—Saint-Martin, which was in excellent order, and la Prée, which could not be put to equally good use.

Toiras did his utmost to prevent the English from effecting a landing. On 26 July a battle took place on the spit of land known as the pointe des Sablonceaux in which both sides fought bravely. Eventually the French commander, who was heavily outnumbered and anxious to keep his garrison in being, ordered the retreat to be sounded, withdrew his remaining troops to the safety of Fort Saint-Martin, and asked for a truce to bury his dead. Buckingham granted his request and paid tribute to those who had given their lives fighting to defend the honour of their king. The duke later boasted that this engagement had cost France the flower of her nobility, and it was certainly true that among the slain there were some who belonged to the most distinguished families in France. They included Restinchères, Toiras's brother, and scions of the families of Noailles and Chantal; the last of these was the son of the foundress of the Order of the Visitation (who thereafter prayed constantly for the salvation of his soul) and also the father of the future marquise de Sévigné.[7]

The small-scale siege warfare which now began on the island was conducted with chivalry but without mercy. Throughout the entire summer
Toiras and Buckingham faced each other. The former was immured in
his fortress without sufficient supplies to hold out for long, but bent on
doing so until help reached him from the mainland. The English commander was loath to waste troops by launching a costly assault which
would win him no advantage that was not bound to be his sooner or later
when the French garrison was reduced to starvation. He barricaded himself in his camp; to his rear he enjoyed unrestricted use of the sea and was
in communication with La Rochelle.

The arrival of the English had caused a division of opinion within the
town. The hotheads hailed the landing of an English expedition on the
Isle of Ré as aid sent from Heaven to assist them in their difficulties with
the king's government. Their only thought was to make common cause
with England. Eight hundred volunteers set out for Ré to offer their services to Buckingham, with Loudrières, the *sénéchal* of Aunis, at their
head. But despite this example set by one of the king's officers in desert-
ing his post the town council of La Rochelle hesitated to come to a
decision. Possibly it would not even have welcomed Soubise (who had
landed with the English expedition and brought proposals from
Charles I) had it not been for Soubise's mother. The old duchess of
Rohan's devotion to the Huguenot cause was certainly heroic but her
stout heart was not matched by her wisdom. It was she who ensured that
her son was admitted to La Rochelle, enabling him to exert all his eloquence on the townsmen and organise propaganda in favour of his cause.

Two parties which drew their support from different social categories
thus came into being in La Rochelle. The bourgeoisie and the office-
holders stood for loyalty to the king of France. Admittedly their attitude
was conditioned by thoughts of their wealth and property and by a
desire to avert the impending storm, but they had at least some political
judgement which the others had not. The common people, inspired by
confused hopes that they would be relieved from their miseries and that
the Kingdom of God was about to be established, followed the lead of
enthusiastic pastors and unruly nobles.

Although the king's government was not taken unawares by the English landing, it did find itself suddenly forced to assume obligations
which were greater than envisaged. To crown everything, Louis XIII
had fallen seriously ill at Villeroy and was incapable of leading the army
himself. It was placed under the command of the duke of Angoulême
and mustered around La Rochelle to keep the town under observation.

Richelieu himself was far from idle. Boats had to be assembled to dispatch reinforcements to Toiras, and in the meantime to keep him supplied. Ten thousand crowns (thirty thousand livres) were offered to the first ship's captain, whether a seaman or not, to transport fifty barrels of corn, flour or biscuits to the fort of Saint-Martin-de-Ré (24 August). In accordance with contemporary tactics (or rather with tactics since time immemorial), preparations for war went on at the same time as negotiations both with Buckingham and with the citizens of La Rochelle. The latter were sufficiently emboldened to demand that Fort-Louis be demolished and put forward ridiculous proposals 'such as the king would only hearken unto if he had already lost two battles'.

This state of affairs continued until the Rochelais impulsively opened fire on the duke of Angoulême's army on 10 September. Two days later the king, who had recovered from his illness, set up his general headquarters at Aytré. The war against La Rochelle was now part and parcel of the war against England, but the initial objective remained the same —to force Buckingham to raise the siege of Saint-Martin.

Everyone knows the memorable story of the siege of La Rochelle. Compared to it the siege of Saint-Martin-de-Ré seems, historically speaking, a very minor affair; yet there is scarce an episode that gives a clearer picture of some aspects of the character of French nobles and soldiers in the time of Louis XIII.

With Richelieu's hand writing the actual words, the king had called upon Toiras and his troops to endure 'when occasion requires all the extremes of hardship and discomfort that men of valour devoted to his service can and should bear'. They obeyed him simply and with complete loyalty. Nowadays we pay attention to the little man's contribution to history, whereas for a very long time it was only the great or the influential who attracted the historian's attention. The three messengers whom Toiras dispatched to the royal camp and who plunged into the water naked to swim to the mainland were humble men of the people. Only one of them, Pierre Lanier, reached the shore, and there for decency's sake he put on the shirt that he had brought with him rolled round his head like a cap.

When Buckingham called upon him to surrender, Toiras replied in knightly fashion that if he were to do such a thing he would feel himself unworthy of the duke's favours.* Boats carrying supplies reached Saint-Martin on several occasions, but the quantity they brought was too

* In the course of the siege the two men exchanged courtesies, melons and scented orange water. (Treasure p. 102)

small. Finally a larger flotilla approached the island on the night of 7/8 October. Toiras had previously declared that he would be unable to hold out after this date, but the almost complete success of this convoy enabled him to prolong his resistance until the arrival of another fleet and a relieving army.

An old sea captain named Beaulieu-Persac, who had joyfully re-enlisted, fell into the hands of the English. 'You must be devils,' Buckingham declared, 'or else you must be men under sentence of death who have chosen to risk your lives keeping this fort supplied so as to escape punishment.' 'My lord,' answered Persac,[1] among our nation we do not use condemned persons to perform deeds of valour for we contend with each other for the honour of participating therein.'

The royal army, consisting of some twenty thousand men, had taken up fixed positions around La Rochelle. The king had entrusted the government of the realm north of the Loire to Marie de Medici so that he could join the army in person. He had with him his brother, Angoulême, Schomberg and Bassompierre. Richelieu employed a team of experienced subordinates to carry out difficult assignments. Churchmen like the bishop of Mende, the abbot of Marsillac, and Sourdis, bishop of Maillezais, showed a real talent for military organisation. They combed the Atlantic ports and creeks and rivers along the coast and up the Loire as far as Nantes, collecting every boat, pinnace and lighter they could lay their hands on, including even old disused hulks which could be turned to good account in the present emergency.

At Paris, Bérulle, who had recently been made a cardinal, was negotiating with the Spanish ambassador, the marqués de Mirabel, for the dispatch of the Dunkirk fleet and the escort of French ships on their way from Holland.

To Condé who was to be sent to fight the rebellious Protestants of Languedoc, Richelieu explained his plans at some length. He was now bent on the destruction of La Rochelle (6 October): 'The Huguenots must be broken. If Ré holds out it will be an easy task. If Ré falls it will be more difficult to destroy them but it will still be feasible [*faisable*] as well as necessary in that it will be the sole remedy for the loss of Ré—for otherwise the English and the Rochelais will be united and powerful. Whether Ré is saved or lost, we will have to carry the war into England for we shall in this way prevent the English from extending it into the interior.' Such was Richelieu's new programme.

In the event Ré was saved. An army of twelve hundred men under Schomberg was landed on the island at the end of October and Toiras exultantly led it into battle. The roles of the two antagonists were now reversed and it was Buckingham's turn to find that supplies were running low. He sensed, too, that there was no spirit left in his army, whose morale had been sapped by its inactivity. He had to raise the siege and saw no alternative but to re-embark his troops—a difficult operation which was saved from turning into a rout by a favourable tide.

But although Buckingham sailed away there was no guarantee that he would not return. Before he did so the town of La Rochelle, now in open rebellion against Louis XIII, must be destroyed. It did not represent an English enclave on French soil, for even in rebellion the citizens asserted their loyalty to their king. But La Rochelle was England's ally. Indeed it was almost a bridgehead-designate for further expeditions.

The king and Richelieu (who was put in direct command of the army), as well as their generals Marillac and Bassompierre, were not apparently disposed to take La Rochelle by assault. It was a fortified town with strong defence works in good condition and manned by troops who were animated by a fierce determination to resist the enemy. By land the town was already invested by the king's soldiers. Between their entrenchments and the city walls lay fields and gardens which were still being cultivated and could provide food for a few weeks. To this could be added the fish caught at sea and the shell-fish to be found in the bay. By sea supplies could still reach La Rochelle and at quite an early stage the cardinal thought of cutting all communication between the town and the open sea. After examining several plans, including those submitted by Targone, an Italian inventor, he decided in favour of the scheme put forward by Métezeau, the king's architect[8]—a mole running across the bay and sufficiently distant from the town for the latter's guns to be unable to prevent its construction. The mole was to be made up of blocks of stone and masonry roughly put together and flanked by blockships [*navires murés*] that is to say, by hulks filled with stones and limestone which would be deliberately sunk there. A gap was to be left in the middle of the mole to allow the sea to pass through without dashing itself too violently against it and carrying away the whole construction. Small boats would be able to slip through the breach easily enough; but it would be impossible for ships of any size to get past. Out at sea or in nearby creeks the royal fleet would be on guard ready to oppose any squadron sent to relieve the town. In this way La Rochelle would eventually be forced to capitulate. Isolated from the rest of France by land, and cut off from the sea by the blockade the people would either have to submit or die.

Work on the mole began in October and was continued doggedly throughout the winter. From January onwards the blockade became effective. It was of little consequence that within the next few months a twenty-five-ton English cutter eluded the gunfire from the royal forces and sailed into La Rochelle with tidings from England and the draft of a treaty which was accepted by the inhabitants, 'albeit without prejudice to the loyalty and obedience that they owed to the Most Christian King their natural and sovereign lord'. A few weeks previously a new town council had been elected in the traditional manner and Admiral Jean Guiton had been chosen as the new mayor. There can be no doubt as to his local patriotism and Protestant fervour, even if he did not express them on assuming office in the way long depicted by popular legend.*

There had been a shortage of food in the town for a considerable time. Although some households still had stocks in reserve, only a small range of produce was available in the markets. It was in poor condition and only obtainable at exorbitant prices. Attempts had been made to send away those of the population whose presence served no useful purpose [*bouches inutiles*], and some of them contrived to escape by sea. However, the poor wretches who managed to drag themselves towards the royal army's lines were turned back by the king's troops. In February an epidemic broke out which lasted for some weeks.

The royal army was well paid and issued with strict instructions to respect the lives and property of the civilian population in whose midst the camp lay. Chaplains reminded the troops in their sermons of the seriousness and holy nature of the war upon which they were engaged. It was undoubtedly one of the best-disciplined armies of its day and was proudly paraded before the famous Spanish general Spinola when he travelled across France in January. He admired the mole and spoke to the king, who was present with his troops, in the most complimentary terms.

But all that could be obtained from Spain was the 'appearance' of help. After assembling in the Gulf of Morbihan, a Spanish fleet commanded by Don Fadrique de Toledo had approached La Rochelle in November. Since Buckingham's forces had left some time ago, it was not much use for the time being—a state of affairs which gave it an excuse for sailing away again. As he wrote in the *Testament politique*, Richelieu remained convinced that the Spaniards neither wanted La Rochelle itself to be cap-

---

* He is said to have driven his dagger into the council table exclaiming that he would in like manner thrust it into the heart of the first man to talk of surrender. (V.L.T.)

tured nor desired a successful outcome to the French king's affairs. Indeed he believed that cardinal de la Cueva[9] had promised England not to send any help to the French which could possibly reach them in time.

All over Europe, anyone who feared the prospect of France becoming powerful at sea sensed the significance of the struggle and realised that this was more than one of those wars between a ruler and his rebellious subjects which were then so frequent an occurrence. Soon we shall see the king of France contending with other revolts—revolts whose historical importance has long been overlooked. But what was happening at La Rochelle seemed a serious matter to every Power in Europe. Venice offered her services as mediator both to England and to France. Her ambassador in London heard Buckingham prophesy that France would eventually lose her maritime trade and be engulfed in civil war for many a year to come.

Richelieu, who did not lose sight of the general picture, would have welcomed an earlier end to the siege for this very reason. On learning that it might be possible to force an entry into La Rochelle through a gate known as porte Maubec, he tried to take possession of it by surprise and pour eight to ten thousand men into the town. Had the attempt succeeded La Rochelle would certainly have been forced to surrender; but it failed miserably (12 March). The effect was to increase the hopes of the citizens that an English fleet would come to their rescue. For two months they waited for its arrival. But when at last the fleet appeared in the middle of May under the command of Buckingham's brother-in-law, the earl of Denbigh, it was a crushing disappointment. Denbigh found the king's forces on land and at sea far too powerful for him to risk an engagement, and did not even succeed in getting supplies through to the town. He sent a message to the citizens advising them to open negotiations with Louis XIII immediately, for perhaps the presence of an English fleet would induce the French king to offer more generous terms. The Rochelais begged the earl at least to make some sort of demonstration. He confined himself to firing on the siege works of the king's army as he sailed away.

The people of La Rochelle were still bent on resistance. They sent a messenger to Charles I imploring further help. But their sufferings during the summer were terrible. The food they ate bore witness to the effects of the siege. Donkey or dog meat became luxuries; grotesque recipes were used, such as pieces of leather boiled in tallow. It was appalling to see the effects of undernourishment on the people as they passed by, pale, yellow and as emaciated as corpses. Yet the sentries showed astonishing endurance, taking their turns at the times laid down even if they subsequently collapsed from exhaustion. Sickness went untended, and people died at a rate that came to be accepted without causing an outcry.

The town council did not reply to the king's demands for surrender. The citizens managed to obtain some news from England, and the most stout-hearted of them still clung to their hopes. But many were beginning to reach the end of their patience. There were a number of desertions and cases of people escaping to the royal camp. Among the common people the mutterings of revolt were gradually growing louder. The town authorities knew that there was no way out, that the king was bound to insist on surrender. In the last resort he might pardon the inhabitants and guarantee them their property as well as their lives, but the town's privileges would be abolished. Those who knew something of European affairs had good reason for thinking that this was the way that rebels were generally treated. Many of the privileges enjoyed by the kingdom of Bohemia had vanished for ever during the repression which had followed the battle of the White Mountain. In addition, a number of individuals had been singled out for punishment. Heads had fallen and fortunes had been penalised by ruthless confiscations. The only hope for the Rochelais still seemed to lie in a last attempt by the English to come to their rescue. It was becoming more and more difficult to sustain the confidence and resolution of the wretched people, who found nothing but scenes of horror awaiting them when they awoke each morning. Moreover the attitude and behaviour of the population varied enormously. Real heroism and Christian charity were to be found side by side with tenacious egoism and a mean-spirited and typically bourgeois preoccupation with questions of social precedence and etiquette.

At the end of September an English fleet appeared out at sea. The bells of the town rang joyfully. The fleet was under the command of the earl of Lindsey and carried an expeditionary force of five thousand men— far too small a number to try conclusions with Louis XIII's army, which was four times as large. On board were Soubise and Laval, the two Huguenot leaders who represented La Rochelle at the court of Charles I, and also an English diplomat named Montagu, who had been involved in these matters since the previous year.* Montagu had been employed on negotiations with foreign Powers, and as a result of his intrigues had

---

* For an account of Walter Montagu's life, see the D.N.B. In the spring of 1627 he had tried to induce the duke of Rohan to join in a grandiose scheme for a league against Louis XIII between England, Lorraine and Savoy.

been abducted from the duchy of Lorraine and imprisoned in the Bastille. Eventually, however, he had been released. It was Lindsey's task to break the blockade of La Rochelle by hook or by crook and to land supplies for its population. By the time the expedition left England Felton's knife had done its work and Buckingham had been dead for several days.

The English fleet first cast anchor at Chef de Baie and then on two occasions offered battle. But since the French fleet was both larger and stronger the English ships manœuvred cautiously, being anxious not to court disaster. The engagements which took place did little damage to either side and decided nothing. In short, after more than a year's hostilities, the tide of war was now beginning to turn against the aggressors and from now onwards the victory of Louis XIII seemed inevitable. Lindsey left it to Montagu to begin negotiations with the French, which were approved by Soubise and Laval, as being the only way of saving the people of La Rochelle from an even worse fate. From the towers of the city the latter had watched the English fleet's manœuvres and realised how things stood.

The Rochelais sent delegates to the king. They were received by Richelieu with that mixture of haughtiness and deference which that consummate artist in deportment considered appropriate to the occasion: their rebellion was heinous but their resistance had been heroic. Deep down the cardinal admired the audacity with which, for all their desperation of mind and wretchedness of body, they still insisted on their privileges and demanded guarantees for Soubise and the old duchess of Rohan. To dispose of their last remaining illusions, he confronted them with their compatriots who had come with the English fleet. He promised them the king's pardon and the free exercise of their religion—no more. The rest of their demands would not even brook discussion. The delegates accepted his offer and returned to La Rochelle. Two days later they reappeared, bringing with them the town's capitulation and an appeal for mercy which they delivered to Louis XIII in person.

Richelieu had scored an even greater victory than was realised. He had been obliged to agree to Montagu's departure for England and had been very much afraid that he would return before the town had surrendered. Although Montagu's presence would not have made any real difference, the cardinal disliked the idea of the king of France appearing to negotiate with, or pardon, his subjects through Charles I's good offices. In the event the king's triumph was complete and unconditional.

Catholic worship, which had for long been excluded by the city's privileges, was immediately re-established in La Rochelle. On All Saints

Day the king made his entry into the town through streets where the people knelt as he passed amidst cries of 'Long live the king'. He proceeded to the Church of Sainte-Marguerite, where the *Te Deum* was sung. Sourdis, the archbishop of Bordeaux and former bishop of Maillezais,* had carried out the ceremony of purification on the previous day and Richelieu had celebrated Mass there the same morning. Shortly afterwards La Rochelle was made a bishopric. It was offered to Father Joseph, but like St Bruno before him he refused a bishop's mitre.[10] In Paris the newly built Church of the Petits Pères was dedicated to Our Lady of Victories.[11] The religious aspect of the king's victory was given great emphasis—a step which seemed all the more necessary because the Protestants in the Cévennes and Languedoc were still in revolt. However, it is impossible to take the view that the government's only object in embarking on the war and prosecuting it with such ruthlessness had been to carry out a successful crusade. It constituted the major episode in a drive to liberate France's seaboard and make the king powerful at sea—an operation that England had attempted to thwart.

That the price which had to be paid for this achievement should have been the destruction of France's foremost seaport may nonetheless seem astonishing. As Michelet put it, La Rochelle had been a source of terror to the Spaniard and of envy to the Dutchman.[12] Four years later when she visited the town, Anne of Austria saw no more than 'the shadow and ghost of La Rochelle'.[13] Its walls and fortifications, including Fort-Louis were ruthlessly razed to the ground. The forts at Saint-Martin on the Isle of Ré were likewise demolished so that no enemy landing on the island would be able to seize the stronghold which Toiras had so valiantly defended. This wholesale destruction of coastal fortifications showed that here too the old mediaeval France, that patchwork of especial customs and privileges, was on the retreat. It represented yet another step towards the unification of the realm under the monarchy. To replace La Rochelle a new port was being built which symbolised the dawning of a new era in France's naval history—the port of Brouage.

The capture of La Rochelle was quite as much a victory for the *dévot* party as for the monarchy. The *dévots* generally and Father Joseph in particular had undoubtedly encouraged the cardinal in his resolve to continue the siege until the town surrendered from exhaustion; and although it was not for them to lay down, or even to suggest, the peace

*This was Henri d'Escoubleau de Sourdis who succeeded his older brother François as Archbishop of Bordeaux on the latter's death in 1628.

terms—by trying, for example, to limit the scope of the king's pardon —they had cause to rejoice that the power of their opponents had been so gravely weakened. To their way of thinking the obvious thing to do was to continue the war until the Huguenot party had been completely destroyed; this meant that the Protestant risings in the south should now be dealt with once and for all. One of the chief men in the *dévot* party was Marillac, the keeper of the seals, a far-sighted statesman who was well informed about the internal situation and the state of French finances (the siege of La Rochelle had cost about forty million livres). In addition to his religious aims, Marillac favoured a policy of peace and reform. He thought in terms of a general internal reorganisation of the realm by means of new enactments which he wanted to see vigorously and systematically enforced. In the following chapter we will examine the arguments upon which this attitude was based. For the moment it is sufficient to say that they were many and not ill-founded. But Richelieu, although he too took these arguments into consideration, held that affairs in Europe were of more pressing importance. He had been compelled to concentrate on one problem at a time, and for as long as La Rochelle was under seige he had wished to devote his energies to the siege alone; but he had continued to follow the course of events outside France. For example, he received a visit from a French agent, Hercule de Charnacé, who described to him the power of Gustavus Adolphus, the young king of Sweden—a new protagonist in the struggle which was taking place in northern Germany.

What had been happening whilst Louis XIII was endeavouring to reduce La Rochelle?

The war in the Empire continued to pursue its course. A few salient features could be distinguished from the tangle of personal, dynastic, economic and religious interests that were already involved in the struggle. The war was still a conflict between the claims of the house of Austria to supreme dominion over Germany and the determination of the German princes to preserve their independence in accordance with the spirit of the old Germanic constitutions. It was still a contest between Catholicism—represented by the emperor, the duke of Bavaria and the Rhenish archbishops—and Protestantism, whether Lutheran or Calvinist. The king of France could not accept the triumph of Spain's ally, the house of Austria, without injury to his own position; but if the German princes and the Protestant cause were victorious he would also be faced with grave dangers, for the princes stood for feudalism and the German Protestants were of the same religion as his rebellious subjects. Yet another complicating factor was Spain's war against the United Provinces, since its successful outcome would lead to the re-establishment of a more powerful Spanish dominion on France's northern frontiers.

However, it appeared very unlikely that any such clear-cut decisions would be reached in the near future. The probability was that the war would last for a long time yet, with varying fortunes for both sides. None of the combatants possessed enough or sufficiently well-armed troops to bring the war to a rapid conclusion. Their armies invariably consisted of regiments of mercenaries which were recruited each spring; by the time winter set in these regiments had more or less broken up, leaving them with only a reduced number of effectives. They supported themselves by looting and committing outrages, and were commanded by ambitious leaders to whom the actual war mattered much more than the cause for which they were fighting; nor could these commanders be relied upon by those who employed them. In short, the Spanish army was virtually the only one that could be described as a disciplined force. But this is not to say that the other armies counted for nothing. They were above all a source of terror to the population of the areas where they had established themselves. The rich Germany of the sixteenth-century merchant cities was being steadily obliterated—eroded by the passage of troops, sucked dry by a succession of occupying armies, consumed by conflagrations.

The disorder prevalent in Germany constituted a temptation to neighbouring countries. It was for this reason the king of Denmark had signed alliances with England, the Lower Saxon Circle and the United Provinces in 1625 and embarked on the conquest of the bishoprics on the Weser which he wished to secure for his son. His military operations were undertaken in conjunction with the two German Protestant generals, Mansfeld and Christian of Halberstadt, whose armies, thanks to English and French subsidies, still remained in the field in western Germany. Their main objective was the reconquest of the Rhenish Palatinate from the Spaniards and Bavarians, followed by the reinstatement of Frederick V; for it was now two years since a general electoral meeting, or *Deputationstag*, had punished the former king of Bohemia for his rebellion against the emperor by confiscating his hereditary principalities and transferring them, together with his electoral title, to the duke of Bavaria.*

---

* The *Deputationstag* or 'general electoral meeting' [the term used by Dame Veronica Wedgwood in her book on the Thirty Years War] should be distinguished from the

But at this moment, when Denmark was entering the war, the Emperor Ferdinand was able to bring forward fresh forces ready for action. At the end of 1625 he made an agreement empowering one of his subjects to raise an army on his behalf. The new general was a Czech Catholic named Albert of Valdstejn, or to give him his German name, Albrecht von Wallenstein. Much has been written about this extraordinary man, one of the most remarkable personalities of his age.[14] Historians have often depicted him as a typical condottiere, but such a bald definition fails to provide the key to his complex character.

Wallenstein was endowed with exceptional intelligence, and was also a man of some learning; but although brilliantly gifted, his mental processes were confused and irrational to the highest degree. Astrology was his passion and he fell increasingly under its spell. We should think of him primarily as belonging to a social and cultural climate which was at the time quite alien to western Europe. He was a Czech or, to put it more appropriately, a Bohemian; and the geographical position of his homeland combined with his heredity and his previous career to place him at the meeting-point of a number of different cultural influences originating from Germany, Italy and central Europe, from the Renaissance, the Reformation and the Counter-Reformation. The Reformation known to him was that peculiar to Bohemia—a curious synthesis of the Hussite, Lutheran and Calvinist creeds. He was also familiar with those immense estates which made the magnates to whom they belonged almost like independent rulers: men to be reckoned with by the monarchs of the great European states. Wallenstein's own vast landed possessions were of recent date having been acquired by adroit speculation in property formerly held by Protestants and rebels which had been confiscated after the battle of the White Mountain. It enabled him to offer the emperor—himself too poor or too ill-served to meet the expenses occasioned by the war—the money and the soldiers which he needed.

Although he was the king-emperor's general, Wallenstein maintained relations with Czech émigrés outside Bohemia. The realm from which they had fled was apparently subjugated, but the spirit of revolt was still alive beneath the surface. As duke of Friedland in Bohemia, he organised his domains like a miniature state, complete with its capital at Jičin;[15] but he realised, too, that he would have the opportunity of carving out more than one principality for himself within the Empire.

From 1625 to 1628 Wallenstein's career as general and conqueror was

---

Reichstag or Imperial Diet. Its members consisted of the electors and a certain number of princes. (V.L.T.)

to carry him through north Germany to the shores of the Baltic. His campaigns were distinguished not so much by an exceptional talent for strategy or generalship as by a capacity to take advantage of the opportunities that were offered him. In April 1626 he beat Mansfeld at Dessau on the Elbe while Tilly defeated the king of Denmark at Lutter (27 August). He next proceeded to reconquer from the Danes and Germans first Silesia (as a result of which he became duke of Sagan and Glogau) and then the duchies of Mecklenburg. Finally he was charged by the emperor with the task of building a fleet and securing the necessary bases on the Baltic. The power of the Habsburgs now extended along its shores, and the Baltic trade was of vital concern to England, Sweden, Poland and Russia, as well as to the United Provinces. But as yet there was no fixed unity of purpose between Madrid and Vienna, for the emperor neither could nor would involve Germany in a war against the Dutch.

Nor did Wallenstein succeed in taking Stralsund, despite his boast that he would do so 'though it were surrounded with a wall of iron and bound with diamond chains to Heaven'. It was defended by a Danish garrison and saved by the intervention of Gustavus Adolphus, who had hitherto been campaigning in Poland. But this setback in no way impaired Wallenstein's power. The emperor appointed him 'Admiral of the North and Baltic seas'* and awarded him the title of duke of Mecklenburg in place of the former dukes, who were declared dispossessed.

From afar off Richelieu watched the progress of this extraordinary adventure. He scarcely had the means of opposing it, but he knew that it was not only the Protestants who were alarmed by the expansion of imperial power. Following a tradition dating back to at least the beginning of the century, he had maintained friendly relations with the Wittelsbachs of Bavaria, and he was sure that although Duke Maximilian was a Catholic and had benefited from a Catholic victory, this did not make him any the less fearful of the emperor. The cardinal had thus some grounds for thinking that the Empire was not yet at Ferdinand's mercy, and that the German princes were quite capable of causing him plenty of trouble before acquiescing in his absolute power.

Richelieu's main preoccupations served to remind him of the headway that Spain had been making in Europe: her advance must be brought to a halt.

A few weeks after the Peace of La Rochelle, Richelieu drew up an

---

* His official title was *General der ozeanischen und baltischen Meeres.*

'Advice to the King' dated 13 January 1629 which set forth his political programme.[16] Neither programme nor policy was new; his object was to summarise the situation as it then stood and the main tasks that had to be undertaken.

At home the war against the Protestants in Languedoc, Rouergue and Guyenne had to be brought to an end, the people must be less heavily taxed (a point which the reader should bear in mind) and the *paulette* should be abolished. In addition the Parlements must be curbed. Abroad, 'the first thing to be done is for this realm to make itself powerful at sea, which gives access to every country in the world'. Evidently the question of sea power was still exercising Richelieu's mind more than any other—at least in theory. Next, to keep Spanish power in check France's frontiers must be fortified, whereas within the realm any strongpoints which did not serve to defend French territory should be demolished. France must also be in a position to come to the help of any victims of Spanish oppression. Nevertheless it was necessary to avoid 'the kindling of an open war against Spain so far as lies in our power. We should consider the possibility of edging forwards cautiously and covertly towards Strasbourg to acquire a means of entry into Germany, towards Geneva so that it can serve as a bastion on France's frontiers [*un des dehors de la France*] and towards Neufchâtel [*sic*]. The latter could be purchased from the duc de Longueville in order to overawe the Swiss cantons[17] and ensure that they will always act as a barrier between [*sépareront*] Germany and Italy. We could likewise consider penetrating into Franche-Comté and Navarre, since they are adjacent to France and rightfully hers. But we should only engage in these operations gradually over a long period of time, unobtrusively and with great circumspection.'[18]

Richelieu's memorandum thus puts forward a number of limited short-term objectives which would enable France to put into effect by degrees, as circumstances permitted, a larger plan for rounding off her frontiers at the expense of Spain. At this date no mention is made of the Netherlands; nor is there any reference to what were later called the natural frontiers of France, or even to Lorraine—although its ruler, Duke Charles IV, was a dubious character who needed to be closely watched, for it was never possible to be sure whether he was pro-French or pro-Spanish. The memorandum gives only one indication that the cardinal was aware of this last danger: Metz must be fortified.

The reason for Richelieu's action in opening up such prospects before his master's eyes by means of this remarkable memorandum was that Louis XIII would need to give his mind to them in the course of a fresh expedition—an expedition upon which he was to embark immediately, that would take him far away from France, and necessitate postponing the conclusion of the war against the Huguenots until the following spring.

During the siege of La Rochelle the duke of Mantua, Vincenzo II di Gonzaga, had fallen gravely ill and realised that his days were numbered. However, he had time to put his affairs in order by nominating his cousin, Charles, as heir to all his territories. The latter was none other than the duke of Nevers, who belonged to the French branch of the Gonzaga family. Pending Nevers's arrival his son, the duc de Rethelois, who was already in Mantua, was to act as lieutenant general, and to guard against the possibility of any dispute Vincenzo II arranged for him to marry his niece and only close relative. The marriage between the young princess of Mantua and the duc de Rethelois took place on the night of 25/26 December. On the following day Vincenzo breathed his last.

Three weeks later Charles de Gonzague, duke of Nevers, took possession of his inheritance. But Vincenzo's heir found himself exposed to all sorts of difficulties. The hasty marriage of the young princess gave rise to protests. Not only had it been celebrated when her uncle was at death's door, but in addition no attempt had been made to obtain the consent of the emperor and the king of Spain, who now that Vincenzo II was dead were the young princess's closest relatives and guardians. Nor was this the only complication. The late duke's principality consisted of two distinct territories, each subject to different legal dispositions. Whereas Mantua was an imperial fief and could only pass to the duke of Nevers if he was invested with the duchy, inheritance of the marquisate of Montferrat, which lay close to Piedmont, could be claimed through the female line. The emperor refused to invest the duke of Nevers with Mantua. As for Montferrat, the king of Spain and the duke of Savoy had already agreed to put forward their own claims, derived from their female forbears, and to divide the marquisate between them.

The Spaniards, making the most of their alliance with France and taking full advantage of her preoccupation with La Rochelle, began to besiege Casale, the chief town of Montferrat. It was defended by a Mantuan garrison and a few French troops under the command of the ex-duellist Beuvron,* who, although he did not dare to return to France as things stood, was anxious to recover his good name.

As soon as La Rochelle had fallen, Richelieu adjured Louis XIII not to

*See above, p. 165

jeopardise his prestige any longer by failing to come to the rescue of a petty prince who was his ally. Marie de Medici, who detested Nevers, and some of the *dévots*, swayed by their sympathy for Spain or by their eagerness to dispose of the Protestants once and for all, advised against the expedition; but not all of them. Father Joseph for one had long been linked with Nevers, for the latter, as head of the Christian Militia, was closely associated with the Capuchin's grandiose anti-Turkish schemes. In short Richelieu's view prevailed.

'I am no prophet,' wrote the cardinal in December 1628, 'yet I think I can assure Your Majesty that provided no time is lost in putting this plan into execution, you will raise the siege of Casale and restore peace in Italy in the month of May; if you then return with your army to Langue-doc, you will reduce all those parts to your obedience and impose peace there in the month of July. In such sort that, as I hope, Your Majesty will be able to return to Paris victorious in the month of August.'[19]

Louis XIII meant to command the army himself. At one stage there had been talk of giving the command to his brother, but Gaston was once more behaving intolerably. His wife had died giving birth to their first child, a daughter later to be known as 'La Grande Mademoiselle', and for the past eighteen months he had been a widower. Now he had fallen in love with the duke of Nevers's daughter, Louise-Marie de Gonzague, and despite the opposition of the king and the queen mother he proposed to marry her.

On 15 January Louis XIII left the capital. It was mid-winter. He left Marie de Medici to act as regent in his absence, and she was delighted to exercise power once more—although she was surrounded by men upon whom the king could rely. He granted an amnesty to all Huguenots who had taken up arms against him but were prepared to submit immediately. At a *lit de justice* he called upon the Parlement to register a grand ordinance known to history as the Code Michau.* This celebrated compendium of earlier decrees was the work of Marillac, the keeper of the seals. Concerned as it was with almost every imaginable topic, it represented a real attempt to regulate the internal affairs of the realm: questions of police, justice, civil and domestic rights, public morals; the authority of the State in matters of armament and military equipment, trade on the high seas and the formation of trading companies—these were some of the subjects dealt with by the Code. With regard to the last of these, the undertakings given to nobles participating in such companies should be noted; and commoners were promised that they too would be ennobled

*The Code Michau is considered more fully below, pp. 264–5.

if they maintained a ship of between two and three hundred tons for not less than five years.

The same undertaking was given to wholesale merchants who had held office as aldermen and consuls.[20] These provisions were in accordance with what the cardinal had himself written a few months earlier in the margin of a memorandum: 'Offer incentives to engage in commerce and give merchants higher status.' By making trading an honourable occupation he hoped to stimulate French commerce and make it easier for the realm to grow rich. It was an idea that opened up prospects of a great stride forward. Access to the ranks of the nobility would no longer depend solely upon a man's military achievements or upon his service in the king's administration, which he could join by purchasing an office. Now he could be sure of obtaining the same privileges by engaging in commerce which was proclaimed an occupation that was useful to the monarchy. In this way work, at least in its higher forms, was reinstated in its proper position, for only the retail merchant and the shopkeeper were still inescapably penalised by the stigma of plebeian status. In a society in which hereditary prejudices and the caste system were still exceedingly powerful, these provisions must be considered as bold and generous as they could be. To the traditionally-minded, however, it may well have seemed that henceforth money counted for as much as honour. Admittedly in this context money could be equated with work; but it could also be equated with luck, and perhaps with trickery.

The cardinal had not yet been in power for five years; but how full those five years had been! How much had been accomplished is particularly evident if one considers the little achieved during the ten hectic years that lay between the meeting of the Estates-General and Richelieu's admission to the Council.

We have seen that Louis XIII set off for his campaign without waiting for the coming of spring. He was accompanied by Richelieu and quite a large military staff. In order to reach Casale it was necessary to cross the passes into Savoy and these had been barricaded by Duke Charles Emmanuel, both because he was proud of his position as an independent ruler and because he wanted a good price for allowing the king's troops access to his territory. The French army was thus obliged to force its way through the Pass of Susa on 6 March; although fighting was only on a small scale, a Spanish regiment was put to rout, flags were captured and some officers were taken prisoner. On 11 March Charles Emmanuel's heir, the prince of Piedmont, arrived to open negotiations.

He undertook to hand over the fortress of Susa to Louis XIII and to allow supplies to be sent to Casale. A few days later Don Gonzalo de Córdoba, who commanded the Spanish troops besieging Casale, raised the siege and promised not to engage in any hostile action against the new duke of Mantua. For his part Louis XIII protested that he had no intention of carrying the war into Spanish territory and would make no acquisition that was detrimental to 'his uncle of Savoy': it was enough that he had shown his strength and restored the duke of Mantua to his rightful position.

Susa, where the king and cardinal had set up their headquarters, was now the scene of a family reunion. Louis XIII was visited by his sister, the princess of Piedmont. It was ten years since they had last met and for the first time Christina was expecting a child. Everyone pretended to be overjoyed, as if the happy event would constitute a new link between the two families;* in the meantime the princess herself, who was as vivacious as she was elegant and beautiful, helped to bring about a reconciliation between the erstwhile enemies.

For the whole of April Louis XIII remained at Susa to receive ambassadors from Florence, Genoa and Venice.† The little Italian states declared that, thanks to the French king's démarche, they felt their liberties were now secure. Indeed, this enhancement of French prestige was precisely what Richelieu had hoped to achieve, quite as much as a victory in the field. Leaving Toiras to guard Casale, Louis XIII returned to France in order to reduce Languedoc as quickly as possible.

It was the duke of Rohan who had been responsible for fostering the rebellion in Languedoc; but in this fresh war of religion the towns belonging to the Huguenots proved incapable of withstanding the royal army. Nowhere was Rohan able to organise serious resistance. Privas attempted to hold out; whereupon the king's troops burnt and sacked the town and, despite the fact that they were fellow-countrymen, put the inhabitants to the sword. This horrible episode constitutes a blot on Louis XIII's whole reign. Richelieu claimed that it was all the result of an unfortunate misunderstanding and that no orders had been issued to this effect. But at the same time as the sack of Privas the king's generals had been given strict instructions to ravage the suburbs of Montauban, Castres and Nîmes. This policy of 'causing a havoc', as it was then called,

* The child was born on 27 July 1629 and christened Louise-Marie-Chrestienne. (V.L.T.)

† It was also at Susa that peace was concluded between England and France during this month.

involved setting fire to houses, felling trees, trampling down crops and gardens and making them unusable. Such a policy certainly ensured that the Protestants did not persist in their rebellion, but it also meant that the same horrors that armies of mercenaries were perpretrating in Germany and Bohemia were introduced into France and inflicted by French soldiers on French families.

One after the other the Huguenot towns submitted—Anduze, Sauve, Alès; and it was from the last of these that Louis XIII issued the Edict of Pacification of 27 June granting peace to his rebellious subjects. The Edict had then to be ratified by the Parlement of Toulouse and accepted by Nîmes and Montauban, both of which were patently hostile. Louis XIII, whose duties obliged him to return to Paris, left Richelieu behind to restore order in Languedoc and Guyenne. The cardinal was to be assisted by the duke of Montmorency, the governor of Languedoc, 'seeing the authority that he hath in this country both in respect of his office and of the people's long acquaintance with his father and forefathers'.[21] The services of three marshals were also at Richelieu's disposal—Bassompiere, Schomberg and Marillac.

The method which the cardinal adopted for restoring order was very simple. The local authorities were invited to make their submission so that their town could benefit by the terms of the Pacification, and in the case of fortified towns such as Nîmes they were further promised that they would be spared the annoyance of a garrison. The most obstinate of them, like Montauban, he terrorised into submission by embarking on ravaging operations and sending a strong army towards the town. Bearers of flags of truce were told that hostages must be handed over as a pledge that the Edict would be observed.

The Edict of Alès reflects the increased authority of Louis XIII. It was not a treaty such as his predecessors and he himself had had to make with the rebels of previous years, but a pardon graciously granted by the king in his mercy and humbly received by his subjects. It was duly registered by the Parlement of Toulouse after the submission of Montauban. The Grace of Alès neither suppressed nor rendered inoperative the main provisions of the Edict of Nantes, but it did annul most of the privileges associated with it. The military privileges allowed to the Huguenots were abolished; but these had been granted by letters patent appended to the Edict of Nantes, not by the Edict itself, and it was therefore easier to revoke them. Moreover, if it was now laid down that the fortifications of the towns concerned were to be razed to the ground, at least the king agreed to this being done by the inhabitants themselves.

In addition to this provision, the king, 'calling to mind his hopes that his Protestant subjects would return to the Catholic Church so that unity of religion might be re-established within his realm', reintroduced the Catholic priesthood and Catholic worship in all those places where they had formerly existed. Thus opportunities were provided for the recovery of lost souls and for the campaign for a general conversion to Catholicism which the *dévots* so earnestly desired; but in the meantime Protestant worship remained authorised wherever it had previously been legally celebrated and members of the Reformed Church continued to enjoy liberty of conscience and freedom to practise their religion. They kept their pastors, their churches and their cemeteries. They could reside anywhere throughout the realm and they could take up a new abode wherever they chose except at La Rochelle and Privas or on the islands of Ré and Oléron. In these places Protestants were allowed only if they already lived there, the main concern of the government being to prevent the re-establishment of large Protestant communities through an influx of newcomers.

Finally we should note that the rebels were pardoned; no investigation was made into the past, no punishment was meted out for the deeds that had been done. Moreover, not only was personal property guaranteed, but anything which had been unjustly confiscated was restored to the rightful owners. The modern reader may be surprised that there was no promise of compensation for damage or devastation. Such an idea was alien to the seventeenth century so far as the bourgeoisie and the common people were concerned: not, however, in the case of a great noble. Despite proof of his collusion with Spain, the duke of Rohan was neither tried nor imprisoned nor punished, and was awarded 'one hundred thousand crowns in reparation for the damage done to his houses'.[22] Admittedly he and his brother had been granted a million livres by the previous treaty, so that this time a slight reduction was made. Furthermore he was escorted to the sea coast and forced to reside outside France; but it was rare for an exile not to be given the right to return to the realm if he showed signs of mending his ways.

To sum up, the Edict or Grace of Alès abolished the political privileges of the Huguenots, namely their military power and their political assemblies, but not their legal privileges, for there were still special courts [*Chambres*] to see that the Edict was enforced. In addition the religious guarantees given to them were left untouched. Richelieu wrote that these terms were far more favourable to the Huguenots than they could have dared to hope. In August, after making his solemn entry into

Montauban and just before his departure in order to return to court, the cardinal sent Louis XIII a victory bulletin: 'Now it can truly be said that the springs of heresy and rebellion have run dry. . . . Everything bends in submission to your name.' Thus the seal was set on a major undertaking and on a struggle which had lasted for several years. In consequence Protestantism had not merely been destroyed as a political force within the realm; since any recourse to violence by the Huguenots seemed henceforth futile, it had also been condemned to die of a kind of suffocation in a country where the Catholic monarchy had become too strong for it and where, in theory at least, the Catholic Church had begun to recover all the ground that she had lost.

However France was as yet far from secure. From now onwards the news from Italy began to give cause for alarm. The emperor had still not agreed to the investiture of Charles de Nevers as duke of Mantua, and his troops were entering the Italian peninsula. Spinola was assuming command of the Spanish troops in the Milanese. The duke of Savoy was posing as the victim of France and showed no readiness whatever to carry out the terms of the Treaty of Susa. As early as July Richelieu foresaw that 'to be in a position to prevent affairs in Italy from going badly we must be ready to enter either Savoy or Piedmont as occasion may require'. He still hoped that there was 'a considerable likelihood that peace will be attained without war (i.e. without a general war) and this should be our objective'. However, it is quite clear that at this date the cardinal regarded the emperor and Spain as virtually France's enemies, just as the English had been two years earlier. He felt that now that the Huguenots had been crushed, now that France was mistress of her own shores and in a position to develop her sea power, it was essential for her to protect her allies in Italy if she was to play the part of a Great Power in Europe.

What Richelieu needed was the king's confidence and harmony within the government. The first was forthcoming but the second was increasingly lacking. During his absence the letters exchanged between him and the queen mother had been as deferential and amiable as could be desired, and when he joined the royal family at Fontainebleau in September the cardinal went to pay court to her. But Marie de Medici adopted an offensively frigid tone when speaking to him in the presence of the large gathering who were watching them, and when he presented his staff of officers to her the only one to whom she offered congratulations was the maréchal de Marillac, the brother of the keeper of the seals. On two occasions the king had to intervene to bring about a reconciliation between his mother and his minister, who began to talk of going into retirement. The politeness with which they once more began to treat each other failed to disguise their estrangement. Some of the Council disapproved of Richelieu's policy. Bérulle, the other cardinal who was a member, and the keeper of the seals were at the head of this hostile faction. They refused to bother their heads about events in Italy, which in their view were concerned with questions of precedence or prestige that were of no practical importance; and they were apprehensive about engaging in ventures which threatened to cause a breach between France and Spain, thus causing dissension in the Catholic world. They considered it dangerous for the king to be required to leave the realm at a time when the most urgent task was to pacify it. They were alarmed by the continual outbreaks among the populace. They demanded that the government press on with the conversion of the Huguenots and the reintroduction of unity of religion. Feelings grew so violent that when Cardinal Bérulle died suddenly at the beginning of October at the relatively early age of fifty-three, it was rumoured that Richelieu had had him poisoned. The rumour was widely accepted as true. People said as much openly in Paris and Rome, and Richelieu had to write to Father Bertin of the Oratory to clear himself, at the same time as he instructed the latter to obtain from the pope a particular favour on his own account—a dispensation from reciting his breviary.[23]

The king's personal authority and prestige, which had been enhanced by his recent victories, inspired such respect that it was not easy to get rid of Richelieu. Did Louis XIII in fact feel any affection for him? We know of several particularly affectionate letters from the king to the cardinal written during this period. They are short and to the point and have nothing in common with the messages overflowing with devotion and loyalty that Richelieu was in the habit of exchanging with the queen mother—messages which prove nothing except that the customs of the time included excessive politeness and exaggerated hypocrisy. No doubt Louis XIII's friendships with his successive favourites, Barradas, Bassompierre and Saint-Simon, were more ardent—although he did not allow these favourites any political role, for he remained sufficiently master of himself not to allow the passing fancies that marked his private life to encroach upon his task as king. But he had faith in the cardinal's talents and was touched by his unflagging zeal, thanks to which he himself was invested with a glory that gave him infinite pleasure. Around him the king could see so many examples of blatant selfishness—his own brother for instance!

Gaston of Orleans still clung to his plan for marrying Princess Louise-Marie de Gonzague, and the opposition of the queen mother and Louis XIII only served to whet his impatience. For some time Marie de Medici kept the princess prisoner in the château de Vincennes, only releasing her after she had promised to join her father in Italy immediately. Filled with bitterness, Gaston left France and took refuge in Lorraine. The court there was a hot-bed of intrigue and a permanent haven for malcontents from France: first Mme de Chevreuse, now the king's brother. Judged by the standards of the time, Gaston's action was a serious matter, for it upset the proper order of things. Even after a king had attained his majority it was only when he was surrounded by all the princes of the blood and assured of their loyalty and eagerness to obey him that the monarchy seemed triumphant and securely established. It followed that Monsieur must be induced to return to France. The scatterbrained fellow tried to bargain demanding an increase in his apanage, in particular in some of the frontier provinces which it would have been most unwise to entrust to his charge.

Marie de Medici vouched for the king's good intentions towards him: 'You can feel complete confidence on that score in view of what I write, which is a definite fact [*chose très véritable*],' she wrote to Monsieur in a letter dictated by Richelieu, 'I entreat you by the love that you bear me, for I could no longer live if I thought that there was a rift between two persons so dear to me as the king and yourself.'

At the end of November Richelieu, who was once more in the ascendant in the Council, secured a decision that the war in Italy was to be resumed: but the negotiations with the duke of Orleans made it impossible for the king to leave Paris. The cardinal requested that he himself be put in command of the expedition with the title of lieutenant general, 'representing the king's person in Italy'. This meant that even the marshals were his subordinates. Never had Richelieu risen so high. According to Father Griffet the courtiers told each other jokingly that the only power the king had kept for himself was the power of curing the king's evil.

In fact the power which Louis XIII thus conferred upon one of his servants was not so very unusual for the age in which he lived; we have only to think of the favours that Ferdinand II was lavishing on Wallenstein at this time. But it was a step impelled by extreme necessity and taken under circumstances of the utmost gravity. And bearing in mind the ideas and behaviour current at the time, let us also give thought to the savage jealousy which Richelieu's promotion awoke in the minds of his possible rivals, and remember that there were only two methods that they could use to destroy a favourite who enjoyed such influence and prestige: they had either to tarnish his reputation in his master's eyes or to kill him. As he travelled south from Paris with the king's good wishes and the specious congratulations of the queen mother and of Marillac's clique ringing in his ears, Richelieu realised that henceforth both these threats were suspended over his head.

Louis XIII was also to rejoin the army as soon as he was assured of his brother's return to France. Monsieur did obtain an increase in his apanage, but in a form that did not endanger the security of the State. However there is no object in boring the reader with details of these transactions. The important point to remember—as Georges Pagès pointed out in a substantial and authoritative article to which we will revert later[24]—is that contemporary Frenchmen varied in the degree of urgency they attached to the various problems that were simultaneously claiming their attention. Marillac and his followers were alarmed by the disorder they observed within the realm, whereas Richelieu, who had been so taken up with plans for reform at the outset of his ministry, no longer paid attention to anything except general policy and affairs in Italy.

'In Richelieu's view the realm was "peaceful" so long as Monsieur did not stir up civil war there in connivance with a foreign Power,' observes Pagès.[25] The young prince's comings and goings assumed the utmost importance in the cardinal's eyes. He does not seem to have regarded them as a mere incident in court life: on the contrary he feared them as a complicating factor in the foreign policy by which he strove to counteract Spanish ambitions.

Being exclusively absorbed with his military preparations, which necessitated moving troops from Grenoble to Susa, the cardinal was scarcely in a position to keep an eye on internal affairs, although Marillac and Bullion kept him informed. But Richelieu was becoming more and more deeply absorbed in the underhand struggle against the house of Austria. One sees him defending France's allies in Italy so that Louis XIII's prestige there counterbalances the king of Spain's; greatly exercised about Switzerland and Venice; advising that strong forces be kept permanently in Champagne, because of his fear that Wallenstein might divert some of his troops there, ostensibly in response to the complaints of Monsieur or the duke of Lorraine.

At the same time, although the weather was at its worst for campaigning, Richelieu embarked on operations in Italy. He had with him some excellent commanders in the shape of Marshals Créqui, la Force, Schomberg and Toiras, the last of whom was given the task of supplying and defending Casale; he also had experienced servants in Servien and Feuquières, the latter being a relative of Father Joseph.

But the cardinal met with an obstacle at the outset: the bad faith shown by the duke of Savoy. The duke was playing a double game. He told the Spaniards under Spinola in the Milanese that he had only signed the Treaty of Susa in the previous year to prevent the French from continuing with their expedition. To the French, on the other hand, he made out that he was ready to carry out the terms of the treaty. However, he did nothing of the kind. He neither provided supplies of corn as promised nor did he order his troops to join forces with the French army. He began building fortifications at Avigliana which were bound to inconvenience the French if they were forced to retreat. He avoided taking part in negotiations himself, sending his son, the prince of Piedmont, to offer trivial excuses.

Richelieu decided to cross the river Dora and push on as if he meant to march on Turin. He advanced as far as Rivoli. The abuse shouted by his famished soldiers as he passed them in his coach left him in no doubt as to their angry resentment: 'Even so they should be forbidden to say such stupid things,' he told an officer. On hearing that a thousand of the duke's men had just left the fortress of Pinerolo to the south and that it was now denuded of troops, Richelieu sent Créqui and la Force to besiege it ('I beg you to exert yourselves to the uttermost') and hastened there himself. On Easter Sunday, 29 March 1630, the fortress fell into the hands of the French. It was both a pledge of the duke of Savoy's good behaviour and a gateway into Italy, just as Geneva was to serve as a gateway into Switzerland and Strasbourg into the Empire. For Pagès the seizure of Pinerolo was 'an event of capital importance not only in the history of Louis XIII's campaigns in Italy' but also in the general history of France and of Europe. 'It was the capture of Pinerolo,' he writes, 'which compelled Louis XIII to make a definite choice between two policies.' These two policies were opposed to each other: the first was favoured by Richelieu, the second by Marillac. 'It was hardly likely that the Spaniards would agree to leave Pinerolo in French hands without fighting. The capture of Pinerolo did not necessitate their abandoning the siege of Casale; unmistakably and for the first time it raised the issue of peace or war with Spain.'

Pagès makes use of a long memorandum from Richelieu to the king now in the archives of the Ministry of Foreign Affairs, which has only been partly published. In this memorandum the fateful choice that has to be made is clearly set forth. Richelieu has learnt from a papal legate, an abbé named Giulio Mazarini (such is Mazarin's first appearance on the historical scene), that there will be no peace in Italy unless Pinerolo is restored to Savoy. But if the French keep and fortify Pinerolo, then 'the king has made the most important acquisition that it is possible for him to make and will be well placed to become arbiter and master of Italy'. This will inevitably mean war with Savoy but the military outlook is highly favourable and there are good prospects of victory. The cardinal admits that having been completely out of touch with affairs at home for several months he is in no position to say whether the internal peace of the realm (which depends upon Monsieur) and its financial resources will allow France to embark on war: 'but', he declares roundly, 'if the decision is in favour of peace it must be made promptly without losing a moment while the king's name is held in high repute abroad. *If the king resolves upon war we must give up all thought of repose, retrenchment and reordering of the realm's domestic affairs.** If on the other hand the desire is for peace, we must give up our ideas about Italy for the future.'

Let us stress, as Georges Pagès has done, the serious implications attached to each alternative: either glory in Italy and the abandonment of any reform within the realm, or peace in Italy and renunciation of a foreign policy worthy of a Great Power. This memorandum is dated 13 April. At the time Louis XIII was at Troyes, where he had met his brother and effected a reconciliation with him. He was on his way to join the army, accompanied by the two queens. His health was none too good but he agreed to follow the advice of Bouvard, his physician, and submitted to a series of purges and enemas. His melancholy humour seemed to be on the wane. He had begun to pay court to his wife and it looked as if there were some hopes of a dauphin. Was he going to agree to this new campaign in Italy?

Continuing on his journey, the king reached Dijon on 26 April. It was there that he received Richelieu's memorandum of the thirteenth. Possibly there had already been other communications from the latter. Before leaving the two queens and the Council at Dijon, Louis XIII declared that he was inclined to favour the cardinal's policy even if he was not as yet openly bent on adopting it. On 10 May he joined Riche-

---

* *Si le Roi se résout à la guerre, il faut quitter toute pensée de repos, d'épargne et de règlement du dedans du royaume.*

lieu at Grenoble. Together they examined the peace proposals put forward by the papacy, but these offered such favourable terms to the duke of Savoy, and such inadequate guarantees to France, that both men considered them unacceptable. An imperial army under Collalto was now besieging Mantua, and a Spanish army under Spinola was besieging Casale. In other words, both the duchy of Mantua and the marquisate of Montferrat were threatened, and France's ally, the duke of Nevers, was being treated as an enemy by the house of Austria. Was this the moment for France to give up Pinerolo and Susa? On the contrary, she must prepare for war.

Nevertheless Richelieu considered that war was only possible if peace was assured within the realm. However, he felt that once the queen mother and Monsieur had given their consent the situation at home behind the French army would be secure. He agreed to go to Lyons where Marie de Medici had ended her journey. He saw both her and Marillac. The clash of opinions between the two men was now brought into the open. Marillac advised making peace in Italy and gave his reasons: the danger of exposing a childless invalid like the king to a fresh campaign, the danger of taking him away from a realm which was a prey to disturbances and required his presence. The internal situation was, in fact, the core of the argument. Marillac pointed to 'the miseries and afflictions of the people of France, who languish in such exceeding great poverty as passeth belief'. He spoke on behalf of the common people, who were breaking into revolt because they could endure their sufferings no longer. It was essential to put an end to their miseries and to re-establish conditions that would favour a general return to Catholicism throughout the realm. 'Piety and justice, the two pillars upon which a state rests, are still very frail, and although they are striving to regain their strength they can only recover if there is peace.'

Richelieu retorted by referring to his memorandum from Pinerolo: 'You know that the reply that I received to my dispatch was that the king had chosen the more valorous course [*le parti le plus généreux*] and was on his way to attack Savoy.' Then he replied to the arguments advanced by Marillac, which he seemed to equate with generalisations such as everyone concurred with and such as are put forward whenever there is any question of war: 'One cannot wage war without trials and tribulations [*grandes incommodités*]. This is not merely true of this particular occasion but applies equally to any other, for war is one of the scourges wherewith it pleaseth God to chasten mankind.' He went on to deny that public opinion could be invoked as a factor for determining French policy. He made this denial with all the pitiless arrogance of a great noble, with the harshness of a ruthless champion of the interest of the State [*une rigueur de raison d'État sans merci*]: 'That the common people are averse to war is not a considerable reason (meaning a reason worth considering) to make us favour peace, for they are often quite as aware and apt to complain of necessary hardships as of those that are avoidable. They are as incapable of knowing what is useful to a state as they are ready to flinch and quick to bemoan their lot [*se douloir*] when faced with hardships which have to be borne if worse evils are to be avoided.'[26]

The attitude of both sides is quite clear. The minister who is a layman talks of piety and justice; the minister who is a priest and bishop uses language that smacks of force and authority. Besides, added the cardinal, if peace were made on dishonourable terms it would not last for long and France would be exposed to lengthy wars in the future—an argument which enabled him to end by expressing a hope which a government is always ready to hold out to public opinion when it has decided to ignore it: 'We shall only wage war to obtain peace, whose light to all appearances will shortly be made more manifest than it is now.' A vague enough promise in all conscience! Pushed to its logical conclusion, it contradicts the statement in Richelieu's memorandum from Pinerolo that if the decision was in favour of war all thought of repose, retrenchment and reordering of the realm's domestic affairs would have to be abandoned.

The cardinal won the day. Marie de Medici also declared herself in favour of this necessary war. Was this pure hypocrisy on her part, or was she temporarily convinced of its necessity? Or was she afraid of opposing the king? Whatever the reason, her apparent consent was enough for the time being.

But to understand the nature, if not the value, of these two policies that weighed in the balance the people and the State, we must turn back to some earlier events which we have hitherto deliberately refrained from mentioning so as to make it easier to follow the development of Richelieu's work as a statesman. We have in consequence lost sight of the French people; but the time has come to see what 'their poverty such as passeth belief' entailed, and whether their miseries did not amount to more than 'hardships which have to be borne if worse evils are to be avoided'. Afterwards we will return to the sequence of events during 'the year of tribulations' as Richelieu called it—the year which ended with the Great Storm and the Day of Dupes.

CHAPTER SIX

The Misery of the People and the Glory of the State

THE GREAT nobles, the Protestants, the house of Austria: Richelieu acknowledged that these were major obstacles to the establishment of his power by dealing with them at length in his memoirs and in the *Testament politique*. He chose to enlighten posterity about these three items in his programme in particular, encouraging historians to credit those whose opposition delayed the success of his policy with evil intentions and sinister schemes; but from 1624 to 1630—six years during which the cardinal's government was consolidating its position—internal opposition was not confined to political resistance by the great nobles and the Huguenots. The realm was also the scene of popular movements, riots and revolts, sometimes local, sometimes embracing a wide area, and requiring repression by force of arms. Only in recent years have a few historians paid attention to them—first Georges Pagès then Boris Porshnev and Roland Mousnier.[1] Their existence was well known, but no one bothered to take an interest in the nature of these disturbances or to consider their impact on general policy.

The archives provide a mass of information about these popular risings against royal taxation. Peasants would arm themselves, make their way in larger and larger bands to the neighbouring town, and attack the officials concerned with public finance, who, since they represented the central government, were held responsible for any fresh taxes.

We must know something of economic conditions in France during this period if we are really to understand the causes for these risings. From 1605 until about 1630 the price graphs show a tendency towards an increase in the price of wheat and staple cereals. This does not mean that a rise occurred regularly and invariably from one year to the next, but it does signify that there was a very marked rise in price over the period as a whole. The state of the market in cereals throughout a large part of Europe is not alone sufficient to account for this development,* which was partly linked with an actual weakening of the *livre tournois* due to

* In this connection it should be noted that there was a marked difference between prices in France and the United Provinces and prices in Mediterranean countries (i.e. Spain and Italy). (V.L.T.)

general monetary causes—namely an insufficient supply of good money (gold and silver) and an influx of copper coinage, mainly of Spanish provenance. Thus good money tended to be reserved for external trade and for the use of merchants in the big cities. The mass of the population only possessed coins of base alloy, whose value had naturally depreciated. Clearly if the demands of the king's tax collector increased under conditions such as these, the common people (including as they did a large number of day labourers) sank into a most dreadful state of poverty. They only needed a few determined leaders to believe that their sole chance of salvation lay in revolt.

Agrarian risings are neither peculiar to the reign of Louis XIII nor to France. They had occurred in the time of Henry IV, and they occurred in other countries in Europe—in fact wherever the countryside was engulfed in the same overwhelming poverty. Even so, the Russian historian Boris Porshnev takes the view that the revolts studied by him present certain original features. They are risings which are leaderless at the outset and the rebels adopt as their chiefs men who tend to belong to the fringe of society—adventurers or ruined gentry. Until they have taken possession of the local town where the administrative centre of the area is located or won the support of the urban proletariat within its walls, these risings have no chance of success. To suppress them the king's officials call upon the army or upon the nobility from whom its officers are recruited and who can levy regular forces in the area. However, the bourgeoisie in the towns, who are also concerned with the maintenance of public and social order, are anxious about their property and the appointments which they hold from the king. They ally themselves with the nobility and dispatch their militia against the insurgents. In theory the bourgeoisie ought not the make common cause with an absolute and feudal form of government which rejects them and lumps them together with the populace; none the less the bourgeois plays his part in defending and rescuing this reactionary system, adopting as his own the cause of those who have property or draw income from land.

As against this view, Georges Pagès earlier drew attention to the fact that the king's ministers in general, and Marillac in particular, were often alarmed by the tacit complicity of local authorities, and even of the Parlements, in such disturbances. Either because they were faint-hearted and feared popular reprisals, or because they wished to induce the government to have second thoughts and give up its extortionate fiscal demands, judges and mayors tended to show no great zeal when it came to repressing a riot. But we cannot really understand what occurred in such cases without studying some specific examples.

Map 5 North Italy

It would seem that scarcely a year went by without disturbances of this nature breaking out somewhere. There were outbreaks for instance in 1616 and 1618. On 17 January 1624 the king's Council decided to open an inquiry into a riot which had taken place at Rouen on 16 and 17 November of the previous year and had not been followed by a serious investigation on the spot. In Poitiers, at the end of November 1624, the people attacked the house of Hersan, the notary royal,[2] firing shots and throwing stones at his windows. There was a fresh outbreak of violence at the hostelry of the Moulin Vert where the clerks of Sieur Antoine Feydeau were staying.* Feydeau was the *adjudicataire général des Aides de France*, and his agents had come to Poitiers to collect the tax known as a *huitième* payable on wine sold retail.[3]

In May of the same year Guyenne was convulsed by a far more serious rising in the area of Figeac and Cahors. The peasants banded together, their ranks swollen by detachments of soldiers whom they had found at large in the countryside. They contrived to form an army of sixteen thousand men—although this figure is necessarily approximate and extremely difficult to verify. Their leaders were a reader of horoscopes named Dois, and Barreau, a ruined nobleman from Gramat. They looted and ravaged the farms and country properties belonging to the *élus*[4] in the district. Yet, like Boris Porshnev, one wonders whether a careful distinction was made between the property of officers of the revenue and property that belonged to any wealthy person. Was this only a revolt against the tax collector, or was it also a rising against rich landlords generally?

The army of peasants (the term *croquants* was already in use)[5] arrived before the gates of Cahors demanding that the *élus* be handed over or that the gates be opened, for they thought they would find reserves of food within the town: otherwise the surrounding country would be ravaged. Nowadays the population of a French town includes a large number of officials, employees and workers who come from other parts of France, and a man's wealth is often derived from investments in remote and impersonal commercial concerns. It therefore requires some effort for us to form a clear picture of an urban community in the seventeenth century. A town and its population were then closely linked with the neighbouring countryside. There the inhabitants owned landed properties

---

* These two examples of popular unrest are mentioned in the article by Georges Pagès. Those that follow are taken from the book by Boris Porshnev. (V.L.T.). [It should be noted that Professor Tapié's references are to the Russian edition of this book— See n. 1]

which provided them with income in kind in various forms. The produce from their land was essential for their livelihood, and they valued it very highly. As for the *élus*, they bore little resemblance to modern tax inspectors, most of whom have no roots in the part of the country where they carry out their duties. The *élus* were almost invariably natives of the area where their employment lay, and in addition they were landowners. For the bourgeois there was no worse threat than the ravaging of the estates that lay outside and around the town in which he lived. Some of the citizens of Cahors were prepared to come to an understanding with the rebels and to allow them within the walls—all the more so because the common people of the town were also in a state of ferment and evidently ready to take up arms. But others, who were made of sterner stuff, decided to hold out until the royal army arrived. The latter appeared under the command of the maréchal de Thémines, the governor of the province, and the vicomte d'Arpajon; en route its numbers had been swollen by nobles who belonged to the local feudal levy. The horde of rebels was unable to make a stand; they allowed themselves to be butchered like cattle. Their leaders were handed over, the one to be beheaded at Figeac and the other to be hanged at Cahors. Order reigned once more in the district of Quercy. Aultry, the intendant of justice in Guyenne—later to be known as Séguier, the keeper of the seals and chancellor—held an inquiry, and in 1625 the *élus* were awarded compensation by the king's Council. There were also disturbances in the area of Montauban.

In April 1626 there was a riot at Troyes, where the warehouses for storing corn were looted. In August 1627, in the same town, the house of Sieur Bertault, the receiver of municipal customs dues [*deniers d'octroi*], was sacked together with adjoining houses belonging to members of his family. This episode occurred following the publication of an edict relating to the *gabelle*, Bertault's house being situated close to the salt warehouse. Was it because some people had a private grudge against him, or was it simply a dastardly outrage? At all events, Bertault complained that the mayor and aldermen had winked at these attacks upon his property and allowed them to be perpetrated under their very eyes.[6]

On 29 May 1628, at Amiens, a mob besieged the inn where an important personage was staying. François de Pomereu was a magistrate of high rank in Paris who had been commissioned to induct some newly appointed officers of justice. In this case the issues involved are complicated, but they enable us to see the clash of interests that could arise in a French community of days gone by which was still not very noticeably imbued with respect for royal authority or concern for the public weal. The officers of the local *présidial* had been the first to show their hostility to Pomereu's commission three months previously. The creation of additional offices was both useful to the Treasury and welcome to those bourgeois who intended to purchase the new appointments; but to the officials who were already installed in their offices it seemed an obnoxious measure, for the competition that they would now have to face from newcomers would diminish their authority and pecuniary resources, as well as reducing the value of existing appointments. In consequence no attempt was made to contradict the rumour that taxes were going to be imposed on all sales of goods. The riot that took place was as much bourgeois as agrarian or plebeian in character. It was the master craftsmen and the merchants who were the first to get together; the lower orders made up the rank and file. As for the town council, it made no move. The duc de Chaulnes, Luynes's brother, who was the governor of Picardy, was powerless to intervene. Pomereu had to take to his heels, run across gardens and jump on his horse. He later made out that the bourgeois militia had tried to catch him and fired on him, and that a furious mob, ten thousand strong, had chased him shouting the most shocking abuse 'even against the sacred person of our king'. Undoubtedly there was a good deal of exaggeration in all this. A crowd of that size in full cry after one man would have torn him to pieces if it had not been kept in check by the authorities and the soldiery. But the popular character of the riot is immediately apparent. The authorities at Amiens had not been sorry to give a royal commissioner a good fright and to force him to take himself off with his commission in his pocket.

In June 1628 there was a riot at Laval. This little town was the capital of Western Maine, and the canvas and linen cloth industry provided a large part of the population with a livelihood, not only within the town itself but also in the neighbouring countryside, where the men and women used to spin flax and hemp for the workshops in the winter season. Moreover it was the first district liable to the *gabelle* on the way inland from Brittany. Whereas in Brittany the sale of salt was free from controls because it came from the salt marshes, in Western Maine the population was obliged to purchase a fixed minimum quantity of salt which was stored in government warehouses and sold at an exorbitant price—*le sel du devoir*.[7] The government had to make money wherever possible, and its financial needs had recently led to the creation of new controllers and inspectors of linen cloth and canvas. The people of Laval rose in revolt; they blamed everyone. The riot became a revolution. The local tax receiver [*receveur des tailles*][8] was roughly handled, the staff who supervised the operation of the *gabelle* were pushed and hustled. A mob of raiders set off for Vitré in Brittany to make a clean sweep of the salt warehouses, shouting that they meant to lay in stocks that would last for ten years. During the next few days the stolen salt was brought to the market place in Laval in large quantities and everyone helped himself.

In February 1630 there was a rising at Dijon known as the Lanturlu revolt.[9] In May there were riots at Caen, in June at Lyons, in July and August at Angers. The realm was in a state of disorder. How else can one describe such a situation?

In the words of Georges Pagès: 'It is easy enough to say that Marillac's main object was to divert the king from a warlike policy that was dangerous to the Spanish and Catholic cause; but it would be much less easy to prove that his fears as keeper of the seals were not justified by the facts.'

Nothing could be further from the truth than to suppose that Marillac stood for old ideas, for a feudal conception of the realm that was opposed to the innovations which formed part of Richelieu's programme. On 15 July 1630 he wrote: 'Revolts are breaking out all over France and the Parlements punish none of them. The king has appointed judges to try such cases and the Parlement obstructs the execution of their judgements, so that revolts are given sanction. I do not know what the outcome is likely to be in view of the frequency of these disturbances, of which we receive fresh notification almost daily.'* All this was no more than a statement of fact. As for the attitude of the Parlements, it was in no way due to a feeling of compassion for the miseries of the populace. It was caused by other factors, which have been well brought out by Mousnier.[10]

Neither the cardinal nor the keeper of the seals was in favour of the *paulette*. They would have liked to suppress it in 1630, but the war made this impossible because of the expense that it entailed. Effiat, the superintendent of finance, had to call upon office-holders to advance sums that were altogether exorbitant—amounting to twenty-five per cent of the value of their appointments. He tried to divide the opposition, and to win over those holding posts in the financial administration whom he knew to be richer and readier to part with their money, by conceding that in their particular case the *paulette* would continue to operate. But the magistracy and officers of justice protested, claiming that they should

---

* '. . . *je ne sais pas ce qu'il faut espérer ou appréhender de cela, vu même la fréquence de ces émotions dont tous les jours quasi nous avons un nouvel avis*'.

continue to enjoy the same advantages as the others. Consequently they too allowed to benefit by the *paulette*—although not on the same conditions as formerly, and without the government abandoning its demand for a loan. The Parlement of Paris not only forbade all its members to contribute, but enlisted the support of the Parlements in the provinces. Together they embarked on a sort of strike in the administration of justice at the very moment when the authority of the law was as much required as force of arms to deal with popular disturbances. Thus the people and the bourgeoisie, although not inspired by common interests but only preoccupied with their own concerns, combined to throw the realm into confusion without any regard for the king's orders or for general political considerations.

Richelieu was not deterred by this alarming situation. He rightly believed that eventually the government would be able to come to terms with the officers of the magistracy. After all, they could not push their revolt too far since their very existence depended on the king's authority; in reality they were merely resorting to blackmail. But what was his reaction to the outbreaks among the common people, who had been driven to the limits of their endurance? It will be said that they represented a far bigger threat to him and his policy, and this is certainly true; but a statesman as intelligent and widely informed as the cardinal, for whom no detail was ever too small, was quite capable of seeing the connection between one thing and another. He knew better than anyone that a government does not make war without money ('a matter for the superintendent of finance' as he put it), that it cannot have money without taxes, and that there are no taxes if the population does not agree to pay them or is unable to do so. Ultimately it was upon the good people of Figeac and Laval that the government had to rely if France was to defeat the duke of Savoy and hold her own against Spain.

Richelieu was surely convinced that this was so, but his attitude went a stage further. He envisaged setting up an emergency administration [*un régime de salut public*]. In his eyes the lower orders were not in a position to judge, let alone to discuss, the sacrifices expected of them. If the *Testament politique* declares that the ultimate basis of a king's power lies in his possessing the affection of his subjects, it also declares that 'the French people are capable of anything provided that those who are in authority over them are capable of showing them where their duty lies'. In other words, it is enough for princes, ministers, governors and officials to be loyal for everything to take place in an orderly manner. A population that is effectively supervised is always obedient.*

This is the place to put forward a theory: it is no more than a theory of course, but it is a reasonable supposition to make and perhaps it will seem more plausible when we turn to follow the cardinal's interest in commercial affairs during these years and observe the development of his economic policy in relation to Turkey, Muscovy and the West Indies. Through the agency of a few rich men who were to help him form trading companies, did he not hope to procure for France fresh sources of wealth which would provide her with extra revenues and profits over and above those provided by agricultural labour?—for we must remember that feudal revenues and the money that the landlord, whether noble or bourgeois, derived from his land were produced by the labour of peasants, whether copyholders or day-labourers. If additional sources of wealth were available there would be far less need for the government to bother about popular resentment, which would subside of its own accord thanks to the increased circulation of money within the realm. Possibly some such hope coloured Richelieu's thinking and affected his decision not to devote too much time to current difficulties which could be corrected in the long run; in that case the whole problem would consist in estimating the length of time that would be required.

At all events, there can be no discussion or theorising about the choice that was made in the spring of 1630. From this date until the end of the reign, revolt was endemic within the realm. The king and the cardinal were to be condemned to pursue a policy which, although by no means foolhardy (for in certain respects it achieved a number of concrete and enduring results of great value), was astonishingly daring. But they were far from being free to do everything they wanted; and in particular their policy was never to succeed in resolving the contradiction between the misery of the people and the glory of the State.

We have seen that an expedition against Savoy had been advised by Richelieu, desired by Louis XIII and, in appearance at least, favoured by the queen mother. It was to be short and crowned with speedy success. Until the very last moment the pope tried to intervene to prevent a conflict; but Mazarin, who had already visited Lyons and whom everyone spontaneously decided was likeable and fascinating, with a marvellous grasp of the situation, was unable to take with him to Grenoble any reasonable offer from the duke of Savoy. The latter demanded that Pinerolo be returned to him. He might as well have said nothing at all. Ac-

---

* *Un peuple bien encadré obéit toujours.*

cordingly Louis XIII set out at the head of a large army, accompanied by Marshals Créqui, Bassompierre and Châtillon. On 17 May the king took possession of Chambéry, and a few days later of Annecy. At the end of the month Rumilly fell. It had been defended by the duke of Savoy's second son, Prince Thomas. Before the end of June, according to Father Griffet, the king found himself master of all Savoy proper except the citadel of Montmélian. The French held the [Little] St Bernard and its approaches; the road to Italy seemed clear.

But Louis XIII had three enemies to deal with—the duke of Savoy, who had lost part of his possessions, the king of Spain's general, Spinola, who was besieging Casale, and the imperialist general, Collalto, who was besieging Mantua. Mazarin, who had been instructed by the pope to restore peace in Italy as soon as possible, became increasingly active as a go-between. The French were no longer invariably convinced of his good faith; some muttered that his main object was to gain time in the expectation that circumstances would favour the Spaniards. In fact it seems far more likely that Mazarin's private sympathies, now that he knew Richelieu, were already, in his own interests, pro-French.

While king and cardinal directed operations and arranged for forts to be constructed, Marillac's party at Lyons resumed their open criticism of the policy that was being pursued. To restore unity within the government, Richelieu wished to arrange for an interview between the king, the queen mother and the keeper of the seals, who could meet him en route at Grenoble. However, Marie de Medici made use of a slight indisposition as an excuse for staying where she was. This meant that Louis XIII had to go to Lyons; nevertheless he ordered Marillac, whose duties as keeper of the seals obliged him not to leave the king's person, to rejoin him at Grenoble—the object being to keep Marillac away from the queen mother and to ensure that he took part in the negotiations with Mazarin so as to make him realise all the difficulties that they involved. But the plague had broken out in the south of France. First it was reported in Provence, then it spread to the Alps and began to attack the king's army. Six thousand men left the ranks. Quite apart from this, the army should have been dispatched into Italy without delay if the troops were to live off the harvest there. Abroad it was well known that there were differences of opinion within the King's Council. In short, it looked as if Louis XIII's expedition against Savoy, for all its triumphant beginnings, was turning out badly.

The king now assumed command of his troops with a view to marching into Italy. At Saint-Jean-de-Maurienne, which he reached on 4 July, he received a visit from Mazarin. Louis XIII reiterated that his only object was to ensure the duke of Mantua's security and the tranquillity of Italy, and he complained that his opponents had still failed to make any proposals. How could he reply to people who did not talk? But while the French army, now reformed and refreshed, was crossing the passes into Italy and winning the battle of Avigliana, the king fell ill. He had to resign himself to leaving Saint-Jean, and early in August he arrived back at Lyons. In the meantime news arrived of a notable victory by the emperor's forces: Mantua had fallen.

From this moment Richelieu felt less confident. In view of what had happened it looked as if Marillac was right. The latter had stopped at Grenoble, but declared that he would obey the king and join him at Saint-Jean though at the peril of his life.*

The cardinal now felt that everything was giving way beneath his feet. At the end of July he wrote to Marillac: 'If Mazarin returns with reasonable terms there will be no difficulty about concluding a satisfactory peace, for such is already our resolve, nor have we ever desired anything else.'[11] This statement may not have reflected all Richelieu's thoughts on the subject, but it did provide his rival with proof of his conciliatory attitude.

It remained to be seen whether France would have to be satisfied with a guarantee from the king of Spain alone in respect of the duke of Mantua. Richelieu admitted that the government was on the horns of a dilemma which he had foreseen from the outset but was now no longer so certain of resolving: 'Unfavourable peace terms will injure the king's reputation, which could have a number of disastrous consequences for the State. On the other hand it must be borne in mind that we are committing ourselves to a large-scale war in Italy in order to keep what we have won; such an operation cannot be undertaken without heavy expenses and will call for the exercise of much care and vigilance by those taking part. Few of them, I find, are capable of this.'

However, there was always Toiras, who was still holding out in Casale—Toiras of whom it was already said that just as St Roche had ensured his own canonisation by dint of working miracles,[12] so M. de Toiras would become a marshal of France by dint of performing notable feats of arms.

But feelings of enmity towards the cardinal were emerging on all sides. A personal quarrel flared up between him and the duke of Guise.

* By contemporary standards Marillac, who was born in 1563, was already an old man.

The latter gave vent to defamatory remarks about Richelieu; he had to be reminded that there were courts of law to settle disputes between private persons and that an attack on the king's minister was an attack on the authority of the king. Early in August Richelieu was so conscious of the threats levelled against him that he no longer even dared to write directly to the king or queen mother.* And when towards the middle of the month he too decided to leave Saint-Jean-de-Maurienne in order to rejoin the court at Lyons, he dispersed the gentlemen in attendance upon him and set off with only a very small suite. No longer attempting to conceal the danger of plague which he had denied during the previous weeks, the cardinal proceeded to Grenoble, where he had himself disinfected. His return has about it something of the doleful atmosphere of a retreat.

The cardinal's withdrawal from Saint-Jean-de-Maurienne was rendered yet more painful by the fact that he had embarked on an extremely important venture in the field of diplomacy. Let us see what had been happening in Germany.

Wallenstein's victories had strengthened imperial power within the Empire to such an extent as to cause uneasiness to all the German princes, whether Catholic or Protestant. The latter had particularly cogent reasons for alarm. The king of Denmark, seeing that he was unable to realise his ambitions, had withdrawn from the struggle and made peace with the emperor by the Treaty of Lübeck (22 May 1629). This was a severe blow to the adherents of the Reformed religion, since its effect was to deprive them of one of their more powerful allies. Nor was this all. Once rid of his main adversary in Germany, Ferdinand II had published on 6 March 1629 the Edict of Restitution. This was one of the most important events of the Thirty Years War. It was a kind of religious peace settlement extended by the emperor to the whole of the Empire. Two years earlier, in his capacity as sovereign of Bohemia, Ferdinand had imposed on the kingdom of St Wenceslas[13] a constitution which abolished the former privileges of the Protestants. Now he re-established the position of the different religions in Germany as it had been in 1555, thus obliging Protestant princes or lords who held property which had been taken from the Catholic Church since that date to restore it to ecclesiastical ownership. Seventy-four years, almost three-quarters of a century, had elapsed since the Peace of Augsburg, during which the secularisation of

---

* His letters were addressed to their secretary, Claude Bouthillier, who was a member of the Council. (V.L.T.)

Church property by Lutherans or Calvinists had profoundly altered the religious and territorial layout of the Empire. Moreover, during this time these secularised possessions of the Church had been handed on to direct or collateral heirs, sold or mortgaged. Their present owners were by no means all of them responsible for their secularisation; far from it. By way of comparison let us take the case of the nationalised property sold during the course of the French Revolution, and let us suppose that instead of the conciliatory provisions of the Concordat of 1801 and the Charter of 1814 the government of the country had decided on legislation of a very different character and at a much later date—around 1860. In other words, let us assume that at some such date in the middle of the Second Empire the order had been given for the ownership of land to revert to the status quo of 1789. The imperial edict of 1629 attempted to do something that was equally impracticable, and reflected just the same revolutionary determination to put the clock back.

It is easy to understand the fury that the edict provoked—a fury which was, however, mitigated by the prospect of the inextricable tangle of law-suits and legal arguments that would inevitably follow its publication and serve to gain time. Moreover intemperate decisions provoke reactions of the same nature. Already a new protagonist for the Protestant cause was emerging—Gustavus Adolphus, the young king of Sweden, who had for some years been engaged in war against Russia and Poland. His country was small but rich in iron ore. He was in process of turning it into the foremost territorial and military power of northern Europe. He had conquered a number of strongpoints bordering on the Baltic and built up a well-equipped army composed of Swedes and mercenaries, an army that was staffed with able officers and animated on the whole by a sense of religion and a spirit of devotion to the Protestant cause. Gustavus Adolphus was young and ambitious; he was also intelligent—though when one looks at some of the portraits of him one is hardly inclined to think so, a statement that applies not so much to the painting by Van Dyck as to a bust by Georg Petel which represents him as a gigantic, almost bestial-looking man with an extremely small cranium and enormous eyes that seem to be starting out of his head.*

The king of Sweden seemed to be prepared to enter Germany and assume the role of armed champion of German Protestantism. He had made overtures to the king of France and to the United Provinces—in fact to any power which he knew to be the natural enemy of the Habs-

---

* Van Dyck painted portraits of both Gustavus Adolphus and Wallenstein without ever setting eyes on either of them.

burgs—offering his services in return for subsidies and guarantees. It will be remembered that during the siege of La Rochelle Richelieu had listened to the reports of a French agent whom he had sent to Gustavus Adolphus. At the time the cardinal had confined himself to examining the situation. As has already been stated, he calculated that an attempt by the emperor to establish his hegemony in Germany would alarm even the Catholics, and especially the duke of Bavaria, who, although the main beneficiary of the victories over the Protestants, was little inclined to pay for the final triumph of Catholicism and the house of Austria with the loss of his independence. It was not long before Maximilian of Bavaria began to feel jealous of Wallenstein and to hate him. The latter's real plans were not precisely known and it would have required some skill to find out what they were, for Wallenstein himself was far from having a clear idea of what he wanted. The emperor's generalissimo was an incalculable personage with an unbridled imagination. He chose to announce that after defeating the Protestants he would turn his forces against Islam, liberate the Christian peoples of the Balkans, and within three years crown the emperor at Constantinople. He also declared that there ought to be only one emperor (meaning one ruler) in Germany in the same way as there was only one king in France, and allowed it to be rumoured that he intended to enter Champagne at the head of his army. Wallenstein did not approve of the Edict of Restitution, which constituted a possible threat to his own interests and to those of several princes with whom he maintained good relations. Yet the emperor's only chance of enforcing his edict lay in his making use of the power that Wallenstein's army still placed at his disposal.

Ferdinand II believed that the time had come to make sure that the house of Austria reaped the fruits of his victories. He had already arranged for his son Ferdinand to be recognised as king of Hungary, which meant that the latter would be called upon to exercise power as such on his own death. Now he wished to ensure that his son would likewise succeed him as emperor by having him elected as king of the Romans. With this object in view he summoned a meeting of the electors at Regensburg.

Richelieu thought that the divergence between these different policies and ambitions would enable France to thwart the emperor's plans. She could deal him a direct blow which would indirectly strike at Spain. The Catholic princes must be weaned from their alliance with the house of Austria. Marcheville was entrusted with a preliminary mission to the electors. He was to point out to them the danger of the Habsburgs becoming all-powerful, which represented a threat to German as well as to Italian liberties. He was to reiterate to all and sundry that the only reason why the king of France was fighting in Italy was to defend the independence of the Italian princes. Louis XIII wished to deliver Germany as well as Italy from the oppression of the house of Austria. His policy was clearly conducive to peace in Europe.

But none of the cardinal's advisers knew Europe as well as Father Joseph. At the end of June Richelieu decided to send him to the meeting at Regensburg. Since it was impossible to invest the lowly Capuchin with the status of an ambassador, a career diplomat was chosen as head of the mission. Brûlart de Léon, who had distinguished himself in negotiations with the Swiss cantons, was thus to outward appearances the only responsible French representative. The task that awaited him and Father Joseph was a formidable one. It was to induce the princes of the Empire to adopt a policy of veiled but uncompromising opposition to every proposal made by the emperor. The latter's position was to be weakened by persuading him to disband Wallenstein's army and by securing the rejection, at least for the time being, of his request for his son's election as king of the Romans. Lastly if possible the French envoys were to bring about the withdrawal of the Spanish troops occupying the Palatinate—ostensibly to facilitate general disarmament. As far as negotiations with the emperor himself were concerned, they were instructed to press for the investiture of the duke of Mantua and the promise of a general settlement.

Even so, neither Father Joseph nor Brûlart was given authority to conclude peace in Italy, which was still under negotiation with Mazarin. On the opposing side the only qualified representatives were Collalto and Spinola (acting for the emperor and the king of Spain respectively) and Christina's husband, Victor Amadeus I, the new duke of Savoy, who had just succeeded his father. But nothing came of these negotiations, and it was said by many that Spinola's jealousy of Collalto's victory at Mantua made him favour delaying tactics until such time as Toiras was forced to capitulate for lack of men and supplies, leaving him with no alternative but the surrender of Casale to the Spaniards. We know that by the end of August Richelieu had begun to wonder whether he could still count on a French victory. He allowed the French representatives at Regensburg to embark on negotiations concerning Italian affairs. 'We are sending you powers to conclude an unrestricted peace [*la paix non limitée*],' he wrote on 24 August to Father Joseph and Brûlart de Léon.

Both men had already done their work well. They had incited the

German princes to ask the emperor to disband his army as a first conciliatory gesture and as a step towards a general peace. Father Joseph had
met Wallenstein and persuaded him to accept this measure, pointing out
its necessity to secure peace but adding that if peace could not be preserved he would soon be given fresh opportunities to cover himself with
glory. The emperor's generalissimo certainly did not allow himself to be
convinced by the Capuchin's arguments; but he did not indulge in any
outburst. His enemies were astonished by the way that he accepted his
disgrace and withdrew to Friedland, his Czech principality. However,
in his heart of hearts he was filled with rage and harboured dark plans for
vengeance. 'The emperor and all his house will live to rue the day that he
inflicted this affront upon a gentleman,' he declared.[14] He knew very
well who had been the authors of his ruin—the duke of Bavaria, the
Catholic electors, the French, and lastly the clique of Jesuits led by Father
Lamormain, Ferdinand II's confessor, whose influence over the emperor
was considerable.

Wallenstein fell back on his astrologers, who discovered undoubted
astral signs that his turn would come whatever the means he employed to
this end. Owing no allegiance to either church or sect, he professed the
opinion that a man's conscience was a matter for God alone and that his
attitude to God depended on his religion. From this date he ceased to be a
whole-hearted supporter of the imperial and Catholic cause; but this was
not at first realised by those around him.

Once Wallenstein had been sacrificed, Ferdinand II saw nothing to
prevent his son's early election; but at this point the German princes
became evasive and the emperor, with Father Joseph's manœuvres in
mind, remarked with some justification that the Capuchin had managed
to cram all six electoral bonnets inside his cowl.*

However, the emperor's ministers tried to compensate for the setbacks
they had suffered by making the most of France's difficulties in Italy.
They pressed Brûlart de Léon and Father Joseph to agree to a settlement
of all outstanding differences including those in Italy, indicating that
they would make no concessions other than in this context. The French
diplomats felt that they were being asked to go too far. It seemed to them
that they were being pushed into exceeding not only their powers but
also the undoubted intentions of their government. Worst of all, the
emperor's ministers were calling for an undertaking that France would
refrain from interfering in German affairs by assisting German princes

---

* The number was six because the seventh electoral bonnet belonged to the emperor
himself in his capacity as king of Bohemia. (V.L.T.)

against the emperor. This necessitated reopening the question of the three bishoprics [Metz, Toul and Verdun] and including the duke of Lorraine in the proposed treaty; but at least the treaty provided that the duke of Nevers should at last be invested with the duchy of Mantua.

After much negotiation and considerable hesitation, Brûlart and Father Joseph appended their signatures to the treaty on 13 October. So general was the desire for peace in France that Bouthillier, one of Richelieu's best servants, showed the utmost satisfaction when the document reached him. He immediately set to work on a proclamation announcing the good news in Louis XIII's name and inviting the whole realm to rejoice at it.

Richelieu was at Roanne when the couriers handed him the text of the treaty. He flew into a violent rage, asserting that the ambassadors had exceeded their instructions. Anyone could see that they had agreed to discuss matters which had nothing whatever to do with the points at issue. What was the point of the clauses about Metz, Toul and Verdun—an old question which had remained dormant for nearly eighty years?* Why was the duke of Lorraine included in the treaty when France was not at war with him? Most important of all, the main clause whereby Louis XIII promised to remain neutral in Germany was both unacceptable and shameful. This clause alone was enough to ruin the entire policy that had been pursued for the past twenty-one months, a policy which Richelieu had defended against all comers. It was also enough to ruin France's credit in Europe, for if he forsook all his allies in this way the king would never be able to retrieve a single one of them later. The conclusion to be drawn from all this was self-evident: the negotations would have to begin all over again; as it stood, the treaty would under no circumstances be ratified.

That the treaty was not of much value was true enough; but the French negotiators had not committed themselves completely. They had indeed signed it, but with some verbal reservations, pointing out that they were not altogether certain that they could accept all its provisions. After all, if people like Bouthillier were mistaken in their reactions did this not go to show that if the worst came to the worst the treaty was worth accepting? Did it not enable France to extricate herself more or less satisfactorily from the Italian imbroglio, in so far as it recognised the

---

* In fact the question of Metz, Toul and Verdun was not particularly dormant for it was not to be definitely settled until the Treaties of Westphalia were signed eighteen years later. (V.L.T.)

duke of Nevers's rights over Mantua, which were the sole cause of the war in Italy?

But the Mantuan succession had never been more than a pretext for pursuing a policy which aimed at enhancing French prestige. Such a policy was clearly useful, but it was also dangerous. The difficulties that had been encountered had proved to be even more numerous than anticipated, and the explanation for Richelieu's firm and haughty language at this stage lies in the fact that by the end of October 1630 the situation appeared to him to have righted itself after the terrible ordeals through which he had passed. It is to these ordeals that we must now turn.

It must seem as if we have rather lost sight of the part played by Louis XIII in connection with these events. The truth is that although we are quite well informed about his activities as king and about the way he spent his time during the summer of 1630, his thoughts and opinions elude us. We know that up to his departure from Saint-Jean-de-Maurienne there was a close community of ideas between the king and the cardinal. When urged to choose between two policies, Louis XIII had shown a clear preference for the policy which carried with it the promise of greater glory for his State and offered him personally opportunities for more dazzling feats of arms. He was fond of warfare, and a war that necessitated fighting abroad appealed to him more than campaigning against his own subjects. If Marie de Medici and Marillac to outward appearances came to support a policy of which they did not approve, which they were prepared to undermine, and against which they had advanced fresh arguments as soon as it ran into difficulties, it was because they knew that the king had made it his own.

At this time Louis XIII was greatly attached to Saint-Simon, although he did not allow him to take part in the conduct of affairs. For several weeks he was fully bent on entering Italy himself, but his health let him down. The plague had broken out at the places where he stopped for the night on his journey, but the king behaved as if he was quite unperturbed. When told that the village where he was staying was infected, he merely expressed the hope that his hostess's house would be spared and prepared himself for a good night's sleep. At Saint-Jean-de-Maurienne attacks of fever left him exhausted, but he recovered reasonably well. The queen mother and Marillac were in a constant state of alarm about his health, and Richelieu went to considerable trouble to reassure them. Louis XIII submitted to the treatment prescribed by Bouvard, his physician. The latter, who was very much aware of his responsibilities, ordered purges and bleedings, specifying that he was 'retaining enemas for the back entrance'. By the time the king decided to rejoin the court at Lyons he was thoroughly run down—well one day and ill the next. Henceforth he was no longer in command of the situation, and everything that he heard said around him, although it did not shake his confidence in Richelieu, aroused doubts in his mind as to whether the project upon which they had embarked would turn out well. The first impalpable shadows of disgrace seemed to hover about the figure of the cardinal; but he had only to appear in person for them to vanish.

Soon the news from Italy improved. Early in September a truce was arranged at Casale. Richelieu hoped that it would allow enough time to reinforce the army, so that fighting could be resumed with the odds in France's favour if peace was not secured. His enemies on the other hand thought that an armistice of this nature would be prolonged until peace was signed; to them it meant quite simply that a dangerous venture had been brought to an end. The death of Spinola on 23 September made this seem all the more likely. Did not Spinola's death mean that the main obstacle to peace had disappeared?

Suddenly the king, who had seemed in quite good fettle for the past few days, again fell a victim to fever. It was thought to be just another attack like the last. No one was alarmed since it was felt that at Lyons he could be looked after under the best possible conditions, even though there had been some outbreaks of epidemics in the town. But far from subsiding the fever increased, and no remedy seemed to have any effect. The physicians could not understand it. To all intents and purposes they gave up treating the patient and let Nature take its course. It was a course that led to the grave. Public prayers were offered and the supreme consolations of the Church were brought to the dying man. His entourage was deeply moved. The man whose life was drawing to a close was a consecrated king. For all his personal weaknesses, his taciturn disposition, his haughtiness and his violent outbursts, Louis XIII commanded universal respect, and in some cases affection, because of his courage, because of the impression that he gave of living not so much for his own sake as for the sake of a great task.

To the common people the king's impending death seemed like a personal affliction visited upon each family. At court a new reign implied inevitably a change of policy, and men's eyes turned to watch the cardinal. For several months his enemies had been working to bring about his downfall and fortune had apparently forsaken him, but he had always succeeded in re-establishing his position and overcoming his adversities. This time the inexorable approach of Louis XIII's death heralded the end to the drama. Under king Gaston, France would again fall into the hands of the queen mother, and the queen mother detested Richelieu.

On the morning of 30 September no one expected Louis XIII to last out the day. Then suddenly, at the end of the afternoon, the king discharged a large quantity of pus through his anal passage. Almost at once the crisis abated, and as night came down he fell into an undisturbed sleep. The terrible menace of death receded as mysteriously as it had come, and even more rapidly. Present-day medical knowledge enables us to diagnose an abscess which had formed in the intestine and then burst of its own accord without the attendant danger of peritonitis.

One has only to read the letter which Richelieu wrote to Schomberg on the same evening to measure the extent and genuineness of his sorrow when he thought that he was going to lose 'the best master in the world', and his immense joy on realising that the king was out of danger. Such a display of feeling disposes of the myth of a tyrannical minister who had made the king's fortunes his own and reveals the real friendship of man for man that existed between Louis XIII and the cardinal at this time.

The king's recovery meant that the cardinal's policy was also secure. What remains uncertain, for this kind of secret eludes the historian, is whether the king, while his illness was at its height, had been convinced by his entourage that the policy he had been pursuing was a bad one. For many years Louis XIII's confessor had been Father Suffren, a Jesuit, whose opinions inclined towards those of Marillac. In the belief that the king would be called to meet his Maker within a few hours, Father Suffren may well have told him that he had not fulfilled his obligations as a ruler in a proper manner, pointing out that his duty was to relieve his unfortunate people and to secure the triumph of the Catholic religion, not to try to win glory abroad in a war against other Catholic princes. Louis XIII had also had some conversations with the two queens. May he not have undertaken to live on better terms with them in the unlikely event of his recovery and promised that he would no longer invariably pay heed to the cardinal and even that he would remove him from the conduct of affairs? And since the king was expected to die, may they not have striven while he was at his last gasp to win his approval for the policy that his successor would adopt? Duplicity was one of the hallmarks of government, and the political principles laid down by Machiavelli were still generally accepted, only slightly mitigated by Christian scruples.

During the return journey from Roanne, which was made by boat down the Loire, professions of mutual goodwill and respect and marks of signal courtesy were freely exchanged between the cardinal and the royal family. No doubt this was all so much double-dealing, but at least it restored Richelieu's freedom of action. In the matter of the Treaty of Regensburg we can well understand his acting as he did in rejecting a solution which he might have accepted three weeks earlier when, wherever he looked, he had seen nothing but grounds for despair. Now he had begun to recover his nerve. In effect there was no need of a treaty to set the seal on the success achieved by his negotiators in Germany. Their efforts had already borne fruit by weakening the position of the emperor in the Empire, by depriving him of his army and by leaving him to face an uncertain future.

As for Italy, negotiations there were still in progress. Mazarin continued to devote all his skill towards obtaining from the duke of Savoy and the Spanish commander (now Don Gonzalo de Córdoba) terms that Louis XIII's plenipotentiaries, Marshals Effiat, Schomberg, la Force and Marillac, would be able to accept. In the meantime the truce was due to expire shortly, and a well turned out and better equipped French army was ready to embark on hostilities. In its ranks there was a young colonel who had only recently entered the king's service, a viscount named Henri de Turenne. He was the younger son of a princely family of foreign extraction and his mother, the dowager duchess of Bouillon, had handed him over as a kind of hostage to safeguard the principality of Sedan against any danger of confiscation. Thus Turenne was to have his first experience of warfare in the very same area as that in which Mazarin was endeavouring to score his first diplomatic triumph.

On 26 October the French army began its march towards Casale. The walls were already in sight when a horseman appeared in the midst of a cloud of dust, riding hell for leather and waving a white sash. 'Halte! halte! pace! pace!' he was shouting. It was Mazarin. By resorting to persuasion, by dint of quibbles and slight alterations, he had succeeded in obtaining peace terms that were acceptable to everyone. The Spaniards undertook to withdraw their troops from the town of Casale and the whole of Montferrat if the French would agree to evacuate the citadel and restore to the duke of Savoy those of his territories which they had occupied. There was no longer any question of the emperor refusing to invest Charles de Nevers with his Mantuan possessions, but until he did so the strongpoints evacuated by French and Spanish forces were to be temporarily handed over to the duc du Maine, Nevers's oldest son.

This was a far more satisfactory settlement than that signed at Regensburg, for it did not create the same dangerous connection between affairs in Italy and affairs elsewhere. In addition, it had been obtained by simply deploying French forces without even the risk of prolonging the war.

Thus France's Italian venture, which had filled so many months with its complications, came to an end before winter. Only statesmen and diplomats were in a position to appreciate its results, for they related essentially to foreign policy and the king's prestige in Europe. It had aroused no great enthusiasm among public opinion. French policy in Italy had been a terrible drain on an already burdened Treasury, which had been completely depleted in consequence. It had been necessary for the government to resort on an even wider scale to those deplorable financial expedients which any sensible bourgeois knew to be thoroughly pernicious: loans from *partisans*,* financiers and private individuals at high rates of interest, the creation of numerous additional offices, an increase in the *taille*, and all this in an impoverished country where the currency was steadily depreciating and where the cost of living continued to rise. In short France was heading for disaster, and the cardinal seemed to be delighted. His train of personal attendants, the immense revenues which he drew from his continually enlarged domains, the number of abbeys *in commendam*† and priories which he did not scruple to accumulate in his own hands for all his sacred office, all these provided Richelieu's enemies with ample grounds for righteous indignation. Certainly Richelieu was scrupulous about asking the pope for the necessary dispensations when he infringed a rule, and very often he advanced considerable sums to the Treasury from his own coffers. But it would be naïve to put forward these precautionary measures or pecuniary sacrifices as an argument in his favour. So far as dispensations were concerned, the pope used to be fairly accomodating for reasons of political necessity, and eventually granted everything for which he had been asked. As for loans to the Crown, when the rich men who made them were in a position to know the date on which receipts from taxation were due to reach the Treasury or to discuss arrangements for their own reimbursement, their generosity turned out in the long run to be extremely profitable to themselves.

Thinking of all the trials that had faced him during the year, Richelieu

---

* See chapter 1 n. 30.

† 'An individual was said to hold a benefice *in commendam* when its revenues were granted to him temporarily during a vacancy . . . Gradually the term came to be restricted especially to benefices which a bishop or other dignitary held more or less permanently along with his see.' (Cross)

in a letter to Bouthillier, called the year 1630 the year of tribulations. Perhaps he believed that he was reaching the end of his ordeals when the most terrible crisis of all broke upon him—the crisis which he himself referred to as 'the great storm'.[15]

The cardinal felt this storm gathering strength around him; but his enemies took care to lull his suspicions. He had suggested that he and his close relatives—his niece Mme de Combalet, his sister Mme de Brézé and his uncle La Porte, a commander of the Knights of Malta—should surrender all the appointments which they held in the queen mother's household, since she no longer seemed to appreciate their services; but he had been requested not to pursue the matter.

After a long absence the court re-established itself in Paris for the winter. Marie de Medici returned to her beautiful residence, the Luxembourg; but as the Louvre and the Palais Cardinal were not yet ready for occupation owing to repairs and alterations, Louis XIII installed himself in the town house in the rue de Tournon which had formerly belonged to Concini, and Richelieu moved into a small house known as the Petit Luxembourg, a short distance from the queen mother's palace. They were thus all located in the same district of Paris.

On the morning of Sunday, 10 November the cardinal presented himself at Marie de Medici's palace to pay his respects. He was surprised to learn that he would not be admitted to her presence, that she was conferring with the king and that she did not wish to be disturbed by anyone. He realised immediately that they were engaged in deciding his own fate. Closed or guarded doors confronted him at every turn, but with wonderful presence of mind Richelieu remembered that there was one route to the queen mother's apartments which might still be open. From the sacristy of the chapel a staircase led to a closet which communicated directly with Marie de Medici's chamber. There would be no one to stop him. If the queen mother had merely omitted to bolt a single door all the other precautions she had taken would be fruitless. Softly the cardinal moved forward. One after the other each door yielded to the touch of his hand. In a few minutes he had reached the queen mother's chamber.

The respective attitudes of the king and queen left the cardinal in no doubt. Marie de Medici was voluble and triumphant. Louis XIII looked gloomy and deeply shaken. The sheer audacity of Richelieu's intrusion froze them for a moment into stillness. He seemed to take advantage of the surprise which he had given them: 'I am sure that you were speaking of me. Come, admit it, Madame.' The queen mother began to deny it: 'Not at all!' she cried. Then she burst out: 'Why yes! We were indeed speaking of you and saying that you were the most ungrateful and wickedest of men.'[16]

Marie de Medici was aware of the indefinable aura of prestige and charm which emanated from the cardinal's person, and she knew that the king always surrendered to it in the end. What point had she reached in her conversation with Louis XIII, and what exactly had she demanded of him? To judge from certain features of the scene which subsequently took place, she had not yet obtained full satisfaction. Despite efforts made after the event to mislead opinion as to the import of this conversation between mother and son, it is hard to believe that it did not take the form of a point-blank demand from the queen mother which was tantamount to calling for Richelieu's dismissal. Perhaps the queen mother proposed stripping Richelieu and all his family of their appointments in her service, or perhaps she refused to appear at meetings of the Council so long as the cardinal continued to be present. Perhaps she called for nothing less than Richelieu's complete removal from office —possibly accompanied by his arrest. These distinctions of emphasis were to be made later when Marie de Medici wished to keep up appearances after she had lost the battle; but they do not affect the main picture. The queen mother was doing her utmost to bring about a major decision. She had already become excited in the course of speaking to her son. Now surprise and vexation, allied perhaps with a panic-stricken fear of losing everything at the very moment when she was nearing complete victory, combined to deprive her of the remnants of her self-control.

Red in the face, gasping for breath, her massive frame choking with emotion, the queen mother began shouting abuse at the cardinal, upbraiding him not only with his conduct of affairs but with his private life. A torrent of scandalous court gossip drowned all reasoned argument. When Louis XIII intervened to calm her, exclaiming 'Madame, what are you doing, what are you saying?' she turned on him, accusing him of preferring a lackey to his own mother. Richelieu, his nerves stretched to breaking-point, fell on his knees and dissolved into tears. The queen seized the opportunity to yell that his tears were only playacting, that he could weep to order as everyone knew. Then suddenly she herself was overcome by tears. Trembling violently, she continued to shout in a voice shaken by sobs. The scene was becoming hideous. Louis XIII was deathly pale, as if about to faint. He asked the cardinal to withdraw, bowed to his mother and himself left the room.

When he reached the main courtyard of the palace, the *cour d'honneur*, the king found Richelieu already there. The cardinal bowed deeply as he passed in a last act of homage and entreaty to his master. But the king did not even vouchsafe him a glance and got into his carriage. Richelieu had no alternative but to return home. His close associates pressed him to flee at once, to avoid certain arrest. He could shut himself up in the citadel of Le Havre, where he held the governorship; from there he would be able to escape abroad by sea. But Richelieu still hestitated, although he felt that it was the only course left to him. . . .

Marie de Medici, still dazed by the scene that had taken place, no longer knew what to think. Those who had witnessed the king's departure and had seen how Louis XIII had ignored the cardinal's mute entreaty, assured her that she was now mistress of the situation. Marillac began to prepare for the formation of a new government. Courtiers who had not attached themselves so closely to Richelieu's fortunes as to be doomed to share in his downfall hastened to assure the victorious party of their eagerness to be of service, attempting to make sure of their tenure of the offices that they had hitherto held or to solicit new appointments. There was a sudden surge towards the men who now enjoyed power—a revolting spectacle but, however squalid, one of the commonest features of political life in every age.

Louis XIII had returned to the house in the rue de Tournon in a state of great emotion. After reaching his chamber he tore open his doublet with a single movement of such violence that the buttons flew off. Saint-Simon came to join his master and did his best to calm him. Gradually Louis XIII recovered his composure. He pondered over the criticisms that he had heard levelled against the cardinal; he thought of the great task which they had undertaken together, and all the hopes and pains that they had shared.

Some historians have declared that Louis XIII felt that the queen mother's headstrong behaviour was an insult to his majesty as king and that he pictured to himself the sort of government he would have if, without the cardinal's influence to act as counterbalance, he surrendered to the overt ambitions of a woman who was incapable of taking a long view despite her experience of affairs—a woman who would always have Gaston and many others intriguing at her back. And what exactly did Louis XIII think of Marillac? Was he not inclined to feel doubtful about the services that a man approaching seventy years of age would be able to render him? Did he perhaps recall the trying time that he had had in the past with ministers who were too old? But these are riddles which

The young Louis

The declaration of Louis' majority, 1614

Marie de Medici after the siege of Ponts de Cé

Cardinal Richelieu

Louis XIII

Petrus Davet Sculpsit. 1649

Ce grand Roy, dont voicy l'adorable visage,
Vainqueur de ce bas Monde au Ciel est remonté.
A genoux donc Mortels! que tout luy rende hommage;
Ou redoutez sa foudre, ou loüez sa bonté.

Gustavus Adolphus

The King at Eaux de Forges

the historian is not called upon to solve, since a person's innermost thoughts are a closed book to him.

Yet it is certain that Louis XIII, unlike some writers since his day, cannot have failed to realise the nature of the conflict—a conflict which extended beyond personalities and still represented a clash between two different policies, the one directed towards building up France's greatness abroad, the other focused on internal reform. The clash between the two was sufficiently serious to give rise to hesitations in the king's mind and to battles within his conscience. And once again in this fresh crisis Louis XIII opted for the policy of the cardinal. He left Paris for Versailles in the course of the afternoon and sent Richelieu an order to join him there. A second, moving interview took place between the two men. On the very same day that the queen mother had demanded the cardinal's dismissal the king restored him to his confidence: 'Remain by my side and I will protect you against all your enemies.' It was indeed, as Bautru said, the Day of Dupes.[17]

The cardinal's reinstatement did not put an end to the difficulties that he had to face, nor did it set a term to the plots which were to be devised for his destruction up to the very last months of the reign. Historians have been guilty of the grossest exaggeration in giving the impression that the Day of Dupes marks Richelieu's final triumph. Nonetheless, it is an un-doubted fact that it constitutes a turning-point in the history of the reign. After the Day of Dupes foreign affairs were the government's chief preoccupation and the mainspring of its policy until the end, while France herself was condemned to do without any general reform and to remain virtually set in her traditional mould. All that was asked of her was that she should pay and obey. The misery of the people was henceforth accepted as the price that had to be paid for the glory of the State.

Louis Batiffol, who pieced together the detailed story of these hours of turmoil with his usual meticulous scholarship and acute psychological insight, placed great emphasis on the part played by Louis XIII's personal will.[18] He was a true king. If he had been the mediocrity tyrannised over by his minister and fluctuating between the pull of different influences that many people have made him out to be, matters would have taken a very different turn. It was he and he alone who saved Richelieu because he saw that the cardinal was the best servant he had. He had not been impervious to the arguments put forward by the opposition, but the latter forfeited its reputation by its plots against the king's chief minister. From then onwards Louis XIII regarded this party as a bunch of people bent on stirring up trouble and decided 'of his own motion', as Richelieu put it, to deal with them as they deserved.

Michel de Marillac was dismissed instantly. The king ordered him to go to Glatigny, near Versailles, to await his orders; he then removed the seals from his custody and had him confined at Châteaudun, where the old man died two years later of grief and shame. His successor was Châteauneuf. It was not long before the cardinal's opponents saw in him a possible rival to their enemy—only for fresh intrigues to lead to his downfall also.

Marshal Bassompierre had allowed himself to become involved with Marillac's party. His military titles and the friendship that the king had vouchsafed him did not save him from the Bastille. But first and foremost Louis XIII remembered that the brother of the ex-keeper of the seals, Marshal Louis de Marillac, was in command of the army in Italy and was thus in a position to bring troops into France and stir up rebellion. This, however, was only a conjecture on the king's part: it was enough for him to send Marshal Schomberg an order to arrest his colleague. Schomberg contrived to carry out this task in a way which was respectful yet firm, but did not omit to treat Louis de Marillac with the deference that his high rank required.

The sequel is less edifying. Determined at all costs to destroy those of his servants who had incurred his displeasure, Louis XIII handed the marshal over to a special court which discovered that earlier in his career he had been responsible for embezzling funds when building operations being carried out on his orders at the citadel of Verdun, and that his subordinates had been guilty of perpetrating various outrages upon the local population. Lapses such as these were of course reprehensible, but not uncommon among professional soldiers—even the best of them, or those most loyal to the king. They were part and parcel of the low standards of behaviour current at the time and exemplified the lack of good order within the realm; they were also a symptom of that lack of civic sense [*ce sens insuffisant de l'État*] which was to remain until the end one of the weak points of the ancien régime.

Often the government would close its eyes to this sort of behaviour or else try to strike terror into the hearts of the culprits by making an example of one of them. But the maréchal de Marillac would not have been singled out in this way if it had not been for the Day of Dupes.

For eighteen months he defended himself step by step against his judges. It does not seem that Richelieu was involved in the affair or that it represented a vendetta on his part; the king's obstinate determination was alone quite sufficient. Eventually, on 8 May 1632, the marshal was condemned to death. Of his twenty-three judges, thirteen called for the death penalty while ten merely recommended exile or imprisonment for life. This slender majority of three in favour of a sentence which the government itself desired entitles us to feel some doubts about the fairness of the trial. Two days afterwards the marshal was beheaded on the Place de Grève.

The position with regard to the queen mother was more delicate. It hardly seemed possible to remove her from the government, and for a number of reasons Louis XIII was perhaps unwilling to do so. Through the good offices of Bagni, the nuncio, and Father Suffren, he tried to effect a reconciliation between his mother and Richelieu. The latter showed no objection to making his peace with her, but once again the situation was complicated by the duke of Orleans. Like a coward, the king's brother forsook in her adversity the mother who had so often compromised herself for the sake of his whims: he was one of the first to congratulate Richelieu on his victory. To seal their friendship he demanded fantastic rewards for his favourites, Puylaurens and Le Coigneux. He wanted the first to be made a duke and the second a cardinal. As these rewards were not forthcoming, he left the court at the end of January 1631 and fled to Orleans. After a few months he removed himself from Orleans to Besançon, on Spanish territory—an open act of rebellion.

After his brother's departure the king withdrew to Compiègne with the two queens and his ministers. He was in search of the calm which would enable him to restore order around him. There he had everyone he needed under his control and far removed from intrigues. He even went so far as to have recourse to the good offices of Marie de Medici's physician, Vautier—an intriguer who had long been used by the Marillacs, and whom the queen mother herself considered to be the only person in the world with a real knowledge of her health. The king's aim was to bring about a definite reconciliation between the queen mother and the cardinal and, in accordance with the customs of the time, to induce them to sign a declaration that they would live on good terms with each other. But Marie de Medici rejected the proposal and categorically declared that she would no longer attend meetings of the king's councils.

Now Louis XIII wanted to reassert his authority within the realm in order to cope with the increasingly serious position abroad. The great storm was over, but tranquillity was far from restored. The country was still racked by disturbances. Grave decisions had to be taken. In the absence of good relations between himself and the queen mother, Richelieu felt that the only solution was for them both to leave the government. He proposed that Marie de Medici be requested with every possible mark of respect to stay away from Paris and the court; he himself would withdraw to his estates.

The king and Council rejected the cardinal's suggestion that he should retire and forced him to agree to remain in office. As for the queen mother, it was Louis XIII alone who decided on the measures to be taken concerning her. He requested her to take up her residence at Moulins, of which she held the governorship. He dispersed her suite of attendants and had Vautier imprisoned in the Bastille. Then he himself returned to Paris.

For some time Marie de Medici continued to live at Compiègne. She was under surveillance but in no way treated like a prisoner. Despite pressing requests to leave for Moulins, where she could look forward to an agreeable stay now that the château had been repaired, she kept on postponing her journey on the plea of ill health. She was, in fact, haunted by the fear that instead of being escorted to Moulins she would be taken to Marseilles and made to go back to Italy. By dint of continual haggling she delayed matters until mid-July. In reality with the connivance of her chaplain and one of the officers of her guard, she was making preparations for her escape. One evening she left Compiègne before the gates of the town were closed, on foot and heavily veiled. After joining the small escort waiting for her in the country, she took the road to the north. Her objective was La Capelle, for she believed that once there she would be able to continue negotiations with the king, free from all danger.

But the queen mother found that the gates of La Capelle were shut. Although it was not actually known that she was thinking of moving to La Capelle—for if this eventuality had been foreseen the guard at Compiègne would have been doubled and steps would have been taken to make it impossible for her to leave at all—there had been some doubts as to the loyalty of the officer who was in command there during his father's absence. The latter, the marquis de Vardes, had therefore been ordered to resume his command in person: being loyal to the king, he obeyed. He reached the town just in time to refuse admittance to the gentleman who was travelling a few hours in advance of the queen mother. As she was frightened of being overtaken, and her escort even more so, Marie de Medici and her followers had no alternative but to make for Avesnes, the nearest town in the Spanish Netherlands.

The queen mother arrived at Avesnes on Sunday, 20 July, less than two days after leaving Compiègne. In quitting the realm she was also making her exit from the stage of history. It had certainly not been her intention to set a frontier between herself and the king, for she had dreaded the thought of having to leave France more than anything else. She who loved power and display was laying herself open to the risk of losing both irretrievably by crossing into a foreign country during a flight that was precipitate and ill prepared. The trouble-makers amongst her entourage had simply reckoned that from La Capelle she would be able to resort to a form of blackmail because the French government would be alarmed by the fact that she was close to Spanish territory; but far from circumstances falling into line with their calculations, everything had combined to confound them.

The first result of the queen mother's flight was a reconciliation between the king and the Parlement of Paris. The latter had continued to demand that the *paulette* be restored on the conditions obtaining previously, and had even dared to show its sympathy for the duke of Orleans. In May Louis XIII had held a *lit de justice* and exiled several magistrates. Richelieu had intervened to bring about their return to his good graces. But after his mother's escape from Compiègne the king needed the Parlement once more. He reintroduced the *paulette* in its favour, as he had already done in the case of the *Chambre des Comptes* and other courts. By making this concession he ensured that those who were office-holders of long standing would remain obedient to him for a long time to come, whilst retaining the means of creating new offices according to his needs.

The king gave orders for a declaration against the queen, his mother, to be registered by the Paris Parlement. It stated that she had departed the realm in order to join Monsieur and together with him to put herself in the hands of the Spaniards. 'But,' the king added, 'I do not fear them and will prevent them from doing me any harm.' As for the cardinal, 'I have always profited from his counsel, whereas if I had followed the advice that others wished to give me all my affairs would be ruined. Whoever loves me will love him.' The king had already written to the duke of Orleans on 14 July concerning Richelieu's zeal: 'I would not deserve to be called "the Just" if I did not acknowledge it. . . . You will realise once and for all that I have entire confidence in him and that in everything which has occurred he has done nothing except on my express command, [which he has obeyed] with the most scrupulous fidelity.' The king's letter also contains this ruthless but vitally important remark which expresses the official view of the internal condition of the realm: 'Your followers maliciously exaggerate the misery and want of my poor people, who matter more to me than anything else.'*

On Louis XIII's orders, those who had aided and abetted the flight of the queen mother and the duke of Orleans, or who had joined the latter in Lorraine, were then declared disturbers of the peace, agents of the enemy and guilty of high treason. The queen mother's offices and revenues were confiscated.

From now onwards Marie de Medici, almost penniless, less capable than ever of seeing where her true interests lay, and always given to trying to solve her difficulties by intrigues which no one could take seriously, ceased to play an important part in European affairs. She never obtained her son's permission to return to France, and died in 1642 forgotten and in poverty. Hers was a strange destiny. For twenty-two years this woman of only moderate abilities, devoid of both breadth of understanding and warmth of heart, had occupied a leading place in the government of one of the chief states of Europe. She had been gorged with money and endowments; drawing prestige from the reputation and popularity of the late king, her husband, and the reigning king, her son, she had been no queen dowager living in eclipse on the memories of another era but a sort of perpetual regent and second sovereign of the realm. Indeed she had continued to share the throne with Louis XIII: for the king's ministers, especially Richelieu, as well as for foreign ambassadors, office-holders and even the king's subjects, the queen mother was a person of real importance, whereas the reigning queen, Anne of Austria, who was younger, cleverer and more attractive, counted for nothing either in the country or in its government. A woman gifted with intelligence as well as ambition, like Catherine de Medici, would have realised this and would have done everything to safeguard her position. A generous-hearted woman with Christian principles would have found that the country's difficulties and the poverty of its population provided her with opportunities for good works and would thus have become a popular figure—if in fact one does become popular through having good intentions and doing good. But Marie de Medici was covetous and narrow in her outlook; she did not care for France—only for the power and wealth that France gave her. She left behind no monument, no title to fame, so that today it requires an effort of mind to picture to oneself the extent and duration of her power. But her departure made Louis XIII's

* *Les vôtres exagèrent avec très mauvais artifice la misère et la nécessité de mon pauvre peuple, qui m'est à cœur sur toute choses.*

reign simpler for him; it clarified and strengthened his authority. In September the king made Richelieu a duke and peer of the realm.[19]

After the year of tribulations, the succeeding year, 1631, was to some
extent a year of recovery. The king of France's reply to the Treaty of
Regensburg which he had rejected and which had aimed at putting a
stop to French intervention in the Empire, was to renew his alliances in
Germany. The treaty concluded by Hercule de Charnacé with the king
of Sweden at Bärwalde on 23 January came perhaps a little too late for its
terms to be altogether in line with Richelieu's hopes, for Gustavus
Adolphus had already been too successful. Now the latter brazenly
imposed his own conditions. He obtained the subsidy for which he had
asked—a subsidy which the French would have liked to reduce to a
lower figure. The treaty specified that he was to be paid a million livres
annually from 1 March 1631 to 1 March 1636 in return for an undertaking to maintain an army of thirty-six thousand men. The Swedish
king also promised to respect the Catholic religion wherever it was established—not, as Richelieu suggested, to authorise its practice everywhere. It was only with some reservations that he agreed to regard the
Catholic League as neutral—a proviso which did not alter the fact that
his alliance with France enabled Gustavus Adolphus to pursue his conquests in Germany. Nor did Richelieu's preference for keeping the terms
secret prevent Gustavus Adolphus from publicly boasting about them.

The king of Sweden had already occupied Pomerania by exploiting
the weakness of its aged duke, Bogislav XIV, who had no heir. He now
succeeded in overcoming the hesitations or neutral leanings of Brandenburg and Saxony, although these had been re-emphasised at the Protestant Convention at Leipzig in February 1631. The elector of
Brandenburg authorised him to occupy certain vital strategic points in
his territories—Landsberg, Küstrin, Frankfort-on-the-Oder and Span-
dau—the Swedish king's object being to obtain control of the chief
rivers; and when in the month of May 1631 Tilly seized Magdeburg in
pursuance of the Edict of Restitution, the Protestant states of north Germany promptly drew closer to their new champion. The capture of
Magdeburg was indeed one of the most notorious episodes of the Thirty
Years War. The town was sacked and set on fire;* scenes of horror took
place which at once gave rise to violent polemics within the Empire and
throughout all Europe. Yet if the event was followed by the fresh out-

---

* *Un sac de ville, un incendie.* Professor Tapié does not suggest that the town was deliberately set on fire, nor does this appear to have been the case.

break of religious warfare in Germany, this did not mean that the spirit in which the two sides rallied round their respective flags allowed no scope for intrigue and personal ambition. The researches and publications of the Czech historian Pekař have shown that during the summer of 1631 Wallenstein established relations with Gustavus Adolphus through the agency of a Bohemian émigré named Sezima Rašín.[20] Daring plans were considered which involved the seizure of the emperor's personal dominions, while he himself was to be driven into Italy. These negotiations were confidential and carried on in the background; no doubt there were many other secret dealings of this nature that have not yet come to light.

As for Richelieu, he had no intention of resorting to alliances with Protestant Powers without anything to counterbalance them. This is proved by his conduct with regard to Bavaria. Many historians have mistakenly believed that his aim was purely and simply to bring about the revival of the Protestant party in Germany; and some of them have praised his tolerance or indifference in matters of religion, while others have blamed him for sacrificing the interests of his Church. This is a serious error. Richelieu's aim was to raise up enemies against the emperor, and he accepted them as and where occasion offered.

In the meantime he still had the same bias in favour of the Catholic states of west and south Germany. An alliance with Bavaria was signed at Munich on 8 May and countersigned at Fontainebleau on the thirtieth. It was a defensive alliance for a period of eight years. The king of France undertook not to give either direct or indirect assistance to any attack on the territories of the elector of Bavaria, who gave a like promise to the king of France. This meant that Catholic Bavaria would be protected from attack when hostilities developed in the Empire as a result of French subsidies—or so it seemed.

Richelieu still hoped to ensure that the Swedish armies and those of the Catholic League (namely Bavaria and the three ecclesiastical electors) treated each other as neutral. The Protestants were annoyed by this cautious policy, while Wallenstein was to call Louis XIII even more of a Jesuit than the king of Spain. As for Gustavus Adolphus, as early as 1629, at the time of his initial negotiations with Charnacé in Sweden, he had declared: 'I see well enough that whoever is not Bavaria's friend is no friend of yours'.

Still, the main point had been won: Ferdinand II was unable to undertake any further action in Italy. By the Treaties of Cherasco (6 April 1631) he pledged himself to recognise the duke of Nevers's claims to

Mantua and Montferrat, and this time no mention was made of France's relations with the German princes. To all intents and purposes he allowed her a free hand in the Empire. With a curious lack of foresight at such a time and in such circumstances, the emperor confined himself to procuring the withdrawal of French forces from Italy whilst promising that Spanish and imperial troops would do likewise; but Richelieu contrived to avoid evacuating Pinerolo and ensured that it would remain in French hands by means of secret agreements with Savoy (March–October 1631 and May 1632).

Thus the cardinal's policy was at last crowned with success. The threat from England and the menace from Spain had been lifted from French territory. France had freed her coasts from the mortgage of foreign domination; she had intervened in affairs outside her frontiers. She had administered a check to the power of the house of Austria in northern Italy as much by tenacious diplomacy as by force of arms without dissipating her military resources in large-scale battles. At court Richelieu's enemies had been brought low. Henceforth no Power in Europe could disregard the king of France, whose power and reputation were rising fast.

Part Three

The Interest of the State
(1630–43)

CHAPTER SEVEN

France under Richelieu

FROM 1630 ONWARDS the cardinal's authority over the realm was sufficiently firmly established for us to be justified in calling it the France of Richelieu. The entire country was now in subjection to his policy—a policy to which Louis XIII indefatigably gave his consent, approval and support. But this should not be taken to mean that France was henceforth as Richelieu wished her to be. On the contrary, whether each class is considered separately or whether the realm is taken as a whole, France was never to be unreservedly subject to the cardinal or even won over to his side. Moreover the administrative system, the organisation of the country, was very far from corresponding with the ideal entertained by a minister who at the outset had envisaged such large-scale reforms. Had he in fact completely abandoned the idea of introducing these reforms? By no means; but everything was subordinated to the overriding need of raising enough money to meet the expenses of French diplomacy from year to year, and from 1635 onwards to support the financial burdens of war.

Richelieu himself admitted that he understood nothing of financial affairs; he meant that he was neither an expert in accountancy nor able to envisage new sources of income. This being the case, he confined himself to obtaining the necessary money directly from Effiat and Bullion, the superintendents of finance, relying upon their zeal to devise the ways and means of raising it.

Nothing is more revealing than the oft-quoted note which he addressed to Bullion in 1635, after he had had three years' experience of the latter's abilities as superintendent of finance: 'I fully admit my ignorance of financial matters and realise that you are so well-versed in the subject that the only advice that I can give you is to make use of those whom you find most useful to the king's service, and to rest assured that I will second you in every way I can.'[1]

This was tantamount to giving Bullion carte blanche. But as ordinary revenues (which were derived from the principal tax, the *taille*, and from Crown lands) remained far below expenditure, the Treasury continued to rely mainly on those financial expedients which offered the biggest returns but were also the most injurious—that is to say loans from financiers [*traitants*], the continual creation of additional offices, and the maintenance of the principle of hereditability in connection with offices generally.

The abuses from which France was suffering were thus not merely prevented from disappearing; they were strengthened, nay multiplied. Richelieu himself took refuge in a contradiction which the *Testament politique* admits, or at least fails to conceal. The people ought not to be over-taxed for they were being ruined, and it was only fair, as well as in the interest of the State, that there should be 'such proportion between what the sovereign derives from his subjects and what they are able to give him as does not occasion notable hardship'. But the sums demanded in the shape of taxes steadily increased. The warrant [*brevet*] authorising the levy of the *taille* provided for an annual average of about 35 million livres; however together with the supplementary levies which were added to it, what was called the *taille* amounted to more than 39 million livres in 1635 and nearly 41 million livres in 1636.[2] The figure rose under the impact of war to more than $45\frac{1}{2}$ million livres in 1638 and nearly 44 million in 1639.

In a general financial statement of 1639 drawn up for the cardinal, revenue derived from taxation—namely receipts from the *taille*, the tax-farms and Crown lands—amounted to nearly 79 million livres; but about 47 million livres which had been charged to the account of the local tax receiving offices and paid out by them had to be deducted from this total. Only the difference between these two sums actually reached the Treasury. Admittedly this taxation was needed to meet the expense that the war entailed, but it was also required to pay the interest on the new debts which the government had incurred, and the salaries of the office-holders, whose number had increased inordinately. The greater the number of office-holders (or of privileged persons), the smaller the number of people liable to the *taille*.* Thus an increasingly heavy burden of taxation fell upon a static or declining number of tax-payers. In addition, the more money the State demanded, the less remained for the tax-payer's use. What was the point of telling a populace reduced to penury that it should make investments, improve its methods of cultivation and risk its savings in some enterprise, when it was almost impossible for people to save any money at all? But this is to give no more than a superficial picture of the situation.

---

* Hence the edict of 1634 which imposed severe penalties on those who sought to evade payment of the *taille* through pretending to noble status by various expedients—in particular by claiming to hold an office that entitled them to noble rank. (V.L.T.)

The worst feature of the French economy during these years was its disorder.

Like many of his contemporaries, Richelieu held that the prerequisite of a kingdom's wealth was its possession of a sound currency in gold and silver. Unlike Spain, France possessed only a small quantity of precious metal; she could only acquire it by exporting more than she imported, and in particular by ensuring that her trade was conducted by her own nationals and by eliminating foreign importers and even exporters. However, the king's subjects had to be reasonably prosperous if they were to produce more, turn their products into finished articles and export them in their own ships. It was always the same problem. Nor was this the only difficulty. There were two currencies in general circulation, namely gold and silver, and the ratio between them varied from one country to another. In France it had hitherto tended to be lower than in the principal neighbouring countries. This meant that it had hitherto been to the advantage of foreigners to obtain their gold there and reduce France's own holdings. But the situation altered after 1630: within a few years there was a considerable increase in the number of gold coins as compared to silver, thus exceeding the ratio then prevailing in both Spain and the Netherlands. The danger now was that there would be an exodus of silver from the realm rather than an exodus of gold. The latter may have had the effect of hampering a certain number of financial operations, but the flight of silver had a very different and far wider impact, for a scarcity of silver signified a shortage of the metal that was used for the vast mass of private transactions. This shortage coincided with a series of crises in the cost of living, especially after such localised hardships as the disastrous harvest of 1630. In consequence the actual devaluation of the currency occurred a long time before the official devaluation which the government was at length compelled to put into operation in order to stabilise the monetary position within the realm.

Excessive taxation, a shortage of currency, foreign competition and a rising cost of living—such were the vicious economic conditions with which Richelieu was faced during his ministry, conditions with which he was unable to grapple unless given a period of peace. For reasons of a different kind he could neither desire nor prepare for such a breathing space.

But in order to understand the France of Louis XIII's day one must never lose sight of the fact that she was an essentially rural country. It might almost be said that her rural character explains everything, whether good or bad—including very probably the exceptional stamina of the population as a whole. Although it is far from easy to determine the exact proportion, a large number of the French people lived within an enclosed economy, obtaining sufficient for their needs from the land that they possessed and cultivated without incurring any outlay. No doubt these needs were reduced to the minimum, and such people lived in conditions which we would nowadays call extreme poverty; in fact even the most dismal conditions in the most backward parts of present-day France would scarcely form a parallel. No doubt, too, there existed a far higher proportion of vagabonds and beggars not merely than in our day but than in the past two hundred years. However it was not only the peasantry who lived in this way. A large proportion of the country gentry [*noblesse campagnarde*] and of the urban bourgeoisie relied on their country property for their sustenance, the food with which it provided them often comprising revenues that were paid in kind [*rentes en nature*] as well as produce from their own estates and gardens. One would have to draw up tables of family income and expenditure during the period in order to prove this point, and the items of which they would have consisted are seldom ascertainable; but unless one makes this assumption, one can hardly explain how so many people managed to live with so little actual money at their disposal. This restriction in expenditure on staple items has been overlooked by historians, but it constitutes a major, indeed a vital phenomenon in the economic climate of France at the time. It alone explains the fact that despite the narrow margin between income and outgoings there was still a little left over for investment—generally in land or in revenue from land [*rentes sur la terre*] and, higher up the social scale, in offices or in certificates of mastership in a craft guild [*lettres de maîtrise*], always assuming that everything had not been swallowed up in taxes. But there was a reverse side to the medal —the economic stagnation of the greater part of the population, and the absence of pecuniary resources such as would have enabled it to break out of existing conditions.

It would be quite untrue to say that there was no middle class in France in Richelieu's day; it consisted of those of the bourgeoisie who were craftsmen or whose background was partly rural. But such people were denied opportunities for self-advancement or for buttressing the State or industry as they were to do in the nineteenth century. Nevertheless there were some fortunate exceptions among them—men who succeeded in breaking out of the economic stalemate thanks to a particularly favourable combination of circumstances. There were already some people in France who had amassed considerable fortunes; admittedly they were few and far between, but throughout the reign their ranks were swelled by newcomers. As a general rule they had grown rich through trade.

It was the merchant of every grade who was best placed to make money. In a country as rural as seventeenth-century France, in which nothing was completely dissociated from the countryside but which was not exclusively pastoral and agricultural in every respect, there were countless people who managed to sell a little and already a considerable number who contrived to sell a lot. Such occupations, and the industry and ingenuity of those engaged in them, offered opportunities for saving money which enabled a family to rise slowly from one generation to another, and in some cases to attain a social level that implied a considerable degree of power in economic terms. As well as those who rose there were of course many who fell, for there are always unlucky people in every age and they are more numerous than the others.

In many cases wealth, or an increase in wealth, was acquired by large-scale transactions in goods and money. The merchants and shipowners in the largest towns and ports, like the Legendres of Rouen, who imported exotic products from overseas: the money-changers who tapped and distributed the flow of ready money, some of whom were only engaged in this activity on a modest scale: the farmers and sub-farmers of seigneurial dues:* the financiers who farmed taxes for the government [*traitants*]:[3] certain officers of finance, and in particular the collectors-general [*receveurs généraux*]:[4] all such people were rich—indeed richer, especially in liquid assets, than the direct owners of land. Yet a wise man would generally include land among his investments. An estate provided the foodstuffs which constituted an essential element in every family budget at all points of the social scale. An even more important consideration was the fact that ownership of land was linked with noble status. Given the contemporary outlook, it gratified a man's vanity. Consequently it is not surprising to find that, as shown by the examples studied by Roland Mousnier, some magistrates in the Parlements held one third of their fortune in landed property, one third in *rentes*[5] and one third in offices.

However offices, too, could be good investments in certain cases. Mousnier has traced the rise in their price in his fascinating book.[6] It varied greatly as between one category and another, and from one district to another; but the value of higher appointments increased far more rapidly than the value of landed property or than the profits that could be made in commerce and industry. Over a few years the price of the

* Namely the *amodiateurs* who used to obtain a lease for the collection of the various dues, tolls etc that were imposed throughout a given seigneurie (V.L.T.)

office of counsellor in the Parlements of Paris or Rouen rose nearly seven times as fast as the price of goods and raw materials. While many people were the victims of economic stagnation and workmen and day-labourers were sinking into a state of acute misery compared with the beginning of the century, the magistrates of the Parlements saw their fortunes automatically increasing. We can thus appreciate the financial power of their families, and the many opportunities that they enjoyed for making good investments.

The great nobles who owned vast estates and whose pomp and ostentation dazzled the popular imagination were also regarded as rich, and rightly so if one considers the capital value of their landed possessions. But what expense they indulged in and very often what debts they incurred, how dependent they were on court appointments to balance their budgets, which generally showed a deficit! Nevertheless there were some families in court circles which had done very well for themselves.

In his book *La Vie quotidienne du temps de Louis XIII* Émile Magne gives an account of the possessions of Mme de Montglat, the king's former governess, who ended her days in 1633 in a little two-storeyed house close by the Louvre. Her style of life was modest, but even so she had five servants and a coach hung with embroidered crimson velvet and drawn by two brown horses. She had endowed her daughter with the marquisate of Montglat, but kept for herself the important seigneurie of La Ferté-Gaucher and a dozen fiefs and manorial estates. She had sufficient money in reserve to continue making quite large investments in what would nowadays be called securities; but instead of being shares or bonds issued by industrial concerns, they took the form of dues imposed on letters patent confirming appointments or making fresh appointments to offices in the county of Auvergne. She sold the patent [*brevet*] giving her this right in 1609. In 1626 she purchased the farm of the *aides* and *domaines* of Provins, entrusting the actual farming of these revenues to sub-farmers.[7] We also find Mme de Montglat making loans to private persons, whether rich, like the king's bastard brother, the comte de Moret, or of only modest means, like the peasants who lived on her estates. Admittedly in this particular case we are concerned with an elderly woman without any expensive commitments who looked after her property wisely; but was her position in fact so exceptional? Would it not have been easy to find a number of dowagers who, like 'Mamanga', were comfortably off?

Those who had capital could be almost certain of investing it profitably, because money was in short supply and the urgent need of hard cash made itself felt in all walks of life. In view of this widespread shortage of money, anyone who was in a position to lend did not have to wait long for a borrower who might offer his pewter or even lowlier possessions as security. As for the *traitants*, who were in a position to lend large sums, what power was theirs! Some of them might be denounced as thieves and bloodsuckers, battening on people and State alike; and popular opinion might be outraged by the extortionate rates of interest that they charged—20 per cent [*le denier cinq*] or 25 per cent [*le denier quatre*] as against the legal rate of 5 per cent [*le denier vingt*]. The fact remained that it was necessary to have recourse to their services. Officials forced to pay over to the Treasury increased contributions from their salaries: great nobles feeling the pinch as a result of their military expenditure or outgoings at court: even the State itself when its reserves were depleted: all of these had to look for money wherever it was to be found. When the cardinal had promised large subsidies to the United Provinces or the king of Sweden or the German princes, or when contracts had suddenly to be negotiated to supply and maintain France's steadily expanding armies in time of war, it was to these men that the government had to turn for help. They were the people who had the money, who were willing to lend it and who, in so doing, grew richer still.

Richelieu would greatly have preferred that this money should not lie idle or merely be employed in usury; he would have liked to see it being used in order to bring about by indirect means an increase in the prosperity of the entire nation. He undoubtedly had some ideas on economic affairs derived from contemporary writings on the subject, from memoranda and reports drawn up at his request—ideas which he used to discuss with experts but which he revised in the light of experience. In his study of Richelieu's economic policy mentioned earlier in this book, Henri Hauser traces their evolution and gives an account of the cardinal's endeavours and of his démarches in a number of widely different fields. But to write as he does at the end of his work that Richelieu cared less about extending France's frontiers by war than about making her rich by a policy of peace and commercial expansion is to overlook the fact that it was Richelieu who had induced the king to opt for a warlike policy.[8] Admittedly his advocacy of this policy was not prompted by brutal imperialism, by a thirst for grandeur or even by his own personal predilection for conquest and military glory. Nevertheless he did observe an order of priorities in his actions. He thought that a prince had to be powerful to be respected by his subjects and by foreigners—powerful that is to say by virtue of the strength of his armies, for in his own words: 'The most powerful state in the world cannot boast of enjoying peace and security if it is not prepared to guard itself at all times against unforeseen invasion and sudden surprise.'[9] Since he thought the need for France to be able to defend herself or to intervene abroad was more imperative than her need for internal reform, the cardinal had no alternative but to wait for peace before turning his attention once more to internal affairs. This is certainly the meaning of the *Testament politique*, which is full of allusions to the opportunities that peace would bring, and of hopes that it would soon materialise. But none of this came to pass and Richelieu's ministry, far from leading to peace, was followed by seventeen more years of war (1642–59). We must never forget that although he encouraged many acts of initiative and embarked upon a large number of projects, the cardinal was never able to carry them through far enough to produce appreciable results for the realm as a whole.

His first concern was with trade by sea. The *Testament politique* treats commerce as a by-product of sea power. Richelieu was convinced that France produced a sufficient quantity of foodstuffs and raw materials for the needs of her population. In his opinion the only products she had to purchase from abroad were spices and luxury goods, and some of the latter she was quite capable of manufacturing herself. Referring to Spanish, English and Dutch cloth he declared that 'we can make cloth of equally good quality if we import wool from Spain as these two latter countries used to do'. On the other hand he thought that foreign countries were unable to do without French products—wine and salt, canvas and hemp, corn on occasions, and also chestnuts, plums and nuts for the northern countries. The tragedy was that foreigners were everywhere superseding Frenchmen; there were now positive foreign colonies in some French ports, like Bordeaux, and at Nantes there was even a quarter known as Little Holland.[10] These foreigners were carving out a commercial monopoly for themselves. Not only did they import into France their own goods or goods shipped from elsewhere, but they also exported French products. They even made the nearby population work for them to supply what they needed for their trading activities. For example the Dutch used to call upon carpenters in the area of Nantes to repair their ships or to make casks for them; they owned and leased vineyards in the Loire valley, and lent money to vine-growers who were in financial straits.

The cardinal was therefore eager to redeem French commerce from its mortgage to foreigners. In future the products required by France's customers abroad were to be transported in French rather than foreign ships, and they were to take on cargo for the return journey. He was consequently in favour of forming trading companies in the same manner as the Dutch.[11] This was the purpose of the *Compagnie des Cent Associés ou du Morbihan*, which represented a continuation of earlier projects. Magistrates who were also engaged in business, like François Fouquet, the father of the future superintendent of finance, and monks like Father Joseph, who held that trading and missionary activity were interconnected, took an interest in the new company, which was to enjoy exclusive trading rights over the territories of New France (Canada) and over any islands which it might conquer and colonise, while those of its members who were commoners were automatically to acquire the privilege of hereditary nobility. But the towns of Brittany protested against the creation of a dangerous monopoly, and the obstacles placed in the way of the company's formation caused such delays that it was never actually established.

The scheme then reappeared in an enlarged form. A new company, with the title of *Compagnie de la Nacelle de Saint-Pierre fleurdelysée*,[12] was to be given two free ports, one on the Atlantic coast, the other on the Mediterranean; it was to set up trading establishments and manufactories in the chief towns of France and to dispatch twelve well-equipped ships to Canada with four hundred families to form a settlement.

Finally, in 1628, Richelieu decided to found a third company, the Company of New France, which took over in part the programme of its predecessors, just as its backers may perhaps have included some of the members of the earlier companies. It was under the direction of Isaac de Razilly, a gentleman of Touraine whom we have had occasion to mention previously. He was a friend of Father Joseph and came from a family of seafarers who had undertaken a number of long voyages. Richelieu set a high value on their services and on the information with which they provided him.

However, the question of La Rochelle having caused a breach between England and France, the war between the two countries spread to the St Lawrence. Quebec was lost and Samuel Champlain, the pioneer of French colonisation in Canada, returned home. But in 1632 France's sovereignty over Canada was restored by the Treaty of Saint Germain-en-Laye, and in the same year two French squadrons, one of them commanded by Razilly, escorted Champlain back to the territory which he had made his domain. Quebec, Montreal and Trois-Rivières[13] were rebuilt or founded, journeys of exploration were undertaken, and Catholic missions were also active. The latter were to leave a deep mark on the colony and determine its subsequent spiritual complexion, the different orders even vying with each other in their zeal to win converts.

Razilly's eyes turned to Acadia,[13] but he did not have time to implant French influence there for he died in November 1635. A few weeks later Champlain himself breathed his last at Quebec.

Other French settlements had begun to spring up in the islands of the Caribbean. For the privateers of St Malo and Dieppe voyages to far-off places in search of adventure were still a traditional occupation. Two gentlemen named Esnambuc and Roissey set sail from Dieppe and reached St Kitts in 1625. There they found that they had been preceded by a small colony of Huguenot refugees, who were engaged in buccaneering and selling tobacco to the Dutch; nor were they at all disconcerted by the presence of a band of English privateers commanded by Thomas Warner.* In due course they returned to France to solicit the king's patronage; whereupon Louis XIII and Richelieu authorised the formation of the *Compagnie de Saint-Christophe et des îles* to carry on trading operations in those waters. But the English and French settlers on St Kitts fell out with each other, and a small squadron had to be dispatched to the rescue of the French. Then, in 1630, a Spanish fleet bound for Brazil paused on its way to sack the settlements, whose growth had begun to cause alarm at Madrid. Despite this setback Esnambuc managed to restore the island's prosperity, and Richelieu, whose interest was aroused by what he had done, enlarged the original company, which became the *Compagnie des îles d'Amérique*. The new company was given exclusive trading rights as well as sovereignty over any territories which it conquered, but the latter were to owe allegiance to the king of France, who was also to exercise supreme judicial functions.

The story of the formation of these companies seems straightforward when its successive stages are summarised as above, but in fact there can be few histories that are so complicated, especially if considered in detail —not so much to bring out their picturesque aspect as to reveal the clash between the different interests involved. The only way to promote the development of a colony, and the only way to compete with the English, Spanish and Dutch, all of whom were better armed for colonial trade and exploitation, was to found a company. But the men who had put up the money were out to make profits, and their demands did not always coincide with the immediate interests of the settlers. The French colonists

* See his biography in the D.N.B.

on St Kitts, for example, preferred to sell their tobacco and cotton to Dutch ships, which called there frequently, and sent only inadequate quantities to France. In France itself the small shipowners or ships' captains were ferocious individualists and highly critical of the trading companies whose privileges threatened them with ruin. Thirty or forty years later Colbert was to meet with the same difficulties.

The capital which these companies had at their disposal did, however, enable them to embark on large-scale ventures beyond the capacity of isolated individuals. They began to recruit a labour force of Frenchmen willing to settle in the colonies for three years. An excellent book on these 'volunteers' has recently been written by Gabriel Debien, a leading authority on the history of the West Indies. They left France by the hundred under circumstances that are of great interest to the student of French social history during those years: they included day-labourers with hopes of acquiring the land that they lacked in France, debtors seeking to pay off their debts, and young men tempted by the hope of learning a trade or simply by the prospect of adventure. For the most part their lot was wretched, sometimes indeed barely distinguishable from slavery; but it was this labour force of white men which cleared the land and built settlements on Guadeloupe, Martinique and St Kitts, on Tortuga,* and even at this early date on Santo Domingo. It was the period of small-scale cultivation—primarily of tobacco. Towards the middle of the century a new era began with the advent of the sugar mill and of capitalist exploitation of a different type involving the use of black labour. Thus the foul blot of slavery which France was striving to eradicate in the Mediterranean appeared among the islands of the Caribbean.

French colonies were also established at a number of other points: in the area between the Amazon and the Orinoco, on Cape Verde Island, in Senegal and Gambia. Several companies, based on Rouen, Dieppe and St Malo, were responsible for these settlements. At the end of the reign a settlement named Fort-Dauphin was founded on the coast of Madagascar, where a company whose governor was the duc de la Meilleraye took possession 'in the king's name of that island and of the isles adjacent thereto'.

When we consider the way in which the France of Richelieu's day expanded beyond her own frontiers to the four points of the compass, we can measure the extent to which his maritime policy was successful. We see the outlines of a French empire beginning to take shape, although admittedly they are only tenuous. Above all, France's colonial vocation

* A small island that lies off the north coast of Haiti.

was confirmed and strengthened during these years and henceforth she was never to show herself unmindful of it.

Canada, which was suitable for both colonisation and missionary activity, interested Richelieu because, as stated in the *Testament politique*, the fur trade did not involve the use of gold since it was carried on 'by bartering such articles as scissors, knives, sheathes, penknives, needles, bill-hooks, hatchets, watches, hatbands, shoulder-knots and all other kinds of court haberdashery'. But for a long time the cardinal's anxiety to prevent precious metals leaving the realm made him adopt a reserved attitude towards French commerce in the Mediterranean.

He was under the impression that it was uniquely concerned with luxury goods such as silks, Persian carpets and porcelain from China, which the Marseilles seamen used to pay for in gold and silver. The Marseillais managed to convince him that this was not the case: admittedly some luxuries were imported, but the goods that came from the Levant —silks, cottons, wax, Turkey leather and rhubarb, as well as several other drugs—were absolutely indispensable to the realm. Nor did ships sail to the Levantine ports in ballast;[14] they carried timber and hemp. On the return journey they used to unload a number of eastern products at ports on the coast of Sicily as well as at Naples, Genoa and Majorca, and so in the end it was not French but Spanish coins that were used.[15]

Richelieu was converted by these arguments. He also noted that the import of silk and cotton yarn served to supply the manufactories of Lyons and Tours and made it possible for France to export the finished products to Flanders, England and Germany.

However, trade in the Mediterranean was greatly harassed by the Barbary corsairs of Algeria and Tunisia. The people of Marseilles liked to boast that thanks to the manœuvrability of their small craft they had no difficulty in evading the attacks of the corsairs, while the heavy Venetian ships were easily captured—a state of affairs which partly explained the decline of Venice. However, the little ships of Marseilles often fell victim to pirates too. Richelieu entered into negotiations with the Barbary corsairs through the good offices of a Corsican named Sanson Napollon, who had succeeded in reviving the French trading post near La Calle known as Bastion de France.* As a result twenty-four boats were allowed to carry on coral fishing almost regularly, and arrangements were made for the export of leather, wool, horses and even corn to Provence. The Marseillais accused Napollon of showing partiality to Genoa, which

---

* La Calle is situated near Bône in Algeria close to the Tunisian frontier. The fortified trading post called Bastion de France had originally been established in 1552.

had suzerainty over Corsica, but Richelieu continued to trust him.

The cardinal would have liked to set up a trading post in Morocco similar to Bastion de France, both to protect French interests and to hold in check the pirates of Salé.* Mogador seemed to him to meet the needs of the case; but his hopes remained unfulfilled. Two journeys made by Razilly did at least lead to the signature of a treaty with the Shereef Abd-el-Malek in 1631. As Hauser has aptly put it, this treaty introduced the Turkish system of capitulations into Morocco:[16] a preferential tariff for French merchants, the establishment of a French consulate and freedom of religion for the French king's Catholic subjects. However, French trade with Morocco tended to languish after 1635.

Directly he ralised that France's Mediterranean trade was in fact profitable to her, Richelieu was eager to obtain information about possible commercial openings not only at Constantinople but also at Alexandretta†and Aleppo in the Levant itself. Des Hayes de Courmenin was ordered to carry out an investigation in 1626, but met with such hostility from Harlay de Césy, the French ambassador in Constantinople, that he had to return to France. The cardinal who was determined to get rid of middlemen, was bent on arranging direct contacts between France and Aleppo, where there was a French consul and where ships from Marseilles used to call, although such visits were not organised.[17] This aim was combined with another. Father Joseph's associates were hostile to Turkey and thought of opening up relations with Persia. A Capuchin named Father Pacifique de Provins made a journey there in 1628–9, and published an account of it on his return. Persia was the enemy of Turkey, and the shah was disturbed to see that caravans returning from India and China were crossing Asia Minor to reach the ports of the Levant. To deprive the sultan of his customs revenues, the shah put pressure on the caravans to find an alternative outlet for their wares. The ports on the Indian Ocean offered such an outlet; indeed English and Dutch ships used to call there to wait for Asian merchandise. Around 1629 it occurred to Richelieu that Persian trade could be deflected towards the Caspian and from there, by making use of the great rivers of Russia, goods could be conveyed either to Archangel or to Narva on the Baltic—a port situated on territory recently occupied by Sweden.

But to reach France from Narva it was necessary to pass through the Baltic Sound, where the king of Denmark imposed such heavy dues that since the beginning of the century French ships had almost completely

* Known to the contemporary Englishman as Sallee.

†Alexandretta is now known as Iskenderun.

given up using this northern route. Possibly to compensate for the setback that he had met with in the Levant, Courmenin was charged with a
mission to Denmark in 1629. He was to put Christian IV in fear of the
French adopting Archangel as the terminus to the new commercial route
across Russia, but he was also to make it clear that if Denmark would
agree to impose only moderate customs dues they would prefer the route
via Narva. Christian IV and his Council must have known very well that
the route via Archangel, although relatively easy for the English, would
be difficult if not impracticable for the French. Probably it was not this
consideration alone so much as general feeling of confidence in French
economic recovery which prompted them agree to award France very
advantageous rates by a treaty dated 14 July 1629. Immediately French
trade in the Baltic came to life again. Courmenin also made his way to
Russia, and in November signed a commercial treaty with Tsar Michael
Fedorovich; but there was no longer any question of the transit of merchandise from Persia and the east. The French merely obtained favourable terms for the purchase and sale of goods at Archangel, Novgorod
and Moscow.[18]

Richelieu's 'great scheme', as Hauser calls it,* namely the establishment of a link between the east and the seas of northern Europe by
way of Russia, had ended in failure—if, that is to say, it was ever taken
seriously, which is open to doubt. It is one thing to open up a new route
and try out an ingenious and novel idea; it is another to deflect a regular
stream of commerce from its traditional course. In short, it would have
been dangerous to injure the interests of the Levantine ports and the
shipowners of Marseille.

On the other hand these plans for opening up commercial relations
with remote parts of the world, these new ventures launched in every
direction, are a clear indication of Richelieu's determination to make
France rich by means of foreign trade, and to direct such of her people's
energies as were not claimed by war and such money as remained after
the collection of their taxes towards the fulfilment of a great task.

In the *Testament politique* Richelieu suggested a method by which the
slowness or inadequate resources of the shipyards of the merchant navy
could have been quite quickly remedied. The king was to sell ships to
shipowners annually at a moderate price; they were to undertake to
make use of these ships for trading purposes and not to sell them outside
the realm. Within a few years France would have a large merchant fleet

---

* *Le grand dessein de Richelieu.* The phrase is suggested by the so-called *grand dessein* of
Henry IV, referred to on p. 65 above.

which in the event of war would be put at the king's disposal just as it was in England. Yet these ingenious expedients, and the attractive prospect of making large profits by engaging in commerce—a prospect rendered yet more inviting by the award of noble rank to those who did so —could not achieve results without the economic stimulus provided by an increase in prosperity among the population. To bring this about stabilised prices and a durable reform of the currency would have been necessary. Nor could anything be achieved when those who did have capital to invest were continually being pressed by the superintendents of finance to lend money to the State, to supply the king's armies in time of war or to buy offices.

And thus we are led to the following conclusion. It remains to the honour of Richelieu that he boldly singled out France's new interests and tried to find a way of invigorating her economy and revitalising her wealth; but by clinging to various disastrous practices imposed on him by the realm's military and financial requirements, he thrust her back into the rut from which he sought to pull her. It is not for the historian to decide whether Richelieu's policy might have yielded better results if it had been conducted differently. His task is confined to stating the contradictions implicit in that policy and to showing how it defeated its own object through certain courses of action that stemmed from it.

There was thus to be no essential transformation in the economic life of France during these years—years that were dominated by her covert and overt conflict with Spain. However, the cardinal certainly did not ignore the progress made in certain fields that could be beneficial to internal trade, and indeed to France's external trade also. For example he took an interest in the silk manufactures of Tours, a town for which he had a particular affection. Not only was it close to his duchy but in addition it was thoroughly French. The cardinal undoubtedly had some acquaintances there, and he thought it a more reliable town than Lyons, which lay close to the frontier and was rather cosmopolitan, owing to the number of foreigners who passed through—Italians or citizens of the Empire.

Tours is awarded a whole paragraph in the *Testament politique*: 'Plush of such fine quality is made there that it finds a ready market in Italy and Spain and other foreign countries. The plain taffetas which are likewise manufactured there are sold in such quantities throughout France that there is no need to try to sell them elsewhere. The red, violet and yellow velvets to be found there are finer than those of Genoa. It is almost the only place where silk serge is made; as for the watered silk of Tours, it is as excellent as that obtainable in England, and the gold cloth of middling standard made there is of better quality and cheaper than that of Italy.' These exquisite products from the workshops of Touraine must not however make us overlook the good steady output of standard cloths from the cloth-makers of Normandy and Berry.

The cloth known as *drap du sceau* derived its name either from the first manufactories established at Saint-Benoît-du-Sault near Le Blanc, or from the seal affixed to pieces as they left the workshops at Châteauroux and Bourges, both of which lay close to the open plateaux specially reserved for sheep. But in the seventeenth century it was also manufactured by the craftsmen of Rouen. Rouen's proximity to the sea and its easy communications with Paris stimulated the growth of this industry. Moreover Normandy was a rich province. Fortunes based on land were more common there than elsewhere and the ample revenues that it yielded encouraged investment in both offices and manufactories. At Romorantin there was a flourishing trade in miller's cloth, while Châlons and Chartres produced finer fabrics with invisible stitches, short-nap cloth being in demand for mourning or for clothes worn on official occasions. This, however, did not alter the fact that a well-stocked wardrobe would include clothes made of foreign as well as French fabrics—fabrics produced in Flanders, Italy or Spain, holland from the Netherlands, serge from Florence or Segovia.

Linen and hempen cloth were still being woven in Normandy and Maine. Workshops in Auvergne and at Beauvais produced tapestries depicting foliage or human figures, and Richelieu hoped that they would compete with the Flemish tapestries so prominently displayed in the residences of the nobility and even in the more unassuming houses of the bourgeoisie. He therefore favoured the royal manufactory known as the *Savonnerie*, which had been established during Henry IV's reign in the galleries of the Louvre and in which children from almshouses were employed.[19] Similarly he wanted to revive and extend the glass industry which provided gentlemen glass-makers with employment to some extent all over France, but particularly in the Argonne—for by engaging in this occupation they escaped both destitution and loss of rank.[20] But the glassware produced was of no more than ordinary quality—such as the window-glass exported to the countries of northern Europe. Fine glass and mirrors were still obtained from Venice and it would seem that there was no alternative source of supply elsewhere. The interior of any house above the borderline of poverty included a Venetian mirror, whether large or small. Here again Richelieu had hopes of fostering a national industry and attempted to set up new manufactories in Picardy or at Paris; a licence dated 1634 was granted to Eustache Grand Mont and Jean Antoine d'Anthonneuil with this object in view.

The network of communications bequeathed by Sully continued to be used for the transport of merchandise within the realm; the network was improved but no great changes were introduced, no new overall plan was envisaged. Public works were the responsibility of the *trésoriers de France*: in other words, within each *généralité* the upkeep or repair of communications was controlled from a central office over which they presided.[21]

Only one reform in this field was of major importance—a reform which set the seal on the efforts of the monarchy for more than one hundred and fifty years by helping to bring road traffic more fully under the authority of the Crown, and to turn the postal and relay system for the hire of fresh horses into a royal service or a service under the king's control.

In 1630 the administration of this service was entrusted to one or more superintendents of the posts, whose offices were specially created for this purpose, their subordinates, the masters of the posts, being also office-holders. These officials carried the organisation of the postal system a stage further by farming out certain sections of it to others. As usual, the creation of new offices met a public need as well as helping the government in its financial difficulties. However in this particular case it was at least followed by the organisation of a stage-coach system with regular times of departure, the collection and distribution of letters and parcels at post offices, and the establishment of a uniform scale of charges for carriage.

Nevertheless waterways were still in many cases preferable to roads as a means of transport. For this reason, Richelieu considered linking various rivers by means of canals after to some extent obtaining reductions in the tolls imposed on river traffic—a most complicated affair, partly because of the tangle of riparian rights that were involved and even more so because of the way in which a river bank can alter very rapidly within a few years unless kept under supervision. The first to be completed was the Briare canal between the rivers Loing and Loire, on which work had begun in the time of Henry IV. There were also several plans for joining the Atlantic to the Mediterranean by means of the Burgundy canal, or by a canal in Languedoc which was later to be built by Riquet.[22]

No great effort of the imagination is needed to picture a day in Richelieu's life as minister—a day spent in discussing an enormous range of topics. His relations with Monsieur and the great nobles remained a constant worry. It is easy for us who look back after a lapse of three centuries and live under a very different system of government to adopt a patronising attitude towards these questions of personalities, but the fact remains that it was impossible to govern the realm unless the various factions were kept in check. In addition to this perpetual problem there were countless other matters that claimed the cardinal's attention: instructions to be sent to the king's ambassadors, news from abroad that would have direct bearing on his policy, steps to be taken in connection with the army, negotiations with the Parlement—for upon its august magistrates depended the registration of the king's edicts and the enforcement of the law. We can also imagine him listening to the proposals of some engineer or inventor, approving them in principle and thinking to himself that they were as desirable as a general reduction of the *taille* —a matter to which he devoted much thought and to which he often used to refer. But Richelieu knew very well that none of this could be done yet awhile. There were other matters that were more pressing —matters that were vital and would brook no delay. He would have to wait until times were quieter—if indeed they ever became so. On many points the cardinal's answer must have been similar to that which he gave in a letter to one of his ablest servants, Sourdis, the archbishop of Bordeaux: 'It will not be possible to carry out work on the port this year, but next year we will work wonders.'[23] Was this a promise or was it simply a pious hope? In the meantime, somehow or other the realm continued to live from hand to mouth.

Did the cardinal at least give France a better administration by means of a few important legislative measures? One is inclined to think so when one recalls the great ordinance of 1629, which was registered by the Parlement of Paris at a *lit de justice*, but soon aroused a chorus of protest from office-holders. This edict was the work of Marillac, the keeper of the seals; it took form of a collection of earlier ordinances and regulations that had been adopted by the Estates-General and the Assemblies of Notables. Gabriel Hanotaux regards it as 'the first French code of law', and after noting the favourable references to it in Richelieu's memoirs, he expresses the opinion that its main provisions were in conformity with the cardinal's views.[24] It is certainly true that, concerned as it is with every aspect of the administration with the evident intention of making it more just, more logical and more fair, the code contains many clauses which do in fact coincide with Richelieu's opinions; but they could also be said to reflect the views of any minister conscious of the role that the State should play, as well as of the abuses for which the privileged were responsible. It is easy to point to a large number of the code's provisions which have the effect of strengthening the State's authority, by asserting its sovereignty in financial matters, and in matters connected with the armed forces and police. For example governors, officers and nobles are forbidden to levy sums of money or other contributions either in their private capacities or on account of the appointments and powers which they hold in the provinces. They are also forbidden to enrol soldiers, accumulate reserves of arms and powder, fortify towns and castles or hold open or secret assemblies. In short, they are prohibited from engaging in any activities which could prepare the way for a civil war.

But our main concern is not so much to commend the code's provisions as to determine to what extent people paid attention to this admirable corpus of regulations, and to what extent it was enforced. In both cases there seems no doubt that the extent was very limited. The fact that the code was known as the 'Code Michau' (this last being a nickname derived from Michel de Marillac's Christian name) soon showed that it was not taken too seriously. In his book *La Monarchie d'Ancien Régime* Georges Pagès noted that when the Parlement stopped enforcing the code after the keeper of the seals had fallen from power, Richelieu made no attempt to compel it to do so.

The Code Michau was thus a useful compilation, but it contained nothing that could be called a new system. Moreover, like any other reform its success depended upon the realm returning to a normal state of order. To Richelieu's mind the only way of securing this under circumstances that made it more and more precarious, was to have recourse to servants who were loyal to his policy. He tried to swell their numbers in a variety of ways. Like many others since his day, he made use of his family, which he did his best to extend by arranging marriages for his relations. This is the explanation for the marriage alliances made with the houses of La Valette and Gramont in 1634 and with Puylaurens, Monsieur's unworthy favourite. There is a sentence in Richelieu's correspondence which forms an eloquent commentary on this policy: 'Your son,' he writes to the comte de Gramont, 'will tell you that to gratify your desire to remain within my kinship (of which he has informed me) I am giving him one of my cousins in marriage; she is as closely related to me as the other, with this one difference, that she brings him a larger dowry in return for the courtesy and sincerity with which he has borne himself in my respect.' In other words instead of Mademoiselle de Pontchâteau being awarded to the compte de Guiche, as the latter had been led to hope, she was, on second thoughts, given to Puylaurens; de Guiche was to make do with Mlle de Plessis de Chivray and a larger dowry. The preferences of the interested parties counted for nothing; all that mattered was the actual bargain.

Richelieu's relations did indeed provide him with some able lieutenants who helped him to carry out his policy. His system of clientele also included the secretaries of state, several of whom were bound to him by the kind of personal ties that bind a loyal servant to his master, as in the case of the two Bouthilliers, father and son. The latter, who was known as 'Monsieur le jeune', reappears later in this book under the name of Chavigny.[25]

The use that Richelieu made of intendants may be said to have been governed by the same attitude. It is a mistake to suppose that it was he who created the office, or to imagine that his government did anything new in this connection or made continuous use of intendants. Indeed it is only very rarely that we can, as Georges Pagès puts it, 'issue a birth certificate' to any institution belonging to the ancien régime. It had been recognised practice in previous reigns to entrust a master of requests with a special mission for a specific object. He might be charged with a commission of inquiry in matters of finance or justice, or even be empowered to take a decision or pass judgement in the king's name whilst provisionally suspending the authority of the officials on the spot. The need to control provinces which were a prey to disturbances or rebellions, and to see that they knew and obeyed the king's will, impelled Richelieu to issue such commissions frequently to men upon whom he could rely. But so as to define the extent of their jurisdiction, these commissioners were generally styled 'intendants of justice', 'intendants of police' or 'intendants of finance'. Sometimes they were given all three designations simultaneously, but 'intendant of justice' seems to have been the one which was most frequently used. It constituted a sort of title which appealed to the recipient's vanity, for the name 'commissioner' carried with it less prestige; however, whichever name was used, commissions were sometimes issued for a long period extending to several years.

Georges Pagès thought that Richelieu preferred commissioners to intendants because of his doubts as to the consequences of delegating excessive power or authority. In the *Testament politique* the dispatch of a commissioner with only a short-term commission to control the administration of financial and judicial officers is described as sound practice on the part of a government. Moreover, intendants of justice did not correspond directly with the cardinal but with the keeper of the seals.

However, subject to these qualifications, there seems no doubt that Richelieu's government did make good use of intendants. In due course we will see them in action after the outbreak of disorders in the provinces, and we will examine the part that they played. One has only to mention them to think of Isaac de Laffemas, 'the cardinal's hangman'. The face that looks out at us from the portrait painted by Michel Lasne is so hard as to be almost repulsive. Laffemas was certainly merciless in his execution of justice, but other intendants showed not only more humanity but also more understanding of the complex situations with which they were confronted. Given the fact that the intendants were the trustworthy servants of a chancellor who was loyal to Richelieu and obeyed his orders—as Séguier was*—they were directly or indirectly Richelieu's men. It is undoubtedly upon this quality of personal loyalty that the stress should be laid. Richelieu wrote a great deal in favour of an ideal of government that he was unable to put into practice. Certainly he realised the need for and desired a well-administered realm in which every office that fulfilled a properly conceived function would *ipso facto* function efficiently. But we must never lose sight of the fact that he held power during an abnormal period given over to war and rife with continual revolt which compelled him to act in a great hurry. In the last resort one must admit that he governed by means of men far more than by means of institutions.

And yet the France of 1630 and her society had undergone very profound changes during the previous ten years—changes which could never have occurred without the growth that took place in the importance and influence of certain social groups. It follows that the historian who attempts to offer a general interpretation of Louis XIII's reign and age must guard against two possible errors.

The first into which he is liable to fall when he considers the magnitude of what was achieved in certain spheres, both at home and abroad, is to overestimate the strength and solidity of the system. He is tempted to credit the government with a mastery over the course of events which it did not possess, and to represent the country as a whole as obedient, co-

---

* Séguier succeeded Châteauneuf as keeper of the seals in 1633 and became Chancellor in 1635.

operative and peaceful when it was in fact nothing of the kind. In short, he is in danger of painting a picture of the age which is both too flattering and too glorious.

The other error to which the historian is prone is to concentrate exclusively on listing the defects and imperfections of the age: a minister exposed to continual plots against his policies and his person, a sickly and childless king wooed by rival factions, a Machiavellian court, ill-defended frontiers, a stagnant economy, an insane taxation system and an exhausted populace despairing of relief from its miseries and ever ready to break into revolt. This approach ignores the fact that, quite apart from the revival of French prestige abroad, the reign of Louis XIII witnessed one of the greatest intellectual achievements in French history. It was during this period that a civilisation began to flower which was to continue to grow in the succeeding reign, imposing on the world in the second half of the century the model of French classicism. This development was neither a miracle nor was it due to the determination of a few individuals, nor can it be ascribed to the fortunate coincidence that a few men of genius happened to be alive at the same time. It was, rather, a slow process of ripening which took place in the sheltered conditions that certain circles of society were able to offer thanks to the encouragement and the security that they provided.

A preliminary explanation is to be found in the intellectual legacy of the sixteenth century, as a result of which culture and an interest in the achievements of the mind had been established as a tradition. This tradition had been given fresh life by the expansion of education at what is nowadays called the secondary level. Colleges run by Jesuits and Oratorians gave their pupils an education that drew abundantly upon the literature of the ancient world—an education which encouraged them to express and define their thoughts and invited them to adopt noble deeds and lofty sentiments as their personal ideals. In contrast to the colleges the universities immersed themselves in scholarly speculations which were only of interest to a small number of initiates. They were not expected to serve as repositories of culture, nor were they called upon to revise their methods. Their jurists and theologians were either regarded as men of learning or treated as pedants. Whether respected, ridiculed or ignored, their influence remained limited.

Intellectual life had begun to flower elsewhere—among fashionable circles in the capital. Great nobles at court who lived in lavish style were glad to include men of letters among their clientele. Among the following of great aristocratic families like the [Gondi de] Retz, the Liancourts, the Montmorencies, the Longuevilles and the Soissons were to be found writers such as Saint-Amand, Théophile de Viau, Chapelain, Rotrou and Corneille himself.

The nobility not only protected men of letters and provided them with a public; through their ideas, their way of life and their tastes they also to some extent inspired the literature of the age, which allowed such scope to romance and displayed such sympathy for heroism and honour. But the writers of the day were mostly bourgeois who came from families that belonged to the office-holding class or to the trading community. They brought with them not only their particular talents, the hard core of originality which was part and parcel of their individual temperaments or genius, but also the tendencies that were native to their social background—a sense of order and the habit of pursuing arguments logically or in minute detail, combined with realism and a capacity for hard work. The contact between these two different worlds in literary circles helped to form contemporary taste.

It was in Paris that this contact was established, and it is easy to see why this was so. Paris enjoyed relative security during Louis XIII's reign and could therefore fulfil her role as capital without interference. She was not attacked by foreign armies, nor was she exposed to civil war or serious disorders. Paris was at one and the same time aristocratic, bourgeois and proletarian, a city where the different classes rubbed shoulders with each other, where the government was almost permanently located, where the magistracy and officers of the Parlement and municipality enjoyed great prestige. Life there flowed past interminably in all its prolific variety. It was Paris that dictated the fashion and enhanced or destroyed reputations. It was at Paris that literature flourished, and it was there that writers hailing from the provinces received the ultimate recognition of their merits, for the provinces had grown accustomed to accepting the capital's pronouncements.

Nowadays literary historians tend to apply the adjectives 'baroque' or 'romanesque' to the age of Louis XIII. These words are used to indicate the existence of a number of different trends and of an intellectual climate that allowed ample scope for individual inspiration and fanciful imagination; they also signify a general liking for grandeur, for animation and for spectacle, attributable to the influence of Italian and Spanish literature, and more particularly to that of Marino and Góngora with their love of elaborate affectation.[26] French logic and realism, which formed part of the legacy bequeathed by the Middle Ages and which had cut across the attitudes of mind imposed by the Renaissance, exercised an active influence on this riotous mass of material, striving to introduce more order and moderation. In consequence a new spirit emerged which maintained a balance between these many conflicting tendencies and helped to prepare the way for classicism. There is nothing stiff or constrained about this period. Indeed, its humanism is modern, for far from slavishly applying rules imposed from abroad, writers of the day were concerned with interpreting the characteristics of society about them. Never was literature more full of life.

The first name that we must single out is that of Malherbe. He held the post of court poet, with the task of commemorating the great achievements of the reign. He was made much of at the Hôtel de Rambouillet, and it was he who laid down the laws for the purification of the French language and for a new prosody. He waged war on words in everyday use because of the imagery which they conjured up; thus the use of the word *pouls* was condemned owing to its possible association with *pou*, and *poitrine* was inadmissible because it was also used in connection with veal. He campaigned against expressions that had a provincial flavour or smacked of local dialect, and against barbarous archaisms. He shunned tricks and pedantry, for he wanted a literary language that was clear and precise, in which every idea would have its *mot juste*. His disciple Racan tells us that Malherbe used to call the porters of the Port-aux-Foins[27] his language masters, but this was only a witty remark or figure of speech. His poetry, written in a style that is strained, not to say forced, strives to create an impression of grandeur; the inadequacy of his poetic imagination or emotional power is redeemed by the nobility and eloquence of his tone. As Antoine Adam has rightly said, Malherbe is the French representative of the baroque by virtue of his genuine feeling for the sublime—a feeling which inspires the verses he devoted to the glorification of Louis XIII and his reign.

Malherbe's disciples greatly extended the field of his influence. They included Racan, who was gifted with more spontaneity and feeling than his master, and Maynard, a skilful poet who maintained the same unwavering standard but whose range was limited. At first Malherbe met with opposition from that delightful but disturbing character Théophile de Viau, although the latter's attitude was rebellious rather than hostile. He was fully conscious of Malherbe's achievement and merits, but was bent on giving free rein both to his varied inspiration and to his own individual manner of expression. Théophile de Viau was a free-thinker who loved and possibly worshipped Nature. He claimed the right to sing her praises as he chose, in lines that were supple yet spontaneous, to write poetry whose emotion was unencumbered by metaphor. Because of this

his poems were to be spurned by the Hôtel de Rambouillet; but for the same reason the Romantics were to be enchanted by them and to pay well-deserved tribute to a poet of genius.

Régnier, who was regarded as Malherbe's antagonist, objected to the latter's action in setting up Parisian salons and aristocratic coteries as arbiters of literary taste. He turned uncompromisingly to plebeian society in the towns. In his satires he describes the characters and behaviour of his day crudely and with verve, taking an evident delight in shocking susceptibilities.

In short, it is scarcely an exaggeration to speak of a conflict between one school of literature devoted to the noble and the ideal and another which in varying forms depicted Nature and Life in terms that expressed an instinctive love of them while at the same time steadfastly refusing to submit to hard and fast rules or preconceived ideas. The success achieved by anthologies of light erotic verse (*Muse folastre, Muses inconnues, Muses gaillardes, Cabinet satyrique, Parnasse des poètes satyriques*), which continued to appear until banned by the Parlement in 1623, but were still being read long after that date even in Anne of Austria's entourage, proves that taste was by no means uniform. If the romantic delicacy of *L'Astrée* gave fresh delight to each generation,* the severe criticism of aristocratic society and the accurate portrayal of contemporary behaviour to be found in Charles Sorel's celebrated novel *Francion* (1623) also scored a lasting success. Nevertheless, it was at this time that the company that graced Mme de Rambouillet's salon reached the height of distinction.

The life and soul of this circle was Voiture,† a fastidious poet and a subtle conversationalist whose badinages sparkled with delightful and original ideas. The cult of 'the precious' entailed the avoidance of any expression that was in everyday use; it necessitated a quest for metaphors which made it possible to translate a common-place into something noble. It implied the rejection of facility and required discrimination, that is to say selection, in all fields and the cultivation of everything that could lend refinement to one's thoughts and daily activities. In each of these ways, therefore, preciosity represented a victory over the uncouth behaviour which still prevailed in the outside world.

Mme de Rambouillet's town mansion in the rue Saint-Thomas-du-Louvre stood only a few steps away from the palace, where the crowd

---

* This pastoral novel by Honoré d'Urfé was published in instalments between 1607 and 1627.

† ' *"L'âme du rond" est Voiture*'. The term used to be applied to him as a kind of nickname.

('how ill-spoken, how lacking in decorum') still used to swarm around the king. For all the indefinable irritation aroused by its excessive fastidiousness, her salon occupies a vital place in French history. It was there that the language which was to conquer the world acquired its suppleness and polish. The exquisite courtesy and refined manners, the elegant cult of Woman, the taste for delicate distinctions and for things intellectual—all these were qualities that were fostered in Mme de Rambouillet's circle. It is their possession of the last of these attributes which has enabled the élite, indeed almost the majority, of the French people to act for nearly three centuries as representatives of a civilisation particularly distinguished for its subtlety and refinement.

Writers such as Malherbe, Voiture, Balzac, Racan, Conrart and Vaugelas, together with nobles, courtiers and even statesmen, came and went in Mme de Rambouillet's *chambre bleue*.[28] Even more striking is the fact that three great literary figures, Chapelain, Conrart and Balzac, were among those who frequented her salon, for they have been described as the triumvirate which reigned over literature in Richelieu's day. Not one of them left behind a work destined for immortality, but their scrupulous regard for purity of language led them to impose a censorship upon every form of literature, a censorship inspired by canons of taste that were both exacting and liberal. It was their meetings and discussions, of which Richelieu was informed by Boisrobert, the rather unsavoury prior of Saint-Saturnin de Nozay[29] who was also an elegant court poet in his entourage, that gave the cardinal the idea of an Academy which would guard and regulate the French language and act as the arbiter of literary merit.

The cardinal loved letters. That he wrote admirable prose is apparent from the precision and clarity of his language and the polished turn of his sentences, which endow his reports and official letters with such vigour and elegance—quite apart from the *Testament politique* or the memoirs which bear his direct imprint. However, Louis Batiffol has maintained that Richelieu was only interested in making himself understood without regard to formal beauty and without any concern for literary effect as such. Even so, the cardinal undoubtedly had very good taste and enjoyed exercising it. He had a particular fondness for the stage. In an age when the theatre was coarse and disparaged, he wished to bring about its rehabilitation through a better choice of subject matter and a more dignified approach to the presentation of performances which would have restored the actors themselves to their proper place in society.

For all these reasons the cardinal wanted the reign of Louis XIII, who was himself both painter and musician, to be a period of brilliant literary and artistic achievement such as had been witnessed during the great reigns of Antiquity and at the courts of the Renaissance. In addition he desired to discipline language and thought in the interests of good order and for political considerations. He knew that ideas are derived from books, and he liked to guide the direction that they took. He was well aware that writers were a potential danger in that they were patronised by various coteries which were far from being entirely at his devotion, and he realised that there would not be room for all of them in the Bastille.* He saw no great harm in curbing intellectual independence when it threatened to degenerate into disorder, and was no great believer in the beneficent effects of uncontrolled freedom upon inspiration.

In consequence, despite opposition in certain quarters we find Richelieu adroitly transforming Conrart's and Chapelain's circle into one of the most original of French institutions: the Académie Française founded in 1635. His action in so doing represented a step towards the triumph of a literature governed by rules which respected the authority of the ancient writers.[30]

In the world of the theatre, which interested Richelieu most, a change likewise occurred in about 1630. True, it was not a complete transformation; the typically baroque partiality for theatrical display—namely intricate plots involving improbabilities and marvels, a blend of the tragic and the comic, and a succession of changes of complicated scenery—was to persist far longer than has since been supposed. But even those who had begun by writing tragi-comedies, pastoral comedies or pastoral tragi-comedies, now followed a different course. They made a point of adopting reason as their guiding rule, or of conforming with the rules laid down by learned Italians of the sixteenth century. Mairet's preface to *Silvanire* (1631) was a manifesto in their favour, and in his tragedy *Sophonisbe* (1634) he proceeded to put their rules into practice. The way was now open for the portrayal of character on the stage. Corneille, whose comedies had attracted attention and won favour and who had succeeded in his use of the baroque theatrical idiom, secured the first great triumph with *Le Cid* (1636). His play gave rise to a wrangle over literary doctrine and caused a stir both at court and in the capital; but it also gave unquestionable proof of its quality as a masterpiece.

Posterity was to associate the name of Corneille with that of Descartes,

* Like the Tower of London the Bastille was used for state prisoners, generally persons of distinction. As a prison it compared very favourably with the Châtelet or the Conciergerie.

for in the year following *Le Cid* there appeared the philosophical disser-
tation *Discours de la Méthode*, in which the search for truth was subordinated to the dictates and proper use of reason. *Cogito ergo sum. The
Discourse on Method* represented a breach with scholasticism. Its underlying aim was to capture the reality and the existence of God by means of
an essay in apologetics through the intuitive deduction of evidence of an
intellectual nature.

Richelieu would have glowed with pleasure if he had been able to
foresee the future and to realise the lasting glory that would belong to the
age that was his. For him it was enough to feel that great works were
emerging into the light of day and that the reign of Louis XIII already
enjoyed the reputation of an age of great intellectual achievement.

Admittedly government initiative alone could neither produce geni-
uses nor foster the rise of a classical school of literature; yet its activities
did contribute to an improvement in the lot of writers and, although not
responsible for the development of intellectual life, consecrated it and
invested it with a lustre that only a government could supply. The essential change is the general development of aptitudes and the increase in
general enlightenment that took place during these years. Antoine Adam
is sufficiently convinced of the existence of this trend to write: 'In 1640
every cultivated Frenchman could reason better than in 1600 . . . and he
could express his thoughts with more accuracy and with more subtle
shades of meaning.'[31]

It was not the intelligence of the French people that had improved in
the past forty years but their way of using it. A comment such as this contains a wealth of implications. It shows us that society in France was now
qualified to appreciate anything of a high standard. It directs our attention to a problem which has hitherto scarcely been touched on—the
problem of public opinion. The tenacious opposition that Richelieu's
policy continually met with, and the many forms that this opposition
assumed are now becoming increasingly clear to us. With the help of the
valuable lists of sources so patiently compiled by Louis André,[32] it is possible to form some idea of the vast quantity of pamphlets and tracts that
each party put out in defence of its cause; but we are ill-informed as to
the impact of all these arguments on contemporary opinion. Until they
have been subjected to the kind of detailed study that will enable us to be
more definite on this point, it is not unreasonable to suppose that a very
large number of people, especially among the middle strata of the bourgeoisie, without unreservedly supporting the cardinal's policy, came to
subscribe to some of the ideas which that policy invoked—ideas such as

the overriding interest of the State, and the necessity for public order guaranteed by the Crown.

Consequently Richelieu went to considerable trouble to enlighten and influence public opinion so as to win over to his side as broad a section of the élite of the nation as possible. He was not concerned with the mass of the people, who were still illiterate and unaccustomed to see further than their local and short-term interests; nor was Richelieu mistaken in thinking that their readiness to submit to authority would in any event depend on the local notables and officials who were responsible for them. However, even if the common people could be ignored it was still necessary to bring influence to bear on the minds of the bourgeoisie and nobility in both Paris and the provinces. The cardinal sought to instruct and win over the literate and thoughtful elements among the nation by every means at his disposal. To *Le Mercure François* an official organ with only a small circulation, he added *La Gazette*, a news-sheet which was the ancestor of the modern French newspaper. This step was suggested by the physician Théophraste Renaudot.

Since notices concerned with business matters were printed side by side with reports of domestic and foreign news, any reader of the *Gazette* inevitably acquired more information from it than he had been looking for in the first place. What could be more striking than this note, written by Louis XIII in the margin of one of Richelieu's dispatches? 'I think that it would be a very good thing to print this news in the *Gazette* to show everyone that it is they who are attacking us.'*

Like his minister, the king realised the importance of public opinion and was appealing to it.

Paris was also being transformed before the eyes of a generation which had known her as the mediaeval city she had been in the days of the League. This is not to say that the capital suddenly lost its mediaeval appearance or inconvenient characteristics. Throughout the seventeenth century the streets of Paris were to remain uncleansed of their accumulation of mud and filth. The rudimentary scavenging service barely skimmed the surface of the mire every morning, and day by day it was replenished by the droppings of horses, mules and donkeys, the discharge

---

* Avenel, Vol. IV, p. 610. Richelieu to the king, 20 September 1634. The answers in the margin and at the end are in the king's handwriting. The king was referring to the arrest near Leucate on French territory of Don Juan de Menesses, the governor of Perpignan, who was attempting to reconnoitre by night the roads and defences in the vicinity. (V.L.T.)

of household slops and the overflow from latrines emptying into the gutters. Some overcrowded quarters in the centre of Paris—that is to say the Île de la Cité and the area around the Hôtel de Ville up to the Châtelet,[33] the Quartier de Saint-Germain-l'Auxerrois and, on the Left Bank, the Place Maubert and the Quartier Saint-Victor, to the east of the Abbey of St Germain-des-Prés[33]—still kept their networks of little dark streets which ran between houses built of cob and stone and topped with high gables. But the building of new districts had begun in the reign of Henry IV. The latter used to enjoy watching the embellishment of his palace with its waterside gallery which followed the course of the Seine extending in the direction of the Tuileries. The river formed a gap that admitted light and good clean air as it flowed through the dark city.

A new bridge between the rue Dauphine and the water-pump known as the Samaritaine[34] connected the two banks of the river and straddled the tip of the Cité. No houses were built upon it. Its principal ornament was to be the statue of Henry IV mounted on a bronze horse.[34] Close by, the light and airy Place Dauphine[35] opened out between handsome brick mansions ornamented with stone, while in the Quartier du Marais[36] not far from the rue Saint-Antoine another and far more spacious square, the Place Royale, was becoming the meeting place for elegant society and the scene of open-air entertainments such as tilts, jousts and tourneys. Building went on steadily there during Louis XIII's reign. The new houses surrounding the Place Royale aroused the admiration of foreigners, their magnificence emphasising their dissimilarity from the tottering, ramshackle buildings in the old quarters of the city. The bright colours of the façades, the pleasing contrast between the red bricks, the white stone beading and the dark blue slates of the roofs, the tall windows giving access to the light, the majestic appearance of the porches, whose surfaces were decorated with reliefs, gave these houses the air of small palaces inhabited by aristocrats and members of the bourgeoisie.[37]

Marie de Medici, who was endowed with pensions and perquisites [*prébendes*] on such a scale that she was as rich as all three previous queen dowagers combined, had desired a residence where she would be able to display to the full the pomp and splendour appertaining to her station. She instructed Salomon de Brosse to build her a palace in the Italian style. The site chosen was an elevation on the Left Bank, a short distance from the university quarter and on the outskirts of the town, so that one could keep in touch with the latter while at the same time enjoying the fresh air and open spaces of the neighbouring countryside. This palace was the Luxembourg. Salomon de Brosse and the French architects of the time turned to Italian architectural treatises for their guide and model. From them they acquired a liking for columns and pilasters which give a triumphal framework to apertures, for applying reliefs to surfaces, for domes or flattened cupolas which serve to crown an edifice with spaciousness and dignity. All these features were incorporated into Marie de Medici's palace. There is something almost sublime about its entrance lodge. At the further end, and on either side of a spacious court-yard where the coaches used to turn, annulated columns and pilasters rose to the height of the three storeys of the palace and its wings; the lines of windows formed a balance which gave an impression of solemn harmony. Rubens was called upon to undertake the decoration of the galleries. In a series of animated compositions steeped in warm golden light the master of baroque painting commemorated allegorically the main events in the queen mother's life. The garden contained a charming fountain and a grotto, also triumphal in style and adorned with a pediment and armorial bearings. How often in her ill-contrived and unfortunate exile the old queen must have pined for the Parisian palace that had been built for her—one of the fairest in Europe!

At the Louvre extensive alterations were in progress, and at the end of the reign Sublet de Noyers, the Superintendent of Fine Arts, recalled Poussin from Italy to decorate the state rooms of the palace.[38] During this time Richelieu purchased a whole quarter of Paris adjacent to the rue Saint-Honoré and arranged for the old houses with which it was crowded to be pulled down. Richelieu's architect, Jacques Lemercier, built on this site the Palais Cardinal, now known as the Palais Royal. Adjoining it was a sumptuous playhouse with a trompe-l'œil ceiling by Le Maire and two tiers of superimposed balconies with gleaming balusters of gold.[39]

New churches were springing up; old churches were being given new façades. In the rue Saint-Antoine the Jesuit architects Martellange and Derand built a church for the society's use which, like the Gesù in Rome, had no side-aisles.[40] The intersection of nave and transepts was crowned by a dome, and they endowed their church with a magnificent three-storeyed façade whose solemnity was enlivened by the felicitous grouping of its columns, volutes and scrolls. It is akin to the façades built by della Porta in Rome, but has an even greater affinity with the façade of Saint-Gervais—the work of Salomon de Brosse or Métezeau.

As rector of the Sorbonne, Richelieu was anxious to beautify the old college and ordered Lemercier to build a church whose spacious cupola, crowned by a lantern with its cross aloft in the sky, was to remind everyone of the cardinal who lay buried beneath the dome. In contrast the graceful dome of the Chapel of the Visitation suggested a bud that was about to open. The chapel was situated in the rue Sainte-Antoine only a short distance from where the Jesuit church stood in all its noble splendour. In designing it the architect, François Mansart, had taken as his model that great circular building, the Roman Pantheon; but he had reduced it to modest proportions, making it more suited to prayer and meditation by the sisters of the order whose name the chapel bore.

Was this a new style of architecture? Contemporaries did not give it a name; throughout the seventeenth century whatever was built was merely said to be in a modern style. Nowadays we often pursue our quest for labels and definitions too far, and in this case it is not easy to find the right one. Some have been tempted to use the term 'Jesuit style' (often in a slightly derogatory sense) when speaking of the churches of the period, and to refer to the palaces as 'in the classical style'. Others, because it is a style that always retains an original and fanciful character, call it 'baroque'. But do these adjectives really have much value? Instead let us try to apprehend the type of art and the underlying artistic purpose that corresponded with the tastes and way of life of the French people around 1630. It is no longer the art of the Renaissance, although still largely inspired by Italy. Yet it is not as austere as the first architectural creations of the Counter-Reformation in Rome, any more than it is in keeping with the sumptuous magnificence of the Rome of Urban VIII, which prepared the way for the dazzling display under Innocent X and Alexander VII, when Rome became truly wedded to the baroque. French architecture of the 1630s tries to follow the dictates of order and clarity, and represents a blend between logic and a fondness for the sublime which evolves with apparent smoothness (for we forget the quarrels between rival schools) into the supreme majesty of the French classical style. But as yet France's architects produced nothing as grandiose or imperial as was to be built under Louis XIV. The style of Richelieu's day is somehow more measured, more graceful perhaps. It seems to represent a pause before embarking on a style which is more blatantly categorical. In a very real sense it is an offshoot of French Gothic. For the old forms and traditional spirit still commanded allegiance; was not the cathedral at Orleans completed in the Gothic style at this time?

To think of the Paris of the 1630s is to conjure up a picture of a city with many of its quarters gutted and bristling with scaffolding; there is an air of bustle and the continual sound of saws and hammers. Louis XIII's capital must often have looked like a building yard, with men everywhere feverishly at work—much like the Paris of Napoleon III in the last century, when it was being rebuilt in accordance with the plans of Haussmann and Viollet-le-Duc.

But it was not only at Paris that building was going on. The cardinal's *duché-pairie* in Poitou had to be provided with a residence worthy of him. At Richelieu a regularly laid out town came into being beside a château, and gardens began to take shape although they remained incomplete at the time of the cardinal's death.* When Gaston of Orleans settled in Blois after his departure from Lorraine—later we will see what happened to him in the interval—he decided to pull down the existing château in the Renaissance style and to replace it with an airy and well-proportioned palace. The only wing that was actually built certainly deserves admiration; but today the visitor cannot but regret that the price that had to be paid for the construction of this graceful building was the needless destruction of other things of beauty. Finally, let us not forget some buildings of a different kind—those constructed at Brouage to compensate for the demolition of La Rochelle and of many other fortifications whose destruction was accepted as being in the interests of the State and of the realm's internal security.

The painting of the period reflects a wide variety of inspiration and taste, ranging between the two extremes of Rubens, with his baroque exuberance, and Poussin, the presiding genius of the classical school.[41] Between these two poles stand Simon Vouet, a baroque painter of Italian inspiration, and Philippe de Champaigne, whose unforgettable portrait of the cardinal seems the very embodiment of absolute monarchy. In the provinces, where the Gothic tradition was still alive, painting was characterised by a grave and simple realism, as can be seen from the pictures of Tassel, Robert Tournier, and that astonishing artist from Lorraine, Georges de la Tour, whose studies of illuminations by candle-light endow it with a beauty as great as the light from the stars. In the Faubourg Saint-Germain artists from the Netherlands formed a French school which painted realistic pictures of everyday life. Baugin and Linard belonged to this school, but the greatest of them all was to be Louis le Nain. Other masterpieces of this period are the etchings or en-

* Richelieu's building activities in Paris and Poitou remind us of the transformations for which Wallenstein was responsible in Prague at about this time. He had an old quarter of the town completely demolished in order to make room for a palace built for him by the Italian architect della Spezza. [On this subject see chapter 9 of Professor Tapié's book, *The Age of Grandeur.*] This predilection for florid architecture, this desire to live in a sumptuous setting is a distinctive characteristic of seventeenth century Europe and is one of those features of its civilisation which may be described as baroque. (V.L.T.)

gravings of Abraham Bosse, Jacques de Bellange and Callot. They are as eloquent a commentary on the society of their day as contemporary manuscripts, for the subjects they depict range from the dandies who haunted the gallery of the palace to hairy peasants and plundering soldiery, victims and perpetrators of the horrors of war.[42]

Sculpture, on the other hand, tended to cling to a single style. It adhered to the Renaissance tradition, even when Simon Guillain tried to achieve perfect accuracy in his statue of Louis XIII, which only hints at a lordly gesture and omits any attribute of royal majesty. This is not the place to discuss the religious iconography of the period, which is still regrettably overlooked, although there are innumerable churches with a reredos or an altar dating from this time. The art of Louis XIII's reign is both varied and charming in all its different aspects, and provides yet further evidence of the diversity of the France of his day.

During the past fifteen years the reform movement within the Catholic Church had continued to make headway. It was encouraged by the government, partly no doubt on grounds of general policy but even more so because the men who actually governed the country—the king, Richelieu and Marillac—were earnest Christians who wanted heretics to be converted and desired to see an improvement in moral standards. In their eyes the success that had attended their projects was a mark of divine protection. They welcomed the impression made on public opinion by the capture of La Rochelle and by the king's sudden recovery from his illness at Lyons in 1630. We have already mentioned the dedication of a church to Our Lady of Victories [in thanksgiving for the first of these events, the second gave rise to an action that was inspired by similar motives] after a considerable delay in issuing letters patent authorising the foundation of a new establishment [*institut*] for nuns which was to be dedicated to the adoration of the Blessed Sacrament, Marillac made up his mind to do so, 'being moved thereto by God in gratitude for the king's recovery, which His Majesty himself ascribed to the Blessed Sacrament'.[43]

Nothing could be further from the truth, however, than to suppose that the realm had been definitely won back to the Faith and to sound moral principles, or to imagine that now that the political power of the Huguenots had been destroyed the government was actively engaged in suppressing heresy. A return to religious unity did, it is true, form part of Richelieu's programme for internal reform; but this programme had been abandoned for reasons of general policy. More than once the cardinal felt obliged to restrain Marillac's eagerness to obtain conversions, and among the many factors that contributed to their estrangement we may include the cautious attitude of the one as opposed to the zealous enthusiasm of the other. For example Marillac advised taking a series of harsh but legal measures against the Protestants of Dauphiné. Richelieu replied as follows: 'All these proposals seem to me excellent, but I am not sure whether they are opportune in the light of existing circumstances. I am afraid that these new provisions, however praiseworthy their intent, will not help to consolidate the peace prevailing in Dauphiné to which the minds of the population are now affected; nor am I sure whether it is wise to take this step at a time when we are engaged in war outside the realm.'[44]

These words, written in 1630, reveal an attitude to which the cardinal consistently adhered right up to the end of his ministry and which assured the Protestants of a relative degree of toleration. In consequence, although we who look back from a distance are apt to consider the reign of Louis XIII a golden age of French Catholicism (as indeed it was), to the contemporary *dévot* or zealous Catholic it could well have seemed a disorderly and godless era, with a government that was over-lenient to the Huguenots and almost accommodating in its attitude towards heresy and irreligion. To him Richelieu's government seemed dangerously preoccupied with temporal affairs, while its interest in spiritual matters was no more than lukewarm. Admittedly there were a number of police regulations in existence which are sufficiently linked to their day and age for us to find them surprising. Thus butchers' shops had to be closed during Advent and Lent, blasphemy and duels were forbidden and the Church's Feasts of Obligation were a public event. But to the *dévots* it seemed that to set a bad example had become the general rule. Protestants had the right during periods of abstinence to buy meat at the butchers' shops in Charenton.[45] Unbelievers made their purchases after nightfall at the back of a shop belonging to some butcher or tripe-seller who appreciated their custom as a slice of good luck. As for blasphemy, it was the general practice. The streets echoed with swear-words and those who were supposed to enforce the relevant edicts were the first to infringe them.* In addition to profanity, licentious and coarse behaviour was a regular feature of urban life and even of life at Court. Paris

---

* Not to mention those who were supposed to set an example! When Richelieu anxiously enquired whther Monsieur had given up swearing, Chavigny replied that there was a distinct improvement for now he only did so when he lost his temper. Avenel, Vol. v, pp. 14–15, May 1635. (V.L.T.)

swarmed with every kind of rascal. At one end of the scale there were the black sheep of respectable families—a type of person with whom the duke of Orleans used to consort when so inclined; at the other there were the common thieves, whom the watch tried in vain to curb and who made the streets singularly unsafe after nightfall.[46] Gambling dens and bawdy houses were numerous. Buffoons and tumblers paraded their obscenities before passers-by of all ages. Pornographic literature was stealthily passed from hand to hand. Behaviour in provincial towns was possibly a little less unbridled but in the countryside degenerated into brutish licentiousness and superstition.

To those who were burning to win souls the moral reformation that remained to be accomplished seemed an enormous undertaking. On several occasions St Vincent de Paul allows his discouragement to show through his correspondence. If he organised missions to distant lands with earnest hopes of their success, it was because he was a prey to immeasurable anxiety about the future of France and Europe for all their Christian heritage. To give impulse to new Christian communities in outlandish countries was a kind of *quid pro quo*.

Thus even amongst the apostles of a Catholic revival there was no unity of purpose. And yet the movement or rather the forward surge that we identified at the beginning of the reign did not come to a standstill. New souls felt the touch of Divine Grace and all through these years continued to respond to the infectious example set by the first reformers. The period has been described as an age of saints. This is an obvious exaggeration—the result of over-estimating what was achieved and also of a failure to realise that Christian perfection is far too difficult to attain for saintliness to be symptomatic of a whole cycle of years or of a whole society. But that there was at this time an accession of the Supernatural and for certain privileged persons a sense of God's presence which at times assumed concrete form and became as it were tangible, that there was a continual outpouring of Divine Grace: these are facts which the most dispassionate critic cannot fail to recognise. Propagandists, proselytisers, reformers, all of them either received a mysterious call or else discerned in some accident of circumstance the signs that prescribed their course of action.

Spiritually these people were giants; but they were not perfect. The Church has not seen fit to canonise all of them but each of them knew what it was for the soul to be caught up into another world. Let us take some examples.

A sermon preached by a Capuchin—incidentally a man of rather dubious character—had such an effect on Jacqueline Arnauld, the youthful abbess of Port-Royal otherwise known as Mère Angélique, that it made her decide to restore strict observance of the [Cistercian] rule within her convent: God acts by whatever means He chooses. On 8 September 1615, the Feast of the Nativity of the Virgin, during Vespers at Saint-Merry, her mother, Mme Arnauld, felt herself transported in spirit into the presence of Our Lord Jesus Christ. In May 1627 the duc de Lévis-Ventadour had a vision and realised that he must devote his life to works of faith. One has only to read the letters of St Vincent de Paul and the papers left by Mère Angélique, Bérulle or Saint-Cyran to perceive throughout the same scrupulous readiness to acknowledge and obey God's will, and the astonishing clarity of judgement that enables someone to relinquish a task undertaken thoughtlessly out of vanity, and accept its failure as a favour from Heaven.

So the work went on. Mère Angélique not only disciplined Port-Royal but also succeeded in introducing reform into other religious houses, at Maubuisson, at Gif, and at Tart in Burgundy. She helped to found an order of nuns dedicated to Divine Adoration whose essential function was to be the worship of the Blessed Sacrament.* On meeting with some hostility to her plans for reform from the abbots of Cîteaux, she tried to place her convents more directly under the diocesan authority of bishops who were better able to understand the reasons for, and nature of, her actions.

The task that this woman of quality was called upon to assume was a formidable one. It involved restoring the common ownership of goods and reviving the system of election, for the sake of which she resigned her position as abbess and became an ordinary nun: it necessitated banishing family influences from the cloister and ensuring that only those whose vocation had been tested were allowed to take vows: it required the introduction of poverty and simplicity everywhere. This task Mère Angélique proceeded to carry out, first at Port-Royal-aux-Champs and then at Paris, where her convent of Cistercian nuns was established from 1625 onwards. She received the help of her parents and their large family, which was to produce another great abbess in her younger sister Mère Agnès, as well as several nuns. After them came her youngest brother, the theologian; destined for a stormy career, he was one day to be known as 'the great Arnauld', and as the author of *De la fréquente Communion*.†

* See p. 280 above and n. 43.

† Antoine Arnauld 1612–94.

Although she had a mistrust of 'the worm of vanity' that was inherent in 'love of noble lineage', Mère Angélique entertained relations with the aristocracy—namely the Longuevilles, who were related to the king, and the Gondi de Retz, who belonged to the same family as the archbishop of Paris.* She was acquainted with Mme de Ligny, the pious sister of Séguier, the future chancellor. By her influence and example she helped not only to impart more fervour to the spiritual life of her day but also to impress upon it certain features which were to leave their mark on French Catholicism.

For Mère Angélique the world and the kingdom of God were virtually incompatible. She admired Mme de Ligny for saying: 'How I pity my brother! I pray God that he be driven from Court, for I know not how it be possible otherwise for him to be saved.'† Although she waged war on over-scrupulousness, Mère Angélique denied herself the sacraments and approved of others doing so, especially in the case of the Eucharist; nevertheless she encouraged the spread of sacramental worship. In the abbé de Saint-Cyran she found a spiritual director after her own heart. To his mind it was imperative to avoid all social intercourse in order to lead a truly religious life, for religious life and secular life were things apart.

Such was the heroically Christian spirit of the community of Port-Royal which by about the middle of the reign was in process of achieving complete self-mastery. This was not yet Jansenism; indeed the history of Jansenism scarcely belongs to Louis XIII's reign except for its earliest stages and the imprisonment of Saint-Cyran in 1638 on Father Joseph's advice. But the essence was already there before the name—the austere, grim religion and the indestructible virtues which the Jansenist movement was to welcome, propagate and defend.

Richelieu was by no means unsympathetic to these attempts at reform, provided that reversion to strict observance of the monastic rule was not used as an excuse for criticising the active life or for condemning those who by virtue of their calling continued to live in the world and were obliged to work out their salvation in it. His pluralism has been denounced as scandalous, and it is certainly difficult to feel altogether happy about the increase in his wealth which aroused such indignation

* The see of Paris was elevated to an archbishopric in 1622. (V.L.T.)

† One has only to think of the many temptations to which a man in high office can be exposed in any age—temptations that threaten his honesty, integrity, sense of justice, impartiality and moral standards—to find Madame de Ligny's attitude a great deal less amusing or exaggerated than it may at first appear. (V.L.T.)

amongst his contemporaries. Yet there is nothing to disprove the possibility that in seeking to secure the generalship of the great orders for himself Richelieu was thinking of the urgent need to put a stop to the no less scandalous quarrels that were breaking out at this time between conservatives and over-zealous progressives.* May he not have been trying to find a way of imposing his arbitration on both sides rather with a view to encouraging the correction of past abuses? At all events Father Valerio, the Visitor of the Carmelites, wrote to Rome in 1639: 'The cardinal is very devout and uses the Church's wealth to good purpose in erecting sacred buildings and in giving alms. His influence conduces to God's service among the orders of which he is general as well as in the churches of France.'[47]

The demands of monastic life were such as to exclude a vast field of activity, which thus lay open to other ardent spirits. St Vincent de Paul thought of 'the poor people (who) are incurring damnation from ignorance of the things necessary to salvation and for want of confessing their sins'. 'If His Holiness only knew of this deficiency,' he wrote in 1631, 'he would have no rest till he had done his utmost to set it to rights.' St Vincent de Paul wanted to form a congregation of missionary priests who were to go and preach in the countryside, avoiding the towns which were provided with sufficient clergy; they were to subordinate themselves to the local *curé* during the time that the mission was functioning in his parish. The congregation, which had originally taken up its residence at the Collège des Bons-Enfants, established itself permanently at the Priory of Saint-Lazare.[48] From this new centre the beams of St Vincent de Paul's evangelising movement radiated in all directions. He concentrated on educating and training the clergy so that they in their turn could preach and give spiritual leadership to the people.

At the retreats conducted for ordinands and at the Tuesday Conferences—which from 1633 onwards were regularly attended by parish priests, deacons and sub-deacons [*jeunes clercs*], as well as by a large number of clergy who were passing through Paris[49]—St Vincent de Paul used therefore to spend comparatively little time on teaching doctrine and far more on instructing his audience how to preach clearly and in a way that was suited to the occasion. He constantly insisted on the need for preaching to be effective. 'How did the apostles preach? In language that was plain, homely and simple. That is how we must preach. We

---

* Richelieu was elected abbot of Cîteaux in 1636. A collection of texts concerning the strictness with which Cistercians observed their rule has been published by Father Zakar and some of them can be used to support this theory. (V.L.T.).

must speak in an ordinary way, plainly and in simple homely terms so that everyone can understand and reap the benefit.'

In Mgr. Calvet's words, he gathered into his hands 'a sheaf of the most varied activities'. The material and moral poverty of the people touched him to the heart. He felt called upon to relieve their distress, both to do honour to Christ who was present among the sick and the poor, and because of his concern for their souls, which needed strengthening amidst their sufferings and misery. He managed to find volunteers willing to do charitable work on a full-time or part-time basis. Among the Parisian bourgeoisie he secured the help of a widow, Mlle Le Gras.* Such people always seem to come from the same milieu, for this lady, known to history as Sainte Louise de Marillac, was the niece of the keeper of the seals. At the time she was a sick and deeply worried woman who lived in the Quartier de Saint-Nicolas-du-Chardonnet, a parish which thanks to Froger and Bourdoise had acquired a reputation for piety. Vincent de Paul induced her to lead a life of regular devotional simplicity that was free from scrupulosity; for example in a letter written in April 1631 he points out that to refrain from receiving Communion because of interior difficulties is to give a handle to the Devil, the enemy of Holy Communion. With her he organised the charitable associations that were copied in the provinces. Around Louise de Marillac there gathered a group of women belonging to bourgeois families connected with the sovereign courts [*bourgeoisie parlementaire*]—women who had the sterling virtues of their class and felt the need to give practical expression to their faith: Mme la Présidente Goussaut, Mlle du Fay, Mlle Pollalion, Mme Séguier. These ladies, who were joined by the duchess of Aiguillon, busied themselves in visiting, distributing alms and comforting and caring for the sick at the Hôtel-Dieu. Vincent de Paul provided them with assistants in the shape of girls of town or country background on whom he imposed a very simple rule of life.[50] The latter were not nuns but sisters living in the world,† who were attached to a parish and in theory not connected with any other church; instead of devoting their lives to prayer they tried to acquire holiness by serving the poor.

At the same time Vincent de Paul was busy recruiting and training priests for foreign missions in North Africa, where he had himself been a

---

* Women who belonged to the bourgeoisie bore the title Mademoiselle; only those who were of noble status or who had married a man who was an *officier* had the right to be styled Madame. (V.L.T.)

† *Ce furent des religieuses dans le siècle.* The term 'religious' then signified enclosed nuns who did not leave the cloister.

captive, and in countries where Richelieu's trading companies had secured a foothold. He was also active in encouraging the creation of diocesan seminaries. Year by year the part that he played and the scope of his activity grew steadily larger. His appeals for help reached the ears of the great men of the day: the king, the two queens and the cardinal all came to know him. This man of the people accustomed to dealing with the country folk he loved so well, threaded his way between all sorts of political factions of whose rivalries he was well aware, and between classes which were mutually hostile. The respect with which he treated those in authority was untinged by flattery or fear. He was not a social reformer, nor did he aspire to become one; but although he was not yet the eminent political and national figure that he was to become during the Fronde, he already occupied a very important place in the country in Richelieu's day. He instilled into society around him the charity, justice and orderliness that it so sorely needed. He alleviated the personal misery of countless individuals, saved or prolonged lives, raised the standard of the élite, instructed, encouraged and comforted the common people and accomplished so many and such different things that his astonishingly racy and stimulating personality seems to rise above the contradictions of his age.

However the name of Vincent de Paul must not be allowed to overshadow all others. Bérulle had died in 1629; but despite this the French Oratory, which continued to follow the paths mapped out by its founder, remained a flourishing organisation. This was the great period of Jean Eudes's missionary activity. Congregations in both Paris and the provinces were converted by his sermons and used to listen spellbound to his preaching. The work that he was eager to accomplish both for himself and for others was so urgent and called for such sacrifices that the need for intercession seemed greater. Eudes besought the faithful to call upon the Blessed Virgin to help them, to unite their hearts to those of Jesus and Mary. He was, it has been said, a Marian theologian in an age when devotion to the Virgin was beginning to revive, accompanied by sufficiently sound doctrine to prevent the return of the confused superstitions of earlier days.

But the inescapable need remained what it had always been—an educated body of clergy with exemplary standards of behaviour. Ignorance and routine were still the main obstacles to religious reform in France, and these apostles of reform were in no position to eliminate them in every part of the realm. The education of the priesthood and the organisation of seminaries were immense undertakings. Alain de Solminihac, the saintly bishop of Cahors, did not succeed in turning his seminary into a permanent institution. A large number of similar projects met with failure, and for this reason Jean Eudes was soon to leave the Oratory in order to found a congregation specially intended for the training of candidates for the priesthood. Nor was it until the end of the reign that Jean-Jacques Olier, after several unsuccessful attempts, took up his residence in the parish of Saint-Sulpice, then on the outskirts of Paris, where he was later to found an inter-diocesan seminary that was to become one of the most radiant centres of French Catholicism.[51]

I would have liked to pause here to draw a map showing the state of religion in France in the middle of Louis XIII's reign; but there are too many details that we still do not know. Also the religious situation is too fluid; positions shift from year to year, and as one focal point of the reform movement comes to life another dies out. Moreover some parts of France which are now considered strongholds of the Catholic tradition were not then imbued with a devotion to the Faith. Brittany and the present-day Vendée are cases in point. It was during this period that Father Maunoir and Michel le Nobletz were carrying out their missionary work in Brittany, while Grignion de Montfort did not reach the Vendée until the eighteenth century.[52] Alternatively, other areas which might equally be described as staunchly Catholic, such as Alsace and [the French province of] Flanders did not yet form part of the realm.

Nevertheless, it was at this time that the France of the ancien régime became pronouncedly Christian, and this was due to men and women who were Louis XIII's subjects and Richelieu's contemporaries. The difficulties with which they had to contend may best be gauged by remembering the errors into which certain over-zealous spirits fell and the spiritual confusion in which others were floundering.

The unanimous respect that has surrounded St Vincent de Paul's memory up to our own day has not been extended to another project somewhat similar to his own—at least in its purpose. The duc de Lévis-Ventadour, a great noble who had taken part in the wars against the Protestants in Languedoc, had the idea of founding a company whose principal aim would be 'within the general spiritual compass of the Church to do as much good as possible and to avert as much evil as possible at any time, in all places and with respect to all persons'. Worship of the Blessed Sacrament, the culminating point of Catholic doctrine, which heretics challenged and free-thinkers ridiculed or despised, was to serve as the rallying point for all the new society's adherents; they were to bring help to every case of distress of which they came to hear, to find out about any scandalous behaviour and to ensure that action was taken to correct it.

Priests who proved unequal to their pastoral duties, monasteries and convents with lax standards, heretics and free-thinkers of all kinds were to be the particular objects of the society's attention; as Raoul Allier has said, its members were expected to bring pressure to bear simultaneously on the judiciary, the administration and the court. Ventadour and his advisers, several of whom were monks or bishops, were convinced that their association would only be powerful and effective if it operated secretly. Indeed there were grounds for fearing that a society whose proposed field of activity was so large and ill-defined as to amount to a claim to control and govern everything would meet with opposition from more than one quarter: from the bishops, who were extremely jealous of their authority and for this reason perpetually at loggerheads with the religious orders because of the latter's dependence on Rome; from the magistracy and office-holders, who were only accountable to the king and his ministers; and finally from the government itself.

However it was also extremely difficult to set up such an organisation all over the country without at least the tacit sympathy of those in authority to protect its freedom from interference. Louis XIII was given the necessary information by his confessor, Father Suffren, and approved the secret assemblies held by the Company of the Blessed Sacrament 'for the glory of God, the relief of the poor and the good of His Majesty's estate; provided that one of the Company's members known unto him shall acquaint His Majesty from time to time with the most weighty of their proceedings at the said assemblies'. The king invited Jean François de Gondi, the archbishop of Paris, to bless the company but the archbishop was unwilling to commit himself at this stage. Urban VIII, who received a similar invitation, bestowed a general blessing such as was appropriate for an ordinary association devoted to pious activities. With its prestige vaguely enhanced by these signs of patronage, the society began to grow. It was directed by a presiding committee, but neither the Parisian nor the provincial associations knew who its members were. Among those who belonged to the Company were court nobility, high-ranking magistrates, officers in the administration, secular priests and bishops; but regular clergy were not admitted because of the vow of obedience that they had taken to the superior of their order. Vincent de Paul was a member from 1635 onwards. During Louis XIII's reign the Company certainly gave its support to charitable works, although it is impossible to identify everything that it initiated or to assess the results of its activities. But it enmeshed the whole realm in an inquisitorial network and thus, after an existence lasting for a number of years, it eventually became an object of suspicion. Its secrets were exposed and the memory that it left behind was an odious one.[53]

Beneath the apparent revival of active loyalty to the Church there remained many irreconcilables—people who found even less satisfaction in the rigours of Protestantism than they found in the Catholic Church. In reality Protestantism was on the wane. It still had some strongholds in certain areas but it no longer exercised any attraction. In the jostle of fashionable and urban life it was not unusual for the Reformed Church to lose some of its supporters; far removed as they were from their traditional bases, they were like lost children—lost in a seething mass of Catholics who now had the upper hand. Catholic clergy were more numerous and better informed and Catholic religious writers, bishops and preachers included men of outstanding talent, while in the monasteries and convents and among the Catholic laity there were men and women who were bold and zealous proselytisers. However this is not to deny that many an ostensible victory for Catholicism amounted to no more than 'occasional conformity'*—to use a modern expression. In particular there was still quite a strong trend towards free-thinking [*libertinage*]; freedom of morals existed too of course, but that is to be found in every age.

In literary circles and among fashionable society there existed secret sects whose members were encouraged to repudiate religion and the established social order, to seek happiness in the world's pleasures and in surrendering to Nature—quite contrary to the ideal that was to be proclaimed in the stanzas of *Polyeucte*.[54] Their objects and opinions are openly expressed or hinted at in certain contemporary works.

After a narrow escape from being burnt for his opinions, Théophile de Viau died prematurely in 1626. With him there disappeared an example of the amatory libertine referred to above.† From 1630 onwards a different kind of free-thinking emerges, to which Pintard, the latest historian to deal with the subject, has given the name 'scholarly scepticism'.‡ Humanists, mathematicians and philosophers began to meet regularly at each other's homes or at the house of some wealthy patron to discuss their researches and exchange ideas. The 'Académie putéane' which used to meet at the house of the brothers Dupuy (both of them historiogra-

* *conformisme saisonnier.*

† *Théophile de Viau . . . l'un des représentants de ce libertinage galant.*

‡ *Libertinage érudit.*

phers) is a case in point.* Were such people free-thinkers in the modern sense of the word? Yes, in so far as they were bent on preserving their independence of judgement instead of merely kow-towing to Christian doctrine, which incidentally they did not study deeply; yes again, to the extent that they made a point of cultivating the pagan philosophers of Antiquity, while some of them at least set out to study Nature in a spirit of inquiry that reflected a desire for explanations which the Churches did not provide. Humanists and philosophers—that was what they claimed to be. Owing to the contacts which they formed abroad through travel or correspondence (for example with Dutch and German writers and with rationalists at the University of Padua), they came under a wide range of different influences. Membership of the group was equally varied, including as it did lukewarm Catholics like Gaffarel, Protestants with advanced views like Diodati and Prioleau, and champions of pagan humanism like La Mothe le Vayer, the author of *Dialogues faits à l'Imitation des Anciens* (1630–1) and an anti-rationalist sceptic who went to considerable trouble to keep up the appearance of being a Christian. Yet another member was Gabriel Naudé, who was librarian to a series of cardinals. Naudé had imbibed Machiavelli's views whilst residing in Italy, and aimed at offering rational explanations for facts which had hitherto been regarded as supernatural.[55]

These humanists dreaded the possibility of falling foul of the Sorbonne and the Parlement. They were careful to avoid breaking with Church doctrine, and in any case their fluctuating beliefs and deeply rooted scepticism made them disinclined to resort to negation as a weapon against it. But some of their disciples were more daring, and cultivated a scepticism which may be described as flamboyant and which expressed itself in parody or burlesque. Amongst them frolicked that ingenious and eccentric figure, Cyrano de Bergerac.† Meanwhile their friend, the Provençal Gassendi, waged open war on Aristotle and was preparing to enter the lists against Descartes. To the arguments of reason Gassendi opposed a philosophy of the senses, but his main achievement was to formulate a subtle compromise, paradoxical though it may seem, between Christianity and the ethics of Epicurus.

The fact that none of this intellectual activity gave rise to scandal probably goes to show that it was confined to small circles which were themselves under the aegis of people who wielded considerable influence. It

* The Latinised version of the name Dupuy was Puteanus.

† *Ils ont des disciples plus hardis, dans un libertinage qu'on pourrait dire flamboyant, cette bohème des burlesques où s'ébat l'ingénieux et fantasque Cyrano de Bergerac.*

also suggests that public opinion was for the most part unaware of these scholarly pastimes.

On the other hand a far more rudimentary, indeed primitive, form of belief was to be found all over the realm and especially in country districts: the belief in witchcraft and magic. Although the Catholic authorities waged war on these beliefs as superstition, many people were incapable of distinguishing between the various aspects of the supernatural. In every unfavourable manifestation of Nature, in every mischance that befell themselves or their families, they saw the Devil's handiwork. He was everywhere, he assumed a variety of forms and he was greatly to be feared. He might act himself or he might use as his instruments some unhappy creatures whom he had tracked down when they were troubled or in distress. He might answer the summons of those who wished to surrender themselves to him—those who, departing from the path of virtue and good order, were plunging into the murky underworld of witchcraft. E. Delcambre has recently published a book on the concept of sorcery in Lorraine in the sixteenth and seventeenth centuries which is based on official records of trials for witchcraft preserved in the archives.[56] It appears that the miseries inflicted on Lorraine by the constant ravages of war encouraged outbreaks of witchcraft there. But phenomena of the same kind were common to the whole realm. They either went on continually but underground, or else they occurred in sudden and intense outbursts. These witches' sabbaths [*manifestations qu'on attribuait au Malin*] were a hotch-potch of different elements—relics of primitive spirit worship, pagan rites which still persisted tenaciously and were blended with distortions or parodies of Christian rites, promptings of individuals and in some cases mental derangement. It is particularly interesting to note that there was a general consensus of opinion among both judges and accused as to the reality and satanic origin of the acts committed. Wizards and witches were tortured to force them to disclose all their actions and give details of their pact with the Devil; no one had the slightest doubt that it was all horrifyingly true.

The authorities of the Church had great difficulty in pointing out to the clergy the dividing line between Christian doctrine and magic in all its countless manifestations. Priests were called upon to exorcise evil spirits, but many of them used to flirt with satanic mysteries. This partly explains the trial of Urbain Grandier, a *curé* of Loudun—a trial for which Richelieu has been held responsible.

Urbain Grandier held the living of Saint-Pierre and a canon's stall at the collegiate church of Sainte-Croix.* He was in the prime of life and a good-looking, intelligent and learned man. Clerical celibacy weighed heavily upon him. He had written a serious treatise attacking it in principle; and in practice he allowed himself liberties which involved him in difficulties with his parishioners and his bishop. By dint of appealing to the Parlement of Paris and his archbishop, he managed to escape unscathed from several suits brought against him in lay and ecclesiastical courts; but the very fact that he was lucky appeared suspicious.

In the meantime a rumour began to spread that some of the sisters at the Ursuline Convent in Loudun were possessed by devils. The Mother Superior, Mme de Belcier, was reported to be one of the victims and so was Mme de Razilly, a nun who belonged to a family which was closely connected with Richelieu's own. Grandier had nothing to do with this convent, but its spiritual director, Canon Mignon, was one of his enemies. It was probably he who was the first to form suspicions. During the exorcisms the nuns were cross-examined, and named the curé of Saint-Pierre as the author of the evil spells cast upon them. In so doing they were yielding either to suggestions that had been put to them or to the workings of their own imaginations after pieces of malicious gossip had reached their ears.

Meanwhile Richelieu had sent a royal commissioner to Loudun to supervise the demolition of the château, choosing for the purpose a magistrate whom he regarded as loyal. The latter was a *conseiller d'Etat* named Laubardemont. He arrived to find the town and district in a turmoil over the affair of the possessed women, and he informed the court accordingly. He was immediately instructed to arrest Grandier and institute proceedings against him. Soon even more peremptory orders were issued by Séguier, the new keeper of the seals: the king commanded that a strict inquiry be made into all the misdeeds with which the curé had been charged and a commission was to be set up to judge the case. While this was going on the *Chambre de l'Arsenal* [57] at Paris was condemning to death another priest, named Bouchard, who had been found guilty of practising magic. We may therefore allow that the instructions which he received from the keeper of the seals encouraged Laubardemont to pass a similar sentence.

Grandier protested that he was innocent and agreed to exorcise the nuns himself in the presence of the bishop of Poitiers; but he found him-

---

*A collegiate church is endowed for a body of canons, but is not, like a cathedral, the seat of a bishop.

self confronted by women convulsed with hysteria, who abused and provoked him. Despite his firm and reasonable defence he was held responsible for this shocking scene. Finally, on 18 August 1634, he was condemned to death, put to the torture and burnt alive. To the last he asserted that he had nothing to confess, that he had committed no act of sacrilege or sorcery.* With his last remaining strength he implored God's mercy, expressed repentance for his other sins and forgave his enemies.

The case of Urbain Grandier was to remain a notorious episode throughout the centuries. Richelieu's enemies and the Protestants threw the blame on to him, charging him with carrying out a personal vendetta.[58] Whether or not the cardinal believed that the nuns really were possessed has little relevance to history, but it seems probable that in allowing Grandier to be condemned he wished to 'make an example' of him.[59] But that a man could be tracked down with such blatant unfairness so that an example could be made of him, that he could be tortured and burnt alive on the strength of his evil reputation for acts which he had certainly not committed, yet in accordance with what was still the due process of law—all this serves to reveal the mediaeval and arbitrary nature of justice in Richelieu's day. The horror which Grandier's trial and death aroused in public opinion even at the time shows that people already felt that there was no defence for justice such as this. A century later Father Griffet, the historian of Louis XIII's reign, displayed considerable embarrassment at this point in his narrative, which he only circumvented by taking refuge in a lame excuse: 'It is certain', he wrote, 'that the sentence was pronounced on evidence that would not be admitted today, but it was then the custom for all courts of justice to accept such evidence.'[60]

The tragic fate of Urbain Grandier, which was shared by many other innocent victims, did at least have the merit of making men's consciences uneasy and of preparing the way for the advancement of reason and justice.

A contrast between magnificence and dire poverty, between things that were beautiful and things that were infamous—such was the France that

---

* His steadfastness, which moved the crowd, was taken by some as yet another sign of his guilt. It was noticed that he shed no tears. 'His eyes remained dry and hideous as before' wrote Father Tranquille. Note that inability to shed tears was reputedly a consequence of making a pact with the Devil (*cf.* Delcambre, op. cit., vol. ii, p. 265) (V.L.T.).

witnessed the political triumph of Richelieu; and such she was to remain, without marked changes, when called upon both to watch and to play her part in the great ventures to which king and cardinal were increasingly to commit her.

CHAPTER EIGHT

Obedience at Home and War Abroad

IF NO POWER in Europe could henceforth disregard the king of France,* this did not mean that Louis XIII and Richelieu were in a position to control the course of events. For a long time to come the best they could do was to adapt themselves patiently to circumstances. In all probability Richelieu continued to take the view that war between France and Spain was inevitable; but he certainly did not intend to embark upon it yet. He merely sought to prevent a situation from arising in Europe that would offer Spain too many initial advantages: hence his interest in the affairs of the Empire. Over the years the alliance and kinship between the two branches of the house of Austria, far from weakening, had been strengthened by new bonds. The emperor's son Ferdinand III, king of Hungary, had married the Infanta Maria, sister of Anne of Austria and Philip IV of Spain. The latter's minister, the count-duke of Olivares, continued to regard the union of the two courts as fundamental to his policy.

In return Richelieu was bound to oppose the establishment of Austrian hegemony within the Empire. At the very least it was essential to neutralise Germany and foster resistance to the emperor's plans. The cardinal consulted Father Joseph continually on the subject. The Capuchin's incautious behaviour at Regensburg had not tarnished his reputation. He was still the man who knew Germany best, and in his case there was none of that disquieting sympathy for the Habsburgs to which the *dévot* party was always prone—a sympathy that was inspired by religious motives but which was devoid of political insight.

Yet Father Joseph too was endeavouring to protect the Catholics in Germany. He would never have agreed to the conquests made by the Counter-Reformation being sacrificed for the benefit of the Protestants. For all his hostility to the emperor he was benevolently disposed towards the German Catholics, and his most pronounced sympathies remained in favour of Bavaria. He saw that there was a case for making use of Gustavus Adolphus, but he also mistrusted him. He expressed his opinion of the alliance with Sweden in a memorable sentence: 'Such expedients must be used in the same way as poisons: a little acts as an antidote and an

---

* See p. 243 above.

excess is fatal.'* He hoped that the Treaty of Bärwalde, which provided for subsidies and commercial exchanges but was not as yet a formal alliance, would make it possible for Swedish forces to be used against the emperor without giving rise to fresh dangers.

In the event these dangers materialised in the summer of 1631. Thanks to the alliances that he had succeeded in obtaining in north Germany, the king of Sweden was no longer a Protestant crusader advancing at the head of a band of loyal and dedicated subjects to champion the Reformed religion. He had certainly given fresh evidence of his qualities as a soldier, but his army had been swelled by undisciplined and marauding German mercenaries, while his staff included Czech refugees who stubbornly clung to the hope of restoring Frederick, the Winter King, to the Bohemian throne.

Soldiers, generals, politics, all seemed to be caught up in a whirlwind. The people of Germany, victims of every pillaging army and living only in fear for the morrow, were ready to put up with anything. Conditions were turning in favour of violent courses of action pursued by men who were prepared to go to any extreme; the odds were worsening against the patient, temporising, moderate approach preferred by Richelieu.

On 17 September 1631 the Swedish king's cosmopolitan army routed Tilly's Catholic army at Breitenfeld near Leipzig. Tilly decided to fight because he saw that his army was starving, disorganised and on the verge of breaking up. He thought that its only hope lay in risking battle. But the fortunes of war favoured Gustavus Adolphus, and the German historian Ranke was right in saying that Breitenfeld avenged the battle of the White Mountain. Never had the emperor suffered such a defeat since the time when he had restored his hereditary authority over the Habsburg lands,† and made the whole empire conscious of his power. The order that had been established and given its final form by the Edict of Restitution was now directly challenged. Ferdinand II had already sustained a diplomatic setback at Regensburg, but it had not affected the basic position. This time he met with a military disaster and henceforth, as Georges Pagès has observed, 'it was the king of Sweden who called the tune'.

From the electorate of Saxony Gustavus Adolphus could have advanced on the hereditary lands of the house of Habsburg.‡ For reasons

---

* *'Il faut se servir de ces choses ainsi que des venins, dont le peu sert de contrepoison et le trop tue.'*

† *les États patrimoniaux;* ‡*les États héréditaires.* As Professor Tapié points out in his chapter 'The Habsburg Lands 1618–57' in N.C.M.H. iv, these states (which largely consisted

Map 6 Lorraine, Alsace and the Rhineland

that remain obscure, he refrained from doing so; possibly a wise sense of caution was responsible, for by marching on Prague and Vienna without sufficiently securing his rear he would have run the risk of being cut off from the Baltic.[1] In the event, he preferred to turn towards central Germany, leaving the army of his ally the elector of Saxony to make for Bohemia, which it entered without encountering resistance. The Saxon army was commanded by Arnim and accompanied by a large number of Czech exiles who demanded the return of their former estates, harassed the new owners and threatened the monasteries.

The Swedish king himself marched towards Thuringia and Franconia. He occupied in succession Erfurt, a dependency of the archbishop of Mainz, and Würzburg, whose bishop, monks and nuns had already taken refuge in precipitate flight. Then he entered Rothenburg, followed by Aschaffenburg in November. Next the capital of the Empire, Frankfurt-am-Main, opened its gates after vainly pleading its duty to the emperor and begging to be allowed at least neutral status. Crossing the Rhine, the Swedish army penetrated into the archbishopric of Mainz, which was garrisoned by Spanish troops. The latter soon abandoned Oppenheim and also Mainz itself, into which Gustavus made his entry towards the end of December. In the meantime the duke of Lorraine's troops had evacuated Worms and Heilbronn. Everything was melting away before the Swedish advance.

During this time the king of Sweden's allies were active in various other parts of Germany. The landgrave of Hesse-Cassel seized Minden, the dukes of Mecklenburg, who had previously been stripped of their territories by Wallenstein, resumed possession of Rostock and Wismar. Everywhere Gustavus Adolphus declared that he came not as an enemy but as a liberator to rescue Germany from every form of oppression. He made a show of treating monks with courtesy and of saving or sparing the lives of non-combatants; he loudly announced that looting was forbidden. In reality he could no longer maintain discipline in his armies. The country they overran was rich, with well-stocked shops and cultivated fields. They proceeded to sack everything. The churches contained not only art treasures of the German Renaissance but also large numbers of votive altars made of precious materials which owed their existence to the taste for baroque art implanted by the Counter-Reformation. At

---

of territories that form part of the modern state of Austria), belonged to one family and had one suzerain but in several cases were governed by cadet branches of the house of Habsburg. It will also be remembered that Ferdinand II had converted the kingdom of Bohemia into a hereditary Habsburg possession in 1627.

Würzburg shrines and reliquaries were carried off as booty together with twelve life-size statues of the apostles in solid silver, while the king took possession of the bishop's plate. As for the armourers' shops, they were stripped bare. Herds and flocks were driven in from the surrounding countryside in such large numbers that they were sold in the markets at ludicrous prices. There were stories of assaults on nuns, and the Catholics, reduced to terror by this Protestant invasion, sent desperate appeals to Rome in their distress.

During the autumn of 1631 Richelieu was primarily occupied with the flight of Monsieur and the latter's intrigues in Lorraine. He seems to have relied on Father Joseph in matters of policy where Germany was concerned. At all events it was Father Joseph who drew up the instructions for the ambassadors who were sent into the Empire. These were Charnacé, who was to work for the preservation of neutrality between the king of Sweden and the Catholic electors, and two agents who were placed under his orders—Melchior de Lisle, the French resident at Strasbourg, and Saint-Étienne, Father Joseph's nephew. However, it is almost impossible to believe that Father Joseph was pursuing a policy of his own which differed from that of the cardinal. We are ill-informed as to their opinions during these weeks. Perhaps they did not yet fully realise the decisive nature of events in Germany.

Richelieu's main concern was to hasten Monsieur's return to the realm and to keep the duke of Lorraine's court at arm's length. Nancy was a hotbed of intrigue, and Duke Charles IV was giving armed assistance to the emperor. The duke had two sisters: the first was Henriette, princesse de Phalsbourg, an ambitious, pushing woman who found consolation for her husband's absence in Germany in the arms of Puylaurens; the second, Marguerite, was virtuous and devout but rather naïve and lacking in personality. She contemplated Monsieur with wide, admiring eyes, and her sister, who saw a career for herself as sister-in-law of the heir to the French throne, took it into her head to arrange for their marriage. As for Monsieur, he was scarcely capable of living under the same roof as a woman without compromising her.

The cardinal knew of this marriage project through intercepted letters. He wished to make himself master of Lorraine in any event. As well as giving the emperor's troops and the Spaniards access to Champagne, the duchy's network of roads offered the French an easy means of entering the Rhineland and Alsace. Although there was not as yet any question of committing the king's forces so far afield, it was essential to be able to move them there when the need arose. An imperial garrison had been stationed at Moyenvic in Lorraine since 1629. In December 1631 an army under the king's command and accompanied by the cardinal advanced in the direction of the town, whereupon the garrison withdrew. Charles IV had to accept Louis XIII's terms. By the Treaty of Vic (6 January) he agreed to hand over the fortress of Marsal for three years, to allow French troops freedom of passage through the duchy and not to enter into any alliance prejudicial to France.

Monsieur could have taken advantage of his brother's approach to effect a reconciliation. Instead he preferred to rejoin the queen mother at Brussels. No one knew at the time that on 3 January, before his departure, he had secretly married Princess Marguerite; the cardinal of Lorraine had issued the licence and given a Cistercian the necessary powers to solemnise the marriage.

With the question of Lorraine provisionally settled, it seemed an appropriate moment to come to a decision regarding Germany. The matter was discussed at a Council meeting on 6 January—the same day as the signature of the Treaty of Vic. According to Lepré-Balain, Father Joseph's official biographer, most of the king's ministers were in favour of making use of the troops available to invade Alsace. Richelieu certainly felt that it would be a good moment to strike a vigorous blow at the house of Austria and was inclined to adopt the same attitude; but Father Joseph argued strongly against it. The Catholic electors must not be left in the lurch, he declared, nor must the king of Sweden be allowed to triumph so completely in Germany that he would be able to carve out a Protestant empire for himself there. Louis XIII postponed his decision. The next day Richelieu announced that there would be no immediate invasion of Alsace and that efforts would be continued to establish a state of neutrality between the Catholic electors and Sweden. The cardinal dispatched his brother-in-law, the marquis de Brézé, to Mainz with instructions to sound Gustavus Adolphus as to the use that could be made of the French king's forces. It was hoped that he would reply by calling upon Louis XIII to invade Italy and Alsace whilst himself undertaking to attack the emperor in the hereditary lands. In that event Brézé was to be careful not to discourage him; he was merely to extract a promise from the Swedish king that he would in future refrain from oppressing the Catholic electors. In addition he was to suggest that Gustavus Adolphus should hand over to the French king several of the towns which he had seized from the Catholic League until such time as their future could be finally determined at a meeting of the Imperial Diet. The main point was 'to procure so far as may be the king of Sweden's speedy departure to assail the house of Austria in Bohemia, Austria and other its hereditary lands'.

Even so, care would need to be taken not to allow imperial or Spanish troops to reoccupy any territories evacuated by the king of Sweden. Brézé and Charnacé were to induce the electors of Mainz, Cologne and Trier to put forward the ideal solution of their own initiative and without the suggestion appearing to come from the French king: it was that Louis XIII himself should assume the protection of their chief fortresses and garrison them with his troops. Thus Spanish domination and the disquieting presence of the Swedes would be superseded by a French occupation—purely as a temporary measure of course. Whatever the outcome, by using her alliance with Sweden to carry the war into the hereditary lands of the Habsburgs and her alliance with the German Catholics to dominate the left bank of the Rhine, France would both protect herself from a threat to her own territory and involve the emperor in difficulties on every side. This policy might sooner or later bring about the end of Habsburg domination within the Empire, which in turn would make it difficult for Spain to continue her war in the Netherlands against the United Provinces. But Richelieu did not yet allow himself to be beguiled by these dazzling possibilities.

An advice dated 1 February 1632 concludes by expressing the opinion that for the time being Louis XIII should not break off normal relations with anyone; he should merely have troops ready to take advantage of the opportunities which time might offer. In short prudence remained the watchword, for only a cautious policy could prepare the ground so that when the time came to intervene France would be able to do so under favourable conditions.

But what difficulties lay ahead! For the French diplomats were now to find themselves dealing with a changed Gustavus Adolphus, with a man hardened in his ambition by his overwhelming success. He was not scared of France, nor was he in the least disposed to become a mere instrument of French policy. He had not the slightest intention of complying with demands that prevented him from taking action against the Catholic League. Brézé and Charnacé met with a very hostile reception, despite the Swedish king's previous liking for the latter. Almost at once Gustavus flew into a rage. He asked the ambassadors whether they brought peace or war. In his eyes the Catholic League was nothing but a bunch of double-dealing rogues and traitors. He was perfectly aware that they were intriguing with the emperor and supplying him with men and money. The French ambassadors received this tirade with the utmost composure, in order to avoid a breach of relations and keep the alliance intact.

The Swedish king's apprehensions were certainly justified, for the Catholic League did not favour a neutral policy any more than he did; indeed its intentions were the reverse of pacific. On 28 February Tilly's army recaptured Bamberg and drove Horn and his Swedish troops out of the town.

A few days later Gustavus Adolphus decided to leave Mainz. He entrusted the surveillance of his conquests in the Rhineland to a German prince who had only recently entered his service. This was Duke Bernard of Saxe-Weimar, later to show himself one of the best generals of his day and a political intriguer whom no one could afford to treat lightly.

The king of Sweden now marched towards central Germany to meet a new enemy. Wallenstein had returned to the fray—on what conditions we shall see shortly. However since Gustavus was withdrawing from the Rhine on his own initiative and proceeding in the direction that Richelieu desired, French policy recovered its freedom of action in respect of the ecclesiastical electors and the duke of Lorraine. In April Richelieu was thus in a position to exchange reassuring remarks with Navaze, the Spanish chargé d'affaires. He paraded his good intentions and drew attention to French moderation, pointing out that France had only occupied Susa and Moyenvic to safeguard her security, without attempting to use either of them as a springboard for offensive operations that would have caused alarm in Italy or Germany. In June a fresh treaty with Lorraine, signed at Liverdun, placed the fortresses of Clermont-en-Argonne, Stenay and Jamets at the disposal of the French. In the following month the elector of Trier placed a number of towns under Louis XIII's protection, and an army under Marshal Effiat set off to occupy them.[2] These temporary safeguards for her security, which were likely to be of distinct value in the future without being excessive as immediate requirements, represented the most that France could hope to gain, for civil war had once more broken out within the realm in answer to Monsieur's call to arms.

In 1631 popular outbreaks had occurred in Paris, Bordeaux, Poitiers, Marseilles, Orleans and Aix.* They were in part at least the result of par-

* For the outbreak in Paris, see Moote, p. 62. A riot in Poitiers and a serious revolt in

ticularly depressed economic conditions and of a deplorably bad harvest in that particular year. But the insurrection with which we are here concerned was due to other causes also. This time an entire province—nobility, bourgeoisie and common people—rose in revolt against the king's authority, refusing to obey him even though the interest of the realm as a whole required that the province in question should contribute towards common expenses. Its insubordination is to be explained by the fact that the newly introduced measures for levying taxes were prejudicial to its ancient privileges. The rights of the province clashed with the rights of the realm.

It was now two years since Richelieu had begun his attempt to introduce the *élus* into the fiscal administration of Languedoc as he had done in Burgundy. In other words, he wished to subject the province to direct collection of taxes by government officials instead of asking the provincial Estates for a contribution. From the government's point of view such a step offered two advantages: it facilitated the creation of fresh offices, and it assured the Treasury of a better return from the province. The government had already been obliged to put down a rising in Burgundy for this very reason and there were therefore good grounds for expecting some unrest in Languedoc. The governor of the province was Duke Henri II of Montmorency, a marshal of France and the brother-in-law of the prince of Condé. Although the king and the cardinal had loaded him with honours and lavished attentions upon him, they had not bestowed upon him the office of constable, which it was his ambition to hold as his father had done. The duke had not opposed the introduction of *élus* into the dioceses* despite the fact that the honorarium which he had been accustomed to receive when taxes were voted by the provincial Estates would be abolished under the new system. Perhaps he wished to show himself exceptionally well disposed towards the government in a delicate situation. It was the Parlement of Toulouse which refused to register the king's edict. Local opposition crystallised more or less everywhere. The arrival of these new officials threatened to reduce the value of appointments that had been created previously.

The duke willingly took part in negotiations with refractory elements in the province, and a compromise was agreed upon: instead of *élus* the government was to send commissioners into each diocese to apportion

---

Aix-en-Provence are described and analysed in Mousnier-Pearce, pp. 40–1, 43, 323; *cf.* Treasure, p. 140.

* In Languedoc a diocese was not only a unit of ecclesiastical administration but also a sub-division of the provincial administration.

the *taille*,[3] and these commissioners were not to collect any tax unless it had been authorised by letters patent issued by the provincial Estates. The latter were summoned to meet at Pézenas on 12 December 1631 with this object in view.

In view of the unrest in his province, the queen mother's supporters now made a dead set at the duke of Montmorency. Her party was still very powerful in France, for public opinion remained undecided. The cardinal had certainly a large number of adherents and loyal servants among the high-ranking officers of the army (such as Schomberg and La Force), among a section of the nobility, among the clergy and probably to an even greater extent among the office-holding class; but there were some from each of these categories who criticised his policy and continued to hold him responsible for the country's sufferings and their own personal difficulties. They were sorry that the king supported him and were still attached to the queen mother and Monsieur, whom they regarded not as rebels but as victims. Above all, the iniquitous trial of Marshal Marillac who seemed to be wantonly subjected to all kinds of indignities aroused grave misgivings. It encouraged a general feeling that even the most outstanding services were no protection in the event of disagreement with the cardinal's policy.

Although Richelieu owed his strength to his clientele, this same clientele was also responsible for raising up enemies against him. The brutality of men like Isaac de Laffemas, and the arrogance of bourgeois upstarts who were in a position to humiliate everyone else thanks to the authority they derived from the cardinal, caused deep offence everywhere. Some chance of circumstance could suddenly snap the tie of loyalty or make a man switch his allegiance from one party to the other. Montmorency was very far from being the cardinal's enemy. Not so long ago, at the time of the king's illness at Lyons, when Richelieu had been in serious danger, he had offered him refuge in Languedoc. But the duke's wife, Marie-Félicie des Ursins, who belonged to one of those great international families with connections in several different countries, was related to the queen mother.* This beautiful and fearless woman induced her husband to throw in his lot with the opposing side —the more easily since Montmorency was himself almost a kinsman of the royal family and cherished feelings of warm friendship for Monsieur. D'Elbène, bishop of Albi, one of Monsieur's supporters, who enjoyed great credit with Montmorency, arranged for his brother, the abbé

---

* des Ursins is the French form of the Italian name Orsini. The Duchess, who was Marie de Medici's niece, was born in Rome.

d'Elbène, to come from Brussels in disguise bringing with him specific proposals for the duke's consideration. He declared that Monsieur had supporters all over the realm and would shortly put himself at the head of an army to be provided by the Spaniards and the duke of Lorraine.

The restlessness of Languedoc during the spring of 1632 was duly noted by the royal commissioners, and they reported it to the cardinal. However, Richelieu did not believe that the duke would let himself be inveigled into joining Monsieur. He thought it only fair to warn him of the suspicions aroused by his behaviour, but was content to accept Montmorency's reassuring professions of loyalty.

The queen mother and Monsieur had sent threatening letters to Marshal Marillac's judges and announced that they would be revenged upon anyone implicated in condemning him to death; and in July 1632, a few weeks after the marshal's execution, Montmorency was definitely committed to the conspiracy. He was well aware of the grave risk that he was running, since he talked of offering his services to Gustavus Adolphus if the plot miscarried and he forfeited the king's favour. This is yet further evidence of the strange medley of politics and personal ambitions that was to be met within a milieu which had remained feudal. What could possibly attract a provincial Catholic nobleman like Montmorency to the side of the Protestant king of Sweden except a last remaining hope that there was still somewhere where he would be treated in accordance with his rank?

Montmorency had made a point of advising Monsieur to await the signal from him before bringing troops into the realm, for a premature invasion would ruin everything; but like the bungler he was, Monsieur paid no attention. In mid-June he made his appearance at the head of an army of foreign mercenaries. He counted on winning over French garrisons in the course of his advance, and issued a proclamation summoning the realm in the king's name to rise and deliver Louis XIII from the tyranny of his minister—a political fiction such as invariably accompanied wars of this nature. He marched on Dijon, expecting that the disaffection which had recently broken out there would come to life again and assist his cause. But the gates of the town were closed against him, and Their Excellencies of the Parlement informed his messengers that they could not pay heed to any order which did not emanate directly from the king. Henceforth the only ally on whom Monsieur could count was the governor of Languedoc.

Towards the end of July Montmorency resumed negotiations with members of the provincial Estates at Pézenas. To the king's representatives he announced that he would propose to the Estates the appointment not of commissioners but of *élus*. The employment of commissioners had been accepted by everyone, and the duke knew very well that his proposal would arouse unanimous opposition. When the astonished representatives protested, he had them arrested together with the archbishop of Narbonne, a declared and loyal supporter of the cardinal who was to preside over the meetings of the Estates.

On 22 July 'the Estates of Languedoc, being assembled at Pézenas', invited the duke to join them in an indissoluble union 'for the execution of the king's service and the relief of the province', and asked him to take immediate military precautions 'until such time as orders were received from the king'. Cloaked in a form of words, this was tantamount to a declaration of civil war. The Parlement of Toulouse had no illusions on the subject, refused to approve the declaration and staunchly maintained its loyalty to the king. The bishop of Mende likewise remained loyal, although his fellow bishops of Albi, Lodève, Uzès and Saint-Pons promised that their cathedral towns would open their gates to Monsieur's troops. Richelieu considered that the presence of Louis XIII at the head of an army was essential if the rebellion was to be crushed. It was arranged that selected regiments from Picardy and the Paris area should be sent to join the royal forces already in the south-west. At a *lit de justice* Louis XIII ordered a declaration to be registered by the Parlement of Paris pronouncing anyone who gave assistance to his brother guilty of high treason; but Monsieur himself was offered the prospect of returning to the king's favour and the restoration of his apanages and pensions, if he undertook to submit within six weeks and disband his troops.

In mid-August the king left Paris. He had not yet reached Lyons when he heard of the victory won by his forces. On 1 September a battle had taken place at Castelnaudary. The army of Monsieur and Montmorency had consisted of 3000 horse and 2000 foot, but most of them were foreign mercenaries. Marshal Schomberg's troops, though far less numerous (1200 horse and 1000 foot), were better officered and better trained. Montmorency was a prisoner, while the king's half-brother, the comte de Moret, who had joined Monsieur's party, was among those who had lost their lives.

Certain episodes in this strange battle are worth recalling, so faithfully do they reflect the colour of the age and reveal the stubbornness with which feudal standards of conduct had lingered on. The governor of Languedoc, armoured and helmeted like a knight, took part in the battle personally and fought to the utmost of his ability using both sword and pistol. He broke through to the seventh rank of the royal army. He was wounded in the face and blood was pouring from his mouth when his horse rolled to the ground, almost crushing him beneath its weight. 'A moi, Montmorency!' he was shouting. The king's officers, who had realised that it was the duke because of the gallantry he had displayed, acted as if they did not mean to take him prisoner at once so as to leave his own soldiers time to come and retrieve him. They wanted him to be spared the shame of capture and the danger of retribution at the king's hands.[4]

All this was reminiscent of a tourney, but the fiction could not be prolonged for the rank and file would not have understood. There was no alternative but to make the duke prisoner. The wounded man was in such a sorry state that for several days rumour had it that he was dead—a rumour which was welcomed in the king's entourage. Alive, the duke was an embarrassment and if God had taken the matter into His own hands it would have been considered a satisfactory end to the whole business. But Montmorency survived.

After entering Languedoc, the king proceeded with the pacification of the province. He behaved generously in suppressing the *élections* which had been the cause or the excuse for the rising, and in maintaining the privileges of the Estates. Then, when calm had been restored, he gave orders for the duke to be moved from Castelnaudary to Toulouse where the Parlement was commissioned to institute proceedings against him. There was no dilly-dallying about the trial. The prisoner was only allowed to argue about points of detail. The mere fact of having engaged in battle against the king's forces at Castelnaudary was enough to justify the death penalty. Every conceivable attempt at intercession was made on the duke's behalf—by his wife (although she too was a prisoner), by the princesse de Condé (who was deeply attached to her brother), by the duke of Angoulême, by Anne of Austria, and by Monsieur, who, now that he was in process of negotiating with the king on his own account, tried to make Montmorency's reprieve one of his main terms. From abroad the queen mother, the duke of Savoy and the pope also appealed for clemency. The duke was a man of thirty-seven—in the prime of manhood, yet young enough to offer hopes of his rendering the king many services in time to come. There were other arguments in his favour as well as his age—the greatness of his name, his personal qualities, his illustrious connections. All these considerations could not but make the death sentence seem a terrible punishment if the king still insisted on its being carried out.

Nor was Louis XIII left in any doubt as to the attitude of the common people. Whilst staying at the archbishop's palace in Toulouse he heard the mob below the windows shouting: 'Pardon him, pardon him, have mercy on him.' Richelieu did not seem to be as ruthless as the king, or else he knew he could safely pretend that he was not deterring Louis XIII from exercising his clemency.

On 30 October the duke was examined for the last time in the presence of Châteauneuf, the keeper of the seals—a part for which the latter was singularly ill-cast, since he had been brought up in the following of the Montmorency family and it was to them that he owed the beginnings at least of his own good fortune. The sentence pronounced was that the duke should be executed immediately and that his property should be confiscated. Through the intercession of the king's confessor, Father Arnoux, Montmorency had already arranged for the verdict to be postponed for one day. He had made use of this last period of respite to confess his sins, to receive communion and to draw up his last will and testament. Clearly he had expected to be condemned to death, and his only resolve was to make a fitting end.

Monsieur de Charlus, the captain of the king's Guards, who had taken away the duke's decorations and marshal's baton in order to give them to Louis XIII, took the opportunity to try to make the inflexible king weaken: 'Ah sire!' he cried, throwing himself at the king's feet, while all those present also fell on their knees in tears, 'will not Your Majesty pardon Monsieur de Montmorency, whose ancestors served your predecessors so well? Grant him pardon, sire!' 'Nay,' said Louis XIII, 'no pardon shall be granted him and he needs must die.'

The courtyard of the Hôtel de Ville was the place appointed for Montmorency's execution. All the gates were closed. Soon the duke entered. He paused for a moment before the statue of Henry IV, his godfather, then committed himself to the hands of the executioner. He died with the great courage for which he was everywhere known and admired, animated by a truly Christian spirit of repentance. Father Arnoux went to tell Louis XIII that God had received the duke into Heaven as one of his saints. The body was buried at Saint-Sernin at about nine o'clock in the evening. Thus ended the house of Montmorency.[5]

The story goes that when the news of the duke's death reached Madrid, Cardinal Zapata asked the French ambassadors, Barraut and Bautru, what in their opinion had led to the conviction of such an exalted personage. 'His mistakes,' answered Bautru in Spanish. 'No,' replied the cardinal, who wished to use the event to point a moral, 'it was the weakness of your present king's predecessors.'[6]

Olivares used very much the same language. All Europe realised that the king of France's authority weighed heavily upon his subjects as it had possibly never done before. Indeed, who knows whether royal authority was not strengthened everywhere in consequence, and whether the precedent set by Montmorency's execution was not to prove fatal to Wallenstein? Charles I of England was also experimenting with absolute government at this time. The power of monarchs was becoming preponderant.

As for Monsieur, he had accepted his brother's conditions and signed an agreement at Béziers. He secured quite good terms, managing to save his friend Puylaurens and some of his servants, although there were others, such as Le Coigneux, whom he left to suffer the due process of the law. He had taken particular care not to reveal that he was married to Princess Marguerite; indeed he even mendaciously asserted that he had gone no further than to promise that they would be betrothed. However, the king and the cardinal found out the whole truth. From that moment Puylaurens thought that he was lost, for he had only been pardoned in return for a promise to reveal everything about the marriage and he had denied that it had taken place. He prevailed upon the duke of Orleans to leave the realm once more, and early in November the prince and his friends escaped from Tours. Montmorency's execution gave them an excuse for stirring up public opinion. Monsieur wrote that he had been promised that the duke would be pardoned and that by deceiving him in this matter the government had deprived him of any guarantee that he himself was safe. He returned to Brussels and resumed his propaganda.

This fresh escape by Monsieur was a serious matter. It threatened to nullify all the benefits that Louis XIII and Richelieu thought they had derived from their successful repression of civil war and the exemplary punishment of Montmorency. The presence of the duke of Orleans abroad at a time when France was yet again to be faced with grave dangers from beyond her frontiers: the promises he could make and the pledges he could offer to foreign Powers: the means that he still possessed of stirring up trouble within the realm: all these were factors that handicapped the king's policy and prevented the government from relaxing its grip, forcing it to uphold its authority by stern measures, to insist on obedience everywhere, and to subject the whole population to the ruthless control of agents upon whom it could rely.

Barely a few weeks after Montmorency's execution news of another death spread through Europe. On 16 November the king of Sweden was killed fighting victoriously against the imperial army at Lützen in Saxony.

These unexpected tidings reached Richelieu at a particularly trying time. He had been unable to rejoin the king in Paris; instead he lingered in Saintonge, tortured by attacks of rheumatism and by a retention of urine which for several days endangered his life. He was frantically worried by Monsieur's flight, by affairs in Lorraine and in the Netherlands, and by the behaviour of Marshal Toiras. The latter's older brother had been implicated in the conspiracy, and he himself was threatening to leave the king's service. Nevertheless Richelieu affected the utmost composure: 'If the king of Sweden had postponed his death for six months,' he wrote to Louis XIII on 15 December, 'it seems likely that your Majesty's affairs would have been more secure.' But, he added, if prompt action were taken no harm would ensue.[7] What had been happening in Germany during the past few months?

The thread of events had become remarkably tangled. To reduce everything to broad outlines is far from easy when the true picture is made up of a mass of small individual actions, each with its own particular significance; but the attempt must be made if we are to thread our way through the labyrinth.

The war within the Empire dominated everything. This was not a war consisting solely of battles that only concerned the armies involved and left the civilian population unscathed. On the contrary, it was an appalling experience for everyone. The passage of troops was signalled by looting, by the requisitioning of supplies, and by the imposition of ransoms. There was not a prince or owner of a fief or domain who did not tremble for his estates, his money, his buildings, his food supplies or his household belongings. Now that imperial authority was crumbling, every man felt that his only hope of safety lay in negotiating with a person stronger than himself, whether it was the warrior advancing towards him or someone further off who could afford him protection and avert the approaching storm by threatening reprisals. So ineffective were its institutions that one might almost say that the Empire no longer existed; and yet its greatness remained a powerful influence in men's minds. We cannot equate this feeling with German patriotism in the modern sense of the term. It was, rather, a deep-rooted faith in an order of things which men hoped and expected would be rebuilt from the ruins in which it lay.

Germany, divided, hewn in pieces, torn asunder, had become a passage-way for armies. The whole country longed for peace. Thanks to his alliances with the chief Lutheran or Calvinist states of the Empire, Gustavus Adolphus had assumed the leadership of a Protestant coalition against the emperor and the Catholic League. But he was a foreigner, owing his strength to his conquests and his arms. Although his victorious entry into a town would be greeted with cheers, he did not win the hearts of the people. The figure of the dreaded conqueror passes by in transitory power.

His faithful henchmen, his Swedish generals, the German and Czech refugees who had joined him, Frederick V the Winter King, Count Thurn, who had taken a leading part in the defenestration of Prague fourteen years previously—all of them had placed their last hopes in Gustavus Adolphus. But, as he was well aware, he could not count on a like loyalty from his two principal German allies, the electors of Saxony and Brandenburg. They or their ministers were still in communication with the imperial court and were watching for the first opportunity to stop the war on terms favourable to themselves.

Despite this the situation seemed so grave to the emperor's entourage in Vienna that many of them favoured resorting to a desperate expedient. There was only one man who could be matched against the king of Sweden—Wallenstein. No sacrifice would be too great to bring about his return.

Ever since the emperor had dismissed him as if he were a lackey Wallenstein had been residing either at Jičín* or in his sumptuous palace at Prague, brooding the while over the means of obtaining his revenge. During the year 1631 he had offered his services to the elector of Saxony and to the king of Sweden; but since he was a prince of the Empire,† the services which he offered were those of an ally who meant to be treated as an equal. He spoke of imposing on Ferdinand II a peace which, in essence, would have restored the conditions that had existed in the Empire prior to 1618 whilst reserving the lion's share for himself.

In the event Wallenstein received little encouragement from Saxony and thus remained open to appeals from elsewhere. Those of the emperor's advisers who believed in Wallenstein's military genius and thought that he alone could save the day, succeeded in their plea for his recall. Ferdinand II swallowed his pride and besought his ex-generalissimo to come to his rescue.

The financial conditions to which the emperor agreed were exorbi-

* Capital of the duchy of Friedland; see p. 193 above.

† Wallenstein had been made a prince of the Empire in 1623.

tant. Wallenstein's debts to the Bohemian Treasury were cancelled. He was promised new estates both in Bohemia and in the Empire, and awarded the duchy of Glogau to compensate for his loss of the duchy of Mecklenburg. In return he agreed to resume supreme command of the imperial army within three months. He was given complete control of operations, and full powers to treat with Saxony if occasion arose.

The Saxon army still occupied Bohemia. Negotiations were immediately opened with Arnim, its commander, but Wallenstein found him unresponsive and soon had to resort to action. His troops had been reformed and were well equipped and reliable. In the spring they scoured Bohemia and swept it clean of Germans.

That Wallenstein did not try to crush the enemy is not surprising, for his cautious attitude was in accordance with the strategy of the day. It is far more astonishing to note that after achieving this success Wallenstein took no further initiative. He did no more than observe the situation, allowing Gustavus Adolphus, after his victory over Tilly's army at the crossing of the Lech, to ravage Bavaria and enter first Augsburg and then Munich, where Frederick V strutted jubilantly at the Swedish king's side, relishing the triumphal march through the capital of the prince who not so long ago had stripped him of his possessions.

However the king of Sweden did not remain in Bavaria for long. He moved northwards in the direction of Nuremberg. Wallenstein had slowly established his position on the outskirts of the town, joining forces with Maximilian's troops, who had been incapable of protecting their homeland. Instead of launching an offensive against Gustavus to bring him to a halt, Wallenstein allowed him to make the next move. Nevertheless the Swedish attacks spent themselves in vain against the resistance of the imperial army.

But at the same time negotiations between the two sides were resumed, and from now on it was Gustavus who took the initiative. Through the intermediary of an officer from the imperialist army whom he had taken prisoner and now returned to Wallenstein, the Swedish king offered peace terms which they would be able to impose jointly. Everything confiscated from the Protestants would have to be restored to them, and the Lutherans were to be granted liberty of worship throughout the Empire. Sweden was to receive Pomerania, and Brandenburg, which had a claim to that territory, was to be awarded compensation in the form of two bishoprics.* Wallenstein himself would obtain a duchy in Franconia.

* Halberstadt and Magdeburg.

For reasons which remain mysterious Wallenstein declined these proposals, saying with truth that he held no powers to treat with Sweden
and that it would take too long to refer them to the emperor. Nevertheless witnesses have declared that Gustavus did not break off negotiations
when he left Nuremberg, and that this time he meant to advise Wallenstein to seize the Bohemian throne.[8]

Meanwhile there was a battle to be fought. The two armies resumed
their march northwards, and on 16 November they met at Lützen. The
imperial army was put to rout and one of Wallenstein's best generals was
killed; but so too was the king of Sweden. Wallenstein withdrew to
Bohemia to regroup his forces and punish the officers responsible for his
defeat.

However, it was the disappearance of Gustavus Adolphus that mattered more than anything else. 'There was not room for two cocks on the
same dunghill,' Wallenstein was to say. Vanquished or victorious, he
had survived the other great protagonist and no one called him to
account for the loss of the battle now that he stood alone.

The death of Gustavus Adolphus opened up the possibility of a complete
change in Europe. The coalition of which he had been the moving spirit
might dissolve without any need for Wallenstein to overthrow it. In that
event would not the restoration of peace in Germany leave Spain free to
attack France when she chose? Richelieu measured the extent of the
danger. To meet it the realm had to be made secure against any threat of
invasion from the Netherlands or the east. It was more imperative than
ever for France to hold Lorraine.

But this was a delicate matter, for it was advisable to keep up appearances, especially in the eyes of Europe. Lorraine to the west of the Meuse,
'Barrois mouvant',* was considered as a fief of the French Crown, while
the rest, 'Barrois non mouvant' and Lorraine proper, which earlier had
been attached to the Empire, had been independent since 1542 with the
exception of certain territories: Pont-à-Mousson, Clermont, Hattoncha-
tel and Blamont. This made it necessary for France to try to avoid alarming European opinion by brutal measures in territories which were not
under French suzerainty. Richelieu felt himself capable of acting with
the necessary caution and moderation so far as these territories were concerned; but he had a far less firm grip on affairs in Germany.

In reality France could only boast two alliances within the Empire:

* *mouvant* means feudally dependent.

firstly her alliance with the king of Sweden, who was dead and whose army was still regarded as a foreign army in the areas that it occupied; and secondly her alliance with Sweden's enemy, the elector of Bavaria, who had been driven from his capital, forced back towards Austria and placed under Wallenstein's protection. Wallenstein's protection—what a delusion!

As always, Richelieu shared out the work among his various assistants. Without surrendering his right to keep an eye on affairs and make the final decisions, he put Father Joseph in charge of the necessary negotiations and left him to handle the details. The latter decided to send Feuquières on a fresh mission to Germany.

Gustavus Adolphus left no children old enough to succeed him—only a little girl of six called Christina, for whom her mother, the widowed queen, was to act as regent. But Oxenstierna, the chief minister and chancellor of Sweden, was still in Germany and so too were the Swedish forces. The latter, which were scattered over the Empire, consisted of troops in Alsace and Swabia under the two Swedish generals Horn and Banér, a small force in Silesia commanded by the Czech émigré Count Thurn,[9] and finally the armies of the German generals William of Hesse-Cassel and Bernard of Saxe-Weimar.

Oxenstierna was not inclined to abandon his master's handiwork. He reverted to his combined programme of war for the Protestant cause and war against the house of Austria until such time as the emperor was defeated. But he had first to reckon with Saxony, whose policy would govern that pursued by Brandenburg.

Although John George, the elector of Saxony, was opposed to Habsburg and Catholic hegemony within the Empire, he had no intention of allowing Germany to fall under the sway of foreigners. His enemies used to say that he had secret leanings towards Austria and Spain, but this was arrant nonsense for John George had no liking for Catholics. However, he made no secret of the fact that he did not want to destroy imperial power. He would have preferred a peace which guaranteed an equilibrium between Lutherans and Catholics—a division of influence in which the two Great Powers would have been himself and the emperor. With Swedish help he had prevented Ferdinand II from dominating all Germany. Now he was quite ready to come to an understanding with him to expel the foreigner, or at least to withdraw from the war once he had obtained adequate compensation. To all intents and purposes this was the solution that he brought about by the Treaty of Prague two years later.

In the meantime the death of Gustavus offered John George an increased measure of independence, and Dresden became the centre for negotiations that might lead to a German peace—which would certainly not be the same as a peace arranged by Sweden.

Historians have not sufficiently emphasised the important part played by Dresden in events at this time. If French historians have been particularly deficient in this respect, it is no doubt because none of the threads were so to speak in French hands. Nevertheless it was there that the future of French foreign policy was being decided. If the war came to an end in Germany the emperor would once more be free to help Spain, German mercenaries would again be available to fight elsewhere and prosperity would return to lands which now lay desolate, thus enabling them to supply Spanish armies. Under such circumstances it is only too easy to see the dangers with which France would immediately be faced in the Netherlands, in Italy, in fact at every strategic point where, without openly participating in the war, she was at present holding her enemy in check.

Oxenstierna hastened to put in an appearance at Dresden only a few weeks after the death of Gustavus. By demonstrating his firm resolve to continue the war he may well have prevented the elector of Saxony from making peace; but he had saved the alliance rather than strengthened it, and he had to look for further support elsewhere.

He found it further to the west. At Heilbronn in February he made a treaty with the four circles of Franconia, Swabia, and Upper and Lower Rhine.* Both Feuquières and an English ambassador were present at the birth of this new league, of which Sweden assumed control, but the French diplomat also applied himself to maintaining existing alliances. From Heilbronn he travelled to Berlin and Dresden, where he visited the electors to strengthen their determination to continue the fight.

Winter was now over and further battles could be anticipated. It seemed as if Wallenstein had done everything possible to ensure that any fresh fighting would be of a formidable nature, for he had spent several months re-forming his army in Bohemia, refusing to risk it in action whatever was happening around him. He had not stirred when advised of the warlike preparations of the duke of Feria, the Spanish governor of Milan, who was preparing to invade Alsace in order to force Horn and his Swedes to raise the siege of Breisach; and he categorically rejected the appeal of the elector of Bavaria, who had been forced back on Regensburg and was complaining that he could not reconquer his duchy single-

* *Rhin électoral et Bas-Rhin.*

handed. At Vienna Wallenstein's behaviour was not merely beginning to cause disappointment; it had begun to seem suspicious.

We are now approaching one of the strangest phases in the history of the Thirty Years War, which has baffled historians by its extraordinary complexity and aroused the interest of poets and dramatists by its daring: Wallenstein's conspiracy.

Is it possible to throw full light on this conspiracy? During the hundred and fifty years that have elapsed since Schiller with an artist's genius and intuition breathed new life into this amazing story, German, Swedish and Czech historians have ransacked the archives, published countless documents and greatly enhanced our critical understanding of events; Hallwich, Pekař and Srbik have also produced their admirable works. Some of these writers—like Srbik forty years ago—have credited Wallenstein with a far-reaching political plan; they have portrayed him as a man who strove for peace in accordance with the methods and ideas of his day. In their view Wallenstein, because he possessed the largest army in central Europe, believed that he alone was capable of establishing an order of things in Germany such as would be acceptable to Catholics and Protestants alike. He sought to convince his opponents of this. In short he wanted to inspire fear by means of his power but arbitration was his aim rather than warfare.

However, other historians (and their arguments are very convincing) have maintained that Wallenstein's only object was to wreak his revenge on the emperor and the duke of Bavaria, whom he would have liked to have at his mercy. At first he thought that the help of Saxony and Brandenburg would be sufficient for his purpose; but, as we have seen, the elector of Saxony's one desire was to come to a reasonable understanding with the emperor. If he was almost sorry to have been dragged so far in the Swedish king's wake, this did not mean that he was prepared to let himself be towed along behind the duke of Friedland, whom he mistrusted. Wallenstein had therefore no option but to go a stage further and negotiate with Sweden and France, despite the fact that they were foreign Powers for whom he had no liking.

Along the Rhine political, religious and dynastic interests had combined to create a situation which was already intricate enough; but as we leave the river's banks in company with Feuquières and draw near to Dresden, Prague and Vienna, we enter a world of inextricable complexity. Louis XIII's monarchy had to contend with a considerable degree of opposition, but how can France be compared with central Europe, where fortunes had been ruined, restored and then ruined again by fifteen years of revolution, forfeiture and war: where conditions in every class had been turned topsy-turvy: where countless human beings had lost their lives? These fifteen years had left a trail of hunger and bitter hatred everywhere. If this book were a history of the Thirty Years War it would be necessary to try to recapture each trend of opinion, each individual attitude;[10] but in a history of Louis XIII and Richelieu we must confine our attention to matters directly relevant to their policy.

The overtures that were made to Feuquières at Dresden enable us to measure the extent to which France had regained prestige in Europe, for they show that now no large-scale plans were laid without regard to her. First a Saxon general, Franz Albrecht of Saxe-Lauenburg, came to voice his grievances against the elector and to offer his own and his army's services. He was followed by Count Vilém Kinský, a Czech refugee who had been living in Dresden for several years. The latter informed Feuquières that Wallenstein was deeply disappointed by imperial policy and was thinking of turning on the emperor with his army and forcing him to make peace. He asked whether France would assist Wallenstein in this undertaking and allow him to take the first indispensable step of restoring the independence of the elective monarchy of Bohemia. The man to be chosen as king would be Wallenstein himself.

Here we must pause for a moment and ask ourselves how a Czech refugee who was a Protestant and an enemy of the emperor could act as spokesman for Wallenstein, who was both a Catholic and the emperor's general. Did this scheme for setting up a king of Bohemia seem at all a likely possibility?

It was in Bohemia that the war had begun, and ever since the country had known no peace. While its monarch had remained in Vienna successive armies had invaded the realm. Order and security had never been really restored. Some districts had been virtually abandoned, and estates had ceased to be cultivated. Elsewhere, as in Friedland, landowners who had been more fortunate were busy introducing new methods of farming which offered a high yield. Some had grown rich: others had been ruined: and intrigues were rife throughout the entire aristocracy. It was not so much a matter of attachment to a given cause as of each man's concern to protect his own fortune or particular position. The climate was a strange one. In speaking of it historians still make use of such words as 'adventurers' or 'condottieri', but it is time these hackneyed terms were dropped. The type of man we are discussing was not the leader of a band of mercenaries. Indeed Wallenstein himself was a great deal more than a mere condottiere. The state of mind we must try to visualise and which was stimulated by events in Bohemia was more the product of the Italian Renaissance than of mediaeval chivalry. Ideals and simple faith were less in evidence than *virtù*, the heady taste for daring exploits and risks that offered the prospect of a dazzling reward.[11] The Imperial Knights [*Ritterschaft*] of Germany a hundred years previously[12] had not possessed the same culture or will for power as these Bohemian nobles whom it would be far more accurate to describe as baroque cavaliers.

Of these nobles Kinský was one. Exile though he was, he still maintained connections with Wallenstein's camp. He and the emperor's generalissimo had mutual relations among the great families of Bohemia —feudal magnates who were loath to submit to absolutism and cherished nostalgic memories of another age not so long ago when the elected monarch had neither made laws nor raised an army without the consent of great nobles like themselves. The same type of great landowning aristocracy, imbued with the same opinions, was to be found in Poland and Hungary. That the schemes of Wallenstein's entourage should have included the idea of restoring the old Bohemian constitution, and that the same idea should have featured in these simmerings of revolt was therefore in no way absurd.[13]

Nor did Kinský's overtures meet with a discouraging reception from Feuquières. The French diplomat agreed without more ado to answer the six questions contained in a memorandum that Kinský submitted to him.* He said in effect that the king of France would provide the duke of Friedland with subsidies and armed assistance if he were to declare himself against the emperor, and would gladly support his plan for restoring the constitution and having himself elected king of Bohemia. There remained, however, the delicate question of Bavaria. Feuquières made it clear that the French king was under certain obligations to the duke of Bavaria, whom he regarded as his ally: he would not therefore take any initiative to Maximilian's detriment. Nevertheless, if the latter persisted in espousing the emperor's cause he would have to assume the responsibility for his decision and for its consequences.

After giving this answer Feuquières sent a report of what had occurred to his government and awaited instructions. It was now the middle of June 1633.

Wallenstein regarded these negotiations as merely exploratory; he did not mean to embark on rebellion without formal undertakings from France and Sweden. If his secret intrigues came to light, the way was still

* This memorandum was written in Italian. (V.L.T.).

open for him to prove to the emperor's advisers that it was Oxenstierna who had made the first advances and that Kinský had spoken without authority.

The French reply to the overtures reported by Feuquières was dispatched on 16 July after a session of the Council at Saint-Germain. They were favourably received, and messages were sent to Wallenstein and Kinský: if the duke of Friedland undertook to raise 35,000 men against the emperor, France would pay him large subsidies amounting if necessary to a million livres, as well as pledging her help and that of her associates. To this message Wallenstein returned no answer. At about the same date he told some emissaries from Oxenstierna that it was not yet time to act. Moreover he was mistrustful of foreigners and would have preferred to come to an understanding with the Saxons. Twice he granted them an armistice and tried to tempt them to terms. He proposed that the imperial army should join forces with the Protestant princes to drive all foreigners out of the Empire, be they Swedish, Spanish or French.

German historians have seen in this proposal a great plan for national liberation; but we may doubt whether any scheme as coherent as this really existed in the generalissimo's mind. It is more likely that (as the Czech historian Pekař has argued) Wallenstein had by this date succumbed to nervous exhaustion caused by the strain of a life spent subject to the wear and tear of military operations and filled with risks. True, he had still the same upright carriage and imperious manner of speech. He remained the most powerful man in central Europe, apparently capable of turning European politics upside down. But he no longer possessed the admirable mental balance displayed by Richelieu, which enabled the latter to stage such an astonishing recovery on more than one occasion. Wallenstein was sinking into superstition. He sought the clues to his future course of action in the stars, listened to the prognostications of his astrologers and wore amulets.

When Feuquières exchanged views with Oxenstierna at the end of August, the Swedish chancellor said with a good deal of wisdom that although no opportunity should be overlooked he thought it unlikely that their dealings with Wallenstein would have a successful outcome. Nevertheless the two allies decided to act in conjunction, and dispatched observers to Silesia. Feuquières's representative, Du Hamel, was however issued with a special directive which clearly reveals the aims of French policy as seen by Father Joseph and his following: he must take care to prevent the Protestants from turning Wallenstein's schemes exclusively to their own account, nor must they be allowed to injure

French interests and the cause of Catholicism. After this Feuquières returned to France to ask for fresh instructions.

It was Nikolaï, the Swedish resident at Dresden,[14] who summed up the situation better than anyone: 'Given the ambition and daring of the man, all this is not to be dismissed as nonsense. But the chancellor is right to feel doubtful about the outcome, for it will not be long before Friedland is regarded as a villain by any honourable person, either for his behaviour towards his own master or for his treatment of ours.'

By this time the Spanish and imperialist faction at the court of Ferdinand II was beginning to grow suspicious.* The Spanish and Bavarian ambassadors dispatched alarming reports to their respective courts. The emperor himself sent Count Schlick, his chief of staff [*maréchal de camp*], on a mission to Wallenstein's army.[15] He begged the generalissimo to stop shilly-shallying and embark on hostilities. Schlick conferred with Wallenstein's principal lieutenants, the two Italians Gallas and Piccolomini. They discussed the possibility of Wallenstein being prevented from retaining his command through illness or for some other reason, and considered the possibility of replacing him.

During the course of 1633, although he could easily have destroyed the forces of the enemy, Wallenstein had granted them one breathing space after another in a way that was frankly incredible, allowing Bernard of Saxe-Weimar's army to advance as far as Regensburg. At the end of the year he withdrew once more to his winter quarters in Bohemia. He now tried to resume his dealings with France and Sweden. Somewhat presumptuously, Kinský wrote to Feuquières on 1 January 1634 as if it was quite the usual thing to renew negotiations after a lapse of six months. This time, he declared, the duke of Friedland was resolved to act: the moment had come for a treaty of alliance to be signed and ratified. Kinský then left Dresden, boldly made his way into Bohemia, despite the fact that he was an exile, and joined Wallenstein at his camp at Pilsen.† Other messengers had been sent to the Swedes, to the Saxons, even to Bernard of Saxe-Weimar. The conspiracy was assuming larger proportions. Was it destined to come to a head?

No, for already Wallenstein's army was slipping from his grasp. Piccolomini, his Italian subordinate, was young, crafty and eaten up with ambition. He had divined more fully than his fellow officers that Wal-

---

* This faction, led by the emperor's son Ferdinand III king of Hungary and the Spanish Ambassador, had been opposed to Wallenstein's recall in the first place.

† Now Plzeň.

lenstein was preparing to commit a monstrous act of treachery but no longer had the strength to carry it through. From that moment Piccolomini thought he would make a great name for himself by coming forward as the saviour of the imperial cause. He warned Vienna. Although unable to reveal everything, he said enough to convince the emperor of the danger. But Ferdinand II, who was extremely scrupulous, was loath to destroy his generalissimo without a hearing. He said nothing to his son the king of Hungary or to the Spanish ambassador, who were Wallenstein's personal enemies. After ordering prayers to be said in monasteries and convents for the success of an important undertaking, he addressed himself to Gallas. He sent a patent appointing him commander-in-chief and gave him the order to arrest Wallenstein as a traitor at the appropriate moment and have him brought to Vienna. If there was no alternative Gallas could put him to death (24 January).

A few days previously Wallenstein, sensing the uneasiness of his officers, had summoned his generals and colonels to Pilsen and obtained from them a fresh pledge of loyalty to himself. It was arranged for this pledge to be conveyed to the regiments stationed on the frontiers so that it could be signed by the officers who had been unable to come to Pilsen. For the next three weeks there were two imperial generalissimos side by side in the camp at Pilsen. The first was fully engaged in plotting treason against his sovereign; the second, though loyal to the emperor, was a traitor to his erstwhile chief and bore on his person an order for his dismissal.

Eventually Wallenstein was apprised of the threat that was hanging over him. In a panic he precipitately abandoned his army and fled to join Bernard of Saxe-Weimar. Whatever happened he was lost. In his negotiations with the Saxons, the Swedes and the king of France he had consistently claimed the supreme command for himself should a rebellion take place, but what possible hope had he of retaining such a position once he put himself in their hands?

Wallenstein shut himself up in the stronghold of Eger.* There on 25 February 1634 he was basely surprised and murdered by a handful of ruffianly mercenaries.[16] Early in the same month Louis XIII had given surprising evidence of his faith in a scheme that had been repeatedly queried as unsound, by ordering Feuquières to conclude the treaty with Wallenstein. And on the very same day as the latter was murdered regiments of the emperor's army commanded by Czech officers rose in rebellion at

---

* Now Cheb. (V.L.T.).

Opava* in Silesia. Amidst shouts of 'Vivat Friedland' they swore allegiance to the king of France as the new king of the Romans—an episode which haunts the imagination and is evoked in a masterly fashion by Jaroslav Durych, a modern writer.[17]

Thus Wallenstein had met his end, like Gustavus Adolphus before him. With the dissipation of the mirage of his conspiracy, France and the Habsburgs were left face to face in Europe as the only two contestants capable of implementing a policy. It was becoming more and more difficult for Richelieu to postpone France's entry into the conflict indefinitely if he was to avert the collapse of the Protestant party and an imperialist victory.

Although the cardinal mentions Wallenstein in his memoirs, he does so in a way which is studiously vague. He preferred not to inform posterity of his failures. In fact, however, it seems clear that he did not conduct the negotiations with Wallenstein himself. Being occupied with more immediate questions, he left them to Father Joseph and his group. The Capuchin and those about him were above all anxious to prevent such a serious revolution from taking place in the Empire without French participation. But did they really expect it to succeed or want it to succeed. They had realised that the triumph of Wallenstein could hardly fail to constitute a Protestant riposte similar in its effects to an overwhelming victory by Gustavus Adolphus. It was a prospect that caused them some anxiety. However, they were not to find the course of events subsequent to the conspiracy any more reassuring.

As if Wallenstein, far from promoting had delayed the peace for which the peoples longed, the German Lutheran princes, after a half-hearted offensive in north Bohemia, resumed direct negotiations with the emperor. This was the way of bringing the war to an end that they preferred above all other; and Richelieu realised that his entire policy would founder unless France, instead of subsidising foreign generals, herself entered the war as a belligerent. But for this he was not ready.

As we have seen, the intrigues of the ducal house of Lorraine with Monsieur and the imperialists had provided the French with an excuse for intervention. Richelieu had extorted from Cardinal Nicolas François an admission that the marriage between the duke of Orleans and Princess Marguerite had been both celebrated and consummated. In August 1633 the Parlement of Paris proclaimed the confiscation [*saisie*] of 'Barrois mouvant'. Next Louis XIII, advancing from Bar-le-Duc, began to

* Formerly Troppau.

besiege Nancy. In September at Laneuveville Duke Charles IV handed over one of the quarters of the capital and renewed his promise not to take part in the war in Germany without the approval of France. However, Nancy was still disinclined to admit the French.

The royal forces resumed their march along the valley of the Moselle. The king captured Charmes and La Force Epinal. At Charmes, on 20 September, Charles IV consented to a fuller occupation of his capital and agreed to demolish its walls. He then decided to abdicate in favour of his brother, Cardinal Nicolas François. The latter, who was only in minor orders, renounced his ecclesiastical dignities to marry his cousin, Princess Claude.[18] The house of Lorraine seemed to be hemmed in on all sides, and Richelieu would have liked to hold its members as hostages; nevertheless they eventually succeeded in escaping to Tuscany—first the princess of Phalsbourg and then Nicolas François and his wife. As for Charles IV, he had entered the emperor's service.

France was thus left with a free hand in Lorraine. The Parlement of Paris brought an action against Duke Charles for abducting the heir to the throne, and shortly afterwards followed this up by calling for the annexation of the whole of Lorraine and the establishment of a supreme court [*cour souveraine*] at Nancy (September 1634). French magistrates were installed there and all the territories which comprised the former duchy of Lorraine were brought under its jurisdiction with the exception of Barrois, which retained its own judicial administration in the shape of the court of Saint-Mihiel: the latter was set up as a Parlement under a French president, but its magistrates were natives of Lorraine as before.

The whole of Lorraine was thus in the king's hands, and henceforth he considered it a province of his realm. But although the duchy had been annexed, this did not mean that it had been subjugated. The new regime was to meet with vigorous opposition from the population, which was still wedded to the autonomy that it had enjoyed previously. The Jesuits fostered the feeling of hostility towards the French, denouncing their alliance with German heretics as scandalous. It was necessary to make use of all sorts of ingenious arguments to meet these charges, and to appease or win over public opinion by showing respect whenever possible for local customs and traditions.

Moreover, the problem of Lorraine, which had been too hastily dealt with, was a more serious matter than a dispute between Louis XIII and an adjacent vassal—although the French would have been glad to present it in that light. In reality it was an international matter. Henceforth the pope, the emperor and the king of Spain were all to make it one of the conditions of a general peace treaty that the duchy should be restored to its previous rulers. This was why Lorraine was eventually to elude France's clutches at the Peace of Westphalia. But in 1634 the French government's only thought was to secure a firm grip on an area that was required for the security of the realm and for the development of strategic operations towards the east.

On the other hand, several towns and seigneuries in Alsace had placed themselves under French protection, preferring it to Spanish or Swedish protection, which, for political or religious reasons, seemed more fraught with danger for themselves. Here again matters had not gone smoothly, for France had had to reckon with the susceptibilities of her ally; in the case of Philippsburg she was even obliged to challenge Swedish control of a Swedish acquisition.[19]

At all events there passed into French control Montbéliard, which belonged to the duke of Württemberg; the towns of Bouxwiller and Ingwiller; Neuviller in the seigneurie of La Roche [*le ban de la Roche*][20]; Saverne and Hohbar, from which it was possible to keep a watch on the whole of the plain below; and finally Haguenau and Colmar. The road was barred to possible incursions from the east, while communications between the Netherlands and the Spanish-dominated territories of Franche-Comté, Austria and Italy were singularly inconvenienced. All in all it was a fine achievement, of which Richelieu was entitled to feel proud. But he still required two more safeguards: the maintenance of the alliances that France was supporting within the Empire against the Habsburgs and the return home of the heir to the throne.

A few months after Wallenstein's death, and without the emperor abandoning his conciliatory attitude towards Saxony, the new imperial army expelled Bernard of Saxe-Weimar from Regensburg (July). It then effected a junction with the forces which Philip IV's brother, the Cardinal-Infante Ferdinand, had brought from Milan. Thanks to the superiority in numbers which they now enjoyed, and to the resolute leadership of their commanders, the Catholic armies inflicted a severe defeat upon the Swedes at Nördlingen near Donauwörth in September 1634.

Understandably, the effect of this victory was to strengthen the determination of the electors of Saxony and Brandenburg to bring about a reconciliation between themselves and the emperor. Within a few months they achieved their object by the preliminary agreement of Pirna (24

November 1634), which was followed by the Peace of Prague (30 May 1635). By the terms of the Peace Saxony acquired the provinces of Upper and Lower Lusatia, now severed from that Bohemian kingdom whose former splendour Wallenstein and his friends had sought to resurrect; she also gained four bailiwicks [*bailliages*] of the bishopric of Magdeburg.[21] A compromise was reached over the question of confiscations, 1627 being fixed as the determining year that was to govern the tenure of lands within the Empire.[22] The amnesty granted by the Peace of Prague was extended to all princes who resumed their allegiance to the emperor.

Was this to be the signal for the complete disintegration of the Protestant party? Might not the Swedes also abandon the struggle, finding that the odds were now too uneven? In fact Oxenstierna did not seem to lose heart completely—only he could no longer continue the fight and support his allies of the Heilbronn League unless France played a more effective part in the war.

But Richelieu did not yet feel sure enough of the internal tranquillity of the realm, or of the quality of the French army which would have to be used if France were to adopt such a course. It proved impossible to raise sufficient volunteers at home. Troops had to be recruited in Germany, and from among German Protestants at that: 'To levy so many Huguenots [*sic*] is vexatious,' Richelieu observed, 'but few good men are to be found'; and he endeavoured to counteract this drawback by staffing such troops with Catholic officers. These military matters were of the utmost interest to Louis XIII. In the margins of Richelieu's reports can be seen frequent jottings in the king's hand: 'Bon', 'Tout cela est très bon', 'Il est très à propos'. King and cardinal were jointly and closely associated with one and the same policy.

Although he was trying to prevent the Protestant leagues within the Empire from disintegrating, Richelieu did not want to begin hostilities there. He was afraid of strengthening the Protestant party in Germany in a way that would endanger his policy as a whole, and of alienating the German Catholics. He was also afraid of indirectly enhancing the emperor's prestige, for if Louis XIII's forces penetrated too far into German territory there was a risk of their being regarded as a conquering army, and this would arouse feelings of hostility towards France. However, Oxenstierna had been doing his utmost to tempt the French to action. He suggested that Louis XIII's troops should take over from the Swedish forces in west Germany, while Sweden and her allies undertook the conquest of Silesia and the hereditary lands. At about the same time proposals of a somewhat similar nature were made by the United Provinces and their commander-in-chief, the Stadtholder Frederick Henry, prince of Orange. The latter offered to carry out the conquest of the Spanish Netherlands in conjunction with France, and to partition the conquered territories with her. Richelieu considered this also a dangerous venture. He was afraid that there would be difficulties later if France and the United Provinces became neighbours. His preference was for the erection of a 'barrier' between them in the form of an independent state. In other words he already had an inkling of the eventual solution—a buffer state, an independent Belgium.

In this critical situation Richelieu's greatest strength lay in his remarkable poise. In his case ambition and daring did not degenerate into megalomania. Although he realised their limitations, the slender means at his disposal neither discouraged him nor deterred him from action. The prestige enjoyed by France was due to his own achievements, but it did not dazzle him and he would have no truck with rash ventures which might impair it. If we analyse the cautious way in which the cardinal made his preparations, we are almost tempted to take his caution for timidity. Yet it is here that his greatness as a statesman is revealed, rather than in sensational exploits such as others would have hastened to attempt had they been in his place. As a result his conduct of policy seems to be invested with a strength and a human quality which evoke the same feelings of satisfaction as a classical work of art.

It was of the need for intervention in the Netherlands that Richelieu was thinking far more than of an expedition into Germany. To lift a well-known expression out of its context, Brussels was a pistol aimed at France's heart. The metaphor is melodramatic but none the less justified. Spain had under her control in Brussels two pawns of incalculable value —the queen mother of France and the heir to the French throne. The danger seemed all the greater because the aged governor of the Netherlands, the Archduchess Isabella Clara Eugenia, had died in 1633. The archduchess was not only the daughter of Philip II of Spain but also the grand-daughter of Henry II of France. She was proud of her French connections, and although undoubtedly a good Spaniard, she was far from being a bitter enemy of France. But now a new governor was about to succeed her. This was the Cardinal Infante, who had recently gained experience as a soldier on the battlefield and who was taking up his new appointment in a belligerent frame of mind. Richelieu contrived to bring about Monsieur's return to France in October 1634 before the Cardinal Infante's policy had borne fruit, by dint of lavish promises to the prince and to his following; nor did he hesitate to marry his cousin Mlle de Pontchâteau to Puylaurens. No one knew better than he that the latter was a man of lax morals and mercenary outlook, as well as a liar; but to restore order within the royal family there was no woman whom he would not have been ready to cast for Iphigeneia's sacrificial role.*

Monsieur left Princess Marguerite behind him in Brussels. On 5 September the Parlement of Paris had declared the marriage null in that it had not been validly contracted—meaning that it had not been contracted with the consent of Louis XIII, who had the disposal of his brother's person. But this Gallican pronouncement came into collision with the uncompromising attitude of the papacy, which took its stand on the rules relating to matrimony laid down by the Council of Trent. The papal view was that as the marriage had been freely entered into by the interested parties and had also been consummated, it was well and truly valid. In vain did the General Assembly of French clergy express an unfavourable opinion on this point in 1635. Both Princess Marguerite and the Holy See continued to protest against the Parlement's ruling. As for Monsieur, although ready enough to flaunt his liaison with a bourgeoise named Louison Roger throughout the length and breadth of his apanage [*douaire*] of Blois, he eventually came to appreciate their obstinacy, for after all it gave him the upper hand over his brother. He succeeded in making use of it to obtain further concessions.

The cardinal had, as it were, reformed his ministry. He had removed Châteauneuf, the keeper of the seals, who was suspected of intriguing with Mme de Chevreuse and the princes of Lorraine, and replaced him by Séguier, a zealous and loyal servant who was later to become chancellor. The other members of the government consisted of the two superintendents of finance, Bullion and Claude Bouthillier;[23] the latter's son Léon, born in 1608, whom Richelieu loved for his 'youth and happiness' and who became secretary of state for foreign affairs with the title of comte de Chavigny; Servien, the secretary of state for war; and Father Joseph and his collaborators, who 'should know the present state of German affairs better than anyone'. Together they made a strong team —a group of experienced subordinates who, although not perfect or invariably on good terms with each other, showed themselves attentive and vigilant in the execution of their duties. The king and the cardinal used to entrust them with both information and the power to take action, while reserving for themselves the right to make the final de-

---

* Iphigeneia, the daughter of Agamemnon, was sacrificed by her father at Aulis in the hope of obtaining a favourable wind to carry the Greek fleet to Troy.

cision. In short this was one of the good governments of French history.

The autumn of 1634 and the spring of 1635 were taken up with continual diplomatic negotiations—negotiations which were difficult and laborious and led to no more than compromises. However the main point was achieved in that the king of France was still the moving spirit in a coalition against the emperor and the king of Spain; and this coalition was still in operation despite the restoration of peace in Germany by the agreement with the electors.*

The Franco-Dutch Treaty of 8 February 1635 provided for an offensive and defensive alliance. The Belgian provinces of the Netherlands were allowed three months in which to stage a rebellion against Spain with the help of France and the United Provinces. If they failed to take advantage of this opportunity, the two allies were jointly to proceed with the conquest of the Spanish Netherlands, which were to be divided between them on terms that were to be settled later.

The negotiations with Sweden were hectic. Oxenstierna still clung to his idea of dragging France into war with the emperor in Germany. Richelieu, or rather Father Joseph, who was ready to assume the responsibility for German affairs provided his advice was heeded, wanted to arrange for an offensive by Banér's Swedish army towards Gmünd and Austria, and a guarantee that neither Power would make peace without the other; but he jibbed at breaking with the emperor. If absolutely necessary, he was prepared to agree to a formula which drew a somewhat artificial distinction between the Austrian territories, the rest of the Empire and the emperor as such: 'contra Austriacos' or 'contra Austriacos Germaniae'.

In April 1635 the Swedish chancellor visited Paris and Compiègne, where he signed a treaty. In fact this treaty contained no more than the promise of an alliance, which was made conditional on a breach of relations between the French king and the house of Habsburg. It recognised the Swedish occupation of the archbishopric of Mainz and the bishopric of Worms, and provided for the restoration of Catholic worship in areas where its free exercise had been affected by recent Protestant conquests, as well as guaranteeing freedom of worship to the Protestants themselves. If no mention was made of the towns in Alsace, this was because a previous treaty with the League of Heilbronn had already provided France with facilities for exercising her protection over them.[24] Richelieu could consequently declare himself satisfied with the terms of the new treaty with Sweden. Oxenstierna returned from Compiègne

* See the reference to the Preliminaries of Pirna on p. 325 above.

highly pleased with the French king, and there was every reason to suppose that he would behave like a good ally.

France was soon to embark on open war. In March 1635 Spanish troops had entered Trier and seized Philip von Sötern, the archiepiscopal elector, despite the fact that he had placed himself and his city under Louis XIII's protection. In acting thus Spain had flung down a challenge which France could not fail to pick up. We can reasonably assume that the Spanish government realised as much, but chose to provoke war at the earliest possible moment in order to put an end to the invidious situation which had enabled France to make conquests with impunity without allowing Spain the opportunity to prevent her from doing so. Richelieu continued to feel extremely anxious about the conditions under which the war was to be fought, and very probably would have preferred to postpone matters; but the insistence of the United Provinces and Sweden made this impossible. Moreover, a war in the Netherlands could at least remain localised for some time and would not inevitably lead to the breach with the emperor which the Swedish armies were eagerly awaiting.

Admittedly in accepting the pretext for declaring war that Spain had given her, France was allowing herself to be ensnared by a political manoeuvre; however it also gave her the opportunity to come forward as the defender of a German prince and thus as the protector of German liberties, whereas a French offensive in Germany such as Oxenstierna had advised could all too easily have seemed a provocative gesture.

Nor was this all. The Italians could also be drawn into the orbit of French protection in the same way as the petty states and towns along the Rhine. It could be pointed out that it was only the French occupation of Pinerolo and Casale that safeguarded the liberties of the Italian princes and neutralised the Milanese by preventing Spanish forces there from taking any action against small neighbouring states. Such was the significance of the policy which in July 1635 culminated in the Treaty of Rivoli between France and the dukes of Savoy and Parma. It was a considerable achievement, although the terms of the Treaty fell short of the hopes the French had entertained of forming an anti-Spanish league composed of all the states of north Italy.

For all these reasons the decision to open hostilities in Flanders—a decision which was dictated by events rather than adopted by Richelieu of his own free will—deserved to be regarded as 'offering advantageous prospects', and as an act of 'courage conjoined with wisdom'. It was with these words that Richelieu justified his decision in the 'Succincte narration'.

The declaration of war was made with solemnity, in the chivalrous manner of the Middle Ages, and clothed in the due ceremonial forms which were now employed for the last time. On 19 May the king's herald-of-arms, a Gascon officer by the name of Gratiollet, made his appearance in Brussels wearing a herald's cap and holding a herald's baton in his hand. He was preceded by a trumpeter who sounded the chamade.[25] Although the Cardinal Infante did not receive him in audience, he watched the way in which Gratiollet went about his delicate task with the sympathy of one nobleman for another. Amongst the multitude that had assembled around him, the French herald scattered copies of the royal declaration of 12 May 1635 bearing Louis XIII's signature and countersigned by Servien.[26] Then he made his announcement:

'I come to seek you out on behalf of the king my master, my only sovereign lord, to give you to understand that whereas you have not seen fit to set at liberty My Lord Archbishop of Trier, an elector of the Holy Empire, who placed himself under His Majesty's protection when he could not obtain it from the emperor or from any other prince: and whereas contrary to the dignity of the Empire and to the law of nations you thus hold prisoner a sovereign prince with whom you are not at war: His Majesty maketh known to you his resolution to have recourse to arms to obtain satisfaction for this offence which importeth each and every prince of Christendom.'

His task completed, the herald left the city and took the road back to France. On reaching the last village that lay in Spanish territory he dismounted from his horse, fastened the manifesto to a post and ordered his trumpeter to sound the chamade once more.

This trumpet blast, wafted across the plain of Flanders by the spring breezes of May, announced the opening of a war between France and Spain that was to last for twenty-four years (1635–59). Seen as an event in world history it was a fratricidal struggle between two nations which were both of them Christian and Catholic. But if we judge it in accordance with contemporary ideas and the position of Europe at the time, it was an inevitable duel between two Powers. The one stood for its own hegemony; the other, under Richelieu's ruthless yet sagacious leadership, was to defend not only its territorial integrity but also, despite the many contradictions in its policy, the right of European states to be subject to no one save their own natural rulers. It was a right which meant to them what freedom means to us.

CHAPTER NINE

The Great Ordeal
(1636–38)

THE DECLARATION of war on Spain which we have been taught by a long historical tradition to regard as quite natural—as if it came at the right moment for Richelieu to carry out the third item in his programme*—in fact involved great risks and was dictated by the over-riding pressure of circumstances. It was essential to stop the anti-Habsburg coalition from dissolving and to prevent the conclusion of a peace whose terms would have been dictated by the house of Austria. Indeed one can scarcely call it a coalition for it was little more than a convergence of two alliances, the first binding France and the United Provinces, the second France and Sweden. Between them stood the army of Bernard of Saxe-Weimar who was not to be linked to the French cause for some months.

So general was the desire for peace in Germany, however, that it would have been dangerous for France to admit that she was turning her back on it. For several years pope Urban VIII had been indefatigable in proposing his own good offices to arrange a settlement. If a war between Catholics and Protestants represented a grave threat to the Church's interests, an extension of the struggle involving warfare between the most Christian king and the Catholic king was a calamity that beggared description, for France and Spain were the two powers that Rome most needed. This reversion to the conflicts between Francis I and Charles V, this rent in the unity of Catholicism, was an appalling danger for the papacy, the more so because the French king would be forced to strengthen his alliance with the Protestants—Sweden, the United Provinces, and the German Lutherans and Calvinists. Not only this, but England might be led to intervene and act as arbiter. In that event only Turkish intervention would be needed for the disaster to be complete.

Here let us mention in passing that Richelieu's accommodating attitude towards heretics was the argument that the Spaniards used to cast a slur upon France. It is therefore rather piquant to note that those who have credited the cardinal with a distinct partiality for alliances with

* See p. 140 above.

Protestant powers or almost acclaimed his indifference to religious considerations, his Machiavellianism and his lack of sympathy for the general interests of the Catholic world at a time when the Counter-Reformation was at its height, have merely adopted somewhat uncritically the statements put out by Spanish propaganda.

In reality it was now impossible for the cardinal to escape from the paradoxical difficulties and inconsistencies in which circumstances had involved him. He declared war only a few weeks after the French king and the emperor had given their consent to the opening of general peace conferences and he did not reject the pursuance of negotiations; but his attitude in no way signified that he was not seriously bent on war. On the contrary in any diplomatic discussion there could be no better argument than a recent victory demonstrating a country's armed strength and arousing the enemy's fears as to the consequences when its forces were yet stronger.

Richelieu also knew full well that he was embarking upon war under difficult conditions. He had not been able to secure the necessary supplies for his troops in advance and he appreciated the dangers to which this could lead: 'In the course of history many more armies have perished for lack of bread and good administration [*police*] than through enemy action', he wrote. 'I can bear witness that all the military enterprises which have been undertaken in my time have come to naught for this reason alone.' He mistrusted the generals and higher officers in the French army many of whom seemed to him of doubtful worth. In addition he had but small confidence in the French soldier. In the *Testament politique* the cardinal was to pass a severe judgement on him, a judgement coloured by his bitter experiences during the early months of the war:

'There is no people in the world so little suited to war as ours. The frivolity and impatience which they show in the most minor tasks are two characteristics which, to my deep regret, only serve to emphasise the truth of this assertion. Although Caesar said that the Franks [*sic*] were skilled in two things, the art of war and the art of speech, I confess that hitherto I have been unable to understand on what grounds he credits them with a talent for the first since patience in toil and hardship, so necessary in warfare, is but seldom found amongst them.'[1]

Should we then emphasise the contrast between French military weakness and the strength and renown of the Spanish army? The truth is that to explain the one or the other it is not enough merely to think in terms of the permanent moral qualities of the two peoples. In expressing his surprise at Julius Caesar's opinion, the cardinal for all his perspicacity was showing a respect for the testimony of the ancient sources which was ill founded and excessive. He apparently believed that a people's genius is fixed once and for all whereas in fact the evolution of history compels it to undergo considerable changes. The entire period of the Roman Empire and all the Middle Ages had elapsed since Caesar's day. How could they have failed to modify the conditions under which the people of France lived as well as their tastes? A thousand years of a civilisation which was more rural than urban lay heavy on the seventeenth-century Frenchman with all the weight of a soil that in other respects offered him so much. If he no longer possessed the first of the two qualities which Caesar attributed to his ancestors was this not due to the fact that he had become essentially a husbandman and a peasant? The peasant will fight to defend his home and his property if absolutely necessary; but unlike the soldier he is not a man with an urge for adventure and travel. Consider for example the French expeditions to those new lands across the Atlantic—Canada and the West Indies. It was the merchants who led the way in colonising them, but peasants from every province of France were invited to take part. To this call they responded, though only in small numbers; and in what frame of mind did they do so—in the spirit of the Conquistadors? Not at all. They were simply attracted by the prospect of new lands to clear, by the hope of exercising their original occupation in better conditions than at home. Woodcutters and tillers of the soil thought only in terms of continuing their association with forest and field.

The seventeenth-century Spaniard on the other hand was essentially a nomad reared in a land given over to grazing and the seasonal migration of flocks. For this reason it was easy for him to become a soldier and a conqueror. Differences of the same order could be observed between the nobility of Castile and the nobility of France. True, they formed a military caste in both countries. Moreover the French nobleman's addiction to sword-play is demonstrated by his fondness for duelling and it was only a short time since he had served his military apprenticeship in the wars of religion. But these martial exploits were carried out close at hand or within the confines of the tilt yard—for in the case of the French noble the decisive influence was his affection for his ancestral manor. He would return there to supervise building and repairs, to collect his rents, to live off the land and from the chase. In the words of a writer who himself belonged to the same class he went there to enjoy 'power and seclusion'.* Although the French country gentleman

* 'Puissance et solitude'. The writer was Chateaubriand. (V.L.T.)

wore a sword he remained attached to the land.

The same is scarcely true of the *caballero* or hidalgo.* Not wars of re-ligion but the reconquest of Spain from the Moors or the epic of the Conquistadors had been the most recent experience of his caste. Like the flocks of the Mesta,† the chief source of wealth in a country given over to pasture and mining, the hidalgo was essentially mobile, always avail-able and ready to embark on distant expeditions.

For half a century the duel between France and Spain was to be one between a nation of peasants steadily growing acclimatised to war, who acquired or rediscovered in the process the martial prowess they had shown in bygone days, and a nation of soldiers that took to warfare as its favourite occupation.

At the outset the advantage seemed to lie with Spain. In the long run it was to be a different matter, for Spain, as we shall see, was already faced with growing economic difficulties and her reserves of wealth were des-tined to run dry more quickly than those of France, The resources of an arable country were to be more regularly replenished than those of a country devoted to the raising of livestock.

But in 1635 the only relevant factors were those that obtained at the outset. Consequently it was vitally necessary for war to appear as the only solution so far as France was concerned—otherwise the king would have suffered a severe blow to his reputation in Europe for daring to embark on hostilities with his country in such a position. This situation has been admirably defined by George Pagès: 'No unity of command, strategic conditions which were at best mediocre, and financial resources that were lamentably inadequate.'[2]

The cardinal's decision was certainly not based on expectations of an easy victory but he faced the danger that beset the realm from without, firmly bent on remaining at his post.

The declaration of war on Spain may be said to usher in a new phase in the history of the reign and of the ministry. Neither Richelieu's memoirs nor the *Testament politique* nor his correspondence divulge his thoughts completely, for the cardinal without being insincere meant what he wrote for posterity to serve as a lesson in politics. In true Cartesian style

---

* I have here translated the French word *cavalier* into its Spanish equivalent *caballero* which in the seventeenth century meant 'a knight, a member of the lesser aristocracy as distinguished from a noble'—Elliott, p. 578. The terms *caballero* and *hidalgo* were then interchangeable—see the same author's *Imperial Spain*.

† A guild of Castilian sheep-farmers.

he emphasises the extent to which reason and will can provide statesmen with political rules and principles and assist them in their task. Admittedly in his letters, in which he tried to instil fresh courage into his colleagues, Richelieu did not disguise the difficulties that a course of action entailed; but he always used to point out that they could be overcome. Both by temperament and of set purpose as well as by virtue of necessity he generated a universal feeling of confidence. Whatever the circumstances of the case he used to focus attention on any gratifying result and adopt a deliberately optimistic attitude.

One is often inclined to believe that the course of events was under Richelieu's control to a greater extent than was the case. Moreover, for us to acknowledge as we look back centuries later that the cardinal was far from able to put his programme into full effect, that he continually had to make do with compromise arrangements and that the evil which he succeeded in arresting at one point often reappeared at another, involves no depreciation of his qualities; if anything the reverse is nearer the truth. This superlative architect of French unity and absolute monarchy failed to do everything that he wanted and often did things which he had not reckoned on doing. In the event the structure which he left, although undoubtedly imposing, was in many respects incomplete and fragile. It is no doubt true that Richelieu had always thought that open war with Spain was bound to come sooner or later; but it is highly likely that he would have preferred to choose the time himself and would only have embarked upon hostilities with a tried army and a disciplined and a willing country behind him—in short under the very conditions that conventional and superficial histories have long told us were already established.

As we have seen, the truth is that the cardinal had realised as early as 1630 that his programme for internal reform would have to be sacrificed in favour of foreign policy. He had the integrity and the strength to reveal to Louis XIII the choice that had to be made and to win him over to his own way of thinking. Then he had to face a dangerous conspiracy by his enemies only to emerge from the crisis stronger than ever. Even so this did not mean that he had completely overthrown and destroyed the party led by the queen mother, the two Marillacs and Monsieur; still less did it mean that he had prevented opposition from recurring. From then onwards he devoted all his efforts towards stopping the war in Germany from spreading to France's frontiers and to French territory. The occupation of Lorraine if not the greatest of his achievements was at all events the one in which his plans were most fully realised. While leaving Father

Joseph and his associates to deal with the details and complexities of negotiations with the Empire and in particular with the negotiations with Wallenstein, the most important of them all, the cardinal had kept a careful eye on events in Germany. He was determined to prevent any peace from being concluded on terms dictated by the Habsburgs and to make sure that the house of Austria's enemies did not relax their vigilance. Richelieu's attention was never completely diverted from Italian affairs; but although he tried to encircle the Milanese and to prevent Italy from falling under Spanish sway it is evident that from about 1632 onwards Germany, the Netherlands and Lorraine assumed an increasingly important place in his preoccupations.

The cardinal's health, which had never been good, had been further impaired by the ministrations of the so-called doctors [*médicastres*] of his day and constantly interfered with his work. We referred above to the optimistic tone of Richelieu's letters. Only rarely does he complain and when he does it is usually about his ailments—his piles, his retentions of urine, the attacks of fever which have prostrated him for several days or several weeks. On several occasions there are signs that he is feeling dejected and he refers to his need to retire from office. It is easy enough today not to take these allusions seriously; yet what they reveal is the exhaustion of a man at the end of his tether even if this exhaustion was fortunately only transient.[3]

In these circumstances what could be more absurd than to suppose that Richelieu could be everywhere at once and concern himself with every single detail? His very role as minister was nothing less than one long negotiation and when the *Testament politique* emphasises the necessity for continual negotiations the statement should not be taken as applying solely to diplomacy. To control general policy the cardinal used to issue broad directives to everyone responsible for its execution and he always acted as arbitrator in the event of any disagreement. But he had to hand over what we would nowadays call large sectors to trusted colleagues, especially after 1635.

Finally, once hostilities had begun the cardinal had neither time nor opportunity for thinking of anything else except at odd moments and almost surreptitiously. Henceforth it was foreign policy, that is to say diplomacy and war, that claimed his attention. He had to leave the internal government of France to others, namely the superintendents of finance and the chancellor. In other words it was for them to extract the money and to see that order reigned within the realm—two immense and terrifying tasks as we shall see. Any large-scale reforms were out of the question, indeed less feasible than ever. To obtain what it could from the population, from institutions and from existing usages, was the most that the government set itself to achieve.

The first encounters in the field went in France's favour. A fine army, 35,000 strong, and commanded by marshals de Brézé and Châtillon, advanced on the bishopric of Liège and won a clear-cut victory over the Spaniards at Avein. Troops under the duke of Rohan, who had been restored to favour and was popular with the Swiss cantons, occupied the passes of the Valtelline while forces under cardinal La Valette advanced to the help of Bernard of Saxe-Weimar. But this was all. Abruptly the fortunes of war changed.

Instead of linking up with the French army in Flanders the prince of Orange simply left it to take up its quarters in Belgium. Unpaid and without victuals its regiments took to battening on the inhabitants, ransacking the houses, outraging the women and committing all kinds of misdeeds. Their aristocratic officers, disappointed at the lack of fighting, and feeling that there was no point in their remaining where they were, gaily decided to return home without bothering themselves any more about their men.

In Lorraine the people had shown themselves ill-disposed to French rule. The war provided them with an excuse for breaking into revolt and several towns declared for the former duke who approached the frontier at the head of an imperial army. The duc de la Force and the old duke of Angoulême had evident difficulty in carrying out defensive operations and Louis XIII was impatient to go there himself to put the situation to rights. Richelieu, forced to stay behind by illness, felt uneasy about the idea but was not in a position to oppose it. He therefore let the king go but took the precaution of ensuring that Louis XIII was at least accompanied by Séguier and Chavigny, ministers upon whom he could rely, while himself retaining Servien and the two superintendents. At the beginning of October the king entered Saint-Mihiel; but he had not enough troops to clear the duchy and expel duke Charles IV, who had entrenched himself at Rambervillers where he had recently been reinforced by Gallas's army. Admittedly other French and allied forces were also entering Lorraine for cardinal La Valette and Bernard of Saxe-Weimar were on their way back to France after penetrating as far as Frankfurt-am-Main and then carrying out a daring retreat, thus evading Gallas. But their men were tired. They had operated too far away from their supply bases and often they had been short of bread and munitions.

They had had to eat turnips and rank vegetables and had been forced to burn their baggage because it delayed them on the march. In addition they had lost a large number of their effectives. The enemy was in a strong position and, although Louis XIII had in fact superiority in numbers, he was dissuaded from risking battle in such dangerous conditions. He returned to Paris having suffered quite a blow to his pride. However the enemy armies although under shelter were also ill supplied and as there were no winter quarters available for them on the spot they withdrew towards Germany. Lorraine remained in French hands.

The French took advantage of the opportunity to make definite arrangements for retaining Bernard of Saxe-Weimar in their service. By a treaty concluded in October Louis XIII took him on his payroll with the right to employ him wherever he thought fit. On the other hand France undertook to recognise Bernard's claim to Haguenau and the landgravate of Upper Alsace[4] and entrusted him with the defence of Alsace, for at one stage there had been fears that it would be impossible to maintain French garrisons there any longer. Whereas Richelieu already regarded Lorraine as a territory that had been permanently annexed to the realm he was as yet only interested in Alsace for strategic reasons; in his eyes it was simply a line which it was important to hold since otherwise it would certainly be occupied by the Spaniards.

In Italy the operations carried out by the duke of Savoy and the maréchal de Créqui did not achieve any decisive results, while at sea the Spaniards, taking advantage of French weakness, seized the Îles de Lérins[5]—a step which gave rise to fears that it might be followed by a landing in Provence.

In this highly dangerous situation Richelieu exerted his full energy. It is surprising to see the difficulties that he met with from the superintendents of finance. Whilst taking care to humour their susceptibilities he bombarded them with demands for the sum required for the upkeep of the king's armies, for the orders and money which had to be sent to the intendants attached to these armies to purchase corn and pay the troops. Although it is true that some of the superior officers were lacking in drive and daring—like 'that old fogey Angoulême', as Richelieu used to call Charles IX's elderly son, refusing to make any allowance for his age —the main problem in these military operations was financial. It was for lack of money and for no other reason that the fine army which had invaded Flanders had disintegrated within two months to Richelieu's intense chagrin. The army operating on the German front had narrowly escaped the same fate as was shown by the case of a young *maréchal de camp* named Turenne who had been reduced to selling his pewter to make ends meet.

Quite apart from the growing recalcitrance of the superintendents of finance there was no certainty of a satisfactory outcome even when they did promise to take action. For example letters of exchange did not arrive in time and the merchants who had contracted to supply the armies [*munitionnaires*]⁶ used to carry out their business dealings as if they were entitled to go on making profits indefinitely and as if soldiers' lives and the safety of the realm did not depend upon their diligence. 'I have some difficulty,' the cardinal wrote to the maréchal de Brézé, 'in inducing Messieurs des Finances to agree to what must be done—although it is relatively easy to overcome their opposition since they are most devoted to his Majesty's service. But their good resolutions are not always translated into action—a fact of which I am often only apprised by the evil consequences that arise therefrom.'

During the winter of 1635–6 Richelieu seems to have been continually concerned with keeping the armies supplied. Servien, the secretary of state for war, threw the responsibility for the military reverses of the past few months on to Bullion attributing them to lack of money. But to raise a hand against Bullion was out of the question and it was Servien who was sacrificed; he was exiled to Angers.

Whereas Richelieu had to display great patience and tact in his dealings with the ministers of finance, he held that the government should show itself merciless in punishing officers and that the best way to keep the people of Lorraine submissive was to intimidate them. An officer of noble birth who deserted must be hunted down. 'In my opinion,' Richelieu wrote to the king as early as 4 August, 'all officers who have gone absent without leave should immediately be deprived of noble rank and proclaimed unworthy and incapable of holding any honours, dignities and charges. All provosts and officers of justice should be ordered to seize them wherever they may be and have them tried in accordance with the severity of the regulations. Truly I fear that there will be mass desertion from the colours unless harsh measures like these are adopted.'

Feudal levies were summoned from among the nobility in the provinces to provide cavalry and reminded that men of noble birth owed the king three months' military service within the realm and forty days' service abroad. Lorraine however was held to be French territory and service there was to be reckoned as service within the realm. This being the case, it followed that the officers of justice and townsmen in Lorraine who had rejoined the duke's party could be dealt with as traitors.

After the capitulation of Saint-Mihiel there had been much indignation in the army about Louis XIII's treatment of the garrison. Some did not hesitate to say that it must have been men who belonged to the *noblesse de robe* like Séguier and Chavigny who had advised him to act thus —men who could give such advice with impunity since they did not bear arms and ran no risk of being involved in open rebellion or of being obliged to throw themselves upon a victor's mercy. However if these ministers did in fact encourage the king to show himself obdurate they were following strict instructions given them by Richelieu. It was precisely because he was sure that they would be amenable that the cardinal had arranged for them to accompany the king.

Louis XIII had allowed the inhabitants of Saint-Mihiel to keep their property except for a few men of whom he intended to make an example.

'Provided that what you advise me the king has decided is carried out to the letter,' Richelieu wrote to Chavigny on 6 October, 'that is to say that some of the inhabitants whom the king has designated are punished as an example—such as the president [of the Parlement] if present—and that the others pay a ransom of 100,000 crowns in return for their lives: provided also that the leaders are held prisoner at Metz and Verdun, that all the soldiers are sent to the galleys and that the Parlement's jurisdiction is transferred to the Supreme Council: and provided that the walls are razed to the ground: all will go well.'

As for the soldiers, although you have only chains for 150 of them, all the others must be sent securely bound with ropes to some safe place, with a good escort and two reliable provosts who will not release any of them in return for money.'[7]

Richelieu recommended that if there was a risk of a town being impossible to hold or serving as a base for a fresh rebellion it should be destroyed: 'The more houses that can be demolished the better; when there is not time to reduce them to this condition they must be set on fire and thoroughly burnt.' All this was written by the cardinal in cold blood in his study at Rueil—several days distant by courier from the places on which he was passing sentence.[8] Even the deputies of the Convention who formed the Committee of Public Safety did not call for more terrible measures.* Is it surprising then that the peasants of Lorraine should have taken to the woods in wild panic whenever soldiers approached, that some districts were reduced to indescribable misery and that it was

---

* The Committee of Public Safety came into existence in April 1793, seven months after the election of the Convention. Both lasted until 1795.

an engraver from Lorraine, Jacques Callot, who bequeathed to posterity the most appalling pictures of the horrors of war?

In acting thus Richelieu believed that he was adopting the best method of preventing the war from dragging on for ever, for he did not want a long war and was still ready to grasp at an opportunity for peace. Nevertheless France had to be in a position to continue the fight and for this fresh financial resources were essential.

Richelieu had for long realised, if only as a result of the information which the keeper of the seals used to receive from the provinces, that where the poor were concerned the limit to the amount of taxation they could endure had already been reached if not exceeded. Nor did he deem it possible to ask for heroic sacrifices from the wealthier taxpayer. In 1633 the duke of Épernon had written: 'I can assure you that distress is everywhere so universal and prevalent amongst all classes that, unless some respite be now given, the helplessness of the people cannot but move them to some dangerous resolution.'[9] In reply to appeals of this nature Richelieu could say with truth that he was fully convinced of the dangers caused by extortionate taxation. He declared as much in the *Testament politique*, stressing the evil consequences peculiar to his day—the stagnation of commercial activity accompanied by the ruin of the country gentry [*noblesse campagnarde*] and an abrupt halt in the recruitment of officers for the king's army. Moreover if goods became expensive it would no longer be to the advantage of foreigners to make their purchases in France. There would be a risk of France becoming a country which was 'full of the fruits of the earth but bereft of gold and silver . . . It is not possible continually to increase the charges imposed by taxation, for taxes raise the cost of living to the prejudice of the country gentry, whose revenues do not increase and who can no longer send their children into the army to serve their king and country as is incumbent on them by reason of their noble birth.' The cardinal admitted further that the king could not increase taxes to suit his own convenience without being answerable to God for so doing, and that the only justification for levying these taxes lay in there being a good reason for them.

In existing circumstances additional expenditure was logically imperative and extra taxation was therefore justifiable. The superintendents of finance had tried to obtain more money by very modest increases in local impositions—surtaxes of the type that the consumer is apt to grumble a little about paying, but eventually pays all the same because he does not want to go without the goods in question and because the additional expense is not excessive. In wine-producing districts attempts had been made to impose on tavern-keepers a tax of a crown per hogs-head [*barrique*], while an imposition of a sol per livre payable on all sales of goods had been introduced throughout the realm.[10]

But these measures had met with more serious resistance than had been anticipated. Riots had broken out in Bordeaux on two occasions—in May and June 1635. The mob had armed themselves. D'Aguesseau, the first president of the Parlement there, wrote to Séguier reporting that the people had shouted 'Long live the king' and some of them had declared that they would pay his Majesty whatever tax it pleased him to impose upon them provided that it did not apply to wine. Order had only been restored through the intervention of the armed forces stationed in the province under the duke of Épernon, the town militia [*milice bourgeoise*] being inadequate for the purpose.

Richelieu had been obliged to give way. 'The edict relating to the tavern-keepers will not be enforced,' he wrote to La Valette on 11 August 1635, 'and if there is some other edict which is injurious to the province we will show similar consideration.' As for the imposition of a sol in the livre Sublet de Noyers, the intendant, declared that to enforce it at Amiens was quite out of the question: 'In the light of the especial knowledge I have acquired of the extreme poverty of this people,' he wrote to Séguier on 9 January 1636, 'and of the strange inward motions to which their great distress can lead them, I consider it to be in the king's service, if his affairs make it necessary to impose this tax, that it should at least be deferred until a more timely season. The mere fear of it has already been enough to bring half the town's trade to a halt and has stricken more than three thousand workmen, some of them being reduced to beggary and death. If I say this, Monseigneur, it is because I have seen it.'[11] Elsewhere the effect of the imposition was not to cause unemployment but to encourage profiteering. In March 1636 Richelieu complained to the *lieutenant civil* of Paris that 'under colour of this imposition of a sol per livre an article which used to be sold at 50 sols and which in view of the imposition should now be sold at 52 sols 6 deniers is offered for sale at 60 or 75 sols. I have heard quoted as an example the pieces of silk of which ladies nowadays make neckerchiefs.' The price of boots and shoes rose to exorbitant heights.

This did not alter the fact that a period of general deflation had begun. The price of cereals was dropping and there was a slump more or less everywhere. Soon the monetary edicts of March and June 1636 were to devalue the livre, the value of the *livre tournois* being reduced to eight grammes sixty-nine of fine silver. Trade was beginning to come to a standstill; there seemed every likelihood of unemployment, economic distress, and a poor return from taxes. In vain did the cardinal issue orders and call upon subordinates 'to work wonders'. Administrative catch-phrases could not alter the facts.

Since any means of extricating the realm from these straits was worth attempting, we must not be surprised to find Richelieu going so far as to authorise experiments like those carried out by Father Du Bois, an unfrocked Capuchin, who undertook to transmute base metals into gold. Was he going to rescue the Crown from its financial difficulties by such an expedient?

It was Father Joseph who recommended this curious individual in all seriousness. An experiment was carried out in the king's presence at the Louvre in the course of which two musket balls were changed into an ingot of fine gold. But this astonishing achievement probably repre-sented the most that the alchemist could do. Richelieu began to grow im-patient for Du Bois was always finding some excuse or other. Eventually he did get to work; but it was not long before everyone had had enough. Du Bois was put on trial and condemned to death for practising magic, counterfeiting the coinage and other crimes.[12]

Experiments like these were not referred to again nor were they recorded for posterity. In the meantime several million livres were needed. However it seems clear that despite the poverty of the country and the limited amount of money in circulation, the government was convinced that there were reserves in existence—belonging of course to the bourgeoisie—which could be tapped by resorting to the creation of offices. In this way it was hoped to raise at least fifteen million livres. Of course this step involved the government in another vicious circle for there was a serious danger of its causing resentment among the office-holders and the magistracy who had hitherto been relatively docile. They would not omit to point out with a good deal of truth that the effect of fresh creations would be to lower the status of offices generally: that a step of this nature would have more far-reaching consequences than a temporary tax imposed as a wartime measure and would impose heavy burdens on future budgets: that a mass irruption of less experi-enced newcomers into judicial, fiscal and administrative posts threatened to reduce the authority that officials had hitherto enjoyed throughout the country. Indeed such arguments were advanced and on several oc-casions. However we can only suppose that they failed to carry convic-tion and were even regarded as lame, for quite apart from having to meet the expenses caused by the war at all costs the government believed that it would succeed in raising the required sum. In fact a large number of the well-to-do among the population were by no means averse from holding more offices. Their desire was kept alive as much by a liking for honours as by a mercenary outlook. The income from the capital invested in an office was certainly considered an attraction but a far more cogent argument in their favour was the fact that office provided entry to the ranks of the privileged and to the nobility. As Georges Lefevbre has very aptly put it, 'perhaps the most original feature of French society was the importance of venality of office'.[13] One can sense as much at this particular moment when the government had to count on the sale of offices to provide the means for continuing the war and saving the state and when so many bourgeois families were eager to benefit from the latest series of promotions.

For example we find Louis XIII urging the magistrates of the Parlement not to raise difficulties about admitting as a counsellor a young man in whom he is interested: 'The person with whom I am concerned is the son of my principal physician; I ask you for the love that you bear me to show him favour.' On this occasion the king handles the old magistrates carefully; being anxious to avoid creating a hostile attitude to the new counsellor he does not give them orders and sets out to make himself positively amiable.

This is the explanation for the mass of forty-two edicts submitted to the Parlement of Paris at the end of 1635 and registered at a *lit de justice* —not without numerous complaints especially from the counsellors of the *Chambre des Enquêtes* who were the youngest and the most unruly. We cannot analyse all these edicts here; but we must at least give some idea of the shower of new offices that descended on the bourgeoisie:

In the Parlement of Paris an extra *président à mortier* and further counsellors, Counsellors of Requests and Masters of Requests.[14]

In the *Chambre des Comptes* new appointments included eight Masters, seven revisers [*correcteurs*] and ten auditors of accounts, controller-binders of accounts and an official wax-heater.

To the *Cour des Aides* was added a complete third chamber.[15]

In the *Grand Conseil* two presidents were appointed (who were exempted from the rule that they should be Masters of Requests) together with ten councillors, not to mention other offices.[16]

Eighty-four more offices with the title of *Sécrétaire du Roi* were established,[17] new officials were introduced into the *Cour des Monnaies*[18] and new offices were created in every *bailliage*, *présidial* and *sénéchaussée*.

A Parlement was set up at Metz, a *présidial* at Rodez and another at Brioude.

An *élection* was established at Cognac and a new *trésorier de France* instituted in each *bureau des finances*.[19]

In every *bailliage, sénéchaussée* and seat of a *présidial*, a *conseiller honoraire* was installed—an office which was not merely made hereditary but was even transmissible through the widow—while each town or parish [*communauté*][20] was provided with a public prosecutor [*procureur du Roi*] and a clerk of the court [*greffier*]. The list is an interminable one.

Other edicts provided for increases in salaries which were made hereditable; for, as mentioned earlier in this book,* if an office-holder agreed to the immediate payment of a sum representing an arbitrarily fixed increase in the value of his appointment the Treasury in return used to pay him a higher salary and the office became hereditary, its tenure being prolonged on the same terms as had obtained during the holder's lifetime.

The government also decided on certain increases in taxes which taken as a whole assured the Treasury of a substantial return although they apparently only required a very modest additional contribution from each taxpayer. But until such time as they had been collected the officials of the relevant tax-receiving offices were expected to advance the equivalent to the Treasury without delay.

The officials concerned were unable to avoid these exactions; nor, all things considered, did they wish to do so. Payments which ensured that an office-holder's appointment was hereditable seemed to him well worth making, for all the energies of the bourgeoisie tended to be devoted to turning offices into family possessions that could be passed on to the next generation. The only question that possibly requires an answer is: where did these officials find the necessary money?

It is highly likely that reserves of ready money were greater than supposed. Hoarding was common practice and explains the quantities of gold and silver stowed away in some hiding place which would miraculously appear at the right moment. Little is known as yet of the history of domestic economy during the Ancien Régime but it must contain many examples of this characteristic feature of peasant thrift or avarice. However it was not necessary for the office-holder himself to have these secret reserves in his possession; it was enough for him to be able to have access to them by borrowing from those to whom they belonged, whether relatives, neighbours or persons subject to his administration

* See p. 56 above.

with an interest in obliging him, or again merchants or traders for whom debts of this nature were good investments.

Rentes sur le clergé and loans to the State were ceasing to inspire confidence. It was better for a man to lend money to a person whom he knew, for it was easier to keep track of an individual's solvency.[21] There were no public banking facilities and in their absence the government, whose opportunities for raising money abroad were also limited, resorted to the fiscal measures we have described as a means of mobilising capital that lay idle. Indeed one might almost say that it was creating this capital, starting from the level of small savings, and using the financial reserves of the king's subjects, however modest, to serve the national interest.[22]

Nor should we overlook the fact that the transactions in ready money which resulted from increases in taxation could be profitable to the officials concerned. Seventeenth-century French coins by virtue of their composition lent themselves to all kinds of operations that were far from honest but which were too easy to carry out and too widespread not to tempt others as well as coiners. Even the latter were by no means all of them rogues. They included people of considerable standing as is shown by the surprising list of names printed in Georges d'Avenel's book: the duke of Angoulême (admittedly through an intermediary), La Vieuville, at one time superintendent of finance, and Roannes, who was a duke and a peer of the realm. The debasement of the coinage, though a criminal offence in law, was in practice more like a rather shady transaction or a chemical experiment that excluded any assay of the coins used; since coins, which were struck with the hammer and not provided with milled edges, were neither perfectly round nor of identical shape it was easy enough to pare away a few particles. 'Better results could be obtained with the help of various essences,' writes Georges d'Avenel: 'people used to dissolve and debase both gold and silver; for gold coins use was chiefly made of an *aqua regia*.[23] Its effect was to reduce their weight by approximately a quarter or a fifth but without altering the portrait.' The result was that everyone including those guilty of the practice used to suspect that coins had been tampered with and eventually they were only accepted according to their weight. But there was nothing to prevent an officer of the revenue who was not over-burdened with scruples from paying the sums demanded of him by the Treasury in coins that were underweight while insisting that taxes be paid to himself in coins of the full weight; he could keep the latter in his private coffers as a refund on the advances he had made to the Treasury. The difference in value represented a clear profit for himself.

Richelieu committed to paper the most admirable maxims on the need for the State to set a good example by its own honesty; but since the conduct of the State with its flagrant exactions and arbitrary proceedings was a far from edifying sight for officials and subjects alike, we must not be too surprised by these deplorable practices caused by financial difficulties, while remembering that to explain them is neither to excuse nor to justify them.

But having made this point let us be careful not to give too one-sided a picture of the bourgeoisie by only mentioning their personal interest in the creation of offices and the increase in salaries and taxes. It is by no means certain that they were deaf to the pleas of common sense and the national interest put forward by the government. Naturally they did not lose sight of their own advantage for to expect people to show self-abnegation on such a heroic scale would be unwise at any time; perhaps however they were readier to pay heed to the government's arguments than the other classes. In 1632 the jurist Cardin Le Bret published his *Traité de la Souveraineté du Roi*. In this treatise he sets forth in the clearest and most convincing way the doctrine of royal absolutism which means to him not only the sovereign's personal power but also the exercise of this power in the service of the State.

'The king is sole sovereign in his realm . . . and sovereignty is no more divisible than a point in geometry.' (I, 9.)

'The only aim of kings should be to make their people happy and to enable them to enjoy all manner of felicities.' (IV, 15.)

The noble serves the king because he is supreme lord and because the hierarchy of dependants joining man to man and vassal to overlord culminates in the king's person. The cleric honours the king as the Lord's anointed who has been consecrated at Rheims and shares in the greatness of the Church. As for the common man who is ready to cry 'Vive le Roi' even when taking part in a riot, if he has not himself set eyes on the king —and a far larger number of his lowly subjects had seen Louis XIII than we are apt to suppose—he thinks of him rather confusedly as a superior being whose duty it is to protect him, a being who must be besought, invoked and feared rather in the same way as God and the Saints.

But what of the bourgeois of the sixteen-thirties, of the eight years 1635–43, the last and most difficult years of the reign? Did he not hold rather a different view even if it led him to adopt a similar attitude of obedience and acquiescence? Nourished as he was on the teaching of the jurists and either permeated with the Catholic spirit of the age or—if a Protestant—mindful of the disciplinary lessons contained in the Bible, did not the bourgeois acknowledge royal authority as an order of things that was in conformity both with the law and with the will of God? And was he not also more receptive to such notions as national independence, the safety of the realm, the public welfare, the regulation of private interests, in short to the idea of the State? To his way of thinking the king wielded a power without which all society would collapse. Significantly it was to some members of the bourgeoisie (the magistrates of the Parlement of Paris) that Louis XIII delivered a speech in which he tried to make them realise that the general interests of the realm, France's place in Europe, the freedom of her territory and the independence of her people were at stake and must take precedence over all personal considerations, even those of the king himself:

'The money for which I ask is not for frivolities or foolish extravagance. It is not I who speak to you but my State and its needs: those who gainsay my wishes do me greater injury than the Spaniards.' After the chancellor had expounded the necessary arguments, Louis XIII reverted to the terms he had already used; they have the same directness and simplicity as Henry IV's manner of speaking and form a curious contrast to the celebrated and more regal formula of Louis XIV. 'It is not I who speak to you but my State.'[24]

We have reached the year 1636. What is its essential significance in French history—that it was the year of *Le Cid* or that it was the year of Corbie? This is not the place for pointless arguments as to the date of the very first performance of the tragedy—whether it took place on 7 January 1637 as seems most likely or whether it occurred in the last weeks of 1636.[25] It remains unquestionable that *Le Cid* was written in 1636 and that during the same year the loss of Corbie on the Somme left the Compiègne road open to enemy outriders and caused a panic in Paris in face of the threat of Spanish invasion. Its recapture in November was both a victory and a profound relief.

It may seem strange that the public had no sooner recovered from this call to arms than it extended an extraordinary welcome to a work which although undoubtedly French bore marked traces of Spanish spiritual influence: 'No spectacle had ever before aroused so much attention.' But to imagine that public opinion was unaffected by military events on the grounds that not everyone was a combatant or that only the nobility and soldiers recruited for the purpose were interested in the outcome of a battle would be to misunderstand the seventeenth century. War had a direct impact on the lot of the people; although they did not, as we do, live in a country completely exposed to attack from the air, its repercussions were felt far deeper within the realm than history has often given us to believe. Nevertheless there is one point which deserves to be noted for it is very characteristic of the spirit of the age.

The war was not a clash between two ideologies but between two policies pursued by peoples who both accepted the same ideology. It was a war between states and in each case public opinion and the nation identified themselves with the state; but there was no inevitable collision, no all-embracing conflict between the fundamental outlook of the two peoples. At this time the French genius was being fertilised by the genius of the Mediterranean peoples of Spain and Italy. The war between France and Spain was a war between nations that were Latin and there is nothing surprising about the success achieved in Paris by a drama featuring Spanish characters and avowedly modelled on a Spanish play.

The greatness of the state, loyalty to one's prince, prowess on the battlefield—these were ideas that appealed equally strongly to Frenchmen and Spaniards. But they did not conclude as a result that since they thought alike they would do better not to fight each other. On the contrary it was because they thought alike that they were engaged in a contest which was chivalrous in principle if not in practice. Likewise neighbours engaged in a law suit did not decide to abandon it on the grounds that they both belonged to the same religious denomination or to the same town or class. Moreover none of this prevented publicists from charging the enemy with breaches of international law so as to shock public opinion; for example we find the French accusing the Spanish soldiery of flagrant attacks on private property or churches. What age does not accept its own inconsistencies?

But the two nations, closely linked as they were in so many respects by their economic relations and intellectual tastes, did not hate each other. On either side men fought the war to which their rulers had summoned them for the sake of a policy of which they were not themselves the judges. In carrying on the fight loyally they were doing their duty with the thought that the peace for which they yearned would return before long.

Yet the war was to continue until 1659 and we may reasonably assume that this struggle lasting for twenty-four years did not further the development of the spiritual affinities between the two nations. Was it for this reason that Italian influences were far more apparent than Spanish in the France of Mazarin's day? The spiritual kinship between France and Spain, strikingly obvious at the outset of hostilities and so strangely in evidence in the year 1636 when the contest between the two Powers became so crucial, must have diminished perceptibly and progressively with the prolongation of the war.

There was however one Power which seemed to hold aloof from everything that was happening—England. Absorbed with arrangements for the establishment of an authoritarian government—for this is the time of Laud and Strafford and Charles I's attempt at absolute rule[26]—she had taken no part in the war on the Continent. But the king and his advisers were none the less quick to take precautions against the danger of a maritime alliance between France and the United Provinces. Charles I made this danger an excuse for extending ship money, hitherto confined to towns on the sea coast, to the whole realm;[27] and there were grounds for fearing that England might draw closer to Spain with whom she had made peace in 1630. Richelieu therefore endeavoured to win her over to the French side tempting her with the suggestion of an offensive and defensive alliance.

In France the winter of 1635–6 was occupied with warlike preparations and drawing up plans of campaign. It was decided to remain on the defensive on the Netherlands front, but to take the offensive on all other theatres—in Germany with the troops of Bernard of Saxe-Weimar,[28] in Franche-Comté, in Switzerland, in Italy and even at sea where French fleets were to operate under the command of the archbishop of Bordeaux and the bishop of Nantes, both of whom combined the role of admiral with that of churchman.*

But the tide of events turned against France. The money that had been expected took some time to reach the King's coffers yet it remained essential to keep France's armies supplied at all costs and to avoid running the risk of losing Alsace 'on which depends the successful outcome of both the war and the peace'.[29] There Haguenau was in danger. In Italy Toiras was dying. In Franche-Comté the siege of Dôle was proving a difficult task for the prince of Condé and Colonel Gassion. In May Richelieu considered the situation very alarming and suggested that Louis XIII make a vow to the Virgin Mary: 'to redouble your Majesty's devotion to the Mother of God cannot but produce very good results'. 'I believe that the more your Majesty clings to God the more your Majesty's affairs will prosper.' In July the king asked the bishops to arrange for the Forty Hours Devotion to be held in all churches throughout the realm[30] together with sermons to remind the people that the

---

* *Cf.* the career of the late Admiral Thierry d'Argenlieu.

government's only object in waging war was to procure for them a long period of peace when efforts would be made to alleviate their lot.

As we shall see these sermons were not persuasive enough. At the same time the storm which it had been hoped to avert broke upon the realm. The Spaniards under the command of the Cardinal Infante realised that the ill-manned northern frontier would not hold out against attack. In a few weeks they broke through its defences. First Le Câtelet and then La Capelle surrendered to them without a blow. On 4 August they crossed the Somme. Simultaneously they invested the fortress of Corbie whose commander surrendered at the end of a week. Croatian outriders suddenly appeared in the area of Compiègne; they belonged to the army of Johann von Werth, an Imperialist general whom Richelieu had at one time thought of recruiting for the king's service in the same way as Bernard of Saxe-Weimar.

At the same time the French were obliged to raise the siege of Dôle. Troops had to be transferred hastily to Picardy and others dispatched to Angoumois which had broken into revolt. The French front in Burgundy was thus likewise depleted and gave way. Fortunately the small fortified town of Saint-Jean-de-Losne, situated on the road leading into the province, put up an astonishing resistance, thereby winning for itself the noble title Saint-Jean-Belle-Défense. But the breach in the northern front endangered the whole realm.

The pusillanimous behaviour of the officers who had surrendered fortresses to the enemy was denounced by Louis XIII in violent terms: 'Dastardly behaviour! Treason! Shameful surrender!' There were agonised fears that Amiens might fall and it was a position of the utmost importance. The comte de Soissons's army was not strong enough to save Picardy. Villages were evacuated, mills and bakehouses smashed to make it more difficult for the enemy to continue his advance. The river Oise was no longer safe and the boatmen only used it at night. The alarm was raised in Paris, for during the nine-days' siege of Corbie the capital itself had to be put in a state of defence. Had the enemy forces reached Paris quickly they would easily have taken it by assault for the erection of new buildings and the gaps made by streets had torn great holes in the old fortifications at several points.

But at this juncture when several provinces were in revolt, Paris stood firm and the population behaved admirably. The king, Richelieu, Bullion and Father Joseph all set an example by their self-possession. There was indeed some murmuring among people on the days when things were at their worst, but at the sight of their leaders passing through the streets outwardly calm and with their courage intact the humbler sort broke into cheers. All traces of arrogance between the different classes disappeared. The Parlement, which continued to block the admission of newly appointed officials to their offices and to carp at Richelieu's administration, nevertheless granted enough money to pay two thousand men. Money was also forthcoming from the guilds and religious communities while the maréchal de la Force enrolled volunteers for military service at the Hôtel de Ville. When the wardens [*jurés*] of the cobblers' guild came to the Louvre to offer the king their services Louis XIII embraced them.* It was truly one of those occasions in the history of Paris when the capital was the incarnation of French resistance.

This firm attitude made it possible to re-form an army of thirty thousand men. At the same time the prince of Orange, who had been warned that Paris was in danger, gave notice of a large-scale attack upon the Spaniards in the Netherlands. The Cardinal Infante afraid of being caught between two fires came to the conclusion that it was impossible for him to pursue his offensive deeper into France. In September after entrusting the government of Paris to the queen, Louis XIII, accompanied by Richelieu and Monsieur, took the road to the north to reconquer the towns captured by the enemy. In November Corbie was retaken.

It would be pleasant to take the view that the dangers which threatened France were now over; but the history of this grim year was not confined to the great recovery in which Parisian patriotism had played so large a part.

The behaviour of the ill-paid, under-fed French army in Flanders towards the Belgians was only too liable to be repeated by other French soldiers in their dealings with their own compatriots. Whenever the government had to take the decision to maintain an army at the expense of the population, with vague promises to reimburse the towns and villages concerned, it was to all intents and purposes handing over an entire district to devastation.[31] This was what happened in the frontier provinces of Picardy and Burgundy in 1635 and 1636. There was no longer any difference between the king's soldiers and the soldiers of the enemy; they all plundered in the same way. And when they had gone they were followed by the agents of the revenue who had come to collect fresh taxes. But since the people had nothing left, how were they to pay them?

* This picturesque incident is the more illuminating because the cobblers of Paris had a reputation for indulging in street-corner politics and for general rowdiness. (Magne, p. 38.)

As always there were some who profited from the general misery; when a regiment needed horses or arms, shady middlemen used to procure them, charging exorbitant prices. In Picardy officers who had been given the task of obtaining wood for the army found deserted villages whose inhabitants had fled to the nearby forests. They had given up attempting to defend their fields which were left exposed to the ravages of the soldiery.

On 1 May 1636 Louis XIII gave Séguier the strictest instructions to put a stop to the outrages committed by the military and to see that those responsible for recent disorders in the countryside were punished even if they belonged to the royal household. In addition he pressed for steps to be taken to punish both swearing and blasphemy—which were prevalent not only in Paris but throughout all France—as well as robbery, murders and duels: 'You need have no fear of any pardon interfering with the course of such justice as you may deem to be necessary.'

The blasphemy that bore witness to the rumblings of discontent among the populace and the increase in crime were both symptoms of the chaos into which the overwrought people were sinking while the enemy was assailing the frontiers of the realm. The Spaniards brought other calamities in their train; an epidemic of plague broke out in Picardy and Burgundy. In Picardy at the end of 1636 the corpses of men and animals were found lying abandoned in houses and stables.[32] Séguier's papers contain complaints from commissioners and officials in almost every province in the realm. Even if we are cautious and allow for some exaggeration, we cannot allow for much, as the misery of the people is described in identical terms in letters from one province after another. In Auvergne the armies raised for the king's service ravaged everything in their path and witnesses declared that even bands of pirates sallying forth from the four corners of the globe would not have committed worse outrages. The people were at the end of their tether. Risings broke out in the towns and in the plain.

How was the government to cope with internal complications of this nature? For at this point other factors intervened. Who represented the king and defended his authority—the governor of the province and his troops, the royal commissioner, the local Parlement, or the officers of the *bailliages* and *sénéchaussées*?

Another conflict was grafted on to the popular struggle, a conflict between provincial authority and the absolutism of the Crown, represented by the commissioners or intendants. For example at the time of the riots of 1635 in Bordeaux a rumour was current that the duke of Épernon, the governor of Guyenne, had allowed the rising to gather strength so as to have the honour of repressing it and in order to show Paris that he was indispensable. Any warning from him would have to be given due heed by the government, otherwise the worst might happen; and if the worst came to the worst only he would be capable of restoring order. Whether there was any truth in this rumour hardly concerns us here; what matters is that it was accepted as true and seemed likely enough.[33] Richelieu affected to give no credence to slanders of this sort and it is quite possible that he did not believe them. But it is equally possible that he took care not to investigate them too closely, so great was his need of the duke of Épernon.

The duke of Ventadour, the governor of the Limousin, wrote to Séguier the chancellor in connection with the new impositions asking him to send a special intendant to the province, but incognito 'so that the people be not alarmed by his coming forasmuch as it is certain that those dwelling in country districts are overmuch inclined to licence and revolt'. What was the duke's object in making this request? Was he not attempting to limit the intendant's prestige while at the same time keeping his authority in reserve?—for the intendant or commissioner was liable to be called upon to arbitrate in local disputes and sometimes his mediation was successful.

In June 1635 a riot broke out at Périgueux; barricades were erected in the streets and some people were killed. The common people laid the blame on the mayor. The intendant Verthamon handled the discussions with four of their representatives with some skill giving them to understand that his commission already 'empowered him to give orders to mayors and consuls so that if they were persons who were not liked by the people, there was no reason for the latter to accept them'. The people of Périgueux tried to induce Verthamon to remain longer in the town more as a safeguard and as their protector than as a hostage: at least that is what Verthamon asserted. Thereupon he tried to compose the quarrels among the bourgeoisie and to put them all in their place. He came to be regarded as a saviour and when he passed along the street, the townspeople, both men and women, would exuberantly rush to embrace him while some few who were still mistrustful would warn him that if he failed them they would certainly pay him out. 'You may see from this, Monseigneur,' observes Verthamon, 'the kind of negotiations that are needed to prevent an explosion in this town.' 'Negotiations'—Richelieu's word and the hallmark of his policy.

In a province like Brittany, which was jealous for its privileges and where particularist feeling was very strong, the various forces in opposition to the government egged each other on. There were the provincial Estates which voted taxes, and also the Parlement at Rennes which, although a royal court, was still an assembly of Bretons if not a Breton assembly. Indeed its magistrates were quite as obstinately Breton as the deputies of the Estates. When the king asked them to fix the amount of a loan to the Treasury, the figures they suggested were ridiculously inadequate (summer 1636). At this point the population of Rennes rose in revolt. The province that was exempt from any tax on salt was afraid that the government meant to introduce the *gabelle*, thus destroying its privileged economic status. In this case the commissioner was less fortunate than his colleague at Périgueux whom the people had welcomed as a protector against the officers of the revenue: the only apparent explanation for his arrival in Brittany was to threaten the ancient liberties of the province. 'Long live the king but no *gabelle*,' shouted the people of Rennes, adding however; 'Let us kill the commissioner and all have a piece of him.'[34]

This furious outbreak lasted for three days. Estampes the commissioner held that the local magistrates were partly to blame: they had been tardy in obeying the king's orders and had set a bad example. 'The only possible course is to install a good garrison in the town,' he wrote to Séguier, 'and to make the inhabitants afraid they will lose their privileges and the Parlement will be transferred elsewhere.' However order was restored by the governor, the duc de Brissac, who was quite a popular figure.

Before appearing at the meeting of the provincial Estates at Vannes a few weeks later in October 1636, Estampes met Richelieu's cousin, Monsieur de Pontchâteau. As a good Breton the latter was as devoted as anyone to the maintenance of the province's privileges; but as a good and zealous servant of Louis XIII he was also anxious for the king's dignity not to be profaned and for his subjects to obey him.[35] He agreed with the commissioner that the direst threats should be issued in the king's name —the object of course being to prevent the outbreak of disturbances that would make it necessary to put them into practice.

Sometimes an intendant could serve as a valuable source of information for the government by acquainting it with conditions in the provinces, and could protect the population very effectively by intervening on its behalf. Early in 1637 to ward off the Treasury's difficulties the financier Montauron (to whom Corneille was to dedicate *Cinna*) proposed raising a forced loan of three million livres from towns in the *généralité* of Bordeaux. The Bordelais was held to be one of the richest districts in France because of its wine trade, and orders were given accordingly. Verthamon, who had rejoined the duc de la Valette as intendant attached to his army, wrote to Séguier that seriously to contemplate introducing such a measure was out of question: it was all a piece of wishful thinking by people in Paris who did not know what they were talking about. Nothing was more contrary to the king's interests than to commit him and his authority to a course of action that would meet with insuperable resistance. 'I shall disregard every kind of danger when it appears that by so doing I may render the king useful service, but not in a case such as this which would put his authority and the obedience due to him overmuch in jeopardy to no purpose.'

Verthamon was himself well informed about Guyenne where he had functioned as an intendant for several years. He knew how things stood. It was quite true that the Bordelais sold approximately fifty thousand hogsheads of wine per annum at twenty crowns a hogshead but this did not mean that a total of three million livres went straight into the vine-growers' money-bags. The English buyers did not pay entirely in coin; part of the sum was paid in kind. As for the payments in cash they were of necessity immediately invested in two types of outlay. Firstly, preparations for the forthcoming grape harvest were a costly business which could not be undertaken without ready money. Secondly, as the Bordelais produced only wine, all the food that its population needed had to be bought from other provinces. In consequence although the Bordelais was rightly accounted a wealthy district and although it was undoubtedly more flourishing economically than neighbouring areas such as the Agenais and Périgord, there was by no means as much money in circulation as might be supposed by someone who was not on the spot. Montauron had only to come and see for himself: he would soon be convinced of the futility of his schemes. The taxes on table wine were arousing the populace and the mere fear of seeing them imposed would be sufficient to cause risings without the people even waiting for the edicts to be enforced.[36]

We can see from this what a variety of services the intendants could render. Their knowledge of a province—where unlike the office-holders their private interests were not at stake—meant that their opinions deserved to be taken seriously. They were thus in a position to prevent the government from making blunders. But since it was the government which in the last resort made the decisions, it was for the intendant to ensure that the king's orders were obeyed by showing himself persuasive in his dealings with the local office-holders who were expected to set a good example and by adopting an attitude towards the population which tallied with the latter's particular mood. Basically the only thing that mattered to Louis XIII, Richelieu and Séguier was the result; the intendant himself was the best judge of how to achieve it. Commissioners and intendants in the provinces were conducting the equivalent of the negotiations that the cardinal was conducting all the time with the royal family, the great nobles, the ministers of finance and foreign diplomats. Their patient work in all its manifold forms was slowly instilling obedience into the entire realm. Day by day their labours were paving the way for the unity of France and building up the structure of absolute government.

We have seen that while fighting was going on at Corbie revolts were breaking out among the peasantry in the south-west. These risings, which died down intermittently only to flare up again, were to last until the summer of 1637.

It was in April 1636 that the first disturbances occurred around Angoulême in the *châtellenies* of Barbezieux, Chalais, Montmoreau and Blanzac. Order seems to have been quite rapidly restored, thanks to the prompt and energetic action of Soubran, the lieutenant of Angoulême.[37] But when La Fosse, the commissioner sent to investigate, arrived at Angoulême in June he found the town in a state of great alarm. On Friday 6 June, market day, about four thousand peasants led by their parish priests had burst into the little town of Blanzac shouting that they were going to kill the tax collectors [*gabeleurs*].[38] They were armed with harquebuses and pikes and as they had no drums village fifers and fiddlers marched at their head. They had arrested and searched a surgeon from Bergerac. Finding that he was carrying letters which seemed to them suspicious they stripped him naked, cut off his arm, led him bleeding around the market place and finally murdered him. After this they had returned to their homes.

At Angoulême there were fears of private acts of vengeance, of the looting and burning of country houses. In consequence the leading personalities of the town such as the dean of the cathedral, the lieutenant general of the *présidial*[39] and the mayor advised La Fosse not to carry out his Commission. The later asked the government in Paris to send troops and explained why the situation was so serious: the peasant army included large numbers of trained soldiers who had already borne arms in the various attacks on La Rochelle: contact had been established between one *châtellenie* and another over a very wide area extending as far as the Bordelais: there were stocks of arms and powder everywhere. In short the peasants had the means for waging a real war which might well reduce the towns in the area to starvation. However in appealing for the armed help that was so sorely needed La Fosse felt impelled to add that he had no alternative: his natural inclination was towards a feeling of 'very great compassion' for 'the exceptional miseries of this people'.

Richelieu duly dispatched some troops but it was at this moment that certain regiments had to be relieved because of the siege of Dôle. Faced with conflicting needs he had to give priority to requirements on the frontier.[40]

The revolt was put down by force but attempts were also made to pacify the population by certain concessions. Some relief was afforded the people in the towns by abolishing the tax of a sol per livre; but this scarcely satisfied the rural population which used to buy few manufactured articles and which suffered primarily from the petty dues and the imposts on wine. The arrival of the tax-farmers charged with their collection was signalled by the tolling of bells summoning peasants in the surrounding villages to take up arms. The nickname *croquants* generally given by townsmen to the rebellious peasantry was regarded by the latter as an insult. An artisan from Angoulême was murdered at La Couronne in June for having uttered the word. This incident took place on a market day when nine or ten thousand men armed with muskets, pitchforks and pikes had assembled in the little town. They had come to make a show of force threatening to cut off food supplies to Angoulême and to burn the houses of the tax collectors* on the outskirts of the town; but they eventually went away without attempting anything.

In July and August the revolt spread to Saintonge, Aunis, Poitou and Limousin. On several occasions the authorities agreed to treat with representatives of the peasantry and promised to intercede with the king for the withdrawal of the edicts imposing the taxes. But although the insurrection appeared to have died down during the winter it came to life again in the spring. It now extended over 'Gascony, Guyenne, Périgord, Quercy, Languedoc, Limousin, Saintonge, Aunis, Angoumois, Poitou, Berry, Marche, Bourbonnais and Nivernais—in other words over an immense expanse bounded approximately by the Loire and the Garonne', an area which, as Boris Porshnev has pointed out, represented a quarter or possibly a third of what was then France; the insurrection thus spread far further afield than the Jacquerie in the four-

* See n. 38.

teenth century which is often referred to as the largest peasant revolt in French history. * However this vast area was not in the grip of one huge insurrection; it was more a question of revolts flaring up around various focal points located here and there. Probably there were contacts and influences at work between one point and another but the threat to the king's authority was not an insuperable one.

The revolt in the south was however alarming in that it forced the government to draw upon troops which were holding the enemy in check. After effecting a landing from the sea a Spanish force had gained a foothold in Guyenne. But the Spaniards did not show signs of intending to launch a large-scale attack. They fortified their position and dug themselves in. The army of the duke of Épernon and his son, the duc de la Valette, kept them under observation without attempting to dislodge them. However in May La Valette had to move north towards Périgord. The rebels there had chosen as their leader a member of the local gentry named Antoine du Puy de la Motte de la Forêt. Later this makeshift general declared that he had been coerced into accepting the role and that, if he had refused, the *croquants* would have murdered him and his family. But for all this La Motte de la Forêt showed himself to be quite a good organiser. He issued a manifesto explaining that he was taking up arms not against the king but to deliver the district from extortionate taxation that was being imposed without the king's knowledge. He made the peasants in all the neighbouring countryside hold themselves ready to answer the first call to arms with their weapons and supply of powder and shot permanently to hand. He limited the size of his army to ten thousand men but saw to it that the discipline that prevailed in its ranks was as good as that of a regular army, if not better. With this force he occupied Bergerac—an operation in which he was aided and abetted by the common people of the town, while the bourgeoisie adopted a passive attitude apart from about a hundred of them who fled to avoid casting in their lot with him.

Moreover La Motte de la Forêt maintained order in the town that he had occupied. He forbade all looting and acts of violence; he invited the clergy to have prayers said for the success of the rebellion and to report to him cases of blasphemy and scandalous behaviour. He also appealed to other localities in Périgord, bidding them refuse to pay the duties levied on wine and new impositions and urging them to join in a strike against the payment of all taxes. The leader of the *croquants* was thus launching a

---

* The Jacquerie was confined to an area to the north and east of Paris, extending little further than the borders of Picardy and Champagne.

fiscal war; indeed it was rather more than this for he declared that the district would no longer pay taxes to which it had not given its consent. In short a territory which was a *pays d'elections* and thus subject to royal administration was to enjoy once more the autonomy of a *pays d'états*. The régime set up by this country gentleman may have offered the people the prospect of some temporary alleviation of their lot but it did not represent a step towards the future; on the contrary it was leading them back into the past.

This state of affairs lasted for several weeks. Then three thousand of the king's troops under La Valette approached the town of Bergerac. Immediately, as if he had nothing to gain by battle despite the disparity in numbers, the commander of the peasant army opened negotiations with the officers of the king's forces. To the young duc de Duras he proposed disbanding his troops if the king's pardon were promised to all.

Perhaps the *croquants* would have obeyed him; but a rising broke out among the artisans of Bergerac. A certain Magot vehemently denounced their nobly born chief as a traitor, and offered to lead them in continuing the fight. A battle took place; but this time it was La Motte de la Forêt and the bourgeoisie of Bergerac who joined forces. Helped by the erstwhile refugees from the town who were now returning under the protection of the king's soldiers, they attacked Magot and his new followers and won an easy victory. Magot having been killed, the *croquants* dispersed and on 8 June the duc de la Valette made his entry into the once more submissive town of Bergerac.

Other popular outbreaks occurred at Cahors (where the local authorities and the bourgeois militia clashed with the artisans), at Sainte-Foy (where the rising was led by a notary royal) and at Eymet. There was certainly considerable disorder but when the royal army arrived everything subsided quite quickly. La Valette could congratulate himself on having restored order throughout Périgord and on having put down the most serious rebellion that had been seen in those parts for very many years.

This insurrection had certainly been more serious than an ordinary outbreak caused by poverty. Nevertheless it proved that even when taught a smattering of discipline and some elementary principles of warfare the provincial population was not capable of very much, and that everything yielded to the king's authority. In Paris there had been some speculation as to whether the Spaniards who were known to be watching these movements carefully had encouraged them from the outset. This does not seem to have been the case. But if civil war had spread and become organised it would inevitably have led to foreign intervention and this additional complication could only have involved the people in further suffering and bloodshed.

Following in the steps of the king's army came the king's justice. A general pardon was granted because common sense required it and because it was the best method of bringing the insurrection quickly to an end. But as was customary the worst culprits were excluded, some being hanged and others condemned to the galleys. As was explained by the judges of the Parlement of Bordeaux who were sent to the scene of the revolt after its collapse, there was nothing that made a greater impact on men's minds. Terror had the last word.

With difficulties such as these to face it is scarcely surprising that Richelieu did not reject the idea of ending the war at the earliest possible moment by means of negotiations. He could hardly oppose the principle in view of the attitude of Rome, for Pope Urban VIII was urging all the belligerents to make peace. But whereas Richelieu had no intention of coming to terms without his Protestant allies, the United Provinces and Sweden, the pope did not wish to be involved in dealings with heretics. The cardinal wrote with some humour that the Holy Father's mediation would constitute an excellent opportunity for enhancing his prestige with the Protestants: Urban VIII remained unshakeably resolved to ignore them.

In consequence Richelieu agreed to the opening of a congress at Cologne to which he sent delegates; but he also asked for passports for the Dutch representatives to enable them to cross Spanish and Imperial territory. The Spaniards were in no hurry to agree to this request. They were afraid that if they were to issue the passports they would be appearing to recognise the United Provinces as a sovereign power for, despite their secret negotiations with the Dutch, they still affected to regard them as rebellious subjects. In any case the congress, being only partly attended, was incapable of undertaking anything.

However Richelieu was not averse to secret negotiations with Olivares.[41]

Contacts had been established as early as 1636. In 1637 there were dispatched to Madrid almost simultaneously Father Bachelier, a Minim who was ostensibly sent to fetch some relics of St Isidore for the queen,[42] and the baron de Pujols, a gentleman from Flanders. The latter was rather an odd character and something of a trickster. Richelieu suspected him of being a double agent but nevertheless made use of his services. He remained at Madrid for several years, being accepted by Olivares as the unofficial negotiator for France.

Spain no less than France had good reason not to desire a long war. Together with all Europe she was involved in a general price revolution. Not only had prices been falling sharply since 1630 but, in addition, as has been revealed by the researches of the American historian Earl J. Hamilton into seventeenth-century Spanish economic history, the entire reign of Philip IV was a period of decadence for Spain generally and especially for Castile.[43] The country was suffering from the disastrous consequences of a whole series of circumstances to which no attention had been paid in previous years. Too many young men had emigrated to America, too many fortunes had been invested in religious foundations: the economic expansion of northern Europe had raised up formidable competitors to Spanish commerce and closed outlets to both the agriculture of Castile, which was already in decline, and to its industry. The cost of living in Spain was invariably very high and the country did not produce enough for the needs of its population. Nor did she possess an industrious middle class such as constituted the driving force in French society. The population did little work. Life among the upper strata of Spanish society was splendid and ostentatious but among the swarming mass of poverty-stricken nobility the only occupation that was viewed with favour was the profession of arms. Theirs was a class that bred good officers and officials but it was incapable of restoring the country's economy.

Quite apart from the number of clergy and monks, which was very large in relation to the country's resources, Spain had to support the dead weight of an indigent and largely idle population. There were too many shepherds and not enough tillers of the soil: too many poor and too many vagabonds who were either content to bask in apathetic poverty beneath the heat of the summer sun or else plunged into a life of adventure or banditry thus increasing the trend towards insecurity and disorder. To a greater degree than in other lands there were strange affinities between the poor nobles and the brigands. Spain was a country of dazzling splendour, mighty in arms and glorious in its achievements; but she was also a country that was slowly growing poorer, where misery was widespread.

Finally deliveries of gold and silver from America decreased steadily from 1630 onwards and the inflation of copper coinage began. It was to be the great blot on Philip IV's reign and the cause of irreparable damage. Like the king of France, Philip IV found himself at the mercy of the financiers, for the Spanish state was heavily in debt. The count-duke of Olivares was a great minister and an opponent worthy of Richelieu. He was too intelligent not to assess the dangers that a prolonged war entailed for Spain; too shrewd a politician not to realise what was at stake in the struggle and not to be afraid of adding to his difficulties.[44] He considered stopping the war but only on advantageous conditions. He preferred a truce to a definite peace for what he needed was a breathing space. Richelieu also wanted peace but wished to know what the terms would be, making it clear that in any event he did not mean to part with Lorraine.

Olivares could not consent to the enemy gaining such a strategic advantage and consequently the secret negotiations came to nothing. However both sides kept them alive or left the door open for their renewal while carefully concealing the need for peace that impelled them to do so and watching for signs that the other was weakening. At the same time each of the two ministers continued to wage war as best he could. Somewhat strangely for France a matter of State became caught up in this web of secret intrigue during the summer of 1637—the correspondence of the queen with the enemy.

Louis XIII and Anne of Austria had contrived to keep their marriage going after a fashion. They had not drawn closer to each other with the passage of time but nor had they drifted further apart, for the king was still desperately eager for a son. However he did not love the queen and he needed to love someone. He dreamed of a relationship that was imbued with feelings of tender affection on both sides. Yet Louis XIII was rather moody and easily disenchanted; when the object of his chaste yet passionate devotion failed to comply with his standards of perfection he would turn to worship a different idol.

The king's great friendship for Saint-Simon cooled a little in 1635 when he fell in love with Mademoiselle de la Fayette, one of the queen's maids of honour who was a kinswoman of the bishop of Limoges; and when Saint-Simon advised him to make her his mistress he dealt a fatal blow to his own position. On the contrary it was the purity of this seventeen-year-old girl that appealed to the king. He was troubled that he who was beyond her reach should be her first and perhaps her only love. Richelieu was well aware of the king's qualms, for Louis XIII had confided in him on an occasion when he had spent the whole night weeping. The cardinal had reason to fear Mademoiselle de la Fayette since her extreme piety had led to her becoming involved with the faction that opposed the war, complained indignantly of the misery of the people and denounced France's alliances with Protestant powers.

He was not at all sorry therefore when Louise de la Fayette became frightened as to what might be the outcome of her relationship with the king and began to talk of entering a nunnery. However she took some time to make up her mind. Those in her immediate circle made out that they were testing her sense of vocation and some tried to induce her not to renounce the world, hoping that Louis XIII would become insistent, that she would eventually give way, and that if she was established as the king's favourite the cardinal would be kept in check.

These calculations were wide of the mark for they failed to take account of Louis XIII's fastidious and intricate psychological make-up. Recoiling from the prospect of committing a sin the lovers parted company early in May 1637. 'Alas! I shall see him no more,' moaned Louise de la Fayette as she left the king. She withdrew to the convent of the Order of the Visitation in the rue Saint-Antoine where Louis XIII obtained permission to visit her. The friend whom he had loved and sacrificed would pray for him; without hope of earthly reward she would continue to be his inspiration and his gentle intermediary with God.

Richelieu was alarmed both by the void left by Louise de la Fayette's departure and by the continuance of her secret influence. He would gladly have found a new friend for the king if he could have counted on her belonging to his party. Two other maids of honour seemed to him fitted for the part: Mademoiselle de Hautefort whose grandmother, the ambitious Madame de la Flotte, was ready to further his scheme, and Mademoiselle de Chémerault. But Louis XIII found the latter 'too ill-natured and overmuch a mischief maker', and although more kindly disposed towards Mademoiselle de Hautefort he clung to his resolution not to commit himself to anyone as he had promised Mademoiselle de la Fayette. He had made it his aim to live as good a life as he could in this world 'that he might enter paradise at the last'.[45]

All through this crisis the queen had become more and more isolated. At the same time she was separated from her best friend the duchess of Chevreuse who had been banished to Touraine. The poor woman took refuge in pious practices, paying frequent visits to the convent of the Val-de-Grâce in the rue Saint-Jacques.[46] However Richelieu's police soon became certain that these periods of retreat were not spent entirely in prayer. Quite by chance they gained possession of a letter to the queen from the marqués de Mirabel, the Spanish ambassador in Brussels. This letter was apparently in the nature of a reply. It was evident that Anne of Austria was corresponding with the enemy.

Louis XIII was informed; but the art of dissimulation was carried to extreme lengths at court and for several weeks neither the king nor his minister gave any indication of their discovery to the queen. Patiently they devoted themselves to weaving a web around her. Possibly it was the ill-natured and mischief-making Mademoiselle de Chémerault who put them on the track of Anne of Austria's go-between. The latter was a member of her household named La Porte, a man of thirty-three who came from Anjou and whose duty it was to carry the queen's cloak for her.[47]

On the evening of 10 August when La Porte came out of a house in the quartier Saint-Eustache as if going for a quiet stroll he found the street blocked by a large carriage. Before he had time to notice it some men leapt on him and bundled him inside. A few minutes later he was in a cell at the Bastille. It was known that he bore on his person a letter from the queen to Madame de Chevreuse and when he was searched it was found without difficulty.

La Porte was one of those staunch Angevins for whom loyalty to one's master or mistress is an inflexible rule. When taken to the Palais Cardinal and brought before Richelieu on the following day he merely said that the letter concerned was the first to have been entrusted to him and that he had been carrying it quite innocently. After all for the queen to write a letter to Madame de Chevreuse was not such a serious matter and clearly someone had to be responsible for its delivery. However La Porte was informed that it was not as simple as that: it was known that in the course of 10 August he had tried to hand the letter to a gentleman named Monsieur de la Thibaudière who had refused to accept it. But La Porte obstinately refused any further explanation and allowed himself to be taken back to the Bastille. The investigation now took a different turn.

Anne of Austria was at this time with the king at Chantilly. At the Val-de-Grâce the nuns saw the archbishop of Paris and Chancellor Séguier arrive at their convent. The two men demanded to be taken to the abbess. The latter tried to excuse herself on the grounds that she was indisposed but finally agreed to receive them. Louise de Milly or, to give her her religious title, Mère de Saint-Etienne, came from Franche-Comté: in other words her sympathies were Spanish.

'Comtois, surrender!'

'Not I, i'faith'.*

The abbess was to demonstrate the obstinacy that belonged to the natives of another province.[48] Although the archbishop enjoined her to

---

*'Comtois, rends-toi! Nenni, ma foi'. See n. 48.

tell the exact and sacred truth she took refuge in vague replies. She was pressed to say what the queen was in the habit of doing when she was at the Val-de-Grâce, whether she used to write letters and whether she received any visitors. The abbess replied that she knew nothing, that she neither used to follow the queen into her chamber when she retired there nor into her parlour.

An elaborate search was carried out but nothing was found except some papers of no importance.[49] The archbishop announced to the nuns that he had no choice but to depose their abbess. A physician was hastily summoned. He declared that Mère Saint-Etienne's state of health was not such as to preclude her making a journey and the over-discreet mother superior was immediately installed in a carriage which conveyed her far away from her convent.

On 14 August Séguier betook himself to Chantilly where he saw the queen. In answer to his questions she denied that she was in correspondence with a foreign power. The chancellor appeared to be satisfied with this reply but he left the queen deeply shaken.

Next day, 15 August, after receiving communion the queen sent for Le Gras, her secretary, whom she trusted implicitly. She asked him to go and see the cardinal on her behalf and to tell him that she swore on the Blessed Sacrament that she had not been conducting any forbidden correspondence. Le Gras delivered the message but reported to the queen on his return that he had failed to convince the cardinal who must therefore be in possession of definite information.

Anne of Austria made up her mind to speak to Richelieu in person and asked him to come and see her.

The interview took place on 17 August. The queen tried to justify herself and to depict the correspondence that she had kept up with her Spanish relations as quite innocent. Respectful but unbending the cardinal listened readily to what she chose to tell him. 'There is more to it than this Madame,' was his only comment. Little by little the queen, now cornered, began to make disclosures that became increasingly serious. Yes, she was in correspondence with her brother the Cardinal Infante, with Madame de Chevreuse and with England. She used to give the letters to La Porte who passed them on to Auger, the secretary at the English Embassy in Paris. The latter dispatched them to Gerbier his colleague in Brussels and he in turn handed them over to the Spanish ambassador the marqués de Mirabel: these letters were not only concerned with family news: on the advice of Madame de Chevreuse the queen also used to pass on political information: she had reported Father Bachelier's mission, she had said that care should be taken not to let England and France form an alliance—an eventuality that Spain had every reason to dread. Anne of Austria could not but admit that she had not behaved like a queen of France but had intrigued against the policy of the king her husband. She did not try to excuse herself. Like the king's subjects she was beginning to discover the overriding claims of the State and the necessity for obedience. Moreover she knew full well that in Spain queens consorts were kept aloof from public affairs and punished for actions far less presumptuous than hers; in her own country she would have been confined to a nunnery, perhaps for years. She was in tears and completely shattered. 'How kind you are, Monsieur le cardinal,' she repeated several times. She wanted to take Richelieu's hand but he refused out of respect for her station.

The cardinal sent a messenger to request the king's presence. As minister he felt that, since the queen appeared to be convinced of the error of her ways, a reconciliation between husband and wife was imperative in the interests of the monarchy. He interceded for the queen with Louis XIII, asking him to pardon her, but the king was not disposed to be merciful.

A memorandum was drawn up at once recording what the queen had confessed and the conditions laid down by the king. Anne of Austria was no longer to correspond with Madame de Chevreuse, her entourage was only to consist of persons of whom the king approved, and she was not to visit a convent without his permission. The signatures of the royal couple were then appended to this strange treaty, a copy of which is preserved in the Bibliothèque Nationale.

It remained to extract a confession from La Porte. He was cross-examined and informed that the queen had told all; but sensing that she had only done so under pressure he still refused to say what he knew, denying for example the connection with Auger although the queen had admitted it. He remained steadfast despite the threat of torture and his courage aroused the cardinal's admiration.

The queen, worried as to the fate of her faithful servant, decided on 22 August to make a further declaration which was however only concerned with certain details of her system of correspondence. She revealed that she had made use of La Porte not only to carry letters but also to write them. She admitted that she had given him a cipher to write to Mirabel which she had subsequently burnt and that Madame de Chevreuse had put her in touch with the duke of Lorraine. Then on 25 August she wrote to La Porte herself telling him there was no point in concealing anything for all was known. But even when brought before Laffemas the obstinate man was still anxious for the safety of his queen. What did her letter prove, he asked—perhaps someone had dictated it to her? He declared that he would only speak if the queen's order to do so were delivered to him by one of her officers on whom he could rely: Monsieur de la Rivière.

The latter was summoned; whereupon La Porte admitted that he had handed some letters to Auger. But by this time the whole story was known and it was becoming discreditable to persecute a man of humble birth who although he had aided and abetted activities that were treasonable had shown such noble constancy to the queen. His inquisitors forbore to trouble him further.

No great effort seems to have been made to lay hands on another of the queen's accomplices, the duchesse de Chevreuse, who was dangerous in a somewhat different way. Perhaps the government would have done better to show more energy where she was concerned. The queen was able to warn her what was happening. In his biography of this beautiful and scheming woman Louis Batiffol gives an extremely vivid account of her flight from the priory of Couzières to the Spanish frontier.[50] Apart from one stage in her escape when she made use of a carriage lent to her by Monsieur de Marsillac—later to inherit his father's title of duc de la Rochefoucauld and win fame as the author of the *Maxims*[51]—the duchess made almost the entire journey on horseback and wearing a man's clothes which made her look like a handsome young page. She displayed a fearlessness which was positively heroic although she was not only compelled to make an exhausting journey in disguise but was also handicapped by a feminine indisposition. On her way she met with a staunch friend in Monsieur Malbâti, the *procureur* of Cahuzac.* Although he had no idea who she was, he went out of his way to help her with the Christian simplicity that was so often to be found among goodhearted people in the France of those days.

Malbâti accompanied the duchess on the last stages of her journey. When it came to an end she was safe but on enemy territory; nor was she to return to France in Richelieu's lifetime. She thus became yet another pawn in the hands of the enemy and remained a constant danger. But her absence simplified the life of the king and queen together and meant that something positive had been achieved by the cardinal's intervention.

Difficulties, defeats, victories: such was the tangled pattern of events in the course of this doleful year.

* For the functions of a *procureur* see chapter 10, n. 27.

During the month of March France had suffered a major setback in the Valtelline and once again it had been caused by shortage of money. The duke of Rohan had not received the sums he needed for the upkeep of his army, and the Grisons seeing his difficulties had decided that it was simpler to come to terms with the Spaniards who were now disposed to be more obliging. In consequence the French had been forced to evacuate the passes. So great was Rohan's fear of the king's displeasure that he took refuge in Geneva; yet this time the government knew that he was neither responsible nor at fault.[52]

The loss of the Valtelline threatened to compromise the king's policy in Italy. Further dangers loomed up on the Italian horizon in the autumn of 1637 when France's two allies, the duke of Mantua and the duke of Savoy, died within two weeks of each other. Neither ruler left an heir who had attained his majority and although in Savoy the regency fell to Louis XIII's sister Christina, her authority had to be defended against her two brothers-in-law both of whom were pro-Spanish: indeed one of them, Prince Thomas, commanded an army in the Netherlands. For Richelieu France's acquisitions in Italy were as important as Lorraine. The two fortresses of Casale and Pinerolo not only guaranteed the safety of her south-eastern frontier; they also prevented the Spaniards from holding the Italian peninsula at their mercy.

Of similar importance was the recapture of the Iles de Lérins which the Spaniards had fortified during the eighteen months that they had occupied them. A fleet under the archbishop of Bordeaux and his lieutenant Harcourt transported troops there to besiege the enemy. The siege lasted for two months until the middle of March. Rather than engage in battle with the French ships mounting guard, the Spanish fleet tried to retaliate a month later by effecting a landing at Saint-Tropez. But the attempt miscarried. Henceforth the French were sufficiently masters at sea to re-establish their Mediterranean trade. They even ventured to send a small expedition to Algiers to open negotiations with the Barbary corsairs. In this they did not succeed but the essential point had been achieved. Spanish control of the islands off France's Mediterranean coast had been brought to an end.

Since the spring it had been planned to launch offensives in several directions, with a view to restoring the military situation by attacks in the Netherlands and fresh operations in Alsace and Franche-Comté. Here the exploits of Bernard of Saxe-Weimar were to put fresh heart into France's Swedish and German allies. After recapturing Saverne in 1636 he succeeded in halting an offensive by the duke of Lorraine at

Gray-sur-Saône in August 1637. He then advanced at high speed across Franche-Comté carrying the war to the banks of the Rhine. Crossing the river at Rheinau he established a bridgehead on the right bank; but he had to withdraw on encountering the formidable Johann von Werth and took up winter quarters in the bishopric of Basle.

In the north Cardinal La Valette occupied Landrecies. However his opponent the Cardinal Infante resisted stoutly; it was evident from an intercepted letter that he thought his position extremely dangerous but he did not lose heart on that account. While the French were besieging La Capelle he launched an attack on Maubeuge, which was defended by the vicomte de Turenne. The latter was still only a young man but his skilful resistance left no doubt as to his qualities as an officer and the brilliant future that lay before him. In addition to these operations the Dutch under the Stadtholder Frederick Henry captured Breda. The Spanish forces in the Netherlands were beginning to feel the strain of a war on two fronts.

In the south of France the war also went amiss for the Spaniards. But it was not their fear of the duc de la Valette that made them abandon their fortified positions at Saint-Jean-de-Luz and the duke's recent victory over the *croquants* did not absolve him from harsh criticism. His inertia was contrasted with the dash shown by the duc d'Halluyn who had checked a Spanish attempt to mount an offensive in Languedoc by a brilliant victory at Leucate. Louis XIII rewarded Halluyn with a marshal's baton and the title of duc de Schomberg—the title under which his father had won fame.

The necessity of fighting to defend her own frontiers had forced France to reduce somewhat her activities in Germany. By her treaty with Bernard of Saxe-Weimar she had to all intents and purposes handed over Alsace to him. Nevertheless Bernard's army, subsidised as it was by Louis XIII, was the only force at France's disposal in the Empire, the only means she possessed of reminding the German princes of the effectiveness of her protection. Of these virtually the only one who was still her ally was the landgrave of Hesse-Cassel. The house of Austria was reaping the benefits of the peace of Prague. Now that the emperor had re-established his alliance with Saxony and Brandenburg and asserted his authority over Bavaria and the ecclesiastical electors (it will be remembered that Sötern the elector of Trier was his prisoner)[53] he was in a position to call an electoral meeting at Regensburg in September 1636.

The emperor was now to have his revenge for the outcome of an ear-

lier meeting held in the same spot when Father Joseph had prevented his
son's election as king of the Romans and secured Wallenstein's dismissal.
This time the electors promised to give the Imperial Crown to the king
of Hungary[54] and thus when Ferdinand II died in February 1637 the succession of his son Ferdinand III took place unchallenged. The emperor
would also have liked to win his vassals over to an anti-French policy at
Regensburg and set the example himself by declaring war on Louis XIII.
However the electors would not go as far as this; as we have seen, they
preferred peace. They declared themselves ready to make overtures to
France and Sweden but resolved not to come to terms with them unless
both powers abandoned all the territories that they occupied in the
Empire. This was equivalent to demanding that France evacuate Alsace,
Lorraine, the three bishoprics of Metz, Toul and Verdun and possibly the
places she held in north Italy which was a fief of the Empire. In other
words Richelieu's policy of carefully avoiding an immediate breach
with the emperor while claiming the right to protect German liberties
suffered a very serious setback.

Sweden herself, all too precariously linked to France, had given up
attempting to hold Worms and the territories of the archbishopric of
Mainz where she had for long seemed firmly established. Her forces had
withdrawn to Mecklenburg from which Banér launched an offensive in
the autumn of 1636. On 6 October shortly before Louis XIII's recapture
of Corbie he won a great victory at Wittstock. As the German historian
Bruno Gebhardt has observed, this victory revealed the shortcomings of
the Treaty of Prague. The Lutheran electors had been in too much of a
hurry to disarm before they were sure that there was no risk of their
being attacked by foreign troops. Brandenburg and Saxony both lay
open to Banér whose army advanced ravaging everywhere. A spearhead
penetrated as far as Erfurt, and in the summer of 1637 Banér was planning to seize Leipzig when the return of the imperial armies which had
remustered at Torgau made him feel that the threat to his own troops was
too great to be ignored. On his retreat northwards he met another imperialist army at Landsberg; but he managed to escape from it by a strate-
gem which gave the impression that he was in full flight towards Poland.
His wife and some of the baggage were in fact sent in that direction but
the bulk of his army fell back on Pomerania. In these operations Banér
had shown himself to be a general who upheld the high military reputation of Gustavus Adolphus, but the fruits of his brilliant victory at
Wittstock were lost.

Admittedly the imperial commanders had been compelled to divide their forces and the fact that they had to deal with two opponents of the calibre of Banér and Bernard of Saxe-Weimar made their task a formidable one. Although the two generals were geographically too far apart to attempt to meet, they still contrived to help each other by supporting each other's operations from a distance. But for all this, in 1637 it had been the house of Austria that had gained the upper hand in the Empire.

From this Richelieu concluded that although peace was no doubt still highly desirable and no opportunity grasping it should be overlooked, the general outlook hardly gave grounds for thinking that it could be obtained on favourable terms. The fight would therefore have to be continued with redoubled vigour and France's first aim should be to win victories. But whether victorious or unsuccessful, long or short, the war was steadily becoming more and more unpopular in the realm. While the cardinal was bent only on continuing the struggle, Louis XIII began to lend a sympathetic ear to those who spoke to him about the state of public opinion, first drawing his attention to the sufferings of his subjects. Louis XIII was no craven spirit but a soldier king who loved army life, was always ready to expose himself to fire and in winter-time was not averse to making plans for the forthcoming spring campaign. But he was deeply concerned to carry out to the full his duty as king. In consequence he thought not only of his own glory but also of his mission—a mission which made him answerable for the personal sufferings of his people. Whilst admiring Richelieu, Louis XIII suspected that he tended to disregard this aspect of the situation. Besides, the cardinal was only a minister, a servant whose duty it was to obey. God asked more of the king; on him devolved the fearful responsibility of giving orders which were just.

Louis XIII's spiritual qualms, far from being lulled, were kept alive by the confessor whom he had chosen, Father Caussin of the Society of Jesus —to such an extent indeed that dissension between the king and his minister appeared likely to break out at any moment.

Richelieu noticed the over-frequent and rather mysterious conversations between Louis XIII and Father Caussin and their embarrassed faces when he came upon them unawares in the course of an unexpected visit. The month of December when the Feast of the Immaculate Conception of the Virgin Mary was celebrated, when devotions were held in respect of Advent and in preparation for Christmas, provided Father Caussin with all too many suitable opportunities for influencing his penitent. He spoke to the king of his mother reduced to financial straits by

the cardinal's intransigence, of the Protestant alliances which were causing the Catholics in Germany so much suffering, of the churches that had
been sacked and the convents that had been desecrated. Above all he
spoke to him of his people reduced to destitution and ground down by
taxes—his people whom God had committed to his charge as if they
were his children. For Louis XIII this was the most effective argument of
all. 'Ah! my poor people,' he would groan with genuine sorrow, adding
however, 'I cannot as yet relieve their sufferings because of the war to
which I am committed'.

The cardinal needed the Jesuits and did not wish to antagonise the Society whose influence at the Holy See was all powerful by giving offence
to one of their number. He decided to play his cards carefully. He wrote
to the general of the Jesuits protesting his good intentions but at the same
time took it upon himself to point out to Louis XIII that Father Caussin
was going beyond his terms of reference and exceeding his powers as the
king's confessor. Once again the cardinal carried the day. Father Caussin
was disgraced and Father Sirmond also a Jesuit but old and peaceably
inclined replaced him for Christmas.

A few days previously, on 11 December, Louis XIII had signed a
solemn undertaking which placed his kingdom under the protection of
the Virgin Mary. He besought her to intervene so that France could have
peace once more. He promised her to invest the Feast of the Assumption
with a particular magnificence and to celebrate it in the capital with a
procession. The other dioceses were to follow the example of Paris if the
bishops thought fit.

Such is the origin of the *procession du Voeu de Louis XIII*—an observance which in certain provinces has been preserved as a tradition to this
day.* Its rustic ceremonies are performed at the height of summer when
the threshing of the corn sets the seal on the agricultural year and when
the vine-grower can already estimate the harvest of grapes that his vines
will very shortly yield.

This act of devotion to the Virgin has often been misconstrued. Historians have failed to realise that it was in accordance with the advice
which Richelieu had been giving Louis XIII for several months and that
this advice was inspired by personal faith or by the desire not to allow the
Spaniards the privilege of appearing as the only nation in Europe that
was fervently devoted to pious practices. It has also been asserted that the
king's vow was connected with a specific favour that he had asked to be
granted him—the birth of an heir. This was not the case at all. The only

---

*It is held for instance (on 15 August) at the Eglise du Suquet in Cannes.

object that Louis XIII had in mind in making his vow was the restoration of peace and of conditions that were more favourable to the temporal and spiritual welfare of his realm.

And yet it was at this very time that there came the promise of the child hoped for and awaited for twenty-two years. Father Griffet tells us of a winter squall which took the king unawares on Sunday 5 December while he was visiting Louise de la Fayette at the Convent of the Visitation. On that particular evening he had intended to spend the night at Saint-Maur but the weather became so appalling that the journey had to be abandoned.[55] Where was he to go? The king's suite of rooms at the Louvre had not been prepared for him but the queen's apartments were known to be ready; not only this but she herself was known to be there. The most sensible solution was to request her hospitality. The king, who was at first opposed to the idea, gave way and within a few minutes he was at the Louvre. After drying himself in the warm he dined with the queen. Brought closer to each other by the intimacy of the occasion husband and wife spent the night together and nine months later a dauphin was born.

Father Griffet is a well-informed writer and his story has so much charm that it would be sad indeed if it were not true. But is it true?—for there can be no unimpeachable authority for an episode like this! Since her experiences of the previous August the queen had been obliged to submit to a kind of exile at Court, and the king had developed an interest in Mademoiselle de Hautefort. She was an alluring fair-haired beauty but a domineering creature—too domineering to replace the gentle affectionate Louise de la Fayette. However Louis XIII used to credit his idols with virtues that were not always confirmed by experience and for the time being Mademoiselle de Hautefort seemed to him the perfect friend for whom he had never ceased to long. Even so such a friend was not and was not to become a mistress. The queen for all his lack of affection for her remained his wife and even in disgrace she did not lose her rights as such. It follows that we cannot be sure that the evening of 5 December 1637 did bring about an exceptional reconciliation between king and queen. After all, although the private lives of princes are never entirely divorced from history and the dividing line between the important and the trivial is far from easy to draw, where they are concerned, it is utterly pointless to go on discussing these marital details indefinitely. What mattered were the queen's fresh expectations of a child which this time were not to be disappointed. The birth of a dauphin ousted the incorrigible Monsieur from his position as heir to the throne, thus reinforcing the king's personal authority both at home and abroad, together with that of the minister whose every act had been carried out on his orders or in his name.

Thus the years of ordeal when even the safety of the capital had been in jeopardy drew to a close under divine protection, with the promise of the greatest boon that could ever have been expected for the cardinal's policy and Louis XIII's dynasty.

CHAPTER TEN

The Fight to the Death
(1639–43)

WHILE SHE was engaged in war with the house of Austria France had to bear in mind the situation in Europe and in the world around her and adapt her efforts accordingly.

The difficulties that faced her were not peculiar to her alone. For several years the world had been passing through a bad period economically. For example there had been a marked fall in the price of cloth at Milan since 1636 which is very revealing of the general trend since cloth was a product that occupied an important place on the international market. Likewise the number of trading ships passing through the Baltic Sound was decreasing and the price of wheat and rye on the market at Amsterdam (another large centre for commercial traffic) was barely beginning to recover from the abrupt fall of the early 1630s. Everywhere there was a contraction in the capital available for expenditure or investment, and financial hardship.

To these conditions was added the intolerable scourge of war. The mere task of attempting to reintroduce a little order into areas where war was no longer raging was in itself a full-time occupation. In the opening pages of his masterly study of the domain of Kost in north Bohemia, the Czech historian Josef Pekař describes the Emperor Ferdinand III leading a procession of atonement at Mladá Boleslav to inaugurate a reign which he desired to be peaceful. The sanctuary is once more in Catholic hands. Around it the people are busy repairing the ruins that bear witness to the devastation inflicted on the district by the soldiery. Although the war had not come to an end within the Empire, they cling to the hope against all odds that no more armies will descend upon them. Money is beginning to pass from hand to hand once more at fairs; capital is being invested again. Those who can still raise the money are buying up cheaply estates that have been abandoned. They have started to put the land back into cultivation, to repair the buildings, to reassemble the peasant labour force and re-stock the farms.

All over the Empire a similar process could be seen at work. The people were beginning to take heart. They believed that they were

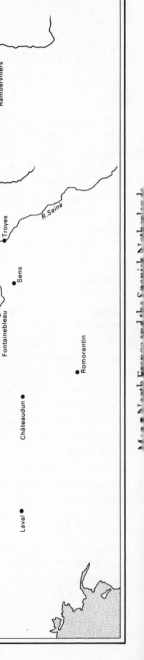

Map 7 North France and the Spanish Netherlands

going to enjoy peace and quiet once more. In a situation which was as a whole unfavourable this was enough, indeed more than enough. On the other hand the Spanish government had to accept the fact that under these conditions only very limited help would be forthcoming from Germany in the future.

As for the Spanish colonies they no longer sent sufficient quantities of gold and silver to the mother country whose monetary difficulties grew steadily worse. Furthermore a breach had been made in Spain's overseas empire. The Dutch had seized north Brazil which had been in Spanish hands since the annexation of Portugal. The régime set up at Olinda by John Maurice of Nassau made the colony more productive and it was the Dutch who reaped the benefit. For Spain the loss was of greater consequence than the loss of a fortress in the Netherlands.

Under circumstances such as these the governments concerned were likely to become more favourably inclined towards peace, both sides showing themselves ready to adopt a more accommodating attitude. During the first few months of 1638 Richelieu proved very willing to carry on secret negotiations with the enemy but his main object was to find out on what terms hostilities could be ended. He instructed Estrées the French ambassador in Rome to approach his opposite number Trautmannsdorf, the emperor's representative. He also took an active interest in the news that Pujols sent from Spain according to which Olivares desired to resume negotiations.

But the cardinal only embarked upon this policy with the utmost caution for his primary concern was to ensure that the coalition which he had formed did not disintegrate. He was well aware of the Swedish court's desire for peace and had little confidence in the Swedish ambassador in Paris, the jurist Grotius—a man of learning but an indifferent politician and a dubious ally.[1] The cardinal believed that Sweden would be prepared to agree to peace provided the emperor recognised her right to Pomerania which was occupied by the Swedish army and whose last duke, Bogislav XIV, had died recently.

However France could not allow Swedish negotiations with the emperor to take place outside her control for, if Sweden were to withdraw from the war before France, might there not be a risk of Bernard of Saxe-Weimar following her example? Richelieu's attitude towards the United Provinces was somewhat similar. He had spies and informers working for him everywhere and knew full well that although Spain still affected to regard the Dutch as rebels she was making overtures to the Dutch government. He had no wish to allow himself to be caught unawares by a general desertion on the part of his allies. With supreme skill he did not exclude the possibility of peace; but he wanted the terms to be settled first and took as much trouble over trying to form new alliances as he did over maintaining the old. For this reason he was greatly preoccupied with England.

The political situation in Britain was extremely complex. Charles I's attempt to impose his absolute authority over England and Scotland had caused him to sacrifice foreign policy to domestic policy for several years —a course of action which was the exact opposite to that followed by Richelieu. He was now beginning to meet with such difficulties from his subjects, especially in Scotland, that he would have welcomed a diversion abroad. He could intervene in the final stages of the war either by drawing closer to Spain or by gravitating towards France. His dynastic interests impelled him to uphold the cause of his nephews the princes palatine. Their father the former king of Bohemia was dead. He had been deprived of the territories he had inherited as elector Palatine ever since he had been placed under the ban of the Empire. Was the punishment inflicted on the father now to be extended to the sons? Elizabeth, queen of Bohemia, begged her brother the king of England to give them his support. Nor was Richelieu himself averse to pleading their cause —without however going so far as to make it one of the prerequisites of a general peace treaty or to bracket it with French claims to Lorraine and Pinerolo. Above all he tried to induce England to join a fresh alliance with Sweden, the landgravine of Hesse-Cassel[2] and the United Provinces. He wanted thirty of Charles I's ships to co-operate in patrolling the Channel so as to harass if not cut Spanish communications with the Netherlands or even to join in carrying out the conquest of fortified towns in the Netherlands: Dunkirk for example.

It would be a gross exaggeration therefore to suppose that Richelieu was completely converted to the idea of negotiating a general peace treaty at the beginning of 1638 although he must have thought that the time was drawing near for preparations to that end. Above all he did not want to look as if he was begging for peace, as if he desired it at all costs and was even prepared to jettison France's Protestant alliances—which was what his political opponents at home wished to do. He took care to preserve the control over events which he had succeeded in acquiring by this date—an achievement which as yet owed nothing to French arms and was unquestionably due to his own diplomacy.

Richelieu's increased confidence in France's military strength was one of the reasons for his attitude. This confidence was excessive, as events were to prove. However in the early months of 1638 he looked forward optimistically to the forthcoming campaign on land and sea.

He was to all intents and purposes 'minister for the navy'. As he himself put it, 'Monsieur de Noyers is responsible for the war on land and I am responsible for the sea.'[3] The fleet had been reorganised and now consisted of forty-one ships of which the most important, *La Couronne*, drew two thousand tons and carried a crew of five hundred and five men. The majority were of between one hundred and five hundred tons with crews ranging from a hundred to two hundred. In addition there were galleys, fire ships and store ships. In short the French navy was now a powerful fighting force.

France's land forces consisted of six armies: an army in Flanders under the maréchal de Châtillon: a second in Picardy and Champagne commanded by the maréchal de la Force: Bernard of Saxe-Weimar's army in Alsace, soon to be joined by Guébriant: the duc de Longueville's army in Franche-Comté: the army of the prince of Condé in Guyenne: and finally the maréchal de Créqui's army in Italy. With these forces at her disposal it looked as if France need no longer fear a repetition of the disasters of 1636. Richelieu issued a stream of orders for strengthening Brouage and the forts on Ré and Oléron. He felt sufficiently confident to resume his plans for overseas trading companies; in fact he was not far from thinking that the war at sea had been won.

Thanks to the skill of the comte d'Avaux, the French ambassador in Germany, a treaty was signed with Sweden at Hamburg in mid-March 1638. Its main provisions were favourable to France. Avaux had made no rash promises about Pomerania. The alliance was renewed for three years during which France was to pay Sweden an annual subsidy of one million livres. Since it did not seem possible for Protestants and Catholics to combine in the same peace negotiations, it was proposed to continue negotiations between France and the house of Austria at Cologne while discussions between Sweden and the emperor were to be opened at Lübeck. In the meantime the two allies were to continue the war synchronising their offensive operations. This was tantamount to saying that the movements of Banér's army would be co-ordinated with those of Bernard of Saxe-Weimar and that war would break out again in the Empire whenever France and Sweden chose.

At the end of January Bernard of Saxe-Weimar had begun the siege of Rheinfelden but an attack by Johann von Werth dislodged him from his positions. The Imperialists thought that they had saved the town when

Bernard suddenly reappeared and without warning fell upon their quarters. The battle was short but decisive. France's ally was victorious and gained a valuable prize in the shape of Johann von Werth himself and his best lieutenant, the Italian Savelli. A month later, Rheinfelden having surrendered, Bernard of Saxe-Weimar advanced on Freiburg and occupied it on 11 April. His next step was to invest Breisach. The town lay on the right bank of the Rhine and thus both shielded Alsace and commanded the roads leading to the Palatinate from Austria and Italy. If well defended, it could hold out for some time. An Imperial army with some Bavarian contingents came to its rescue. However, at least these forces would not be available to resist a Swedish invasion of the Empire.

On the Netherlands front the maréchal de Châtillon had begun to besiege Saint-Omer. In the south-west Condé's army advanced towards the Franco-Spanish frontier and laid siege to Fuenterrabía. A fleet under Sourdis—who was both admiral and archbishop of Bordeaux—was to support Condé's operations by sea.

Fortified by these achievements Richelieu had replied to Spanish advances by sending Pujols the draft of a truce. He wanted it to be of long duration and to be extended to all the belligerents. It was to be established on the basis of a *status quo* but France and Spain would be able to exchange some of the towns they had captured in the Netherlands and Italy. Discussions with a view to a general peace were to be held immediately.

Olivares sent a representative to negotiate whom Richelieu allowed to enter France. This time it was a person of distinction, Don Miguel de Salamanca.[4] He first had an audience with Chavigny but demanded an interview with the cardinal himself. The latter agreed and the two men met in great secrecy in a church at Compiègne on 14 May.

However, each tried to avoid committing himself and to manoeuvre the other into submitting proposals that were as specific as possible. The most flattering compliments were conveyed to the cardinal from Olivares to which he replied with equally elaborate courtesies. He and Salamanca went so far as to envisage the three Catholic monarchs combining in a war against the Turks when peace had been concluded—for this perpetual dream of a crusade against the Infidel dating from the Middle Ages still occupied men's minds. But in the meantime Salamanca had to admit that he was not authorised to speak on the emperor's behalf and Richelieu made no secret of his absolute refusal to make concessions in respect of two points: France would not give up either Lorraine or Pinerolo and she would not act independently from her allies. With regard to the Dutch, Olivares demanded that they hand back Brazil in return for an indemnity. Richelieu expressed doubts as to whether this was feasible. On the following day a second meeting was devoted to German affairs (namely Württemberg and the Palatinate)* but to no purpose. With fresh exchanges of courtesies the two men parted without having decided anything.[5]

Richelieu was not sorry for he was counting primarily on successes in the field. But it was here that the most crushing disappointments lay in store for him. The war was to reveal the internal weakness of France's armies. As a case in point let us take the farcical behaviour of Richelieu's brother-in-law, the duc de Brézé, who seriously asked to be relieved of his command and given permission to return to Milli, his estate in Anjou, because the season for melons was approaching and he wanted to eat some so as to be in good fettle for hunting in the autumn. Far more serious was the fecklessness shown by the maréchal de Châtillon. Whilst besieging Saint-Omer he forgot about a canal which the Spaniards were using to supply and reinforce the garrison. Richelieu wrote him a devastating letter on 12 June: 'To be brief, even if Saint-Omer were another Ostend, the king would still be bent on victory'. Alas! under pressure from the armies of Piccolomini and Prince Thomas of Savoy, Châtillon had no alternative but to raise the siege and withdraw. In Italy the maréchal de Créqui was killed while carrying out a reconnaissance and cardinal La Valette who was sent to succeed him met with a defeat at Vercelli.

But the worst blow of all was the shocking débâcle at Fuenterrabía during the summer. On 22 August after a victory over the Spanish fleet in the Bay of Guatari, Sourdis had landed soldiers who then joined forces with the army commanded by the prince of Condé and the duc de la Valette. Richelieu was expecting to hear that Fuenterrabía had fallen when he learned that the French had made no attempt to storm the town after a breach had been made in the defences; instead they had allowed themselves to be defeated and on 7 September the whole operation had ended in a panic-stricken rout. Several hundred dead, wounded and prisoners had been left behind. 'I am so grieved about Fuenterrabía that it will kill me,' wrote the cardinal.

The prince of Condé when called upon to explain the disaster made some very grave accusations against the duc de la Valette. He asserted

---

* Like the elector palatine the duke of Württemberg had been excluded from the Peace of Prague. It will be remembered (p. 325 above) that he had previously placed Montbéliard under French protection.

that the duke had persistently refused to storm the town although the mine had been effective and at a council of war several officers had thought that an immediate assault was feasible. La Valette had made some highly alarming remarks; for instance he had said that his guards were paid by him not by the king and that he meant to be sparing in the use he made of them. During the retreat he had been seen laughing boisterously on the pretence of reassuring the men by putting a good face on it.

What was one to think? Instead of coming forward to justify himself La Valette had taken ship for England. In addition to being a duke, the son of the duke of Épernon, and the brother of cardinal La Valette, he was Richelieu's nephew by marriage. His illustrious birth and connections made the scandal worse; but no less tragic was the fact that twelve thousand men had retreated in disorder before an enemy force only seven or eight thousand strong. As Richelieu himself observed, 'There must have been some arrant bad captains among them.' In short the army believed capable of winning the decisive victories that would enable France to dictate the peace terms had proved to be composed of generals who were none too reliable, officers who were no more than mediocre, and troops who were lacking in discipline. In mid-September Richelieu had to have the brother-in-law of Feuquières executed at Amiens on the charge of intriguing with the Cardinal Infante. Thus he was unlucky enough to discover the same weaknesses both among his own kinsmen and among those of Father Joseph.

The defection of La Valette gave rise to one of those merciless trials through which king and cardinal sought to stifle public opinion by threatening it with their justice. After all the pattern of events at Fuenterrabía, or at least the circumstances under which the retreat had taken place, were not fully known. The prince of Condé had thrown the responsibility on to the duc de la Valette but his account was far from dispassionate and he did not produce any absolute proof. The case against La Valette ought to have been heard by the Parlement of Paris to say the least; but since the king was the source of all justice and the chief justiciary of the realm he could as legitimately convene an extraordinary commission to deal with the trial. That formed by Louis XIII and chancellor Séguier consisted of dukes and peers of the realm, *conseillers d'État*, *présidents à mortier* and the dean of the Parlement. The latter, an old magistrate named Pinon, showed visible disapproval of the procedure but when pressed by the king eventually replied with an irony that was impeccably respectful. 'Sire, since you order me to do so. I agree with these findings.'

Louis XIII explained his views to the judges. The arguments which he put forward deserve repetition for they reveal his outlook, his knowledge of his senior officers (which was quite considerable), his conception of a soldier's duty and the personal reasons for his severity. In the same way as Charles V during his discussions with the Imperial Diet on religious questions had frankly admitted that he was no theologian before suggesting the solution which was to his mind most compatible with the public interest, so Louis XIII now explained that he did not profess to be a trained lawyer and could not therefore follow the magistrates in their discussions on matters of form. What mattered to him was the ill will and undisciplined conduct of a general under specific circumstances in time of war: 'I shall say no more than this and in my own words: the duc de la Valette is not on trial for cowardice or for ignorance of the duties appertaining to his rank. He understands these very well and is not devoid of courage for I have myself seen him bearing himself bravely in several passages of arms. But he did not want to take Fuenterrabía . . . he could not have acted as he did except on a jealous impulse for which there can be no valid excuse whatever.[1] The duke was condemned to death in his absence and executed in effigy.

Richelieu's hopes that the capture of Fuenterrabía would counterbalance the setback at Saint-Omer had been wide of the mark. During the summer he had established himself at Saint-Quentin to decide which fortress was to be besieged. Hesdin and Arras were out of the question and the French had to confine themselves to recapturing Le Câtelet. This operation was carried out, although with some difficulty, on 14 September. Even so the year had been wasted and the cardinal wrote to the king without much optimism: 'We must watch the frontiers more closely than ever. I hope that the disorder which exists in your Majesty's armies this year will beget good order in the year that is to come.'

But at least he drew some consolation from the knowledge that galleys under the command of his nephew Pontcourlai had fought a successful engagement off Genoa which, together with the victory won by Sourdis, had enhanced the reputation of the French navy generally. 'I am overjoyed by these victories of his Majesty,' he wrote to the faithful Chavigny, 'and it gives me great content to see that his fleet which is my especial charge is doing its duty.' The cardinal went on to elaborate on this statement with some ingenuity: 'if the sea is more favourable [to our arms] this year than the land, I believe the advent of Monseigneur le Dauphin to be the cause thereof in that it has brought [God's] blessing on the element where the dolphins hold their sway.'[6]

In resorting to this imagery Richelieu was expressing his joy at the immense assistance that events—which as a Christian he saw as God's plans—had perhaps afforded his policy. On 5 September, slightly later than the physicians' forecast, Queen Anne gave birth to the long hoped-for child—a child whose very birth seemed almost a miracle and what was more a son: Louis-Dieudonné. Richelieu who was engaged in supervising the seige of Le Câtelet was unable to return to Court at once. As soon as he arrived he made a point of informing everyone through an article in the *Gazette* of the transports of joy that had seized him on seeing the king and queen in the dauphin's chamber and 'between the father and the mother that wondrous child, the object of his hopes and the ultimate fulfilment of his happiness'.

The birth of the dauphin was a matter of interest to all Europe. The main weakness of the monarchy of Louis XIII had been caused by the uncertainty as to who would succeed him. From the moment that the succession to the throne in the direct line was assured order was restored and the king's authority revived. To the seventeenth-century mind deeply imbued with respect for the monarchy but also apt to see signs and portents in every occurrence the birth of the dauphin seemed like a blessing from heaven, a renewed consecration of Louis XIII's greatness.*

Indeed it seemed to symbolise even more than this. A few days after the birth of the future Louis XIV a little girl was born at Madrid—the Infanta Maria Teresa who was to become his wife in 1660. If one were to apply present-day standards one would be inclined to say that the oddest thing of all was that Richelieu and Olivares immediately began to think in terms of an eventual marriage between the two children as a pledge of peace between the two crowns; but in point of fact there was nothing odd about their doing so. The statesmen of the day did not think differently from their contemporaries. They too looked for signs and portents; and since everything that occurred had a deep significance might not 'the coincidence of these two births', as Chavigny put it, 'one day bring about a great union and great good for Christendom'?

Secret negotiations were resumed between Paris and Madrid through the good offices of Pujols. Perhaps Richelieu, shaken by the lesson that events in the field had taught him during the year, worried by the inefficiency of the financial administration, and worn out by his perpetual wrangling with the superintendents (who always replied by emphasising the difficulties they encountered in finding money and made promises which they did not keep) was once more thinking of peace. The evi-

---

* A second son was born two years later in September 1640. (V.L.T.).

dence for this hypothesis is to be found not so much in the answers sent to Pujols or in the renewed requests to the nuncio to procure passports for the Dutch from the Spaniards, as in three lines written at the bottom of a private letter. A saintly churchman who was a friend of Saint Vincent de Paul had interceded with the cardinal on behalf of prisoners held for civil offences—people committed to prison for debt were treated like criminals in accordance with the harshness of the times. Richelieu recommended him to the chancellor; but impressed by his visitor's holiness he picked up his pen again after signing the letter and wrote: 'I beg you to redouble your prayers for peace. So sincerely and fervently do I long for it that I do not hesitate to ask God to punish those who impede it'.[7] What was the cardinal's motive for writing thus? Was he trying to convince a person who had some influence in certain circles of his good intentions? Or was he actuated by something which was more simple and more humane—a twinge of conscience, an appeal to Heaven?

However, Richelieu's resolve only to agree to an advantageous peace did not weaken on that account. In mid-December the siege of Breisach came to an end and Bernard of Saxe-Weimar took possession of the town. The news of this success had not yet arrived when one winter's evening whilst staying at Rueil as the cardinal's guest Father Joseph collapsed. He had already had a paralytic stroke in May during the conversations with Salamanca. This time the seizure was so violent as to preclude any hope of survival. Summoned in haste to the bedside of the dying man Richelieu tried to make his last moments happy by telling him as if he had just received the dispatch for which they had been hoping: 'Father Joseph, Breisach is ours.'

With the Capuchin the cardinal lost not only one of his most loyal servants but also one of his ablest associates in every aspect of his policy. He had often admitted him to meetings of the Council and considered him his best possible successor in the event of his own demise. For this reason he had particularly asked that of the two cardinal's hats to be awarded to France by the papacy the first should be conferred on Father Joseph without delay and the second be bestowed on the abbé Jules Mazarin whose skill in international negotiations he valued more and more highly. But as the Holy See took as long as possible to accede to Richelieu's request, the 'grey Eminence' died still wearing his coarse woollen scapular. He had certainly occupied a very important place in French foreign policy for more than twenty years. It would be going altogether too far to suppose that there would have been no Richelieu without this exceptional man, both mystic and realist, imaginative and cautious, humble and ambitious, a blend of sweetness and bitterness; but it is none the less true that without him certain matters would have turned out very differently.

Father Joseph had, therefore, a large share in the victory at Breisach. Not only did it give the French command of the Rhine valley but it also made them virtually masters of south Germany for it placed the valley of the Danube at least under their surveillance.

The Spaniards had hoped that a setback at Breisach would make the French more favourably disposed to peace and in Madrid the fall of the town was taken as an indication that the outlook for 1639 was stormy and menacing.

Both sides braced themselves for the struggle and from now on events followed a rather strange rhythm which was to last until the end of the reign. It has often been said even in the best books on the subject that from 1638 onwards there was a progressive improvement in the realm's affairs and that Richelieu could henceforth devote all his attention to a war which was punctuated by one victory after another. But this is yet another of those over-simplifications which bear little relation to the facts. Secret peace negotiations were never interrupted; they can be followed in minute detail in Canon Leman's book *Richelieu et Olivarès*. Both the French and the Spanish governments were equally desirous of peace but each accused the other of bad faith—possibly with genuine conviction—and each continued to do the other as much damage as possible. In fact it was a matter of proving to the enemy that one was in a far stronger position than himself so as to obtain favourable terms for an armistice or a peace.

The way to achieve this was not only to win victories in the field but also to foment difficulties for him by seducing his allies or by intriguing with the opposition that he had to contend with at home. The result was that each spring the war came to life again despite the great difficulty involved in finding the money and the men to form fresh armies.

It should be added that Richelieu had a very bad reputation in foreign courts. Even the ambassador of one of France's allies like Grotius, the ambassador for Sweden, used to send back reports on French affairs which were almost invariably unfavourable to the cardinal.[8] Olivares was not alone in thinking that 'he was the prime mover in all the persecution and injuries that afflicted Christendom and everything he said was manifest trickery'.[9] Relations with Rome were deplorable. The nuncio in Paris declared that he would not have been treated worse at

Constantinople and only Mazarin pleaded in favour of Richelieu's good faith. In Holland the prince of Orange had little liking for him. Of Louis XIII's sisters, the queen of England and the duchess of Savoy, the animosity of the first towards Richelieu was stimulated by her mother, for Marie de Medici spent the winter of 1638–9 in London.[10] Neither sister trusted him. They regarded him as a tyrant, the author of all the dissensions that divided the royal family and the chief obstacle to the restoration of peace in Europe.

The capture of Breisach neither gave France a lasting advantage nor guaranteed her tranquillity. Bernard of Saxe-Weimar who did not always receive his subsidies at the appointed times meant to obtain recognition of his own right to the towns which he had conquered for France claiming them as outright possessions. In short he saw himself as duke of Alsace in the same way as a few years earlier Gustavus Adolphus had suggested that he make himself duke of Franconia. There was a distinct danger that Bernard would try to come to an understanding with the emperor on the subject. How could France have tolerated an arrangement that left him as duke of Alsace? Not only would she have lost the Alsatian towns which could be used as bargaining counters in negotiations for a general peace, but also Bernard would inevitably have become favourably disposed to the duke of Lorraine since it would have been far more to his advantage to have a petty prince for a neighbour than the kingdom of France. It is in complex situations of this nature that Richelieu's merits as a statesman are most strikingly apparent. To a greater extent perhaps than anyone else in Europe he had a gift for discerning all the consequences of a situation. For this reason he was never satisfied with a settlement, however favourable and reasonable it might appear at first sight, in which he sensed some element of potential danger.

At the end of the year Bernard of Saxe-Weimar died. It was difficult to say whether his death was a blow or a blessing: on the one hand France lost the services of the finest general left in Europe after the death of Gustavus Adolphus, but on the other there was the continual risk that he might desert her at any moment. There was no lack of candidates to succeed him. Charles I's nephew, the prince palatine, tried to go and take command of Bernard's army but was seized whilst crossing France. He was imprisoned at Vincennes until the outlook became clearer.[11]

The French managed to retain Bernard's troops in their service and induced them to accept the maréchal de Guébriant as their chief. This meant that France was still in a position to continue the war in the Empire. Banér had launched a new offensive which penetrated as far as

Bohemia; he established himself in the former duchy of Friedland and in his train came the Czech émigrés still clinging to their hopes of recovering their former lands, for, in the words of one of their compatriots, the game was not yet over and the dice still lay upon the table.

In Italy France was faced with further difficulties. The little duke of Savoy, Francesco Giacinto, had died in October 1638. His mother the Duchess Christina had been entrusted with the regency by her husband's will, but Victor Amadeus had failed to provide for the possibility of his son's dying before he had attained his majority and for the new problems regarding the succession which would then arise. The little duke was survived by a younger brother. Was his mother to act as regent on his behalf also? Such an assumption was promptly challenged by his two uncles, Prince Thomas and Cardinal Maurice—both of whom were popular in the duchy, far more so than their sister-in-law. However as we have seen their sympathies lay with Spain; indeed they were intriguing with the marqués de Leganés the governor of Milan.

Christina was not 'a disloyal Frenchwoman' but she was growing impatient with the kind of protectorate that her brother's government was exercising over her son's dominions. She had for long maintained in her entourage a Jesuit named Father Monod whose sympathies were Spanish. Ever since the French had decided to arrest him and remove him to the fortress of Montmélian she had borne a particular grudge against Richelieu. It must be admitted that this antipathy was mutual. Richelieu used to refer to her as 'that wretched woman' complaining of 'the heedlessness of her actions' and 'the incontinence of her tongue' and denouncing her rashness and ingratitude. She showed no readiness to follow his advice that the chief fortresses of Piedmont, Nice and Savoy itself should be strongly garrisoned or occupied by the French. As a result of her obstinacy Piedmont went over to the side of her brothers-in-law in the spring of 1639. Turin alone remained in her hands and on 18 April the town was invested by Prince Thomas. The duchess who had only some Swiss troops at her disposal withdrew into the citadel and waited for the French to come to her rescue. Thanks to their protection she made good her escape; but the situation seemed so grave to the French that Cardinal La Valette who commanded the king's forces in Italy thought it wiser to conclude an armistice for two months on 14 August. Immediately Sweden and the United Provinces became alarmed, pretending to believe that France was working for a separate peace.

In September Louis XIII travelled to Grenoble to reprimand his sister. He found her in tears and in a recalcitrant frame of mind. She felt that she was being virtually called upon to surrender her powers into her brother's hands and flatly refused to commit the person of the young duke to French keeping, despite the offer to bring him up with every possible honour in the dauphin's household. Richelieu was so incensed that he seriously considered leaving Christina to her fate and negotiating with her brothers-in-law whom he thought of winning over from Spain by unprecedented concessions.

In Italy therefore events had largely gone in Spain's favour. But in the autumn she was to suffer a crushing defeat at sea. A large Spanish fleet was surprised in the Channel by the Dutch admiral Tromp; it was driven to take refuge in English waters and destroyed by him off Dover. Elsewhere victories and defeats counterbalanced each other. The French suffered a reverse at Thionville in Luxembourg[12] but on 19 July the prince of Condé took Salces in Roussillon—although in November it was to be the scene of his defeat. Most important of all was the capture of Hesdin in Artois on 29 June. Louis XIII himself took part in the siege. He was full of admiration for the valour shown by La Meilleraye, the Grand Master of the Artillery, who was directing operations. 'He is well worth those dotards of ours,' he would say, alluding somewhat unkindly to the two old marshals Châtillon and La Force. However the comment was true enough. One day the king stood in the breach and himself presented La Meilleraye with the baton of a marshal of France. Louis XIII was a typical French noble. Although he could be heartless on occasion he was gracious and charming when he felt that he had been well served and nothing gave him more pleasure than the valour of his officers in the field.

The rise of a new favourite dates from the siege of Hesdin. Cinq-Mars was the son of Effiat, the deceased superintendent of finance. He was nineteen years old and of attractive appearance. He had been picked out by Richelieu who thought that he would make a pleasant companion for the king. The latter was meeting with repeated disappointments in his platonic friendship with Mademoiselle de Hautefort—or rather with Madame de Hautefort to give her the designation to which her appointments in the queen's service now entitled her.

Father Griffet explains the beginning of the king's friendship with Cinq-Mars in the aptest terms: 'This minister who had an intimate knowledge of the king's character knew that he needed a favourite with whom he could converse unreservedly. He would have been very glad if he himself had been the sole person to occupy such a position; but he had found by experience that the king wished to have someone other than his minister as a confidant and that while he gave him his complete confidence in respect of the government of his realm, his Majesty was unable to bring himself to associate with him on those familiar terms that give life its charm.' In November Louis XIII told Madame de Hautefort that she must no longer pretend to his affections for he had given them entirely to Monsieur de Cinq-Mars.

According to Chavigny the new favourite depended entirely on the cardinal. The king had never before had such a violent infatuation for anyone. He bestowed on him the office of Grand Equerry of France;* Chavigny observed with a smile it was not a bad beginning for a young man of nineteen.

Men to fight and money to pay them—it was always the same story. But these were Richelieu's two vital needs and only the nation could supply them. The rest was his affair and depended on him alone subject to the king's approval. However both men and money were becoming increasingly difficult to find. The search for the former was even extended to foreign countries. Richelieu urged Bellièvre, the French ambassador in London, to organise levies in Scotland, pointing out that Charles I ought to sanction them to prove his good will, for if he aimed at winning French confidence or wanted to remain 'equally neutral' he could not overlook the fact that there were several Scottish and Irish regiments in the Spanish army. To preserve a balance there should therefore be approximately the same number of these troops in the French army. Moreover as there was a danger of rebellion in Scotland it would be in the king's interest to favour these levies since in this way the number of men liable to take up arms against him would be correspondingly reduced. In short Charles I was invited to encourage his subjects to emigrate so as to be able to dominate Scotland the more easily when it had been depleted of its fighting men. It was quite a Machiavellian argument. The cardinal returned to the charge more than once repeating to Bellièvre that 'we will find the money provided we can be sure of having the men'.[13]

In France itself the recruiting officers found that their task was made more difficult by the exhaustion of the population. They had to turn to the large towns where recruits cost more. However in the towns there

---

* *Grand Écuyer de France.* This appointment explains the nickname 'Monsieur le Grand' by which Cinq-Mars became known at court and which is sometimes used in the course of this chapter. The equivalent appointment at the English Court was Master of the King's Horse.

were more ways of pressing men into service, whereas in the country they could take to their heels. In 1639 Richelieu envisaged the recruitment of two thousand men in Paris:[14] 'recruitment'—already almost the same thing as calling to the colours, that is to say mobilisation, for the men who had enrolled in the two previous years were to be made to re-enlist by decree. Master craftsmen would be expected to submit the names of those who had borne arms since 1635 to the mayor of Paris [*prévôt des marchands*], and they would then be taken off to the army by the *gentilshommes du Roi*.[15] Admittedly each soldier was to be paid four crowns in accordance with the principle that the army consisted of mercenaries who hired out their services voluntarily. But in reality these men were being forced to serve as soldiers. Recourse was had to the crafts in the towns because the commissioner of a quarter[16] was in a position to draw up a list of the men employed in each shop or workshop. The trend was thus away from a professional army and towards compulsory military service. This was not a deliberate substitution but a change that was due to pressure of circumstances. By innovations of this nature Louis XIII's government was diverging more and more from the traditions of the Middle Ages and beginning to approximate to the government of a modern state.

Richelieu kept on repeating that there would be enough money. He maintained that it was far easier 'for *Messieurs les financiers* to find the money than for him and Monsieur de Noyers to find the men since a hoard of money does not vanish whereas a muster of soldiers disperses immediately without pay'.[17] The cardinal was very conscious of the ill effects of an incompetent and dishonest financial administration and he did not think that the government could demand money of the king's subjects regardless of the circumstances under which it was being paid. He fully realised that the system of farming out taxes made the tax farmers rich (although the government could not do without them) which would at the same time reduce the population to penury. His journey to the frontier in 1636 had brought him into contact with the grim realities of the situation. The people of Abbeville had agreed to a tax on wines the proceeds of which were to be devoted to the town's fortifications; however they themselves were to undertake its collection. In the event the tax-farm had been taken away from them, and the tax itself, to which they had consented for only a limited period, had been made permanent. Again, the population of Saint-Quentin had contributed fifty thousand livres towards the cost of their fortifications on condition that they paid no tax on wine; nevertheless the tax in question had been imposed upon them.

Richelieu took a very grave view of these breaches of faith. He felt certain that they reflected the desire of the hard-pressed superintendents to oblige some tax-farmer [*traitant*]; but in the meantime 'his Majesty is forfeiting the good repute of his given word; the people are not only losing heart but also their affection for the king: the towns are forfeiting their security and hence the realm likewise—all this to gratify a man like Barbier or some other financier [*partisan*]' (21 August 1638).[18] With regard to contracts for supplying the armies, or the administration of the king's revenues by officials who also derived substantial profits from their fees, the cardinal knew for certain that one and all were doing their best to line their own pockets. 'Peculation is so frequent,' he declared, 'that it could not be more so.'

Even the superintendents whom he used to say were devoted to the king's service did not seem to Richelieu altogether free from suspicion. If this did not apply to Bouthillier, whom he trusted,* it was certainly true of his attitude towards Bullion. When the latter requested him to ask the king for a gratuity in respect of his son's marriage, Richelieu replied with a criticism of his conduct which leaves one wondering how it was that Bullion continued to hold office thereafter. The cardinal requested him to limit his fortune to the possessions which he had at present and not to expect any increase in the future. He bade him revert to the earlier procedure now no longer current whereby no cash disbursements were made unless three copies of the particulars were drawn up: indeed it would be better still if Bullion were to make out four copies, the last being for the cardinal himself. And finally . . . but here we must let Richelieu express himself in his own words, for a dressing-down such as this should not be merely explained or summarised: 'in the fourth place [the sieur de Bullion] is to apply himself to the reform of the finances and the relief of the people with as much care as he devoted to his personal affairs before he was charged with those of the public. He is requested to do this not only because the public interest requires it but also so that he may one day be as rich in heaven as he is on earth—which is the most salutary wish that a person who loves him as I do can have for him.' (10 January 1639)[19]

Clearly Richelieu did not entertain many illusions about his team of ministers; but he evidently thought that there would be no great advant-

---

* Richelieu had entrusted Madame Bouthillier with the education of his orphaned niece Mademoiselle de Maillé-Brézé. It was this niece who married into the royal family through her alliance with the duc d'Enghien. (V.L.T.)

age in replacing them and that newcomers would be no better.

By dint of harrying everyone in the civil administration and the army, by adopting a benevolent attitude at one moment and a threatening attitude at another even in respect of gratuities which he had previously to a certain extent sanctioned or tolerated, he forced people to stay alert and kept things moving after a fashion. It would probably be going too far as well as unjust to suppose that the superintendents did not know their job or that they neglected financial reform. They were trying to defend the currency and stave off bankruptcy. But it would have been a matter of reforming the whole fiscal system and that depended at the very least on a firm balance between income and expenditure—an impossibility in time of war.

Nevertheless Richelieu did intend to carry out such a reform. Not only is it mentioned in the *Testament politique* but in 1639 he had a statement of the realm's receipts and expenses drawn up by Galand the older, the secretary of the *Conseil de direction des finances* 'in order subject to the king's good pleasure to frame a good plan for restoring the finances which is to be put into execution as soon as may be'. However peace was still a prerequisite for such an undertaking. It was even proposed to suppress the *taille* and the *gabelle* and to allow salt to be sold and consumed freely; but as against this a tax would have been imposed on salt throughout the realm which would have been similar to the tax of a sol per livre on all sales. Richelieu anticipated that these two indirect taxes, which would have become the Treasury's chief source of revenue, would yield thirty million and twelve million livres respectively. But we do not know what was the basis for this forecast and the whole scheme never got beyond the realm of wishful thinking. Obviously it would also have been necessary to bring about a fairer distribution of the burden of taxation among the different classes of French society; but this was incompatible with the privileges and the general organisation of the realm. Here the position of France was in no way peculiar, for more or less the same conditions prevailed in the other states of seventeenth-century Europe.

For the time being therefore the only way of finding more money was to increase existing taxes, either by raising the *taille* or by adding new indirect taxes to those already imposed. But the *taille* always fell on the same people. The government tried to ensure that it was paid by resorting to oppressive measures. The principle of *solidité* or collective responsibility, whereby the inhabitants of a parish were declared jointly and severally responsible for a payment, was applied generally.[20] This meant that not only those who failed to pay were punished with imprisonment but also those who, having paid themselves, refused to assume the tax burden of their insolvent neighbour. As for the new indirect taxes, the dues imposed on the sale of goods, they inevitably led to an increase in the cost of living and brought trade to a standstill. Moreover the unavoidable practice of entrusting the business of collection to tax-farmers (sometimes professional financers and sometimes royal officials) who would promptly pay a large sum of money into the Treasury, made such dues even more iniquitous. The common people in town and country alike being solely conscious of their own plight (and who shall blame them?) were only too ready to imagine that it was the tax-farmers who were responsible for these indirect taxes, and that they had petitioned for their introduction in order to make fortunes for themselves.

Under these conditions a revolt in the provinces was no longer a matter for surprise. This was 'the great mischief'* that Richelieu mentioned more than once to the superintendents without further explanation as if he was afraid of calling the calamity he foresaw by its real name. Why did it first erupt in Lower Normandy? Did the region of Avranches, where the revolt began, still harbour memories of earlier insurrections in the time of the League? The truth is that there was scarce a province of France where the past had not left a tradition of civil war —in some cases because they had been Protestant, in others because they had supported the League, or, going further back in time, because they had been Burgundian, Armagnac or Breton. The slightest reversion to calm and peaceful conditions was sufficient to efface such memories or at least to keep them within bounds. But as soon as distress became acute once more there was a resurgence of angry resentment accompanied by confused legends of the wars of former days. The sudden turn of events in the summer of 1639 was simply due to new threats of taxation causing a furore in a region which had been harassed with taxes for some years and had reached the limit of its endurance.†

Around Avranches as in all districts that bordered on the sea, salt was not a royal monopoly and the *gabelle* did not operate.[21] The local people used to collect it in the salt pans of the bay and largely depended on this

---

* *'Le grand inconvénient'*.

† The ensuing account of the revolts which occurred in Normandy during the second half of 1639 may be usefully amplified by reference to chapter 5 of Roland Mousnier's *Peasant uprisings in seventeenth-century France, Russia and China* translated by Brian Pearce and published in England in 1971 (referred to elsewhere in this book as Mousnier-Pearce).

occupation for their livelihood.[22] They formed a small private and independent world with its own particular customs; the energy of the population was tried by the difficulties of its daily life—lashed by the wind from the open sea where Mont Saint-Michel girdled with ramparts bore its abbey aloft in the sky. They were rude folk, half seafarers and half landsmen, and something of this quality was reflected in the behaviour of the people of Avranches. Outsiders, 'les horsains', were unpopular. That they should come to buy, bringing money into the district and contributing to its prosperity, was wholly reasonable; but it soon became intolerable that they should be sent to announce fresh taxation which would bring Avranches into line with Normandy and the rest of the realm. In the spring of 1639 the news spread that the government was going to forbid the use of white salt and introduce the *gabelle*.[23] For the people who worked in the salt pans this would have meant ruin. Ten or twelve thousand would have lost their means of livelihood or have seen it threatened. Fear worked upon the popular imagination. Feelings of mutual mistrust and old grudges undoubtedly existed among people who knew each other: all the more reason for a stranger to be an object of suspicion even if he belonged to a place which was no more than seven or eight leagues away or exercised his profession there. Any traveller was suspected of being an agent of the revenue. This was the tragic fate of Charles de Poupinel, sieur de la Besnardière, an officer of justice at Coutances who ventured into Avranches on 16 July on a matter connected with his official duties and in no way concerned with the *gabelle*. There were shouts of 'Gabeleur!' 'Monopolist!'. He was pursued and beaten to death in the street by a mob which treated his body with merciless savagery. The women came and gouged out his eyes with their spindles. He had to be buried at night but the people found his grave and an inscription was placed there threatening a like fate on anyone who came to the town to introduce the new taxes.

The governor of Avranches, the marquis de Canisy, had enough men and arms to defend the château but lacked sufficient forces to patrol the plain and prevent rebels from mustering; he was therefore quite powerless to stop the revolt from spreading and becoming organised. Within a few weeks all Lower Normandy was in rebellion. The movement reached the towns spreading through Pontorson, Saint-Aubin and Mortain as far as Vire and Domfront. At the same time a peasant army recruited from one village after another was forming in the countryside under the leadership of gentry and priests. Church bells sounded the tocsin summoning the people to muster. Placards were set up in the

market towns announcing that the whole area would be liberated from
the new taxes. The movement claimed to be led by a mysterious chief,
Jean Va-nu-Pieds or John Go-barefoot and the name Nu-Pieds was
proudly adopted by these new-style *croquants* in the same way as the
rebels in the Netherlands had assumed the name of Gueux or Beggars in
the previous century. They also called themselves the Army of
Sufferers—'l'armée de souffrance' or 'l'armée des souffrants'. Who was
Jean Va-nu-Pieds? Possibly it was only a name, a symbol based upon
memories of John the Baptist, a popular saint in the France of bygone
days, the forerunner of Christ and of a better era. 'Fuit homo missus a
Deo cui nomen erat Joannes'. 'There was a man sent from God, whose
name was John': such was the motto of the rebel army.[24] It has a clerical
tang about it and some have maintained that the general who issued his
orders 'from his camp near Avranches' may well have been Jean Morel
the *curé* of the parish of Saint-Saturnin on the outskirts of the town;
others have pointed to a nobleman the sieur de Ponthébert. The leader's
orders were countersigned 'les Mondrins' which according to some was
Jean Morel's nickname. In the language of the coast the term 'mondrins'
was applied to the little mounds of sand left by the sea at low tide.

However this may be, a well-organised rebel army was soon in being.
Its officers were inevitably drawn from the gentry who were to some
extent used to giving orders and conducting a war. The rank and file
were required to muster with their arms at the appointed places and to
observe strict discipline. By the end of autumn their numbers had risen to
twenty thousand men.

It was not long before the headquarters of the Va-nu-Pieds grew
bolder; not content with promising to abolish all taxes introduced since
the time of Henry IV the leaders called upon all Normandy to join the
revolt. In a series of curious manifestoes in rhyme they urged every class
of society to participate—the nobles to wreak vengeance for the hu-
miliations they had suffered, the bourgeoisie and the *rentiers* in revenge
for the endless extortions they endured. They conjured up the memory
of those who had made their name in history by battling against tyranny
—men such as Brutus and Catiline. Appeal was made to other provinces—Brittany and Poitou; nor was the capital itself overlooked.

> *Vous, Paris, qui tenez le premier rang au monde*
> *Montrez votre valeur au secours des souffrans,*
> *Assistant de vos forces une troupe féconde.*

'If Paris had hearkened to this appeal,' writes the Russian historian

Porshnev, 'the revolt of the Va-nu-Pieds would have developed into a political revolt by all France against tyranny: in other words it would have become the Fronde. But the Fronde did not come until ten years later. The revolt of the Va-nu-Pieds was one of its dress rehearsals.'[25]

This is a very sweeping statement. There is no denying that the revolt of the Va-nu-Pieds was a serious matter and that it has since been too often neglected by historians as if it were no more than a minor outbreak incapable of affecting Richelieu's authority for long; whereas in fact it was a movement of such dimensions that it all but threw the realm into confusion and made it difficult to continue the war abroad. But this is no reason for over-estimating the impact of the rebels' eloquent appeals. We must begin by picturing to ourselves the rebel army with its troops composed essentially of peasants and give first place to the state of mind, one might even say to the psychology, of these men. No doubt the rising of the Va-nu-Pieds is a prelude to the Fronde. But long after the Fronde there was another civil war in France—the war of the Vendée; and when one studies the peasant revolts of Louis XIII's day a comparison with the latter becomes inevitable. Despite the interval of a hundred and fifty years one is struck by the features these movements have in common. Admittedly the motives for taking up arms were not the same but the nature of the conflict presents marked similarities.

In each case the country people of a certain region rise in revolt because new laws constitute a threat to their customs or mode of life and they cannot imagine living in any other way. They respond to the summons of their priests and their gentry for they are used to listening to the former and look upon the latter as their natural leaders. This rural population can form an army that is all the more formidable because it is helped by the lie of the land which becomes its most valuable ally. Wood, fallow, and farm, indeed the whole countryside, aid and abet its every move. The peasant army is thus able to establish its ascendancy quite quickly over a given area, subjugating it and terrorising its inhabitants. The towns are occupied without much difficulty for the bourgeois guard generally puts up a poor resistance in the face of the rebels' furious onslaught. Henceforth a major military operation such as the victorious march of the royal and Catholic army towards Granville is not beyond their powers.[26] But we must bear in mind that successes of this nature were like sudden attacks of fever. Precisely because they hold land and are passionately attached to their soil, peasants in rebellion cannot bring themselves to leave their holdings for months on end. Even when fighting on their home ground the Vendéans of 1793 liked to devote part of each week to warfare and part to their rural occupations. If ever some large scale operation took them away from their native province their only thought was to return there as quickly as possible. Similarly the army of the Va-nu-Pieds did not leave Lower Normandy and we must be careful not to be too hasty in concluding that because Paris was mentioned in the rebel manifestoes there was a real possibility of a general rising throughout the realm. Instead of listening to the bombast put out by the leaders let us concentrate on the rank and file.

And this in turn brings us to another characteristic of agrarian risings: for all their stamina it is never long before the peasants show signs of tiring. The war is unleashed with terrible fury but the organised impetus behind it does not maintain its momentum. The leaders of the Vendée rebellion also announced that they were going to march on Paris and to this day there are still historians in sympathy with their aims who deplore their failure to do so. But it is well nigh impossible to prove that the Vendéans were really able to march on the capital; and even if they had reached Paris it is more than doubtful whether they could have maintained their position. By their very nature peasant risings are bound to degenerate into guerilla warfare which regular armies are bound to overcome in the long run. But only in the long run. The fact remains that a guerilla war extending over several years can be a terrible thing capable of producing far-reaching consequences in the region where it erupts. The insurrection in Lower Normandy was now to be accompanied by increasingly serious disturbances in the rest of the province.

Among the most odious of the recent fiscal measures were an increase in the duty on dyed fabrics and the appointment of controllers of dyeing charged with the task of visiting manufactories to inspect pieces of material and single out those liable to the new tax. The most obvious results had been a halt in production, and unemployment in the workshops. The people of Rouen were incensed and ready to seize the first opportunity of giving vent to their anger. In addition the governor of Normandy, the duc de Longueville, was absent, as he was in command of an army on the frontier. If not a popular figure he was at least respected and feared; indeed as he watched the rebellion gaining ground Richelieu was to declare that Longueville's value to the king in Normandy was becoming patently obvious and that his lieutenants had ruined everything through their failure to follow his example. The governor of Rouen, the comte de Guiche, was also absent from his post for the same reason. In short there was no strong authority in the town. The archbishop François de Harlay maintained that since the chief cause of the trouble lay in its lack of a governor Rouen should not be blamed for having governed itself badly. The parish clergy did not conceal their disapproval: ' 'tis most horrible and pitiful to hearken to the poor country folk who forsake their habitations and seek refuge in the woods because they can no longer provide what the king is pleased to require of them,' declared a *curé* of Rouen in the course of a sermon. As for the magistrates of the Parlement they resented the recent creation of a *Cour des Aides* at Caen as a threat to their own position. They held that the enforcement of collective fiscal responsibility and the imprisonment of people who had paid the *taille* on the grounds that their fellow citizens had failed to do so (generally a sign of destitution not of recalcitrance) were contrary to justice. The *procureurs*, claiming to be people of limited means and contrasting their station with the opulence of the magistracy, refused to pay the taxes imposed on their offices; rather than do so they preferred to cease carrying out their duties.[27] In effect they embarked on a kind of strike which brought legal proceedings to a standstill and this in a region where litigation was a frequent occurrence and where large numbers of people had laid suits to secure a refund of money or to remedy some complexity of long standing. The *procureurs* blamed especially Hugot, the *receveur-général des droits domaniaux*,[28] asserting that it was he who had negotiated for taxes to be imposed upon them. The *rentiers* for their part complained that they had not received the interest due to them each quarter, only to be told by le Tellier de Tourneville, the *receveur des gabelles*,[28] that he had not a penny of the king's revenues left in his coffers. In short there were complaints everywhere—among the legal profession, amongst manufacturers, tradesmen, and artisans, in the liberal professions and among the rural population. As for the collective responsibility for the payment of taxes it was enforced all over the province whose population was either reduced to hardship or to downright misery. It was nothing short of a general crisis.

The storm broke at Rouen. When the first official sent to enforce the edict on dyed cloth made his appearance he was done to death on the square outside the cathedral. For four days (20, 21, 22 and 23 August 1639) gangs of young men joined in sacking the houses belonging to the tax-farmers. The first president of the Parlement called upon the bourgeois militia and local gentry to intervene but by no means all of the bourgeoisie responded to his appeal. On the contrary many of them set upon the first harquebusiers they happened to meet. A captain was pursued right into the church of Saint-Ouen and murdered there and a service of purification had to be held before it could be used again for public worship.[29] The attacks of the mob were chiefly directed against the *bureaux des aides* and the offices of the excise on hides and cards, in fact against everything which was associated in the people's eyes with the vexatious taxes they hated so much.[30] A certain Gorin, the son of a cutler and himself a clock-maker, assumed the leadership of the rising and gave himself out to be the lieutenant of Jean Va-nu-Pieds. He raised the old cry against injustice: 'Haro, mon prince, on me fait tort!' and the first word was distorted by the people into the name Raoul.[31] An attack was made on the house occupied by Tourneville who was besieged there together with his household. Two counsellors from the Parlement intervened and succeeded in delaying the sack of the house thus enabling Tourneville to make his getaway in disguise. Before escaping he threw the money due to the king down the privies and into the well —evidently despite his earlier denial there was some after all. As a shot fired from one of the windows had killed a child in the crowd, the first president of the Parlement announced that an inquiry would be held into the acts of violence perpetrated by the persons barricaded in Tourneville's house.[32]

For all this the Parlement did help to calm the tumult, partly through the courageous behaviour of its magistrates who appeared in a body wherever the danger was greatest, thus eventually overawing the hooligan element, and partly through its pronouncements. At the same time in the suburbs the bourgeois defended their houses by force of arms and Gorin was arrested. With the town in a state of upheaval the canons of Saint-Ouen cancelled their traditional procession which was due to be held at about this date, while the Jacobins* made haste to remove from their door the large escutcheon bearing Richelieu's coat of arms which had been erected there for some time. This was not the moment to parade the cardinal's friendship; the emblem which had hitherto caused them to be treated with respect would only serve now to attract popular violence.

Disturbances occurred more or less everywhere—at Bayeux, for example, and at Caen where the artisans led by a street-porter named Brasnu laid siege to the houses of the bourgeoisie. The turmoil spread all over Normandy. In a letter written from Langres on 28 August to Bouthillier, the superintendent of finance, the cardinal threw the responsibility on to the Council: 'I know of the disorders at Rouen but I know

---

* This was the name popularly given to the Dominicans whose house in the rue St Jacques in Paris dated from the thirteenth century. (Marion, *Cross*)

not what is the remedy since it is impossible to provide the troops for which we have been asked if we are to avoid ruining the king's affairs completely and abandoning France to the foreigner. Moreover even if we were willing to expose ourselves to such a risk you could not have the troops in less than two months whereas the harm that we would suffer in consequence would not be so slow in declaring itself.

'I confess that I do not understand why you do not give somewhat more thought to the consequences of the decisions made in your *Conseil des finances*. It is easy to avert even the most incurable diseases; but once they occur they cannot be remedied'.

The cardinal expressed a similar opinion in a letter to the Council: evidently he had no illusions as to the mischievous nature of the policy that had been pursued to date. To his mind neither the *gabelle* nor the summoning of feudal levies from among the Norman nobility (which was under discussion) nor the tax on the well-to-do[33] were reasonable measures. In his view all of them only constituted grounds for revolt. 'I know full well,' he wrote 'that *Messieurs les surintendants* will immediately say that nothing is achieved by doing nothing, and that necessity compels them to do many things which they would themselves condemn at any other time. But I beg them to believe that measures which can deliver not only loyalties but also strongholds to our enemies are to be condemned at any time.' And again: 'We must endeavour to restore the situation in Normandy as best we may by a mixture of dexterity and caution; for to count on troops being available for the purpose is quite out of the question at the present time.'

Yet to demand money from the superintendents and condemn almost every method of raising it—the new taxes because they caused revolts, the aid of the financiers because it made them scandalously rich: to assert that it was the government's fiscal measures which were responsible for the outbreaks and to refuse the soldiers who would have quelled them: to expect an obedient population while conducting a war that was the source of all its ills: such an attitude on Richelieu's part had something inhuman or superhuman about it, and one can understand that his ministers in their desperation felt that the only thing left for them to do was to dash out their brains against a wall. One can also understand the continual danger of the realm rising in rebellion, given a leader to organise it; and some had already begun to whisper to a number of different persons (who certainly did not include the makeshift generals of the Va-nu-Pieds) that they were well-fitted for such a part.

Richelieu's colleagues did not dare tell him everything. In October

1639 Bouthillier writing in confidence to his son Chavigny admitted the full extent of his despair: 'I have never been so overwrought as I am now, with such a revulsion from business and an unutterable feeling of sorrow when I consider the situation in which we find ourselves. I shall explain myself more fully when we meet, God willing. Expenditure of ready money amounts to at least forty millions; the *traitants* are forsaking us and the people are unwilling to pay anything whether the taxes be old or new. We are now at our last gasp* and no longer in a position to choose between good advice and bad. And I fear that our war abroad will degenerate into a civil war. His Eminence will find some remedy when he sees how matters stand but I must confess that for my part I am at my wits end [*bien empêché*] and can see no light.'[34]

What could be done except to wait for a miracle from the man who literally demanded the impossible?

Although the towns in Normany were gradually regaining their calm, the army of the Va-nu-Pieds still controlled the area of Avranches and kept Canisy penned within his fortress. The magistrates of the Parlement, content with a return to everyday peaceful conditions, were in no hurry to restore order as the king's Council understood it. For example they left in disorder the tax-farming offices which had been looted during the riots, and pretended that they were unable to provide the officials concerned with new premises—a task which they left to the *Cour des Aides*. Nor did they show much eagerness to institute proceedings against the rioters whom they had arrested. What were they waiting for? For better times, for peace perhaps, and for the past to be forgotten. The government in Paris was soon convinced that the revolt of the Va-nu-Pieds would not have lasted so long and the disturbances in the towns would not have occurred or been so serious if the magistrates of Rouen had not been so tolerant and given the impression that they excused the rebels but regarded the representatives of royal authority as insufferable. The king's Council decided to crush the rebellious province in the king's name. As there was a risk of French soldiers tending to feel sorry for the wretched people, the main task of repression was given to Colonel Gassion since he commanded foreign troops. The latter entered Lower Normandy as if it were enemy territory where they could do as they pleased with impunity. The Va-nu-Pieds could not stand up to opponents of this calibre. They fell back on Avranches and were quite quickly dispersed. The town was given over to the soldiery who indulged in an orgy of

---

* *'Nous sommes maintenant au fond du pot'.*

hanging and looting while their commander was complimented on his severity.

An unprecedented punishment fell upon the Norman capital. Chancellor Séguier obtained from the king an especial commission vesting him with exorbitant powers both civil and military which made him temporarily a sort of viceroy for Normandy, at one and the same time chief justice and constable. He was even authorised to punish rebels without trial by a mere order given by word of mouth. When news of this decision reached the province the people realised the fresh miseries that lay in store and the fearful calamity that was going to descend upon them after the few weeks of respite they had enjoyed.

The year 1639 was drawing to a close. During this particular Advent which in the France of former days was observed as another Lent, as a time devoted to prayer and penance, the churches of Rouen were even more crowded than usual. François de Harlay, the archbishop, exhorted his flock to resign themselves to their lot but encouraged them to put their confidence in the king's mercy. He too did not consider the people overmuch to blame and still hoped that a signal gesture of submission, a public display of repentance would be rewarded with a pardon such as had not been invariably refused to the Protestants in the past.

At the end of December Séguier arrived at Gaillon[35] accompanied by fresh troops. A deputation representing the aldermen and Parlement of Rouen called upon him to pay its respects. It met with an extremely ungracious reception. The archbishop sent word that he proposed to await the chancellor kneeling at the gates of the town and to renew his promise that his people would obey. It would have been impossible to leave a gesture of this kind unanswered; nor would it have been fitting for the representative of the Most Christian king to give a flat refusal to one who spoke to him in God's name of meekness and gentleness. It followed therefore that such a confrontation must be avoided. The archbishop was accordingly requested not to bestir himself and informed that 'religious pomp and ceremony could not be allowed to affect the issue or regarded as relevant in this particular context'.

On 2 January 1640 amid a silence that betokened a subjected city Séguier entered Rouen. From the door of his coach he listened to an address delivered by the lieutenant of the *bailliage* begging him of his goodness to safeguard the people of this the second city of the realm. His only answer was a stern look. He immediately took up his residence at the royal abbey of Saint-Ouen which was a direct dependency of the Crown. He was thus dispensed from any debt of hospitality to the citizens of Rouen. Two days later the chancellor announced his decision. The Parlement and the town council were suspended. Instead of the former there was to be a commission composed of counsellors of the Parlement of Paris under the direction of Tanneguy Séguier a kinsman of the chancellor and a *président à mortier*. This commission was to administer justice and hold an enquiry into the recent disturbances. All the taxes which had been contested were reintroduced. With regard to the tariff on dyed cloth, the charges that clothiers and dyers would be called upon to pay were back-dated to 7 June 1639, this being the day on which the *Cour des Aides* had registered the edict under pressure. The town council of Rouen was provisionally replaced by a commission to be nominated by the chancellor which was to take over the administration of the city. Soldiers were to be quartered on the inhabitants who were also to provide their pay. In addition Rouen was to pay an indemnity of more than a million *livres* and compensate the tax farmers* who could submit their complaints for examination.

These directions were followed by the proclamation of 8 January which laid down that the urban population was to be disarmed and hand in its weapons. It made magistrates responsible for any delay in carrying out orders and warned them that they would be treated as accomplices if unable to produce evidence of their zeal. Leaving the town of Rouen dazed by these conditions Séguier proceeded to Lower Normandy to meet Gassion's army. At Caen he replaced the *présidial* by a commission; at Bayeux and indeed everywhere he carried out his task with the same frigid severity. Officials and bourgeois were declared answerable for any outbreaks in the towns and nobles made responsible for disturbances that were reported on their fiefs.

In the Cotentin in March Séguier summoned the nobility to meet him.† They came in large numbers. He spoke to them ruthlessly but adroitly enough. He knew that those present had been to a greater or lesser extent involved in the rising of the Va-nu-Pieds. He pointed out that they had acted misguidedly and that their authority as nobles and landowners was in fact bound up with the authority of the Crown. For them to allow a rebellious rabble to have the whip hand was clean contrary to their interests.

Some of his listeners ventured to say in reply that disturbances could break out suddenly without their being able to prevent them. Séguier

---

* '*Les traitants et les fermiers*'.

† The Cotentin is the Cherbourg peninsula.

retorted by quoting the actual words of the proclamation which specified that if they had acted in accordance with their duty and had done
what lay in their power they could not be held to blame. But since any
appraisal of their behaviour was bound to be highly arbitrary this was
tantamount to saying that no one would be safe if there were further outbreaks in the district.

Normandy was delivered over to a reign of terror. But the harshness
of the punishment, ostensibly inflicted as a warning to others, had no
effect on public opinion. On the contrary it did not prevent the outbreak
of serious disturbances in Moulins during the year 1640. There is no
doubt whatever that the whole realm had had more than enough of the
war and that people were only waiting for a saving opportunity to be
quit of it.

Henceforth, as the reports of Grotius to his government testify,
Richelieu's enemies among the king's entourage and abroad were convinced that a change of policy would be welcomed by most of the population and that all France would join in any scheme bold enough and
well enough led to topple the cardinal from his throne. This is the
explanation for the last plots of the reign. But there was the king to be
reckoned with. Despite some scattered instances of a few hotheads
inveighing against the king, the authority of the Crown and the person
of the monarch, those two reflections of God's power, were too unanimously respected and revered and seemed too much part and parcel of
the world order for the French monarchy—and therefore Louis XIII, its
living embodiment—to be in danger.[36] One could of course argue from
what was happening in England at the same date. But the history of the
English revolution is the story of the slow erosion of royal prestige. It
proves on the contrary that even in the midst of civil war, and even in the
eyes of his rebellious subjects who had taken up arms against him,
Charles I for long remained a consecrated king vested with a supernatural authority.

Thus everything depended on Louis XIII; and although the king often
had occasion to feel exasperated with the cardinal he was obdurate
whenever he thought that his authority in the State was involved and
very conscious of the prestige derived from victories in the field. It still
seemed to him that in both these respects no one had served him so well
as the cardinal.

The position of Spain was not such as to give France cause for envy. The
Council of State at Madrid had given up all hope of receiving more

wholehearted support from the emperor. Olivares would have liked
Ferdinand III to launch an invasion of France, or to dispose of Sweden by
a separate peace so as to be free to join forces with the Spaniards. But the
emperor had recalled his general Piccolomini to Germany after the
latter's victory at Thionville. Henceforth Olivares saw that he could no
longer count on his ally and his sole concern at the beginning of 1640 was
to avoid another spring campaign at all costs. 'The sign that God wishes
for peace to be made is that He is visibly depriving us of the means of
waging war. We are in most grievous straits and the emperor's plight is
worse than ours since he is without any government whatever, without
good order or the means of obtaining it and unable to rely upon the
loyalty of his vassals or the diligence and zeal of his ministers. In fact all is
lost (En efecto, todo perdido).'[37] The Council of State shared this view
and admitted that the only course was to renew negotiations with France
with the firm intention of reaching an understanding. And it is probable
that these negotiations would have succeeded if Richelieu had been of a
like mind.

However, despite events in Normandy, the cardinal had begun to feel
more hopeful, especially since Tromp's victory off Dover. The prospects
that he saw unfolding before him at the same date form a contrast to the
desperate picture of Spain's position painted by Olivares. 'It is an affair of
such importance to complete the destruction of the Spanish navy and
thwart their projects for transporting soldiers from Flanders to Spain and
from Spain to Flanders that everything possible must be done to achieve
this end,'[38] he wrote on 22 December 1639 to Estrades, the French ambassador at the Hague. 'Admiral Tromp with thirty ships is undoubtedly
able to complete the task that he is about to undertake. Spur on his Highness the Prince of Orange, their Excellences of the Estates and the Admiral himself.'[39] He pointed to the desperate plight of the Spanish navy,
to the Cardinal Infante arranging for the shattered remnants of the fleet
to be repaired in England and at Dunkirk and endeavouring to purchase
boats everywhere even in Holland where care would have to be taken to
ensure that the Spaniards were not allowed to reap such an advantage
through an oversight. The cardinal no longer hesitated even to 'propose
a number of different ventures' with a view to carrying out at least one
which stood a good chance of success. He talked of a joint operation by
the Dutch and French fleets off the Spanish coast, at Gibraltar, or in the
area of the Azores and the Canary Islands. 'By making use of the forces of
the West India Company and part of the king's fleet we could even
undertake some operation in the Indies or against Cartagena or Porto

Bello at both of which the Spanish fleet calls every year, or against the fleet itself.'[40]

The revolt in Scotland freed the cardinal from another anxiety. Although he thought it unwise for France to become too deeply involved there[41] and felt that it would possibly be dangerous to weaken Charles I's position he knew that henceforth it would be beyond the latter's power to intervene seriously abroad. Even if the king of England was of no assistance to France it was equally certain that he would give no help to Spain.

Richelieu was on the point of seeing his exertions as 'Minister for the Navy' crowned with success before any of his other activities. Spain had made use of the sea to dominate the world and it was the sea that ensured communications between the scattered components of her Empire; but now freedom of the seas was secure and it was there that France's formidable enemy was to be brought to bay.

In any case, the alliance between France and the United Provinces was renewed for the operations of 1640. Richelieu was always haunted by the fear that his Dutch and Swedish allies would be alienated if his secret negotiations with Spain came to light and was therefore in no great hurry to reply to proposals from Madrid. When the Spaniards offered to send a small mission composed of three people he raised objections: it was far too large and would arouse suspicions. In short it was not until June when hostilities were engaged on several fronts that the cardinal received the Spanish emissary Jacques de Brecht[42] in a modest country manor house near Compiègne. He adopted a haughty attitude towards the terms which Brecht put forward despite the fact that the Spanish proposals regarding Lorraine were very moderate. In particular he rejected the pressing demand that he should induce the Dutch to relinquish north Brazil in return for an indemnity of three or five millions. Although he kept up appearances by fulsome and insincere declarations of his devotion to Olivares, the cardinal allowed the negotiations to dissolve into thin air as in 1638.

These negotiations had ceased to have much relevance. The summer of 1640 was marked by a series of French victories of which the most brilliant was the capture of Arras. After a laborious siege lasting several months the French entered the town on 10 August. The king was present with his nobility and Cinq-Mars or 'Monsieur le Grand' as he was known gave proof of his courage. In Italy Turin was retaken from the Spaniards.

These were unquestionably major successes but they were costly in men and money. Nor should it be imagined that once these strongholds were taken there was no further risk of their being lost again. Nothing was more difficult than the retention of a town that had been captured from the enemy. An army could break up owing to grievances over its pay or victuals, or because of an inadequate bread ration. Much care and energy were required to keep one's hold on an occupied town and the task of safeguarding Arras, Turin and Casale whose loss the Spaniards felt so keenly, was a source of great worry to the cardinal.

Nevertheless the year had been an exhausting one for Spain. Her population was as over-burdened with taxes and as worn-out as that of France. It was a question of which country would be the first to collapse. Spain—that is to say the kingdoms and territories of which Spain was composed*—had not the same degree of unity and cohesion as France. Cracks were beginning to appear in the whole structure. Provincial loyalties were kept alive by the existence of local Estates and of legislation peculiar to each territory. Portugal had been linked to Spain by a purely personal union since Philip II had succeeded to the inheritance of the last king of the house of Avís in 1580.†

But he had set aside the pretensions of the Braganzas, another branch of the Portuguese royal family. At the end of 1640 the duke of Braganza supported by a conspiracy in which Richelieu's agents were involved laid claim to his rights and was proclaimed king at Lisbon by the Cortes with the title of John IV. In the capitals of Europe officials began to search the archives for legal and rational arguments that could be propounded to the king of Spain to justify recognition of the new régime. Moreover Brazil was a dependency of the Portuguese crown.

A province of Spain likewise broke away. The principality of Catalonia had become utterly exasperated by the heavy military obligations it was made to assume for the defence of the adjoining territory of Roussillon. The Catalans asked the king of France to protect them, offering to recognise him as count of Catalonia, and a delegation arrived at Saint-Germain. Louis XIII promised his assistance and undertook not to make peace without including Catalonia; but the province could only be reached by sea, for Roussillon remained loyal to Philip IV and its strongholds were stoutly defended by his army.

Spain was on the decline and her allies showed themselves correspondingly less and less eager to support her. Charles IV of Lorraine felt that he would do better to come to an understanding with France. As for

* Castile, Aragon, Valencia, Catalonia, Navarre, Vizcaya, Galicia and Portugal.

† This dynasty had ruled over Portugal since 1385.

Richelieu he thought that it would be a good thing if the duke could be won over and the question of Lorraine settled before a general peace was negotiated. He allowed Charles IV to travel to Paris and on 29 March 1641 a treaty set the seal on their reconciliation. The duke was restored to his states and acknowledged that he held Barrois as the vassal of the king of France. He definitely surrendered Clermont, Stenay, Jamets and Dun and agreed to the temporary occupation of Nancy. Most important of all he undertook not to make any alliance with France's enemies and promised to assist her against Spain. Lorraine thus regained her separate status but was brought under French tutelage to an extent that made her more like a vassal state than an independent duchy. At a solemn ceremony Charles IV confirmed his promises by an oath sworn on the Gospels. However, on the previous day, he had lodged a formal protest with a notary declaring the oath that he would be taking null and void on the grounds that it was being extorted from him under pressure.

Richelieu attached great value to this diplomatic achievement. He must have felt that he was giving foreign opinion a proof of French moderation and would be laying Spain open to the charge of acting with futile obstinacy in continuing the war; otherwise it is difficult to account for his being hood-winked and for his readiness to trust Duke Charles once more.

In Germany the emperor had summoned a Diet to meet at Regensburg during the summer of 1640, counting upon it to give him aid.* Piccolomini had forced Banér to withdraw from Bohemia but the Swedish general had thereupon entered Germany and at one time it was thought that he meant to march on Regensburg and break up the Diet. The latter discussed with the emperor plans for a general pacification of the Empire. It proposed fixing 1618 not 1627 as the determining year for a territorial settlement.† In practice this would have involved reverting to the *status quo ante bellum* and would have assured the Protestants of substantial advantages. On the other hand the emperor would still have benefited from his consolidation of the hereditary lands.‡ Without waiting for agreement on all these points the Diet granted a subsidy of one hundred and twenty Roman months for the upkeep of an army which now ceased to be merely the emperor's and became the army of the Empire.[43] The fact was that a strong peace party was emerging—a party comprising princes of both religious denominations—which was inclined to come

* The last meeting of the Imperial Diet had taken place in 1608.

† *Cf.* p. 326

‡ See note on pp. 297–9

to an understanding with Sweden in return for a few territorial concessions in Pomerania.

Richelieu wanted to keep Sweden and Hesse-Cassel in the anti-Habsburg coalition and by an agreement made in June 1641 he obtained an undertaking from his allies that they would not make a separate peace. He did not reject peace in principle but merely sought to conclude it with the princes of Germany individually rather than with the emperor. Above all he wished to avoid treating with the latter in his capacity as head of the Empire.

In Brandenburg a new ruler was beginning his reign. This was Frederick William, later known as the Great Elector, who for forty years was to occupy an important place in European affairs. A change in the composition of his government was followed by the disgrace of his chief minister, Count Adam zu Schwarzenberg, a Catholic and favourably disposed to the emperor. Brandenburg now prepared to sign a truce with Sweden.

The continuation of the war on a general scale was thus becoming increasingly unlikely everywhere and the conflict was beginning to resolve itself into a duel between France and Spain. France was beginning to get the upper hand but could she maintain the effort required of her? Both French and Spanish governments were struggling to defend their currencies. In March 1640 a royal edict issued from Saint-Germain created a national gold coin—the louis, worth ten *livres tournois*. Throughout the year the superintendents busied themselves with arrangements for the conversion of small coins into this new currency. In Madrid the government tried to revalue the maravedí. But it was impossible for these operations to be effective for as long as the financial haemorrhage caused by the war continued unchecked.

In the last days of 1640 Bullion, the superintendent of finance, admitted the straits in which he found himself just as his colleague Bouthillier had done in the previous year. Thirty-two million francs were needed if the expenses for 1641 were to be met and there seemed to be no alternative but for the government to commit itself yet again to the *partisans*. In addition to a tax of a sol per livre which an Italian financier Paleologo[44] professed himself ready to negotiate, the government envisaged tapping the wealth of the clergy. The intention was either to impose the *taille* on all clergy who were not of noble status, or to introduce a tax on church benefices equivalent to a third of their revenues. Mere rumours on the subject provoked immediate complaints to Richelieu from parish priests in the capital and the cardinal did not conceal his fears of a fresh outbreak in Normandy. Meanwhile Bullion died 'of a creeping gout*'. So unpopular was he in Paris that the news of his death was greeted with joyful demonstrations in the streets and his family had to arrange for him to be buried after dark. There was also talk of an investigation being made into his fortune before allowing it to pass to his heirs and it was said that the king might confiscate part of it.

But this did not solve the problem of balancing the budget; and whether Richelieu's policy was to be carried through to a conclusion or brought to a halt while its results were still in doubt depended on this problem's solution.

The rumours were correct. The time had come to turn to the clergy and call upon them to make an exceptional contribution. A declaration of 1639 had recalled that the use of *mortmain* which had been conceded to the clergy was purely and simply an act of grace on the part of the Crown. The king finding himself compelled to resort to a number of exceptional measures for the maintenance of his armies could annex to his domain and alienate for his own profit all church property on which amortisation dues had not been paid, for these were still owing.[45] However, to avoid having recourse to outright confiscation the king would be satisfied with the payment of an amortisation tax on all property acquired by the Church prior to 1620. With this end in view all clergy and incumbents throughout the realm were to be compelled to submit to a commission set up for the purpose 'a most true and perfect declaration in inventory of the houses, inheritances, ground-rents, tithes transferred to lay persons, [*dîmes inféodées*][46] and generally of all rights and landed property whether noble or common of which they stand in possession, of every title and condition whatsoever'.[47]

The memoirs of Montchal who was notoriously hostile to Richelieu† describe the 'outcry' to which this decision gave rise among the clergy. Some passages read like a polemic written at the time of the Combes ministry towards the beginning of this century.[48] It was said that it would henceforth be impossible to ensure the continuance of ministrations at pious foundations and that consequently there would be a more whole-sale suppression of Masses than had occurred even in Calvin's day: it was said that the holding of services would be interrupted in numerous parishes, that the property of the Church was the property of the poor and the dead, that religion was being despoiled and that the conse-

---

*'*une goutte remontée*'

† Charles de Montchal, archbishop of Toulouse 1589–1651.

quences of these disgraceful proceedings would be momentous. The clergy had hitherto been well-behaved and loyal. Would they in their turn now be driven into opposition? Richelieu believed that he could ignore their complaints by relying on some of the bishops. In 1640 the Assembly of Clergy was summoned to meet at Mantes and the cardinal was careful to ensure that the important posts were held by those prelates who were most devoted to him. Although he was nominated president as he had been in 1635 he himself did not appear at the Assembly's sessions but he made every effort to keep a firm hold on the leading-strings. Some bishops were bold enough to raise objections. They were promptly exiled to their dioceses. They protested that this constituted a violation of the rights of the Gallican Church. Eventually the clergy made a grant of four millions.[49] Richelieu declared that this outlay was necessary both for the State and for the Church, issuing mysterious threats of other measures which might be even more injurious to the liberties of the clergy 'for I know what *Messieurs des Finances* would like to do'. That it was necessary for the Church remained unproven, but that it was essential for the State was self-evident. There was no longer any other way of meeting the expenses of a war in which the contest was becoming more and more desperate.

It was vital to guard against any possibility of resistance which appeared to have some legal basis. The early months of 1641 witnessed the humiliation of the Parlements. On 21 February the Parlement of Paris was compelled at a *lit de justice* to register a terrible edict which forbade the sovereign courts to take any cognisance of affairs of State, of administrative or financial matters, and of questions of government, or to discuss or issue pronouncements on such topics without the king's express commandment. The edict declared 'that a monarchical state cannot suffer any hand to be laid upon the sovereign's sceptre or that any share his authority. The power concentrated in the king's person is the source of a monarchy's glory and greatness and the foundation upon which its conservation rests.' It followed that the Parlement of Paris and the other sovereign courts had only been established to dispense justice. However, their right of remonstrance was not abolished; it was regulated by Article 5, and reduced to mere representations connected with the verification of edicts, the words 'we neither can nor may' being excluded from the formula as 'injurious to the prince's authority'.

At the same time several counsellors who had proved refractory in the past few months found that their appointments were cancelled and abolished. The king reserved the right to provide for their reimbursement as he saw fit. The Parlement was forbidden to allow these counsellors to attend its sessions and the king's subjects were prohibited from recognising them as judicial officers.

Talon, the advocate general, delivered quite a dignified speech appealing to the king to display his justice and goodness instead of his anger but his protest was no more than a matter of form intended to safeguard the Parlement's prestige, and Richelieu took it as such. Louis XIII was obeyed. Thus the king's authority had now been defined and proclaimed, and nobility, Parlement, officials and clergy all bowed their heads before it. Not only had it been defined and proclaimed but, most important of all, it was backed by force. Never before had the power of the Crown extended over so wide a compass.

It was at this time that the Cardinal Infante declared that the Spanish and Imperial armies were so reduced in numbers as to be incapable of undertaking anything: 'There is only one resort left to us,' he admitted, 'it is to build up a following in France and try with its help to induce the government in Paris to show itself amenable'.[50] In other words outside the context of the battlefield the two antagonists were making use of the same weapons to fight each other. Just as France was stirring up trouble in Catalonia and Portugal, so Spain was attempting to foment a rising inside France.

In 1640 the behaviour of the king's half-brother the duc de Vendôme had aroused suspicion. In the spring of 1641 the comte de Soissons, a prince of the blood, the duke of Guise, and Turenne's older brother, the duc de Bouillon, who was also prince of Sedan on the French frontier, combined in a plot which was supported by Spain and backed with Spanish subsidies. In the summer, an army based on Sedan and reinforced by a detachment of imperialist troops under Lamboy, advanced into France. The maréchal de Châtillon attempted to bar its way but on 9 July he was put to rout at la Marfée. However at the end of the battle the comte de Soissons was among the slain. The circumstances of his death are somewhat mysterious; but it is not improbable that it should be attributed to one of the cardinal's spies who had infiltrated into the ranks of the enemy and who recognised the count as he was in the act of raising the visor of his helmet because of the heat.

In the meantime Louis XIII advanced on Mézières, captured Donchery and threatened Sedan. The duc de Bouillon made haste to submit and sue for pardon which was granted him. The duke of Lorraine, faithful to the restriction that had accompanied his oath but not to the oath itself, had once more taken up arms against France. His duchy was accordingly reoccupied by the French in the course of a rapid campaign. In addition, several strongholds on the northern frontier were captured—Lens, La Bassée and Bapaume. The Spanish garrison at Bapaume was given the right to evacuate the town without interference—only to be attacked en route by Saint-Preuil the governor of Arras who was unaware of the terms on which it was being allowed to withdraw. Despite the magnificent services that he had previously rendered, he was beheaded at Amiens as an example to others because he had caused the king to break his word.

For all this it would be a complete fallacy to suppose that French arms had definitely prevailed or that Richelieu's policy had carried the day. Everything was still precarious. A revolt like that of the comte de Soissons was no longer a belated echo of intrigues at Court and among the nobility. On the contrary, it threatened to challenge everything. The young count was extremely popular. When Louis XIII wanted to institute proceedings against his corpse it was pointed out to him that whatever happened Soissons would still be Louis de Bourbon, the king's cousin and a prince of the blood, and that it would be nobler on the king's part to behave magnanimously. The count's body was accordingly brought back to France to be handed over to his family and receive a decent burial.

Father Carré, one of Richelieu's agents, did not disguise the fact that 'if Monsieur le comte had not been slain he would have been welcomed by half Paris. Indeed such is the general feeling of all France that the whole country would have rallied to his side because of the tax of a sol per livre and other vexations that the *partisans* inflict upon the people who are greatly discontented.'[51] This general discontent evinced by public opinion was a grave matter in a country that was still in ferment. Even Normandy, crushed and rigorously suppressed though she was would gladly have risen in rebellion. Signs of unrest were observed in the Cévennes. But the revolt of a single isolated province was not enough in itself to be decisive. It was necessary for some great personage to give the signal and for the movement to be supported by an army such as only Spain could provide. The dukes of Bouillon and Lorraine were semi-foreign princes and would scarcely do more than play a useful part as allies. A prince of the blood had far better chances of success. Now that Soissons was dead it was not unreasonable to think of the king's brother once more.

And so the incompetent Gaston was yet again to act as sponsor to an attack by those of Richelieu's enemies who were among the king's closest associates.

The friendship between the king and 'Monsieur le Grand' was a very stormy one. This was always the case where Louis XIII's affections were concerned. The king was touchy and dictatorial and he expected the person whom he loved to correspond in every particular with the idealised picture he had built up in his imagination. As soon as the chosen favourite departed from this ideal there were sudden quarrels and emotional scenes followed by solemn reconciliations, and the exchange of written assurances that neither had ever loved the other so much or would ever again give the other cause for complaint. This curious performance was repeated with Cinq-Mars from the very first weeks that he was in favour.[52] But this time the causes for disagreement lay deeper.

Richelieu had been driven to distraction by the incessant quarrels which had been a feature of Louis XIII's friendship with Madame de Hautefort; but if he thought that Cinq-Mars would be conducive to the king's peace of mind he was singularly deceived. The ordeals through which he had passed and the passage of time had altered the king's character and worn away the childlike or juvenile trust in others that had made him submit to the influence of Luynes, of Barradas, perhaps also of Saint-Simon, and which at the time of the siege of La Rochelle had drawn him close to Richelieu himself. Louis XIII was approaching the age of forty. After a reign fraught with dangers the maturity that comes with middle age lay more heavily upon him than upon most men of his years. The king felt happy when a charming young man who could have been his son responded with a good grace to the interest which he showed in him.

But Louis XIII did not succeed in suppressing his critical faculties or his clarity of judgement, neither of which was really compatible with his emotions. He had too much experience of men not to be irritated by the glaring defects in the character of 'Monsieur le Grand'. Marshal d'Effiat's son had all the qualities of a badly brought up young man of good family. He could be brave enough no doubt but he used to brag and show off at every turn. At first Louis XIII would listen to him laughing; but he very soon lost patience for he did not understand irony and was incapable of a light-hearted retort. On various occasions he snapped at 'Monsieur le Grand' in public and bade him hold his tongue. Everybody was left on tenterhooks. It was difficult for anyone to witness the discomfiture of the king's favourite without feeling uneasy, for he and the king were sure to be reconciled on the morrow and Cinq-Mars would be certain to make those who had observed his humiliation pay dearly for it.

Louis XIII wanted his friends to be always at his beck and call, always affectionate and ready to share his tastes. But apart from warfare and hunting, his interests were already those of a man who was growing old and liked a quiet life, who was scrupulous in his religion and economical in his expenditure. Neither church music nor pious books were of much interest to 'Monsieur le Grand'. He was young, little worried by scruples, and inclined to dissipation. Above all he had a craze for lavish expenditure and extravagance of dress. At the outset as Grand Master of the Wardrobe he had tried to provide the king with new clothes only to be roundly rebuked for his pains, for Louis XIII, who took little trouble over his appearance, always considered his wardrobes quite adequately stocked and set an example in Spartan simplicity. Matters became progressively worse when his favoured position as the king's Grand Equerry enabled Cinq-Mars to live in grand style. Not only did he spend all his money but he ran up debts. Companions of his own age inveigled him into joining them in their pleasures. He frequented places of amusement, he was constantly to be seen at the Marais, he gambled, he paid calls on Marion de Lorme, the fashionable courtesan of the day.[53] When the king woke early to go hunting and looked for his favourite companion, 'Monsieur le Grand' needed the whole morning to sleep off the dissipations of the night before. His licentious way of life shocked the king profoundly. Instead of the fond friend who was to fill his life with sweetness and charm, he found a young rake whom any father would have taken to task.

But how could the king discipline a youth whose head he had turned by heaping honours upon him and before whom he had so often humbled himself? Cinq-Mars, who was not over-blessed with intelligence or finer feelings, very soon began to behave insolently. He would defy the king, resort to sulking, and take a great deal of persuading before he recovered his good humour. Many of these petty squabbles took place in front of Chavigny who was more or less given the task of patching things up afterwards. But from 1640 onwards it often fell to Richelieu to play the fearful part of arbiter and mentor and this for two reasons. Firstly, he had been responsible for this tempestuous friendship from the outset and was supposed to have some influence over 'Monsieur le Grand'. Secondly, Louis XIII, who thought of him as a wise friend, trusted him completely and for fifteen years had never concealed from him any of the troubles of his private life. But by assuming this role Richelieu incurred the animosity of Cinq-Mars. Forgetting to whom it was that he owed his rise to favour, the latter eventually came to believe that he would have a far better hold over the king if the cardinal were not always there between them. Moreover, in the course of more than one scene when his irritation made him say all kinds of stupid things 'Monsieur le Grand' had happened to make some unfortunate allusions to the king's partiality for his minister. They left something of a mark on Louis XIII's mind. Richelieu was not infallible. He had made a bad investment and now he was in danger of losing everything and of being lost himself as a result of the young man's favoured position.

Early in 1642 Cinq-Mars who had taken part in the conspiracy of 1641, although only unobtrusively and cautiously, plunged more deeply into the plot. He repeated what everyone was whispering—that Richelieu would continue to reject peace indefinitely because it was the war alone that made him indispensable. Louis XIII, still tormented by qualms for having made his people suffer or for having delayed the reconciliation of Christendom, appeared to listen to these remarks. Cinq-Mars reminded him that first and foremost he was the king and proposed opening secret peace negotiations with Rome and Madrid. So far as is known Louis XIII had never before resorted to secret diplomacy behind Richelieu's back. He felt inclined to give it a trial. Cinq-Mars suggested that the mission be entrusted to a young nobleman named de Thou, the son of the historian.*

Montglat's memoirs report something more alarming. Cinq-Mars suggested that Richelieu should be assassinated. The king was horrified and answered that he would be excommunicated since Richelieu was both a priest and a cardinal. This was certainly a reason for him to reject his favourite's suggestion, but was it the only consideration that weighed with Louis XIII? Admittedly Montglat's memoirs do not constitute conclusive evidence: but there is a document in existence which is more disquieting. During the trial of Cinq-Mars Louis XIII wrote a strange letter to chancellor Séguier as if to prevent possible disclosures by the accused. He explained that on occasions when he was in an ill humour he might well have complained about the cardinal and allowed Cinq-Mars to continue with his evil talk. 'But when he went so far as to tell me that it was time to be quit of my said cousin† and to offer to do the deed himself, I

---

* Jacques-Auguste de Thou 1553–1617, whose great work *Historia sui temporis*, later translated into French under the title of *Histoire universelle*, is an invaluable authority for the French Wars of Religion.

† Etiquette prescribes that cardinals should be deemed the cousins of emperors and kings. (V.L.T.)

was filled with horror and revulsion at his wicked thoughts. I know that I have only to say as much for you to believe it, but no one can seriously think that this was not the case; for if the Sieur de Cinq-Mars had obtained my approval for his wicked schemes he would not have leagued himself with the king of Spain against my person and my State.'[54] Altogether rather an embarrassing defence.

To try to understand the whole situation we must cast our minds back to the murder of Wallenstein on the emperor's orders. It was certainly an extreme interpretation of these orders but the fact remains that they did not exclude putting Wallenstein to death without trial. We must also bear in mind that in the seventeenth century an all-powerful king was on certain occasions master of the lives of all his subjects and allow for Louis XIII's shattered health and the possibility of a momentary lapse of will-power on his part. And lastly, since we know nothing for certain about this episode, we must take care not to draw any conclusions from it.

Cinq-Mars later denied that it had been planned to murder the cardinal but his accomplice Fontrailles maintained the contrary and Richelieu went through the agony of believing that there was a plot against his life in which the king was implicated.

At the same time as he strove to win the king's consent to the cardinal's ruin, Cinq-Mars embarked on another scheme, this time of a treasonable nature. His idea was to come to an understanding with Olivares and win Spanish backing for a sort of *pronunciamento*. In essence Soissons's plan was revived but this time it was in favour of the duke of Orleans. When Philip IV's minister received a visit from a French gentleman—namely Fontrailles—he was amazed by the proposals submitted to him. Who was this prince of the blood, he asked, who could obtain possession of a town on the frontier and muster an army there? And who were the two leading members of the nobility who were ready to vouch for the conspiracy? It was explained to him that the prince of the blood was Monsieur and that the great nobles in question were the duc de Bouillon and Louis XIII's favourite, Cinq-Mars. Olivares demurred, pointing out that Monsieur was no longer heir to the throne; but being aware of the widespread discontent in France he said to himself that, after all, with Spain herself in such a plight, he would be running no great risk in giving this scheme a trial.

Accordingly Olivares signed the treaty. It specified that the rights of the king, queen and dauphin would not be infringed. The duke of Orleans was to act as lieutenant-general of the realm[55] while the provinces were rallying to his side and he was to proclaim a truce with Spain.

Olivares was to provide the troops required initially and subsidies amounting to twelve thousand crowns per month.

For the French the main object of the campaign of 1642 was to besiege Perpignan, the chief town of Roussillon. Although both men were in such a precarious state of health that rumours had been current in Europe for several weeks that neither of them had long to live, Louis XIII and Richelieu left Paris without waiting for the end of winter. At Lyons Louis XIII reviewed an army of fifteen thousand foot and fourteen thousand horse which was to advance against Perpignan under the maréchal de la Meilleraye. It seems that Cinq-Mars had intended to make use of the king's stay at Lyons in order to attempt some action against the cardinal but refused to assume the responsibility in the absence of his eminent accomplices the duke of Orleans and the duc de Bouillon. Neither of them appeared at Lyons, the duc de Bouillon remaining at Turenne in Auvergne where he was preparing to rejoin the army in Italy as one of its commanders.

The royal retinue left Lyons and continued on its journey. But Richelieu, who was becoming increasingly ill, had to stop at Narbonne. One of his arms was incapacitated by abscesses. He felt extremely worried at having to part from the king, himself a sick man and, as the cardinal knew, surrounded by men who were his personal enemies. From Perpignan the faithful de Noyers and Chavigny kept Richelieu supplied with a constant flow of information; but amongst the king's entourage it looked as if Cinq-Mars was in full favour and all-powerful once more despite continual fluctuations in his relationship with his royal master. The cardinal was confined to bed, his body afflicted with sores and his imagination tormented with suspicions; but his mind was as clear as ever. He wondered if all his work was in jeopardy and went through agonies. He guessed that the duc de Bouillon was involved in the intrigues against him and greatly feared that he would induce his uncle the prince of Orange to follow suit. In May he wrote to Estrades instructing him to give the latter a true picture of the situation: 'You must know that Cinq-Mars has formed a conspiracy against me and wishes to take my place beside the king.' He was overjoyed to receive a reassuring reply. The prince of Orange had declared that if the cardinal had not been at the head of affairs in France he would already have accepted the king of Spain's proposals and come to terms with him. The prince had displayed such abhorrence at the ingratitude of Monsieur de Cinq-Mars that Richelieu could certainly count on his friendship.

Eventually the cardinal was able to travel from Narbonne to Arles where he expected to be able to stay more comfortably. It was there that he received a copy of the treaty between Cinq-Mars and the Spaniards.

How did this document come into Richelieu's hands? Father Griffet was inclined to think that it had been procured by Marshal Schomberg whom Cinq-Mars had hoped to win over to his side: Schomberg who was thus strongly enough placed to be free to choose between the two parties decided in favour of the cardinal. Other writers have suggested that the queen who was still in Paris had received information about the treaty from Spain or Flanders: feeling that she was in too weak a position to risk arousing suspicions once more she hastened to forewarn Richelieu so as to demonstrate her loyalty.[56] In Avenel's opinion it was Pujols who was responsible, but canon Leman has refuted this theory for Pujols did not enjoy sufficient credit at the Spanish Court for him to have been able to steal the treaty or discover its terms. But in any case what does it matter who Richelieu's informant was? 'God is coming to the king's aid with miraculous discoveries,' wrote the cardinal to de Noyers. No doubt the remarkable network of espionage which Richelieu maintained throughout the length and breadth of Europe was the instrument whereby the miracle had been effected.

Louis XIII, who was by now too ill to stay at Perpignan, decided to take the waters at Montfrin.[57] On the way he stopped at Narbonne and it was at this stage of his journey on the evening of 12 June that he was visited in great secrecy by Chavigny who had been to see Richelieu. Chavigny handed the king the damning agreement with Spain. Louis XIII was appalled. Deeply conscious as he was of his royal greatness the idea of a treaty with the enemy, of a plot to transfer the government of the realm to his brother was more than he could bear. He had believed his favourite capable of many misdeeds but not of this. He at once gave orders for all exits from the town to be sealed and for Cinq-Mars to be arrested. The wretched man had been warned and it took the whole day to discover the house where he was hiding and to lay hands on him. Louis XIII never saw him again; yet even on the following day he still wondered whether it could all be true. He questioned de Noyers to make sure that there was no possibility of a mistake, that there had been no confusion of names. 'What a fall for Monsieur le Grand,' he kept repeating. He was so sad at heart, he seemed so weary and disconsolate that his ministers began to cast about for someone who could help him to recover from the blow. Only one person seemed to them to fit the role—that charming, adroit and invariably successful man whom Richelieu had to some extent chosen to replace Father Joseph. 'The sooner Monsieur le cardinal de Mazarin can be here the better it will be.' Out of the ruins of Cinq-Mars's career Mazarin rose to favour.

Cinq-Mars and de Thou were condemned to death and beheaded at Lyons. The execution of de Thou aroused some feeling for he had been privy to the conspiracy rather than an active participant. But he had himself declared that foreknowledge of such a plot and failure to divulge it amounted to complicity in an act of high treason and it was proved that he knew of the treaty with Spain. Monsieur had taken refuge at Annecy in Savoy and Richelieu would have been delighted to learn that Monsieur's sister, the duchess Christina, was also implicated. As was the custom Gaston obtained the king's pardon, for it was in the interest of the State as then understood that it should be granted him; but even so it was an outrageous custom. How many young men had paid with their lives for the conspiracies which he had sanctioned and to which he had lent his name! Yet he himself had risked virtually nothing by sponsoring them for he could be sure of a resounding triumph if they succeeded and of going unpunished if they miscarried. However, such were the rules of the game and public opinion accepted the fact that the king's brother remained immune.

The duc de Bouillon, who had been arrested whilst with the army in Italy like the maréchal de Marillac before him, also came to terms with the king by dint of placing the principality of Sedan under French protection.

While these events were taking place Marie de Medici died at Cologne.

On his return to Paris the cardinal set about making his own position more secure and overwhelmingly powerful than it had ever been. He began by tendering his resignation in the certainty that the king would not accept it; but before agreeing to remain in office he dictated his terms and demanded a new mandate. Frankly, there was some dirty dealing. At Richelieu's instigation, Chavigny hinted at certain secret matters revealed by Cinq-Mars which had been kept from the king.

The cardinal asked Louis XIII for a written undertaking to have no favourites outside his council, to listen to its advice, to authorise its members to express their views with complete freedom and not to communicate its deliberations to anyone else. The king also had to agree to a number of changes in the composition of the royal household involving the removal of several officers whom Richelieu considered suspect. For a few days Louis XIII hesitated; then he agreed to everything. Perhaps it was the proposals in respect of foreign policy which clinched matters, for the king cannot have felt any reservations about signing the haughty conditions relating to the war. He declared his intention of rejecting any peace that did not leave France in possession of her conquests and guarantee her Lorraine, Pinerolo, Roussillon, Breisach and the Alsatian towns bordering on Lorraine.[58]

The general situation had become markedly favourable to France. She had repulsed the Spanish threat on her northern and south-western frontiers while her other armies dominated north Italy and kept the Empire constantly on the alert. Perpignan had capitulated early in September and Salces surrendered shortly afterwards—victories which almost erased memories of the defeat suffered at Honnecourt in May.[59] Despite the death of Banér in 1641 the Swedish army had remained intact and Guébriant had taken command until the arrival of Torstensson, Banér's successor. The year 1642 was punctuated by two victories in the Empire. In January Guébriant won the battle of Kempen in west Germany and towards the end of the year a second battle was gained by Torstensson on the already celebrated field of Breitenfeld—a victory which was followed by the Swedish occupation of Leipzig.

At the end of December 1641 France and Sweden had concluded a preliminary agreement with the Empire providing for the opening of two peace conferences in March 1642—one at Münster to be attended by representatives of the Catholic Powers, while the other for the Protestants was to be held at Osnabrück. There were good grounds for assuming that France, fortified by her exertions and her victories, would enjoy great prestige at these conferences. The opening date had not been observed but the French were content to wait in the knowledge that they were in a strong position.

Thus Louis XIII and Richelieu found themselves still in agreement over the main issue in matters of policy but the fearful crisis which had centred on Cinq-Mars had left cruel wounds in the hearts of the two men who had been friends for so long.

It seems well established that Louis XIII's last letter to Richelieu was the note written from Saint-Germain on 21 November 1642 which is now preserved in the archives of the Ministry of Foreign Affairs. It is surprisingly cold; indeed throughout the copious correspondence between the king and his minister such a tone is quite unprecedented. This time Louis XIII does not even make use of some polite formula such as 'I give you good day' which he often used to add hurriedly in his own hand at the end of a letter. There are none of those touching and artless phrases which used to be so frequent a feature of his letters and were simply an expression of friendship: 'I observed today as a festival (i.e. 'I received Communion') and said a prayer for you.'* No, there is nothing of the kind in this last letter; it is just a thoroughly impersonal minute.[60]

This then was how matters stood between them, even though they had made their peace some days previously, when on 29 November Richelieu became increasingly troubled by a pain in his side. Pleurisy set in and he grew more and more feverish. On 2 December the physicians were unable to prevent the illness from gaining ground and announced that it would prove fatal. Beside the cardinal's bed were the secretaries of state talking to him even now of public affairs. His dutiful and gentle niece, the duchesse d'Aiguillon, looked after him with devoted care. The king could not omit to visit him and act as if he had forgotten his resentment. Louis XIII was a natural gentleman and when some light nourishment was brought to the dying man he made a point of offering it to him with his own hand. But first and foremost he was a king and he listened to Richelieu's last words of advice, promising to retain the secretaries of state—including Chavigny whom he had begun to detest—and to appoint Cardinal Mazarin as chief minister. It is not unlikely that, as was said at the time, he assumed a jaunty manner on leaving the room and elected to display a marked interest in the tapestries that decorated the gallery. However this may be, Louis XIII did not return to Saint-Germain but took up his residence at the Louvre there to await the cardinal's death. On 4 December the latter passed quietly away. He had enquired of the physicians as to his condition and had asked the *curé* of Saint-Eustache, his parish, to give him the last sacraments. It is said that Cospéan, the bishop of Lisieux and former bishop of Nantes, one of Richelieu's ablest servants, was surprised by the cardinal's serenity which he attributed to a lack of spiritual self-perception. 'Profecto nimium me terret magna illa securitas.' ('Truly I find his great composure exceedingly alarming.') But was the bishop right to feel so shocked? What reason is there for thinking that the cardinal's peace of mind was not genuine or that he was not sincere when he declared in the presence of the Blessed Sacrament that throughout his ministry his only aims had been the welfare of religion and of the State? By now he no longer seemed to be suffering greatly and his exhausted body must have experienced such a feeling of lassitude.

'He was not beloved by the people,' said Father Griffet, 'and I have known old men who still remembered seeing the bonfires that were lit in

* '*J'ai fait ma fête aujourd'hui où j'ai prié le bon Dieu pour vous.*'

the provinces on tidings of his death.' December 1642 to May 1643: Louis XIII was to reign without Richelieu for only a few months.

In January came the news of the disgrace of Olivares. The cardinal Infante had been dead for over a year.[61] The scene was changing but nevertheless preparations went on for continuing the war which Mazarin declared to be the king's main concern. However, Louis XIII was never again to make his appearance among his soldiers. In March he too fell ill and soon he extorted from his physicians the admission that they already considered his case to be hopeless. Both in his own day and in ours there has been considerable discussion among experts as to the nature of his illness. Apparently its symptoms are compatible with the last stages of tuberculosis of the intestines.

For several weeks, however, Louis XIII held out. He had thus time to make the necessary arrangements. Almost reluctantly and under Mazarin's influence he nominated the queen as regent and appointed the duke of Orleans lieutenant-general; but both were tied to a Council of Regency which included the prince of Condé, Mazarin himself as chief minister, and the secretaries of state. In short Louis XIII meant to keep at the head of affairs the same team of ministers as he had inherited from Richelieu, even after his own death.*

Lacking Richelieu's arrogance the king made no attempt to conceal his uneasy conscience and his fears that he had not acted rightly. Marie de Medici's body had been brought back to France during the winter and he publicly expressed his regret for having treated her so ruthlessly. He decided to recognise his brother's marriage to Princess Marguerite and urged Gaston to invite her to join him, recommending that they should live together as man and wife after a fresh marriage ceremony had been held to dispose of any suspicions as to the regularity of their union. He pressed the elderly maréchal de la Force not to end his days as a heretic. As the dauphin had only been baptised privately [*ondoyé*] he gave instructions for the remaining rites to be performed.[62] The ceremony took place on 21 April: Mazarin was the dauphin's godfather while his godmother was the princesse de Condé. When the little boy was brought back from the chapel the king called him to his bedside and asked him:

'And what is your name now?'

'My name is Louis XIV, Papa.'

---

* As is well known, the Parlement annulled these arrangements after the king's death at Anne of Austria's request and gave her full powers as regent. However one change in the team of ministers was made a few weeks before the king's death: Sublet de Noyers was disgraced and Michel le Tellier replaced him as secretary for war. (V.L.T.)

Louis XIII smiled. 'Not yet, my son, not yet, but soon perhaps if it be God's will;' and he added 'Mercifully grant, O Lord, that he reign in peace after me as a true Christian. May he always have before his eyes the maintenance of thy holy religion and the alleviation of his people.'

The relief of his people from their miseries remained the chief concern of the dying man. More than once he blamed himself to his confessor Father Dinet for his shortcomings in this respect: 'Ah! My poor people,' he would sigh, 'I have caused them much suffering because of the great and weighty affairs with which I have had to contend.' When his hopes of recovery were revived by a slight increase in his strength, Louis XIII declared that in two years he would restore France's prosperity, for next year he would make peace and in the following year he would disband his army. He also said that he would put a stop to immorality and suppress duels; when the dauphin had attained his majority he would abdicate and retire to Versailles with four Jesuits with whom he would converse about salvation; hunting would be his sole recreation and he would only indulge in it in moderation.

The king was never to go hunting again; but in its stead there was still music. He ordered musicians to sing and play to him as he lay in bed and he composed a *De profundis*.[63] He was in great pain and passed his time in prayer. Bishops and priests visited him frequently. One and all were edified by his faith but none more than Saint Vincent de Paul who was later to declare, 'Since I have been on earth I have not seen anyone make a more Christian end.'[64]

The story goes that at the beginning of May, whilst semi-conscious, Louis XIII had a vision of the battle of Rocroi. He told the prince of Condé that the Spaniards were entering the realm in force but that his son the duc d'Enghien would bar their way and vanquish them.[65]

On 10 May the king's illness grew worse. There was probably a secondary development of acute peritonitis and he experienced increasing difficulty in breathing. On Thursday 14 May, Ascension Day, Louis XIII asked for the Prayers for the Dying to be read to him. Shortly afterwards he lost consciousness and early in the afternoon he died. It had been on the same day, 14 May, and at about the same hour that his reign had begun thirty-three years earlier.

Conclusion

THEY RESTED, the one in the crypt at Saint-Denis, the other beneath the dome of the Sorbonne, those two great actors whose departure left the stage not empty, but peopled with figures of lesser stature. Within the realm only the hope of peace could compensate for the excessive strain to which the French people had been subjected. The effort required of it had exceeded the capacity of the nation. The extension of the war and the increased financial burdens resulting therefrom had impaired and curtailed the programme of reform which Richelieu had considered so indispensable at the outset of his ministry sixteen years previously: not only this but it had caused fresh calamities. France was thus an unhappy country with the majority of her people reduced to a penurious and care-worn existence. But to try to establish whether their sufferings were worse in 1643 than in 1610 or 1620 would be quite futile, for any estimate of individual or general hardship is necessarily highly relative, depend-ing, as we would say today, on the degree of awareness of their miseries evinced by those concerned.

Yet exhausted and discontented though she was, there is no denying that the France of 1643 was a far stronger state with more resources at her disposal, a state that was more respected and feared both in Europe and throughout the world, than the disorderly kingdom of 1624; and it is likewise unquestionable that the élite of French society were more numerous and of greater political, moral and intellectual distinction.

Should the credit for this achievement be given to the government which ruled France during the period? Its trend had been towards abso-lutism—that is to say, in every sphere the authority of the king and of those who acted on his instructions (no longer merely in his name as had recently been the case) had asserted itself at the expense of the privileges that had hitherto guaranteed individual and corporate liberties. That there were less of these in the realm at the end of Louis XIII's reign seems certain. For a medley of liberties, which existed side by side but were unconnected with each other and sometimes mutually incompatible, was substituted the concept of collective solidarity with a common end in view—the good of the State.

It must be realised that these traditional liberties or privileges, for the

428

most part only enjoyed by small groups who were thus kept in a state of stagnation without prospects and without the means of developing or exploiting their resources, bore no resemblance to the liberty known to us, which offers every man access to a higher position in society, assuring him of a happier lot and enabling him to acquire a more exalted sense of his own destiny. By harnessing the entire nation to the king's service and to the service of a more powerful state the absolutism of Louis XIII and Richelieu freed France from her mediaeval shackles and opened up wider horizons for every Frenchman.

For let there be no mistake about it: the France of Marie de Medici's Regency and Louis XIII's early years which took the place of the rehabilitated kingdom of Henry IV was an easy prey for others. In 1643 there may well have been many holders of fiefs both lay and ecclesiastical, many magistrates and officers of finance, many merchants and shipowners, who looked back regretfully to the years gone by when the Crown's interference had seemed less oppressive, when their daily actions had gone virtually unchecked and when their profits had seemed more secure. And what of the peasant, whose labour provided a vital motive force and upon whose back the entire structure rested? Yet would any of them have been much better off if they had lived out their lives in an enfeebled kingdom under an inert government?

France's rights to several of her provinces were still in dispute. The house of Austria had not forgotten its persistent claims to Burgundy and it was not very long since Calais had slipped from England's grasp. Brittany had been annexed to the French Crown barely a century previously. On the eastern frontier the title-deeds to Metz, Toul and Verdun had not yet been validated. The incorporation of Béarn into France and the improvement in the strategic position of Lyons through the acquisition of Bresse and Bugey had only recently been effected by Henry IV. It is highly likely that if France had continued to be rent by factions she would sooner or later in one way or another have been drawn into a European war which would again have led to the invasion of her territory and have been followed by her dismemberment.

Without committing ourselves to arguments based on assumptions and on events which did not take place, we cannot overlook the fact that there was no longer a French navy in 1610. France was economically dependent on Dutch, Spanish and English merchant ships and thus in a sense a blockaded country. One cannot but realise that, if she had been left to her own devices and her population had been allowed to drift along in a way of life which at the best of times hardly bore witness to a general state of peace and well being, her position would have increasingly degenerated into that of a vassal state whose subjects worked for the benefit of foreigners. It would be utterly fatuous to suppose that the governments and subjects of neighbouring states would have continued to respect the frontiers of a country which had become such a tempting bait, or that they would have felt any compunction about disrupting her inertia or interfering in her internal quarrels. Disintegration or survival: these were the alternatives with which France was confronted. Louis XIII and Richelieu chose survival.

That a state could only be strong in so far as its neighbours were weak does not argue a very high standard of international morality: such however were the conditions that prevailed at the time. For France the progressive weakening and depopulation of Germany through the catastrophic war which raged unceasingly upon her territory, the economic crisis which cut short the relative prosperity of Spain and the internal quarrels that absorbed England in each case represented a stroke of good fortune. This is not to say that the misfortunes of France's neighbours are necessarily the prerequisite of her own greatness as if there were some perpetual and irrevocable law linking the two: to claim this as a so-called lesson that history teaches us would be both odious and absurd. The divisions that rent seventeenth-century Europe despite the many arguments in favour of unity and solidarity implicit in her civilisation, and the absence of any alternative to war—although we have already seen the sufferings and destruction that it caused both victors and vanquished—are fearful blots on an age which is in many respects singularly attractive. It is undoubtedly these features of the seventeenth century which are most repugnant both to the Christian conscience and to the classical ideal of reason. But we must not forget to emphasise the importance of the word 'then'. In carrying out his task of interpretation, the historian can only take into account the conditions that prevailed at the time. No state was then powerful or wealthy enough to create around itself a climate of peace and economic progress. But a state with the necessary determination could at least safeguard its territorial independence and itself put its natural resources to good use. It is here that Richelieu's merit lies; the merit of Louis XIII lay in his realising that in Richelieu he had a minister who served him well.

The results speak for themselves. The France of 1643 is far larger than the France of 1610, extending well beyond the valley of the Somme to the plateaux of Artois whose chief towns are in her grasp. She dominates Lorraine and Alsace, Metz, Nancy, Colmar and the bridges over the upper Rhine. She has a foothold in Italy, she occupies Roussillon, and protects Catalonia. By her alliance with Portugal she has driven a wedge into the Iberian peninsula. The revival of her seapower enables her to trade in the Mediterranean, the Atlantic and northern seas. She has colonies in Canada and the West Indies whose inhabitants 'they being of French descent or even savages converted to the Christian faith and professing the same shall be deemed and reputed natural-born Frenchmen capable of holding and receiving any office, honour, inheritance and donation without being required to obtain letters of declaration or naturalisation'.[1] There are French trading posts on the Senegalese coast and on Madagascar. In less than twenty years France has become a country of greater importance in the world than ever before.

Although he did not possess the qualifications of an economist and financier, Richelieu had a broad enough outlook to interest himself in problems which any other statesman in his position might almost have felt justified in regarding as outside his competence. As a ruler Louis XIII subscribed to certain general ideas on monarchical authority and religious unity, while in his private capacity he had a good acquaintance with military matters and a love and knowledge of music; but it is unlikely that he would have taken much interest in the evolution of the French economy—certainly a great deal less than Henry IV, who had at least shown signs of wishing to know more about the subject and flashes of insight. Richelieu's exceptional intelligence enabled him to perceive that France's greatness would depend not merely on the power that territorial expansion and the better defence of her frontiers would bring, but also on the more efficient use of her resources and the degree of skill that she showed in exporting her goods throughout the world. Thanks to his initiative France, a country with an agrarian and feudal economy, began to engage in commercial capitalism—the new and productive form of economic activity which had given a lead first to the Spaniards and then to the Dutch and upon which was soon to be founded the greatness of England as a world power.

The war had an adverse effect on France's attempts to develop her overseas trade just as it did on all her other efforts towards recovery—although it was probably somewhat less marked owing to the growth of her navy. But it is evident that from 1624 to 1642 Richelieu attached the utmost importance to her commercial expansion because as Henri Hauser has observed, he was inspired by 'a broad and lofty vision of France's economic destiny' and had 'the future in his mind's eye'.[2]

From the social point of view it was a tragedy that the beneficial effects of this expansion did not make themselves generally felt whilst it was actually in progress. A small number of people became rich but they tended to be men who were already prosperous and had sufficient means to risk a stake in commercial ventures. The large fortunes which were built up only made more cruelly apparent the gulf between the financiers (the direct beneficiaries of the political system) and the mass of the nation. Not only was there no revolution in agricultural techniques but, in the provinces that rebelled or were situated near a war zone or bore the brunt of the voracious tax demands of the Crown, the miseries of the population increased.

France succeeded in re-establishing her prestige abroad within the space of a few years and if agreement could have been reached on satisfactory peace terms in 1636 or 1637 it would possibly have been followed by a very rapid improvement in the standard of living of her population and a fairer distribution of prosperity among the different classes of French society. This is only a hypothesis for we would need to be better informed of contemporary world economic conditions than we are at present; but there can be no doubt that the prolongation of the war was a catastrophe for everyone and Richelieu, who never abandoned his efforts to restore peace, fully realised as much.

Even so one cannot but admit that this deplorable war meant ruin for France's enemies even more than for France herself, and that she was the only country in Europe to reap advantage from it. From 1637 to 1642 the miseries of her population become more and more appalling and sometimes she seems to be skirting the very edge of the abyss. But at the same time what increased prestige is hers, what power she enjoys, how many conquests she has made, how many pledges she has obtained in a Europe that is well aware of her difficulties and watches her slightest weaknesses with relish! The many and fearful sacrifices required of her were thus not accepted in vain.

In his book *Strange Defeat* Marc Bloch makes this memorable observation; 'There are two categories of Frenchmen who will never really grasp the significance of French history: those who refuse to thrill to the consecration of our kings at Rheims and those who can read unmoved the account of the Festival of Federation.' And he adds with profound wisdom: 'I do not care what may be the colour of their politics to-day.'[3]

Certainly the worst mistake that can be made in connection with history is to search the past for attitudes that may serve as models to be copied today, and to fail to realise that the greatness of certain men or events is bound up with their exceptional intelligence and effectiveness *within the context of their age.* A whole segment of French history lies beneath the symbol of the coronation at Rheims; an entirely separate phase stems from the gesture symbolised by the *Fête de la Fédération*, and between them is the Revolution.[4] Richelieu was one of the architects of his country's greatness because he harnessed the latent energies of French society, which in his day was monarchical and religious, to the pursuit of a definite programme.

During the nineteenth century in particular with its Parliamentary government and liberal outlook—an age prolific with achievement and worthy of respect to which we of the twentieth century are sometimes ungrateful—Richelieu and seventeenth-century France were often wrongly credited with ideas and sentiments which were quite alien to them. The existence of an anointed king was not an annoyance or a sort of impediment to Richelieu's activities as minister, nor yet a potential danger to which he learnt to adapt himself; on the contrary it was the necessary condition on which he acted as minister at all. Although he was ready enough to make use of all sorts of Machiavellian maneouvres, to dissemble and resort to trickery, it is indisputable that Richelieu believed with all his heart and soul in the lofty and religious character of the institution of monarchy and held that his sovereign's greatness was somehow divinely ordained. Louis XIII himself who was neither outstanding nor second rate—and who two hundred years later if he had been allowed to follow his personal inclinations would have made a good regimental officer in the Algerian wars[5] or, had he reigned as king, a very adequate constitutional ruler—shared Richelieu's faith in a mission of which he was only the instrument. It was this faith alone which enabled him to remain equal to his task, and invested him when occasion required with an authority that compelled obedience.

As we have seen, such obedience was not easily won since it called for the sacrifice of personal interests by no means all of which were unreasonable or ignoble. But society as a whole was religious and saw a close connection between the concept of kingship and that of God. Rebels met their end fortified by the sacraments of the Church and acknowledging in their last confessions that their act of rebellion had been a sin. Royal authority was always invested with divine authority; whenever opposition to the king was inspired by something more noble than private interests and those who led it sought to invoke some principle, it was generally to religion that they turned so as to ascertain whether the king's policy was not drifting into courses detrimental to the Catholic cause.

This religious conception of the world encouraged a ready acceptance of hierarchies and privileges; not that such an attitude was due to mere obsequiousness or inertia. The Church herself provided the model example of a hierarchy and of an aristocratic society by the very nature of her organisation. The doctrine promulgated by the Council of Trent had linked the Church militant to the Church persecuted and the Church triumphant by means of a series of interventions. The approach to God lay through the Saints and the Virgin Mary; dulia and hyperdulia opened the way to latria.[6] The whole theory which found expression not only in theological works but also in the iconography of churches and in religious images or pictures in private houses reinforced the idea that since the temporal order was a reflection of the divine order it was right and proper for a well-ordered society not to be egalitarian.

The Protestants with their hostility to ritual, with their mistrust of the forms and their devotion to the spirit of Christianity, found in the Bible and in the example set by the Chosen People arguments which justified the same opinions. As for those who subscribed to no religious beliefs —few in number and consisting of small groups—they tended to appreciate their peculiarity as if it was a privilege and were not at all inclined to propagate their emancipated ideas. Did not Cyrano de Bergerac, one of the most emancipated of them all, later write: 'I maintain that popular government is the worst scourge with which God can afflict a state.'[7] One is even apt to wonder to what extent the theories of predestination which were so widely held at the time (somewhat to the perplexity of our own generation) were coloured by this general acceptance of the notion of privilege—although this is not the place to try to answer such a question.

For the way the people of the seventeenth century understood and practised their religion—which is still that of the twentieth century with the same doctrine and the same dogmas—retains its particular character, deriving its distinctive qualities from the codes of behaviour and general conditions current at the time. Admittedly the degree of fervour shown varied from person to person in just the same way as standards of intelligence or types of character; and the fact that the people of seventeenth-century France were religiously inclined did not mean that there were not many lax Christians among them who repeatedly postponed the decision to live in accordance with their principles. However it is not in this context that our chief difficulty lies. The main problem is rather to discover why it was that France, which adhered to the same doctrines as Italy and Spain, did not also adopt the same forms of religious life as these two countries. Why was it that in France ceremonial was less sensuous and less ritualistic, that churches were less overlaid with gilt and less congested with shrines? Why was it that even French mysticism was characterised by a greater concern for logic and clarity?

Many historians believe that these differences are to be explained by the existence of a particularly strong bourgeois element in French society, which had become quite familiar with the jurists and their methods of argument. The writers and thinkers of the day were drawn almost exclusively from this social category: Corneille, Descartes and Pascal all belonged to the bourgeoisie and so too did Racine a little later. Molière's profession as actor puts him in a slightly different position but he too came from a bourgeois family. What was true of the world of letters was also true of the Church: theologians were for the most part of bourgeois stock or moved in bourgeois circles. Two works of the utmost importance belonged to the last years of Louis XIII's reign. The first, the *Augustinus* of Bishop Jansen was published in 1640; the second, *De la fréquente communion* by Antoine Arnauld was written during the king's lifetime and appeared in August 1643. As opposed to the worldly humanistic and subtle religion taught by the Jesuits the two theologians stood for a religion that was more exacting and more austere, that called for a more disinterested love of God and a greater exercise of reason. Their views won support primarily among the bourgeoisie. Admittedly Jansenism lies outside the history of Louis XIII's reign although it was then that the movement was set in train; moreover to draw a hard and fast distinction between an aristocracy which favoured the Jesuit approach to religion and a bourgeoisie converted to Jansenism would be arbitrary and utterly misleading for there were members of each class in both camps. Nevertheless it is important to note the opposition to the Society of Jesus that existed among Catholic circles in France. As an international religious order with an ultramontane outlook the Jesuits tended to work for the introduction throughout Europe not only of the same doctrine but also of the same methods of expressing belief. In France this kind of uniformity was resisted with well-founded arguments. And here we must refer to the attitude of Richelieu himself. While it is undoubtedly true that Richelieu waged war not on nascent Jansenism but on those who were to disseminate it after his death, he was also, with the full weight of his authority as bishop and theologian, one of the most stalwart defenders of the existence of a French Church within an universal Church. Here however we are faced with a problem. When the situation was at its worst and relations with Rome had become extremely tense Richelieu was thought to be planning a definite breach with the Holy See and to intend summoning a national council and having himself proclaimed Patriarch of the Gallican Church (1639). Scotti, the pope's nuncio extraordinary, who had been sent to press for the conclusion of peace but had met with opposition from the cardinal seemed to think that a schism was imminent.

There is no denying that threats to this effect were brandished by Chavigny,—that is to say by one of Richelieu's direct associates—and some of the bishops such as Montchal became alarmed. Séguier the chancellor saw every reason 'for refraining from entering so readily into a breach with the Holy See' precisely because of the misgivings that such a step would arouse among the clergy and in a predominantly Catholic country.[8]

In considering this episode two points in particular must be borne in mind. The first is that the Holy See was a temporal power suspected at the time of working for the Spaniards and that these threats were aimed at the pope in his capacity as territorial ruler in Italy. The second is that Richelieu who was always concerned to establish clear principles which everyone could admit in theory was trying to steer a middle course; as the first order of the realm the clergy had to be brought into subjection to the French crown, but at the same time reform of the Gallican Church must be fostered as part of the Catholic reform movement as a whole. A schism would have compromised his twofold plan at the outset and added to France's dangers.

A work entitled *De Concordia Sacerdotii et Imperii* by Pierre de Marca, which was dedicated to the cardinal and published under his auspices in 1641, upheld the liberties of the Gallican Church and insisted on the necessity for an even balance between the civil power and the primacy of Rome.

And so seventeenth-century France, that deeply religious country owing allegiance to an anointed king, retained far more spiritual independence under Louis XIII's absolute rule than might have been expected in view of the despotic nature of its government in so many spheres and the tremendous effort that was made to force the whole realm to submit to one and the same law. France had not merely been safeguarded from the threat of political and economic subjection to foreign powers: she had also been preserved from the danger of total surrender to ideas and forms of civilisation which she would have accepted indiscriminately. She kept her individuality.

One last feature of the reign deserves to be borne in mind. The edifice erected by Louis XIII and Richelieu was both essential and imposing, but for all its strength it was also imperfect and therefore precarious. For this there were a number of reasons, the first being that the changes introduced by the king and his minister did not have a deep effect on the outlook and behaviour of the French people. It was only respect for the king's authority and fear of punishment that made them accept royal interference over so wide a field and submit to the financial exactions caused by the war. What was achieved was superimposed upon the existing social and economic structure and did not constitute a far-reaching reform of the structure itself. Absolutism was essentially a fact which owed its significance to the presence of two men. Indeed one is almost amazed to find that a part of their work at least was continued after their disappearance from the scene, despite the return to France of men who were Richelieu's enemies and hostile to the policy which Louis XIII had accepted.

That this was so was due to the loyalty of ministers like Séguier who had served Richelieu and were still convinced of the effectiveness of his policies, to the skill shown by Mazarin, to the part played by the financiers in supporting a system of government in which they had staked their money, and to the easing of the economic crisis for a few years: but these are matters which lie outside the scope of this book. However in the absence of a king old enough to make his will respected, it was inevitable that all the social categories and groups whose authority in the State had been reduced—the nobility, the Parlements, the office-holders in the provinces, the corporations in the towns—should have thought in terms of regaining the privileges or concessions they had lost. They reorganised themselves with remarkable speed and as early as the summer of 1643 one can see the warning signs of a crisis which was to take five years to mature and become the Fronde. In particular, personages such as the abbé de Retz, the future Coadjutor,[9] and the duc d'Enghien, whose youth and victories in the field invested him with great prestige[10] quickly attracted a clientele. Groups of writers, enlisting themselves in their train, were soon to work on public opinion and foster the hope that changes were on the way.

Nevertheless there is a great contrast between the France of 1643 and the France of 1610—a contrast that extends to Europe also. Never again was France to sink so low as she had done after the death of Henry IV. Little by little with the passage of time the trials and tribulations of Louis

XIII's reign faded from the living memory, as those who had witnessed and experienced them disappeared from the scene. And as France climbed towards predominance in Europe and, with the Fronde behind her, her powers seemed steadily to increase as if to keep pace with the young king, people began to think well of the previous reign. There seemed no doubt that Louis XIII's reign had at least prepared the way for the triumphant years of the Age of Louis XIV.

Yet further on in time Richelieu was hailed as one of the founders of French unity, as one of those who had most accurately understood and recognised the character and needs of the French nation. People even went so far as to detach him from the age in which he lived and to think of him as a contemporary because he had been a forerunner. In reality he was essentially a man of his time, and no doubt this was where his chief strength lay, since for all his ideals and force of character he was always judicious in estimating the means at his disposal, and in all his work he never lost sight of present realities. Even so, there were in him those qualities that bring honour to mankind in every age, while the France of Louis XIII's day possessed a youth and vigour which enabled her to bear the colossal strain of being severed from a whole portion of her past so that she could be steered towards a glorious future.

Chronological Table

This enlarged version of the chronological table printed in the French edition of Professor Tapié's book is intended as a rough guide for the general English reader. Various original entries have been expanded and a number of additional items have been inserted, most of them referring either to topics of general and cultural interest or to events in British history. Some of the latter have been chosen because, although not strictly relevant to this book, they are sufficiently important to be well known in the English-speaking world and may help the reader to keep his chronological bearings; others have been selected to emphasise a link or to point a contrast between Britain and the Continent; others again have been inserted because they represent small pieces in the jigsaw-puzzle of seventeenth-century European history which interlock with events mentioned in this book.

This table does not, however, represent an attempt to tabulate systematically all the major events in European or British history between 1610 and 1643. For reasons of space, events which took place outside West and Central Europe have been omitted completely, while many of those listed under a particular year have been grouped under headings rather than given in strict chronological order. In the case of events in Britain I have retained the old style of dating.

Among the various books which I have consulted I would like to mention the late Dr S. H. Steinberg's *Historical Tables* and Dame Veronica Wedgwood's two masterly volumes on the reign of Charles I–*The King's Peace* and *The King's War*.

D.McN.L.

1610

12 February	Alliance between Henry IV and the German Evangelical Union.
25 April	Treaties of Bruzòlo between Henry IV and Charles Emmanuel I duke of Savoy.

14 May	Assassination of Henry IV. Accession of Louis XIII (born in 1601).
15 May	Marie de Medici, the queen mother, becomes regent.
17 October	Coronation of Louis XIII at Rheims.

Germany and the Empire: Frederick V becomes Elector Palatine.

1611

Protestant Assembly at Saumur.

Resignation of Sully, Henry IV's superintendent of finance.

Publication of Edmond Richer's work *De ecclesiastica et politica potestate*, which is subsequently condemned.

Accession of Gustavus Adolphus to the throne of Sweden.

Germany and the Empire: Coronation of Archduke Matthias as king of Bohemia.

1612

Growing restiveness of the great nobles under Marie de Medici's rule.

Rise to favour of the Concini (husband and wife).

Germany and the Empire: Death of the Emperor Rudolf II, who is succeeded by Matthias.

1613

14 February	Elizabeth, daughter of James I, marries Frederick V the Elector Palatine.
24 October	Gabriel Bethlen becomes prince of Transylvania.

1614

15 May	Treaty of Sainte-Menehould ends rebellion against Marie de Medici under Condé's leadership.
October 1614 to ⎱ January 1615 ⎰	Meeting of the Estates-General (the last before 1789).

1615

August	Outbreak of second rebellion led by Condé.
November	Marriage of Louis XIII and Anne of Austria, daughter of Philip III of Spain, at Bordeaux.

1616

3 May	Marie de Medici concludes peace with Condé and other great nobles at Loudun.
May–September	Condé in favour.
September	Condé is arrested and a 'Concini Ministry' is formed which includes Barbin, Mangot, and Richelieu.

1617

April	Murder of Concini. Louis XIII seizes power together with Luynes, his favourite. Richelieu dismissed.
December	First Assembly of Notables.
	Germany and the Empire: Archduke Ferdinand of Styria chosen as next King of Bohemia.

1618

	Louis XIII decides to re-establish Catholicism in Béarn.
23 May	*Germany and the Empire:* Defenestration of Prague, signalling the outbreak of the Thirty Years War. Bohemia in rebellion.

1 July   Ferdinand of Styria crowned king of
                                Hungary.

1619

13 March   Execution of Oldenbarnevelt.

30 April   First War between Mother and Son (i.e.
                                Marie de Medici and Louis XIII).

20 and 26 August   Peace of Angoulême.

                                Germany and the Empire: Death of the emperor
                                Matthias. Silesia, Upper and Lower Lusatia, and
                                Moravia join the Bohemian rebellion. Election of
                                Ferdinand as emperor. Frederick V, the Elector
                                Palatine, is elected king by the Bohemian Estates-
                                General. Gabriel Bethlen besieges Vienna.

December   Louis XIII promises armed assistance to
                                Ferdinand (now the Emperor Ferdinand II).

1620

January   Louis XIII withdraws his promise of help,
                                and decides to send an embassy to restore
                                peace within the Empire.

                                Second War between Mother and Son—
                                battle of Ponts de Cé followed by the Peace
                                of Angers.

July   *Germany and the Empire:* The French embassy at Ulm
                                arranges an armistice between Catholic and Protest-
                                ant forces in Germany, thus preparing the way for
                                the Spanish occupation of the Palatinate and the
                                emperor's triumph in Bohemia.

8 November   Battle of the White Mountain near Prague. Flight
                                of Frederick V, 'the Winter King'. Ferdinand II
                                re-establishes his authority over Bohemia.

September to   Louis XIII reduces Béarn to submission.
October

                                Crisis in the Valtelline.

1621-22

31 March 1621	Death of Philip III of Spain. Accession of Philip IV, with Olivares as his chief minister.
	End of the Twelve Years Truce between Spain and the United Provinces.
27 April 1621 to 19 October 1622	Louis XIII's campaigns against the Huguenots are continued until the Peace of Montpellier.
14 December 1621	Death of Luynes.

Germany and the Empire: Ferdinand II puts Frederick V under the ban of the Empire. In Bohemia the leading rebels are savagely punished.

1623

Maffeo Barberini elected Pope (Urban VIII).

England: Abortive negotiations by Buckingham and Charles, Prince of Wales, for Anglo-Spanish marriage alliance.

Germany and the Empire: Ferdinand II bestows Palatinate and electoral title on Maximilian of Bavaria.

1624

April	Richelieu joins the king's Council. La Vieuville concludes an alliance between France and the United Provinces. Negotiations for Anglo-French marriage alliance.
August	La Vieuville dismissed. Richelieu becomes chief minister.
Winter	French intervention in the Valtelline.

1625

27 March	*England:* Death of James I of England. Accession of Charles I, Buckingham remaining chief minister. England declares war on Spain.

23 April   *United Provinces:* Death of Maurice of Nassau, who is succeeded as Stadtholder by his half-brother Frederick Henry.

11 May   Marriage of Charles I and Henrietta Maria, sister of Louis XIII.

English and Dutch ships take part in fighting against La Rochelle.

United Provinces: The Spaniards capture Breda.

Germany and the Empire: Danish intervention in Germany. Wallenstein appointed Imperial Generalissimo and created duke of Friedland.

1626

February   Peace of La Rochelle concluded with the Huguenot rebels of 1625.

5 March   The Treaty of Monzón between France and Spain lays down peace terms for the Valtelline.

The Chalais conspiracy (the first to form around Gaston, the king's brother) is unmasked. Marriage of Gaston (Monsieur) and Mademoiselle de Montpensier.

Numerous popular disturbances in various parts of France.

December (to February 1627)   Second Assembly of Notables. Richelieu's programme for general reform.

25 April   *Germany and the Empire:* Wallenstein's victory over Mansfeld at Dessau.

27 August Tilly's victory over the Danes at Lutter.

1627

Breach between England and France leading to a Franco-Spanish alliance.

July   English expeditionary force commanded by Buckingham lands on the Ile de Ré near La Rochelle.

September	La Rochelle throws in its lot with England.
November	Re-embarkation of Buckingham's expeditionary force. La Rochelle under siege.

Foundation of the Company of the Blessed Sacrament.

Germany and the Empire: Wallenstein and Tilly invade Brandenburg, Pomerania, Holstein and Jutland.

Bohemia proclaimed a hereditary Habsburg possession, with Catholicism the only official religion. Massive Protestant emigration begins.

1628

May	English fleet under Denbigh attempts to relieve La Rochelle.
2 June	*England:* Petition of Right addressed to Charles I by Parliament.
23 August	*England:* Assassination of Buckingham.
September to October	English fleet under Lindsey attempts to relieve La Rochelle.
29 October	Capitulation of La Rochelle.

Italy: Dispute over the Mantuan succession, the claims of the French candidate, the duke of Nevers, being opposed by the Emperor and the Spaniards. The latter besiege Casale.

Germany and the Empire: Wallenstein is granted the duchies of Mecklenburg and appointed Admiral of the Baltic by Ferdinand II but fails to capture Stralsund.

1629

January	Promulgation of the *Code Michau*—an ordinance providing for widespread administrative reform, in answer to the complaints of the Estates-General of 1614 and of the Assemblies of Notables held at Rouen (1617) and Paris (1626–7).

Jan–March	*Italy:* Richelieu advises Louis XIII to intervene in favour of the duke of Nevers' claims. French troops force the pass of Susa and enter Piedmont. Temporary submission of duke of Savoy.
10 March	*England:* Charles I dissolves Parliament and begins his personal rule. Peace with France concluded at Susa in April.
6 March	*Germany and the Empire:* Ferdinand II issues the Edict of Restitution.
22 May	Treaty of Lübeck (Denmark withdraws from the Thirty Years War).
June	In France, resistance by the Huguenots is brought to an end. They are pardoned by the Edict of Alès but lose their political and military privileges.

1630

29 March	*Italy:* Capture of Pinerolo.
July	Death of Charles Emmanuel duke of Savoy, following further reverses at the hands of the French. He is succeeded by Victor Amadeus I, Louis XIII's brother-in-law.
	Fresh trouble with Monsieur. Rising in Burgundy. The *dévots* led by Marillac criticise Richelieu's warlike policy and hostility to Spain.
July–September	Louis XIII sets off to rejoin the French army in Italy, but has to return to Lyons where he falls gravely ill.
July and August	*Germany and the Empire:* Gustavus Adolphus king of Sweden lands in Pomerania. The electors meet at Regensburg. Despite Wallenstein's dismissal (13 August) they refuse to elect the Emperor's son as king of the Romans. Brûlart de Léon and father Joseph, the French representatives, unwisely agree to the treaty proposed by the Emperor providing for a general settlement of disputes between himself and France.

10 November	Day of Dupes. Defeat of Marie de Medici and the *dévot* faction. Triumph of Richelieu.
	England: Charles I makes peace with Spain; he undertakes to mint bullion shipped from Spain and to transport it to the Spanish Netherlands.

1631

	Italy: Settlement of French disputes with Savoy, Spain and the Emperor (Treaties of Cherasco). Mantua and Casale pass to duke of Nevers. France keeps Pinerolo.
January	Treaty of Bärwalde between Louis XIII and Gustavus Adolphus.
May	Treaty of Fontainebleau providing for a defensive alliance between France and Bavaria.
20 May	*Germany and the Empire:* Tilly captures Magdeburg which is set on fire and sacked. Resumption of war in Germany between Catholics and Protestants.
17 September	Gustavus Adolphus defeats Tilly at Breitenfeld near Leipzig. Wallenstein is subsequently recalled by the Emperor.
	Marie de Medici flees from France and takes refuge in the Spanish Netherlands, where she is soon joined by Monsieur.

1632

January	French invasion of Lorraine followed by Treaty of Vic between Louis XIII and Duke Charles IV.
	Secret marriage between Monsieur (a widower since 1627) and Princess Marguerite of Lorraine.
	Germany and the Empire: Further victories by Gustavus Adolphus. Death of Tilly.

Revolt of duke of Montmorency who is in league with Monsieur but is taken prisoner at battle of Castelnaudary, tried and executed.

16 November *Germany and the Empire:* Death of Gustavus Adolphus at the battle of Lützen. Oxenstierna, his chancellor, assumes control of Swedish policy.

England: Van Dyck becomes Court painter to Charles I.

1633

Louis XIII occupies Lorraine.

Jacques Callot's engravings illustrating the horrors of war (*Les Grandes Misères de la Guerre*).

Germany and the Empire: The League of Heilbronn, consisting of Sweden and certain South German Protestant princes, is formed against the Emperor.

Secret negotiations of Wallenstein with the Saxons, the Swedes and the French.

England: Laud becomes archbishop of Canterbury.

1634

French occupation of Colmar.

25 February *Germany and the Empire:* Wallenstein is murdered as a traitor by troops in the Emperor's service.

5–6 September Imperialist victory over the Swedes at Nördlingen. After contributing to this victory a Spanish army from Italy led by Philip IV's brother the Cardinal Infante enters the Spanish Netherlands.

Saxony and Brandenburg make peace with the emperor (Preliminaries of Pirna, 1634, followed by the Peace of Prague, 1635).

First performance of the Passion Play at Oberammagau.

Urbain Grandier, a *curé* at Loudun, is tried and burnt at the stake for witchcraft.

England: First writ of Ship Money issued by Charles I, ostensibly to raise a naval force to deal with pirates.

Milton's masque *Comus* performed.

1635

8 February to 25 April	Richelieu prepares to intervene directly in the Thirty Years War and renews agreements with the United Provinces and Sweden.
19 May	Solemn declaration of war by Louis XIII on Philip IV, king of Spain.
30 May	*Germany and the Empire:* Peace of Prague between the Emperor and the elector of Saxony: other German princes follow suit.
11 July	*Italy:* Treaty of Rivoli between France and the dukes of Savoy and Parma.
October	French agreement with Bernard of Saxe-Weimar.
	Disintegration of the French army in Flanders.
	Séguier, Keeper of the Seals, is appointed Chancellor of France.
	Foundation of the Académie Française.

England: Second writ of Ship Money issued by Charles I, this time addressed to the inland counties as well as to maritime counties and seaports.

1636

Germany and the Empire: Ferdinand II declares war on France; his son Ferdinand, king of Hungary, is elected king of the Romans.

Northern front: Fall of Corbie (August). The enemy advance threatens Paris.

Eastern front: Imperialist troops threaten Burgundy. Siege of Saint-Jean de Losne.

	At sea: The Spaniards seize the Iles de Lérins off the coast of Provence.
6 October	*Germany and the Empire:* The Swedes under Banér defeat the Imperialists at Wittstock.
	Widespread peasant revolts in central and south-west France.
14 November	Recapture of Corbie.
December	First performance of Corneille's tragedy, *Le Cid*.
	England: Third writ of Ship Money issued, making it clear that instead of being an emergency measure Ship Money is becoming a permanent extra-Parliamentary tax. Papal agent received at English Court.

1637

April–May	At sea: Recapture of the Iles de Lérins.
May	Louis XIII's private life: Mademoiselle de La Fayette retires to the convent of the Visitation.
23 July	Northern front: Capture of Landrecies by cardinal La Valette.
	Suppression of popular risings in south-west France.
	Secret negotiations between Richelieu and Olivares.
August	Discovery of Anne of Austria's secret correspondence with the enemy.
Autumn	*Italy:* Deaths of the Duke of Mantua and of Victor Amadeus I Duke of Savoy.
10 October	*United Provinces:* The Dutch recapture Breda.
December	Louis XIII's confessor, father Caussin, acquires too much influence over the king and is disgraced.
	Louis XIII's vow—France is dedicated to the Virgin Mary: inauguration of processions in her honour annually on 15 August.
	Descartes' *Discours de la Méthode*.

Germany and the Empire: Death of the Emperor Ferdinand II, who is succeeded by his son Ferdinand III.

England: Arrival of Bellièvre the new French ambassador. Charles I under pressure to join Franco-Dutch alliance against Spain.

John Hampden refuses to pay Ship Money and is cited before the Exchequer Court; 5 out of 12 of the judges subsequently give judgement in his favour.

Scotland: Charles I's attempt to impose the Book of Common Prayer leads to riots and widespread opposition.

1638

March	Eastern front: Bernard of Saxe-Weimar's victory at Rheinfelden is followed by the siege of Breisach.
15 March	Treaty of Hamburg between France and Sweden.
May	Northern front: The French besiege Saint Omer.
	At sea: Naval victory off the Atlantic coast by Sourdis archbishop of Bordeaux.
5 September	Birth of the Dauphin (later Louis XIV).
7 September	South-western front: French forces put to rout at Fuenterrabía.
	At sea: Naval victory by Pontcourlai on the Mediterranean.
14 September	Northern front: Recapture of Le Câtelet by the French.
4 October	*Italy:* Death of Francesco Giacinto, the young duke of Savoy. The right of the duchess Christina (his mother and Louis XIII's sister) to act as regent for his brother is disputed by his uncles.
	England: Marie de Medici at the English Court.
18 December	Death of father Joseph.

Eastern front: Capture of Breisach by Bernard of Saxe-Weimar.

Scotland: The National Covenant, a religious manifesto calling for a return to the Calvinist Confession of Faith promulgated in 1580, protests against Charles I's attempts to alter 'true religion'. The General Assembly of the Clergy subsequently declares episcopacy abolished. Charles I attempts unsuccessfully to raise arms and troops in the Spanish Netherlands for use against Scotland.

1639

April	*Germany and the Empire:* The Swedish general Banér invades Bohemia.
7 June	Eastern front: French reverse at Thionville.
29 June	Northern front: Capture of Hesdin.
July	South-western front: Capture of Salces in Roussillon by the prince of Condé.
	Trial of the duc de la Valette.
	Rise of Cinq-Mars in Louis XIII's favour.
18 July	Death of Bernard of Saxe-Weimar.
	Revolt of the *Va-nu-pieds* in Normandy—eventually repressed by Gassion.
21 October	*At Sea:* Tromp's victory over the Spanish fleet off Dover, (battle of the Downs).
December	South-western front: Loss of Salces.

England and Scotland: First 'Bishops' War' ends with Charles I promising to submit civil and ecclesiastical differences to a new Scottish Parliament and General Assembly of Clergy.

The latter promptly confirms its decisions of the previous year while the leading Covenanters appeal to Louis XIII to mediate between them and Charles I. Spanish troops as well as bullion now being conveyed through England to Netherlands.

Charles I recalls Strafford from Ireland.

1640

January	Séguier the Chancellor enters Rouen. Normandy is severely punished for its rebellion.
	Germany and the Empire: Banér evacuates Bohemia.
31 March	Introduction of the *louis d'or*.
July	Disturbances at Moulins.
9 August	Northern front: Capture of Arras by the French.
September	Italian front: Harcourt's victories at Casale and Turin.
September	Birth of Louis XIII's second son, Philip Duke of Anjou.
23 September	*Germany and the Empire:* Opening of the Imperial Diet at Regensburg.
October	Assembly of French clergy at Mantes.
December	Death of Bullion, the superintendent of finance.

Spain: Revolutions in Catalonia and Portugal. The Duke of Braganza is proclaimed king of Portugal as John IV.

England and Scotland: Charles I summons the Short Parliament on Strafford's advice in the hope of obtaining supplies to enable him to coerce the Scots. This hope being disappointed, the Short Parliament is dissolved. Charles I's negotiations for a Spanish subsidy in return for permanent English naval escort through Channel of Spanish troop transports are frustrated by the Dutch envoy. A Scottish army invades northern England (the Second 'Bishops' War') and defeats the King's troops. Charles I, compelled to agree to armistice and unable to obtain financial help abroad, summons the Long Parliament, which impeaches Strafford for treason.

Germany and the Empire: Death of George William Elector of Brandenburg and accession of Frederick William, later known as The Great Elector.

Death of Rubens.

Poussin summoned from Rome to act as Court painter to Louis XIII.

Publication of Jansen's *Augustinus*.

1641

England: Lely arrives, Van Dyck dies in London.

23 January
The Cortes of Catalonia proclaims the deposition of Philip IV and appeals for Louis XIII's protection.

French negotiations with the Catalans and the Portuguese.

16 February
Edict issued by Louis XIII restricting the political powers of the Parlements.

Marriage of the duc d'Enghien (a prince of the blood) with Clémence de Maillé-Brézé, Richelieu's niece.

29 March
Treaty between Louis XIII and the Duke of Lorraine.

20 May
Germany and the Empire: Death of Banér at Halberstadt. Guébriant assumes command of his army pending the arrival of the Swedish general Torstensson, Banér's successor.

July
Revolt of the Comte de Soissons, who wins the battle of La Marfée but loses his life (6 July). Submission of the duc de Bouillon.

26 July
Northern front: Capture of Aire-sur-la-Lys by the French.

19 September
Treaty between France and Catalonia.

Reoccupation of Lorraine by the French, the duke having broken the treaty.

9 November
Death of the Cardinal Infante, governor of the Spanish Netherlands since 1634.

22 December
Death of Sully, formerly Henry IV's minister, at the age of 82.

30 December
Mazarin made a cardinal.

England, Scotland and Ireland: Charles I jettisons understanding with Spain in favour of marriage alliance with the House of Orange. He is forced to agree to Strafford's execution, abolition of Courts of Star Chamber and High Commission, and other Parliamentary measures depriving Crown of many of its extraordinary powers and sources of revenue. Laud imprisoned. Catholic rebellion in Ireland followed by massacres of Protestants gives rise to rumours that it had been instigated by the queen. Charles I suspects House of Commons, led by Pym, of plotting her impeachment.

1642

Death of Galileo.

Poussin returns to Rome.

Rembrandt's 'Night Watch'.

Urban VIII condemns Jansen's *Augustinus*.

January	*England:* Charles I enters the House of Commons and attempts to arrest five Members for treason; his plan failing, he leaves London with the queen who sails to the United Provinces to raise money and arms.
17 January	*Germany and the Empire:* Guébriant wins the battle of Kempen; conquest of the duchy of Jülich.
26 May	Northern front: French defeat at Honnecourt.
14 June	*Italy:* Settlement of differences with Savoy.
	Discovery of secret treaty of Cinq-Mars with Spain, followed by his arrest.
	Germany and the Empire: Torstensson's victories in Silesia and Moravia.
3 July	Death of Marie de Medici at Cologne.
August	*England:* Charles I raises his standard at Nottingham—beginning of Civil War.
September	South-western front: Capture of Perpignan (9 September) and Salces (15 September) by the French.
12 September	Execution of Cinq-Mars.
2 November	*Germany and the Empire:* Torstensson wins the battle of Breitenfeld.

November	*England:* Following the battle of Edgehill the Royalists advance towards London as far as Brentford and Turnham Green.
4 December	Death of Richelieu.

1643

17 January	*Spain:* Olivares dismissed.
14 May	Death of Louis XIII. Accession of Louis XIV.
19 May	Northern front: The duc d'Enghien's victory over the Spaniards at Rocroi.

England and Scotland: Henrietta Maria lands in Yorkshire (escorted by Tromp). John Hampden defeated and killed at Chalgrove Field. Solemn League and Covenant concluded between Parliament and the Scots. Death of John Pym.

Table of abbreviations used for works cited in editorial footnotes and numbered notes

Ariès: Philippe Ariès, *Centuries of Childhood* trans. Robert Baldick, (Cape, London, 1962)

Attwater: Donald Attwater, *The Penguin Dictionary of Saints* (Penguin Books, London, 1965)

Batiffol: Louis Batiffol, *Marie de Médicis and the French Court in the Seventeenth Century*, trans. M. King (Chatto and Windus, London, 1908)

Blunt: Anthony Blunt, *Art and Architecture in France 1500–1700* (Penguin Books, London 1953)

Buisseret: David Buisseret, *Sully and the Growth of Centralised Government in France 1598–1610* (Eyre & Spottiswoode, London, 1968)

Burckhardt: Carl J. Burckhardt, *Richelieu and his Age*, vol. II *Assertion of power and the Cold War* vol. III *Power politics and the Cardinal's death* trans. Bernard Hoy (George Allen & Unwin London, 1970–1971)

Clarke: J. A. Clarke, *Huguenot Warrior: The Life and Times of Henri de Rohan 1579–1638* (Nijhoff, The Hague, 1966)

Cross: *The Oxford Dictionary of the Christian Church*, ed. F. L. Cross (Oxford University Press, 1963 ed.)

D.B.F.: *Dictionnaire de biographie française*, 12 vols (Letouzey et Ané, Paris, 1933–74) (in progress)

D.N.B.: *Dictionary of National Biography*, 68 vols and supplements (Smith, Elder, London, 1885–1909)

Doucet:	R. Doucet, *Les institutions de la France au XVIe siècle*, 2 vols (Picard, Paris, 1948)
Elliott:	J. H. Elliott, *The Revolt of the Catalans: a study in the decline of Spain 1598–1640* (Cambridge University Press, 1963)
Evans:	Joan Evans, *Monastic architecture in France from the Renaissance to the Revolution* (Cambridge University Press, 1964)
Evelyn:	*The Diary of John Evelyn*, ed. E. S. de Beer, 6 vols (Clarendon Press, Oxford, 1955)
Gibb:	M. A. Gibb, *Buckingham 1592–1628* (Cape, London, 1935)
G.L.E.:	*Grand Larousse Encyclopédique* 10 vols and Supplement (Librairie Larousse, Paris, 1960–69)
Hanotaux:	G. Hanotaux and the Duc de la Force, *Histoire du Cardinal de Richelieu*, 6 vols (vols 1–2 Firmin-Didot, vols 3–6 Librairie Plon, Paris, 1893–1946)
Hill:	*The Political Testament of Cardinal Richelieu: the significant chapters and supporting selections* translated by Henry Bertram Hill (University of Wisconsin Press, Madison, paperback edition 1965)
Léonard:	Emile G. Léonard, *A History of Protestantism*, vol II: *The Establishment*, trans. R. M. Bethell (Nelson, London, 1967)
Littré:	Emile Littré, *Dictionnaire de la langue francaise* 7 vols (vols 1–4 Pauvert, vols 5–7 Gallimard-Hachette, Paris, 1956–8 ed.)
Lublinskaya:	A. D. Lublinskaya, *French Absolutism: The Crucial Phase 1620–1629* trans. Brian Pearce, (Cambridge University Press, 1968)
Magne:	Emile Magne, *La vie quotidienne au temps de Louis XIII* (Hachette, Paris, 1964 ed.)
Major:	J. Russell Major, *The Deputies to the Estates General in Renaissance France* (University of Wisconsin Press, Madison, 1960)
Mariéjol:	*Histoire de France*, ed. Ernest Lavisse, 9 vols

	(Hachette, Paris, 1911 ed.), vol. VI pt 2 (1598–1643) by J. H. Mariéjol
Marion:	Marcel Marion, *Dictionnaire des institutions de la France au XVIIe et XVIIIe siècles* (Picard, Paris, 1923 repr. 1969)
Matthews:	George T. Matthews, *The Royal General Farms in Eighteenth Century France* (Columbia University Press, New York, 1958)
Moote:	A Lloyd Moote, *The Revolt of the Judges: the Parlement of Paris and the Fronde 1643–1652* (Princeton University Press, New Jersey, 1971)
Mousnier:	Roland Mousnier, *La Vénalité des Offices sous Henri IV et Louis XIII* (Maugard, Rouen, 1946)
Mousnier–Pearce:	Roland Mousnier, *Peasant uprisings in seventeenth-century France, Russia and China* trans. Brian Pearce (George Allen & Unwin London 1971)
N.C.E.:	*New Catholic Encyclopaedia*, 15 vols including index (Catholic University of America, 1967)
N.C.M.H.:	*The New Cambridge Modern History* vol. iv *The Decline of Spain and the Thirty Years War* ed: J. P. Cooper (Cambridge University Press, 1970)
N.E.D.:	*A New English Dictionary*, 10 vols and supplement (Clarendon Press, Oxford, 1888–1933)
O'Connell:	D. P. O'Connell, *Richelieu* (Weidenfeld & Nicolson, London, 1968)
O.E.D.:	*The Oxford English Dictionary*, 12 vols and supplement (Clarendon Press, Oxford, 1933)
Pagès, Fr:	G. Pagès, *La Guerre de Trente Ans* (Payot, Paris, 1939)
Pagès, Eng:	G. Pagès, *The Thirty Years War* trans: David Maland and John Hooper (A & C Black, London, 1970)
Polišenský:	J. V. Polišenský, *The Thirty Years War* trans. Robert Evans (Batsford, London, 1971)

Purcell: Mary Purcell, *The World of Monsieur Vincent* (Harvill Press, London, 1963)

Ranum, *Paris:*   Orest A. Ranum, *Paris in the Age of Absolutism: An Essay* (Wiley, New York, 1968)

Ranum, *Richelieu:*   Orest A. Ranum, *Richelieu and the Councillors of Louis XIII* (Clarendon Press, Oxford, 1963)

Robbins: Russell Hope Robbins, *The Encyclopaedia of Witchcraft and Demonology* (Peter Nevill, London, 1959)

Robert: Paul Robert, *Dictionnaire alphabétique et analogique de la langue francaise*, 6 vols (vols 1–3 Presses Universitaires de France, vols 4–6 Société du Nouveau Littré, Paris, 1953–64)

Roberts: Michael Roberts, *Gustavus Adolphus: A History of Sweden 1611–1632*, 2 vols (Longmans Green, London, 1953–8)

Schwarz: H. F. Schwarz, *The Imperial Privy Council in the Seventeenth century* (Harvard University Press, Cambridge, Mass., 1943)

Shennan, *Government:*   J. H. Shennan, *Government and Society in France 1461–1661* (George Allen & Unwin, London, 1969)

Shennan, *Parlement:*   J. H. Shennan, *The Parlement of Paris* (Eyre & Spottiswoode, London, 1968)

Sutherland: N. M. Sutherland, *The French Secretaries of State in the Age of Catherine de Medici* (University of London, Athlone Press, 1962)

Tapié, *Age of Grandeur:*   Victor-L. Tapié, *The Age of Grandeur: Baroque and Classicism in Europe* trans. A. Ross Williamson, (Weidenfeld & Nicolson, London, 1960)

Tapié, *Habsburg Monarchy:*   Victor-L. Tapié, *The Rise and Fall of the Habsburg Monarchy* trans. Stephen Hardman (Pall Mall Press, London, 1971)

Treasure: G. R. R. Treasure, *Cardinal Richelieu and the development of Absolutism* (A & C Black, London, 1972 paperback edition)

Wiley:

W. L. Wiley, *The Early Public Theatre in France* (Harvard University Press, Cambridge, Mass., 1960)

Zeller:

Gaston Zeller, *Les institutions de la France au XVIe siècle* (Presses Universitaires de France, Paris, 1948)

Notes

1. According to tradition, St Dionysius or Denis was the first bishop of Paris and was executed *c.* 258 on Montmartre, 'the martyrs' mount'. The history of the abbey (to which his remains were translated) goes back to the reign of its founder, the Merovingian king Dagobert I (*c.* 630). The kings of France subsequently became its chief benefactors and adopted its banner as their own, while the saint himself came to be regarded as the patron saint of France. The regalia used in the ceremony of coronation at Rheims (which were also carried at a king's interment) were kept at the abbey of St-Denis and most of France's kings were buried there, including Henry IV himself. According to Evelyn, who gives an elaborate description of it in his *Diary*, the abbey was at this time about six miles outside Paris. *See* N.C.E., Cross, and the short account of Henry II's interment in Lady Antonia Fraser's *Mary Queen of Scots* (Weidenfeld & Nicolson, London, 1969).

2. Philippe Erlanger, *L'étrange mort d'Henri IV* (Paris, 1957): Roland Mousnier, *L'assassinat d'Henri IV* (Paris, 1964). (V.L.T.)

3. The Arsenal was located beside the Seine and close to the Bastille. Together they constituted a sort of royal enclave. Sully (who was grand master of artillery as well as superintendent of finance) had taken up residence at the Arsenal and made it his administrative headquarters several years previously. Henry IV often used to go there from the Louvre to visit him, as on this occasion. In addition, the Arsenal had become a fashionable place of entertainment, a magnificent hall with a double row of galleries having been opened there in December 1609. *See* Buisseret and Batiffol.

4. The post of colonel-general of the infantry which had been created in the 1540s, had been conferred on the duke of Épernon by Henry III in 1584. With the exception of a few units (e.g. the colonel-general of the Swiss Guards at this time was the duke of Rohan —*see* Clarke, p. 18), he thus controlled, at least in theory, all the appointments of officers in the infantry. Henry IV, who considered his powers excessive, had earlier attempted to reduce them. (Mariéjol, pp. 28–9)

The French and Swiss Guards were the only foot soldiers among the household troops. The former dated from 1574, while the Swiss Guards came into existence at the end of the fifteenth century. The Scots Guards were an earlier creation, having been formed as the king's personal bodyguard after the battle of Verneuil in 1424, but by 1610 a number of them were in fact Frenchmen. *See* Doucet, Zeller.

5. R. Mousnier, *Le Conseil du Roi*, p. 35. (V.L.T.)

6. The other sovereign courts (some of which had adjuncts in certain provinces) were the *Cour des Aides*, the *Chambre des Comptes*, the *Cour des Monnaies*, the *Cour du Trésor* and the *Grand Conseil*, most of which are referred to more fully in the notes to chapter 9. With the exception of the last-named, these sovereign courts all normally met in the Palais de Justice on the Île de la Cité, as did the Parlement itself (Shennan, p. 80). A list of provincial Parlements is given in chapter 2, n. 1.

Edicts, ordinances and declarations were all expressions of the king's legislative power.

Whereas edicts tended to deal with one topic, as in the case of the Edict of Nantes, royal ordinances generally covered a wide range of subjects—witness the great ordinance of 1629 popularly known as the 'Code Michau'. Declarations on the other hand were generally relatively brief enactments laying down a principle or interpreting an edict or ordinance previously issued.

7. This monastery, known as 'Le Grand Couvent' and famous as a meeting place for the clergy of France, was situated on the left bank of the Seine in the university quarter not far from the Pont-Neuf. The name 'Grands (or Vieux) Augustins' was applied to the congregations of hermits or friars banded together under the rule of St Augustine in the thirteenth century, as opposed to the congregations of 'Petits Augustins' who followed a reformed rule instituted at Bourges. For the 'Petits Pères' *see* chapter 5, n. 11. (Information supplied by the Rev. J. R. Fox, c.r.; *see* also Mousnier, *L'assassinat d'Henri IV*, and Evans.)

8. The first president of the Parlement of Paris was a prominent public figure whose position secured him membership of the king's council. By this date there were at least seven presidents in the Parlement. Together with the counsellors or ordinary members they constituted the permanent professional element in any plenary session of the Parlement which might be attended by the king, the chancellor and the princes of the blood, as well as by peers and privy councillors—as will be seen from Professor Tapié's narrative.

The Parlement was divided into a number of courts where different types of cases were heard, consisting by this date of five *Chambres des Enquêtes*, two *Chambres des Requêtes* (whose functions are briefly described in chapter 9, n. 14) and one central court senior to them all, known as the *Grand' Chambre* where the plenary sessions of the Parlement were also normally held. The first president presided over this central court, the other permanent members of which had habitually served a preliminary period of apprenticeship for several years as counsellors in one of the other chambers mentioned above—*see* Shennan, Zeller.

9. The peers of France came next in precedence to the children of the royal family. The title and the right which it gave to attend the Parlement's meetings belonged at this stage only to the king's most powerful vassals and six specified bishops. (*See* Shennan, *Government*, p. 26, and Zeller, pp. 90–1.)

10. The Hôtel de Ville was of course the town hall, while the *lieutenant-civil* and the *prévôt des marchands* were roughly equivalent to the chief officer of police and the mayor; but to translate this sentence in such a way would be to give a misleadingly modern impression of the administration of seventeenth-century Paris. In Evelyn's opinion the latter, for instance, was 'an office more resembling our Recorder and Sheriff than Mayor' (vol. iii, p. 638). The *prévôt des marchands* was in theory chosen for two years by a severely restricted electoral college but, in practice, especially from the time of Henry IV, he was the king's nominee (Ranum, *Paris*, p. 56). The appointment was unpaid but carried with it great prestige. According to Magne those chosen during Louis XIII's reign included four presidents and four counsellors from the Parlement, and two *lieutenant-civils*. The importance of the latter post may be gauged by the fact that the salary of a *lieutenant-civil* was fixed at 400,000 livres in 1634 (Marion). Ranum, who refers to him as 'the single most important royal official in Paris though nominally under the Parlement', gives a useful account of his many activities (pp. 53–5).

11. The *lit justice* was a throne covered with cushions upon which the king sat when he presided in person over a session of the Parlement. (Shennan).

12. Mayenne, who died in 1611, had succeeded his brother the duke of Guise as head of

the League after the latter had been murdered at Blois in 1588; but after Henry IV's conversion to Catholicism had helped to bring the League's policy of resistance to the monarchy and acceptance of Spanish help into complete discredit, he had eventually made his submission in January 1596. The League's opposition to Henry IV finally ceased in 1598.

13. For the functions of an advocate general, *see* chapter 3, n. 7. *Bailliages* and *sénéchaussées* were judicial and administrative circumscriptions corresponding roughly in size to the modern French department. The term *sénéchaussée* was more generally used in the south of France.

14. *See* P. Goubert, *Beauvais et le Beauvaisis, de 1600 à 1730*, pp. 31, 69. (V.L.T.)

15. These examples are quoted by R. Mousnier, in *La Vénalité des offices*, pp. 223, 237. (V.L.T.)

16. The *livre tournois* was not an actual coin but a money of account, that is to say a monetary unit used when keeping accounts. The nearest equivalent coin was the franc, which was introduced as a silver coin towards the end of the sixteenth century. As far as coins of low denomination were concerned there were 12 deniers to a sol (or sou) and 20 sols to a *livre tournois*.

As will emerge in the course of this book, 'such moneys of account were convertible into gold and silver but the conversion rate was not fixed. In brief their intrinsic value was variable.' (F. C. Spooner, in the chapter entitled 'The economy of Europe 1559–1609' in N.C.M.H., iii, which contains a table showing the index of devaluation of certain European silver currency systems between 1530 and 1614.) However, for practical purposes Professor Tapié equates 10,000 écus or crowns with 30,000 livres on p. 183 and Buisseret refers to the livre as being valued at three to the écu in 1602 (p. 95).

17. Jean Bodin, 'the Aristotle of the sixteenth century' as Trevor-Roper calls him in a recent essay, died in 1596.

18. Later, exceptions were made to this rule. Men of noble birth were allowed to take part in maritime trade provided they sold nothing retail. (V.L.T.) [For glass-making, *see* p. 487 below.]

19. The French reads as follows: '. . . au tenancier qui lui payait un cens, au fermier et au métayer qui lui versaient ou un loyer en argent, arrondi de redevances, ou des rentes en nature.'

A helpful definition of the status of the *tenancier* and of the *métayer* is given in Brian Pearce's prefatory note to his translation of Professor Lublinskaya's book. Henceforth direct use of the words *métayer*, *métairie* and *métayage* will sometimes be made in this book to refer to a share-cropping farmer, to the land held by him on this basis, and to the share-cropping system of land tenure that was so widespread in seventeenth-century France.

20. The judicial powers possessed by the nobility were divided into three categories—high, middle and low. The first of these is briefly described in note 27. Those who had the right to the second and third could arrest, imprison and impose fines of up to 60 sols and 6 sols respectively. Appeal could however be made to royal justices against a sentence passed by a seigneurial court, which, unless it was the court of a great noble, would generally be presided over by a steward or factor rather than by a professional lawyer. For further details, *see* Mousnier-Pearce pp. 29–30, Zeller, Doucet, Marion.

21. The French here reads '. . . le seigneur prélevait des droits de four, banalités, péages, marchés, moulins.'

22. *Testament politique*, chapter iii, 'De la noblesse' (ed. André, p. 218) (V.L.T.) [*cf.* Hill, p. 20].

23. D'Avenel, *La noblesse française sous Richelieu*, p. 20. (V.L.T.)

24. With superb arrogance the Rohan family motto proclaimed: 'Roi ne puis, duc ne daigne, Rohan suis'. However Henri de Rohan, prince de Léon (1579–1638), the head of the house of Rohan and subsequent leader of the Huguenots, was created a duke by Henry IV in 1603. Two years later he married Sully's daughter (Lublinskaya, Clarke).

25. Lesdiguières, who was born in Dauphiné, a province where the Huguenots were strongly established, was himself brought up as a Protestant and played a leading part in the Wars of Religion there, as well as subsequently championing Henry IV's cause in south-east France against attack from Spanish forces in Italy and the duke of Savoy. Henry IV's choice of this nickname indicates the immense power and prestige that Lesdiguières enjoyed in his native province. The title 'dauphin' had originally been first a personal name and then an appellation given to the counts of Albon which later came to be applied to the general area where their power lay—the territory of Viennois. When Dauphiné was acquired in 1349 by Charles de Valois (later Charles V), the grandson of Philip VI of France, the title 'dauphin of Viennois' was transferred to the French Crown and soon afterwards was permanently adopted by the reigning king of France's oldest son, who continued to occupy a semi-independent position in Dauphiné as 'dauphin' or ruler of the province until 1456.

26. 'In the Roman Catholic Church the term "ordinary" is defined as including . . . all diocesan bishops . . . their officials and vicars-general and, in the vacancy of a see, the vicar capitular or lawful administrator. The jurisdiction of an ordinary extends over his rights of teaching, governing, adjudicating, and administering the Sacraments'. (Cross).

27. *Cf.* note 20 above. Only great nobles had these judicial powers, which included the right to sentence to death in certain cases and gave their courts full jurisdiction as courts of first instance in criminal matters.

28. The provisions of the Edict of Nantes are examined in some detail in Léonard, ii, pp. 167–71. For an excellent short survey of 'the Huguenot problem' after the Edict of Nantes, which draws a valuable distinction between the permanent rights and the temporary concessions granted to the Huguenots by the Crown, *see* G. A. Rothrock's article 'Some aspects of early Bourbon policy towards the Huguenots', in *Church History*, xxix (1960) 17–24.

29. On this subject, *see* Buisseret, pp. 197–9. In the opinion of the English ambassador, Sully was 'not void of learning, both of knowledge of Latin and other studies of humanity; but chiefly in arguing points of religion, whereof he is very ready and confident.'

30. Since Saulnier's name has already been mentioned and it was Paulet who gave his name to the *paulette*, this seems an appropriate place to draw the reader's attention to the contemporary French word *traitant* which appears several times in this translation. Briefly, a financier was known as a *traitant* if he had concluded a tax-farming contract with the government—although, as pointed out by Brian Pearce the translator of Lublinskaya (p. 307, n. 4), the form of the contract signed by a *traitant* differed from that drawn up for a *fermier* proper. He might also be referred to as a *partisan*, another contemporary term which I have sometimes retained, especially if he was a member of a *parti* or financial syndicate. According to Zeller the word *partisan* appears for the first time at the end of the sixteenth century (p. 273). The nearest English equivalent would appear to be 'partner' (*see* Lublinskaya, pp. 236, 242).

31. *See* n. 19 above. For some illuminating comments on the status of the *laboureur* and the *brassier* or *manouvrier*, reference should be made to P. Goubert's article (translated by George Rudé), 'The French peasantry of the Seventeenth Century: a regional example' in *Past and Present*, x (Nov. 1956), and to Mousnier-Pearce, pp. 9–10, 26–7.

32. Great credit is due to Roger Dion for having established that France owes her most celebrated wines far more to reasons derived from historical geography than to such factors as a suitable soil and climate. Ever since the days of the Romans and all through the Middle Ages such wines have been the letters patent which have given the vine its noble status. 'A suitable soil and good exposure are not in themselves sufficient to promote the development of a vineyard;' he writes, 'the natural communications of the area in question must also facilitate the export of the wines it produces to places where they will be consumed.' And, to quote Olivier de Serres: 'If you have nowhere to sell your wine, what is the use of having a large vineyard?' (V.L.T.)

33. Calvet, *Saint Vincent de Paul.* See Vincent de Paul's letter to his mother, dated 17 February 1610. (V.L.T.)

34. Sainte Germaine Cousin or Sainte Germaine of Pibrac was a shepherdess who lived a pious life, ill-treated by her stepmother and in miserable conditions, in the countryside near Toulouse from 1579 to 1601. She was canonised in 1867. (Attwater, N.C.E.)

35. The story goes that Henry IV said to the duke of Savoy, while the latter was on a visit to Paris early in 1600, 'Si Dieu me donne encore de la vie je ferai qu'il n'y aura pas de laboureur en mon royaume qui n'ayt moyen d'avoir une poule dans son pot.' (This version, quoted by A. Poirson in his *Histoire du Règne de Henry IV,* iii, p. 199 (1865), follows that given on pp. 459–60 of the 1823 edition of Hardouin de Péréfixe, *Histoire du Roi Henri le Grand,* a work originally written to glorify Henry IV in the eyes of the youthful Louis XIV.) To credit Henry IV in 1600 with the hope that every *laboureur* in France would be able to have a fowl in his cooking pot before the end of his reign was not altogether unreasonable.

36. Gaston Zeller's recent survey *L'industrie en France avant Colbert* establishes this point very clearly. 'It would really be better to avoid using the word "industry" in connection with pre-seventeenth-century French history,' he writes, 'or at least to try to use it as little as possible'. (V.L.T.)

37. In his *Studies in Economic History,* p. 98, G. Unwin gives the following examples of the 'masterpieces' that were required by various craft guilds in Paris over a period of four centuries. Scriveners used to examine candidates in the casting of accounts and in handwriting and spelling; printers and booksellers tested their knowledge of Greek and Latin; pinners expected them to make a thousand pins; shoemakers required them to make a pair of boots, three pairs of shoes and a pair of slippers; and the 'masterpiece' required by butchers involved dressing for sale the carcases of a cow, a calf, a sheep and a pig. Naturally if a craft was 'free', no fee, 'masterpiece' or guild membership was called for.

38. For a colourful description of the fair at St Germain-des-Prés, which Henry IV took particular pleasure in attending and at which both he and Marie de Medici used to gamble quite heavily, *see* Batiffol, pp. 58–61; *cf.* Ranum, *Paris,* p. 20.

39. Further particulars about these officials are given by Professor Tapié on p. 57 while the *taille* and the *gabelle* or salt-tax are more fully dealt with on pp. 57–9. The object of this note is to explain simply the official titles mentioned in this sentence.

Apart from the provinces of Languedoc, Provence, Dauphiné, Burgundy and Brittany, where the fiscal organisation differed from that described below in important respects, France was at this time divided into some fifteen financial circumscriptions known as *généralités.* Their territorial limits sometimes corresponded with those of individual provinces, but this was not necessarily the case. In each *généralité* was established a *bureau des finances,* a supervisory body, the chief officials of which were entitled *généraux des finances.* These officials consisted of (a) three collectors general (*receveurs généraux*) and

(b) ten treasurers styled *trésoriers de France*. In neither case however did all these officials carry out their duties concurrently. (*See* Buisseret, p. 57.) It was one of the particular tasks of the treasurers to keep an eye on the king's seigneurial rights and extraordinary revenues. (Shennan, *Government*, p. 54.)

Each *généralité* was subdivided into a varying number of *élections*, in which the chief fiscal officers (who were subordinate to the treasurers) were the *élus*. Despite their name the latter were not elected to their offices but had purchased them. The *élus*, of whom there were between ten and twenty per *élection*, after apportioning the amount of *taille* to be collected among the parishes used to entrust the invidious task of collecting it at parish level to persons chosen by the inhabitants themselves.

Provinces in which this system of financial administration prevailed were for the most part known as *pays d'élections*; *see*, however, chapter 2, n. 4. According to Buisseret and Lublinskaya there were at this time about 150 such *élections*.

40. The *baillis* and *sénéchaux* were nominally in charge of the administrative and judicial divisions known as *bailliages* and *sénéchaussées* mentioned in n. 13 above. However, as Professor Tapié indicates later, such appointments had become largely honorary and were generally given to the nobility. It was the lieutenant of the *bailli*, a lawyer, who really presided over the *tribunal du bailliage*; between these tribunals and the Parlements were the courts known as *présidiaux* here referred to by Professor Tapié and described by him more fully on p. 54. As mentioned in n. 6 the *Cour des Aides* and the *Chambre des Comptes* were both sovereign courts. The first tried suits arising out of the collection and farming of taxes whilst the second was primarily concerned with auditing and revising the public accounts. For further details about the above, *see* Doucet, Zeller and Buisseret.

41. The *parties casuelles* have already been defined—*see* p. 13 note. The income derived therefrom was paid to a special treasurer—the *trésorier des parties casuelles*. *See* the interesting figures of receipts from *parties casuelles* between 1600 and 1622 printed in Buisseret (p. 77) and Lublinskaya (p. 230).

42. The origins of this phenomenon have been examined and described at length in Roland Mousnier's book *La Vénalité des Offices sous Henri IV et Louis XIII*, a work of deep and valuable scholarship. (V.L.T.)

43. A translation of the relevant sections of the royal declaration introducing the *paulette* is printed in Shennan, *Government*, pp. 137–8.

44. Mousnier op. cit, p. 58 (V.L.T.)

45. Cardinal du Perron said of Henry IV: 'He hath no ear for either music or poetry wherefore there are none that in his day do excel therein' (quoted by A. Adam in *Histoire de la littérature française au XVIIe siècle*, p. 25); but one has only to read his letters to savour their admirable clarity, sparkle and vigour, and to find vivid references to various aspects of Nature which show the king's sensitive awareness of beauty. He was by no means unperceptive or obtuse. (V.L.T.)

46. The term is used by Karel or Charles of Žerotín, a Czech and a gentleman of Moravia. He is an unusual example of a sixteenth-century humanist and European. Nowadays he is very largely a forgotten figure, but his name will recur later in this book in connection with important events. (V.L.T.)

47. This theatre, as its name implies, occupied the site of a former residence of the dukes of Burgundy. It was located near Les Halles, the public market of Paris. In the sixteenth century it became the only permanent theatre in Paris and from about 1606 a company of professional actors known as *les Comédiens du Roi* or the King's Players was established there—*see* Wiley, pp. 50–1. Wiley, who gives a good description of its appearance at this

time, refers to a brief history of the theatre given in an article published in *The Theatre Annual* for 1947: 'The Hôtel de Bourgogne: France's first popular playhouse', by Charles Niemeyer.

48. Clovis, the first Christian king of the Franks, had been baptised at Rheims and the right of the archbishops of Rheims to crown the kings of France had been recognised by the pope as long ago as 999. In 1179 Alexander III formally declared it to be their exclusive privilege (Cross). Henry IV was crowned at Chartres, but his was an exceptional case —he had only recently declared himself a Catholic and was meeting with active resistance from the League, which at the time still controlled both Rheims and Paris.

49. A fourteenth-century representation of St Louis holding the hand of justice aloft at the end of a staff is reproduced in G.L.E., vi, p. 983.

50. The Holy Phial (*la Sainte Ampoule*) was believed to have been brought by an angel to St Rémi, the apostle of the Franks and archbishop of Rheims, for the baptism of Clovis in 496. Chrism is a mixture of olive oil and balsam; unlike other holy oils, it can be consecrated only by a bishop. (Cross.)

51. *See* Marc Bloch, *Les Rois thaumaturges*. (V.L.T.)

52. *Noel* was a cry of joy which used to be uttered on some public occasion such as the birth of a prince, the arrival or coronation of a king etc. (Littré.)

CHAPTER TWO: The Regency of Marie de Medici

1. In addition to the Parlement of Paris there were at this date Parlements in Toulouse (Languedoc), Bordeaux (Guyenne), Rennes (Brittany), Rouen (Normandy), Dijon (Burgundy), Grenoble (Dauphiné) and Aix (Provence).

2. Pierre Jeannin (1540–1622) was known as President Jeannin because at an earlier stage in his career he had been first president of the Parlement of Dijon.

3. These officials, the *Maîtres des Requêtes de l'Hôtel*, had originally been created to exercise jurisdiction in cases involving members of the royal household; but they were also assistants to the chancellor and as such used to deal with petitions (*requêtes*) from private persons and groups from all over France. In addition to the services they rendered in connection with the King's Councils their legal expertise and loyalty to the Crown made them also particularly well qualified to serve as intendants in the provinces, as later described by Professor Tapié. According to Zeller (pp. 116–17), there were more than a hundred of them during Henry IV's reign.

4. The full title of a *trésorier de France* was *Trésorier de France et Général des Finances*. A brief description of the organisation of a *généralité* and of the role of the *élus* in their *élections* is given in chapter 1, n. 39.

Provinces like Auvergne, Burgundy, Brittany, Dauphiné, Languedoc, Normandy and Provence which had their own Estates (and in most cases their own Parlement also) were known as *pays d'états*; but not every province where provincial Estates existed was in an equally favoured position with regard to direct taxation. As will emerge later in this book, Normandy was particularly unfortunate. Although it had its own Estates, the financial administration was nevertheless controlled by the government and its agents, the *trésoriers de France* and the *élus*. In short, although Normandy was a *pays d'états*, it was to all intents and purposes taxed in the same way as a *pays d'élections*. Sully indeed commented that the Norman Estates were only 'une ombre au prix des six austres', i.e. only a shadow compared to the other six provincial Estates (Buisseret, p. 96). See details of direct taxes paid by Normandy in 1620 given by Lublinskaya (p. 226, n. 4) who contrasts them with the far smaller contributions made by the more fortunate provinces of Languedoc and Provence where the *élus* did not operate. Note also, however, Buisseret's comments (p. 76) on the fiscal commitments of Languedoc for the period 1600–10.

5. A *châtellenie* may be defined in general terms as the lordship of a castle together with its land and jurisdiction; it was also the name given in most parts of France to a subdivision of a *bailliage* or *sénéchaussée*.

6. The *Cour des Comptes* was the same as the *Chambre des Comptes* referred to with the *Cour des Aides* in chapter 1, n. 40. Both these courts had adjuncts in certain provinces—for details of which and for Sully's dealings with them as Superintendent of Finance, *see* Buisseret, pp. 30, 92–5.

7. As the Crown laid claim to provincial customs dues and to a proportion of the duties levied on goods entering towns in many cases, the organisation of something approaching a coherent system of collection was plainly in its interest. The farming of the five main types of customs dues imposed in the provinces around Paris, which were known as the *cinq grosses fermes*, was entrusted to a single tax farming organisation by Sully in 1607 (Matthews, pp. 42–3). These dues should be distinguished from *aides*; one of them admittedly applied to wine, but to wine in transit, not to wine for sale. For details, *see* Doucet, i, pp. 587–94.

8. The palace of the Tuileries which had been built for Catherine de Medici by Philibert de l'Orme was destroyed during the Commune (1871). For the Grand Gallery, *see* Ranum, *Paris*, pp. 69–71, where it is pointed out that Henry IV may have considered it partly as an escape route in the event of a rising in the capital.

9. This prison formed part of the Palais de Justice on the Île de la Cité (for which *see* chapter 1, n. 6). Its chief officer, the *concierge*, was nominated by the Parlement. (Mousnier, *L'assassinat d'Henri IV*, Shennan).

10. Santarelli was an Italian Jesuit. His treatise, which claimed that the pope could depose kings not only for being heretics but for their inadequacy as rulers or for their crimes, was introduced into France in 1626.

11. As the Faculty of Theology generally used to hold its meetings at the Sorbonne it was often referred to by that name.

12. The legend that Henry IV had a great plan for the future of Europe was refuted in an article by Christian Pfister which was published in the *Revue historique* as long ago as 1894. But legends take a remarkably long time to die! How many people, one wonders, still believe in this one? (V.L.T.)

13. The Milanese (in French 'le Milanais') was the name given to the territory of the old duchy of Milan. Strictly speaking the latter still existed with the king of Spain as its duke.

14. These treaties had been signed as recently as 25 April 1610 (i.e. less than three weeks before Henry IV's death) in a Piedmontese village some six miles to the east of Susa which is generally called Brussol or Brusol by French historians. In Italian its name is variously given as Brosòlo, Brusòlo, Bruzzòlo and Bruzòlo, the last of which is the most modern form. The treaties (which provided amongst other things for a joint attack on the Milanese) were signed by the duke himself and by Lesdiguières and Claude de Bullion on behalf of Henry IV who was to ratify the terms within a month. The full text of both treaties (which were drawn up in French) is given in Signor Federico Marconcini's ar-

ticle 'I Trattati di Bruzòlo' published in vol. ii, no. 2 of the Italian review *Segusium* (Susa, December 1965).

15. The reference is to a famous episode in mediaeval history. In 1077 the Emperor Henry IV, who had been excommunicated by Pope Gregory VII in the previous year, made a penitential visit to the castle of Canossa in central Italy where the pope was staying. He waited barefoot outside the castle for three days in the depth of winter before he was given absolution.

16. Daniel Chamier (1564–1621) was the chief pastor of the Huguenot stronghold of Montauban and thus a person of some consequence. He was killed by a cannon ball during the siege of the town in 1621.

17. Sully had had quite a distinguished military career during the Wars of Religion and Henry IV had appointed him Grand Master of Artillery in 1599—an appointment which gave him control of all artillery and ammunition on land and sea. For details see the relevant chapter of Buisseret.

18. The three small towns of Péronne, Roye and Montdidier (all within the province of Picardy) were combined into a single 'government' in the second half of the sixteenth century (Major, p. 18). Governors of such towns were often the king's nominees although under the authority of the governor of the province. The latter was sometimes styled (especially in the case of frontier provinces) lieutenant-general; but a lieutenant-general might also be appointed by the king to a particular province to serve as a check to the power and authority of its governor—*see*, for instance, the case of Luynes, cited by Professor Tapié on p. 95 and the example given by Lublinskaya (p. 244).

19. Avenel, *Lettres, instructions diplomatiques, et papiers d'État du Cardinal de Richelieu*, vol. i, p. 93. (V.L.T.)

20. The successive marriages of Anne, duchess of Brittany, with Charles VIII and Louis XII, and of her daughter Claude with Francis I, had only brought about a personal union between Brittany and the French Crown. It was not until 1532 that an indissoluble union between the two was formally accepted by the Breton Estates.

21. Cîteaux was the mother house of the Cistercian order and Clairvaux one of its most important abbeys.

22. Pierre Blet, s.j., 'L'article du Tiers aux États Généraux de 1614' in the *Revue d'histoire moderne et contemporaine*, 1955, pp. 81–106. (V.L.T.)

23. The Bidassoa, which flows into the Atlantic, has for long partly served as a frontier between France and Spain. In 1659 the Treaty of the Pyrenees was signed on an island situated in mid-stream near its estuary.

24. For a short but laudatory description of du Vair, Mangot and Barbin, *see* Batiffol, p. 200 (note) where their emergence as ministers is attributed to the influence of Léonora Galigaï

25. R. Mousnier, op. cit., p. 341. (V.L.T.)

26. For a good account of the architectural florescence of Rome at this time see Tapié, *Age of Grandeur*.

27. Avenel, *Lettres de Richelieu*, vol. i, pp. 73, 112 (letters written in 1611 and 1613). (V.L.T.)

28. This town, now known as Châtillon-sur-Chalaronne, is situated south-west of Bourg-en-Bresse in the present department of Ain. The principality of Dombes which lay on the east bank of the Saône had been confiscated from Charles, duke of Bourbon, by Francis I in 1523, but was subsequently granted to the family of Bourbon-Montpensier (Purcell, Doucet).

29. Adrien Bourdoise (1584–1655) was a close associate of St Vincent de Paul. For his biography *see* the D.B.F.

30. St Geneviève (422–500) has for long been the patroness of Paris. In particular the diversion of Attila's army from Paris in 451 was attributed to her prayers. The abbey stood partly on the site of the present-day Panthéon. For a description of its great importance at this time *see* Ranum, *Paris*, pp. 21–2.

31. This book has been translated into English under the title *The coming of mysticism 1590–1620* (*see* bibliography at the end of this book p. 514). Marie-Jacqueline Bonette de Blémur (1618–96) was a learned Benedictine nun.

32. The convent of Port-Royal had been established in 1204 on the outskirts of Paris. When Jacqueline Arnauld (who assumed the name of mère Angélique) became abbess at the age of ten in 1602, discipline had declined and the twelve nuns who lived there were lax in their observance. In 1608 she decided to re-establish the Cistercian rule in its full rigour. On 25 September 1609 she gave a dramatic example of her determination to let nothing prevent her from enforcing the rule of enclosure by refusing to admit members of her own family to the cloister when they came to visit her—despite their expostulations from the other side of the entrance gate (or *guichet*).

33. The reference is to the colonies of hermits and monastic communities which flourished in the desert around Thebes in Upper Egypt during the fourth and fifth centuries.

34. Madame Acarie lived from 1566 to 1618. A useful short article about her is printed in Cross. See also the account of her life given in the D.B.F. An English biography is mentioned in the bibliography on p. 542 below.

35. Works concerned with Ange de Joyeuse and Benet of Canfield are mentioned in the bibliography on pp. 510, 542.

36. A. Adam, *Histoire de la littérature française au XVIIe siècle*, p. 94. (V.L.T.)

37. Quoted in Calvet, *Saint Vincent de Paul*, p. 23. (V.L.T.)

38. *The Introduction to the Devout Life* was written by St François de Sales. It first appeared in 1608 when he was 41.

39. St Radegonde or Radegund (*c.* 520–87) was a princess who was born in Thuringia. While still a child she was abducted by the Frankish King Clotaire I (d. 561) who subsequently compelled her to marry him. She later became a deaconess and in about 555 established a nunnery at Poitiers where she spent the rest of her life. It acquired great fame on account of its relics which included a reputed fragment of the true cross and by the time Radegund died the convent which she had founded included many nuns of noble birth. (Note also the reference to a nobly-born abbess of Sainte-Croix de Poitiers in the list of names given by Professor Tapié on p. 82 above). Popular canonisation followed very soon after her death. N.C.E., Cross, Attwater.

40. The Doctors of the Church to whom Professor Tapié here refers included, in particular, St Jerome, St Ambrose, and St Gregory the Great.

CHAPTER THREE: Louis XIII and the Catholic Cause (1617–24)

1. Ed. André, p. 266 (V.L.T.) [*Cf.* Hill, p. 36].

2. For a reference to a *De profundis* composed by Louis XIII see p. 427 below. Aries (p. 62) quotes a passage from Héroard's journal which describes him playing the violin when only seventeen months old, but rightly points out that the violin was not as yet

considered a noble instrument—'it was still the fiddle played for the dancing at village weddings and fêtes.'

3. Avenel, vol. iii, p. 184. (V.L.T.)

4. This institution was founded in 1594 by Antoine de Pluvinel, a Gascon and the author of a celebrated treatise on horsemanship. His academy is aptly described by O'Connell as a kind of cadet school. Pupils were, however, taught social accomplishments such as dancing and the lute as well as the military arts, fencing, etc. Both Richelieu and Father Joseph attended Pluvinel's academy as young men. See O'Connell, Ariès, Batiffol.

5. Father H. Griffet, *Histoire de Louis XIII*, vol. i, p. 209. (V.L.T.)

6. On this edict *see* also Lublinskaya, p. 172, Clarke, p. 66. For Jeanne d'Albret, *see* n. 19 below.

7. *Procureurs-généraux* or attorneys-general were the king's legal representatives in the Parlements and other sovereign courts and acted as public prosecutors on his behalf (Shennan). Like the two advocate-generals who were associated with him, a *procureur-général* enjoyed the same privileges as the presidents and counsellors of the Parlement. Collectively these three officials were known as *les gens du Roi* (Zeller).

8. For the significance of the title king of the Romans see Professor Tapié's comments below. Charles V's brother, Ferdinand (who succeeded him as emperor in 1558), had married in 1521 Anna, the daughter of Vladislav, king of Bohemia and Hungary (d. 1516). The latter was the son of Casimir IV of Poland and thus belonged to the house of Jagellon. His son Lewis who succeeded him in both kingdoms was defeated by the Turks at Mohács in 1526 and perished in the battle. Anna, however, lived until 1547. Since Lewis was childless, Ferdinand as his brother-in-law was a strong candidate for the thrones of both Bohemia and Hungary. He was elected to the Bohemian throne thus becoming the first Habsburg to rule over the kingdom of Bohemia; but in Hungary although he obtained the title of king, and before his death in 1564 induced the Hungarian Diet to crown his son, Ferdinand's share of the kingdom was in fact to be limited to a segment in the west and north which lay next to the Habsburg lands (i.e. Austria) and included much of what is now Slovakia. The remainder of Hungary was either brought under direct Turkish occupation or ruled over by the princes of Transylvania—a state of affairs which lasted until the end of the seventeenth century.

9. The term 'margrave' is derived from the German word *markgraf* which was originally used to denote a count who was military governor of a *mark* or border territory; it thus corresponds with the English and French titles, marquess and marquis.

Counts Palatine were originally high officials in royal service, and the office of Count Palatine of the Rhine dates from the middle of the tenth century; but the holders of this title soon became hereditary rulers, and the Rhenish Palatinate had by this date been ruled over by a branch of the Wittelsbach family for several hundred years. The contemporary English version of the German title was 'Palsgrave'.

10. The background to the Letter of Majesty and its terms are discussed by Professor Tapié in his chapter on the Habsburg lands in N.C.M.H., iv, and on p. 86 of his book *The Rise and Fall of the Habsburg Monarchy*.

11. British and American historians generally refer to Prague Castle by its Czech name Hradčany. For the course of events in Bohemia between 1609 and 1618 see Polišenský.

12. It is interesting to note that Žerotín was the brother-in-law of Wallenstein and the patron of Comenius—*see* Tapié, *Habsburg Monarchy*. For his important political role during these years *see* Polišenský.

13. Francis Gomar (1563–1641) and Jacobus Arminius (1560–1609) were leading theologians at the University of Leyden. The former, who taught at Saumur from 1614 to 1618, was a staunch upholder of Calvin's views on predestintion and bitterly opposed to religious toleration; whereas Arminius and his followers insisted that Jesus Christ died for all men and not only for the 'elect'—a view which had obvious political implications since it meant that Spanish Catholics enjoyed the same opportunities of winning salvation as Dutch Calvinists. In addition Arminius like Luther before him accepted the idea of a Church controlled by the State.

14. The state of Hungary during this period is outlined in n. 8 above. Gabriel Bethlen has for long been known as Bethlen Gábor in the English-speaking world; for instance we find James I's daughter Elizabeth of Bohemia writing in 1622: 'For Bethlen Gabors sending to the Turk I assure you the king [i.e. her husband] did know nothing of it'. (*Letters of Elizabeth, Queen of Bohemia* ed. L. M. Baker, p. 65). However, as Gábor is merely the Hungarian form of Gabriel, to refer to Gabriel Bethlen as Bethlen Gábor is like referring to Winston Churchill as Churchill Winston. Bethlen Gábor is certainly his correct name according to Hungarian usage, but its continued use in English seems unnecessarily misleading.

15. Polišenský notes that it was the knights who suffered most severely from the confiscations in Bohemia but that other sections of the population, in particular the burghers of Prague, were punished by means of fines etc., while Calvinist preachers were expelled from Bohemia in 1621 and all Protestant clergy from both Bohemia and Moravia in 1624. *See* his account of the activities of the confiscation commissions and their catastrophic social consequences on pp. 134–46 of his book.

16. Now Krnov in Northern Moravia. The margrave had been one of the leaders of the rebellion in Silesia and invaded Moravia in 1621.

17. The noble lady in question was Polyxena, the widow of the Chancellor Lobkovic or Lobkowitz who had been largely responsible for the Bohemian Diet's acceptance of Ferdinand as king-designate in 1617. The figure is apparently still widely known by its Italian name, *Bambino Gesù di Praga* (*see* Josef Polišenský *Gesellschaft und Kultur des Barocken Böhmens*, p. 118, a monograph published by the Österreicheische Ost-und Südosteuropa-Institut in Vienna). This lady whose house stood close to the Castle of Prague had earlier extended a helping hand, or rather a helping ladder, to the victims of the defenestration after they had fallen into the moat.

18. '. . . son étonnante *Transverbération de Sainte Thérèse*.' Santa Maria della Vittoria was also a Carmelite church—hence the representation of Saint Teresa who was canonised in 1622. She gives an account of her ecstasy or mystical 'transverberation' by an angel in the twenty-ninth chapter of her autobiography which was written *c.* 1560. To refer to it as a 'legend' as David Maland does when describing Bernini's masterpiece in his excellent text book *Europe in the Seventeenth Century* (Macmillan, London 1966) seems, therefore, rather odd.

19. Henry IV's mother Jeanne d'Albret, queen of Navarre, died in 1572 (the Salic Law applied in France but not in Navarre). Upper Navarre on the south side of the Pyrenees had been occupied by the Spaniards in 1512, leaving less than a quarter of the original territory of Navarre under the rule of the house of Albret. Béarn thus became the largest and most important of its remaining possessions. A useful account of Béarn and its institutions is given in Nancy L. Roelker's book on Jeanne d'Albret (see bibliography, p. 543). Henry IV had already annexed the counties of Foix and Bigorre to the French Crown (Lublinskaya, p. 171) so that by annexing Lower Navarre and Béarn Louis XIII completed the process of absorption.

20. Montgomery had been accidentally responsible for mortally wounding Henry II in a tournament in 1559. He was then Captain of the Scots Guards. He subsequently played a very active part in the Wars of Religion, conducting a brilliant defence of Béarn on behalf of the Huguenots in 1569, but was captured and beheaded as a traitor five years later.

21. In 1621 Daniel Tilenus the theologian to whom Bouillon had entrusted the education of his second son (later the celebrated French marshal Turenne) published a pamphlet under a pseudonym advising the Huguenots to behave like dutiful subjects (*Avertissement à l'Assemblée de la Rochelle* par Abraham Elintus, Paris, 1621). (V.L.T.) [For further details of this pamphlet *see* Clarke, p. 76, where reference is made to W. J. Stankiewicz, *Politics and Religion in Seventeenth Century France*, p. 84]

22. This was a permanent military force known as the *gendarmerie de la garde du roi*. As constituted in 1609 it consisted of 210 mounted men at arms (*gendarmes*) all in theory of noble birth. The king himself was their captain with a captain-lieutenant as his deputy and it was their duty to accompany him everywhere. *See* Marion.

23. The Franciscan Third Order was founded by St Francis for those who lived in the world but wished to try to attain Christian perfection. Tertiaries belong to the Franciscan movement but do not live in communities or take public vows and they remain lay persons. However, their admission and noviciate are governed by rules regarding poverty, temperance etc. *See* N.C.E.

24. In her book *French absolutism: the crucial phase* Professor Lublinskaya, who maintains that this treaty was signed on 15 not on 25 April, puts forward the suggestion (p. 180) that it was the news of its signature (which could reasonably be supposed to have reached the French king about a fortnight to three weeks later) that prompted Louis XIII and Luynes to launch their campaign against the Huguenots early in May 1621 as described above on p. 123. She points out that its effect was to make it unnecessary for France to go to war with Spain over the Valtelline; and in support of her theory she states that it was not until 28 April that the king left Fontainebleau for Orleans and only on 5 May that he moved westwards towards the Huguenot town of Saumur. Her argument is that up to 5 May it would thus have been perfectly possible for Louis XIII to have opted for marching southeast rather than west, in which case his aim would have been not to fight the Huguenots, but to make a warlike demonstration against the Spaniards in Italy; and as evidence that this possibility was a real one she mentions French military preparations during the preceding months, the vigorous protest that Bassompierre, the French envoy to Madrid, had been instructed to make against Spanish occupation of the Valtelline and the advice of Lesdiguières, then Marshal-General of the King's Camps, that war be declared on Spain rather than on the Huguenots.

Unfortunately Professor Lublinskaya does not seem to have consulted Professor Tapié's earlier work published in 1934, *La politique étrangère de la France et le début de la guerre de Trente Ans (1616–21)*, from which it is clear that the Huguenots had already diverted the French government's attention from European affairs some time before the signature of the Treaty of Madrid (pp. 619–20). In his biography of Henri de Rohan, Clarke mentions that the Huguenot Assembly which met at La Rochelle in the winter of 1620–21 had refused to disperse twice in January and February despite Louis XIII's orders, and states that this disobedience provoked a strong reaction in the King's Council. He quotes Rohan as promising his fellow Huguenots in February that he would do all he could to 'appease this storm' and refers to Luynes as 'exhorting the king to go in person and pacify the Huguenot provinces' (op. cit., pp. 74–6). According to Professor Tapié in his work cited above it was with this object in view that Luynes was appointed Constable on 2 April and the king's army left Fontainebleau for Orleans towards the middle of the same month 'résolu d'y faire peu de séjour et de passer outre'. This last passage is a quotation from a letter written by Louis XIII himself on 27 April which Professor Tapié convincingly interprets as meaning that the king intended to embark on his campaign against the Huguenots without delay; and according to Clarke it was in fact on that day that 'the king placed himself at the head of the royal army and marched against the rebels' (op. cit., p. 77).

In view of all this it is impossible to accept Professor Lublinskaya's suggestion that the French government may have contemplated making a warlike demonstration against Spain at this time, nor is there any evidence to support the hypothesis that Louis XIII delayed taking action against the Huguenots until the news of the signature of the treaty of Madrid had reached him. On the contrary, whatever may have been the date on which the treaty was signed, the categorical statement by Professor Tapié (op. cit., p. 620) that, the king did not even wait for news of the upshot of Bassompierre's mission'—a statement which rests on the evidence of two authorities—would seem to be perfectly correct.

25. For details of these changes *see* Lublinskaya, pp. 258–9.

26. The various factors that contributed to the fall of La Vieuville are discussed at some length by Professor Lublinskaya in the last ten pages of the chapter entitled 'The financiers and the absolute monarchy.'

CHAPTER FOUR: Richelieu in the Service of King and Nation (1624–27)

1. Her husband, the nephew of Luynes, was killed at the siege of Montpellier in 1622 and she never remarried. (V.L.T.)

2. H. Hauser, *La pensée et l'action économiques du Cardinal de Richelieu.* (V.L.T.)

3. The French reads as follows: 'Je lui promis (à V.M.) d'employer toute mon industrie et toute l'autorité qu'il lui plaisait me donner pour ruiner le parti huguenot, rabaisser l'orgueil des Grands, réduire tous ses sujets en leur devoir et relever son nom dans les nations étrangères au point où il devait être.' Translations of both this and the two preceding quotations are to be found in Hill, pp. 9–11.

4. *Les principaux poincts de la Foy de l'Eglise catholique défendus contre l'escrit adressé au Roy par les quatre ministres de Charenton*, pr R. P. en Dieu Messire Armand Jean du Plessis de Richelieu, Evesque de Luçon. Poitiers, A. Mesnier, 1617; 2e édition, Paris, Moreau, 1618. (V.L.T.)

5. M. Deloche, *Autour de la plume du Cardinal de Richelieu*, p. 133. (V.L.T.)

6. The origins of this famous church, for long the parish church of the Louvre, go back to the early eighth century when it was called Saint Germain le Neuf. Its present name, dating from about the beginning of the twelfth century, is to be explained by the fact that in addition to Saint Germain or Germanus, bishop of Auxerre, there was a saint of the same name who was bishop of Paris in the sixth century (see chapter 7, n. 33). The former was born *c.* 378 and seems to have visited Britain twice. St Patrick was probably one of his pupils. (Cross, N.C.E.)

7. For details of two other pamphlets written by Fancan *see* Lublinskaya, pp. 265–6. In

giving this title to his pamphlet the author intended to single out L'Hôpital and Bayard as models of disinterested patriotism, the one conspicuous for the political wisdom that he displayed at the outset of the Wars of Religion, the other distinguished for his absolute loyalty to the king and for his chivalrous behaviour and feats of arms during the Italian Wars.

8. '*Sur le parvis de Notre-Dame*'. Carola Oman who gives a colourful description of the ceremony states that a temporary platform was erected for the purpose outside the west door of the cathedral (*see* her *Henrietta Maria* (1939 edition), p. 32). For a description of Notre-Dame and its precincts in 1600, *see* Ranum, *Paris*, pp. 9–10.

9. The name of the first of these islands used to be spelt Rhé, but according to Gibb (p. 265, n.) the modern spelling was already beginning to creep into use at this time. It is some 17 miles long and lies about 1½ miles from the mainland, approximately 5 miles to the west of La Rochelle. Oléron which is roughly twice as large lies about seven miles to the south of Ré.

10. A *maréchal de camp* ('marshall of the camp' in contemporary English) was of the same military rank as a brigadier-general. Originally it had been his primary duty to precede the main body of the army to ensure that the route chosen presented no obstacles and to make arrangements for the next camp (Littré). However he had increasingly begun to act as a chief of staff (Zeller, p. 316).

11. Avenel, vol. i, p. 83. (V.L.T.)

12. Avenel, vol. i, pp. 121–2. (V.L.T.)

13. Avenel, vol.i, pp. 120–1. (V.L.T.)

14. Avenel, vol. i, p. 168. (V.L.T.)

15. Professor Lublinskaya, who makes use of unpublished documentary material in the Saltykov-Shchedrin Library, Leningrad, gives a valuable analysis of the general political background to the Treaty of Monzón and of the widespread anger that it aroused among France's allies.

16. Professor Tapié refers to Chalais's uncle as 'le commandant de Valençay.'

The Order of the Knights of St John of Malta still held very considerable possessions scattered all over Catholic Europe. The Order was composed at this date of seven 'nations' or 'tongues'—three of which (Provence, Auvergne and France) were French. Each 'tongue' was divided into priorates which were in turn sub-divided into commanderies. A member of the Order who had the custody of such a group of estates or manors was therefore known as a commander. A brief summary of the position of the Order in France in the sixteenth century is given in Doucet, ii, p. 759; *cf.* Marion under the heading *Ordres de chevalerie religieuse*. For a short account of Valençay's interesting career *see* Hanotaux, iii, p. 72.

17. There is a place called Maison Rouge which lies about 20 miles to the north-east of Fontainebleau in the present-day department of Seine et Marne. However, the reference here is almost certainly to a house which stood on the left bank of the Seine near Essones and was visited by Evelyn on his way back to Paris from Fontainebleau in 1644—*see* Evelyn, ii, p. 120: '. . . an house cal'd Maison Rouge incomparable for its Prospect, Grott and Fountaines one whereoff rises 50 foote from the ground . . .'

18. The title *secrétaire des commandements* had earlier been given to those secretaries who were allowed to sign a letter on the sovereign's behalf if the latter ordered them to do so. In the second half of the sixteenth century those directly in the king's service generally came to be known as *secrétaires d'état*, although the title *sécretaire d'état et des commandements*

was still frequently used in Louis XIII's reign (Ranum, *Richelieu*, p. 47, n. 1). In the case of the secretary who served the queen mother it is evident that the old title continued to be used (*see* Sutherland, p. 173). For a short account of Claude Bouthillier's career and connections with Richelieu's family *see* Ranum, *Richelieu*, p. 32.

19. Alexandre de Vendôme bore the title of Grand Prior of France, i.e. of the Knights of Malta—*see* n. 16 above.

20. It has since become a convent belonging to the Sisters of the Order of the Visitation. (V.L.T.)

21. The Minims were an order of mendicants founded by St Francis of Paola in the fifteenth century—their name giving emphasis to their cult of humility in regarding themselves as the least (*minimi*) of all those devoted to God's service. One of their vows binds them to abstain not only from meat and fish but also from all dairy produce. The order flourished particularly in seventeenth-century France. Under the French version of his name, St François de Paule, the founder of the Minims had become celebrated throughout France for his austerities and miracles long before his death in 1507, and it was there that he spent the last twenty five years of his life. (N.C.E., Cross)

22. Blaise de Montluc (*c.* 1502–77) served in Italy under Bayard as a young man, was knighted by Francis I and in the reign of Henry II conducted a brilliant defence of Siena. He was a staunch royalist in the Wars of Religion and Henry III made him a marshal of France. A selection from his *Commentaries* edited by I. Roy has recently been published in England (Longmans, London, 1972).

23. The Franciscan Observants or Observantines (so called because they claimed to observe strictly the primitive rule of St Francis) were known as Cordeliers in France because of the knotted cord which they used to wear around their waists.

24. Griffet, *Histoire de Louis XIII*, vol. 1, p. 545. (V.L.T.)

25. H. Hauser, *La pensée et l'action économiques du Cardinal de Richelieu*. (V.L.T.)

26. . . . *en supprimant les grandes charges*. The offices of Constable and of Admiral of France came into this category, the holders of these titles being classified as *Grands Officiers de la Couronne* together with the Chancellor, the Grand Equerry and others (for a complete list *see* Zeller, p. 120). Louis XIII did not of course abolish all these *grandes charges*.

27. Griffet, op. cit., vol. i, p. 530. (V.L.T.)

28. This speech is printed in Avenel, vol. ii, pp. 297 ff. (V.L.T.)

29. Avenel, vol. ii, p. 299. (V.L.T.)

30. It would appear that the towns which Richelieu had in mind were Rouen, Amiens, Troyes, Dijon, Lyons, Toulouse, Bordeaux, Poitiers, Rennes, La Flèche and Pau—*see* Hauser, op. cit., p. 64, n. 2.

31. Hauser op. cit., p. 65. It is interesting to compare Richelieu's views with those of Francis Bacon. In 1611 Bacon wrote to James I as follows: 'Concerning the advancement of learning, I do subscribe to the opinion . . . that, for grammar schools, there are already too many. . . . The great number of schools which are in your Highness's realm doth cause a want, and likewise an overthrow—both of them inconvenient and one of them dangerous; for by means thereof they find want in the country and towns, both of servants for husbandry and of apprentices for trade; and on the other side there being more Scholars bred than the State can prefer and employ . . . it must needs fall out that many persons will be bred unfit for other vocations and unprofitable for that in which they were bred up, which fill the realm full of indigent, idle and wanton people . . .'. (J. Spedding, *Life of Bacon*, vol. iv, pp. 252–3).

32. *See* Hill, pp. 14–19, where Richelieu's views on education are given at greater length.

33. Avenel, vol. ii, p. 303. (V.L.T.)

34. *Cf.* however the explanation Professor Lublinskaya puts forward for the cardinal's reference to a six-year period in the last chapter of her book, 'Richelieu's administration 1625–27'. This explanation is also given by J. P. Cooper, the editor of N.C.M.H. iv, *see* pp. 40–1.

CHAPTER FIVE: The Western Seaboard, La Rochelle and Italy

1. John Viénot, *Histoire de la Réforme française* (V.L.T.)

2. This town which lies to the north-east of La Rochelle is now some five miles from the sea.

3. Ed. André, p. 104. (V.L.T.)

4. Op. cit., p. 75. (V.L.T.)

5. The quotations given here are slightly fuller than those given by Professor Tapié as they have been copied directly from the original document bearing Charles I's signature in the Public Record Office, London (State Papers Domestic, Charles I, vol. lxvii no. 57). This document is entitled: 'Instructions for our right trusty and most entirely beloved Cousin and Councillor George Duke of Buckingham our High Admiral of England.' The instructions were 'given at our Court at Southwick the nineteenth day of June 1627' (the dating is of course old style). Southwick is near Fareham in Hampshire. Charles I was residing there when Buckingham was assassinated at Portsmouth in the following year.

6. H. Hauser op. cit., p. 41. (V.L.T.) [This quotation has been translated rather freely to give it greater impact. The French runs as follows: 'J'ai le coeur tout serré quand je viens à considérer les discours que font de nous tous les étrangers quand ils parlent de la France. Et me disaient: quelle puissance à votre Roi, vu qu'en toutes ses forces il n'a pu vaincre un gentilhomme de ses sujets sans l'assistance d'Angleterre, de la Hollande et de Malte: à plus forte raison s'il avait guerre contre le roi d'Angleterre?']

7. Jeanne Françoise de Chantal (1572–1641), often referred to in the English-speaking world as St Jane Chantal, founded the Order of the Visitation for girls and widows in 1610 with the help of St François de Sales after having herself been widowed nine years previously. *See* N.C.E., Cross, the chapter entitled 'A generation of saints' in Ranum, *Paris*, and the biography by Elizabeth Stropp mentioned in the bibliography at the end of this book (p.542) Madame de Sévigné (1626–96) was of course one of the most famous letter-writers of all time.

8. For a short account of Targone's career see *Enciclopedia Italiana,* vol. xxiii. The family of Métezeau formed a dynasty of architects just as the Couperin family was later to form a dynasty of composers and musicians. The architect mentioned here is Clément II (1581–1652).

9. This was Alonso de la Cueva, marqués de Bedmar, who had become the resident Spanish ambassador in Brussels in 1618. A man of considerable ability, who was hostile to the liberties and privileges allowed to the provinces of the Spanish Netherlands, he acquired very great influence over the Archduchess Isabella, the sole governor after her husband's death in 1621; but he became so unpopular that in 1629 it was necessary to recall him to Spain.

10. Before he founded the Carthusian Order Saint Bruno (*c.* 1030–1101) was offered the archbishopric of Rheims, where he had already won fame as a teacher and been appointed chancellor cf the diocese; but he preferred to withdraw into the mountains and forests near Grenoble and founded the Grande Chartreuse there *c.* 1084. While visiting Italy some years later at the invitation of his former pupil, Pope Urban II, he refused the archbishopric of Reggio, preferring to retire to the wilds of Calabria where he died after founding a hermitage. (N.C.E., Cross).

11. The Petits Pères were discalced (i.e. barefoot or sandalled) Augustinians or Augustinian recollects, a subdivision of the order of Augustinian hermits or friars which spread from Spain into France at the end of the sixteenth century—where they were given the nickname of Petits Pères because the founders of the first congregation in France were short in stature. They were originally established in Paris by Marguerite de Valois. The church of Notre-Dame-des-Victoires here mentioned still survives, but underwent considerable alteration in the eighteenth century. It stands in what is now the Place des Petits Pères. (Information supplied by the Rev. J. R. Fox, C.R.; *see also* Cross and Evans).

12. Jules Michelet (1798–1874), who came of a family of Huguenot extraction, was one of the leading French historians of the nineteenth century. His history of France in nineteen volumes has become a literary classic. Michelet's work as a whole, which covers an enormous range of time and subject, is distinguished by a vivid style and characterised by a mixture of erudition, prejudice and patriotism. *See* Pieter Geyl's penetrating essay in his *Debates with Historians* (Fontana Library, Collins, London 1962).

13. According to Lublinskaya (p. 219 n.) the population of La Rochelle which had numbered 28,000 in 1627 had been reduced to 5,400 at the time of the surrender and many of the survivors died soon afterwards from exhaustion.

14. Of the various books on Wallenstein the most important is that written by the Czech historian J. Pekař (1870–1937),—not so much on account of its length (2 vols) as because of its penetrating judgements and the novelty of its interpretation. Georges Pagès gives a good analysis of Pekař's views in *La Guerre de Trente Ans* (Payot, 1939). (V.L.T.) [This last-named work together with its English translation of which particulars are given on p. 459 is generally referred to by the author's name alone in subsequent notes. Bibliographical details of the Czech and German editions of Pekař's book on Wallenstein and of an English translation of the epilogue are given on pp. 516, 588. For fuller particulars of Pekař's work and of more recent publications relating to Wallenstein see Polišenský, pp. 283–6 and Tapié, *Habsburg Monarchy*, p. 110, where reference is also made to *Wallenstein und seine Anhänger* by the Finnish historian Suvanto (Helsinki, 1963)].

15. For Wallenstein's territorial acquisitions in Bohemia proper after the battle of the White Mountain, see Professor Tapié's *Habsburg Monarchy*, p. 101; p. 519 of his chapter 'The Habsburg Lands' in N.C.M.H., iv; and Polisenský, pp. 155, 181, from which it appears that the nucleus of Wallenstein's duchy of Friedland, which included its capital Jičín, consisted of lands formerly belonging to his maternal uncles the Smiřický and acquired by him in 1623 to protect them from the threat of confiscation. It should be noted that Albrecht Jan Smiřický had been one of the ringleaders of the rebellion of 1618 and that the family were among the greatest landowners of Bohemia.

Professor Tapié also stresses the fact that Wallenstein himself was already by that date a very rich landowner in his native province of Moravia—largely as a result of his marriage earlier to a wealthy young widow who had died leaving him all her possessions. However he seems to have sold his Moravian lands in the same year as he acquired the lands of his uncles in Bohemia (Polišenský).

16. Avenel, vol. iii, p. 180. (V.L.T.)

17. Neuchâtel had come into the possession of the family of Longueville by marriage at the beginning of the sixteenth century. It was converted to Protestantism by Farel in 1529–30. Abortive attempts had been made by its rulers on several occasions to sell the county first to Fribourg and Bern in the sixteenth century and then in 1615, 1618 and 1623 to the duke of Savoy. However, the price asked was too high for the latter's taste. France did not in fact embark on a policy of active interference in Neuchâtel until the male line of the house of Longueville began to show signs of dying out in Louis XIV's reign. *See Dictionnaire historique et biographique de la Suisse*, Vol. v.

18. In translating all this passage I have made some use of the excerpts from Richelieu's memorandum given by Mariéjol (p. 291).

19. Avenel, vol. iii, p. 151. (V.L.T.)

20. A translation of part of this section of the ordinance is printed in Shennan, *Government*, pp. 109–10. Aldermen of towns in the south of France (including Lyons) were usually styled *consuls* whereas in the north they were generally known as *échevins*. Note that the title *consuls* or *juges-consuls* was also borne by the merchant judges appointed by the guilds (or sometimes by the aldermen of the town concerned) to settle disputes between guild members (Zeller, pp. 191–2).

21. Note written by Richelieu in July 1629; Avenel, vol. iii, p. 376. (V.L.T.)

22. Richelieu to Le Mazuyer: Avenel, vol. iii, p. 364. (V.L.T.) [For Rohan's secret negotiations with the Spaniards after Charles I had made peace with Louis XIII by the treaty of Susa, *see* Clarke, Mariéjol, p. 273].

23. The daily recitation of the Divine Office (consisting of Mattins, Lauds, Prime, Terce, Sext, None, Vespers and Compline) was in theory obligatory for all Catholic clergy.

historique, vol. clxxiv (1937). (V.L.T.)

25. Ibid., p. 24, n. 1. (V.L.T.)

26. *See* Richelieu's *Mémoires* (under the year 1630) and Avenel, vol. iii, p. 664 ('Avis du Cardinal en réponse à celui du garde des Sceaux'). (V.L.T.)

CHAPTER SIX: The Misery of the People and the Glory of the State

1. Georges Pagès was the first to stress the significance of these outbreaks in his article, 'Autour du Grand Orage: Richelieu et Marillac, deux politiques' [*see* chapter 5, n. 24] which was based on his researches among documents in the Archives des Affaires étrangères (Mémoires et documents) and in the Archives Nationales (series E). After the Second World War, in 1948, a book by the Russian historian B. F. Porshnev entitled *Popular revolts in France prior to the Fronde from 1623 to 1648* was published by the Academy of Sciences of the U.S.S.R.* In the appendix were printed a number of documents, most of them previously unpublished. The manuscripts used by Porshnev form part of a collection that formerly belonged to the French Chancellor Séguier (1588–1672) which is of exceptional historical value. After various peregrinations the details of which are obscure, this collection of Séguier's papers reached Russia after the French Revolution of

---

* [The French form of this historian's name is Porchnev; but in this translation the English form is invariably used except when specific reference is made to the French edition of his book].

1789 and has remained there ever since. As a source for the historian it is far from being exhausted for it remains to a considerable extent unexplored. (V.L.T.)

2. The function of a notary is to draw up formally such documents as deeds, inventories, and wills in such a way as to establish their authenticity. Notaries were to be found not only serving in the secretariats of the various Parlements where their technical expertise in such matters was clearly of great value, but also in almost every town in France. A notary royal—as distinct from a notary apostolic, for example, who would be appointed by a bishop or archbishop and might be the registrar of an ecclesiastical court—was allowed to carry out his duties only within the area where the court to which he was subordinate exercised its jurisdiction. The proliferation of notaries under the *ancien régime* was partly due to the continual creation of fresh offices by the Crown, but also because, as Zeller puts it: 'Quiconque possédait quelque bien n'envisageait pas de quitter ce monde sans avoir fait donner forme authentique à l'énumération des legs pieux dont, peut-être, dépendait le salut de son âme. Et les contrats de louage de travail ou d'apprentissage étaient d'usage courant' (p. 216). Such an occupation obviously gave plenty of scope for chicanery and for the exploitation of ignorant people.

3. A graphic description of the infuriating nature of these indirect taxes is given by W. H. Lewis in *The Splendid Century* (pp. 85–6). For a short biography of Antoine Feydeau (1572–1627), one of the richest and most powerful financiers of the period who contrived to control two out of the four largest tax-farms in France before ending his career in bankruptcy, see Lublinskaya, pp. 241–2; she also refers to a study by P. Heumann, 'Un traitant sous Louis XIII: Antoine Feydeau', printed in *Études sur l'histoire administrative et sociale de l'Ancien Régime*, ed. G. Pagès (Paris 1938); *cf.* Treasure, p. 65 n. Of the four large tax-farms mentioned above that of the *aides de France* was one, while two more, the *cinq grosses fermes* and the *gabelles de France,* are touched upon in the following footnote but one.

Despite their name the *aides de France* did not apply to the whole realm. 'France' meant the area under the direct rule of the king of France when these taxes were first introduced under Charles V in the fourteenth century—a large area of northern and central France, 'the heartland of France' which included both Poitou and Champagne.

In 1604 the collection of these *aides* had been consolidated by Sully and leased en bloc to a tax-farmer named Jean de Moisset. The adoption of this system resulted in a threefold increase in the yield from *aides* between 1604 and 1624. Large-scale tax farms such as this were styled *fermes-générales*. The lease used to be put up for public auction by the government at periodic intervals and the farm would then be awarded to the person who had made the highest bid who was known as the *adjudicataire-général*. Whether or not this person was acting as a member of a syndicate of financiers the lease was invariably let to him alone. In effect he became the administrator-general of the tax-farm, which he then proceeded to split up amongst sub-farmers who were answerable to him and who worked under his supervision. It was the task of the functionaries known as *commis des aides* to draw up inventories of wine held by wine-producers, vintners etc. Once these were completed the business of collecting the wholesale or retail taxes began. As for the *huitième* despite its name it was not in fact an *ad valorem* tax of an eighth. (For further details *see* Lublinskaya, pp. 236–40; Matthews, 41–5, 158–61).

4. Note that the office of *élu* which was inferior to that of *trésorier de France* (*see* chapter 1, n. 39 above) did not carry with it noble rank but represented the top echelon of the Third Estate. Even so, 'by the middle of the seventeenth century an *élu* would not pay very much less than 10,000 livres for his office' (Shennan, *Government*, pp. 58–9). In addition to apportioning the amount of *taille* payable by each town or parish in his *élection*,

the *élu* possessed certain judicial powers in fiscal matters and charged fees for issuing receipts, confirming accounts etc. He was thus an obvious target for popular animosity.

5. The word *croquant*, which occurs again later in this translation, can be roughly translated as clodhopper. It first appears at the end of the sixteenth century and the theories that have been put forward about its origin are of some interest. In 1593 a peasant rising which quickly became known as 'l'insurrection des croquants' broke out in the Limousin and neighbouring districts. From the account given by J. Nouillac in *Histoire du Limousin et de la Marche* (p. 160) it seems that the rebels adopted the battle cry 'Aux croquants' when launching attacks on their oppressors because it was they who used to scrunch up (*croquer*) the livelihood of the poor. However, as a result of the depredations of the peasant army the term was soon applied by the nobility to the rebels themselves. It thus became a nickname and acquired a new meaning.

From Littré's comments on the origins of the word it is evident that this account is based on that given by de Thou; according to d'Aubigné, another contemporary historian of this period, the term *croquant* was derived from a village called Croc where the first rebels assembled. Littré also draws attention to the word *croquart* used by Froissart.

6. Porchnev (French edition, p. 265) attributes both these riots to hunger and to the price of corn. It should be noted that Troyes is not only situated on the Seine but also lay within the area of the *cinq grosses fermes* to which Professor Tapié refers on p. 59 above (see maps in N.C.M.H. Atlas and Matthews). *Deniers d'octroi* were so called because they were revenues from taxes that were granted to a town for a limited number of years by a *lettre d'octroi* signed by the king. Although they were municipal customs dues, they were often levied by tax-farmers who were in effect royal agents, the proceeds being devoted to public works such as town fortifications which were not necessarily popular. They could be imposed on both corn and flour as well as on salt. (Zeller, pp. 50–1, Marion, and Nora Temple 'The control and exploitation of French towns during the ancien régime' *in History* Vol. li (1966)).

In addition Troyes was subject to the exactions of the tax-farmers responsible for levying the *gabelles de France*, since it lay in the area (comprising much of north and central France) known as the *pays de grandes gabelles* where the salt tax was most onerous (see maps as above). This tax-farm had come into being in 1598; Feydeau was its chief farmer from 1622 to 1624. (Matthews, p. 44; Lublinskaya, pp. 238, 242.)

7. This passage has been expanded to explain the meaning of the term *sel du devoir*. Like Champagne, Maine was a *pays de grandes gabelles*.

8. This official was responsible for receiving the *taille* at the level of the *élection* after its collection in the parishes. (Zeller, p. 279.)

9. This rising, led by the vine-growers of Dijon, who occupied a whole quarter of the town, was prompted by rumours that drinks were to be taxed. The word *Lanturlu* comes from the chorus of a song which was sung by the rebels. Originally it was meaningless, but it developed the sense of a contemptuous or mocking refusal. *See* Mousnier-Pearce, Littré and Robert.

10. *See La Vénalité des Offices sous Henri IV et Louis XIII*, pp. 268–9. (V.L.T.)

11. Avenel, vol. III, p. 774. (V.L.T.)

12. Saint Roch(e) or Rocco (*c*. 1295–1327) seems to have been a native of Montpellier. The largely legendary account of his life credits him with curing innumerable victims of the plague by miraculous means both whilst on a pilgrimage to Rome and during his subsequent travels in Italy. (Cross, Attwater.)

13. This was the official designation of the kingdom of Bohemia. Prince Václav or

Wenceslas had ruled over Bohemia from 921 to 929 when his attempts to spread Christianity among his partly pagan subjects were cut short by his murder. He was subsequently adopted as patron saint of Bohemia and his likeness used to feature on emblems of Bohemian sovereignty such as seals, coins etc.

14. Wallenstein's famous threat deserves to be repeated in the original words used by Arnim (printed by Roberts, vol. ii, p. 682, n. 8). According to Arnim it ran as follows: 'Der kayser mitt seinem gantzen hause soll schmerzlich sehen und empfinden dass er einen cavallier affrontired hab'.

15. Louis Batiffol's account of this crisis in his two books *Richelieu et Louis XIII* and *La journée des Dupes* is both full and well-informed and may be taken as definitive. (V.L.T.)

16. H. Griffet, vol. ii, p. 61. (V.L.T.)

17. Guillaume Bautru, comte de Serrant, who served as Richelieu's envoy to the Spanish Court on more than one occasion was both a friend of Monsieur and a notorious rake as well as a man of considerable intelligence: 'a cunning courtier quite capable of giving to even the most outrageous lies the character and colour of truth.' (Clarke p. 133.) See Georges Mongrédien's article on him in the *Revue des questions historiques*, April 1931.

18. L. Batiffol, *Richelieu et Louis XIII*, pp. 83, 291 ff. (V.L.T.)

19. The Richelieu family estate was elevated into a *duché-pairie* with this object in view. (V.L.T.)

20. According to Burckhardt ii, p. 379 n., where his name is given as Jaroslav Sezyma Rašín, he was appointed to approach Gustavus Adolphus on Wallenstein's behalf by the latter's brother-in-law Adam Trčka (referred to in N.C.M.H., iv, p. 337 as Adam Terzka). Trčka, together with his émigré relative Vilém Kinský, was to play a leading part in the anti-Habsburg intrigues of 1633–4 to which Wallenstein lent his name and which are described in chapter 8.

CHAPTER SEVEN: France under Richelieu

1. Avenel, vol. iv, p. 728. (V.L.T.). [An English translation of this passage is also given by Ranum on p. 136 of his book *Richelieu and the Councillors of Louis XIII* (hereafter referred to as Ranum *Richelieu*)].

2. The *brevet* both authorised the levy of the *taille* and gave details of the total amount that was to be collected:- 'For the direct taxes in the *pays d'élections* the Superintendent [of Finance] drew up a *brevet des tailles* which after being submitted to the king for approval was broken down for an appropriate extract to be sent to each *généralité* [i.e. to each major financial circumscription]'—Buisseret, p. 59. The most important of the supplementary levies to the *taille* was known as the *taillon* or little taille. It was introduced in 1549 to pay for the upkeep of garrisons and soon incorporated into the larger tax. (Zeller, pp. 260, 326.)

3. As mentioned earlier, Brian Pearce, the translator of Lublinskaya, points out (p. 307, n. 4) that *traitants* were distinguished from *fermiers* in that the form of the contracts they signed with the government was different, but that it is not possible to draw this distinction between them in English.

4. As already mentioned, in each *généralité* there was a *bureau des finances* presided over by 10 *trésoriers de France* and 3 *receveurs-généraux*. The latter, one of whom served every three years, supervised the collection of all royal revenues whether ordinary or

extraordinary within the *généralité* and exercised authority over the collectors of particular royal revenues (Shennan, *Government*, p. 54). When sufficient sums had been accumulated to justify their dispatch to Paris under guard, the *receveurs-généraux* would send them to the central treasury after deducting various items of local expenditure and collection-expenses. The latter are unknown so far as the tax-farmers are concerned but in the case of the *taille* it has been estimated that they amounted to about a quarter of the net income. In addition it was the *receveurs-généraux* who paid the salaries of the *trésoriers de France*. As Buisseret puts it: 'Perhaps the weakest point of the local organisation [of the financial administration] was the disinclination of the *bureaux* effectively to supervise their *receveurs-généraux* . . . the financial officials of the provinces formed a compact social group . . . the Normandy estates thus complained . . . that "most of the *trésoriers* are related to the *receveurs* which is why justice is not observed in the administration" (pp. 60, 67).

5. *Rentes* in the sense used here meant broadly speaking either of the following:

Rentes constituées which were interest-bearing loans negotiated between private persons.

Rentes sur l'Hôtel de Ville. There were government bonds backed by the corporations of the cities of Paris, Lyons or Rouen which were put up for sale at irregular intervals.

In each case the transaction (which resembled the purchase of an annuity) had a formal character and it is now realised that *rentes constituées* were a far more frequent form of investment than was previously supposed. Note as further examples of *rentes* connected with institutions the references to *rentes sur le domaine royal* and *rentes sur le clergé* on pp. 106, 347.

6. R. Mousnier, op. cit., pp. 335–6, 342. (V.L.T.)

7. *See* Magne, pp. 145–6. *Domaines* was the generic name given to the king's ordinary and permanent revenues from Crown lands (Matthews, pp. 8, 39, 175). Provins is a small town in the present department of Seine-et-Marne. In effect Madame de Montglat bought the right to farm or levy (a) indirect taxes such as *aides* (imposed chiefly on wine) and (b) various dues, tolls, rents and so forth, in and around the town and seigneurie of Provins; and she then entrusted the actual collection to tax-farmers, who in return paid her a handsome annuity.

8. H. Hauser, op. cit., p. 186. The relevant passage in the *Testament politique* (chapter 9. 'The Power of the Prince', section 6, 'Commerce') runs as follows: 'It is a common yet true saying that just as States often extend their boundaries by war, so they normally grow rich through trade in time of peace.' However, the problem is to make peace secure; the first step is therefore to determine under what conditions it can be regarded as secure or acceptable. It was certainly Richelieu's primary concern that France should extricate herself from her precarious position and bring about a permanent European peace settlement; but he did not believe that he could achieve this aim without first engaging in war. (V.L.T.)

9. *Testament politique*, ed. André, p. 379. (V.L.T.)

10. According to evidence cited by Lublinskaya (p. 127, n. 3) there were 60 rich foreign merchants residing in Rouen alone in 1625–6.

11. Lublinskaya mentions (p. 141, n. 1) that the constitutions of the Dutch trading companies were published in *Le Mercure François* (an official organ) in 1623–4.

12. Lublinskaya points out that the words 'Nacelle de Saint-Pierre' or 'St Peter's boat' are a figurative description of the Catholic Church; the adjective 'fleurdelysée' was of course added to the company's name to emphasise the fact that it was both royal and

French. She adds that 'one of the organisers had the intention of redeeming Frenchmen who had been taken prisoner by the Algerian pirates with money raised by selling exemptions from keeping fast-days. The pope issued such indulgences and it may be that the name given to the company signifies that it was intended to place it under the high patronage of the pope on the one hand and of the king on the other' (p. 284—*see* notes 2 and 4).

13. The town of Trois-Rivières or Three Rivers is situated on the St Lawrence roughly midway between Quebec and Montreal. Acadia, an area which included what are now New Brunswick and Nova Scotia, had been visited by the French in the sixteenth century and Champlain himself had played a leading part in the foundation of settlements there in 1604–5. In 1613 however these settlements were attacked and razed to the ground by English colonists from Virginia. Subsequently a small number of Scottish settlers arrived, only to leave again when Acadia was restored to France by the Treaty of St Germain-en-Laye in March 1632.

14. These ports were collectively known to the French as les Échelles and this is the name that Professor Tapié gives them. The term was also applied to the Levant generally.

15. Compare all this paragraph with Lublinskaya, p. 125, n. 2.

16. These agreements, concluded by successive Sultans of Turkey with the French in particular, and drawn up in Latin, were so called because they were divided into headings or chapters (*capitula*).

17. It was common practice to refer to Aleppo as if it was a port: e.g. in *Macbeth*, Act I, scene iii, the First Witch says:
'Her husband's to Aleppo gone, master o'the *Tiger*,
But in a sieve I'll thither sail'.
The reason for this was probably that, whereas Aleppo was a great city, its port Alexandretta was 'a poore Village built all of straw and durt' where 'the Merchants doe unloade their goods but themselves make haste to Haleppo, committing the care of carrying their goods thither upon Camels to the Factors of their Nation'. The air at Alexandretta was apparently 'pestilent'. (Fynes Moryson, *Itinerary*, vol. ii, pp. 68–9 4 vols., MacLehose, Glasgow, 1907–8.)

18. The port of Narva is situated in Estonia on the southern shore of the Gulf of Finland. The Russians had conquered it in 1558 but lost it in 1581; however, it continued to be an important centre for trade with Russia until the foundation of St Petersburg in the eighteenth century. There were French merchants at Narva in the 1560s but, although a French trading company was given permission to import goods into Russia on payment of only half the import duties in 1587, France's trade with Russia by the northern, i.e. Archangel, route did not amount to much.

It is worth noting that in the second half of the sixteenth century a series of voyages were made by English merchants to Persia across Russia in the hope of developing trade with Persia via Narva, but they were abandoned in about 1580 having proved unprofitable owing to lack of efficient organisation and to the great distances involved. For details see T. S. Willan, *The Early History of the Russia Company 1553–1603* (Manchester University Press, 1956).

19. The manufactory was given this name because it was moved from the Louvre to some premises formerly occupied by a soap factory.

20. [The Argonne is a generally wooded area in north-east France lying between the rivers Aisne and Aire and occupying part of the present-day departments of Marne and Meuse. There appear to have been some 2,500 gentlemen glass-makers in France (Lublinskaya, p. 118, n. 3).]

Loss of status was only incurred when a noble traded in produce or products that were not derived from his domain. But it was admitted that to manufacture glass with the sand from one's own pits or quarries and then to sell it was not strictly speaking very different from the sale of the corn and wine produced on one's own domain; after all corn and wine like glass were subjected to certain processes (such as threshing and fermentation) prior to being offered for sale at the market. (V.L.T.)

21. The *trésoriers de France* were expected to make periodical tours of inspection of their *généralité* in connection with their fiscal duties; to make them responsible for communications also was therefore more sensible than might at first appear. For their role in this connection during Henry IV's reign, *see* chapter 6 of Buisseret.

22. For the construction of canals in Henry IV's reign, *see* Buisseret. Pierre Paul de Riquet (1604–82) spent 14 years (1666–80) constructing the Canal du Midi with the encouragement of Colbert.

23. 28 July 1631, Avenel, vol. iv, p. 184 (V.L.T.)

24. The Code Michau was briefly mentioned above (p. 197). It is printed in *Recueil général des anciennes lois françaises*, vol. xv, pp. 223–344. *See also* the summary given in vol. iv of *Histoire du Cardinal de Richelieu* by G. Hanotaux and the duc de la Force (p. 115 ff). (V.L.T.)

25. For Richelieu's relations with the Bouthilliers, *see* Ranum, *Richelieu*.

26. It has been well said that whereas Tasso is a great poet, Marino is a great virtuoso of poetry. Giovanni Battista Marino (1569–1625) was born and died in Naples but lived in France from 1615 to 1623, being favourably recognised by Marie de Medici. See *inter alia* Franco Croce's article 'Baroque Poetry: New Tasks for the Criticism of Marino & Marinism'—in *The Late Italian Renaissance 1525–1630*, ed. Eric Cochrane (Macmillan, London, 1970) and an early work by Mario Praz: *Secentismo e marinismo in Inghilterra: John Donne—Richard Crashaw* (Florence, 1925).

Luis de Góngora y Argote (1561–1627) was born and died at Córdoba, but for a time held a court chaplaincy at Madrid. 'His light verse was highly esteemed but he was considered to have violated the principles of poetry and language in his long poems *Polifemo* (1612) and *Soledades* (1613–17). In these he elaborated his style by the introduction of numerous Latinisms of vocabulary and syntax and by exceedingly complex imagery and mythological allusions' (excerpt from an article by Christopher Colin Smith in the *Encyclopaedia Britannica*). The fact that both 'marinism' and 'gongorism' have been incorporated into the English language as literary terms gives some indication of the celebrity of these two poets in the seventeenth century; *cf.* the vogue for Euphuism in England after the appearance of Lyly's *Euphues* in 1580.

27. This was a quay close to the Louvre where barges used to unload hay, corn and other commodities.

28. For a description of this famous room where 'Arthénice' used to hold her weekly reunions, *see* Ranum, *Paris*, p. 153 and Magne, pp. 217–8.

29. Located in Brittany in the present-day department of Loire-Atlantique. (V.L.T.)

30. *See* W. L. Wiley's lively essay 'The French Academy' in *The Formal French* (Harvard, 1967). It has been well said that 'from the beginning the Academy had the temperament of a . . . court of law. It was exclusive, self-perpetuating and possessed of a well-defined function.' (Ranum, *Paris*, p. 193).

31. A. Adam, *Histoire de la littérature française au XVIIe siècle*, p. 577. (V.L.T.)

32. L. André, *Sources de l'Histoire de France*, vol. XIV, journaux et pamphlets. (V.L.T.)

33. The Grand Châtelet was the seat of the criminal and civil judiciary for Paris as well as a sort of police station with its own police (*commissaries enquêteurs du Châtelet* and *ser-*

gents du Châtelet). It was presided over by the *lieutenant civil* (mentioned in chapter 1, n. 10). In addition it was a city prison with an extremely grim reputation—for which, *see* Purcell, p. 94. The abbey of St Germain-des-Prés was originally founded in the sixth century and subsequently named after St Germain, the bishop of Paris, who was buried there in 576 (*cf.* note on St Germain l'Auxerrois, chapter 4, n. 6). The fair of St-Germain-des-Prés (*see* chapter 1, n. 38) was held nearby under its auspices. 'Standing almost alone beyond the walls in 1600, St.-Germain still possessed all the characteristics of a medieval stronghold. Surrounded by a wide ditch, high crenelated walls, towers, drawbridges, and gates, the abbey remained as independent of Paris physically as it was legally.' (Ranum, *Paris*, p. 19). Its prison later acquired notoriety as one of the scenes of the September massacres of 1792.

34. The new bridge here mentioned was of course the Pont-Neuf. The statue of Henry IV was erected in 1615. 'At foote of this Bridge is a water-house at the front whereof . . . is the Story of our B. Saviour and the Woman of Samaria powring Water out of a bucket: above a very rare dyal of several motions with a chime [i.e. carillon] etc.—the Water is conveyed with huge Wheeles, pumps, and other Engines, from the river beneath'. 'The Samaritan or Pumpe at the End of Pont Noeufe . . . is, beside the Machine, furnished with unnumerable rarities both of Art and Nature; especially the costly Grotto where are the fairest Corals growing out of the very rock . . . also huge morsels of Chrystals, Ametheists and Gold in the mine . . . with two huge Conchas. . . .' (Evelyn, ii, p. 93; iii, p. 10.)

35. The Place Dauphine was so called in honour of the future Louis XIII when the land for its construction was handed over to the First President of the Parlement in 1607. (Wiley, pp. 14–15.) *See* the illustration on p. 114 of *The Formal French* by the same author. There is an excellent description of the Place Dauphine in Ranum, *Paris*, pp. 73–5.

36. 'In a general way the section of the Right Bank [i.e. the northern bank of the Seine] east of Les Halles to the ramparts and fields and south of the old fortress known as the Temple . . . was called the Quartier du Marais or "Quarter of the Marsh". . . . In it and on immediately contiguous terrain were the first public theatres of the capital; and in close proximity to the theatres lived the actors. . . . The Marais area was unquestionably *à la mode* during the first decades of the seventeenth century. In this lively section of Paris there flourished—along with the halls given over to drama—cabarets, gambling halls and brothels. High society both lived in and passed through it in search of diversion.' (Wiley, pp. 120–1.)

37. *See* the illustrations of the Place Royale reproduced in Wiley (p. 258) and Ranum, *Paris* (p. 76). 'In England Covent Garden (*c.* 1630) is a direct imitation of the Place Royale which may therefore be regarded as the ultimate ancestor of the square development in London, Bath and elsewhere.' (Blunt, p. 117.)

38. On this subject see Claude Michaud's article 'François Sublet de Noyers Surintendant des bâtiments de France' in *Revue historique*, ccxli (Jan.–June 1969). Sublet de Noyers wrote to Poussin in January 1639, '. . . comme j'ai un amour tout particulier pour la peinture, je fis desseing de la caresser comme une maistresse bien aimée, et de lui donner les prémices de mes soins.'

39. See the engraving printed by Wiley who also gives a detailed description.

40. Étienne Martellange (1568–1641) worked as architect-general to the Society in the provinces of Paris, Lyons and Toulouse. This church is now called St Paul et St Louis.

41. 'Poussin lived and conversed with the ancient statues so long that he may be said to

have been better acquainted with them than with the people who were about him.' Sir Joshua Reynolds (quoted in ' "The Realm of Flora" in Keats and Poussin' by Ian Jack in *The Times Literary Supplement*, 10 April 1959).

42. *See* Professor Tapié's comments on Callot's horrifying series of etchings *Les Misères et Malheurs de la Guerre* on p. 342. For Jacques de Bellange, who also came from Lorraine, see the remarks of Otto Benesch in the chapter entitled 'The Ancient and the Gothic Revival in French Art and Literature' from his book. *The Art of the Renaissance in Northern Europe*, which is reprinted in *French Humanism 1470–1600*, ed. W. L. Gundersheimer (Macmillan, London, 1969). Abraham Bosse's mordant engraving '*La Galerie du Palais*' is reproduced and shrewdly analysed by Ranum in his book *Paris in the Age of Absolutism*.

43. *Relation écrite par la Mère Angélique Arnault sur Port-Royal* [ed. Louis Cognet] 'Les Cahiers Verts' vol. ii [Grasset, Paris] 1949. (V.L.T.). [The papal bull instituting the new Order was dated August 1627 and the letters patent were issued in October 1630—*see* p. 128 of the *Relation* and notes 145 and 158.]

44. Avenel, vol. i, p. 833, 6 August 1630. (V.L.T.)

45. Charenton is situated on the Marne to the south-east of Paris. The Edict of Nantes forbade Protestant worship in Paris—hence the construction in 1606 of a Protestant church at Charenton which was easily accessible by river and was then, according to Evelyn, about 6 miles outside the city. The first church was burned to the ground by a Catholic mob in 1621 (Clarke, p. 89); the second and larger church constructed in about 1623 was destroyed at the Revocation of the Edict of Nantes. Léonard estimates the number of Protestants in Paris at this time at 10,000 to 15,000 (see his interesting account of Parisian Protestantism and worshippers at Charenton on pp. 360–3). For a description of the second church (designed by Salomon de Brosse) and of a service there see Evelyn, ii, p. 115.

46. Gangs in Paris bore names such as 'les Rougets', or 'Manteaux rouges', 'les Grisons', 'les Plumets' etc., etc. and used to wear the appropriate clothing. 'Les Frères de la Samaritaine' used to haunt the Pont-Neuf after nightfall. These gangs spoke a thieves' jargon known as *narquois*. *See* Magne, pp. 40–6, where the criminal underworld of Paris at this time is estimated at more that 50,000.

47. Quoted by Pierre Blet, s.j., in his introduction to *Correspondance du Nonce en France Ranuccio Scotti 1639–41* published in the series Acta Nuntiaturae Gallicae (V.L.T.)

48. This was the Congregation or Company of the Priests of the Mission (sometimes known as Vincentians), founded in 1625. The Collège des Bons-Enfants owed its name to the fact that it had been a boarding school for boys. The Priory of St Lazare (also situated in Paris) had been a leper hospital—the Lazarus of the parable having been adopted in the Middle Ages as the patron saint of lepers and beggars. Since this priory became the headquarters of the Congregation those who belong to the latter are also known as Lazarists.

49. In translating *jeunes clercs* as 'deacons and sub-deacons' I have followed Purcell, p. 159, where it is stated that among those who attended the Tuesday Conferences were Olier (mentioned, p. 288), Bossuet, the great preacher of Louis XIV's reign, and the future Cardinal de Retz.

50. Madame Goussaut bore the title of Madame la Présidente because her husband had been a President of the *Chambre des Comptes*. The Hôtel-Dieu was the largest hospital in Paris and stood near Notre-Dame. In his edition of Evelyn's Diary, E. S. de Beer notes that it was not unusual to find from three to seven patients in a bed (vol. ii, p. 101, n. 5).

The girls who undertook this work were turned into a religious society, the Congregation of the Daughters of Charity founded in 1633, whereas Madame Goussaut and her fellows, who made up informal groups, were known as Ladies of Charity.

51. Alain de Solminihac (1593–1659) was consecrated bishop of Cahors (an enormous diocese) in 1637. See N.C.E. The congregation founded by Eudes was called the Congregation of Jesus and Mary. The Society of St Sulpice which was founded by Olier in 1642 aimed at training a zealous clergy especially suited to be directors of seminaries. It took the form of a community of secular priests following a common life, with masters and students working in close association. Priests trained there arrived in Montreal as early as 1657 (Cross).

52. Julien Maunoir (1606–83) was a Jesuit born in the French-speaking part of Brittany, who taught himself the Breton language and from 1640 to 1682 was active in organising and himself carrying out missionary work among the Celtic-speaking population; he also compiled a Breton–French dictionary and grammar (N.C.E.). For Michel le Nobletz, his predecessor (1577–1652), a secular priest who was also of Breton extraction, *see* Ferdinand Renaud, *Michel le Nobletz et les missions bretonnes* (Editions du Cèdre, Paris 1955) in which are printed two of his hymns in the Breton language. St Grignion de Montfort (1673–1716), who was trained at St Sulpice (see previous note), founded both a missionary and a teaching congregation, composed a vast number of hymns and spent most of the 16 years of his priesthood as a travelling missionary in western France. The impact made by the preaching of these three men in Brittany and the Vendée was to some extent comparable with that produced by Whitefield's and Wesley's preaching in eighteenth-century Wales and Cornwall.

53. The Company of the Blessed Sacrament was given its death-blow by Mazarin in 1660 when he arranged for the Parlement to ban its secret reunions. For an interesting account of its outlook, activities and growing unpopularity in the 1650s see the chapter entitled 'A generation of Tartuffes' in Ranum's *Paris*.

54. The reference is to Polyeucte's soliloquy in Act IV, scene ii of Corneille's play of that name written in 1642. This play, which is set in the third century A.D. during the Decian persecution, has been called the greatest of all Christian tragedies. Polyeucte, who is eventually martyred, sets a higher value on constancy to his religion than on his love for his wife, and repudiates the delights of this world as obstacles to those of the world to come.

55. Gabriel Naudé (1600–53) who studied medicine at Padua was subsequently librarian to two cardinals in Rome, one of them being Urban VIII's nephew Cardinal Barberini. In 1642 Richelieu put Naudé in charge of his library and on Richelieu's death he entered Mazarin's employment. He is thus the originator of the Bibliothèque Mazarine.

56. E. Delcambre, *Le concept de la sorcellerie dans le duché de Lorraine au XVIe et au XVIIe siècles*. (Nancy, 2 vols, 1948, 1949). (V.L.T.)

57. This extraordinary commission, composed of *conseillers d'État*, masters of requests and members of the *Grand Conseil*, was set up by royal edict in September 1631 to judge certain crimes involving 'the security of the state', which included conterfeiting the coinage. Despite the Parlement's refusal to register this edict the new court began to function; nor did its procedure and verdicts correspond with established legal practices—e.g. it ordered executions to be carried out by night. The effect, as Shennan points out, was to damage the Parlement's judicial authority. In reply to remonstrances Louis XIII roundly told a delegation of magistrates: 'Vous n'êtes établis que pour juger entre maître Pierre et

maître Jean.' The *Chambre de l'Arsenal* was understandably regarded with widespread hatred and was suppressed by Anne of Austria after Louis XIII's death. (Shennan, *Parlement*, pp. 249–50; Moote pp. 45, 84.)

58. According to the account given by Aldous Huxley in *The Devils of Loudun*, Grandier had rudely claimed precedence over Richelieu in a religious procession through the streets of Loudun while the latter was still bishop of Luçon (pp. 25–6, 169). Robbins refers to a report that he had published a satire which enraged Richelieu; *cf.* Burckhardt, iii, p. 268.

59. Hanotaux-La Force, *Histoire du Cardinal de Richelieu*, vol. iv, p. 278 (V.L.T.)

60. Griffet, vol. ii, p. 534. (V.L.T.)

CHAPTER EIGHT:Obedience at Home and War Abroad

1. For an admirable discussion of the various factors that may have influenced the Swedish king's decision, in which the suggestion is made that his real military objective was still Tilly's army, *see* Roberts, ii, pp. 538–47.

2. Effiat fell ill and died while this was going on. As we have seen he had held the post of superintendent of finance. Effiat's death deprived Richelieu of a loyal servant who had carried out his duties satisfactorily and he subsequently continued to protect the dead man's family (*see* below p. 391). (V.L.T.)

3. '. . . à la place des élus, le gouvernement enverrait dans chaque diocèse du Languedoc des commissaires au département des tailles.' Languedoc was divided into twenty-two such dioceses. As Major puts it (p. 89), 'It would be too much to hope that their boundaries would conform with those of the ecclesiastical dioceses and they did not.' It was the practice for the Estates to divide the total amount of tax required from the province among these twenty-two dioceses; the diocesan assemblies would then in turn apportion the tax to be contributed by each town and parish within the diocese (Mariéjol, pp. 403, 405). This process of apportionment was called *l'assiette et département des tailles*. (Doucet, i, p. 307).

4. *Cf.* G. Hanotaux-La Force, op. cit., vol. iii, p. 376 where the reader is referred to Dom Vaissette's *Histoire du Languedoc*. The account given by Father Griffet (op. cit., vol. ii, p. 304) which is slightly different but similar in character contains several examples of chivalrous behaviour. A sergeant of the guards serving in the royal army named Sainte-Marie condoles with the wounded man and tells him that less than a quarter of an hour ago he had been praying that they would not meet in the fray: he agrees to take charge of a ring which he undertakes to deliver to the duchess. We are also given a description of the Marquis de Brézé coming to greet the duke as he lies prostrate on the ground. 'Courage, sir, 'tis nothing,' he says to console him. He quickly gives orders for the wounded man to be carried to a small farm [*métairie*] and a chaplain and a surgeon belonging to the royal army hasten there to attend to him. (V.L.T.)

5. It was not until 1645 that the duchess of Montmorency, who had become a Sister of the Order of the Visitation at Moulins, was granted permission by Anne of Austria in her capacity as regent to have the duke's body moved there and buried beneath a splendid mausoleum, the work of Anguier. Even so the magnificence of Montmorency's tomb was considered unusual in view of the fact that he had been condemned to death for high treason during the late king's reign. (V.L.T.)

6. Antonio Zapata de Mendoza (1550–1635) was archbishop, first of Burgos and then of Toledo before being appointed inquisitor-general by Philip IV in 1626. This conversation (which is recorded in Part II chapter 5 of Richelieu's *Testament politique*—see Hill, pp. 87–8) must have taken place soon after he had resigned this appointment in September 1632 and become a member of the Council of State. (H.C. Lea, *History of the Inquisition in Spain*, iv p. 309; Elliott, pp. 299–300).

7. For a longer extract from this letter see Burckhardt, ii, pp. 402–3.

8. On this subject, *see* Roberts, ii, pp. 748–51, who takes the view that the Swedish king's overtures to Wallenstein were prompted by the unfavourable military outlook both before and after his unsuccessful attack on Wallenstein's positions.

9. Heinrich Matthias von Thurn, who was born in 1568, had had a good deal of military experience. As a young man he had fought against the Turks and subsequently he had taken part in the fighting against the Hungarian leader Bocskay. In 1618 after the defenestration of Prague he had been elected one of the Supreme Commanders of the rebel army by the Bohemian Estates.

10. Since the publication in 1878 of Charvériat's work, which gives its political and military history but is now out of date, a cogent analysis of the Thirty Years War has been written by Georges Pagès.* Pagès devotes ample space to social conditions without which a proper understanding of the period is impossible.

Georges Livet has opened up the economic aspect yet further with his little book *La Guerre de Trente Ans* (1963) (published in the series 'Que sais-je'). *See also* in the series 'Les Cours de Sorbonne' the course of lectures which I delivered at the Sorbonne from 1963 to 1965. (V.L.T.)

[Details of works in English on the Thirty Years War are given in the bibliography at the end of this book but this seems an appropriate place to mention again two recent works listed there and already referred to in these notes both of which appeared in an English translation in 1971: Professor Tapié's book *The Rise and Fall of the Habsburg Monarchy* and *The Thirty Years War* by the Czech historian J. V. Polišenský.]

11. The Cambridge Italian Dictionary defines *virtù* in the sense that it is used by Machiavelli as meaning 'ruthlessness and determination combined with exceptional ability to conceive and carry through a plan of action'. However this definition seems to omit the qualities of energy and daring which were quite as characteristic of the successful careerist of the Italian Renaissance as ruthlessness and ability. The successful practitioner of *virtù* was thus a virtuoso in a wider sense than is generally given to the word in English; hence also the dictum '*virtù vince fortuna*' which proclaimed the belief that the energies of the individual human genius could prevail over the inhuman logic of fate.

12. The Imperial Knights formed a class which was directly subject to the emperor, not to the territorial princes of Germany. On the eve of the Reformation its two most notable figures were Franz von Sickingen, a successful condottiere, and Ulrich von Hutten, a man of letters who proceeded to adopt Luther's views with enthusiasm. As a class however the Imperial Knights were both resentful and ineffective—resentful because they were being impoverished by the economic and social pressures of the age and by the suppression of private wars within the Empire, ineffective because they were disunited and excluded from any share in the government. The Knights' War of 1522–23 under Sickingen's leadership aimed amongst other things at secularising all ecclesiastical

* [See chapter 5, n. 14. An English translation of this book was published in 1970. Reference is made in these notes to both the English and the French editions.]

dominions within the Empire for the benefit of his own class; but it was not supported by Luther, and the German princes and the Free Cities joined forces to crush it. The deaths of Sickingen and Ulrich von Hutten in 1523 marked the end of any attempt by the Imperial Knights as a whole to play an independent part in German politics. However the career of Götz von Berlichingen, the hero of Goethe's play of that name and of Sartre's *Le diable et le bon Dieu*, offers a good example of the kind of role that an individual knight could still play in Reformation Germany.

13. Unlike Thurn, Kinský had left Bohemia as recently as 1628. For his and Wallenstein's links with great Bohemian families (of which some examples are given in chapter 3, n. 12; chapter 5, n. 15 and chapter 6, n. 20 above) *see* Tapié, *Habsburg Monarchy*, pp. 96, 100–2, 104; Polišenský, 182, 195–8, 201–2. Polišenský describes Wallenstein as a haughty and self-confident Bohemian aristocrat who did not conceal his distaste for Hungarians, Italians and Poles.

14. This was Lars Nilsson Tungel who had occupied the position of Swedish resident in the Saxon capital since December 1631—*see* Roberts, ii, p. 684; Burckhardt, ii, p. 379 refers to him as Laurens Nikolai.

15. Schlick was President of the Imperial War Council (*Hofkriegsrat*)—*see* Schwarz, pp. 139–40. Polišenský emphasises his long-standing hostility to Wallenstein.

16. The ringleaders consisted mostly of Irishmen and Scots. One of them, Walter Leslie, had thereafter a particularly successful career, rising to the position of Imperial Privy Councillor—*see* Schwarz and the D.N.B.

17. In a collection of short compositions entitled: *Rekviem—menší valdštejnská trilogie* [Requiem—a shorter Wallenstein trilogy], published in Prague in 1935.* Historians have hitherto thrown no light on this episode which has been left as a preserve for the literary imagination. No doubt it represents a belated echo of the pledges made to Wallenstein at Pilsen and is to be explained as a false move by a few colonels who were loyal to Wallenstein and believed that his conspiracy had been successful. (V.L.T.)

[Since this note was written by Professor Tapié, Polišenský's book has appeared. *See* his comments on the abortive rebellion of some of Wallenstein's officers in Silesia, pp. 198, 200–1].

18. Minor orders, which include acolytes and lectors, can be considered as stages on the way to priesthood. Clerks in minor orders enjoy ecclesiastical privileges but are not bound to celibacy (Cross).

19. On this subject *see* Burckhardt, ii, pp. 435–8. Note that Philippsburg, a fortress in the Palatinate, lies on the east bank of the Rhine.

20. The word *ban* which is derived from the mediaeval Latin *bannus* or *bannum* means in this context a territory subject to the dominion or jurisdiction of some person (see *Mittel-lateinisches Wörtebuch*, ed. Prinz and Schneider (Verlag C. H. Beck, Munich, 1967)). Since this particular *ban* or seigneurie was situated in a valley in the Vosges where the castle of La Roche stood, the entire area, containing about eight villages (of which Neu-viller was one), and covering some twenty-five square miles, became known as Ban-de-la-Roche, a name which is still applied to the district today. For further geographical and historical details see Baquol's work, *L'Alsace Ancienne et Moderne* (3rd edition revised by P. Ristelhuber, Strasbourg, 1865).

* [This title was chosen because the book was intended to commemorate the tercentenary of Wallenstein's death and Durych had published an historical novel about Wallenstein in three volumes a few years previously. I owe this information to Christopher Lockie.]

21. *Cf.* Pagès Fr. p. 193, Eng. p. 184, and Burckhardt, ii, p. 448. One of the elector's sons also became the administrator of the bishopric.

22. For a fuller discussion *see* Pagès Fr. pp. 194–5, Eng. pp. 184–5, and N.C.M.H., iv, p. 345.

23. Bullion and Bouthillier assumed office together in August 1632 in succession to Effiat (for whom *see* n. 2 above). 'When the superintendency was held jointly as it was several times under Louis XIII, there was no division of duties or authority between the two officers. They worked on the same problems, signed the same documents, often wrote letters in common and advised the King *en conseil* together' (Ranum, *Richelieu*, pp. 143–4). Ranum points out however that until his death in 1640 Bullion was the more influential of the two.

24. For details of these earlier negotiations *see* Pagès Fr. p. 190, Eng. p. 181, and Burckhardt, iii, pp. 51–4.

25. The chamade could be sounded on the trumpet to signify a wish to hold a parley, or, as pointed out by John B. Wolf in his recent biography of Louis XIV, it could take the form of 'a specific drum beat to call a fortress to surrender' (pp. 480, 653). *See also* the examples given in N.E.D. and Littré.

26. We know that as early as the reign of Henry II, after the king had signed a letter, the secretary used to add the date and place and put his signature and sign-manual at the end of a continuation line or near the foot of the page (Sutherland, p. 48). During the reign of Louis XIII 'royal letters were in certain cases valid only when a secretary of state countersigned them.' (Ranum, *Richelieu*, p. 49)

CHAPTER NINE: The Great Ordeal (1636–38)

1. For a translation of the whole passage in Part II, Chapter 9, of the *Testament politique see* Hill, pp. 121–3; *cf.* the excerpts printed in Burckhardt, iii, pp. 123–4.

2. *See* Pagès Fr. p. 201, Eng. p. 191.

3. *See*, for example, the quotation from one of Bouthillier's letters given by Pagès (Fr. p. 184, Eng. pp. 175–6).

4. These territories belonged to the house of Austria. For a brief background *see* Burckhardt, iii, pp. 169–71.

5. These are the two small islands of St Honorat and Ste Marguerite near Cannes.

6. This word, which came into use in the second half of the sixteenth century, was mainly applied to merchants who contracted to supply *munitions de bouche* (i.e. flour, bread, meat, wine, forage etc.) to the armies in the field. *See* Littré, Zeller, Marion. For the names of two prominent *munitionnaires* of Richelieu's day, one of whom at least seems to have been concerned with the supply of munitions, *see* Ranum, *Richelieu*, pp. 105, 108–9.

7. *See* Avenel, vol. v., from which the above quotations are taken. (V.L.T.) [The provosts mentioned here and in Richelieu's letter on p.340 would have been military police officers (*prévôts des maréchaux*). For their powers *see* Marion and Zeller].

8. Rueil is close to St Germain-en-Laye where the king generally resided. At this time it was about 18 miles outside Paris. Of Richelieu's château Evelyn wrote, 'The House is but small but fairly built in forme of a Castle moated about . . . but though the House be not of the greatest the Gardens about it are so magnificent as I much doubt whither Italy have any exceeding it for all varietyes of pleasure.' (vol. ii, pp. 108–9.)

9. Porshnev, op. cit., p. 643 (no. 1 of the documents printed in the appendix, letter to Séguier from Épernon). (V.L.T.)

10. A tax on sales had been imposed as early as the reign of Charles V, but the real ancestor of the 5% surcharge here described was the *pancarte* introduced in 1597 but suppressed by Sully in 1602, for which *see* Zeller, p. 264, and Marion.

11. A longer extract from this letter is given in translation in Burckhardt, iii, p. 281. In the following month Sublet de Noyers was appointed Secretary of State for War in succession to Servien. For details of his career *see* Ranum, *Richelieu*, and Claude Michaud's article cited in chapter 7, note 38.

12. *See* the facsimile of part of a report from Richelieu to Louis XIII, dated 4 December 1636, which is reproduced on p. 144 of Burckhardt, iii. The relevant passages run as follows. 'L'affaire de Du Bois fera un peu de peine estant un esprit fascheux, mais j'espère que le Roy y trouvera son compte. . . . Ou cet homme se résoudra à travailler, ce que je croy qu'il fera de gré ou de force . . . ou il faudra tascher de faire achever ce qu'il a commancé selon les mémoires qu'on a trouvez dans son laboratoire. Je tascheray pour cet effet de m'asseurer dès aujourdhui de deux hommes qui ont travaillé souvent avec luy sans sçavoir le fonds de son secret et je les meneray demain a Rue[i]l avec moy pour y faire faire un laboratoire.' *See also* Burckhardt's comments on Dubois, ibid., p. 142.

13. *Annales*, 1948, p. 261 (V.L.T.). [Moote (p. 6) estimates that there were already about 40,000 judicial and financial officials in France in the early seventeenth century which he equates with one official for every 400 subjects].

14. For details of the various courts (*chambres*) of which the Parlement of Paris was composed at this time and of the number of its presidents, *see* chapter 1, n. 8. The *Chambres des Enquêtes* judged civil cases based on written evidence and criminal cases that did not involve liability to capital or corporal punishment. The *Chambres des Requêtes*, to which the Counsellors and Masters of Requests here mentioned would have belonged, were primarily concerned with judging civil cases involving persons to whom had been granted royal letters of *Committimus* which entitled them to appeal directly to the Parlement of Paris for judgement of their suit without recourse to ordinary tribunals. This privilege was enjoyed by many great personages, monasteries, colleges etc, as well as by the more important office-holders (Zeller p. 178, Shennan, *Parlement*, pp. 37, 39). *Présidents à mortier* were magistrates who held the official status of a presiding judge in a high court, the *mortier* being the black velvet cap that they used to wear on formal occasions. They were of course particularly prominent in the Parlement of Paris.

15. For a brief description of the functions of these two sovereign courts, *see* chapter 1, n. 40. In 1582 the *Chambre des Comptes* in addition to 8 presidents included 48 *maîtres des comptes*, 12 *correcteurs* and 50 *clercs* and *auditeurs* (Doucet, i, p. 190). For an earlier example of the conversion into a venal office of the post of wax-heater (*chauffe-cire*), *see* Zeller, p. 217. Both the *Chambre des Comptes* and the *Cour des Aides* had supreme jurisdiction in civil and criminal cases concerning fiscal matters but the *Cour des Aides* was first and foremost a court, which already consisted of two chambers by 1552 (Doucet, i, p. 197).

16. The *Grand Conseil*, like the Court of Star Chamber in England, was an offshoot of the king's council. Its separate existence dates from the end of the fifteenth century. It was extremely unpopular with all the other courts (especially the Parlements) because the king frequently withdrew cases from them and submitted them to the *Grand Conseil* either because its members would judge them more impartially or because they were more susceptible to his influence. Note that the *Grand Conseil*, whose jurisdiction covered the whole realm, used to meet near the Louvre unlike the other sovereign courts, all of

which had also counterparts in various provinces. (Zeller, Shennan, *Government*, Marion).

17. The *Secrétaires du Roi* were not in fact the king's secretaries at all; although there were a number of them who held clerical posts in the chancellor's office, for example, in many cases these were becoming purely honorary appointments. As they could be purchased they were often held by *partisans* (Mousnier, p. 141), for the title carried with it valuable fiscal and judicial privileges—for which *see* Marion, who states that Colbert later abolished no less than 215 such appointments. Note in particular that according to an excerpt from G. de la Roque's *Traité de la Noblesse* printed in translation in Shennan, *Government*, p. 104, tenure of this office was held to confer immediate hereditary nobility.

18. The *Cour des Monnaies* was concerned with the minting, counterfeiting and devaluation of the currency and cases arising therefrom (Zeller).

19. As the terms *bailliage, présidial, sénéchaussée and élection* have already been explained in the notes to chapter 1, there is no point in redefining them here. It should be realised, however, that an *élection*, although only a subdivision of a *généralité*, had a tribunal of its own which judged cases connected with taxation, and that each *élu* had at least two assistants (Zeller p. 282).

Under Henry IV there had been ten *trésoriers de France* to each *bureau des finances*, five of them serving alternately each year. It will be remembered that there was a *bureau des finances* in each *généralité*—*see* chapter 1, n. 39 and Buisseret, p. 57.

20. 'Villes et villages de France constituent au même titre des communautés d'habitants. . . . Dans les campagnes elles coïncident avec les paroisses.' (Zeller, p. 37)

21. *Cf.* chapter 7, n. 5 above. It is clear however from Marion's comments on *rentes sur le clergé* (pp. 106, 484) that the credit of the clergy was far better than that of the State.

22. See the comments of Roland Mousnier, op. cit., p. 385 and vol. ii of G. d'Avenel's old-fashioned but very informative work *Richelieu et la monarchie absolue*, the quotations that follow being taken from pp. 155, 156. (V.L.T.)

23. 'A mixture of nitric and hydrochloric acids, so called because it can dissolve the "noble" metals, gold and platinum.' (N.E.D.)

24. Griffet, *Histoire de Louis XIII*, vol. ii, p. 818 (V.L.T.)

25. *Cf.* Louis Battiffol, *Richelieu et Corneille*. (V.L.T.)

26. The close association between Laud and Strafford seems to have begun in January 1631—*see* C. V. Wedgwood, *Thomas Wentworth, First Earl of Strafford—a Revaluation*, p. 91 (Cape, London, 1964, paperback edition). It continued despite the fact that in the same year that Laud was appointed archbishop of Canterbury, Strafford, as he later became, was nominated Lord Deputy of Ireland (1633). However Charles I was not Louis XIII. 'He deflected the energy and discouraged the efforts of his two best ministers. . . . The friendship of Laud and Wentworth was cemented by their common frustration. . . . The alliance of the two, had it ever became effective, would have given to the king's government the strength it so gravely needed. But Charles . . . did not care to encourage men who were stronger than he.' *The King's Peace* (by the same author), p. 142 (Collins, London, 1966, paperback edition).

27. Significantly John Selden's *Mare Clausum*, which denied the Dutch claim to freedom of the seas and asserted British sovereignty over the so-called Narrow Seas separating England from the Continent, was officially published at this time. In January 1636,

Sir Kenelm Digby reported that it had reached Paris where according to him it was 'both much esteemed and much envied'—*see* E. W. Bligh, *Sir Kenelm Digby and his Venetia*, p. 197 (Samson Low, Marston, London, 1932).

28. It was at about this time that Father Joseph, who was still very much involved in German affairs, went so far as to point out on the map the lines of march that should be adopted, causing Bernard of Saxe-Weimar to retort in exasperation, 'But, Monsieur Joseph, your finger is not a bridge.' (V.L.T.)

29. These quotations and those that follow are taken from the collection of documents published by Avenel—*see* vol. v, p. 467 ff. (V.L.T.)

30. The Forty Hours Devotion was a continuous period of prayer and supplication which was originally observed at the end of Holy Week in memory of the forty hours of Christ's death—i.e. from 3 p.m. on Good Friday to 7 a.m. on Easter Sunday. During the forty hours the Blessed Sacrament was permanently exposed. This observance was introduced by St Philip Neri in 1548. With the spread of the Counter-Reformation it came to be more widely adopted until it was extended to the whole Roman Catholic world by Urban VIII in 1623. I am grateful to the Rev. J. R. Fox for supplying me with this information.

31. This decision had in fact been taken before France declared war on Spain. *See* the minute of a meeting of the Council held on 28 April 1635 which is summarised by Pagès, Fr. pp. 200–1, Eng. p. 190.

32. Porshnev, op. cit., p. 43. (V.L.T.)

33. For a brief account of the part played by Épernon in the Bordeaux rising of May 1635, *see* Burckhardt, iii, p. 284. These disturbances are described in more detail in Mousnier-Pearce, pp. 45–6.

34. *See* the undated letter to Séguier printed in translation in Shennan, *Government*, pp. 149–50, in which the Parlement of Rennes indignantly protests against the dispatch of an intendant to Brittany. For an example of the vague and apparently limitless powers that an intendant might be granted by the king, *see* ibid., pp. 133–4.

35. Porshnev, op. cit. (*see* the documents printed in the appendix, pp. 659–60). (V.L.T.)

36. Porshnev's book contains some very interesting passages on this subject (pp. 64–5). (V.L.T.)

37. For the definition of a *châtellenie see* chapter 2, n. 5. At this time there was one governor for the provinces of Saintonge and Angoumois; below him was a lieutenant-general for each province, and a *lieutenant du roi* at Angoulême who would have been in command of the garrison there—*see* P. de Lacroix, 'Les Gouverneurs d'Angoumois' in the *Bulletin de la Société archéologique et historique de la Charente* 1875; cf. Mousnier-Pearce, p. xii.

38. It is important to remember that, as Porshnev points out, 'the word *gabelle* came to have a special significance for the poorer classes; it referred not only to the government tax on salt, but also to any illegal and burdensome tax in general, and even to any threat of the imposition of a new tax. Sometimes rumours sufficed to make a crowd rise against an unspecified *gabelle*. . . . The slogan "down with the *gabeleurs*, the monopolists, the *partisans* was equally comprehensible to all" (quoted in *Revolutions in Modern History*, ed. Heinz Lubasz, pp. 10, 14, Macmillan Company, New York, 1966).

39. It will be remembered that the *présidial* was a court senior to that of the *bailliage*. Its jurisdiction thus extended over more than one *bailliage* or *sénéchaussée* with which, however, it was closely connected. The chief justice of a *présidial* might have the title of

president or of lieutenant-general and he might be the same person as the lieutenant of a *bailliage* (Doucet, i, pp. 265–7).

40. *See* the letters from Richelieu to the king written at Conflans on 21 and 22 June 1636 in vol. v of Avenel's collection. The first of these (No. 247) is undoubtedly a résumé of the information given by La Fosse in his report of 9 June to Séguier from Angoulême which is printed in the appendix to Porshnev's book (see no. 10 printed on pp. 652, 654, 655, the first page of La Fosse's despatch being reproduced on p. 653). However, Richelieu describes the rebels as consisting of 'seven to eight thousand men of whom three to four thousand are armed' (this passage is in Richelieu's own handwriting); whereas La Fosse only refers to about four thousand armed men. Did Richelieu perhaps have other sources of information? (V.L.T.) [Part of Richelieu's letter of 21 June is printed in translation in Burckhardt, iii p. 287. The account of the rising in Angoumois given in Mousnier-Pearce, chapter 3, which supplements that given by Professor Tapié, is partly drawn from the report of 9 June mentioned above.]

41. A. Leman, *Richelieu et Olivarès*. On p. 46 the author quotes from a letter dated 5 August 1637 in which Chavigny informs Pujols that 'the revolt of certain of the peasantry, upon which the enemies of this realm counted greatly, has broken up in utter disorder.' (V.L.T.)

42. The reference is to Saint Isidore the Farm Labourer (c. 1070–1130) who worked on a farm outside Madrid. Later he was adopted as the city's patron saint. He had been canonised some 15 years previously at the instance of Anne of Austria's father Philip III. (Attwater).

43. Earl J. Hamilton, *American treasure and the price revolution in Spain 1501–1650*. Harvard Economic Studies, no. 43, 1934. (V.L.T.)

44. That Olivares was already beginning to grow very despondent is shown by his comment in a letter written at the end of the year: 'L'année qui finit a été la plus malheureuse que l'Espagne ait connue depuis un demi-siècle.' In other words Olivares considered the year 1637 to have been the most disastrous that Spain had experienced since the defeat of the Armada. (This quotation comes from a letter to Roose dated 13 December 1637 as printed on pp. 462–3 of *Correspondance de la Cour d'Espagne sur les Affaires des Pays Bas*, vol. vi (Supplement 1598–1700) ed. J. Cuvelier and J. Lefèvre (Brussels, 1937).

45. Louis Vaunois, *Vie de Louis XIII*, p. 472 (V.L.T.)

46. This convent, founded by Anne of Austria herself, owed its name to the fact that the Benedictine nuns whom she installed there came from an abbey of that name near Bièvres to the south of Paris. The present church was not built until after Louis XIII's death, although it was certainly Anne of Austria who was responsible for its construction (G.L.E., Evans, Blunt).

47. La Porte was therefore styled the Queen's *porte-manteau*. He would have carried her cloak in a special bag when she was not wearing it herself; but as the expression 'cloakbag bearer' used by Cotgrave, the contemporary English lexicographer, is extremely clumsy, and the word 'portmanteau' has acquired a different meaning, I have preferred to ignore them both. *See* N.E.D.

48. Franche-Comté, or the Free County of Burgundy, had been seized by Louis XI but, unlike the Duchy of Burgundy, control of it was lost after his death in 1483. As explained by Professor Tapié on p   above, Franche-Comté had subsequently passed into the hands of the Kings of Spain and it should be noted that Philip II's minister Cardinal Granvelle was a Comtois by birth. The old saying 'Comtois rends-toi! Nenni, ma foi' cannot apparently be traced back to any particular episode in the history of

Franche-Comté—although one is tempted to associate it, for example, with the siege of Arbois by Henry IV's troops in 1595 when Joseph Morel, the Comtois commander of the garrison, was hanged by the French for his defiant refusal to surrender. That it was anti-French in origin and not just a tribute to Comtois obstinacy certainly seems likely enough. Significantly the period 1636–46 during which Franche-Comté suffered appalling devastation at the hands of friend and foe alike is generally referred to by historians of the province as 'la guerre de dix ans' and the expression 'méchant comme Weimar' was still in current use in Pontarlier in the nineteenth century. It was a period that was much commemorated in provincial folklore on account of the semi-legendary exploits against the French and their allies of the Comtois guerilla leader Jean-Claude Prost, popularly known as 'le capitaine Lacuzon'. The change in the popular attitude towards France begins in the reign of Louis XIV who after overrunning Franche-Comté twice took definite possession of it in 1678. *See, inter alia,* Lucien Febvre *Histoire dé Franche-Comté,* pp. 175–6, 181–5 (Boivin, Paris, 1912)—a combination of erudition and provincial patriotism written by a rugged individualist: A. Desmesmay, *Traditions populaires de Franche-Comté* (Deis, Besancon, 1838): Émile Fourquet, *Les hommes célèbres ... de Franche-Comté,* pp. 10, 87–8, 114–5 (Séquania, Besançon, 1929).

49. This gave rise to the legend (rather incautiously accepted by Kerviller, Séguier's biographer) that the Chancellor had secretly forewarned Anne of Austria before visiting the convent and that any compromising papers had consequently been destroyed. (V.L.T.)

50. L. Batiffol, *La Duchesse de Chevreuse,* pp. 138 ff. (V.L.T.). [The most recent biography in English is *Marie de Rohan, Duchesse de Chevreuse* by Michael Prawdin (Allen & Unwin, London, 1971].

51. François de la Rochefoucauld (1613–80). The most recent study in English is by W. G. Moore, *La Rochefoucauld, His Mind and Art* (Oxford, Clarendon Press, 1969). Chapter 7, 'Political implications,' is of particular interest to the historian.

52. *See* Richelieu's frantic letter to Bullion of 28 March 1637 from which slightly different exerpts are given in translation in Ranum, *Richelieu,* pp. 149–50 and Burckhardt, iii, p. 190.

53. *Cf.* p. 330 above. Admittedly the elector had been abducted by the Spaniards but subsequently he had been transferred to Vienna on the charge of treason to the Empire. (V.L.T.)

54. As mentioned above (p. 223) this was the title borne by the Archduke Ferdinand. For several years it was to remain the only one that the French were willing to concede him since they pretended to consider the election of 1636 null and void. (V.L.T.)

55. Saint-Maur-des-Fossés lies to the east of Charenton, itself at this time 6 miles outside Paris. The château there (which has not survived) was built in the sixteenth century by Philibert de l'Orme.

CHAPTER TEN: The Fight to the Death

1. The fame of Hugo Grotius as the founder of the science of international law needs no stressing. 'By birth a Dutchman, living as an exile in France, and employed as a diplomatist by the Swedish crown, Grotius was an international man: he stood between nations as he stood also between the warring creeds'—G. N. Clarke *The Seventeenth*

Century, p. 127 (Clarendon Press, Oxford, 2nd edition, 1947). It was his arguments in favour of freedom of the seas which John Selden had attempted to refute as mentioned in Chapter 9, n. 27.

2. This was Amelia Elizabeth, widow of William V, Landgrave of Hesse-Cassel mentioned on p. 371 above. The title of Landgrave (or Landgravine in the case of a wife or woman ruler) had originally been borne by certain German counts who had a number of other counts in subordination to them; but as in the case of the titles of Margrave and Palsgrave (see chapter 3, n. 9) it had merely become a hereditary title.

3. 'M. de Noyers a la charge de la guerre et moi celle de la mer'. Even in a purely administrative context the word *charge* conveys a number of different shades of meaning —office, post, function, responsibility. It will be remembered that, although there was no Secretary of State for the Navy, Richelieu did hold the post of Grand Master and Superintendent General of Commerce and Navigation. The varied activities of Sublet de Noyers as Secretary of State for War are described in the relevant chapter of Ranum, *Richelieu*. Ranum draws attention to 'the very limited functions of the Secretary of the War department' as outlined in the regulations of 1619 (printed in translation in Shennan, *Government*, pp. 132–3) but observes that by the end of the reign the department of war was firmly established (pp, 52–3).

4. His instructions are catalogued in *Les archives générales de Simancas et l'histoire de Belgique*, vol. ii, ed. Maurice van Durme (Brussels, 1966), p. 80, where he is described as the Secretary of State and for War to the Cardinal Infante.

5. A. Leman, *Richelieu et Olivarès*, pp. 51 ff. the mission of Miguel de Salamanca. (V.L.T.)

6. Richelieu to Chavigny, 15 September 1638, in Avenel, vol. vi, p. 176 (V.L.T.) [In French this passage is a play upon words since the word *dauphin* also means a dolphin].

7. Avenel, vol. vi, p. 234 (V.L.T.)

8. Burckhardt, iii, p. 291, refers to Grotius as 'the most independent of all observers'.

9. A. Leman, op. cit., p. 88, n. 2. (V.L.T.)

10. 'She brings with her six coaches, seventy horses and a hundred and sixty in her train: by this you will easily decry her,' wrote one unhappy English official to another, ordered to make hasty preparations for Marie de Medici's arrival. . . . 'Charles I allotted a hundred pounds a day for his self-invited guest's expenses.' (Carola Oman, *Henrietta Maria*, p. 94.) Marie de Medici remained in England until August 1641 during which time she contrived to make herself remarkably unpopular. Another enemy of Richelieu's residing at the English Court at this time was Madame de Chevreuse who appears to have cost Charles I two hundred guineas a week (ibid., p. 93)—although her stay came to an end in 1640. Both her mother and her friend increased the dislike and suspicion with which Henrietta Maria was regarded in England, but were quite powerless to affect Richelieu's position in France.

11. This was Charles Lewis the older brother of the Prince Rupert who was to play a leading part in the English Civil War. For Richelieu's attitude over this matter, *see* Burckhardt, iii, p. 233.

12. Thionville was ceded to France in 1659 and incorporated into the province of Lorraine. It is now in the department of Moselle.

13. Avenel, vol. vi, pp. 88, 238. Letters from Richelieu to Bellièvre dated 16 August and 13 November 1638 (V.L.T.)

14. Avenel, vol. vi, p. 413, Richelieu to Bullion, 5 July 1639. (V.L.T.)

15. For the *prévôt des marchands*, *see* chapter 1, n. 10. The *Gentilshommes du Roi* belonged

to the companies known as the *Cent gentilshommes de l'Hôtel du Roi*—crack troops who formed part of the king's household. Writing of the sixteenth century, Doucet comments, 'C'était là qu'affluaient en temps de guerre les gentilhommes sans emploi qui grossissaient l'effectif jusqu'au chiffre de 1400 ou 1500 hommes.' (ii, p. 628).

16. Paris at this time was divided for administrative purposes into sixteen quarters. The commissioners, who were responsible for police duties, were the agents of the Châtelet which, as already mentioned, combined the roles of law court and prison with that of police headquarters. (Magne, Doucet.)

17. For a longer extract from this letter in translation, *see* Ranum, *Richelieu*, p. 156.

18. Barbier subsequently went bankrupt—see the extract from Bouthillier's letter to Richelieu of 17 August 1641 printed in Ranum, op. cit., pp. 178–9.

19. Ranum, *Richelieu*, pp. 152–3 prints a longer extract from this letter.

20. See Marion under the heading *solidité*, and the complaints of the peasants of Saintonge in Burckhardt, iii, p. 286; *cf.* Mousnier-Pearce, p. 70.

21. '*On jouissait du privilège du sel.*' *See* the details of privileged areas and provinces that were exempt from the *gabelle* given by Marion, pp. 218–19. It was the absence of compulsory purchase which was the main distinguishing feature between a *pays de petites gabelles* like Provence and a *pays de grandes gabelles* like Maine or, for that matter, most of inland Normandy. The parts of lower Normandy which did not belong to this last category were known as *pays de quart bouillon*—a term which is explained in the first sentence of the following note and the second sentence of note 23.

22. The mixture of salt and sand was dissolved in sea-water which used to be boiled until it evaporated, the owners of forests, woods and copses in the vicinity supplying wood for this purpose. In addition to the employment which this industry provided, there was also a considerable trade in salted produce with Rouen and Paris, and large scale smuggling of salt into neighbouring areas which were liable to the *gabelle*—a very profitable occupation—*see* following note. For all this, *see* the article by Michel Caillard 'Recherches sur les soulèvements populaires en Basse Normandie (1620–1640) et spécialement sur la révolte des Nu-pieds' referred to in the bibliography at the end of this book (p. 516). I owe this reference to the kindness of a reviewer for *The Times Literary Supplement*.

23. The white salt produced in the area of Avranches was both of better quality and cheaper than the grey salt generally obtainable at the salt warehouses in regions where the *gabelle* operated. It was in fact table salt. Whereas in the *pays de quart bouillon* the only obligation imposed was that a quarter of the output of salt should be supplied to such warehouses, in the nearby *pays de grandes gabelles* the price of salt had increased considerably between 1627 and 1638. In January 1639 severe orders were issued against salt-smuggling (Caillard, op. cit., pp. 106–7). In a letter to the two superintendents of finance dated 24 July 1639 pointing out the undesirability of putting a stop to the traffic in white salt, the five local *trésoriers de France* wrote as follows, 'Soubz la liberte de cet usage de petit sel blanc tous les taillables [persons liable to the taille] de ces quartiers du Cotentin et du Bocage [in lower Normandy] gaignent leur vie par l'emploi qu'ils ont à entretenir les fourneaux des salines . . . il est grandement à craindre qu'ils ne pourroient payer leur impost des tailles et celuy du sel.' (ibid., p. 143).

24. Pius V had cited the same passage sixty-eight years previously, after Don John of Austria's victory over the Turks at Lepanto.

25. Porshnev, op. cit., p. 367. (V.L.T.)

26. The Vendée rebellion broke out in March 1793—two months after Louis XVI's

execution. Following on its initial success the Vendéan armies styled themselves 'Catholic and royal' and claimed to be acting in the name of Louis XVII. In June they took Saumur and Angers but failed to capture Nantes. Four months later, despite a crushing defeat at Cholet, a Vendéan army accompanied by a mass of refugees succeeded in crossing the Loire at Ancénis, defeated republican forces near Laval, and advanced via Avranches as far as the port of Granville on the Norman coast in the forlorn hope of meeting the English there. However their failure to capture the town quickly proved fatal to the rebels' morale and the siege was raised after only two days.

27. *Procureurs* were the equivalent of solicitors. Although accredited to a Parlement (or to a court such as the Châtelet), they did not belong to it and did not enjoy the same social standing as magistrates. It was the duty of a *procureur* to assist his client by obtaining the services of a barrister or *avocat* (also superior in status to a *procureur*—*see* Zeller, p. 211) and to help the latter to present the plaintiff's case to the court. (Shennan, *Parlement*.) If he was an *avocat-procureur* he would of course carry out both these tasks himself.

28. 'Chaque catégorie de revenus, Domaine, taille, aides, gabelle, avait ses receveurs particuliers.' (Zeller, p. 279.) These receivers were royal officials under the authority of the receiver-general of the *généralité* whose functions are outlined in chapter 7, n. 4.

As a source of revenue the king's domain did not consist merely of Crown lands and the seigneurial rights arising therefrom; it included innumerable rights which belonged to him as sovereign, not only to levy dues on the lands of others but also to charge fees generally and in certain cases to acquire the goods and chattels of his subjects. The king had, for example, the right to a portion of the profits derived from markets and fairs (for which his licence was always required) and to the property that non-legitimised bastards inherited from their father or mother. As we have seen (p. 37) he was entitled to a fee when letters of mastership were issued (for details of such *droits domaniaux*, *see* Matthews, pp. 176–80). He was entitled to certain dues in respect of all forests whether they belonged to him or not. In Normandy he had the right to impose a hearth-tax known as the *fouage*. These are only a few examples—for further particulars *see* Zeller, pp. 250–4; Doucet, ii, pp. 548–53.

Neither the receiver-general nor the receiver here mentioned were themselves responsible for collecting such dues or the *gabelle*, which would be paid over to them by tax-farmers or by their own subordinates as the case might be; but in the case of all such agents or officials Zeller's comment remains valid, 'Fermiers et receveurs s'entendaient souvent aux dépens des finances publiques.' (p. 279.)

29. Saint Ouen (*cf.* the Welsh form Owen) was bishop of Rouen from 641 to 684. The abbey to which his remains were translated and which is mentioned on p. 405 adopted his name shortly afterwards and became an important intellectual centre in the Middle Ages. It was suppressed at the time of the Revolution but the church still exists (N.C.E., Cross).

30. Caillard (op. cit.) gives several examples of riots and complaints caused by the imposition of these duties in Normandy earlier in the reign—riots in which the cobblers and tanners had played a prominent part. It should be noted that, as in the case of the dyed fabrics mentioned above, these duties applied to manufactured goods and that the only people who stood to gain by them were those who had purchased the offices of controller, inspector etc., and those who imposed the levy, i.e. tax-farmers. According to Montchrétien, writing in 1615, about three-quarters of the population of France wore leather shoes (Lublinskaya, p. 116). Even if Montchrétien was exaggerating this was obviously reason enough for the excise on leather goods to be widely resented, quite apart

from the fact that what might have been a highly profitable industry was being hampered and penalised.

31. In theory every Norman who raised this cry ('Haro, my Prince! I am being wronged') thereby acquired the right of having his case referred to the king himself—for details, *see* Mousnier-Pearce, p. 109. It used to be generally held that the word 'haro' was derived from 'ha Raoul', that is to say from the custom of appealing to Rollo or Raoul, the first Duke of Normandy, who was a great lawgiver—*see* Littré and *Oxford Dictionary of Christian Names*, ed. E. G. Withycombe, under Ralph, Raoul, Rolf, and Rollo. It seems clear that the custom of 'crying for justice', which apparently still survives in the Channel Islands, was early established in Normandy if not specifically of Norman origin. *See Encyclopaedia Britannica* under 'Haro, clameur de'.

32. Apparently Tourneville's house was defended by a positive garrison which he had hired for the purpose—*see* Burckhardt, iii, pp. 297–8, where a detailed account is given of this episode.

33. 'La taxe des aisés.' Such a measure, which could take various forms outlined by Marion, was in fact introduced by Mazarin's administration shortly after Louis XIII's death. It had evidently been recently imposed in Normandy when Richelieu wrote this letter—*see* Mousnier-Pearce, p. 89. For its operation in the sixteenth century, *see* Zeller, pp. 271–2.

34. *See* Ranum, *Richelieu*, pp. 145–6; however the letter was not written to the cardinal as there stated.

35. This château, built for Louis XII's minister, Cardinal Georges d'Amboise, archbishop of Rouen, and used as a residence by subsequent archbishops, was one of the first secular buildings in France in which large-scale use was made of Italian decoration and ornament. (*See* Blunt.) Only part of it still survives. Gaillon is situated on one of the two main roads between Paris and Rouen.

36. Writing of popular disturbances during Louis XIII's reign, Robert Mandrou comments '. . . pour un Louis XIII brûlé en effigie à Dijon en 1630 il faut compter par dizaines les "Vive le Roi sans gabelle" '—*see* p. 34 of his article in the *Revue historique* vol. ccxlii (July–September 1969).

37. A. Leman, op. cit., p. 118. (V.L.T.)

38. 'Philip IV had never dared to place too much faith in Belgians or Flemings and he moved troops about frequently, sending Spaniards to the Netherlands and bringing Walloons down into Spain. As a result of the battle of Dover however these constant exchanges became almost impossible.' Pagès Eng., p. 201.

39. The Estates-General of the United Provinces were composed of the representatives of the seven provinces, the leader of the delegation from the province of Holland being the Grand Pensionary. As they were the central organ of the union the importance of the Estates-General was considerable, especially in matters of foreign policy war and defence.

40. Avenel, vol. vi. The West India Company is the same as the Compagnie des îles d'Amérique. (V.L.T.) [Cartagena and Porto Bello are situated in Colombia and Panama.]

41. Richelieu's intrigues with the opposition in Scotland seem to have begun in 1637. In the winter of 1639–40 the leading Covenanters appealed to Louis XIII to mediate between themselves and Charles I in just the same way as the Huguenots had appealed to Charles I to mediate between themselves and Louis XIII during the previous decade. *See* Burckhardt, iii, pp. 155–6; Wedgwood, *The King's Peace*, p. 284.

42. Jacques de Brecht was secretary of the Council for Flanders and Burgundy (i.e.

Franche-Comté) in Madrid. *See Les archives générales de Simancas et l'histoire de Belgique*, vol. iii (Brussels 1968), ed. Maurice Van Durme, for several references to him.

43. In 1521 the Emperor Charles V had been granted 128,000 florins for his Roman expedition and coronation to enable him to pay an army of 4,000 cavalry and 20,000 infantry for one month. From the end of the sixteenth century this sum, known as a Roman month, was treated as a standard unit in making grants for military purposes. In fact the raising of the money would have been spread over several years nor does the full sum appear to have been raised on occasions when such grants were made. (I am grateful to Mr K. J. Leyser for supplying me with this information.)

44. In addition to the branch of this Byzantine family which established itself in Montferrat in the fourteenth century there was another Italian branch in Taranto which apparently moved to Naples towards the middle of the seventeenth century. See *Dizionario Storico-Blasonico delle Famiglie Nobili Italiane*, ed. Crollalanza (Pisa 1886).

45. *See* Marion under the heading *Amortissement*, especially the second paragraph.

46. This was quite a common occurrence especially in areas like south-west France where Protestantism had become strongly established in the sixteenth century (*see* Zeller, pp. 356–7), since the 'transfer' often amounted to downright usurpation. In effect the tithes thus transferred became seigneurial dues paid by tenants to lay persons. *See* Marion, p. 176 for further ramifications.

47. Isambert *Recueil des Lois*, xvi, p. 504 (V.L.T.)

48. Émile Combes (1835–1921), who was Prime Minister from 1902 to 1905, was responsible for the separation of Church and State in twentieth-century France following on the termination of Napoleon's Concordat of 1801 with the papacy and a rupture of diplomatic relations between the French government and the Holy See. His period as prime minister was marked by violent polemics as a result of his policy of contesting the pope's right to intervene in French ecclesiastical affairs, closing Roman Catholic schools, and severely restricting the activities and number of religious orders allowed in France.

49. A decision which was assisted by bribery—*see* Ranum, *Richelieu*, p. 174.

50. Quoted by Pagès, p. 215. (V.L.T.) [*cf.* Pagès, Eng. p. 203].

51. Avenel, vol. vi, p. 830. (V.L.T.)

52. *See* the strange declarations signed by Louis XIII and Cinq-Mars which are printed in translation in Burckhardt, iii, p. 331; *cf.* Philippe Erlanger, *Richelieu and the Affair of Cinq-Mars*, translated by G. and H. Cremonesi (Elek Books, London, 1971).

53. During her liaison with Cinq-Mars she was therefore nicknamed 'Madame la Grande'. For a useful short account of her, *see* under Delorme in the D.B.F. She lived from 1613 to 1650 but none of her letters have survived.

54. Father Griffet, op. cit., vol. iii, p. 504, using as his source the collection [?*Memoires pour l'histoire du Cardinal Duc de Richelieu*] compiled by [Antoine] Aubery. (V.L.T.)

55. In theory this was purely a military appointment (*see* Zeller, p. 85) but in practice it had acquired obvious political implications by the end of the sixteenth century. For instance, Henry III had been compelled to make the duke of Guise lieutenant-general of the realm in 1588; at this time Guise was not only the head of the League, but was also being heavily subsidised by Spain. After his murder, his successor Mayenne entered into open rebellion against the king, but this did not prevent him from assuming the same title.

56. [This is the opinion of both Burckhardt and Erlanger but O'Connell is more cautious]. Louis XIII whose jealousy had been aroused by the affection that the dauphin and the duke of Anjou showed for their mother had momentarily thought of separating

the queen from her children. At Anne of Austria's entreaty Richelieu had intervened to dissuade the king from taking this step. (V.L.T.) [On this subject see the letters printed in translation in Burckhardt, iii, pp. 323–6, 438].

57. Situated in the department of Gard and to the north-east of Nîmes.

58. Excerpts from Louis XIII's memorandum are given in translation in Burckhardt, iii, p. 458.

59. Honnecourt is situated near Cambrai on the Saint-Quentin canal in the department of Nord.

60. The letter is in the Recueil de la réserve des Archives (feuillet 147) and is given below. It was printed for the first time by Vaunois (*see* his *Vie de Louis XIII* p. 547) in modernised spelling which I have also adopted:

'Vous m'avez fait grand plaisir de m'envoyer la dépêche d'Angleterre (laquelle je vous renvoie). Je ne vois pas qu'il y ait beaucoup d'avantage de part ni d'autre, s'il y en a eu, je le tiens du côté du Roi.

Je trouve très bon qu'on continue à Laffemas la commission de lieutenant civil, il s'est trop bien acquitté de cette charge pour ne pas la continuer. Louis.'

[The tone of this letter is perhaps best conveyed by translating it into colloquial English:

'I was very pleased to receive from you the dispatch from England (returned herewith). It does not seem to me that either side has really got the upper hand, but if anything I would say that the King's side is in the better position of the two.*
I quite agree that Laffemas should continue to act as *lieutenant civil*; he has done a very good job and deserves to keep his appointment.

Louis']

I do not think that this letter has much historical interest other than as a curiosity. In the case of a moody person like Louis XIII it is perfectly reasonable to take the view that his resentment against Richelieu (which it is admittedly difficult to deny) would gradually have given way to a renewal of their collaboration over a period of several months. (V.L.T.)

61. When the Cardinal Infante died in November 1641 Louis XIII had ordered his court to go into mourning—Burckhardt, iii, p. 388.

62. At an *ondoiement*, or private baptism, which was carried out shortly after the child's birth, only the essential part of the ceremony would be performed, i.e. the pouring or sprinkling of water by the priest, accompanied by the words, 'I baptise thee in the name of the Father and of the Son and of the Holy Ghost'. The naming of the child, at which the godparents would of course be present, was a public ceremony held at a later date. This procedure which was not infrequently followed in France until quite recent times, was common practice among the French royal family—*see*, for instance, V. Sackville-West's biography of 'La Grande Mademoiselle', *Daughter of France, the life of Anne Marie Louise d'Orléans, duchesse de Montpensier, 1627–1693*, Appendix 1, 'The baptism of royal children.' (Michael Joseph, London, 1959).

63. 'Out of the depths have I cried unto thee, O Lord'—Psalm 130.

* [The battle of Edgehill had taken place on 23 October by the old style of dating used in England, but on 2 November by the new style of dating which had been adopted in France.]

64. *Correspondance de Saint Vincent de Paul*, ii, pp. 393–5 letter of 15 May 1643 to [Bernard] Codoing, Superior [of the Priests of the Mission] in Rome.* (V.L.T.)

65. The battle took place on 19 May, five days after Louis XIII's death. The victor, the duc d'Enghien, had married Richelieu's niece, Clémence de Maillé-Brézé two years previously. This was the niece who had been brought up by Madame Bouthillier at her house at Caves (V.L.T.). [*See* note on p. 394 above. For Caves *see* Ranum, *Richelieu*, pp. 34–5, 180].

CONCLUSION

1. Article 13 of the edict of March 1642 issued at Narbonne renewing the charter of the *Compagnie des Îles d'Amérique*. (V.L.T.) [Letters of Declaration were issued by the government in the king's name. They took the form of letters patent and had the same legal force as an edict or ordinance. *See* Chapter 1, n. 6].

2. H. Hauser, op. cit. *See* the interesting passages in the conclusion on the part played by the cardinal and the value of his economic policy; note also the comparison made by the author between him and Colbert, a comparison which is in Richelieu's favour and apparently rightly so. (V.L.T.)

3. These quotations are taken directly from the English translation of Marc Bloch's book, *L'étrange défaite*, by Gerard Hopkins (O.U.P., 1949)—*see* pp. 166–7.

4. The *Fête de la Fédération*, the Festival of Federation referred to in the preceding quotation, is the great national festival held throughout France on 14 July to commemorate the fall of the Bastille and hence the downfall of the ancien régime. First celebrated in 1790, it symbolises the triumph of the Revolution of 1789 and of the principles of Liberty, Equality and Fraternity.

5. This was the period of the wars against Abd-el-Kader after the French occupation of Algiers in 1830; from 1840 onwards the French army under the command of Bugeaud embarked on the conquest of the whole of Algeria.

6. Whereas dulia is the veneration which should be offered to the saints, hyperdulia ('more than veneration') is due to the Virgin Mary and latria ('complete worship') is owed to God alone.

7. Quoted by A. Adam, *Histoire de la littérature francaise au XVIIe siècle*, vol. ii, 'L'époque de Pascal', p. 115 (V.L.T.)

8. *See* Father Blet's introduction to the collection of documents concerned with Scotti's nunciature, *Correspondance du Nonce Ranuccio Scotti 1639–41*, series Acta Nuntiaturae Gallicae. (V.L.T.)

9. de Retz became coadjutor archbishop (i.e. assistant archbishop) to his uncle Jean François de Gondi, archbishop of Paris, later in 1643.

10. The battle of Rocroi was the greatest French victory since Marignano in 1516 and shattered the legend of Spanish invincibility. At the time the duc d'Enghien was only 22. He subsequently took a leading part in the campaigns in Germany.

* [An English translation of this letter is printed in *Letters of St Vincent de Paul* trans: and ed: Joseph Leonard, pp. 171–4. For a short account of Codoing *see* ibid: p. 543.]

Bibliography

SHORT BIBLIOGRAPHICAL SURVEY

NOTE

The bibliography which follows is a translation of Professor Tapié's *aperçu bibliographique* as printed in the second edition of *La France de Louis XIII et de Richelieu*, published in 1967. In some cases further bibliographical details have been given in square brackets. In addition, if a book mentioned by Professor Tapié was written in or has been translated into English, the English title and publication particulars have been inserted when necessary, and an asterisk has been placed in the margin.

At the end of this translation of Professor Tapié's *aperçu bibliographique* is printed a guide to works in the English language relating to various subjects mentioned in his book. It consists of books and articles written in or translated into English that are not included in his bibliographical survey, many of which have appeared since 1967. For a broad indication of what this guide does and does not contain see pp. 519–20 below.

D. McN. L.

MANUSCRIPT SOURCES AND PRINTED SOURCES

Documentary records concerning Louis XIII's reign are so numerous that their very abundance is sufficient to explain why they have never been fully examined or utilised. For a long time historians were essentially concerned with political history. Now their attention has begun to shift to aspects of history that were previously neglected —economic history, social history and religious history—and there are vast tracts awaiting discovery, not only in the Archives Nationales but in the archives of various ministries, among municipal records, in the archives of religious communities, among notarial records and in the private manuscript collections that have been preserved by a large number of families.

Some idea of the sheer magnitude of the task that lies ahead can be obtained by referring to the series of catalogues compiled by the two historians Émile Bourgeois and Louis Andre and printed in *Les sources de l'histoire de France au XVIIe siècle*. It must also be borne in mind that in the case of both economic history and diplomatic history there are sources to be investigated in foreign as well as French archives. In addition, a vast quantity of French manuscripts are to be found abroad—such as the collection of Séguier's papers in Russia used by Boris Porshnev.

Further information about sources is given in vol vii of the 'Clio' series, *Le XVIIe siècle*, by E. Préclin and Victor-L. Tapié, 2nd ed. (Paris: Presses Universitaires de France, 1949). Of those documents relating to Louis XIII's reign that have appeared in print, the collection assembled by Avenel in *Lettres, instructions diplomatiques et papiers d'État du Cardinal de Richelieu*, 8 vols, (Collection des documents inédits de l'histoire de France, 1853–7) is of prime importance. Even so, this monumental edition cannot be regarded as definitive. The principles by which the editor was guided in making his selection were too narrow by present-day standards and his series needs to be supplemented. A critical edition of the personal correspondence of Louis XIII and Richelieu would be of great value; amongst other things, it would help to increase our knowledge of the collection of manuscripts acquired by the French Ministry of Foreign Affairs some thirty years ago. Some use was made of these documents, though with different objects in view, by Georges Pagès in *La Monarchie d'Ancien Régime* and Louis Vaunois in his *Vie de Louis XIII*. These two works are referred to more fully below. See also Beauchamp, *Louis XIII, d'après sa correspondance avec le Cardinal de Richelieu* (1902); H. de la Ferrière, *Deux années de mission à Saint-Pétersbourg*, 1 vol., 276 pp. (Paris: Imprimerie Impériale, 1867).

The papers left by Richelieu have been published in part in the following: *Maximes et papiers d'État du Cardinal de Richelieu*, ed. G. Hanotaux (Paris, 1880); *Mémoires du Cardinal de Richelieu*, ed. Petitot, 2nd series, 10 vols. (1823); ed. Michaud and Poujoulat, 3 vols. (1837–8); ed. Société de l'histoire de France, 10 vols. (1907–31)—this last edition stops short at the end of 1629.

A critical edition of Richelieu's *Testament politique* by L. André was published in 1947: *Testament politique du Cardinal de Richelieu*, 524 pp. (Paris: Laffont, 1947). [Selections from this edition have been translated and published by Henry Bertram Hill together with an introduction, under the title *The Political Testament of Cardinal Richelieu* (Madison: University of Wisconsin Press, paperback edition 1965)]. It should be studied in conjunction with the articles by R. Mousnier entitled 'Le testament politique de Richelieu' which appeared in the *Revue historique* in January and March 1949.

This is an appropriate place to say something about the authenticity of both the *Mémoires* and the *Testament politique*. There can be no question nowadays of treating them as apocryphal writings composed without the Cardinal's knowledge as Voltaire formerly maintained was the case so far as the *Testament* was concerned. However the actual drafting was partly at least the work of Richelieu's secretaries. Even after the publication of Louis André's edition of the *Testament*, the question still arises: 'Is this really a political testament intended for the king (as the present writer believes) or is it a collection of documents that originated from the Cardinal's private office and was put together by his secretaries?' The whole subject offers plenty of scope for learned discussion but in my opinion one thing can be regarded as certain: like Richelieu's correspondence, the *Testament* can be accepted as a genuine expression of his views.

A vast quantity of miscellaneous information which needs, however, to be used with caution is provided by the memoirs of the period that have appeared in the Petitot collection in the series published by Michaud and Poujoulat, or among the publications of the Société de l'histoire de France, such as the Memoirs of Phélypeaux de Ponchartrain, Sully, Monglat, Bassompierre, Rohan, etc. This is also true of Saint-Simon's work, *Le Parallèle entre les trois rois Bourbons*, of the Memoirs composed by Montchal, archbishop of Toulouse, *Mémoires concernant des particularités de la vie et du ministère de Richelieu* (2 vols., Amsterdam, 1718), and of the Journal of Louis XIII's physician, J. Héroard, which was partly published in 1868 in two volumes under the title *Journal sur l'Enfance et la Jeunesse de Louis XIII*.

In writing this book I have made considerable use of the work of Father H. Griffet, s.J., *L'histoire du règne de Louis XIII, roi de France et de Navarre* (3 vols., Paris, 1768). Here again a certain caution is necessary. Henri Hauser complained of Father Griffet's disdainful silence about a number of topics that are of definite interest to the present-day historian. Obviously one must not expect too much of Father Griffet; but he was acquainted with many documents which have since disappeared and, as Georges Pagès observed, his history must still be considered an important source for the period. Having given these few particulars about sources for Louis XIII's reign, since a complete bibliography is clearly out of question in the case of a book of this nature and size, I will now merely specify the principal works that may be usefully consulted —giving preference to those which have appeared recently.

LOUIS XIII

The character of Louis XIII has attracted the attention of historians perhaps because there is something mysterious about the man once one has seen through the romantic legend depicting him as a weak king, completely dominated by his minister's overwhelming genius.

A number of books about him were written by Louis Batiffol, a historian of great ability, whose interpretation of the documentary evidence is distinguished by keen psychological insight and balanced judgement: *La vie intime d'une reine de France au XVIIe siècle:*
* *Marie de Médicis*, 2nd ed., 2 vols., (1931) [*Marie de Médicis and the French court in the Seventeenth Century*, trans. M. King, (London: Chatto and Windus, 1908)—being translated from the first French edition of 1906]; *Le roi Louis XIII à vingt ans* (1909); *Richelieu et le roi Louis XIII* (Paris, 1934). All these works may still be regarded as authoritative.

L. Vaunois, the author of *Le Roman de Louis XIII* (Paris: Grasset, 1934), later produced *La Vie de Louis XIII* (Grasset, 1944), a chronological account of the king's life based on original research. This is an accurate and detailed biography, containing a wealth of factual information. It concentrates primarily on anecdotes and Court gossip.

Lieutenant-Colonel Romain, *Louis XIII, un grand roi méconnu* (Paris: Hachette, no date —1930?). L. Canu, *Louis XIII et Richelieu* (Paris: Fayard, 1946). Dr Cabanès, *Les morts mystérieuses de l'histoire* (Paris: Albin Michel, n.d.): this gives a diagnosis of Louis XIII's death.

RICHELIEU

Richelieu the man, his family and his entourage are conscientiously studied by Maximin Deloche in *La Maison du Cardinal de Richelieu* (1912); *Autour de la plume du Cardinal de Richelieu* (1920)—essential for contemporary polemics; *Les Richelieu: le père du Cardinal* (1923); *Un frère de Richelieu, le Cardinal Alphonse de Richelieu* (1936).

L. Batiffol's book *Autour de Richelieu* (1937), provides information of great importance about the cardinal's private fortune, one of the main sources of his power and a valuable means of estimating the extent to which his actions were disinterested. See also the same author's *Richelieu et Corneille* (1936) for the cardinal's connections with the world of letters.

The relations between Richelieu and Father Joseph which were first examined by G. Fagniez in his substantial book *Le Père Joseph et Richelieu* (1895) subsequently aroused the interest of an Angevin schoolmaster, Canon Dedouvres, who felt a positive call to come forward as the Capuchin's apologist. Hence a number of admirably learned works which, however, are sometimes excessively uncritical in their approach; the last of these, *Le Père Joseph de Paris, polémiste et apôtre* (2 vols., 1932), embodies the fruits of years of unremitting labour.

Foreign historians have also put forward their own interpretations of Richelieu:
* Hilaire Belloc, *Richelieu* (London, Benn, 1930); Carl J. Burckhardt, *Richelieu* (I, 'Der

* Aufstieg zur Macht', II, 'Behauptung der Macht und kalter Krieg', III, 'Grossmachtpolitik und Tod des Kardinals') [3 vols., Verlag Georg D. W. Callwey, Munich 1961–66. The notes and index to the three volumes were published separately in 1967. The first volume of this biography which was originally published in Germany by the same firm in 1935 was translated into English in 1940 in slightly abridged form by Edwin and Willa Muir under the title *Richelieu, his rise to power*, the publishers being George Allen and Unwin. This translation was reprinted after the reissue of the first volume in Germany in 1961 and translations of the second and third volumes by Bernard Hoy appeared a few years afterwards under the titles *Assertion of Power and Cold War* and *Power politics and the Cardinal's death*, the title given to the entire work being *Richelieu and his Age* (3 vols., George Allen and Unwin, London, 1967–71). This learned but very discursive work should be used with caution. Nor is the index to the English edition (which is divided up amongst the three volumes) up to the standard of the index to the German edition; for example, the name of Gustavus Adolphus is completely omitted from that provided for the second volume.]

* Aldous Huxley, *Grey Eminence* (London: Chatto and Windus, 1941) deals with the part played by Father Joseph [and is also concerned with the English Capuchin, Benet of Canfield]. W. Andreas, *Richelieu (Persönlichkeit und Geschichte)* (Göttingen, 1958).

POLITICAL HISTORY OF THE REIGN

First and foremost must be mentioned *Histoire du Cardinal de Richelieu*, 6 vols. [Paris: vols. 1–2 Firmin-Didot, vols. 3–6 Plon, 1893–1946] by G. Hanotaux and the Duc de la Force. This work, which is a great deal more than a mere biography of the cardinal, tends to develop into a general history of the reign, of contemporary French institutions and of domestic and foreign policy. It was begun in 1893 and launched on an imposing scale that was perhaps over-ambitious. Yet, strange though it may seem in view of its massive proportions, this elaborate study ignores a number of problems, nor are the different volumes of which it is composed all equally reliable and authoritative. It needs to be treated with considerable caution but nevertheless remains indispensable.

Compared with this *magnum opus*, H. Hauser's book *La pensée et l'action économiques du Cardinal de Richelieu* (Paris: Presses Universitaires de France, 1944) seems very slight (194 pp.). However, its importance may be gauged by the fact that it represents the first step towards an economic history of the reign—a history which has yet to be written. It is only an outline, but it is based on sound and recent research and sparkles with intelligence, even if some of its statements do not carry complete conviction.

This is the place to mention also *La Monarchie d'Ancien Régime* by Georges Pagès (Paris, 1926), a work based on careful and thorough research, carried out over a period of years. Pagès's interpretation of the problems involved is both original and profound. His book is essential to a proper understanding of the period, of which he also wrote a short synthesis entitled *Naissance du Grand Siècle (1610–1661)* (Paris: Hachette, 1949).[1]

[1] For the benefit of those who are interested in historical methodology, I should mention that this last book contains an introductory essay on Pagès's work and the historical method he followed in his writings. Anyone who wishes to obtain some idea of how historical methodology has evolved within the past few years should make a point of read-
* ing Marc Bloch's book published after his death, *Apologie pour l'histoire, ou Métier d'historien*, 3e cahier des Annales (Paris: Armand Colin, 1949) (V.L.T.). [This book was

Ernest Lavisse's *Histoire de France* is of course a historical classic. The reign of Louis XIII is covered in vol. vi, written by J. H. Mariéjol and published in 1906. The book is obviously to some extent out of date, but the factual narrative remains of distinct value. It still deserves to be recommended as a work that is sound, clearly written and packed with information. In *La Prépondérance Espagnole* by H. Hauser (vol. ix of the 'Peuples et Civilisations' series under the general editorship of Louis Halphen and Philippe Sagnac) the reign of Louis XIII is considered in the context of the evolution of Europe as a whole between 1598 and 1660. In the *Histoire de France* published by Hachette in 1949 the period with which we are concerned is dealt with by André Latreille. In the 'Clio' series, *Le XVIIe siècle* by E. Préclin and Victor-L. Tapié is primarily intended for students, but the authors make a point of drawing attention to the main problems.

R. Mousnier, *Les XVIe et XVIIe siècles* ('Histoire des civilisations', iv, Paris, 1954, 2nd edition 1964). H. Méthivier, *Le Siècle de Louis XIII* ('Que sais-je?' series 1964). G. Zeller, *Aspects de l'ancien régime* (Paris, 1964).

CONSTITUTIONAL AND ADMINISTRATIVE HISTORY

Le Bret, *De la Souveraineté du Roi* (Paris, 1632). *Recueil des anciennes lois françaises*, ed: Jourdan, Decrusy and Isambert, vol. xvi, 1610–1643.

In addition to *La Monarchie d'Ancien Régime* mentioned above, Georges Pagès published a series of articles on seventeenth-century French administrative history which appeared in the *Revue d'histoire moderne* for 1932 and 1938.

Roland Mousnier is the author of a survey entitled *Le Conseil du Roi de la mort de Henri IV au gouvernement personnel de Louis XIV* ('Études d'histoire moderne et contemporaine', published for the Société d'histoire moderne; Paris: Hatier, 1947) but is above all known for his large scale work *La Vénalité des Offices sous Henri IV et Louis XIII* (Rouen: Maugard, 1946, xxix, 618 pp.). Readers will have seen for themselves how much the present writer is indebted to this masterly study.[1]

G. d'Avenel, *Richelieu et la Monarchie Absolue* (4 vols., Paris, 1884–90). In the review *XVIIe siècle* (the journal published by the Société d'Études du XVIIe siècle) two special issues should be noted: no. 25–6, 'Comment les Français voyaient la France au XVIIe siècle' (1955); no. 42–3, 'Serviteurs du Roi: quelques aspects de la fonction publique dans la société française du XVIIe siècle' (1959).

*   Orest A. Ranum, *Richelieu and the Councillors of Louis XIII: a study of the Secretaries of State and Superintendants of Finance in the Ministry of Richelieu, 1635–1642* (Oxford: Clarendon Press, 1963).

ECONOMIC HISTORY

Ideally, a long list of works should be given under this heading, even though it con-

translated into English by Peter Putnam under the title *The Historian's Craft* (Manchester University Press, 1954; published in the United States by Alfred A. Knopf and in Canada by McLelland & Stewart)].

[1] [A revised and enlarged edition of this work was published by Presses Universitaires de France, Paris, in 1971.]

stitutes a field which has largely been left untouched; but it is only possible here to give a brief selection. The economic history of Louis XIII's reign must necessarily be considered in conjunction with general economic conditions in the seventeenth century: hence the
* value of Herbert Heaton's *Economic History of Europe* [2nd ed. (New York: Harper, 1948]
* and the fundamental importance of Earl J. Hamilton's *American treasure and the price revolution in Spain 1501–1650* (Cambridge, Mass.: Harvard U.P., 1934).

The following are more particularly concerned with France: Henri Sée, *Histoire économique de la France*, i, 'Le Moyen Age et l'ancien régime' (Paris; Colin, 1939); G. Roupnel, *Histoire de la campagne française* (Paris: Grasset, 1932); P. de Saint-Jacob, *Les paysans de la Bourgogne du Nord au dernier siècle de l'ancien régime* (1955)—an admirable book which ranges back into earlier history; M. Vénard, *Une classe rurale puissante au XVIIe siècle: les laboureurs au Sud de Paris* (1955); L. Merle, *La métairie et l'évolution agraire de la Gâtine poitevine* (Paris, 1958); P. Goubert, *Beauvais et le Beauvaisis de 1600 à 1730*, (2 vols., Paris, 1958).[1]

E. Vaillé, *Histoire générale des postes françaises*, vols. ii and iii (Paris: Presses Universitaires de France, 1949–50); Paul Masson, *Le commerce français dans le Levant au XVIIe siècle* (Paris, 1896); H. Hauser, *La pensée et l'action économiques du Cardinal de Richelieu* (mentioned above).

P. Boissonnade, *Le socialisme d'État, l'industrie et les classes industrielles en France pendant les deux premiers siècles de l'ère moderne (1453–1661)* (1927), which must now be supplemented by Gaston Zeller's study, 'L'industrie en France avant Colbert' (*Revue d'histoire économique*, Marcel Rivière, 1950)—a survey which gives much food for thought.

Natalis de Wailly, 'Mémoire sur les variations de la livre tournois depuis le règne de Saint-Louis jusqu'a l'établissement de la monnaie décimale', *Mémoires de l'Académie des inscriptions et belles-lettres*, xxi, no. 2, (1857): of fundamental importance.

Until such time as he has completed the large-scale work on which he is at present engaged, see also the remarkable articles by the distinguished scholar Jean Meuvret that have appeared in various publications, such as 'Les crises de subsistances et la démographie de la France d'ancien régime', in *Population* (1946), 'Circulation monétaire et utilisation économique de la monnaie dans la France du XVIe et du XVIIe siècle', in *Études d'histoire moderne et contemporaine* (Paris: Hatier, 1947) etc.[2]

H. Hauser, *Recherches et documents sur l'histoire des prix en France de 1500 à 1800* (1936); G. d'Avenel, *Histoire économique de la propriété, des salaires, des denrées et de tous les prix depuis l'an 1200 jusqu'en l'an 1800* (Paris, 1894–8): now to some extent out of date as a result of F. Simiand's more recent work on the subject.

---

[1] [This book has since been republished in abridged form under the title *Cent mille provinciaux au XVIIe siècle* (Paris: Flammarion, 1968). Goubert's two recent volumes entitled *L'ancien régime* and covering the period 1600–1750 should also be mentioned here —vol. i, 'La société', vol. ii, 'Les pouvoirs' (Paris: Armand Colin, 'Collection U', 1969, 1973). The first has already appeared in an English translation: *The Ancien Régime: French Society 1600–1750*, trans. S. Cox (London: Weidenfeld and Nicolson, 1973). For other books and articles by Goubert that have been translated see pp. 530, 531, 547 below].

[2] [Jean Meuvret died in 1971. See his obituary in *Revue d'histoire moderne et contemporaine*, xix (January–March 1972). His book on social and economic problems of seventeenth-century French agriculture was unfortunately never published but after his death some forty articles by him, all concerned with some aspect of seventeenth-century French economic history, were collected and published under the title *Études d'histoire*

SOCIAL HISTORY

B. F. Porshnev, *Narodnye vosstaniya vo Frantsii pered Frondoï 1623–1648* (Moscow, 1948) ['Popular revolts in France prior to the Fronde 1623–1648']. For all its wealth of information and despite the fresh questions it raises (after making due allowance for its Marxist interpretation of events), this book is not in fact a social history of the working classes in France in the time of Louis XIII. It first appeared in a German translation and was then translated into French under the title *Les soulèvements populaires en France de 1623 à 1648*, with a foreword by R. Mandrou (S.E.V.P.E.N., 1963).[1] The book gave rise to an interesting controversy in which Roland Mousnier, who contested the validity of its conclusions, put forward solid arguments in favour of his own contention that the popular revolts of Louis XIII's reign were not symptoms of a class struggle. *See*, in particular, R. Mousnier, 'Les mouvements populaires en France au XVIIe siècle', *Revue des travaux de l'Académie des Sciences Morales et Politiques* (2e semestre, 1962) and 'Questionnaire de recherches sur les mouvements populaires de 1483 à 1787', undertaken for the *Centre de recherches sur la civilisation de l'Europe moderne* at the Sorbonne.[2]

G. Roupnel, *Les populations de la ville et de la campagne dijonnaises au XVIIe siècle* (Paris, 1922); G. d'Avenel, *La noblesse française sous Richelieu* (Paris, 1914); P. de Vaissière, *Gentilshommes campagnards de l'ancienne France* (Paris; 1904); Émile Magne, *La vie quotidienne au temps de Louis XIII* (Paris: Hachette, 1964 reprint); E. Levasseur, *La population française*, i (Paris, 1889); Antoine Adam, *Histoire de la littérature française au XVIIe siècle*: contains a wealth of invaluable detail (further reference is made to this book below).

MILITARY AND NAVAL HISTORY

J. Colin and F. Reboul, 'Histoire militaire et navale', vol. vii (1925) of *Histoire de la nation française* [15 vols., Paris, 1920–35], published under the general editorship of G. Hanotaux; L. André, *Michel le Tellier et Louvois* (Paris, 1942); F. de Vaux de Foletier, *Le siège de La Rochelle* (Paris, 1931).

G. Lacour-Gayet, *La marine militaire de la France sous les règnes de Louis XIII et de Louis XIV*, i, 'Richelieu–Mazarin, 1642–1661' (Paris, 1911); Charles de la Roncière, *Histoire de la marine française*, iv (Paris); H. Méthivier, 'Richelieu et le front de mer de Provence', *Revue historique*, clxxxv.

RELIGIOUS HISTORY

There is a tendency even among Catholic historians to underrate Georges Goyau's book

---

économique (Paris: Armand Colin, 1971). See also details of a translation of his article given on p. 530 below].

[1] [For details of sections of Porshnev's work that have been translated into English see pp. 531, 547 below. The French spelling of his name is Porchnev.]

[2] [See also the reference on p. 531 below to an English translation of Roland Mousnier's *Fureurs Paysannes: les paysans dans les révoltes du XVIIe siècle (France, Russie, Chine)* (Paris: Calmann-Lévy, 1967). This book is discussed by Robert Mandrou in an article in the *Revue historique*, ccxlii (July–Sept. 1969)].

Histoire religieuse vol. vi (1922) of *Histoire de la nation française* published under the general editorship of G. Hanotaux. However, those who have sufficient patience to persevere will find this carefully composed survey of Catholic religious life in its many varied aspects of great assistance.

For French Protestantism, see John Viénot, *Histoire de la réforme française* (2 vols., Paris, 1934), which sometimes shows a certain lack of comprehension in its attitude towards contemporary political issues and occasionally tends to become polemical in tone, but is to be commended for its wide range of information, conscientious scholarship and magnanimous outlook.

* H. Bremond's monumental work, *Histoire littéraire du sentiment religieux en France* (11 vols., Paris, 1924–33), is in a class by itself. [The first three volumes of this work were translated into English by K. L. Montgomery under the general title *A literary history of religious thought in France* (London: S.P.C.K., 1928–36). The subtitles of the individual volumes were as follows: i, *Devout Humanism*; ii, *The coming of mysticism 1590–1620*; iii, *The triumph of mysticism—the French school.*]

Vol. ii of *Histoire du catholicisme en France* by A. Latreille, E. Delaruelle and J.-R. Palanque, entitled *Sous les rois très chrétiens* (Paris: Spes, 1960), gives an excellent and
* stimulating summary. See also Daniel-Rops, *Histoire de l'Eglise du Christ*, vol. iv, part ii, *La Réforme Catholique* (1955) [translated into English by John Warrington under the title *The Catholic Reformation*]; vol. v, part i, *Le Grand Siècle des Âmes* (1958) [translated into English by J. J. Buckingham under the title *The Church in the Seventeenth Century* (London: Dent, 1962, 1963)].

In the large-scale History of the Church published under the general editorship of A. Fliche and V. Martin see vol. xviii, *La Restauration catholique (1563–1648)* by L. Willaert (1961). See also M. Braure, *L'Église à l'époque classique (XVIIe et XVIIIe siecles)* (Paris: 'Je sais, je crois' series, 1961).

For further reading, recourse must be had to works of original scholarship or to specialised studies; amongst these should be mentioned: J. Dagens, *Correspondance du Cardinal Pierre de Bérulle* (1936–9) and *Bérulle et les origines de la restauration catholique* (1952).

L. Cognet, *Les origines de la spiritualité française au XVIIe siècle* (Paris, 1949), *De la dévotion moderne à la spiritualité française* (Paris, 1958) *Le jansénisme* (Paris; 'Que sais-je?' series, 1961). J. Orcibal, *Les origines du jansénisme*, i, *Correspondance de Jansénius* (1947); ii, *Jean Duvergier de Hauranne, abbé de Saint-Cyran et son temps* (1948). J. Orcibal, *Saint-Cyran*
* *et le jansénisme* (1961). L. Goldman, *Le Dieu caché* (1955) [translated under the title *The Hidden God* by P. Thody London: Routledge, 1964)]. A. Gazier, *Histoire générale du mouvement janséniste*, (2 vols., Paris, 1928).

J. Pannier, *L'Église de Paris sous Louis XIII, 1610–1621* (Paris, 1921). G. Serr, *Henri de Rohan, son rôle dans le parti protestant 1610–1616* (Aix-en-Provence, no date [1946]). Canon L. Prunel, *La Renaissance catholique en France au XVIIe siècle* (Paris, 1928).

P. Coste, *Le grand saint du grand siècle: Monsieur Vincent*, 2nd ed., 3 vols. (1934) [English
* translation by J. Leonard, *The Life and Labours of Saint Vincent de Paul*, (3 vols., London: Burns, Oates & Washbourne, 1934–6)]. J. Calvet, *Saint Vincent de Paul* (Paris: Plon,
* 1947) [English translation by L. C. Sheppard (London: Burns, Oates, 1953).] M. Riquet, s.J., *Saint Vincent de Paul ou le réalisme de la charité* (1960).

R. Allier, *La Compagnie du Saint-Sacrement* (Paris). A. Bertout, *Les Ursulines de Paris sous l'ancien régime* (Paris, 1936).

E. Delcambre, *Le concept de la sorcellerie dans le duché de Lorraine aux XVIe et XVIIe siècles*

(Nancy, 1948), i, *L'initiation à la sorcellerie et le sabbat* (1948): ii, *Les maléfices de la vie supranormale des sorciers* (1949).

Finally, mention should be made of the extremely important work by P. Blet, s.j., *Le clergé de France et la monarchie*, (2 vols., 1959). See also the same author's *Correspondance du nonce en France Ranuccio Scotti 1639–1641* (vol. v in the series 'Acta Nuntiaturae Gallicae', Paris and Rome, 1965).

LITERARY HISTORY

A new approach is made to the subject by Antoine Adam in his *Histoire de la littérature française au XVIIe siècle* (Paris: Domat), i, *L'époque de Henri IV et de Louis XIII* (1948), ii, *L'époque de Pascal* (1951).[1] See also Henri Peyre, *Qu'est-ce que le classicisme?* (Paris: Droz, 1942); R. Pintard, *Le libertinage érudit* (Paris, 1943); G. de Reynold, *Le XVIIe siècle—le classique et le baroque* (Montreal, 1944); R. Lebègue, 'Le théâtre baroque en France', an article printed in *Bibliothèque d'Humanisme et Renaissance* (Paris, 1942); J. Morel, *La Tragédie* (Paris: Armand Colin, 1964).

HISTORY OF ART

A. Michel, *Histoire de l'art*, vi. E. Mâle, *L'art religieux après le Concile de Trente* (Paris, 1932). E. Lavedan, *Histoire de l'art: l'époque moderne* (in the 'Clio' series). B. Dorival, *La peinture française*, i, (Paris: Larousse). Denise Maynial, *Saint-Paul–Saint-Louis* [a church in Paris] Editions du Cerf, Paris: 'Collection Nefs et Clochers'). L. Hautecoeur, *Histoire de l'architecture classique en France*, i, *L'architecture sous Henri IV et Louis XIII* (2nd ed.).

*   Victor-L. Tapié, *Baroque et classicisme* (Paris, 1957). [The title of the enlarged English version is *The Age of Grandeur*, trans. A. Ross Williamson (London: Weidenfeld & Nicolson, 1960). This book is mentioned in the editorial notes. The translation is of high quality.]

COLONIAL HISTORY

Maurice Besson, *Histoire des colonies françaises* (Paris: Boivin, no date [1931]). Charles A. Julien, *Histoire de l'Afrique du Nord*. G.-L. Jaray, *L'Empire français d'Amérique*. F.-X. Garneau, *Histoire du Canada*, i, (5th ed.). G. Debien, *Un aspect de l'émigration populaire vers les colonies d'Amérique au XVIIe siècle: les engagés partis de La Rochelle* (thèse de la Faculté des Lettres de Paris, 1951).

FOREIGN POLICY

On this subject, see the bibliography to Chapter 3, entitled 'La Guerre de Trente Ans', in *Le XVIIe siècle*, the volume in the 'Clio' series mentioned above, under the heading 'Political History of the Reign.'

*   G. Pagès, *La guerre de Trente Ans* (Paris, 1939) [English translation under the title *The Thirty Years War 1618–1648* by David Maland and John Hooper, (London: A. and C.

[1] [See also the English translation of a work by this author mentioned on p. 544].

Black, 1970)]. G. Livet, *La guerre de Trente Ans* ('Que sais-je?' series, 1963). G. Pagès, 'Autour du "Grand Orage"': Richelieu et Marillac: deux politiques', in *Revue historique*, clxxix (1937). A. Leman, *Richelieu et Olivarès* (Lille, 1938). H. Pirenne, *Histoire de Belgique*, iv. W. Mommsen, *Kardinal Richelieu und seine Politik im Elsass und Lothringen* (Berlin, 1922). L. Batiffol, 'Richelieu et la question de l'Alsace', in *Revue historique* (1921); *Les anciennes républiques alsaciennes* (Paris, 1918). G. Zeller, *La réunion de Metz à la France* (2 vols., Paris, 1926).

Johannes Paul, *Gustav Adolf* (3 vols., Leipzig, 1926–32). Lauritz Weibull, 'Gustave Adolphe et Richelieu', in *Revue historique* (1934). J. Pekař, *Valdštejn 1630–1634* (in Czech, Prague, 1933–4).[1] Heinrich Ritter von Srbik, *Wallensteins Ende* (Vienna, 1920).[2]

* P. Vilar, *La Catalogne dans l'Espagne moderne*, vol. i (S.E.V.P.E.N., 1962) throws fresh light on conditions in Catalonia on the eve of the rebellion revealing that its newly-recovered prosperity was threatened. G. Zeller, *Les temps modernes*, i, *De Christophe Colomb à Cromwell* (*Histoire des relations internationales*, under the general editorship of P. Renouvin, Paris, 1953). The German edition of the *Acta Pacis Westphalicae*, i, ed. Braubach and Repgen (1962) prints many new documents which throw light on Richelieu's political plans between 1635 and his death.

MISCELLANEOUS

Notwithstanding the book by Porshnev mentioned above, A. Floquet, *Histoire du Parlement de Normandie*, vols., iv and v (Rouen, 1841–2) is still of some value for the rebellion of the *Va-Nu-Pieds*. But a fresh approach is made to the whole subject in Madeleine Foisil's typed thesis 'La révolte des Nu-Pieds en Normandie, 1639' (thèse pour le 3e cycle, Paris: 1966).[3]

R. Kerviller, *Le chancelier Pierre Séguier* (Paris, 1874) is still of use but too narrow and

[1] [A German translation of this work, made under the author's supervision, was published in 1937 in Berlin under the title *Wallenstein 1630–1634: Tragödie einer Verschwörung*, the conclusion of which was translated into English and printed in the *Slavonic & East European Review* in 1938. For further details, see below, p. 588.

[2] [A second edition of this book appeared in 1952. In his recently translated work *The Rise and Fall of the Habsburg Monarchy* mentioned in the editorial notes and p. 586 below, Professor Tapié also refers to *Wallenstein und seine Anhänger* by the Finnish historian Suvanto (Helsinki, 1963)].

[3] [The account of this revolt given in chapter 5 of Roland Mousnier's *Fureurs paysannes* mentioned on p. 513 above and recently published in English under the title *Peasant uprisings in seventeenth century France, Russia and China* makes considerable use of this thesis which has since appeared in book form: Madeleine Foisil, *La révolte des nu-pieds et les révoltes normandes de 1639* (Paris: Presses Universitaires de France, 1970). See John B. Wolf's favourable review in *Journal of Modern History*, vol. lxiii, no. 2 (1971).

This is an appropriate place to mention also a long and informative article on disturbances in Lower Normandy already referred to in the notes to the text of this translation: Michel Caillard, 'Recherches sur les soulèvements populaires en Basse Normandie (1620–1640) et spécialement sur la révolte des Nu-Pieds', in *A travers la Normandie des XVIIe et XVIIIe siècles* (3e cahier des Annales de Normandie, Caen, 1963). I would like to thank a reviewer for *The Times Literary Supplement* for his or her kindness in drawing my attention to this article.]

apologetic in its approach. *Lettres et Mémoires adressés au Chancelier Séguier, 1633–1649*, collected and published by Roland Mousnier, (2 vols., Paris: Presses Universitaires de France, 1964).

G. Mongrédien, *Le bourreau du Cardinal de Richelieu: Isaac de Laffemas* (Paris, 1929).

L. Batiffol, *La duchesse de Chevreuse* (Paris: Hachette, 1913); *La Journée des Dupes* (Paris: Hachette, 'Récits d'Autrefois' series).

P. de Vaissière, *La Conjuration de Cinq-Mars* (Paris: Hachette, 'Récits d'Autrefois' series, 1928).

The bibliographical guide which follows refers primarily but not exclusively to topics which Professor Tapié discusses in his book. It is, therefore, largely devoted to France and French civilisation during the reign of Louis XIII and is not intended to cover the Fronde, despite the fact that a number of works are cited which deal with that topic. It will also be found that, whereas a fair amount of space has been allotted to French literature, to the visual arts and to music, ballet, etc., I have cited few works on the history of science and technology in France and have made only a brief selection from the innumerable books on Descartes and French thought generally during this period.

Nor is this guide intended to serve as a comprehensive bibliography for the history of early seventeenth-century Europe although it contains three sections devoted to general European history. As is indicated by its title, apart from some books and articles listed in those three sections or under the headings THIRTY YEARS WAR and TURKEY it does not include works on either Scandinavia or Eastern Europe. Similarly Dutch history as such and for that matter Dutch art have been omitted and there is no list of books on the history of what is now Switzerland. Those listed under the heading GREAT BRITAIN are largely restricted to works concerned with the contemporary English attitude towards Europe (in particular Spain and Italy), with British foreign policy (especially Anglo-French relations) and with British trade in the Mediterranean. The last two sections on MILITARY AND NAVAL HISTORY and TURKEY have been deliberately kept short for reasons of space.

Despite these necessary limitations, without which it would have swollen to unmanageable proportions, I hope that this bibliographical guide will be of some use to anyone who is interested in seventeenth-century Europe and its civilisation—the more so as most of the works that it mentions are of recent date. A list of its contents is given overleaf. I am grateful to J. P. Cooper and K. V. Thomas for reading through the original, shorter version which covered a wider field in considerably less depth, and for making a number of helpful suggestions.

Sainte-Anne-de-Grasse, 1973.

D. McN. L.

A Bibliographical Guide to Works in the English Language concerned with Western, Central and Southern Europe, *c.* 1598–1643, with particular reference to France during the Reign of Louis XIII

Bibliographical Aids

General European Histories

General European Economic and Social History

France, Economic and Social History: Bibliographies and general surveys – Population – Agrarian history and popular risings – Urban history and Social life – Trade and Industry – Financial.

General European Religious History: Bibliographies, encyclopaedias, etc., – General works – Works concerned with particular aspects of European religious history (i, The Council of Trent; ii, The Counter-Reformation; iii, Arminianism; iv, Toleration; v, Scepticism and Free-thought; vi, Witchcraft; vii, Miscellaneous).

France, Religious History: Bibliographies – Catholicism – Protestantism – Jansenism – Scepticism and Free-thought – Witchcraft – Miscellaneous.

France and the French Monarchy: Bibliographies – Introductory surveys – General – Constitutional – Institutions – Absolutism – The Reign of Henry IV – The Regency of Marie de Medici – The Ascendancy of Luynes – Louis XIII – Richelieu – Miscellaneous.

France, Literary History: Bibliographies, etc. – Introductory surveys – General – Poetry – Theatre and Drama – Salons, Academies, etc. – Miscellaneous.

History of Art: Works of reference – Introductory surveys – General – Italy – Spain – Belgium – France.

Music, Ballet and Theatre: Dictionaries, Bibliographies, etc. – General surveys – Miscellaneous – Italy – France – England.

Spain: General surveys – Internal affairs, economic, social, cultural – Rebellion – Institutions – Government and statecraft – Spanish foreign policy – the Spanish Netherlands – the price revolution.

Italy:

The Holy Roman Empire and the Thirty Years War; Introductory – The Empire, General surveys – The Empire, Specialised studies – Thirty Years War, General surveys – Thirty Years War, Specialised studies – Bohemia and the House of Habsburg – Wallenstein – Gustavus Adolphus.

Great Britain: Bibliographies – Britain and Europe, General – British Attitudes to Spain and Italy – Anglo-French relations (i, Guides to sources; ii, Printed sources; iii, Secondary authorities) – English diplomacy in west and central Europe (i, Guides to sources; ii, Secondary authorities) – Commercial relations with Spain and the Mediterranean.

Military and Naval History: Military – Naval.

Turkey

BIBLIOGRAPHICAL AIDS
These are given under the appropriate headings of this guide when feasible. The following is a short list of *general* bibliographies, guides, etc, which may prove of assistance.

Theodore Besterman, *A World Bibliography of Bibliographies and of Bibliographical Catalogues, Calendars, Abstracts, Digests, Indexes and the Like*, (5 vols. inc. index, Totowa, New Jersey: Rowman and Littlefield). The 4th edition of this monumental work, which lists over 117000 volumes, goes up to 1963 inclusive. The earliest printed bibliography according to Besterman dates from *c.* 1470.

A. J. Walford, *Guide to Reference Material* (London: Library Association, 3 vols., 2nd ed., 1966–70). Also an invaluable work containing references to bibliographies in many languages—vol. i is concerned with science and technology, vol. ii *inter alia* with history and religion, and vol. iii with literature and the arts.

Turning now to guides to archives, a series of brief introductory surveys of the libraries and archives of various countries has been appearing in *History*—that dealing with France for example (by M. G. A. Vale) was published in vol. iv (1970).

For anyone about to embark for the first time on original research into the diplomatic history of Western Europe during this period an indispensable book is Charles H. Carter's *The Western European Powers 1500–1700*—one of a series dealing with historical sources published under the general editorship of G. R. Elton (London: Sources of History Ltd., in association with Hodder and Stoughton, 1971). Professor Carter, whose name appears elsewhere in this guide, is particularly well informed about the early seventeenth century. His book, which is concerned essentially with France, Spain, England and the Spanish Netherlands,[1] is neither a guide to diplomatic archives nor an inventory of diplomatic sources—although it contains many detailed references to such works; but it provides an excellent description, accompanied by examples, of the various types of material available to the researcher into diplomatic history including published as well as unpublished documents. There are two particularly interesting chapters on *relazioni* (or their non-Italian equivalent), on news-letters and on the use of cipher; and an illuminating example of the valuable non-diplomatic information that can often be found in an ambassadorial report is given on pp. 115–17.

Daniel H. Thomas and Lynn M. Case, *Guide to the diplomatic archives of Western Europe* (University of Pennsylvania Press, 1959) is useful and well arranged. The thirty-page chapter on France is primarily concerned with the archives of the French Foreign Ministry and refers to manuscripts belonging to Richelieu on more than one occasion.

The International Bibliography of Historical Sciences is a multilingual publication published with the assistance of U.N.E.S.C.O. and based upon the contributions of the various national committees of the International Committee of Historical Sciences, Lausanne. Vol. xxxvi (Paris: Armand Colin, 1970), edited by Michel François and Nicolas Tolu, covers the year 1967 and some publications of earlier years. It contains both numbered entries and details of periodicals. An admirable little publication specifically concerned with the latter is J. L. Kirby's *Guide to historical periodicals in the English language* (London: Historical Association, *Helps for students of History* no. 80, 1970).

Guide to Historical Literature published under the auspices of the American Historical Association (New York: Macmillan, 1961) remains of considerable value. This is an appropriate place to mention also the *Annual Bulletin of Historical Literature* published by

---

[1] Note that a volume on Central Europe and its historical sources is planned for the same series.

the Historical Association, London, which has been becoming steadily more and more comprehensive, and has now (1973) reached the year 1970.

Louis B. Frewer's *Bibliography of Historical Works published in Great Britain and the Empire 1940–45* (Oxford: Blackwell, 1947) has been followed by four successive volumes entitled *Bibliography of Historical Works issued in the United Kingdom* and covering the years 1946–56, 1957–60, 1961–65 and 1966–70 (Institute of Historical Research, University of London, 1957–72). These four volumes, of which the first was edited by Joan C. Lancaster and the remainder by William Kellaway, and which will no doubt be followed by others, were compiled for the sixth, seventh, eighth and ninth Anglo-American Conferences of Historians.

The *Centenary Guide to the publications of the Royal Historical Society 1868–1968 and of the former Camden Society 1838–97* (London: Royal Historical Society, 1968), compiled by A. T. Milne, covers in detail the varied publications for which the Royal Historical Society has been responsible.

Turning to bibliographies more particularly concerned with history from the end of the fifteenth century, note firstly H. M. Adams, *Catalogue of books printed on the Continent of Europe 1501–1600* (2 vols: Cambridge University Press, 1967).

A Bibliography of Modern History, ed. John Roach (Cambridge University Press, 1968), is a one-volume bibliography designed both to supplement *The New Cambridge Modern History* (mentioned below), bibliographies having been omitted from the individual volumes, and to stand on its own as an aid to teaching and research. The book is divided into three sections, of which Section A, covering the period 1493–1648, corresponds with the first four volumes of *The New Cambridge Modern History*. There are, however, no lists of books on music or the visual arts.

This bibliography plainly fulfils a useful function but is inevitably rather sketchy and for the first half of the seventeenth century by no means up to date.

Alun Davies, *Modern European History 1494–1788* (London: Historical Association, 1967) does not claim to be more than a select bibliography but gets quite a lot into its thirty-odd pages. A revised and, it is to be hoped, considerably enlarged edition is due to appear in 1974.

Finally mention should be made of an important venture launched in 1966 by De Lamar Jensen of Brigham Young University, Salt Lake City, with the cooperation of J. H. Elliott of King's College, University of London: the publication of an annual newsletter, 'Historians of Early Modern Europe', which gives details (derived from questionnaires sent to specialists in this field) of doctoral theses and research in progress as well as of recent or forthcoming publications.[1]

In *The English Historical Review*, *The American Historical Review* and *The Renaissance Quarterly* ample lists of recent articles and publications are printed at regular intervals. See also in this connection the important American journal *French Historical Studies*, founded in 1958, in which have appeared a number of articles on seventeenth-century French history; some of these are referred to elsewhere. Articles of interest have also appeared in that deservedly popular magazine *History To-day* but for reasons of space I have not attempted to give details of these. *The Economic History Review* is specifically referred to later in this guide and a number of other learned journals are also mentioned. There is little point in listing here the many other relevant historical periodicals in view of J. L.

---

[1] I owe these details to Professor R. M. Hatton's article, 'Louis XIV: recent gains in historical knowledge' in *Journal of Modern History*, vol. xlv, no. 2 (June 1973).

Kirby's guide mentioned above but five newcomers in particular should be singled out: *Journal of Medieval and Renaissance Studies* (Durham North Carolina: Duke University Press) and *European Studies Review* (Macmillan Journals) the first numbers of which appeared in 1971; *Journal of European Economic History*, published by the Banco de Roma and launched in April 1972; *Viator: Medieval and Renaissance Studies* (California University Press), an annual publication intended 'to embrace all aspects of medieval and renaissance studies between late Antiquity and A.D. 1600', of which the first volume, dated 1970, also appeared in 1972; and *Journal of Peasant Studies* (Frank Cass and Co. Ltd) the first issue of which is to be published in July 1973.

GENERAL EUROPEAN HISTORIES

Details of good standard text books will be found in the short Historical Association bibliography by Alun Davies mentioned above and in subsequent *Annual Bulletins of Historical Literature*; there is no point in repeating them here—although two are referred to on p. 527. An exception should however be made in the case of G. N. Clark, *The Seventeenth Century*, (Oxford University Press, 2nd ed., 1947), a short survey rather than a history and in a class by itself.

In *The New Cambridge Modern History*, vol. iv, *The Decline of Spain and the Thirty Years War*, ed. J. P. Cooper, is directly concerned with this period; but vols. ii, iii and v also contain much that is indispensable to an understanding of the first half of the seventeenth century. See, for instance, in vol. ii, *The Reformation*, the chapter by the late H. O. Evennett entitled 'The New Orders' on the rise of the Jesuits, Capuchins and Oratorians, and in vol. v, *The Ascendancy of France*, Rudolf Wittkower's chapter on seventeenth-century art and architecture. The relevance of vol. iii, *The Counter-Reformation and Price Revolution 1559–1610*, ed. R. B. Wernham (1968), needs no stressing. In the case of vol. iv, one of the most successful in the series, the reader should not overlook the remarkable general introduction by the editor which contains amongst much else of interest a brief sketch of the characteristics of the main European nobilities. Note also that this volume includes chapters on the Scientific Movement, Drama and Society, European expansion in the Atlantic, and Latin America. The titles of chapters dealing with other subjects covered by this guide are given below under the appropriate heading together with the names of the authors.

In the *Fontana History of Europe* series, ed. J. H. Plumb (Collins), the volume for the period 1598–1648 has not yet appeared. J. H. Elliott, *Europe divided 1559–1598*, in the same series (1968), is both admirably compressed and highly readable, with a good short bibliography from which I have profited.

The Age of Expansion: Europe and the World 1559–1660, ed. H. R. Trevor-Roper (Thames and Hudson, 1968) is a large and magnificently produced 'coffee-table' book with copious illustrations of high quality. The contributors are all scholars of standing, such as Menna Prestwich (who writes on France from Henry III to Louis XIV), H. G. Koenigsberger (the author of the chapter on the Thirty Years War)[1] and Henry Kamen (who is responsible for the chapter on Spain). In short, unlike many books of this type, *The Age of Expansion* is well worth reading although, as pointed out by F. L. Carsten in *The English Historical Review* (Jan. 1970), there is a good deal that has been omitted, given its title. In addition much originality is shown in the choice of illustrations and the bibliography is good.

An original and interesting approach is that of O. Ranum in *Searching for Modern Times*, vol. i (1500–1650) (New York and Toronto: Dodd Mead, 1969) which is intended to make 'underlying ambiguities of periodization as apparent and obvious as possible'.

For other relevant titles, see under GENERAL EUROPEAN ECONOMIC AND SOCIAL HISTORY. See also the list of books and articles which are of general constitutional and political interest given under the heading FRANCE AND THE FRENCH MONARCHY (p. 548). In

---

[1] This chapter has been incorporated into the same author's *The Habsburgs and Europe 1516–1660* (Ithaca and London: Cornell University, 1971), which is listed below under SPAIN.

addition, the titles of numerous collections of historical essays that relate to general European history are given in various sections of this guide. An obvious example is J. H. Hexter, *Reappraisals in History* (cited p. 527). In this case, as in some others, I have not listed each relevant essay in the collection.

GENERAL EUROPEAN ECONOMIC AND SOCIAL HISTORY

Even when confined to a single country, this is a subject with endless ramifications and to attempt here to pursue more than a few of them on a European scale is out of the question. *The Cambridge Economic History of Europe*, vol. iv, contains full bibliographies (for a useful review of this volume entitled *The Economy of Expanding Europe in the Sixteenth and Seventeenth Centuries*, ed. E. E. Rich and C. H. Wilson (Cambridge U. P., 1967) see D. C. Coleman in *History*, lii (October 1968).[1] Note also R. G. Albion, *Naval and Maritime History: an Annotated Bibliography* (mentioned under MILITARY AND NAVAL HISTORY below) nearly a third of which is devoted to Commerce and Shipping. *The Economic History Review* prints at regular intervals lists of recent books and articles on economic history, both in English and in foreign languages.

In this guide writings bearing on the economic history or social history of a particular country are mentioned under the appropriate heading: works on Mediterranean commerce and economic affairs are thus listed under FRANCE, ECONOMIC AND SOCIAL HISTORY; SPAIN; ITALY; TURKEY or, in the case of British Mediterranean trade, GREAT BRITAIN. For the price revolution, see also SPAIN. I have considered population studies only in respect of FRANCE. What follows here therefore is a brief and somewhat arbitrary selection of books, collections of essays and articles, mostly of recent date, which deal with some aspects of the economic and social history of this period of European history in fairly broad terms. Inevitably many of the works listed under GENERAL EUROPEAN RELIGIOUS HISTORY are concerned with economic and social history also.

H. Heaton, *Economic History of Europe* (New York: Harper, 2nd ed., 1948), has already been mentioned in Professor Tapié's bibliography. Equally useful is S. B. Clough and C. W. Cole's *Economic History of Europe* (Boston: Heath, 3rd ed., 1952). The second volume of *The Fontana Economic History of Europe* (which covers the period 1500–1700) is being published in parts written by different authors under the editorship of C. M. Cipolla. Those published so far include *European Industries* by Domenico Sella, *European Trade* by Kristof Glamann, *Population in Europe* by R. Mols and *The Emergence of Modern Finance in Europe* by Geoffrey Parker (London: Collins, 1970–73). The complete volume is expected to appear in October 1974.

In vols. iii and iv of *The New Cambridge Modern History*, note the two chapters by F. C. Spooner concerned with the economy of Europe from 1559 to 1650,[2] and J. P. Cooper's General Introduction to vol. iv.

The following contain important essays: *Essays in Economic History*, ed. E. M. Carus-Wilson, (3 vols., London: Edward Arnold, 1954–66), consists of articles that have ap-

---

[1] Vol. v, the exact title of which has not yet been decided, will probably appear in 1975. The proposed table of contents is as follows: Introduction, by C. H. Wilson; c. 2, Fishing Fleets and Ports, by L. A. Harper; c. 3, European Trade, 1500–1750, by K. Glamann; c. 4, European Industry, by H. Kellenbenz; c. 5, European Agriculture to the end of the 18th century, by B. H. Slicher van Bath; c. 6, Banking, Credit and Finance, by H. van der Wee; c. 7, The State and the Economy, by C. B. A. Behrens; c. 8, The Nature of Enterprise, by B. E. Supple. I am much obliged to Mr P. E. T. Davies, of the Cambridge University Press, for supplying me with this information.

[2] Spooner's book, *The International Economy and Monetary Movements in France 1493–1725*, is listed under FRANCE, ECONOMIC AND SOCIAL HISTORY.

peared in *Economic History* and *The Economic History Review*. Charles Wilson, *Economic History and the Historian* (London: Weidenfeld and Nicolson, 1969) includes *inter alia* essays on mercantilism, taxation and the decline of empires. This author's Historical Association pamphlet, *Mercantilism*, was reprinted in 1971. *The Economic Decline of Empires*, ed. Carlo M. Cipolla (London: Methuen, 1970) includes essays by the editor on the decline of Italy, by Vives and Elliott on the decline of Spain, by Bernard Lewis on the decline of the Ottoman Empire, by C. R. Boxer on the economic decline of the United Provinces. *Revisions in Mercantilism* ed. D. C. Coleman, (London: Methuen, 1969), also includes essays by continental scholars. On this subject see also R. C. Blitz, 'Mercantilist Policies and the Pattern of World Trade 1500–1750', in *Journal of Economic History*, xxvii, no. 1 (1967). E. F. Hecksher's *Mercantilism*, which has been revised and reprinted on several occasions since its first appearance in an English translation in 1935, is too well known to require further mention.

For the controversy about 'the crisis of the seventeenth century' (a concept first put forward by Roland Mousnier) see *Crisis in Europe 1560–1660*, ed. Trevor Aston (London: Routledge, 1965) in which are reprinted a number of articles on the subject, most of which originally appeared in *Past and Present*. Among them should be noted the contribution of Mousnier himself. Those by H. R. Trevor-Roper, Michael Roberts and J. H. Hexter are reprinted in collections of essays by these three historians entitled respectively *Religion, The Reformation and Social Change* (London: Macmillan, 1967), *Essays in Swedish History* (London: Weidenfeld and Nicolson, 1967) and *Reappraisals in History* (London: Longman, 1961)—collections which contain other essays relevant to the social and economic history of this period. For details of some of the subsequent contributions to the debate, including Professor Lublinskaya's book referred to below (p. 551), see J. H. Elliott, 'Revolution and continuity in early modern Europe', in *Past and Present*, xlii (Feb. 1969). An outstanding one which should not be overlooked is I. Schöffer, 'Did Holland's Golden Age coincide with a period of crisis?' in *Acta Historiae Neerlandica*, i (1966).[1] The viewpoints more recently put forward in J. H. Shennan, *Government and Society in France 1461–1661*, (referred to more fully p. 547); D. H. Pennington, *Seventeenth Century Europe* (London: Longman, 1970) and A. L. Moote, *The Seventeenth Century: Europe in Ferment* (Lexington, Mass: D. C. Heath, 1970) although more briefly expressed also deserve attention. The subject is far more fully examined in part 4 of Henry Kamen, *The Iron Century: social change in Europe 1550–1650* (London: Weidenfeld and Nicolson, 1971), an important work of scholarship much of it based on original research and including chapters on the growth of capitalism, on the European nobility, gentry and bourgeoisie and on the peasant economy of the period. See John Bossy's review in *Economic History Review* (Aug. 1972).[2] Note also *Preconditions of Revolution in Early Modern Europe*, ed. Robert Forster and Jack P. Greene (Baltimore and London: Johns Hopkins University Press, 1970) which contains *inter alia* essays by Mousnier on the Fronde and by Elliott on the revolts against the Spanish monarchy in the 1640s. H. G. Koenigsberger, *Estates and Revolutions* (New York: Cornell University Press, 1971) is a collection of eleven articles on the sixteenth and seventeenth centuries some of which have some bearing on this subject.

Three more general surveys which are of distinct value for the seventeenth century are:

[1] J. V. Polišenský's article 'The Thirty Years War and the Crises and Revolutions of Seventeenth Century Europe' in *Past and Present* (April 1968) is noted elsewhere.

[2] Maurice Ashley's *The Golden Century 1598–1715* which belongs to the same series but is more concerned with cultural history is listed under HISTORY OF ART.

B. H. Slicher van Bath, trans. O. Ordish, *Agrarian History of Western Europe A.D. 500–1850* (London: Edward Arnold, 1963); G. Renard and G. Weulersee, trans. M. Richards, *Life and Work in Modern Europe from the fifteenth century to the eighteenth century* (London: Kegan Paul Trench and Trubner, 1926); and J. U. Nef, *War and Human Progress* (London: Routledge, 1950). This last named work reprinted in 1963 as a Harper Torchback under the title *Western Civilisation since the Renaissance* is a stimulating and debatable discussion of the role of war in modern European economic and social development.

Note also C. M. Cipolla, *Clocks and Culture 1300–1700* (London: Collins, 1967), *Economy and Society in Early Modern Europe* ed. Peter Burke, (London: Routledge, 1972) consists of eight articles, four of them concerned with the sixteenth-century price revolution, from the well-known French historical journal *Annales* with which the names of Lucien Febvre, Marc Bloch and Fernand Braudel will always be particularly associated. Burke has contributed a useful short introduction on these three French historians in which he also discusses briefly the work of Simiand, Chaunu, Goubert and Le Roy Ladurie. The same historian is responsible for assembling and editing a selection from Febvre's writings, under the title *A New Kind of History* (London: Routledge, 1973). Amongst them is an essay on witchcraft written in 1948. (This subject is dealt with under the heading GENERAL EUROPEAN RELIGIOUS HISTORY). References will be found elsewhere in this guide to English translations of works by Marc Bloch. For Braudel, the reader should consult *The Journal of Modern History*, xliv (Dec. 1972), which contains fanfares in his honour sounded by H. R. Trevor-Roper and J. H. Hexter to celebrate the appearance in an English translation of the first volume of his masterpiece on the Mediterranean world in the time of Philip II (for bibliographical details see under SPAIN). Here it is appropriate to mention the first volume of his *Capitalism and Material Life 1400–1800*, trans. Miriam Kochan (London: Weidenfeld and Nicolson, 1973). See T. Stoianovich's review of the French edition, published in 1967, in *Journal of Modern History*, xli (March 1969)—'A student who does not find it almost unbearably exciting should give up historical studies', comments Max Beloff. This sense of the emotive quality of history emerges from Braudel's own 'Personal Testimony'[1] with its tributes to an older generation of historians and the influence which they exercised upon him—men such as Pirenne, Febvre, Hauser and Bloch. But perhaps his most moving tribute is to an anonymous schoolmaster, 'At school, which I entered late, I had a superb teacher, a man who was intelligent, considerate, authoritarian and who recited the history of France as though he were celebrating Mass.'

In connection with the comments of J. P. Cooper and Henry Kamen on the European nobility in works referred to above, see also J. H. Hexter's 'The Education of the Aristocracy in the Renaissance' in *Reappraisals in History* (already mentioned) and Stuart Woolf's 'The Aristocracy in Transition: a Continental Comparison' in *Economic History Review*, xxxiii, no. 3 (Dec. 1970). The latter article, which was prompted by Laurence Stone's book on the crisis of the English aristocracy between 1558 and 1641, makes the point that 'the view that the western European aristocracies were prohibited from engaging in business whereas their English counterparts were not is far from accurate. What was forbidden on the Continent was the exercise of "mechanical" arts or menial trades. In practical terms, this was not very different from the acceptance of "proper" limits to aristocratic business activities in England.' Woolf goes on to point out that mining, fen

---

[1] Printed in *The Journal of Modern History*, xliv cited above. Note that the collection of essays from *Annales* edited by Peter Burke to which reference has been made above includes one by Braudel on History and the Social Sciences.

drainage and urban development, for example, were perfectly proper activities for a member of the nobility in Western Europe, that the great families of seventeenth-century Andalusia played a prominent part in trading activities, and that an absolutist monarch was quite capable of requiring his courtiers to hold shares in joint stock companies.

FRANCE, ECONOMIC AND SOCIAL HISTORY

BIBLIOGRAPHIES AND GENERAL SURVEYS

In addition to those listed under FRANCE AND THE FRENCH MONARCHY and FRANCE, LITERARY HISTORY see works mentioned under GENERAL EUROPEAN HISTORY and GENERAL EUROPEAN ECONOMIC AND SOCIAL HISTORY. Note also a number of relevant works cited under the headings FRANCE, RELIGIOUS HISTORY; HISTORY OF ART; MUSIC; MILITARY AND NAVAL HISTORY, etc.

Note further that, as mentioned in a note to Professor Tapié's bibliography (p. 512), the first volume of Pierre Goubert's *L'ancien régime* has appeared in an English translation by S. Cox under the title *The Ancien Régime: French society 1600–1750*. It includes short chapters on demography, the nobility, rural and urban society etc.

POPULATION

Although the number of articles available in English on the population of seventeenth-century France is very limited, some idea of the present range of French demographic studies can be gained by consulting the article by Emmanuel Le Roy Ladurie entitled 'From Waterloo to Colyton' in *The Times Literary Supplement* for 8 September 1966.[1] *Daedalus* (the Journal of the American Academy of Arts and Sciences) for spring 1968 contains an excellent study on infant mortality in eighteenth-century France (which gives useful information on sources in Brittany) by Pierre Goubert, and an article on historical demography by Louis Henry. See also in the same journal David Landes, 'The treatment of population in history textbooks'.[2]

See in *Population in History; Essays in historical demography*, ed. D. V. Glass and D. E. C. Eversley (London: Edward Arnold, 1965) the contributions of P. Goubert and J. Meuvret, (trans. Margaret Hilton), 'Recent theories and research in French population between 1500 and 1700' and 'The demographic crisis in France from the sixteenth century to the eighteenth century'. P. Laslett's remarkable essay, *The World we have lost* (London: Methuen, 1965, 2nd ed., 1971), although concerned with English society, makes good use of Goubert's work on the Beauvaisis mentioned in Professor Tapié's bibliography and his article 'Le brassage de la population en France et en Angleterre au XVIIe et au XVIIIe siècles' (*Annales de démographie historique*, 1968) underlines the degree of Anglo-French cooperation that exists in the field of demographic studies. A recent book which I have not read is O. and P. Ranum (eds.), *Popular attitudes towards birth control in pre-industrial France and England* (New York: Harper and Row Torchback no. 1696, 1972).

---

[1] Note also Professor Le Roy Ladurie's *Times of Feast, Times of Famine; a History of Climate since the year 1000*, trans. B. Bray (London: George Allen and Unwin, 1973) which first appeared in France in 1967. His two-volume study, *Les paysans de Languedoc* (Paris: S.E.V.P.E.N., 1966) has not so far as I am aware appeared in an English translation.

[2] All the articles which first appeared in the above number of *Daedalus* have since been reprinted together with eight new demographic studies on other topics in *Population and Social Change*, ed. D. V. Glass and Roger Revelle (London: Edward Arnold, 1972). R. S. Schofield's paper 'Historical Demography: some possibilities and some limitations' (*Transactions of the Royal Historical Society*, 5th series, xxi (1971) cites two important general studies of this subject which have appeared since 1968, by E. A. Wrigley and T. H. Hollingsworth.

AGRARIAN HISTORY AND POPULAR RISINGS

Marc Bloch, *French rural history*, trans. Janet Sondheimer, (London: Routledge, 1966) is a translation of the original version of *Les caractères originaux de l'histoire rurale française* without the supplement added by R. Dauvergne in 1956. English translations of the works of Marc Bloch to date are considered in an article on this eminent historian by R. R. Davies, *History*, lii (1967), 265–86. Elsewhere in this guide are noted translations of two more books by Bloch which have appeared since 1967 (pp. 532, 545).

A balanced approach to a controversial subject which is relevant to this period also is made by Elizabeth S. Teall in her article 'The Seigneur of Renaissance France: advocate or oppressor?', *Journal of Modern History*, xxxvii (June 1965). *Cf.* R. Forster, 'The provincial noble: a reappraisal', in *American Historical Review*, lxvii (1963). Davis Bitton, *The French Nobility in Crisis 1560–1640* (Stanford University Press, 1969) is an interesting but misleadingly entitled monograph—see the searching reviews of Menna Prestwich in *Economic History Review*, xxiv, no. 1 (1971) and of Raymond F. Kierstead in *Journal of Social History*, v, no. 3 (Spring 1972).

P. Goubert, 'The French peasantry of the seventeenth century: a regional example', trans. G. Rudé, *Past and Present* (Nov. 1956) is a masterly summary which is reprinted in Trevor Aston's *Crisis in Europe 1550–1650*, mentioned above. I have not read I. Woloch's general study, *The Peasantry of the Old Régime* (New York: Holt Rinehart, 1970). Olwen Hufton's 'Begging, Vagrancy, Vagabondage and the Law' in *European Studies Review* vol. ii, no. 2 (April 1972) is admittedly concerned with eighteenth-century France but brings out the extent to which, despite all Saint Vincent de Paul's efforts, the poor in the countryside had no special institutions to relieve them, and is particularly illuminating on the seasonal migrant from barren areas such as Auvergne or Savoy. E. Chill's article, 'Religion and Mendicity in seventeenth century France', (*International Review of Social Sciences*, vii (1962)) should also be noted.

This is a convenient place to mention the translation of pp. 280, 282 and 283–99 of the Russian edition of Porshnev's book (referred to in Professor Tapié's bibliography above) which is printed in *Revolutions in Modern European History*, ed. Heinz Lubasz (New York: Macmillan Company, 1966) under the title 'Plebeian uprisings in France preceding the Fronde 1623–48'—although the context of the risings there mentioned is mainly urban. A list of the popular disturbances examined by Porshnev in the course of his book is printed on the opening page.[1] An urban movement that does not feature in this list forms the subject of a scholarly monograph by S. A. Westrich: *The Ormée of Bordeaux* (Baltimore and London: Johns Hopkins University Press, 1972) which also briefly examines the background to the Bordeaux revolts of 1635 and 1643, and estimates that England accounted for one-third of Bordeaux's exports. J. H. M. Salmon, 'Venality of office and popular sedition in seventeenth century France', *Past and Present*, xxxvii (July 1967) 21–43, is a valuable review of the controversy between Messrs. Porshnev and Mousnier (mentioned in Professor Tapié's bibliography) which also considers the attitude adopted by Professor Lublinskaya (see below) and gives details of the quantity of Séguier's correspondence hitherto published by these three scholars. Since this date, as mentioned in a note to Professor Tapié's bibliography, Mousnier's *Fureurs paysannes: les paysans dans les révoltes du XVIIe siècle* (Paris, 1967), has appeared in a workmanlike English translation by Brian Pearce under the title *Peasant uprisings in seventeenth century France, Russia and*

[1] For details of further passages from Porshnev's book that have appeared in English, see p. 547 below.

China (London: George Allen and Unwin, 1971). This translation is referred to several times in my editorial notes. The Russian and Chinese rather than the French chapters of Mousnier's book are given a rough handling in a contribution to *Past and Present* for Feb. 1971 by three American scholars—Michael O. Gately, A. Lloyd Moote and John E. Wills, 'Seventeenth Century Peasant "Furies": some problems of comparative history'.

Note also the penetrating review of both the French translation of Porshnev's book and Robert Mandrou's *Classes et luttes des classes en France au début du XVIIe siècle* by Menna Prestwich in the *English Historical Review*, lxxxi (1966), 565–72, where M. Mousnier's views are also analysed.

URBAN HISTORY AND SOCIAL LIFE

For popular disturbances see previous sub-section.

This is probably an appropriate place to mention David Maland's *Culture and Society in Seventeenth Century France* (London: Batsford, 1970) a useful book, which neglects neither town planning nor landscape gardening.

Howard M. Solomon, *Public welfare, science and propaganda in seventeenth century France: the innovations of Théophraste Renaudot* (Princeton, N.Y.: Princeton University Press, 1972), which is also mentioned elsewhere in this guide, is listed here because of its valuable account of Renaudot's activities as *Commissaire Général des Pauvres* (from 1618) and of his *Bureau d'Adresse* (established *c.* 1630) both of which brought him into close touch with the poorer classes of Paris. 'Henry IV's Paris had a population of at least 400,000 and estimates of chronically unemployed poor ranged as high as 20 to 25 per cent'. *Cf.* two studies of poor relief in sixteenth-century Lyons and Geneva: N. Z. Davis, 'Poor Relief, Humanism and Heresy: the case of Lyon' (printed in *Studies in Medieval and Renaissance History*, vol. v, 1968) and Robert N. Kingdon, 'Social Welfare in Calvin's Geneva', in *The American Historical Review*, lxxvi (1971). Note also Solomon's description of the situation in Renaudot's birthplace, Loudun, and a forthcoming article in *French Historical Studies*: 'Social welfare and the Edict of Nantes: Lyons and Nîmes' by Wilma J. Pugh.

Nancy L. Roelker (trans. and ed.), *The Paris of Henry of Navarre* (Cambridge, Mass: Harvard University Press, 1958), represents a selection from the *Mémoires-Journaux* of Pierre de l'Estoile which stops short at 1599 (the original diary continues to 1611). Miss Roelker rightly claims that l'Estoile's diary does for late sixteenth-century Paris what Pepys' Diary did for Restoration London; her introduction, translation and editorial work are all of high quality.

Orest Ranum, *Paris in the age of absolutism* (New York: John Wiley and Sons, 1968), also the work of an expert, contains interesting illustrations and is one of a recent series entitled *New dimensions in history: historical cities*. See also Ronda Larmour, 'A merchant guild of sixteenth century France: the grocers of Paris', in *Economic History Review* (1967), and, in the same review (1966), N. Z. Davis, 'A trade union in sixteenth century France' (concerned with the printers journeymen of Lyons).

For a notice regarding the *Bibliographie d'histoire des Villes de France*, ed. P. Dollinger and P. Wolff (Paris, 1967), published under the auspices of the International Commission for the History of Towns, see *History* (Oct. 1968), 419.

Marc Bloch, *The Île-de-France*, trans. J. E. Anderson (London: Routledge and Kegan Paul, 1971) is concerned with the origins, extent, geography and archaeology as well as past history of the province which became the heart of France.

In addition to the light thrown on contemporary social life by a number of books listed under the headings FRANCE, RELIGIOUS HISTORY and FRANCE AND THE FRENCH MONARCHY, it is perhaps worthwhile to mention one of a number of contemporary English sources which is of some value. This is *The Diary of John Evelyn*, ed. E. S. de Beer (6 vols., Oxford: The Clarendon Press, 1955). Evelyn was in France or Italy from 1643 to 1647 and from 1649 to 1652 and, although much of the topographical information which he gives was cribbed from contemporary guide books, the importance of the Diary as a source is greatly enhanced by the superlative work of the editor, who not only identifies but also supplies more details about almost everyone and everything Evelyn mentions. See also J. W. Stoye's useful survey, *English travellers abroad 1604–67* (London: Jonathan Cape, 1952). John Locke's journal of his travels in France belongs, of course, to a later period.

Turning to a different aspect of social history, P. Ariès, *Centuries of Childhood* (originally entitled *L'enfant et la vie familiale sous l'Ancien Régime*), trans. R. Baldick, (London: Cape, 1962) is particularly interesting on education although his views in other respects have met with some criticism—see, for instance, N. Z. Davis, 'The Reasons of Misrule: Youth Groups and Charivaris in Sixteenth Century France' in *Past and Present* (Feb. 1971). Another book on the same theme reviewed by Olwen Hufton in *History*, lvi (1971) is David Hunt, *Parents in History: the Psychology of Family Life in Early Modern France* (New York: Basic Books, 1970). The reviewer complains that a great deal is deduced from very little and that, since the author concentrates his attention on the uppermost echelons of French society, and more particularly on Louis XIII's relations with his parents, the title is highly misleading.

TRADE AND INDUSTRY

Note F. B. Artz, *The development of technical education in France 1500–1850* (Cambridge, Mass: M.I.T. Press, 1966), J. U. Nef, *Industry and government in France and England 1540–1640*, (Ithaca, N.Y. and London: Cornell University Press, 1957). The same author's 'Prices and Industrial Capitalism in France and England 1540–1640' is printed in *Essays in Economic History*, i, ed. E. M. Carus-Wilson (cited p. 526).

For the place occupied by the Huguenots in seventeenth-century French industry and commerce see W. C. Scoville, 'The Huguenots in the French economy 1650–1750' (*Quarterly Journal of Economics*, lxvii (August 1953)), the same author's two articles on 'The Huguenots and the diffusion of technology' (*Journal of Political Economy*, lx (1952)) and his subsequent work *The persecution of the Huguenots and French economic development 1680–1720*, University of California Press, 1960): for watchmaking however cf. C. M. Cipolla, *Clocks and Culture* (cited p. 528) Note also Scoville's *Capitalism and French Glass-making 1640–1789* (University of California Press, 1950).

For internal trade, see also D. J. Buisseret, 'The communications of France during the reconstruction of Henry IV', *Economic History Review* (1965). A. P. Usher, *The History of the Grain Trade in France 1400–1710* (Cambridge, Mass: Harvard University Press, 1913) contains much that is still of value. David T. Pottinger, *The French Book Trade in the Ancien Régime 1500–1791* (Cambridge, Mass: Harvard University Press, 1958) covers a much wider range of topics than might be supposed with chapters on censorship, journeymen, strikes, paper-making, book illustration and so on, as well as on the roles of author, printer and publisher and the administration of the book trade. Note, in this connection N. Z. Davis's article on the printers' journeymen of Lyons, cited above.

R. B. Grassby, 'Social Status and Commercial Enterprise under Louis XIV (*Economic History Review*, 2nd series, xiii, no. 1 (1960)) shows Louis XIV pursuing Richelieu's policy of stimulating commerce by ennoblement and attempting to induce the nobility to engage therein.

On French mercantilism, see C. W. Cole, *French mercantilist doctrines before Colbert*

(New York: Richard R. Smith, 1931) and the same author's *Colbert and a century of French mercantilism*, (2 vols., New York: Columbia University Press, 1939). Though narrow in their approach, these books contain much useful information. In L. Rothkrug, *Opposition to Louis XIV; the Political and Social Origins of the French Enlightenment* (Princeton University Press, 1965), Part I gives an interesting, but disputable, account of mercantilism and its opponents, 1576–1683.

Various aspects of French external trade (for which reference should also be made to works listed under NAVAL HISTORY and TURKEY) are examined in the following: W. Kirchner, *Commercial relations between Russia and Europe 1400–1800* (Indiana University Press, Russian and East European Series, xxxiii, 1966). This book includes an essay entitled 'The beginnings of Franco-Russian economic relations 1550–1650'.

D. W. Davies, *A primer of Dutch seventeenth century overseas trade* (The Hague: Martinus Nijhoff, 1961) includes a chapter on France. Two works concerned with piracy and trade in the Mediterranean should be mentioned here: Sir Godfrey Fisher, *Barbary Legend: War, Trade and Piracy in North Africa 1415–1830* (Oxford: The Clarendon Press, 1957) is amongst other things a defence of the Barbary corsairs. See the review by C. R. Boxer in *The Mariners Mirror*, xliv (1958), and compare the attitude shown in A. Tenenti's book, *Piracy and the decline of Venice 1580–1615*, referred to under the heading ITALY. Note that a study of the Barbary corsairs is being prepared by John B. Wolf. Both for the corsairs and for France's Mediterranean trade, Braudel (cited, p. 574) is invaluable.

FINANCIAL

F. C. Spooner, *The International Economy and Monetary Movements in France 1493–1725* (Cambridge, Mass: Harvard University Press, 1972), a revised and extended version of a study originally published in French in 1956, is dedicated to Fernand Braudel, with whom the author had already collaborated in studying prices in Europe from 1450 to 1750 (see *The Cambridge Economic History of Europe*, vol. iv). It is a work of immense learning whose range can be judged from the fact that its 32 graphs are devoted to such topics as prices of copper in Amsterdam, loans to the Spanish monarchy, and monthly totals of exports of silver from Venice to the Levant 1610–14, as well as to wheat prices in Paris and the annual activity of French mints.

M. Wolfe, 'French views on wealth and taxes from the Middle Ages to the Old Régime', *Journal of Economic History*, xxvi, no. 4 (1966), is an interesting survey.

The Fiscal System of Renaissance France by the same author (Yale University Press, 1972) studies the period from the early fifteenth century up to Sully's dismissal in 1611 and concludes: 'To say that the tax system of Richelieu's France owed a great deal to Renaissance France would be to make a gross understatement . . . the chief significance of French Renaissance fiscal history . . . is that the institutions and attitudes of the Renaissance system became a deadly burden in the seventeenth century . . . its ramifications into French society were so deep, its structure so solid, the level of revenues that it produced so vital to the king, that it resisted—apart from a few matters—even the reforming zeal of Turgot'. The appendices entitled 'The Chief Elements of the Tax Machine', which constitute almost one third of the book, contain authoritative accounts, not only of institutions such as the *Bureaux des Finances*, the *Chambre des Comptes* and the *Cour des Aides*, but also of the procedure for levying the *taille* and for farming the *aides*, as well as of the salt taxes, the *domaines* revenues and the network of tariffs and tolls that enmeshed pre-Revolutionary France. Mr Wolfe has blazed a broad, clear trail through this administrative and fiscal jungle and his book deserves high praise.

George T. Matthews, *The royal general farms in eighteenth century France* (New York: Columbia University Press, 1958): a valuable work which is not superseded by that mentioned above and which deserves to be more widely known, especially since it ranges back into pre-eighteenth-century history.

David Buisseret's book *Sully and the growth of centralised government in France 1598–1610* and Professor Lublinskaya's work *French absolutism: the crucial phase, 1620–29*, which are considered more fully on pp. 550–51 below, both contain information of value on this subject, as well as on economic and social conditions generally in early seventeenth-century France. For the government's use of special tribunals to try superintendents of finance (such as La Vieuville), their agents and their subordinates, see '*Chambres de justice* in the French monarchy', in *French government and society 1500–1800*, ed. J. K. Bosher (London: Athlone Press, 1973).

Julian Dent, 'An aspect of the crisis of the seventeenth century: the collapse of the financial administration of the French monarchy (1653–61)' in *Economic History Review*, xx (1967), also gives useful general information on the workings of the financial system. The same author's 'The role of clientèles in the financial élite of France under Cardinal Mazarin' in the collection of essays edited by Bosher mentioned above emphasises that much of the financial chaos and incompetence of the early years of Mazarin's ministry might have been avoided if, like Richelieu, he had had time to build up a clientèle of able and loyal supporters in the administration before Louis XIII's death. Dent's *Crisis in Finance: crown, financiers and society in seventeenth century France* (Newton Abbot: David and Charles, 1973) is an excellent study of the financial administration, of the role of the Paris financiers known as *traitants*, and of their connections with the world at large.

The Journal of European Economic History, vol. i, no. 3 (Winter 1972) contains some notes on French public finance in the seventeenth century by Robert M. Jennings and Andrew P. Trout.

GENERAL EUROPEAN RELIGIOUS HISTORY

BIBLIOGRAPHIES, ENCYCLOPEDIAS ETC.

In addition to those mentioned at the beginning of this guide, the following will be found of particular service:

The Oxford Dictionary of the Christian Church, ed. F. L. Cross (Oxford: Oxford University Press, 2nd ed., 1974) is an admirable publication in one volume, both concise and scholarly. On a larger scale, *The New Catholic Encyclopaedia* (15 vols., New York and London: Mc Graw-Hill, 1967) is also a work of high quality which completely supersedes its unsatisfactory predecessor *The Catholic Encyclopaedia* (1907–14, with a supplement issued in 1922). Both these works give useful up-to-date bibliographical information.

Donald Attwater's excellent little book, *The Penguin Dictionary of Saints* (1965) can be usefully consulted for short biographies of a number of saints whose names are mentioned by Professor Tapié. See also Attwater's second revised edition of A. Butler, *Lives of the Saints* (4 vols., 1956), and note Helen Roeder, *Saints and their Attributes* (cited under HISTORY OF ART).

Details of further works of reference as well as of particular studies are given in Owen Chadwick's pamphlet *The History of the Church: a select bibliography* (London: Historical Association, 3rd ed., 1973) which is, however, decidedly thin on seventeenth-century Europe. It should be supplemented by A. G. Dickens's article 'Recent books on the Reformation and Counter Reformation', in *The Journal of Ecclesiastical History*, xix (Oct. 1968), J. W. O'Malley, 'Recent Studies in Church History 1300–1600', in *The Catholic Historical Review*, lv (1969–70), and Laurence D. Stokes, *Mediaeval and Modern Germany (to 1648): a select bibliography* (London: Historical Association, 1972). The latter, which is confined to works printed in English, gives details of many books which are not uniquely concerned with German history, such as H. J. Hillerbrand, *A Bibliography of Anabaptism 1520–1630* (Indiana: Elkhard, 1962) and *The Mennonite Encyclopedia* (4 vols., Pennsylvania: Scottdale, 1955–59).

Turning to witchcraft and allied subjects, there is no need to mention here earlier standard works of reference other than H. C. Lea's compendium, *Materials towards a History of Witchcraft*, edited and arranged by A. C. Howland (3 vols., Philadelphia: Pennsylvania University Press, 1939).

More recent works include the following:

R. R. Robbins, *Encyclopaedia of Witchcraft and Demonology* (London: Peter Nevill, 1959): to be used with caution; considerable knowledge but presentation confused.

W. Bonser, *A Bibliography of Folklore* (London: Folklore Society, 1961).

An Encyclopedia of The Unexplained: Magic, Occultism and Parapsychology ed. Richard Cavendish, and containing an extensive bibliography, is to be published by Routledge and Kegan Paul in 1974.

GENERAL WORKS

Note the series of essays by various scholars on a wide variety of topics produced by the Ecclesiastical History Society under the title *Studies in Church History* (9 vols., 1964–72, in progress, the publishers being Nelson, London (vols. 1 and 2) E. J. Brill, Leiden (vols. 3–5) and Cambridge University Press (vol. 6 onwards)).

See the volumes of *The New Cambridge Modern History* already mentioned. The chapter on changes in religious thought in vol. iv is by G. L. Mosse.

The Cambridge History of the Bible, vol. iii, *The West from the Reformation to the Present*

Day, ed. S. L. Greenslade (Cambridge University Press, 1963), contains *inter alia* chapters on English and continental versions of the Bible during the sixteenth and seventeenth centuries and its role in the Roman Catholic Church from the time of the Council of Trent.

L. von Pastor, *History of the Popes from the close of the Middle Ages*, (London, 40 vols., 1891–1953; vols. 1 and 2, John Hodge (1891); vols. 3–34, Kegan Paul Trench and Trubner, 1894–1941; vols. 35–40, Routledge and Kegan Paul, 1949–53). For the period covered by Louis XIII's reign, see in particular vols. xxv–xxix inclusive. The translation by Dom Ernest Graf o.s.b. is of a very high standard.

Émile G. Léonard, *A History of Protestantism*, vol. ii, *The Establishment*, trans. R. M. Bethell, ed. H. H. Rowley (London: Nelson, 1967), covers this period and gives full bibliographies. The translation however is not so satisfactory.

J. T. McNeill, *The History and Character of Calvinism* (Oxford University Press, 1954). Note the 78-page bibliographical essay by this author included in the reprint of Williston Walker, *John Calvin* (New York: Schocken Books, 1969). H. R. Trevor-Roper's 'Religion, the Reformation and Social Change' in the collection of his essays published under that title (London: Macmillan, 1967) re-examines and redefines the connection between Calvinism and economic enterprise first postulated by Max Weber. (This essay is also mentioned under the sub-heading Counter-Reformation below).

For a valuable list of the principal books and articles in English that are devoted to this perennially fresh subject, see Stokes, pp. 60–1; there has since appeared L. M. Lachmann, *The Legacy of Max Weber* (London: Heinemann, 1970).

C. P. Clasen, *Anabaptism: a social history 1525–1618* (Ithaca and London: Cornell University Press, 1972). This survey is concerned with Switzerland, Austria and the Czech lands, as well as South and Central Germany. Note also J. K. Zeman, *The Anabaptists and the Czech Brethren in Moravia 1526–1628: a study of origins and contacts* (The Hague: Mouton, 1969)

F. A. Norwood, *Strangers and Exiles: a history of religious refugees* (Nashville, Tennessee: Abingdon Press, 1969): spans the period 1517–1685.

WORKS CONCERNED WITH PARTICULAR ASPECTS OF EUROPEAN RELIGIOUS HISTORY
(i) *The Council of Trent*
Note H. J. Schroeder (ed. and trans.), *Canons and Decrees of the Council of Trent* (St Louis and London, 1941). Only the first three volumes of H. Jedin's *History of the Council of Trent* have appeared to date; the first two have been published in an excellent English translation by Dom Ernest Graf (London: Nelson, 1957, 1961). For the third volume see John Bossy's review in *European Studies Review*, iii, no. 2 (April 1973). Fortunately, however, reference can be made to his valuable summary of the Council's last stages: *Crisis and Closure of the Council of Trent: a retrospective view from the second Vatican Council*, trans. N. D. Smith (London: Sheed and Ward, Stagbooks, 1967).

'The Council of Trent, the *Spiritual Exercises* and the Catholic Reform', an article by Robert E. McNally s.j. (*Church History*, xxxiv (1965)) gives a useful short analysis of the exercises and makes it clear that they were not intended as a manual of popular devotion. Note also L. B. Pascoe, 'The Council of Trent and Bible Study' (*Catholic Historical Review* lii (1967)). For the Council's attitude towards religious music and influence on the greatest composer of sacred music of his day, see H. Coates, *Palestrina* (London: J. M. Dent, 1938).

(ii) *The Counter-Reformation*

B. J. Kidd, *The Counter-Reformation 1550–1600* (London, 1933) is still of service. For biographies of some of its leading sixteenth-century figures, see Chadwick's bibliography (cited above) and that of Dickens (mentioned below); see also Stokes, pp. 52–3, and FRANCE, RELIGIOUS HISTORY.

Note Ellis Waterhouse's essay 'Some painters and the Counter-Reformation before 1600' (cited under HISTORY OF ART).

The following are of more general interest and more relevant to the seventeenth century: A. G. Dickens, *The Counter-Reformation* (London and New York: Thames and Hudson, 1968)—an admirable and perceptive survey with a useful short bibliography. H. O. Evennett, ed. J. Bossy, *The Spirit of the Counter-Reformation* (Cambridge University Press, 1968): the Birkberk lectures and the work of a sensitive scholar. A. V. Antonovics, 'Counter-Reformation Cardinals 1534–90' in *European Studies Review*, ii, no. 4 (Oct. 1972) is a useful corrective to some of Evennett's judgements.

J. Bossy, 'The Counter-Reformation and the people of Catholic Europe' (*Past and Present*, xlvii); concerned essentially with France and Italy, and considered under FRANCE, RELIGIOUS HISTORY. Note also E. Cochrane, 'New light on post-Tridentine Italy: a Note on recent Counter-Reformation scholarship', in *Catholic Historical Review*, lvi (1970–1); A. P. Farrell, *The Jesuit Code of Liberal Education* (1938). Trevor-Roper's essay 'Religion, the Reformation and Social Change' (cited p. 537) which contends that it was 'the Counter-Reformation State which extruded [individual] economic enterprise from society, not Calvinist doctrine which created it . . .' and points to the increase in princely and clerical bureaucracy in countries where the Counter-Reformation succeeded, has some interesting comments on the economic modernity of the Jesuits.

Rudolph Wittkower and Irma B. Jaffee, eds., *Baroque art: the Jesuit contribution* (New York: Fordham University Press, 1972)—a symposium; J. Brodrick s.j., *Robert Bellarmine* (revised edition, 1961); Fr Cuthbert o.s.f.c. [Lawrence Cuthbert Hess] *The Capuchins: a contribution to the history of the Counter-Reformation* (2 vols., London: Sheed and Ward, 1928)—a valuable survey; P. A. Kunkel, *the Theatines in the History of the Catholic Reform* (Washington D.C. 1941).

(iii) *Arminianism*

A. W. Harrison, *The beginnings of Arminianism to the Synod of Dort* (1926). See also *Arminianism* by the same author (1937). A useful article is C. Bangs, 'Arminius and the Reformation' (*Church History*, xxx). Note Trevor-Roper's analysis of Arminian influences at work in his important essay 'The religious origins of the Enlightenment' (printed in *Religion, the Reformation and Social Change* cited above). A recent work on Amyraut is noted under FRANCE, RELIGIOUS HISTORY.

(iv) *Toleration*

Joseph Lecler s.j., trans. J. L. Weston, *Toleration and the Reformation* (London: Longman, 1960): mainly concerned with the sixteenth century. For an analysis of the position in France between 1520 and Richelieu's ministry, see vol. ii, pp. 5–155. H. A. F. Kamen, *The Rise of Toleration* (London: Weidenfeld and Nicolson, 1967) is a good brief survey which covers both the sixteenth and seventeenth centuries.

(v) *Scepticism and Free-Thought*

Seventeenth Century Rationalism, with introduction by N. Cantor and P. L. Klein, in the

Monuments of Western Thought series (Waltham, Mass: Blaisdell, 1969) includes selections from and comments on a number of seventeenth-century figures including Bacon and Descartes. Richard H. Popkin, *The History of Scepticism from Erasmus to Descartes* (Assen: Van Gorcum, 1960) includes a chapter on the *libertins érudits* and two on Descartes. This valuable book is to some extent complemented by J. S. Spink, *French Free Thought from Gassendi to Voltaire*, mentioned under FRANCE, RELIGIOUS HISTORY below. Frances A. Yates, *The Rosicrucian Enlightenment* (London: Routledge and Kegan Paul, 1972). This fascinating study of which only a brief description can be given here, explores the historical background to some tracts published in early seventeenth-century Germany about a fictious hero, Christian Rosencreutz, said to be the founder of a mysterious order or fraternity whose members had the power of making themselves invisible. Doctor Yates examines the European impact of these tracts, notably in Germany and France, and their influence on figures such as Comenius. From the point of view of general European religious history two chapters deserve particular attention, 'The R. C. Fraternity and the Christian Unions' and 'Rosicrucionism and Freemasonry'. Readers of other works by this author will agree with Trevor-Roper, who describes this book as 'brilliant and exciting', that 'no one has done more than she to recreate from unexpected material the intellectual life of past ages'. Two recent works which to some extent complement Doctor Yates's study should be mentioned here: Peter French, *John Dee: World of an Elizabethan Magus* (London: Routledge and Kegan Paul, 1972) and R. J. W. Evans's book on Dee's patron, *Rudolf II and his World: a study in intellectual history 1576–1612* (Oxford, 1973). Note also Trevor-Roper's 'Three Foreigners: the philosophers of the Puritan Revolution' in his book of essays cited above. There is a masterly review of Doctor Yates's book by Evans in *The Historical Journal*, xvi, no. 4 (Dec. 1973).

(vi) *Witchcraft*

An influential contemporary work, the *Compendium Maleficarum* (or 'Handbook of Witches'), compiled by Francesco-Maria Guazzo, a Milanese friar, and printed in 1608, has recently been republished complete with its lurid illustrations (London: Muller, 1970). This book, which quotes from over three hundred 'authorities', soon became one of the standard seventeenth-century demonologies.

Note L. Febvre's essay in *A New Kind of History* (mentioned p. 528 above). Of recent works on this topic, H. R. Trevor-Roper's long and powerful essay 'The European witch-craze in the sixteenth and seventeenth centuries' should be listed first. It is already, and deserves to be, a classic, although it appeared for the first time in book form as recently as 1967 (in *Religion, the Reformation and Social Change* cited above). Like most classics, however, it has since been faulted on certain points, as mentioned below.

J. Burton Russell, *Witchcraft in the Middle Ages* (Ithaca and London: Cornell University Press, 1972) although it stops short at the end of the fifteenth century is far from irrelevant to this period. It also contains some useful judgements on the attitude of Rossell Hope Robbins whose *Encyclopedia of Witchcraft and Demonology*, has already been noted. The author rejects Trevor-Roper's view that witchcraft flourished particularly in mountainous areas and points out that it appeared in the Alps only after witches and heretics had taken refuge there to escape persecution elsewhere. Witchcraft, he asserts, flourished in the Middle Ages wherever and whenever heresy flourished. It was strongest in France, the Low Countries, the Rhineland, N. Italy and the Alpine regions 'with the exception of the last, the richest, most populous, most highly industrialised and most intellectually advanced areas in Europe'. Coming from an historian who has made a particular study of mediaeval religious dissent, these views command respect. The book is based on extensive researches—see, for example, the notes to chapter 9, pp. 338–42. There is also a very full bibliography.

Julio Caro Baroja, *The World of the Witches*, trans. Nigel Glendinning (London: Weidenfeld and Nicolson, 1964) is the work of an author particularly acquainted with the Basque provinces of Spain who has already written a book on magic in Castile in the sixteenth and seventeenth centuries (see p. 101). The first four chapters deal with the general, pre-classical and classical background to the subject; and of the remaining sixteen chapters no less than six relate to witchcraft trials in the Basque Country on both sides of the Pyrenees from the end of the fifteenth century until the seventeenth. For Baroja 'witchcraft in the Basque Provinces was closely linked from the start with its special social structure, and its pagan traditions' (p. 144). Note also the comments, partly shrewd and partly ludicrous, of the French judge de Lancre who was charged by Henry IV with the task of repressing witchcraft among Basques north of the Pyrenees (pp. 158–9). On other areas, the book is regrettably brief though knowledgeable and perceptive. The translation deserves praise. Four of Goya's *Caprichos* are reproduced but, rather unfortunately, there is no map.

Aldous Huxley, *The Devils of Loudun* (London: Chatto and Windus, 1952) is concerned with the case of Urbain Grandier.[1]

E. W. Monter, *European Witchcraft* (New York: Wiley, 1969) is a valuable selection of passages from sources and secondary authorities made by a specialist who has supplied illuminating commentaries; essentially post-mediaeval.

The following studies by the same scholar should also be noted: 'Inflation and Witchcraft: the Case of Jean Bodin' in *Action and Conviction in Early Modern Europe*, ed. Theodore K. Rabb and Jerrold E. Siegel (Princeton University Press, 1969): Monter draws a parallel between Bodin's attacks on Malestroit and Weyer for denying the reality of inflation and of witchcraft respectively and examines his aims and polemical methods. 'Witchcraft in Geneva 1537–1662' in *Journal of Modern History*, vol. xliii, no. 2 (1971).

'Patterns of Witchcraft in the Jura' in *Journal of Social History* vol. v, no. 1 (1971). This article is concerned with two predominantly rural but not unduly mountainous areas which now form part of the cantons of Neuchâtel and Berne; in the seventeenth century, however, they constituted 'an unimportant corner of the Holy Roman Empire, religiously diverse [although French-speaking then as now] and legally fragmented'. Making use of the abundant local records which testify to the fact that at least 500 people were put to death for witchcraft during the period under review, Monter tests some current hypotheses about the history of European witchcraft. The case of the Jura, he points out, makes nonsense of Trevor-Roper's thesis that 'the recrudescence of the European witch-craze in the 1560s was directly connected with the return of religious war'.

'The Jura was certainly a religious frontier area, yet it seems to have had no religious strife at all. On the other hand, Bâle bishopric [i.e. the French-speaking area of the present canton of Berne], which was under almost constant military occupation during the latter half of the Thirty Years War, had practically no trials for witchcraft during that

---

[1] The less said about the recent film on this subject, the better; but the little known Danish film *Day of Wrath*, made in the years following the 1939–45 war, conveys the horrifying atmosphere of a seventeenth-century Protestant witch hunt with marvellous authenticity.

period.' Religious *conflict*, Monter concludes, probably slowed the pace of witch trials; but religious *rivalry* may have increased their tempo.

He adds that, as elsewhere in the Empire, witchcraft in the Jura clearly cut across social boundaries and that the evidence shows that those indicted included quite a substantial minority of men. This article, which is accompanied by maps and tables, is an important contribution to a highly intricate subject.

H. C. Erik Midelfort, *Witch Hunting in Germany 1562–1684: the social and intellectual foundations* (Stanford University Press, Oxford, University Press, 1973). I have not been able to read this book.

For witchcraft in seventeenth-century Finland, see the English summary printed in A. Heikkinen, *Paholaisen Liittolaiset* (Historiallisia Tutkimuksia, Helsinki, 1969).

Note O. Diethelm, 'The Medical Teaching of Demonology in the Seventeenth and Eighteenth Centuries', in *Journal of Historical Behavioral Sciences*, vi (1970).

Finally, K. V. Thomas, *Religion and the Decline of Magic* (1971), although concerned with popular beliefs in England only, has too wide a significance to be omitted from this guide.

(vii) *Miscellaneous*

Alison Hoppen, 'The Finances of the Order of St John of Jerusalem in the Sixteenth and Seventeenth Centuries', in *European Studies Review*, iii, no. 2 (April 1973). Note that this article, which requires no description here, contains a reference to V. Borg, *Fabio Chigi, Apostolic Delegate in Malta (1634–39)* (Studi e Testi, no. 249, Vatican City, 1967). Chigi, who was later elected Pope as Alexander VII, was to play an important part from 1639 onwards in the negotiations which culminated in the Treaties of Westphalia.

FRANCE, RELIGIOUS HISTORY

With a few exceptions books or articles that refer to the period before 1600 have been excluded. For general assemblies of clergy and Protestant assemblies see works cited under FRANCE AND THE FRENCH MONARCHY, pp. 548–9.

BIBLIOGRAPHIES

See under the headings GENERAL EUROPEAN RELIGIOUS HISTORY, FRANCE AND THE FRENCH MONARCHY, and FRANCE, LITERARY HISTORY.

INTRODUCTORY SURVEYS

Note H. F. Kearney's essay 'Religion and society' in J. Cruickshank, ed., *French Literature and its Background* (p. 559) and other general surveys cited there and on p. 546.

CATHOLICISM

Of the three volumes of H. Bremond's *Histoire littéraire du sentiment religieux en France* which have been translated into English (for details, see Professor Tapié's bibliography above), the second and third are directly concerned with the reigns of Henry IV and Louis XIII. They provide the only full accounts available in English of men like Bérulle and Olier as well as of the great abbesses of early seventeenth-century France.

Michael de la Bedoyère, *François de Sales* (London: Collins, 1960). A popular life, whose judgements need to some extent to be corrected by Ruth Kleinman, *Saint François de Sales and the Protestants* (Geneva: Droz, 1962, no. 52 in the series *Travaux d'Humanisme et Renaissance*). This book (reviewed by H. O. Evennett in *History*, xlviii) makes it clear that, despite his gentleness and humanity as a person, St François de Sales did favour coercion of the Huguenots within his diocese by the State.

Note also *Saint Francis of Sales: Selected letters*, edited and translated by Elizabeth Stopp (London: Faber, 1960) and, for his influence on an English Catholic poet, M. F. Bertonasco, *Crashaw and the Baroque* (University of Alabama Press, 1971).

J. Brousse, *The lives of Ange de Joyeuse and Benet of Canfield*, ed. T. A. Birrell (London: Sheed and Ward, 1959). These two lives were published in French in 1621 and translated into English in 1623 by Robert Rookwood, a secular priest. Birrell reprints and edits Rookwood's text, to which he contributes a useful introduction. 'What Sully did for the French economy, Father Benet did for the mystical life'. Note that this English Capuchin also figures prominently in Aldous Huxley's *Grey Eminence*, mentioned by Professor Tapié above (p. 510) in connection with Father Joseph.

L. C. Sheppard, *Barbe Acarie: wife and mystic* (London: Burnes and Oates, 1953): I have not been able to consult this book. The same applies to J. P. Sheedy, *Untrodden paths: the social apostolate of St Louise de Marillac* (London, 1958) and Elizabeth Stopp, *Madame de Chantal: Portrait of a Saint* (London: Faber and Faber, 1962).

On St Vincent de Paul, see, in addition to English translations noted in Professor Tapié's bibliography, Mary Purcell, *The World of Monsieur Vincent* (London: Harvill Press, 1963)—short but useful; J. Leonard (trans. and ed.), *Letters of St Vincent de Paul* (London: Burns Oates and Washbourne, 1937). This selection from the 3300 letters printed in Pierre Coste's 8-volume edition is prefaced by a translation of the chapter by H. Bremond on St Vincent de Paul in vol. iii of his *Histoire littéraire du sentiment religieux*. Coste's valuable notes on each of the letters selected by Leonard are also given in English translation. Note also Maurice A. Roche, *Saint Vincent de Paul and the*

Formation of Clerics (Studia Friburgensia no. 39, Fribourg University Press, 1964).

L. Von Matt and Louis Cognet, *Saint Vincent de Paul*, trans. Emma Crauford (London: Burns and Oates, 1960), a popular work intended to commemorate the tercentenary of the Saint's death, contains a number of good reproductions of engraved portraits, etc, of his vast circle of acquaintances. These included Cardinal de Retz with whose family St Vincent de Paul was closely associated and whose biography by J. H. M. Salmon is listed under FRANCE AND THE FRENCH MONARCHY after the sub-section devoted to Richelieu. For the latter's religious policy generally and in particular his relations with the *dévots* and his clever use of men of religion as his propagandists or trusted agents Church's *Richelieu and Reason of State*, there briefly described, is an invaluable guide. It contains for example a valuable account of Fancan. Church also agrees with Dedouvres (cited p. 509) that in addition to his many other activities it was probably Father Joseph who directed *Le Mercure François* from 1624 until his death in 1638.

Turning now from individual figures to religious orders in seventeenth-century France, two recent works should be noted: P. J. S. Whitmore, *The order of Minims in seventeenth century France* (The Hague: Martinus Nijhoff, 1967—no. 20 in the series *International Archives of the History of Ideas*).

Louis J. Lekai, *The rise of the Cistercian strict observance in seventeenth century France* (Washington, D.C.: Catholic University of America Press, 1968): favourably reviewed by J. McManners in *English Historical Review*, Oct. 1970; *cf.* William F. Church's review in *American Historical Review*, lxxiv, ii (December 1968), 626–7. Note the articles by this author and A. F. Allison listed under FRANCE AND THE FRENCH MONARCHY in the subsection devoted to *Richelieu*.

For the Society of the Blessed Sacrament, see E. Chill, 'Religion and mendicity in seventeenth century France' (cited p. 531) and chapter 11 of O. Ranum's *Paris in the age of absolutism* (cited on p. 532 above). This last work may deal inadequately with sceptics and free-thinkers, as a reviewer has complained, but it gives a most stimulating account of 'a generation of Tartuffes'. J. Bossy's important article 'The Counter Reformation and the People of Catholic Europe' (*Past and Present*, xlvii) is concerned essentially with the rural population of France and Italy. The author points out that the late mediaeval Church had not in fact been 'a parochially grounded institution' and that the effect of the Counter-Reformation was to introduce, through the agency of bishops of the stamp of Charles Borromeo, 'a system of parochial conformity similar in character to that which the contemporary Church of England was seeking to impose—though much more comprehensive in its detail'. The view that dioceses 'should resemble well-organised armies which have their generals, colonels and captains' became more and more widely adopted, and any obstacle to uniform parochial observance met with episcopal hostility. This partly accounts for the antagonism aroused by special fraternities such as the Company of the Blessed Sacrament; it also explains the general disappearance during the seventeenth century of the profaner aspect of religious festivals which had been tolerated in tne Middle Ages—such as eating, drinking, dancing, etc., in churches.

Finally, mention should be made of George A. Rothrock's article 'The Gallican Resurgence after the death of Henry IV', in *The Historian*, xxiv, no. 1 (1961).

PROTESTANTISM

Do not overlook the *Proceedings of the Huguenot Society of London*.

For the Huguenots and the French economy see p. 533 above. Nancy L. Roelker, *Queen of Navarre: Jeanne d'Albret 1528–72* (Cambridge, Mass.: Harvard University Press,

1968): so far as Louis XIII's reign is concerned, this book is valuable for its account of religious and social conditions in Béarn towards the end of Jeanne d'Albret's life.

A very useful and sensible summary of the relations between the Crown and the Huguenots in the first quarter of the seventeenth century is given in G. A. Rothrock's 'Some aspects of early Bourbon policy towards the Huguenots' in *Church History* (1960).

Note Buisseret's book on Sully, and, for an example of an ex-Huguenot in royal service, Solomon's work on Théophraste Renaudot (both mentioned under FRANCE AND THE FRENCH MONARCHY, pp. 550, 556).

J. A. Clarke, *Huguenot Warrior: The life and times of Henri de Rohan 1579–1638* (The Hague: Martinus Nijhoff, 1966): useful biography but rather inadequate on the background to Louis XIII's wars against the Huguenots, for which *cf.* chapter 4 of Professor Lublinskaya's *French absolutism: the crucial phase 1620–29* and David Parker's article 'The social foundations of French absolutism', both mentioned under the heading FRANCE AND THE FRENCH MONARCHY. W. J. Stankiewicz, *Politics and religion in seventeenth century France* (University of California Press, 1960) was unfavourably reviewed, e.g., in *History*, xlvi (1961), but contains useful material.

For the evolution of French Protestantism, in addition to vol. ii of Léonard's *History of Protestantism* already cited p. 537, see Brian C. Armstrong, *Calvinism and the Amyraut heresy: Protestant scholasticism and humanism in seventeenth century France* (Madison and London: University of Wisconsin Press, 1969). Moïse Amyraut, a liberally-minded professor of theology at the Huguenot Academy of Saumur, which after Gomar's departure in 1618 became the centre of Protestant enlightenment in France, was charged with heresy before the national synod of reformed churches in 1637. There is also some relevant material in G. H. Dodge, *The Political Theory of the Huguenots of the Dispersion, with special reference to the thought and influence of Pierre Jurieu* (New York and London: Oxford University Press, 1947). Jurieu, himself the son of a minister, was the grandson of Pierre du Moulin (1568–1658).

JANSENISM

N. J. Abercrombie, *The Origins of Jansenism* (Oxford University Press, 1935) and, in an altogether more popular vein, M. Escholier, *Port Royal: The Drama of the Jansenists* (New York: Hawthorn Books, 1968). Readers of Ronald Knox, *Enthusiasm—a chapter in the history of religion with special reference to the seventeenth and eighteenth centuries* (Oxford University Press, 1950) might also consider Edward B. Ham's review 'Knox on Jansenist enthusiasm' in *Journal of the History of Ideas*, xix (April 1958). L. Goldman, *The Hidden God* is mentioned in Professor Tapié's bibliography.

SCEPTICISM AND FREE-THOUGHT

R. H. Popkin, 'Scepticism and the Counter-Reformation in France' (*Archiv für Reformationsgeschichte*, li) should be noted. Among works cited under GENERAL EUROPEAN RELIGIOUS HISTORY, note J. S. Spink, *French Free-Thought from Gassendi to Voltaire* (London: Athlone Press, 1960), which complements Popkin's book there mentioned, giving a fuller account of the subject from c. 1620 onwards, and offering different interpretations and perspectives.

D. C. Potts, 'French thought in the seventeenth and eighteenth centuries', in *France: a companion to French Studies* (cited p. 559) and A. Adam, *Grandeur and Illusion: French Literature and Society 1600–1715*, trans. H. Tint, (London: Weidenfeld and Nicolson, 1972) are two out of a number of general surveys which discuss this subject. Adam, whose history of French seventeenth-century literature is cited in Professor Tapié's bibliography, has published an anthology of writings by 'libertines'.

F. D. Pickman, *Libertine ideas in the time of Richelieu and Mazarin* (Proceedings of the Massachusetts Historical Society, 1944–7).

J. V. Rice, *Gabriel Naudé* (Baltimore: Johns Hopkins Press, 1939), and a more recent study by J. A. Clarke, *Gabriel Naudé* (Hamden, Conn: Archor Books, 1970) should both be mentioned here.

Note that Naudé appears prominently in the chapter entitled 'The Rosicrucian scare in France' in Frances A. Yates's *The Rosicrucian Enlightenment* (cited p. 539), in which details are also given of Descartes's travels in Germany and Bohemia between 1619 and 1623—travels which account for the rumour after his return to Paris that he had become a Rosicrucian.

Note also Solomon's account of the weekly conferences organized by Renaudot between August 1633 and September 1642 in chapter 3 of his book on that many-sided figure (cited p. 532).

Details of recent books on seventeenth-century science are given in Maurice Crosland's article 'The History of French Science: Recent Publications' (*French Historical Studies*, viii, no. 1, spring 1973). These include Harcourt Brown, *Scientific organisations in seventeenth century France 1620–80* (Baltimore: Johns Hopkins Press, 1934, reissued, New York: Russell and Russell, 1967).

Erica Harth, *Cyrano de Bergerac and the Polemics of Modernity* (New York and London: Columbia University Press, 1970): 'Demonstrates admirably Cyrano's audacity in refuting all miracles . . . in putting on a par revealed religion and superstition and in scorning the authority of orthodox philosophy'—Patricia M. Harry in *The Modern Language Review*, lxviii, no. 2 (April 1973). Another work on Cyrano de Bergerac is listed under FRANCE, LITERARY HISTORY (p. 562).

WITCHCRAFT

See under GENERAL EUROPEAN RELIGIOUS HISTORY.

MISCELLANEOUS

Sir Francis Oppenheimer, *Frankish Themes and Preludes: the legend of the Sainte Ampoule* (2 vols., London: Faber and Faber, 1952–3)—see chapter 1, note 50 above. For a summary of the author's theories see *The Times Literary Supplement*, 1 May 1953. Although attractively written and illustrated, this book is unfortunately condemned by an expert as 'factually unreliable and largely hypothetical' (J. M. Wallace-Hadrill).

Marc Bloch, *The Royal Touch: Sacred Monarchy and Scrofula in England and France*, trans. J. E. Anderson (London: Routledge, 1972). The French original, *Les Rois Thaumaturges*, is referred to in chapter 1, note 51 above.

Ralph E. Giesey, *The Royal Funeral Ceremony in Renaissance France* (Geneva: Droz, 1960, in the series *Travaux d'Humanisme et Renaissance*). Anthony Levi, *French Moralists: The Theory of the Passions 1585–1649* (Oxford University Press, 1964). Terence C. Cave, *Devotional poetry in France c. 1570–1613* (Cambridge University Press, 1968). Joan Evans, *Monastic architecture in France from the Renaissance to the Revolution* (Cambridge University Press, 1964), and its no less scholarly companion volume devoted to the same period, *Monastic iconography in France* (1970).

Note the essays by Febvre and Benesch in *French Humanism 1470–1600* cited under HISTORY OF ART.

FRANCE AND THE FRENCH MONARCHY

BIBLIOGRAPHIES

Some idea of the mass of books and articles devoted to seventeenth-century French history which have appeared in recent years can be obtained by consulting the following, published respectively in December 1965, June 1964 and June 1973 in *The Journal of Modern History*: William F. Church, 'Publications on Cardinal Richelieu since 1945: a bibliographical study'; John B. Wolf, 'The reign of Louis XIV: a selected bibliography of writings since the war of 1914–18'; Ragnhild M. Hatton, 'Louis XIV: Recent Gains in Historical Knowledge.'

Reference should also be made to the admirable 50-page bibliographical introduction to *Louis XIV and the Craft of Kingship*, ed. John C. Rule (Ohio State University Press, 1969) and to the lists of recently published works on French history which are printed at regular intervals in *French Historical Studies* (mentioned above p. 522). Details of the microfilming of certain French records are given in Davis Bitton's article, *ibid.*, vol. viii, no. 1 (spring 1973). See also the bibliographical information given at the beginning of this guide and under FRANCE, LITERARY HISTORY below. J. Russell Major's guide to material in French archives relating to French representative assemblies is mentioned later in this section.

INTRODUCTORY SURVEYS

A History of French Civilisation by Georges Duby and Robert Mandrou, trans. J. B. Atkinson (London: Weidenfeld and Nicolson, 1965) is mentioned here partly because Mandrou is responsible for the second part of the book (extending from the sixteenth century to modern times). His name is mentioned in the editorial notes to this book, in Professor Tapié's bibliography and under FRANCE, ECONOMIC AND SOCIAL HISTORY above. The bibliographical notes contain references to English translations of works cited by the authors and the chapters on the sixteenth and seventeenth centuries are probably the best in the book. See N. Hampson's rather unenthusiastic review in *History*, lii (1967), 126–7.

Note Roland Mousnier's chapter on French institutions and society, 1610–61, in *The New Cambridge Modern History*, vol. iv. D. G. Charlton (ed.), *France: A Companion to French Studies* (London: Methuen, 1972) consists of twelve essays by experts on the history and culture of France since the Renaissance. See Roger Mettam's essay, 'French history and society from 1589 to 1789'. Details of others in this volume which are also relevant are given under the appropriate headings of this guide.

Two surveys for the non-specialist are: John Lough, *An introduction to seventeenth century France* (London: Longman, 1954), which has a deservedly high reputation and makes good use of literary sources; G. R. R. Treasure, *Seventeenth Century France* (London: Rivingtons, 1966): a well-written text book which is, however, rather over-heavily weighted in favour of Louis XIV's reign and sometimes inaccurate.

W. H. Lewis, *The Splendid Century* (London: Eyre and Spottiswoode, 1953) consists of a series of essays on various aspects of French life during Louis XIV's reign, some of which are also relevant to the reign of his predecessor. They are based on wide reading of contemporary memoirs etc., and should be regarded not as historical studies but as literary compositions designed to evoke an atmosphere. In this they are highly successful.

Note also David Maland's *Culture and Society in Seventeenth Century France* mentioned above (p. 532).

GENERAL

J. M. Wallace-Hadrill and J. McManners (eds.), *France: Government and Society* (2nd ed., with revised bibliographies, London: Eyre and Spottiswoode, 1970) contains two lucid and scholarly essays by Menna Prestwich and J. S. Bromley, which together cover the seventeenth century.

J. H. Shennan, *Government and Society in France 1461–1661* (London: George Allen and Unwin, 1969) consists of a 73-page introduction and 82 pages of documents designed to illustrate this theme which have been ably selected and translated by the author, a leading authority on the subject (see his *Parlement of Paris* below). One is left with a feeling of astonishment at the amount which he has been able to fit into so narrow a compass—although inevitably Government is given more emphasis than Society. The reader should not, however, overlook the section entitled 'A seventeenth-century crisis?' towards the end of Doctor Shennan's admirable introduction or the excerpts he gives from Porshnev's book. In short, this is an extremely useful and stimulating little book.

B. F. Porshnev, 'The Legend of the Seventeenth Century in French History', *Past and Present* (Nov. 1955). This is a translation of part of the introduction to Boris Porshnev's book *Popular risings in France prior to the Fronde 1623–48*, first published in 1948 and mentioned above: it represents an attempt by the Russian historian to explain the glorification of the Age of Louis XIV by French historians, beginning with Voltaire, and their failure to undertake 'scientific study of popular movements in the seventeenth century'. Porshnev also joins issue with the views of Pagès and Mousnier regarding the significance to be attached to the purchase and sale of offices. Note that another extract from Porshnev's book which has been translated into English is referred to under the heading FRANCE, ECONOMIC AND SOCIAL HISTORY. For excellent summaries of Porshnev's attitudes generally, see J. H. M. Salmon's article in *Past and Present*, xxxvii (July 1967), 'Venality of office and popular sedition in seventeenth century France: review of a controversy', and Menna Prestwich's review of the French translation of his book in *English Historical Review*, lxxxi (1966), 565–72.

Pierre Goubert, *Louis XIV and Twenty Million Frenchmen*, trans. Anne Carter (London: Allen Lane The Penguin Press, 1970), is mentioned here because not only is Goubert a leading authority on this period of French history but much of what he has to say of the twenty million Frenchmen in this refreshingly original approach to Louis XIV's reign is also relevant to the earlier half of the century. This book was first published in France in 1966. See, however, Professor R. M. Hatton's comments on the inaccuracies and omissions that detract from the value of the English version in her article, 'Translated History: the reign of Louis XIV', in *European Studies Review*, vol. i, no. 2 (April 1971).

Orest and Patricia Ranum (eds.), *The Century of Louis XIV* (London: Macmillan, 1973), one of a series entitled *The Documentary History of Western Civilisation*, also contains much relevant material (in this case well translated) taken from a variety of specified sources, some of them manuscript sources. Note that numbers 1, 8, 9, 47, 51 and 60 include documents belonging to the first half of the seventeenth century. The editors, who are obviously very much at home in their period, have done their work well.

CONSTITUTIONAL

The *Encyclopaedia Britannica* contains a good article on French law and institutions by Messrs Esmein and Doucet. Esmein was the author of *A History of Continental Criminal Procedure with special reference to France* (Boston, 1914) and Doucet was responsible for an elaborate and scholarly study, *Les Institutions de la France au XVIe siècle*, of which I have made use in the editorial notes to this book. See also J. B. Brissaud, *A History of French Public Law*, trans. J W. Garner (Boston, 1915).

F. C. Green, *The ancien régime: a manual of French institutions and social classes* (Edinburgh University Press, 1958) is a useful seventy-page guide which assumes a certain knowledge of French. W. F. Church, *Constitutional thought in sixteenth-century France* (Cambridge, Mass: Harvard University Press, 1941) gives a valuable background. Note that other works by this author are mentioned later in this section (pp. 554, 556).

The following, which are of general constitutional and political interest, have been inserted here since they have also some bearing on the outlook and conditions that existed in seventeenth-century France: J. G. A. Pocock, 'The Nature of Constitutional Thought in Early Modern Europe' (*Colloquium*, v (1966)).[1] J. H. Franklin, *Jean Bodin and the Sixteenth-Century Revolution in the Methodology of Law and History* (New York: Columbia University Press, 1963).

J. P. Cooper, 'Differences between English and continental governments in the early seventeenth century' in *Britain and the Netherlands* (papers delivered to the Oxford-Netherlands Historical Conference in 1959), ed. J. S. Bromley and E. H. Kossmann (London: Chatto and Windus, 1960).

Herbert H. Rowen, 'Kingship and republicanism in the seventeenth century: some reconsiderations' in *From the Renaissance to the Counter-Reformation: Essays in honour of Garrett Mattingly*, ed. C. H. Carter (London: Jonathan Cape, 1966).

H. G. Koenigsberger, *Estates and Revolutions*, and Robert Forster and Jack P. Greene (eds.), *Preconditions of Revolution in Early Modern Europe*: these have already been mentioned (p. 527 above).

G. Griffiths, *Representative government in Western Europe in the Sixteenth Century* (Oxford: The Clarendon Press, 1968) contains documents and commentaries on a large number of European institutions during a crucial period of their history. These include the Cortes of Castile, the Corts of Catalonia, the Parlament of Sicily and the Estates of the Netherlands as well as the French Estates-General and provincial Estates. Huguenot assemblies are added for good measure. Documents are printed in English as well as in their original language unless the latter was French.

Friedrich Meinecke, *Machiavellism: the doctrine of raison d'état and its place in history*, trans. Douglas Scott (London: Routledge and Kegan Paul, 1957—the German original appeared in 1924). For some criticisms see W. F. Church, *Richelieu and Reason of State* (considered p. 556 below).

V. G. Kiernan, 'Foreign mercenaries and absolute monarchy', *Past and Present*, xi (1957), reprinted in *Crisis in Europe*, ed. Aston; see also 'State and Nation in Western Europe' by the same author in *Past and Present*, xxxi (1965).

K. W. Swart, *The sale of offices in the seventeenth century* (The Hague: Martinus Nijhoff, 1949) has chapters on Spain, the Netherlands, England, Germany, Italy as well as on France. For France note also Davis Bitton 'History and politics: the controversy over the sale of offices in early seventeenth century France', printed in *Action and Conviction in Early Modern Europe* (cited p. 540).

INSTITUTIONS

J. H. Shennan, *Government and Society in France 1461–1661* (referred to above) is excellent

---

[1] This author has since produced *Politics, Language and Time: Essays on Political Thought and History* (London: Methuen, 1972).

on the institutions of seventeenth-century France generally. The best and fullest account in English of French financial institutions are, however, contained in M. Wolfe's *The Fiscal System of Renaissance France* and in Julian Dent's work (cited pp. 534–5). *The Parlement of Paris* (London: Eyre and Spottiswoode, 1968) also by J. H. Shennan, is the first book in English to deal with this subject and the first in any language that 'attempts to synthesise the Parlement's multifarious activities and to offer an assessment and interpretation of its overall significance in French history'; see Menna Prestwich's review in *The English Historical Review* (April 1970). Altogether this survey is a remarkable achievement. For A. Lloyd Moote's book, *The Revolt of the Judges*, see under Absolutism, below.

J. F. Bosher in his essay on '*Chambres de justice* in the French monarchy' (cited p. 535) describes these occasional extraordinary tribunals as 'a royal business institution disguised as a court of law'.

For French representative institutions generally during this period see G. Griffiths's study mentioned on p. 548 above. The Estates-General met only once in the seventeenth century and although its role and significance in the second half of the sixteenth century have been studied by a number of British and American scholars, it is hardly surprising that no book has been exclusively devoted to the Estates-General of 1614. Three articles on the subject have, however, appeared in *French Historical Studies*: G. A. Rothrock, 'The French Crown and the Estates-General of 1614', (1960) i, 295–318, and 'Officials and Kings Men: A note on the possibilities of royal control in the Estates General', (1962) ii, 504–10; J. M. Hayden, 'Deputies and *Qualités*: the Estates-General of 1614', (1964) iii, 507–24.

This is an appropriate place to mention a number of works by the American scholar, J. Russell Major. *The Deputies to the Estates General in Renaissance France* (Madison: University of Wisconsin Press, 1960), which includes the Estates General of 1614, is a work of considerable learning which examines the varying systems of suffrage and election, as well as the social background and experience of deputies. It also contains information on the institutions, sub-divisions, chief towns, etc. of the different provinces of which I have sometimes made use in the editorial notes to this translation. See also 'The French Monarchy as seen through the Estates General', in *Studies in the Renaissance*, ix (New York: Publications of the Renaissance Society of America, 1962) and Major's monograph 'French Representative Assemblies: Research Opportunities and Research Published' in *Studies in Mediaeval and Renaissance History*, vol. i, ed. William M. Bowsky (Lincoln: University of Nebraska Press, 1964), a very useful guide to the material available on this subject both in print and in French archives. Note that this study also deals briefly with the estates of territories annexed to France after the death of Louis XIII, with general assemblies of clergy, and with French Protestant assemblies. The author is engaged on a study of the decline of the provincial estates under Henry IV and Louis XIII, and two further articles by him are listed under the sub-heading Absolutism below. Major's views about the 'popular and consultative' nature of the French monarchy in the sixteenth century—the phrase is taken from the opening chapter of his book, *Representative Institutions in Renaissance France 1421–1559* (Madison: University of Wisconsin, 1960)—are however highly controversial. For a reply to them, see R. J. Knecht's pamphlet *Francis I and Absolute Monarchy* (London: Historical Association, 1969). Finally mention should be made of Joseph M. Tyrell's monograph *A History of the Estates of Poitou* (The Hague: Mouton, 1968).

On the intendants, see D. J. Buisseret, 'A stage in the development of the intendants: the reign of Henri IV', *The Historical Journal*, ix (1966), 27–38. The introduction to V. R.

Gruder, *The royal provincial intendants* (New York: Cornell University Press, 1968), a work concerned with eighteenth-century France, gives a brief summary of the use made of these commissioners in the first half of the seventeenth century.

ABSOLUTISM

Roland Mousnier's chapter in *The New Cambridge Modern History* vol. iv, 'The exponents and critics of absolutism' sets the subject in its European framework.

W. F. Church, *The Impact of Absolutism in France* (New York: Wiley, 1969) is a useful short introduction more fully described p. 554 below. Orest Ranum's book, *Richelieu and the Councillors of Louis XIII*, has already been cited in Professor Tapié's bibliography. N. M. Sutherland, *The French Secretaries of State in the Age of Catherine de Medici*, (London: Athlone Press, 1962) may be usefully studied in conjunction with it.

David Buisseret, *Sully and the growth of centralised government in France 1598–1610* (London: Eyre and Spottiswoode, 1968) is a work of fundamental importance (see Nancy L. Roelker's review in *The American Historical Review*, lxxiv, no. 1 (Oct. 1968), 182–3). It not only considers the workings of the fiscal administration, Sully's achievement as superintendent of finance and his respective roles as 'Minister of Works', superintendent of fortifications and grand master of the artillery, but also contrives to give a clear picture of his character, religious opinions and services to the monarchy generally. Note particularly the author's comparison between him and Richelieu on p. 201; unfortunately, the index is inadequate.

Raymond F. Kierstead, *Pomponne de Bellièvre: a study of the King's Men in the reign of Henry IV* (Evanston: North Western University Press, 1968), as its subtitle implies, is not merely an account of the career of Sully's unsuccessful rival and is considered more fully p. 552 below.

J. Russell Major, 'The Crown and the aristocracy in Renaissance France', *American Historical Review*, lxix, no. 3 (April 1964), refers to the seventeenth as well as to the sixteenth century and is particularly interesting on the patron–client relationship. See also his 'Henry IV and Guyenne: a study concerning the origins of royal absolutism', *French Historical Studies*, iv, no. 4 (autumn 1966), 363–83. This article is referred to again later in this section. For a different aspect of the same trend as reflected in the revision of a contemporary treatise see M. P. Gilmore, 'Authority and Property in the Seventeenth Century: The First Edition of the *Traité des seigneuries* of Charles Loyseau' (*Harvard Library Bulletin*, iv (1950), pp. 258–65).

A. Lloyd Moote, 'The French Crown versus its judicial and financial officials 1615–83', *Journal of Modern History*, xxxiv (1962), the same writer's article 'The parlementary Fronde and seventeenth century robe solidarity', in *French Historical Studies*, ii (1962) and Nora Temple, 'The control and exploitation of French towns during the *ancien régime*', *History*, li (Feb. 1966) are all useful surveys which are mainly but not exclusively concerned with developments after the death of Louis XIII. A. Lloyd Moote, *The Revolt of the Judges* (Princeton University Press, 1971) is also primarily concerned with the attempt of the Parlement of Paris to reassert itself during the decade after the king's death but contains two instructive opening chapters on the position of the *officiers*, the role and organisation of the Parlement of Paris and Louis XIII's attitude towards it, which was evidently more hostile than that of Richelieu. The following quotations may help to illustrate these themes. 'The truth is that the *officiers* deftly fashioned their role as "part of the Crown" into a flexible double-edged weapon of offense and defense. On the one hand they had developed the technique of acting against royal interests by feigning ignorance of the King's wishes. . . . On the other they never broke formally with the principle of royal absolutism thereby making it difficult for the monarch to tar them with the brush of treason or rebellion . . .' (p. 12) . . . 'Louis XIII wanted his judges to obey his paternal authority but he wished to act within the framework of the laws of France. He firmly believed that, whenever he overruled his *officiers*, he was not overriding but applying existing laws . . . his greatest assault came in the shape of attacks on their personal freedom and offices' (pp. 42, 50). The book has an excellent bibliography, but the author has been criticised by Julian Dent in *Journal of Modern History* for excessive denigration of Mazarin, and excessive praise of the Frondeur magistrate Pierre Broussel as a result of omitting to consult certain sources in the Archives Nationales.

French Absolutism: the crucial phase, 1620–29 (Cambridge University Press, 1968) is a translation of the second volume of a trilogy by Professor A. D. Lublinskaya. It was originally entitled *Frantsuzsky Absolyutizm v Pervoi Treti XVII veka* and published in Moscow –Leningrad in 1965. The titles and dates of publication in Russia of the other two volumes are as follows: *Frantsiya v nachale XVII veka (1610–1620 gg)* [France at the beginning of the seventeenth century (1610–20)] (1959); *Vnutrenniya politika frantsuzskogo absolyutizma* [The internal politics of French absolutism] (1966). This last volume carries the survey up to 1649.

The English translation of vol. ii of this trilogy by Brian Pearce, who was responsible for the short notice about the Russian original printed in *English Historical Review*, lxxxii (Jan. 1967), 167–8, and has since undertaken the translation of Mousnier's book on peasant uprisings mentioned above, p. 531, is clearly based on wide knowledge and careful scholarship and may be regarded as authoritative. It must have been a formidable undertaking, for Professor Lublinskaya's book does not appear to make many concessions to literary elegance and is packed with detail. Since it has already been extensively reviewed, there is no need to repeat the main thesis of this work here, but a résumé of its contents may be helpful.

The first two chapters (totalling 102 pages) consist of an elaborate examination of the views put forward by (amongst others) Messrs. Hobsbawm, Mousnier, Trevor-Roper, Hexter, Kossmann and Elliott regarding 'the existence, the character and the extent of a "general crisis of the seventeenth century"' (the quotation is from the short foreword to Mr Pearce's translation contributed by the last-named of the above historians). The attitude adopted by Trevor-Roper in the controversy causes the learned authoress to break out in a rash of indignant footnotes. David Buisseret in *The English Historical Review*, vol. lxxxv (Jan. 1970), pp. 124–6, rightly criticises the third chapter on French economic development for concentrating overmuch on Montchrétien's treatise of 1615 and ignoring the work of J. U. Nef.

In chapter 3, note 24 above, I have myself pointed out an unwarranted hypothesis put forward by Professor Lublinskaya in her fourth chapter, 'The suppression of the Huguenot "State within the State"'. For a detailed criticism of Professor Lublinskaya's view that the Huguenots aimed at extending their territory and their rights, see David Parker, 'The social foundations of French absolutism 1610–30' in *Past and Present* (Nov. 1971). Even so this is a masterly survey which argues convincingly that '1620 [the year of Louis XIII's expedition to Béarn] was a turning point in the internal policy of the French government not because the latter ventured for the first time to take determined measures, but because these measures were crowned with success'.

Of the two remaining chapters, the first, 'The Financiers and the Absolute Monarchy' includes a valuable investigation into the background of La Vieuville's appointment as superintendent of finance and subsequent dismissal; while the last chapter, 'Richelieu's administration (1625–27)' is particularly good on the Assembly of Notables. The whole book, which is remarkably free from Marxist jargon, is copiously annotated so that although the going is sometimes heavy, the argument is always clear.

For a very different aspect of royal absolutism, see, under the heading MUSIC below, Robert M. Isherwood, *Music in the service of the King*.

THE REIGN OF HENRY IV

The first quarter of the seventeenth century is beginning to receive increasing attention from historians, but there is still no good modern biography of Henry IV in English. His reign is covered in *The New Cambridge Modern History*, vol. iii.

Charlotte Haldane's *Queen of Hearts: Marguerite de Valois* (London: Constable, 1968) and the English translation of Battifol's book on Marie de Medici mentioned in Professor Tapié's bibliography are adequate but old-fashioned. Henry's ministers however have been better served; in addition to David Buisseret's important study of Sully already mentioned there have appeared of recent years E. H. Dickerman's article in *French Historical Studies*, vol. vii, no. 3 (1972) 'The man and the myth in Sully's *Économies royales*' (considered below) and the same author's *Bellièvre and Villeroy: power in France under Henri III and Henri IV* (Providence, R. I.: Brown University Press, 1971) a monograph concerned with their views rather than their personalities and careers—see De Lamar Jensen's review in *Journal of Modern History*, xlv, no. 2 (June 1973).

Raymond F. Kierstead, *Pomponne de Bellièvre: a study of the King's Men in the Age of Henry IV* (Evanston, Illinois: Northwestern University Press, 1968) is a valuable and more ambitious study of the man who rose to become Henry IV's chancellor and played a leading part in the pacification of the realm before being eclipsed by Sully. In her review in *Journal of Modern History*, xli, no. 4 (1969), Nancy L. Roelker, the leading authority on this period, praises especially Kierstead's account of the disintegration of the League and of the formation of a team of 'King's men' drawn from ex-Leaguers and *politiques*. The book has also some useful things to say on the subject of office-holding and on the initial clashes between the Parlements and the Crown which marked the steady revival of royal power.

For the policy of Henry IV and his successors towards the Huguenots and their attitude to provincial institutions see George A. Rothrock's article cited under FRANCE, RELIGIOUS HISTORY and J. Russell Major's article 'Henry IV and Guyenne' mentioned under the sub-heading Absolutism above. Maurice Lee's study of Anglo-French relations, *James I and Henry IV*, and J. D. Mackie's essay on the two rulers are referred to under the heading GREAT BRITAIN. Note also Roland Mousnier's *The Assassination of Henry IV*, trans. Joan Spencer, cited by Professor Tapié at the beginning of this book (London: Faber and Faber, 1973).

THE REGENCY OF MARIE DE MEDICI

J. Michael Hayden, 'Continuity in the France of Henry IV and Louis XIII: French foreign policy 1598–1615' (*Journal of Modern History*, xiv, no. 1 (March 1973)) maintains that Henry IV's assassination did not in fact bring about an abrupt alteration in the course of French history and that in particular there was no significant change in French policy between 1598 and 1615. This leads Hayden to a careful examination of the evidence regarding Henry's plans during the crucial period 1609–10, from which he concludes that the real target was the imperial position at Cleves, and that the attack on Milan in conjunction with Savoy, had it occurred, would have been at best a sideshow. Henry's aim in short was simply to administer a check to the Habsburgs on the Rhine by ousting them from Cleves, preferably without war with Spain—although it was necessary to prepare for this eventuality. This was in fact carried out by Marie de Medici and her ministers. Hayden makes the important point that the Archduke Albert had already agreed to allow French troops to pass through the Spanish Netherlands before Henry's death and believes that, having succeeded in his object without a general war, the latter would have been very willing to conclude a marriage alliance with Spain as Marie de Medici was to do later: 'Marie de Medici and her Ministers did not provide new solutions; but they should be given full credit for continuing the policies of Henry IV. By so doing they made it possible for France to maintain a strong position in Europe; and European war was prevented long enough for France to begin to solve its internal problems and to prepare for the conflict. Henry IV would have approved'. The argument is ingenious, but it is hard to share the view that France did 'maintain a strong position in Europe' during Marie de Medici's Regency; similarly Major's statement in his article cited above that 'it [the Regency] marked . . . the return to the consultative tradition of the Renaissance monarchy with its respect for the rights and privileges of towns, provinces, estates and social classes' seems to credit a weak government with a more deliberate policy than it really possessed. The ambivalent relations between Marie de Medici and Condé during these years, hinging as they did on his position as First Prince of the Blood, acquire added significance if one consults R. A. Jackson's 'Peers of France and Princes of the Blood' in *French Historical Studies*, vii, no. 1 (1971) and Ralph E. Giesey, *The Juristic Basis of Dynastic Right to the French Throne* (Philadelphia 1961).

Dickerman's important article on Sully's *Économies Royales*, cited above, suggests that he composed the latter between his fall from power in 1611 and Louis XIII's coup d'état in 1617 (although they were not published until 1638) and that they were written in the hope of persuading the young king to recall him to office as he had recalled other former ministers of Henry IV. It is this which explains the distortions and exaggerations of the *Économies Royales* which, for example, represent Henry IV and Sully himself as far more bellicose in their attitude towards Spain than they really were. The author also establishes that it was not Villeroy and others who were responsible for Sully's fall but Sully himself by his arrogance and inflexibility.

THE ASCENDANCY OF LUYNES

Although the rehabilitation of Louis XIII took place a considerable time ago, it has only been of recent years that any credit has been allowed to his first favourite, notably by Professor Lublinskaya. I know of no book or article on Luynes available in English. Nevertheless the traditional notion that he was 'a near-cypher in government who played no role of importance in the shaping of French policy' is no longer generally accepted. 'Continued research increasingly shows Luynes to have been a minister of fair competence, force and influence and to have been the deliberate promoter of policies usually associated with Richelieu (the uniqueness of that greater genius having been successfully imposed upon history with near-Napoleonic cunning)'—C. H. Carter in *The Western European Powers* (cited p. 521 above), p. 271. This quotation broadly reflects Professor Lublinskaya's thesis, and it should be noted that according to J. Russell Major it was in 1621 that *élections*, earlier introduced by Sully, were once more established in the province of Guyenne after having been abolished by Marie de Medici ten years previously.

The fact remains however that no attempt has yet been made to rehabilitate French foreign policy during the period that Luynes was in power and Professor Tapié's careful analysis of the disastrous effects of French diplomatic intervention in the early years of the Thirty Years War is unlikely to be superseded. This monograph is referred to in chapter 3, note 24.

LOUIS XIII

The existence of Héroard's Journal largely explains the exceptional interest taken in Louis XIII's childhood. See, for example, Lucy Crump, *Nursery life 300 years ago: the story of a Dauphin of France 1601–10* (London: Routledge, 1929), P. Ariès, *Centuries of Childhood*, and David Hunt, *Parents in History* (both cited p. 533; these two works also discuss Louis XIII's attitude to children and family life).

Hester W. Chapman, *Privileged persons: four seventeenth century studies* (London: Jonathan Cape, 1966), which contains a short study of Louis XIII, is also primarily useful for his childhood and adolescence.

Meriel Buchanan, *Anne of Austria: The Infanta Queen* (London: Hutchinson, 1936) is an example of that unfortunate hybrid, fictionalised biography, but Martha Walker Freer, *The Married Life of Anne of Austria* (first published in 2 vols., 1864, revised ed., London: Eveleigh Nash, 1912) although old-fashioned and dated is not to be despised, being based on a respectable amount of research. The same may be said of K. A. Patmore, *The Court of Louis XIII* (London: Methuen, 1909), which although it misinterprets the king's character is interesting about his music and contains some little-known illustrations, including one of a four-part song composed by the king.

For the infancy and early childhood of Louis XIV, see John B. Wolf, 'The formation of a King' in *French Historical Studies*, i (1958), which is however primarily concerned with his education after his father's death. This article is reprinted in J. C. Rule, *Louis XIV and the Craft of Kingship* (cited p. 546).

It goes without saying that the main authorities for Louis XIII's activities as king are to be found in the sub-section that follows.

RICHELIEU

Reference should be made to William F. Church, 'Publications on Cardinal Richelieu since 1945: a bibliographical study', printed in *The Journal of Modern History*, xxxvii (December 1965). This author's short study *The Impact of Absolutism in France* (cited p. 550), which is concerned with 'the national experience under Richelieu, Mazarin and Louis XIV' and also contains a useful bibliography, includes both extracts from sources and passages from modern historians such as Pagès, Tapié and Mousnier. See also the bibliographical details given at the head of this section. C. V. Wedgwood, *Richelieu and the French monarchy* (London: Hodder and Stoughton, *Teach Yourself History* series, 1949; rev. ed. 1962): a gracefully-written and perceptive introduction which is inevitably rather brief.

The Responsibility of Power: historical essays in honour of Hajo Holborn, ed. Leonard Krieger and Fritz Stern (New York: Doubleday, 1967; London: Macmillan, 1968) contains an essay on Richelieu by Dietrich Gerhard (with useful notes on books and articles concerned with him, and on the cardinal's writings) which reveals wide knowledge but is clumsily written.

D. P. O'Connell, *Richelieu* (London: Weidenfeld and Nicolson, 1968). Unfortunately not a satisfactory book—for a detailed criticism, see the review in *The Times Literary*

Supplement, 19 September 1968, headed 'Under the Red Robe'—a heading which reminds one that although easy enough to shunt around as a stage-prop in a romantic historical novel, the figure of Richelieu presents formidable difficulties when it comes to serious biography. Carl J. Burckhardt's three-volume biography, *Richelieu and his Age*, is mentioned in Professor Tapié's bibliography and is frequently referred to in the editorial notes. Burckhardt is capable of writing with great insight but this work, useful though it is, is uneven in quality and often maddeningly diffuse.

The following are concerned with various aspects of Richelieu's career and policy which are dealt with in Professor Tapié's book. Orest A. Ranum, *Richelieu and the Councillors of Louis XIII* (mentioned in Professor Tapié's bibliography and often cited in the editorial notes to this book); W. F. Church, 'Cardinal Richelieu and the social estates of the realm', *Album Helen Maud Cam*, ii, 263–70, (Louvain: Études présentées à la Commission Internationale pour l'Histoire des Assemblées d'États, xxiv, 1961); Richard Herr, 'Honor and absolutism: Richelieu's fight against duelling', *Journal of Modern History*, xxvii (1955), 281–5; Orest A. Ranum, 'Richelieu and the great nobility: some aspects of early modern political motives', *French Historical Studies*, iii, no. 2 (1963), 184–204. Louis J. Lekai, 'Cardinal Richelieu as abbot of Cîteaux', *Catholic historical review*, xlii (1956), 137–56, describes Richelieu's manoeuvres to get himself elected as Abbot-General of the Cistercians so as to bring the Order under his control and supervise its reformation. Note also 'The abbatial election at Cîteaux in 1625' by the same author in *Church History*, xxxix. A. F. Allison, 'Richard Smith, Richelieu and the French marriage: the political context of Smith's appointment as bishop for England in 1624', *Recusant History*, vii (1964), 148–211 also refers to the part played by Bérulle. M. Sedgwick, 'Richelieu and the "Querelle du Cid"', *Modern Language Review*, xlviii (1953), 143–50, and O. von Simson, 'Richelieu and Rubens,' *Review of Politics*, vi (1944), are both of interest. For Richelieu's writings see Henry B. Hill's edition and translation of selected chapters from the political testament (already mentioned in Professor Tapié's bibliography) and Church's book referred to below.

Philippe Erlanger, *Richelieu and the Affair of Cinq-Mars*, trans. G. and H. Cremonesi (London: Elek Books, 1971) is the translation of a book which first appeared in France in 1962, under the title *Cinq-Mars*. Erlanger is a lively, prolific and essentially superficial writer who has produced a number of studies of seventeenth-century figures. His works include a recent biography of Richelieu himself in three volumes, also in process of translation into English by Patricia Wolf (New York: Stein and Day, 1968).

G. R. R. Treasure, *Cardinal Richelieu and the Development of Absolutism* (London: A. and C. Black, 1972) is, in contrast, plainly intended for students. Mr Treasure is evidently well acquainted with recent works on the period including this one and is the master of a pleasant style. Unfortunately, there are too many misprints or misplaced accents and also too many factual errors, perhaps as a result of over-haste. Moreover, although the book contains some good individual chapters and paragraphs, as well as a number of penetrating remarks, it tends to lack coherence. As an example of confused presentation, we may cite an unexplained reference (the first in the book and taken from a quotation) to 'the passes of the Val Telline' (p. 33); this is followed on p. 69 by a second reference by the author himself to 'Richelieu's designs on the Val Telline'. It is not until p. 81, however, that the reader is told where these passes were and what was their strategic significance.

Louis Auchinloss, *Richelieu* (New York: Viking Press, and London: Michael Joseph, 1973). This short study, which is not by a professional historian and has no bibliography, contains some interesting and unusual illustrations.

W. F. Church's *Richelieu and Reason of State* (Princeton University Press, 1972) is in a very different category. Church's book is not yet another history of Richelieu's political career but something far more original and useful—an analysis of the concept of reason of state as revealed not only in the cardinal's policies but also in the writings of himself, of his pamphleteers, of jurists such as Le Bret, and of his opponents. In the course of it the author draws upon the rich store of contemporary tracts and treatises. We are thus given careful analyses of such pamphlets as *La France mourante* or the *Mysteria politica*, as well as of Le Bret's treatise *De la Souveraineté du Roy* (singled out here because each is mentioned by Professor Tapié). The last part of Church's book entitled 'Richelieu's efforts to perpetuate the memory of his greatness' is specifically devoted to a detailed examination of the cardinal's memoirs and political testament; but excerpts from his and Louis XIII's correspondence are to be found elsewhere. Nor are such topics as the hostility of Jansen towards Richelieu's foreign policy or the latter's relations with the papacy over-looked. It is to be noted that, unlike Professor Tapié, Church sees Richelieu's influence at work in the trial of the maréchal de Marillac and believes that he also tried to increase the king's animosity towards Montmorency after the duke's abortive rebellion. He is particularly interesting on the changes of attitude of men who had originally supported Richelieu —not only Morgues and Bérulle but also La Mothe le Vayer. Nevertheless the author's verdict is in favour of the cardinal. Discussing his policy towards the Empire and Lorraine, he agrees with Dickmann that Richelieu took the French Crown's traditional rights there seriously, and showed himself fundamentally a man of principle trying to act in accordance with legal principles; and Church concludes (p. 513) 'Richelieu did not secularize modern politics and should not be so judged. He believed himself to be a Christian statesman who was meeting the exigencies of politics with the best available means for the building of Christian France.'

MISCELLANEOUS

Note Marc Bloch, *The Royal Touch*, and Ralph Giesey, *The Royal Funeral Ceremony* (mentioned under FRANCE, RELIGIOUS HISTORY, p. 545).

Certain biographies of some of Richelieu's contemporaries can be helpful for students of Louis XIII's reign, such as J. A. Clarke's biography of Henri de Rohan (cited p. 544). There is no biography of Monsieur available in English, but V. Sackville-West, *Daughter of France* (London: Michael Joseph, 1959) is an elegantly written account of the life of his daughter, 'La Grande Mademoiselle', who lived from 1627 to 1693. The first two chapters carry the story up to 1643: cf. Francis Steegmuller, *La Grande Mademoiselle* (London: Hamish Hamilton, 1955).

Michael Prawdin, *Marie de Rohan, Duchesse de Chevreuse* (London: George Allen and Unwin, 1971) is too slight and uncritical to have much independent value. J. H. M. Salmon, *Cardinal de Retz: the anatomy of a conspirator* (London: Weidenfeld and Nicolson, 1969) is the work of a painstaking scholar but rather uninspiring as a biography.

Other relevant biographies, or studies of contemporary figures and their works, are listed under FRANCE, RELIGIOUS HISTORY and FRANCE, LITERARY HISTORY. However, this seems the best place to mention Howard M. Solomon's *Public Welfare, Science and Propaganda in Seventeenth Century France: the innovations of Théophraste Renaudot* (Princeton University Press, 1972) since Renaudot is best known for his association with the weekly government-sponsored newspaper, the *Gazette*, which began to appear in 1631. The two admirable chapters which Solomon devotes to it can be profitably read in conjunction with Church's analysis of contemporary political pamphlets in his work mentioned above. They contain fascinating insights into what was and was not regarded as news suitable for public consumption. Thus despite the fact that it was Marie de Medici's intrigues which had inspired the royal publicity and propaganda of which the *Gazette* formed a part, and despite the fact that she had taken refuge in the Spanish Netherlands, reports appeared almost weekly in the *Gazette* describing[1] the ballets, intrigues, banquets, bleedings and purgings of her court at Brussels with the same thoroughness as the dispatches emanating from the court at Saint-Germain or at Paris'. We also learn that several articles regarding Monsieur were written either by Richelieu or by Louis XIII himself (pp. 130–31), and that from 1640 onwards English affairs were given particularly extensive coverage for 'by publishing stories about the chaos in England, Renaudot was silently extolling the social and political calm at home' (p. 161). That this was later to prove an unwise and short-sighted policy is demonstrated by Philip A. Knachel's *England and the Fronde: the Impact of the English Civil War and Revolution in France* (Ithaca: Cornell University Press, 1967).

French Political Pamphlets 1547–1648, compiled by R. O. Lindsay and John Neu (University of Wisconsin Press, 1969), is a catalogue of major collections in American libraries. The editors define the term 'pamphlet' as signifying for their purpose 'any publication of 100 pages or less printed in France in French or Latin and of some immediate or contemporary interest'. No less than 6742 titles are listed in this pioneer work, which surprisingly enough is not mentioned in the bibliographies of either Church or Solomon. It is to be noted that the years 1614 and 1615 were particularly prolific in pamphleteering. *Cf.* Doris V. Welsh, *A Checklist of French Political Pamphlets 1560–1644 in the Newberry Library Chicago* (Chicago, 1950).

FRANCE, LITERARY HISTORY

BIBLIOGRAPHIES, ETC.

Reference can be made to journals such as *French Studies* and *The Modern Language Review* for fuller information on works concerned with this subject, or with individual writers of the period. I might add that the literature on Montaigne and Descartes, for example, is enormous and no attempt has been made to deal with it here. (See, however, R. H. Popkin, *History of Scepticism from Erasmus to Descartes* listed under GENERAL EUROPEAN RELIGIOUS HISTORY above.) Vol. iii of *The Critical Bibliography of French Literature* mentioned below devotes a chapter of more than fifty pages to works about Descartes in a number of languages.

Accordingly, only a selection of books and essays on seventeenth-century French literature has been listed below, and although, for example, Corneille and La Rochefoucauld have been included, Pascal and Molière have not.

The recent *Penguin Companion to Literature*, ii, 'European', ed. Anthony Thorlby (1969), which gives short bibliographies, is commendably detailed in view of its size. So too on a larger scale is *The Oxford Companion to French Literature*, ed. Harvey and Heseltine (Oxford University Press, 1959), which contains entries on a number of subjects which are by no means exclusively literary, such as the river Loire. See also *Dictionary of French Literature*, ed. Sydney D. Braun (London: Peter Owen, 1959). *The Oxford Companion to the Theatre*, ed. Phyllis Hartnoll, 3rd ed. (1967) contains *inter alia* a long article on the French theatre and quite a useful short article on Corneille.

R. W. Baldner, *Bibliography of Seventeenth-Century French Prose Fiction* (New York, 1967) cited by J. C. Rule (p. 546 above) presumably supersedes R. C. Williams, *A Bibliography of the Seventeenth-century Novel in France* (New York, 1932). Most important of all is *A Critical Bibliography of French Literature*, general eds. D. C. Cabeen and J. Brody, of which vol. iii, 'The Seventeenth Century', ed. Nathan Edelman, was published in 1961 (Syracuse University Press). This excellent book is a far more comprehensive guide to works on seventeenth-century France generally than might be supposed, for it includes sections on history, social life, trade, religious writers, the fine arts, philosophic and scientific literature etc. According to J. C. Rule, the *Bibliography of French Seventeenth Century Studies*, published since 1953 'for the Modern Language Association [of America] French Group III', also cites works on social and cultural as well as on literary history.

Two useful publications which have appeared since 1961 are Charles B. Osburn's *Research and Reference Guide to French Studies* and his *Guide to French Studies* (Metuchen, N.J.: Scarecrow Press, 1968, 1972). The first of these is to a large extent a bibliography of bibliographies and the second which contains a cumulative index is a supplement to it. Note also Osburn's editorial introduction and the appendices to *The Present State of French Studies*, (Metuchen, N.J.: Scarecrow Press, 1971) which contains seven essays on seventeenth-century French literature by different authors reprinted from various periodicals. Some of these are mentioned below.

Finally, in addition to the catalogue of French political pamphlets mentioned under FRANCE AND THE FRENCH MONARCHY, note the publication of *A Short Title Catalogue of French Books in the Library of the British Museum 1601–1700*, ed. V. F. Goldsmith (London: Dawsons, 1970–73), and A. C. Taylor *Bibliography of Unpublished theses on French Subjects deposited in University Libraries of the United Kingdom* (*French Studies*, Supplementary Publication no. 2, 1964).

INTRODUCTORY SURVEYS

There are many of these and in the list that follows pride of place is given to those that have appeared recently, such as W. D. Howarth's essay 'French Literature from 1600 to 1750', in *France: A Companion to French Studies*, ed. D. G. Charlton (London: Methuen, 1972), which also contains an essay on French thought in the seventeenth and eighteenth centuries by D. C. Potts (mentioned p. 544 above). Howarth, who is Professor of Classical French Literature at the University of Bristol, was also responsible for *Life and Letters in France*, i, *The Seventeenth Century* (London: Nelson, 1965) in which are included texts by some twenty writers together with illuminating commentaries on their relationship to the contemporary scene. J. Cruickshank, ed., *French Literature and its Background*, ii, *The Seventeenth Century* (Oxford University Press, 1969) contains contributions by H. F. Kearney on 'Religion and Society' and 'Social Structure and Social Change' as well as essays by P. France and the editor on Corneille and Pascal. Note also *A Literary History of France*, ii, *The Seventeenth Century*, by P. J. Yarrow (London: Benn, 1967) and W. G. Moore's admirable little book *French Classical Literature* (Oxford University Press, 1961). H. Caudwell, *An Introduction to French Classicism* (London: Macmillan, 1931) is also still of value. Antoine Adam, *Grandeur and Illusion: French Literature and Society 1600–1715* (cited p. 544) is written on a larger scale than these last two works and with different aims in view in that, 'it seeks to exhibit the fundamental relationship that existed between French society in the seventeenth century and the literature it created' and includes chapters on such topics as the social implications of political history. The book is provided with full notes and references and a useful short bibliography. In his bibliography, Professor Tapié pays a generous tribute to Adam's *Histoire de la littérature française au XVIIe siècle*. So far as I know, *Grandeur and Illusion* is the only one of his works to appear in English to date.

In conclusion, two older and more general works should perhaps be mentioned: H. J. C. Grierson, *The First Half of the Seventeenth Century*, one of a series entitled *Periods of European Literature*, was published as long ago as 1906, but its two chapters on French verse and prose and French drama are still of value. B. Willey, *The Seventeenth Century Background* (London: Chatto and Windus, 1934) includes an essay on Descartes. A recent survey of European literature which I have not read is Frank J. Warnke's *Versions of Baroque: European Literature in the Seventeenth Century* (Yale University Press, 1972).

GENERAL

In addition to those mentioned under the sub-heading Poetry, the following collections contain relevant essays: Werner L. Gundersheimer (ed.), *French Humanism 1470–1600* (London: Macmillan, 1969) includes essays by Lucien Febvre and Otto Benesch referred to under HISTORY OF ART. D. R. Haggis (ed.), *The French Renaissance and its Heritage: essays presented to Alan Boase* (London: Methuen, 1968), includes an essay by J. D. Mackie on Henry IV and James VI and I listed under GREAT BRITAIN. I. Buffum, *Studies in the Baroque from Montaigne to Rotrou* (New Haven, Connecticut: Yale Romanic Studies, 2nd series, iv, 1957). J. Brody (ed.), *French Classicism: A Critical Miscellany* (Englewood Cliffs, N.J.: Prentice-Hall, 1966). *The Classical Line: Essays in honor of Henri Peyre* (French Studies, University of Yale, 1967). Charles B. Osburn, *The Present State of French Studies* (cited above p. 558), contains an article by R. J. Nelson, first published in 1965, 'Modern criticism of French classicism'. W. L. Wiley, *The Formal French* (Cambridge, Mass: Harvard University Press, 1967) is a volume of stimulating essays, not exclusively on literary subjects, but mostly concerned with the seventeenth century. That on the French Academy is noted below.

E. B. O. Borgerhoff, *The Freedom of French Classicism* (Princeton University Press, 1950) establishes with the help of well-chosen extracts from the writings of both professional and non-professional men of letters of the day that they were far less the slaves of the 'rules' than is often supposed: particularly interesting on Richelieu's protégé, Chapelain.

The *Journal of Aesthetics and Art Criticism*, xiv (1955), contains a number of articles which attempt to define the baroque from the point of view of different fields. Note in particular H. A. Hatzfeld's 'The Baroque from the Viewpoint of the Literary Historian' together with his article 'Use and misuse of "Baroque" as a critical term in literary history' (*University of Toronto Quarterly*, xxxi (1962)). *Cf.* Henri Peyre, 'Common sense remarks on the French Baroque' in *Studies in seventeenth century French literature presented to Morris Bishop*, ed. J. J. Demorest, (Ithaca, N.Y.: Cornell University Press, 1962) and R. Wellek 'The Concept of Baroque in Literary Scholarship' in *Concepts of Criticism* (Yale University Press, 1963). I owe this last reference to Rule's bibliography. Note that Hatzfeld's *Literature through Art: a new approach to French literature* (Oxford University Press, 1952) contains a valuable chapter on the seventeenth century.

H. U. Stubbings, *Renaissance Spain in its Literary Relations with England and France: a critical bibliography* (Nashville, Tennessee: Vanderbilt U. P., 1970) contains some seventeenth-century material.

Note that a translation of Góngora's *Solitudes* by E. M. Wilson and a selection of his poems, with an introduction by R. O. Jones, have been published by Cambridge University Press (1965, 1966). For Marino, see James V. Mirollo, *The Poet of the Marvellous* (Columbia University Press, 1963) and Franco Croce's essay 'Baroque poetry: New Tasks for the Criticism of Marino and of Marinism', published in *The Late Italian Renaissance 1525–1630*, ed. Eric Cochrane (London: Macmillan, 1970). This essay also contains some interesting comments on Tasso, 'the true ancestor of the Baroque all over Europe'. Ettore Mazzali's essay on Tasso in the same volume is, however, rather heavy going. For the influence of both these poets on English writers, see C. P. Brand, *Torquato Tasso: a Study of the Poet and his Contribution to English Literature* (Cambridge University Press, 1965) and M. F. Bertonasco, *Crashaw and the Baroque* (University of Alabama Press, 1971).

In conclusion, three works should be cited which have an obvious bearing on seventeenth-century French literature: N. Edelmann, *The Attitude of Seventeenth-Century France towards the Middle Ages* (New York, 1946); Clarence Dana Rouillard, *The Turk in French History, Thought and Literature* (Études de littérature étrangère et comparée, no. 13, Paris, n.d. (1940?)); Anthony Levi, *French Moralists: The Theory of the Passions 1585–1649* (Oxford University Press, 1964).

Note also L. M. Marsak, 'The Idea of Reason in seventeenth century France' (*Journal of World History*, 1968).

POETRY

Geoffrey Brereton, the editor of *The Penguin Book of French Verse* vol. ii, is also the author of *An Introduction to the French Poets* (London: Methuen, 2nd ed. 1973) a survey extending from Villon onwards which is of particular value to the student of the seventeenth century because the author, an expert in this field, also discusses such terms as 'classicism' and 'baroque'. Note also the editorial comments in *The Poetry of France 1600–1800*, ed. Alan M. Boase (London: Methuen, 1973). Odette de Mourgues, the editor of *An Anthology of French Seventeenth-Century Lyric Poetry* (Oxford University

Press, 1966), attempts to establish agreed meanings for similarly elusive terms in *Metaphysical, Baroque and Précieux Poetry* (Oxford: Clarendon Press, 1954). Note also R. Winegarten, *French Lyric Poetry in the Age of Malherbe* (Manchester University Press, 1954). For Malherbe himself the latest book is David Lee Rubin, *Higher, Hidden Order: Design and Meaning in the Odes of Malherbe* (University of North Carolina Press, 1972)—well reviewed in *French Studies*, Jan. 1973. *Studies in seventeenth-century French literature presented to Morris Bishop*, ed. J. J. Demorest, (Ithaca, N.Y.: Cornell University Press, 1962) includes essays on Malherbe, Saint-Amant and Corneille.

For a study of late sixteenth- and early seventeenth-century devotional poetry, see Terence Cave's work listed under FRANCE, RELIGIOUS HISTORY. This author has since edited *Ronsard the Poet*, a collection of essays including one by Odette de Mourgues (London: Methuen, 1973).

An essay published in *Seventeenth century Studies presented to Sir Herbert Grierson* (Oxford: Clarendon Press, 1938) deals with Pierre Motin, an early seventeenth-century *précieux* lyrist, quoting passages from his adulatory verses on Henry IV and the future Louis XIII and emphasising his 'metaphysical' style.

THEATRE AND DRAMA

See also under the heading MUSIC.

No student of the French theatre during this period can overlook the work of Henry C. Lancaster and in particular his *magnum opus, A history of French dramatic literature in the seventeenth century* (Baltimore: Johns Hopkins Press, 9 vols (1929–42), reprinted with corrections, 1952.) This monumental work is divided into five parts, of which parts 1 and 2 (representing four volumes) deal with the period 1610–51. Part 5 (vol. 9) is a recapitulation covering the whole period 1610–1700.

In addition to his excellent general survey *Introduction to seventeenth century France* listed under FRANCE AND THE FRENCH MONARCHY and his chapter 'Drama and Society' in *The New Cambridge Modern History*, vol. iv, which also deals briefly with ballet and opera, John Lough is the author of a fascinating study, *Paris Theatre Audiences in the Seventeenth and Eighteenth Centuries* (Oxford University Press, 1957), which corrects some of Lancaster's judgements on their social background.

W. L. Wiley, *The Early Public Theatre in France* (Cambridge, Mass: Harvard University Press, 1960), also a fascinating book, covers the period 1580–1638 approx., the last chapter being concerned with Richelieu's interest in the theatre and patronage of writers. See also Georges Mongrédien, *Daily Life in the French Theatre at the Time of Molière*, trans. Claire Eliane Engel (London: George Allen and Unwin, 1969).

A short but masterly introduction to French dramatic literature during this period is W. G. Moore's *The classical drama of France* (Oxford University Press, 1971), the first four chapters of which cover the first half of the seventeenth century. B. Jeffery, *French Renaissance Comedy 1552–1630* (Oxford University Press, 1969), and Geoffrey Brereton, *French Tragic Drama in the Sixteenth and Seventeenth Centuries* (London: Methuen, 1973) are valuable surveys. In *Robert Garnier and the Themes of Political Tragedy in the Sixteenth Century* (Cambridge University Press, 1969) Gillian Jondorf resurrects a late sixteenth-century tragedian who has been overshadowed by his great seventeenth-century successors.

For Corneille, see chapter 8 in Ranum's *Paris in the Age of Absolutism* (already cited); Martin Turnell, *The Classical Moment* (London: Hamish Hamilton, 1947, reprinted 1964); L. W. Tancock's article 'Work on Corneille since 1945', written in 1959 and reprinted in Osburn, *The Present State of French Studies* (cited above); and above all Robert J. Nelson *Corneille, His Heroes and their Worlds* (University of Pennsylvania Press, 1963), especially the first five chapters. The same author has also edited *Corneille and Racine: Parallels and Contrasts* (Englewood Cliffs, N.J., Prentice-Hall, 1966). Another study of these two dramatists is Gordon Pocock, *Corneille and Racine: problems of tragic form* (Cambridge University Press, 1973). *Studies in Seventeenth-Century French Literature presented to Morris Bishop*, cited above, includes an essay on *Horace* (1640—dedicated by Corneille to Richelieu). Note also M. Sedgwick, 'Richelieu and the "Querelle du Cid"' in *Modern Language Review*, xlviii (1953).

SALONS, ACADEMIES, ETC.

L. Clark Keating, *Studies on the literary salon in France 1550–1615* (Cambridge, Mass: Harvard University Press, 1941), which has oddly enough been overlooked by the editors of both the relevant volumes of *A Critical Bibliography of French Literature*, gives a picture of the situation prior to the formation of Mme de Rambouillet's *salon*.

Frances A. Yates, *The French Academies of the Sixteenth Century* (Warburg Institute, University of London, 1947) a deservedly well-known work, traces in its last chapters the links which connect the academies of the reign of Henry III with the more celebrated foundations of the seventeenth century. Solomon's account of the weekly conferences organised by Renaudot has already been mentioned under the heading FRANCE, RELIGIOUS HISTORY. Note Borgerhoff's book and W. L. Wiley's essay on the French Academy in *The Formal French*, cited above p. 559–60.

In *Fritz Saxl: a volume of memorial essays*, ed. D. J. Gordon (London: Nelson, 1957), Anthony Blunt's essay 'The *précieux* and French art' (also omitted from Edelman's bibliography) breaks fresh ground and is both interesting and an important contribution to the subject.

MISCELLANEOUS

For La Rochefoucauld whose *Maxims* are described by Adam as 'one of the most important and typical works of the century' see the authoritative book by W. G. Moore, *La Rochefoucauld—his mind and art* (Oxford: Clarendon Press, 1969), especially chapter 7, 'Political implications'. Although the *Maxims* were not composed until some years after Richelieu's death it would be a mistake to assume that they were uninfluenced by events prior to 1643, when La Rochefoucauld was a young man. Note also J. H. M. Salmon's article 'Retz and La Rochefoucauld' in *History Today*, xx.

For Cyrano de Bergerac, see Erica Harth's book, cited under FRANCE, RELIGIOUS HISTORY, and E. W. Lanius, *Cyrano de Bergerac and the Universe of the Imagination* (1967).

Finally, to conclude this section with a study of the works of a great French historian who died in 1617, Samuel Kinser in *The Works of Jacques-Auguste de Thou* (The Hague: Martinus Nijhoff, 1966) publishes the results of his exhaustive examination of de Thou's manuscripts in Paris and elsewhere. It appears that the widely used French edition of 1734 of de Thou's *Historia sui temporis* (styled *Histoire universelle*) is full of inaccuracies. Thus no satisfactory edition of this great work exists.

HISTORY OF ART

This subject is not included either in Roach's *Bibliography of Modern History* (cited p. 522) or in vol. iv of *The New Cambridge Modern History* (see, however, the chapter by R. Wittkower in vol. v); and my own treatment of it is admittedly somewhat arbitrary. Of the making of 'coffee table' art books there appears to be no end, and many which refer to this period have been omitted, as have National Gallery and other such catalogues and a number of works on individual artists. I have for instance included books on Rubens, but not on Van Dyck (much of whose working life was spent in England), on El Greco and Velázquez but not on Murillo and Zurbarán; on Poussin but not on Claude le Lorrain, of whom Kenneth Clark wrote in *Landscape into Art*, 'No great artist has inspired so little literature'.

Apart from the works of reference and general surveys cited below, I have not attempted to cover Europe as a whole but have largely confined myself to late sixteenth- and early seventeenth-century Italian and French painting, sculpture and architecture. A few works have been included on Spanish and Flemish art. Art or artists in contemporary Britain, Holland, Scandinavia and Central Europe have been mentioned only incidentally if at all. For art and the theatre see MUSIC and the appropriate sub-section of FRANCE, LITERARY HISTORY.

WORKS OF REFERENCE

The two short dictionaries published by Penguin Books: P. and L. Murray, *A Dictionary of Art and Artists* (1968) and Fleming, Honour and Pevsner, *The Penguin Dictionary of Architecture* (2nd ed., 1972) need no recommendation from me. An earlier but more comprehensive guide which covers the applied arts, paintings, drawings, sculpture, prints, engravings and architecture is Mary W. Chamberlin, *Guide to Art Reference Books* (American Library Association, 1959). This work by the Librarian of the Fine Arts Library of Columbia University contains more than two thousand entries.

Note also Pietro Zampetti, *A Dictionary of Venetian Painters* (mentioned below), and an invaluable reference book for anyone interested in religious art, Helen Roeder's *Saints and their Attributes* (London: Longman, 1955).

INTRODUCTORY SURVEYS

In addition to the first few titles in the useful list of books on art and architecture included in the bibliography of David Maland, *Europe in the Seventeenth Century* (London: Macmillan, 1966), which includes V. L. Tapié, *The Age of Grandeur: Baroque and Classicism in Europe* (cited p. 515 above), the following can be recommended: Maurice Ashley, *The Golden Century 1598–1715* (London: Weidenfeld and Nicolson, 1969) is a useful survey, which is concerned with political, literary and scientific, as well as artistic, developments and thus sets seventeenth-century art in its historical perspective. It has good illustrations and is generally readable apart from the author's irritating refusal to anglicise Christian names even in the case of well-known European rulers. Henri IV for Henry IV is reasonable enough, but to call Philip III and IV of Spain Felipe, Peter the Great Pyëtr, and even William III Willem is a bit much. Kenneth Clark, *Civilisation* (London: John Murray, 1969), which consists of the scripts of a famous series of television programmes by an eminent art historian, contains two admirable chapters that deal with Italian and Dutch art during this period and some superb illustrations. The same author's *Landscape into Art* (London: John Murray, 1949) also contains seventeenth-century material.

A survey of a different kind which is now a classic is Arnold Hauser's *Social History of Art* (London: Routledge and Kegan Paul, 1962; 4 vols.), see vol. ii, *Renaissance, Mannerism and Baroque Art*.

Of the various sumptuously produced general surveys which are concerned with the art of this period, note *The Larousse Encyclopaedia of Renaissance and Baroque Art* (London: Hamlyn) and Germain Bazin, *The Baroque—principles, styles, modes, themes*, trans. P. Wardroper (London: Thames and Hudson, 1968). The author of the latter is *Conservateur-en-chef* of the Louvre.

Sacheverell Sitwell, *Southern Baroque Revisited* (London: Weidenfeld and Nicolson, 1967) is, as its title implies, a survey of the art of the Western Mediterranean which extends into the eighteenth century. Since composers such as Domenico Scarlatti are included for good measure the ordinary reader is left feeling rather sated by the time he reaches the end of this learned work.

K. S. Van Eerde, *Wenceslaus Hollar: Delineator of his Time* (Virginia University Press, 1970, for Folger Shakespeare Library) is a beautifully produced and scholarly work which is of great interest to any student of the seventeenth century, for Hollar, who was born in Prague and died in London, travelled widely in Germany and the Netherlands during his eventful career. In this connection, see p. 592 below.

GENERAL

H. G. Koenigsberger's paper 'Decadence or shift? Changes in the civilisation of Italy and Europe in the sixteenth and seventeenth centuries' (London: *Transactions of the Royal Historical Society*, 5th series x, 1959) is reprinted in his collection of essays, *Estates and Revolutions* (cited p. 527). The importance of this essay may be judged by the extent to which Koenigsberger's views have been adopted by subsequent historians. He maintains that, beginning in the second half of the sixteenth century, artistic achievement in Italy did not decline as generally held, but shifted to fresh fields, away from painting towards architecture and, even more so, towards music. He suggests that a number of political, economic and religious factors were responsible for this change and concludes his essay by considering more briefly the cultural history of other Western European countries during this period. See Geoffrey Parker's thoughtful review in *European Studies Review* vol. ii, no. 3 (July 1972).

Note H. R. Trevor-Roper's illustrated lecture *The Plunder of the Arts in the Seventeenth Century* (London: Thames and Hudson, 1970), H. Murray Baillie, 'Etiquette and the planning of State Apartments in Baroque Palaces' (*Archaeologia*, 1967) and M. Levey, *Painting at Court* (London: Weidenfeld and Nicolson, 1971).

The following, already cited under GENERAL EUROPEAN RELIGIOUS HISTORY, should also be noted: E. Waterhouse, 'Some painters and the Counter-Reformation before 1600' in *Trans. Royal Historical Society*, 5th series, xxii (London, 1972): concerned with Baroccio (*c.* 1535–1612), El Greco (1541–1614) and Caravaggio (1573–1610). This learned and eminently readable paper is full of illuminating 'asides' revealing, for instance, that the Jesuits had little say in the architectural style of their mother church the Gesù, and that El Greco was a friend of Góngora. R. Wittkower and I. B. Jaffee, eds., *Baroque art: the Jesuit contribution*.

See, in addition, the chapter on Calvinism and art in A. Cuyper, *Calvinism* (London, 1932)—referred to by Peter Burke in 'Patrician culture: Venice and Amsterdam in the seventeenth century' (London: *Transactions of the Royal Historical Society*, 5th series, xxiii,

1973), which draws some interesting contrasts between the patronage of the arts in these two cities.

ITALY

In view of the ascendancy of Italian artistic influence during this period, it is appropriate to mention the following: Pietro Zampetti, *A Dictionary of Venetian Painters* (Leigh-on-Sea: F. Lewis, 1969–71, 4 vols.) Vols. ii and iii of this valuable work deal with the sixteenth and seventeenth centuries and contain scholarly introductions.

L. von Pastor, *History of the Popes* (cited p. 537) gives information on papal patronage of the arts. F. Haskell, 'The market price for Italian art in the seventeenth century' (*Past and Present*, April 1959) and *Patron and painter: studies in the relations between Italian art and society in the age of the baroque* (London: Chatto and Windus, 1963). Note also Peter Burke's essay on patrician culture in Venice and Amsterdam cited above.

Anthony Blunt, *Artistic theory in Italy 1450–1600* (Oxford University Press, 1962); S. J. Freedberg, *Painting in Italy 1500–1600* (Harmondsworth: Pelican History of Art, 1970); Walter Friedlaender, *Caravaggio Studies* (Princeton University Press, 1955) and *Mannerism and Anti-Mannerism in Italian Painting* (Columbia University Press, 1957); D. Posner, *Annibale Carracci* (London: Phaidon, 1971, 2 vols.); Ellis Waterhouse, *Italian Baroque Painting.* (London: Phaidon, 1969); John Pope-Hennessy, *Italian High Renaissance and Baroque Sculpture* (London: Phaidon, 1963, 2 vols.); Denis Mahon, *Studies in Seicento Art and Theory* (London: Warburg Institute, 1947) is a work for specialists. A more general survey of artistic developments in Italy during this period is Rudolf Wittkower's *Art and architecture in Italy 1600–1750* (Harmondsworth: Pelican History of Art, revised ed., 1965); in addition note this author's *Gian Lorenzo Bernini* (London: Phaidon, 1955) and also H. Hibbard, *Bernini* (Harmondsworth: Penguin Books, 1965), which does not overlook Bernini's services to the theatre as stage designer etc. (pp. 19, 135–6).

The impact of Italian art on three eminent seventeenth-century figures may be studied in John Summerson, *Inigo Jones* (Harmondsworth: Penguin Books, 1966), Bruce Allsopp's magnificently produced *Inigo Jones on Palladio* (2 vols., Oriel Press, 1973), E. Panofsky, *Galileo as a Critic of the Arts* (The Hague: Nijhoff, 1954) and Kenneth Clark, *Rembrandt and the Italian Renaissance* (London: John Murray, 1966).

SPAIN

In addition to Sacheverell Sitwell's book already mentioned, see: G. Kubler and M. Soria, *Art and architecture in Spain, Portugal and their American Dominions 1500–1800* (Harmondsworth: Penguin Books, 1959) and James Lees-Milne, *Baroque in Spain and Portugal* (London: Batsford, 1960).

E. Waterhouse, whose essay partly concerned with El Greco has already been noted, cites as the best and most recent work on this painter Harold E. Wethey, *El Greco and his School* (Princeton University Press, 1962). Note that Thomas Bodkin, *The Approach to Painting* (London: Collins, 1954) contains short but evocative essays on one of El Greco's studies of St Francis, and on Velázquez's *Las Lanzas* (specifically mentioned by Professor Tapié, p. 149: painted some years after the event to commemorate the surrender of Breda).

A. de Beruete, *Velázquez* (London: Methuen, 1906) remains a standard authority; E. Lafuente, *The Paintings of Velázquez* (London: Phaidon, 1944) contains a useful introductory essay.

BELGIUM

H. Gerson and E. H. ter Kuile, *Art and architecture in Belgium 1600–1800*, trans. O. Renier (Harmondsworth: Penguin Books, 1960) is particularly good on connections between Flanders and Italy and contains a chapter on Rubens, whose international role is stressed in *Rubens, painter and diplomat* (London: Faber, 1932) written by E. Cammaerts while he was Professor of Belgian Studies at London University. The letters of the great Flemish painter have been edited and translated by Ruth S. Magurn—*The Letters of Peter Paul Rubens* (Cambridge Mass: Harvard University Press, 1955)—see Trevor-Roper's review (entitled 'Rubens in Politics') reprinted in his *Historical Essays* (London: Macmillan, 1957). An article on Richelieu and Rubens is cited p. 555 above. For a recent brief study, see Christopher White, *Rubens and his World* (London: Thames and Hudson, 1968). Note also W. Stechow, *Rubens and the Classical Tradition* (Oxford University Press, 1969).

An unusual subject, not only of interest to specialists, is examined in a monograph published in both English and Dutch, *Music in paintings of the Low Countries of the sixteenth and seventeenth centuries*, by P. Fischer (Amsterdam: Donemus, 1972). The first part is concerned with painting in the Spanish Netherlands between 1565 and 1620, the second with the United Provinces between 1600 and 1690.

FRANCE

There is no point in attempting to list the innumerable general studies devoted to French art. Both the best short introduction to art in France during this period and the best survey are by Sir Anthony Blunt—see his essay in *France: a companion to French studies* (already cited) and his *Art and architecture in France 1500–1700* (Harmondsworth: Pelican History of Art, 1957). More detailed studies of architecture are the same author's *François Mansart and the Origins of French Classical Architecture* (London: Warburg Institute, 1941) and Joan Evans, *Monastic Architecture in France from the Renaissance to the Revolution* (cited p. 545 together with its companion volume, *Monastic Iconography in France* which covers the same period).

Lucien Febvre's essay 'At Amiens from the Renaissance to the Counter-Reformation', reprinted in translation in *French Humanism 1470–1600*, ed. Werner L. Gundersheimer (London: Macmillan, 1969) makes use of estate inventories to investigate changes in Christian names, books, domestic iconography and pictures between the end of the fifteenth century and 1600.[1] In the same collection of essays note Otto Benesch, 'The Ancient and the Gothic Revival in French Art and Literature' (referred to in chapter 7, n. 42 above) where an interesting parallel is drawn between the art of Jacques de Bellange and the mysticism of St François de Sales, and two works by this little-known artist are reproduced. Some drawings by another artist from Lorraine, Jacques Callot, who is known chiefly for his series of engravings of the horrors of war, are to be found in Walter Sorrell's *The Mask in the Arts* (cited p. 570).

The publishing house of Skira has been responsible for two magnificently illustrated surveys of French painting which between them cover the seventeenth century, *French painting from Fouquet to Poussin* (1963)—which includes La Tour and Vouet—and *French painting from Le Nain to Fragonard* (1964)—which includes Philippe de Champaigne who, it should be noted, was born and brought up in Brussels. The joint authors of both

---

[1] This essay is also printed in *A new kind of history from the writings of Febvre*, ed. Peter Burke, trans. K. Folca (London: Routledge and Kegan Paul, 1973) referred to on p. 528 above.

volumes, Albert Châtelet and Jacques Thuillier, have been well served by their translators, Stuart Gilbert and James Emmons. For Vouet, see also W. R. Crelly, *The Painting of Simon Vouet* (New Haven: Yale University Press, 1962). The great reputation of Georges de la Tour (1593–1652) dates from the present century and an important exhibition of his works was held in Paris in 1972—see Anthony Blunt's article in *The Burlington Magazine* (August 1972) and the recent and authoritative book by Benedict Nicolson and Christopher Wright, *Georges de la Tour* (London: Phaidon, 1973). The authors identified a hitherto unknown painting by him belonging to a Yorkshire museum early in 1972.

But perhaps an even more impressive publishing achievement is represented by Anthony Blunt's *The Paintings of Nicolas Poussin*, 3 vols., Critical Catalogue, Plates, Text (London: Phaidon, 1966–7), the fruit of more than thirty years of devotion and scholarship, which was preceded by *The Drawings of Nicolas Poussin*—a work for which W. Friedlaender was also responsible (London: Warburg Institute, 1964). A good idea of the range and importance of Sir Anthony's contributions to the history of art generally and to the study of seventeenth-century French art in particular may be obtained by consulting the bibliography of his writings printed in *Studies in Renaissance and Baroque Art presented to Sir Anthony Blunt* (London: Phaidon, 1967). (His essay 'The *précieux* and French art' has already been mentioned under FRANCE, LITERARY HISTORY above.) Among these studies are two which are of particular interest for the light that they throw on Tasso's influence on the visual arts of the period: R. W. Lee, 'Mola and Tasso' and M. Alpatov, 'Poussin's "Tancred and Erminia" in the Hermitage: an interpretation'.[1] Poussin's 'Orion' (in the Metropolitan Museum, New York) is discussed by E. H. Gombrich in *Symbolic Images: Studies in the Art of the Renaissance* (London: Phaidon, 1972). His 'Holy Family on the Steps' (in the National Gallery in Washington) is examined in a fascinating monograph with that title by H. Hibbard (London: Allen Lane, 1973) which contains a chapter on his attitude towards religion. Note also Mario Praz's essay 'Milton and Poussin' in *Seventeenth Century Studies presented to Sir Herbert Grierson* (already mentioned under the heading FRANCE, LITERARY HISTORY)—a short but perceptive study of the Italian influences apparent in the works of these two men which makes some interesting comparisons between them. An article in *The Times Literary Supplement* on '"The realm of Flora" in Keats and Poussin' is referred to in chapter 7, n. 41 above. I have not seen W. Friedlaender, *Nicolas Poussin* (London: Thames and Hudson, 1966) or R. H. Wilenski's *Poussin* (London: Faber, 1958).[2]

For a fuller study of the links between literature and art in seventeenth-century France, see 'The baroque classicism of the seventeenth century' in H. A. Hatzfield, *Literature through Art*, mentioned under FRANCE, LITERARY HISTORY above. Note also C. Goldstein, 'Studies in Seventeenth Century French Art Theory and Ceiling Painting', in *The Art Bulletin* (1965), and G. Savage, *French Decorative Art 1639–1793* (London: Allen and Unwin, 1969) for the evolution of decorative art after the death of Louis XIII. For French furniture see the very useful little book by John Gloag, *Guide to furniture styles, English and French 1450–1850* (London: A. and C. Black, 1972).

---

[1] A recent work on Mola is Richard Cocke, *Pier Francesco Mola (1612–66)* (Oxford: Clarendon Press, 1972).

[2] Further details of recent books and articles about Poussin are given by Hibbard in his monograph cited above.

MUSIC, BALLET AND THEATRE

As in the case of the HISTORY OF ART, a good deal has been left out of this section. Except for the works of reference and general surveys cited below, books on religious music, on individual musical instruments and on musical theory have been ignored.[1] I have, however, included some works on court festivals, the dance generally and the theatre (for the theatre in France see also FRANCE, LITERARY HISTORY).

In geographical terms, the history of music in countries other than Italy or France has been largely omitted. To include works on Elizabethan or Jacobean composers would be superfluous in a guide of this nature; but I have made an exception in the case of John Dowland (1563–1626), the greatest lutanist of his day who travelled widely in Europe and could boast that music composed by him had been published in eight continental capitals.

The reasons for the emphasis given to Italy are easily summarised. Of the great composers of Europe north of the Alps, Sweelinck (1562–1621) and Schütz (1585–1672) studied as young men under Andrea and Giovanni Gabrieli in Venice; while the English composer John Cooper (d. 1626) who also studied in Italy chose to call himself thereafter Giovanni Coperario. It was in Italy too that opera first emerged as a new form of musical and dramatic composition at the end of the sixteenth century.

Finally, it should be noted that the period covered by this guide is the age of Frescobaldi and Monteverdi, both of whom died in 1643. The latter's *Orfeo* was performed at Mantua in 1607, his *Vespers* were published in 1610 and his last and greatest work *L'Incoronazione di Poppea* was produced in Venice in 1642.

DICTIONARIES, BIBLIOGRAPHIES, ETC.

Among various bibliographies should be mentioned H. M. Brown, *Instrumental music printed before 1600: a bibliography* (Harvard University Press, 1965). Among the various musical reviews published, note *The Journal of Renaissance and Baroque Music*.

Grove's *Dictionary of Music and Musicians* (5th ed. by Eric Blom, 10 vols., London: Macmillan, 1954, 1961) is a monumental work of scholarship containing articles from a host of learned contributors. An equally outstanding achievement in one volume by an eminent musicologist, who was also a Fellow of the Royal Historical Society, is *The Oxford Companion to Music* by the late Percy A. Scholes (10th ed. revised by J. O. Ward, Oxford University Press, 1970). (*Cf.* the same author's *The Concise Oxford Dictionary of Music*, 2nd ed., 1966). Unfortunately, unlike Frederick the Great, Louis XIII as a composer does not appear to receive any attention from either. Most of the information about music at the French court in the first half of the seventeenth century is to be found in the articles on Ballet and Opera.

Finally, Oliver Strunk, *Source Readings in Music History* (New York: Norton, 1950) contains valuable material on this period, given in translation.

GENERAL SURVEYS

The following general surveys cover the music of this period pretty fully and are the work of acknowledged authorities. Henri Prunières, *A New History of Music from the Middle Ages to Mozart*, trans. E. Lockspeiser (London: Dent, 1943). This book by an eminent French musicologist, with an introduction by Romain Rolland, is admirably

---

[1] Note, however, the study of Palestrina mentioned in connection with the Council of Trent, p. 537 above.

translated and edited by a leading authority on French music who is himself the author of an outstanding work on Debussy. As well as writing a number of studies of seventeenth-century French music and composers, Prunières was responsible for editing the complete works of Lully. This book, despite its age, deserves to be far better known in the English-speaking world. The bibliography which was revised and expanded by Lockspeiser for the English edition lists many works translated into English or by English writers.

Alec Robertson and Denis Stevens, *The Pelican History of Music* (3 vols., Harmondsworth: Penguin Books, 1969–71) is an admirable publication by two distinguished musicologists.

A more massive survey with which I am not familiar is A. Harman, A. Milner and W. Mellers, *Man and his Music: the story of musical experience in the West* (4 vols., 1969, of which vol. ii is concerned with late Renaissance and Baroque Music. London: Barrie and Jenkins, 1969). Most exhaustive of all is *The New Oxford History of Music*, ed. Gerald Abraham, which is still in progress; vol. iv, *The Age of Humanism 1540–1630*, published in 1968, includes a bibliography of more than sixty pages. A more specialised study is W. S. Newman, *A History of the Sonata Idea* (3 vols., University of North Carolina Press, 1959–69)—see vol. i, *The Sonata in the Baroque Era* (2nd ed., 1968) which has much to say on Italy in the first half of the seventeenth century. G. S. Bedbrook, *Keyboard music from the Middle Ages to the beginnings of the Baroque* (London: Macmillan, 1949) is an excellent little book which contains chapters on the two Gabrieli, Sweelinck and Frescobaldi.

Reference should also be made to the works of the late Curt Sachs, one of the foremost authorities on the history of the dance and on musical instruments—see, for example, his *World History of the Dance*, trans. B. Schonberg (New York: W. W. Norton, 1937).

Note also A. Loewenberg, *Annals of Opera 1597–1940* (2nd revised ed., Societas Bibliographica Geneva, 1955), and Roy Strong's recent magnificent work *Splendour at Court: Renaissance spectacle and illusion* (London: Weidenfeld and Nicolson, 1973) which extends into the first half of the seventeenth century and combines a readable and scholarly text with superb illustrations.

Among surveys which are confined to the music of this period should be mentioned: F. Blume, *Renaissance and Baroque Music* trans. M. D. R. Norton, (London: Faber, 1968) a scholarly short work which does not however supersede Manfred K. Bukofzer's authoritative *Music in the baroque era from Monteverdi to Bach* (London: Dent, 1948). Note, in addition, A. J. Davison, *Historical Anthology of Music* (2 vols., Oxford University Press, 1949–50). The second volume, *Baroque, Rococo and Pre-Classical Music*, begins with an extract from Peri's opera, *Euridice* (1600), and ends with an eighteenth-century song by Francis Hopkinson, who ranks as the first American composer.

MISCELLANEOUS

In addition to H. G. Koenigsberger's important paper first delivered to the Royal Historical Society, 'Decadence or shift?' (cited under HISTORY OF ART), note his subsequent essay 'Music and Religion in Modern European History', published in *The Diversity of History: Essays in Honour of Sir Herbert Butterfield*, ed. J. H. Elliott and H. G. Koenigsberger (Ithaca, N.Y., and London: Cornell University Press, 1970). This essay suggests that music, which more than any other art came to be regarded in the sixteenth century as a means of access to the divine, in due course became a substitute for religion and contributed to a decline in religious fervour. See also the comments of P. Fischer in *Music in paintings of the Low Countries* (cited under HISTORY OF ART) on 'good' and 'evil' music.

The following are perhaps primarily of interest to specialists: D. P. Walker, 'Musical Humanism in the Sixteenth and early Seventeenth Centuries', in *The Music Review* (1941, 1942). M. Mersenne, *Harmonie Universelle: The Books on Instruments*, trans. R. E. Chapman, (The Hague, 1954). For Mersenne, see Isherwood (cited below). The original, a massive work which was concerned with far more than musical instruments and consisted of eight books, was published in Paris in 1636. J. Roche, *The Madrigal* (London: Hutchinson, 1972) includes chapters on the madrigal north of the Alps and on the Italian madrigal after 1600. A. Dolmetsch, *The Interpretation of the Music of the XVII and XVIII Centuries Revealed by Contemporary Evidence* (London: Novello, 1946). S. Paganelli, *Musical Instruments from the Renaissance to the nineteenth century*, trans. A. Rhodes (London: Hamlyn, 1966).

Of more general interest are: M. Dolmetsch, *Dances of Spain and Italy from 1400 to 1600* and *Dances of England and France 1450–1600* (London: Routledge and Kegan Paul, 1954, 1959); Margarete Baur-Heinhold, *Baroque Theatre: A cultural history of the seventeenth and eighteenth centuries*, trans. Mary Whittall, (London: Thames and Hudson, 1967); Allardyce Nicoll, *The World of Harlequin: A Critical Study of the Commedia Dell'Arte* (Cambridge University Press, 1963); Walter Sorell, *The Other Face: the Mask in the Arts* (London: Thames and Hudson, 1973).

ITALY

A. Einstein, *The Italian Madrigal* (3 vols., Princeton University Press, 1949). Valuable on the growing interrelationship between literary meaning and musical style.

In view of the direct connection between court festivals and early opera, this is an appropriate place to mention A. M. Nagler, *Theatre Festivals of the Medici: 1539–1637* (Yale University Press, 1964), which is cited several times in the article mentioned below: H. M. Brown, 'How Opera began: an introduction to Jacopo Peri's *Euridice*', included in *The Late Italian Renaissance*, ed. E. Cochrane, (cited p. 560). This scholarly article by the Professor of Music at the University of Chicago is particularly interesting on the views of Galileo's father, Vincenzo Galilei (died 1591), who urged composers to go to the theatre in order to listen to people speaking to each other and to note the pitch and volume of the voice when a prince spoke to his subject, a gentleman to his servant or a lover to his mistress. Peri (1561–1633), who was a singer and organist as well as a composer, came from the same artistic milieu and was responsible for finishing the music of an earlier opera, *Dafne*, most of which is lost. *Euridice* was written to celebrate the marriage of Henry IV and Marie de Medici (1600) and performed in a small room on one of the upper floors of the Pitti Palace. Brown compares it favourably with the similarly-named work hastily composed by Caccini out of spite in the same year, and considers that the accusations of monotony and dryness which have been levelled against it are undeserved. He points out that it does contain two distinct styles, song and recitative, and concludes, after quoting examples from both words and music, 'The truth is one cannot analyse *Euridice* in abstract musical terms for much of the music is without a meaning independent of the words. . . . If I hesitate to rank it among the acknowledged masterpieces of early opera—and they are only two: Monteverdi's *Orfeo* and his *L'Incoronazione di Poppea*—it is because I feel that Peri's *Euridice* is really *hors de concours*, a "special" work, lacking perhaps the breadth and universal appeal of a genuine masterpiece, but nevertheless brilliantly succeeding in the more limited goals the composer set for it.'

For Monteverdi see D. Arnold and Nigel Fortune, eds., *The Monteverdi Companion* (London: Faber, 1968), a volume of essays by various contributors on the great composer's environment etc., which contains a useful bibliography. Arnold was also responsible for a study of Monteverdi and his music in the well-known Master Musicians series (London: Dent, 1963). The leading authority on Monteverdi is Leo Schrade, formerly Professor of Music at Yale University—see his *Monteverdi: Creator of Modern Music* (London: Gollancz, 1972). A valuable study which has·obvious relevance to the second half of Monteverdi's career is S. J. Worsthorne, *Venetian Opera in the Seventeenth Century* (Oxford University Press, 1954). For the effect of Venetian influence on the greatest German composer of the day, see H. J. Moser, *Heinrich Schütz: his life and work* (Saint-Louis, Missouri, 1959). trans. Carl F. Pfatteicher.

Note, in conclusion, the various writings of E. E. Lowinsky and Claude Palisca on Italian music of the sixteenth and seventeenth centuries. The latter is also the author of a general survey, *Baroque music* (Englewood Cliffs, N.J.: Prentice-Hall, 1968).

FRANCE

The first French academy of music was founded during the reign of Charles IX and formally recognised by letters patent. Although this academy did not survive the 1580s, the crown continued to give active support to music in various ways. It has been suggested that it was as a result of the presence of Italian musicians such as Caccini (see above) at Marie de Medici's court that sung instead of declaimed recitative was introduced into court ballets early in the seventeenth century. By Louis XIII's reign, a permanent body of singers, organists and composers was attached to the royal chapel. It was Louis XIII also who created the first royal chamber orchestra; most of these musicians were members of the *Vingt-quatre violons du Roi*, whose task it was to give concerts, and above all to compose the music for and accompany the elaborate ballets that were such a feature of his Court.

A useful short introduction to French music during this period is contained in Edward Lockspeiser's essay in *France: a companion to French Studies* (already cited); see also the relevant chapters of his translation of Prunières (mentioned p. 568).

The latest and most detailed survey of *ballet de cour* at this time, although written by a Scotswoman from Glasgow University, seems to have appeared only in French—M. McGowan, *L'art du ballet de cour en France, 1581–1643* (Paris: Centre National de la Recherche Scientifique, 1963). Some of the ballets mentioned are referred to in my comments on Isherwood's book below. Here it must suffice to point to the influence of Tasso in the case of one ballet in which Luynes played the leading part. Note also chapter 12, 'La contribution des pères Jésuites au ballet'.

Rather surprisingly, neither of these works is referred to in the bibliography of Robert M. Isherwood, *Music in the service of the King* (Ithaca, N.Y., and London: Cornell University Press, 1973). This scholarly book is largely concerned with the reign of Louis XIV; but the two opening chapters 'Musical philosophy' (in which due space is allotted to Mersenne and Descartes) and 'Music and Monarchy before the reign of Louis XIV' contain much that is directly relevant to the earlier part of the seventeenth century. As the author points out, this is not a history of music in the traditional sense: 'Many historians treat the arts and especially music as the frills of history and relegate them to the periphery of their studies of the past. . . . Musicologists on the other hand tend to write for each other, using a terminology that baffles the historian and the general reader. Moreover, they tend to work from the assumption that musical forms and styles develop according to a logic of their own. . . . Although there are exceptions, neither historians nor musicologists have found a thread tying general historical developments to the history of music'.

Music in the service of the King is an attempt 'to locate that thread during the century when French culture rose to preeminence in Europe and the power of the French monarchy reached its apogee'.

Isherwood is thus concerned not with French music as a whole during the seventeenth century but with the various forms of musical production sponsored by the French monarchy—which included for instance pageants and ceremonies as well as ballets and opera —although the latter was not introduced from Italy until Mazarin's day. The second chapter underlines the cultural debt owed by France to the last two Valois and the use made of court festivals as political propaganda—note, for instance, the elaborate outdoor ballet performed after the fall of La Rochelle and the *Ballet de la Marine* which celebrated Richelieu's revival of the French navy. By the time of Louis XIV's birth (1638), musical *spectacles* had become a state institution. Shortly afterwards Giacomo Torelli, the celebrated Italian stage designer and craftsman (1608–78), was invited to Paris by Richelieu. The *Ballet de la Prospérité des Armes de France* produced at Richelieu's palace in 1641 'was the culmination of a long association between musical *spectacles* and royalism which originated in the Middle Ages. . . . Astute leaders such as Richelieu discovered that the ballet was a useful exercise and a time-occupying diversion for the restless nobility . . . while the monarchy found that the plots of these productions, spun out through *entrées* and *récits*, could convey an image of glory, benevolence, courage and strength to the court sycophants at the Louvre and to the bedazzled bourgeoisie at the Hôtel de Ville' (pp. 112–13). The book is copiously annotated and has a full bibliography.

Wilfred Mellers, *François Couperin and the French Classical Tradition*, (London: Dobson, 1950), is an outstanding work, but inevitably is focussed primarily on the late seventeenth and early eighteenth centuries. James R. Anthony, *French Baroque Music* (London: Batsford, 1973) which is concerned with the history of French music from Beaujoyeulx to Rameau, i.e. *c.* 1581–1733, has unfortunately appeared too late to receive more than a brief mention. The book includes a chapter on music for the lute which was at the peak of its popularity in Louis XIII's reign. For an excellent short criticism and résumé of the contents of what is plainly an important work, see Richard Luckett's review in *The Spectator*, 1 December 1973. This review also contains some penetrating comments on the reasons for which French music of this epoch has hitherto failed to exercise as wide an appeal as Italian or German music of the same period.

ENGLAND

Diana Poulton, *John Dowland* (London: Faber, 1972), the first full-length study of the man and his music, has the added advantage of being the work of a writer who is herself a distinguished lutanist. Despite the flattering receptions he was given in Italy and Germany and the high position he obtained at the Danish Court, Dowland, a convert to Catholicism in his youth who may have later acted as a spy for the English government, never succeeded in obtaining adequate royal recognition in England, and died with his reputation in decline. This learned work not only traces his career but gives details of his translations, his patrons and his friends.

SPAIN

Details of general histories of Spain are omitted, being available elsewhere. The new edition of *Spain: a companion to Spanish studies*, ed P. E. Russell (London: Methuen, 1973), replaces the earlier volume with the same title by the late E. Allison Peers and includes chapters by J. H. Elliott on Spanish history from 1474 to 1700, by the editor on Spanish literature from 1474 to 1681, by O. N. V. Glendinning on the visual arts and by Robert Stevenson on Spanish music. With the exception of a few works, mostly on Cervantes, no attempt will be made here to cite books on the literature of Spain during this period (see, however, the references to Spanish literary influences and to Góngora under FRANCE, LITERARY HISTORY): some works on the visual arts in Spain and the Spanish Netherlands are referred to under HISTORY OF ART. Spanish music has been ignored, as have Spanish and Portuguese colonial history. The Spanish Netherlands and Portugal are dealt with only in relation to Spanish policy. For Milan, Naples and Sicily (other than Koenigsberger's book on Spanish rule in Sicily mentioned below), see ITALY.

GENERAL SURVEYS COVERING THIS PERIOD

Note the chapters 'Spain and Europe 1598–1621' and 'The Spanish Peninsula 1598–1648' by H. R. Trevor-Roper and J. H. Elliott respectively in *The New Cambridge Modern History*, vol. iv, together with Henry Kamen's chapter 'Spain's dominion: problems and policies of a world power' in H. R. Trevor-Roper (ed.), *The Age of Expansion* (cited p. 524 above).

R. Trevor Davies, *The Golden Century of Spain* (London: Macmillan, 1937), covering the period from the beginning of the sixteenth century up to 1621, is a very much better book than its successor, *Spain in Decline* (London: Macmillan, 1957), a short survey of the reigns of Philip IV and Charles II which the author did not have time to revise before his death. Antonio Domínguez Ortiz, *The Golden Age of Spain 1516–1659* (New York: Basic Books, 1971), one of a series on Spanish history edited by J. H. Parry and Hugh Thomas and the work of a distinguished Spanish historian, is favourably reviewed by Richard Kagan in *Journal of Modern History* (March 1973). Before the appearance of the latter, both Trevor Davies's books had already been superseded by J. H. Elliott's *Imperial Spain 1469–1716* (London: Coward Arnold, 1963), a superlative work, and J. Lynch's two-volume *Spain under the Habsburgs* Oxford: Blackwells, 1964, 1969)—see Ruth Pike's review of the second volume 'Spain and America 1598–1700' in *Journal of Modern History*, xlii, no. 1 (March 1970). Lynch's main thesis is that what occurred in the seventeenth century was not so much 'the waning of the Hispanic world as the recession of Spain within that world', largely as a result of a progressive change in the economies of Mexico and Peru. This learned work is particularly good on the economic aspects of Spain's decline, but rather meagre on religious history.

J. H. Elliott in *The Old World and the New 1492–1650* (Cambridge University Press, 1970) discusses the impact of the newly-discovered Americas on sixteenth- and early seventeenth-century Europe with particular reference to Spain. The last of these four lectures considers the extent to which the power and prestige of the Spanish monarchy both at home and in Europe, was believed to depend and did depend upon its American possessions. This little book is a *tour de force*.

Of the writings of the late Jaime Vicens Vives, note his *Approaches to the History of Spain* (University of California Press, 1967), trans. and ed. J. C. Ullman, which contains two essays on Spain under the Habsburgs and *An Economic History of Spain* (Princeton

University Press, 1969), trans. F. M. López-Morillas, based on lectures first published in 1956. This is a remarkable general survey, though already dated in some respects, thanks to work which Professor Vives himself did much to inspire. As already mentioned, essays on the decline of Spain by both Vives and Elliott (see next paragraph) are included in Cipolla's *The Economic Decline of Empires* (p. 527 above).

J. H. Elliott's 'The decline of Spain', an admirable article particularly relevant to the first half of the seventeenth century which appeared in *Past and Present*, xx (1961), was reprinted in Trevor Aston's *Crisis in Europe* (cited p. 527); the same author's *The Revolt of the Catalans* is mentioned below.

It is perhaps appropriate to conclude this sub-section with one of the greatest historical works to be published in this century. F. Braudel, *The Mediterranean and the Mediterranean World in the Age of Philip II*, 2 vols. (London: Collins, 1972, 1973) trans. Siân Reynolds, is not of course a history of Spain at all. Indeed for Professor Braudel national frontiers are irrelevant. Nevertheless Spain and Turkey were *inter alia* two great Mediterranean empires and the mere fact that Philip II's name features in the title given to this immense survey testifies to the range of Spanish power and influence in the Mediterranean world. In his preface to the English translation of Henri Fluchère's book on Shakespeare, T. S. Eliot referred to the problems created for the translator by the 'reciprocal inadequacies' of the French and English languages. All the more credit is due to Siân Reynolds, therefore, for having succeeded in translating a work of such length and complexity into readable and comprehensible English.

INTERNAL AFFAIRS, ECONOMIC, SOCIAL, CULTURAL

J. Klein, *The Mesta* (Cambridge, Mass., 1920) remains the leading authority in English on this subject; *cf.* the decay of privileges pictured in D. R. Ringrose, 'The Government and the Carters in Spain 1476–1700' (*Economic History Review*, xxii).

L. P. Wright 'The Military Orders in Sixteenth and Seventeenth Century Spanish Society' (*Past and Present*, xliii, May 1969). This interesting article investigates the use made by the crown of the Military Orders of Calatrava, Santiago and Alcántara which had been founded in the twelfth century, had acquired vast estates and revenues during the wars against the Moors, but after 1492 had lost their *raison d'être*. Once Ferdinand the Catholic has assumed the Mastership they could be exploited as a means of conferring honours. 'Olivares put *habitos* of the Orders up for sale with the same blithe disregard for public opinion as he had shown in introducing the Portuguese *marranos* into Castile'. Interestingly enough one of those who appears to have obtained a dispensation from the entry requirements was Velázquez as can be seen from his self-portrait in 'Las Meninas'. K. W. Swart, *The sale of offices* (cited p. 548) contains a chapter on Spain. Richard L. Kagan, 'Universities in Castile 1500–1700' (*Past and Present*, xlix (Nov. 1970), observes a decline in the seventeenth century.

On the Moriscos before their expulsion, see Andrew C. Hess, 'The Moriscos: an Ottoman Fifth Column in Sixteenth-century Spain' (*American Historical Review*, lxxiv, 1968). James Casey in 'The Moriscos and the depopulation of Valencia' (*Past and Present*, l (Feb. 1971) argues that much of the land abandoned by the Moriscos after their expulsion was poor in quality and that their departure did not affect the agricultural prosperity of the province as a whole. Its decline did not occur until after 1620, partly as a result of disastrous floods. In addition, 'late marriage, clerical celibacy and emigration by enlistment in the army all made the Christian population of Valencia more vulnerable to economic pressures and depopulation than the Moriscos had been'.

Ruth Pike, *Aristocrats and traders in Sevillian society in the sixteenth century* (Cornell University Press, 1972).

Note I. A. A. Thompson, 'A map of crime in sixteenth century Spain', Henry Kamen, 'Galley service and crime in sixteenth century Spain', and the disagreement between the views of these two scholars in *Economic History Review*, vols. xxi, xxii (1968, 1969).

Marcelin Defourneaux, *Daily Life in Spain in the Golden Age*, (London: George Allen and Unwin 1970) trans. Newton Branch is one of a well-known French series on daily life in past ages intended for the general public.

I owe the following references to Mr J. P. Cooper: C. A. Jones, 'Honour in Spanish Golden Age Drama', in *The Bulletin of Hispanic Studies*, xxxv (1958); *Honour and Shame: the Values of Mediterranean Society*, ed. J. Peristiany (London: Weidenfeld and Nicolson, 1966)—see the contribution of J. Caro Baroja; E. M. Wilson, *Some Aspects of Spanish Literary History* (Oxford, 1966); P. Laín Entralgo and J. M. Lopez Pinero, 'The Spanish Contribution to World Science' (*Journal of World History*, vi, no. 4 (1960–1)) gives a succinct account of Spain's growing intellectual isolation in the seventeenth century; O. H. Green, *Spain and the Western Tradition*, iv (Madison, Wisconsin, 1966) is the last volume of a work which over emphasises Spain's links with European culture, but does give some insights into Spanish attitudes in the seventeenth century.

It is appropriate to end this sub-section with Cervantes. *The Adventures of Don Quixote*, which has been described as the first modern novel and which was published in two parts in 1604 and 1614, brought him instant popularity. There is a very readable translation by J. M. Cohen (Harmondsworth: Penguin Books, 1950). Recent books on Cervantes include *Cervantes: a collection of critical essays*, ed. Lowry Nelson (Englewood Cliffs, N.J: Prentice-Hall, 1969), and Richard L. Predmore, *Cervantes* (London: Thames and Hudson, 1973), a useful account both of the man and of his age.

REBELLION

There is no special study known to me of the Portuguese revolution of 1640 and apart from H. V. Livermore, *History of Portugal* (Cambridge University Press, 1947: this edition is fuller than that of 1966), the only works available in English would appear to be R. B. Merriman, *Six Contemporaneous Revolutions* (Oxford, 1938) and E. Prestage, *Diplomatic relations of Portugal with France, England and Holland from 1640 to 1668* (Watford: Voss and Michael, 1925).

For the revolt in Catalonia, however, there is J. H. Elliott's fine study, *The Revolt of the Catalans: a study in the decline of Spain 1598–1640* (Cambridge University Press, 1963); see the important review by A. Domínguez Ortiz in *Past and Present*, xxix (1964). This book was preceded by two articles in particular that are well worth reading: 'The Catalan Revolution of 1640: some suggestions for a historical revision' in *Estudios de Historia Moderna*, iv (Barcelona, 1954) and 'The King and the Catalans 1621–40' in *The Cambridge Historical Journal*, xi, iii (1955).

INSTITUTIONS

In addition to many of the above-mentioned works see Griffiths, *Representative government* (cited p. 548 above). For the Spanish Inquisition, H. C. Lea, *History of the Inquisition in Spain* (4 vols., New York, 1906–7) remains an irreplaceable source. Henry Kamen, *The Spanish Inquisition* (London: Weidenfeld and Nicolson, 1965) is a valuable piece of historical revision; note also the same author's 'Confiscations in the economy of the

Spanish Inquisition' (*Economic History Review*, xviii) and P. J. Hauben, *The Spanish Inquisition: a Crucible of National Values* (New York: Wiley, 1969): a collection of documents and extracts from authorities such as Lea and Elliott. Pauline Craft, 'Englishmen and the Spanish Inquisition 1558–1625' (*English Historical Review*, April 1972) is a scholarly article on a well-known theme.

GOVERNMENT AND STATECRAFT

J. H. Parry, *The Spanish Seaborne Empire* (London: Thames and Hudson, 1966) should be cited in this connection.

The reign of Philip II lies outside the period covered by this guide. However, H. G. Koenigsberger's fine article 'The statecraft of Philip II' (*European Studies Review*, i, no. 1, Jan. 1971) and his book *The Practice of Empire* (Ithaca: Cornell University Press, 1969), a revised and enlarged version of his earlier monograph *The Government of Sicily under Philip II of Spain* (London: Staples Press, 1951) are too relevant to the seventeenth century not to be mentioned here.

A useful source for the same period is J. C. Davis (ed. and trans.), *Pursuit of power: Venetian ambassadors' reports on Turkey, France and Spain in the reign of Philip II.* (New York: Harper and Row, 1971).

Patrick Williams, 'Philip III and the restoration of Spanish government 1598–1603', in *The English Historical Review*, lxxxviii (1973), emphasises the frequency with which the Councils of War, State and Finance began meeting after Philip II's death, and the extent to which they were reorganised, and also points out that, despite or because of his laziness and irresponsibility, Philip III was better at delegating than his father.

Note also C. H. Carter, 'The nature of Spanish government after Philip II' in *The Historian*, i, and 'Belgian "autonomy" under the Archdukes 1598–1621' in *Journal of Modern History*, xxxvii, no. 1 (Sept. 1964). Further works by this historian are mentioned in the following sub-section.

J. H. Elliott, 'The Statecraft of Olivares' included in *The Diversity of History: Essays in honour of Sir Herbert Butterfield* (London: Routledge, 1970), ed. J. H. Elliott and H. G. Koenigsberger. Not only is any article by Elliott worth reading but also Marañón's biography of Olivares has not, so far as I know, been translated into English.

SPANISH FOREIGN POLICY

The late Garrett Mattingly's brilliant work *Renaissance diplomacy* (London: Cape, 1955) extends into the early seventeenth century. H. G. Koenigsberger's *The Habsburgs and Europe* (briefly cited p. 524) extends from the early sixteenth century beyond the Thirty Years War. Koenigsberger, who treats the latter as a European civil war, is at pains to emphasise the Habsburg triangle of Madrid–Brussels–Vienna, but this admirably lucid survey is essentially concerned with the policy of the Spanish branch. B. Chudoba, *Spain and the Empire 1519–1643* (University of Chicago Press, 1952), an earlier and useful reminder of Spain's importance in Central Europe both before and during the Thirty Years War, met with considerable criticism in some circles for its excessively pro-Spanish bias. Spanish influence at the Imperial court is also touched upon by R. J. W. Evans in his study of Rudolf II (d. 1612), and in J. V. Polišenský's *Thirty Years War* (mentioned p. 586).

The mantle of Mattingly has fallen upon C. H. Carter, author of *The Secret Diplomacy of the Habsburgs 1598–1625* (New York: Columbia University Press, 1966), for which see

Koenigsberger's review in *History*, lii (1967). Other writings by this historian on this period, in addition to his articles mentioned in the previous sub-section, include the following: 'The ambassadors of early modern Europe: patterns of diplomatic representation in the early seventeenth century' (included in *From the Renaissance to the Counter-Reformation: essays in honour of Garrett Mattingly* (London: Cape, 1966) a volume edited by Carter himself); 'The informational base of Spanish policy 1598–1625' (*Journal of World History*, viii, no. 1 (1964))—mainly concerned with relations with England, as is 'Gondomar; Ambassador to James I' (*Historical Journal*, vi (1964)).

A. J. Loomie, the author of *The Spanish Elizabethans* (London: Burns and Oates, 1964), a study of the English Catholic exiles at the Spanish Court, is also responsible for at least two articles on Anglo-Spanish relations during this period: 'Philip III and the Stuart Succession in England' (*Revue belge de philosophie et d'histoire*, ii (1965)) and 'Sir Robert Cecil and the Spanish embassy' (*Bulletin of the Institute of Historical Research*, xlii (1969)). This article defines Cecil's policy as hostile towards Spain up to 1606, but thereafter more friendly (partly because of his uneasiness at the increase in French influence at The Hague), and comments on his coolness towards France and the United Provinces even during the crisis of 1610. For Cecil the betrothal of Anne of Austria to Louis XIII was a severe blow.

Note also C. F. Senning, 'The Carvajal Affair' (*Catholic Historical Review*, lvi).

For further works on or sources for Anglo-Spanish relations during this period see Conyers Read (ed.), *Bibliography of British History: Tudor period 1485–1603* (2nd. ed., 1959), and G. Davies (ed.), *Bibliography of British History: Stuart Period 1603–1714*, (2nd ed., revised by Mary F. Keeler, 1970) (Oxford: Clarendon Press, for Royal Historical Society). An article on commercial relations between the two countries is listed p. 578 and another is cited under the heading GREAT BRITAIN. The last years of Antonio Pérez (d. 1611) as a refugee in England and France are movingly described in Gregorio Marañón, *Antonio Pérez: 'Spanish traitor'*, (London: Hollis and Carter, 1954), trans. C. D. Ley. For Franco-Spanish relations in the early seventeenth century see the study of Philip III's policy towards France, 1598–1610, by A. Eiras Roel in *Hispania*, xxxi.

THE SPANISH NETHERLANDS

Note firstly Geoffrey Parker's *Guide to the Archives of the Spanish institutions in or connected with the Netherlands (1556–1710)* (Brussels: Archives et Bibliothèques de Belgique, 1971). Parker is the author of a highly-praised book which I have not read: *The Army of Flanders and the Spanish Road 1567–1659: the logistics of Spanish victory and defeat in the Low Countries* (Cambridge University Press, 1972) in which the vital importance of the overland communications with the Spanish Netherlands is for the first time fully investigated. An important article by Parker, 'Spain, her enemies and the revolt of the Netherlands 1559–1648', in *Past and Present*, xlix (November 1970), served partly as a preliminary study for his book. Spain's treatment of the Netherlands problem in the seventeenth century, the author finds, differed little from the pattern established under Philip II. Between 1604 and 1607, Spain profited from a breathing space as a result of peace with France and England; when hostilities were resumed with the Dutch in 1621, she was still able to devote all her energies to the war until 1625 because France was again the victim of religious wars and James I was bent on an Anglo-Spanish marriage. However, her attention was then diverted by France's intervention in the war of the Mantuan Succession: any war which involved France became for Spain of paramount importance. Spinola was transferred to Italy and the flow of money sent for military purposes to the Netherlands declined significantly during those years. After the triumphant arrival of the Cardinal Infante in the Netherlands in 1634, it was again France who came to the rescue of the Dutch by declaring war on Spain in the following year. As in 1590, Spain proceeded to give priority to the war against France, the enemy whom she feared the most; but the financial strain entailed sacrifices which Castile's unwilling partners, Portugal and Catalonia, found intolerable. This learned article which includes tables of money received from Spain by the Military Treasurer of the Spanish Netherlands contains some interesting insights into differences of opinion within the Spanish government. The decision to send troops into the Palatinate early in the Thirty Years War was only taken after bitter debate. There were always some councillors who thought the security of Italy more important than the Netherlands, and as late as 1632 Olivares held that the defence of Lombardy was more important for Spain than the defence of Flanders—the former being the nerve-centre of the Spanish monarchy, the latter only an outlying province.

Note also the same author's article 'Mutiny and discontent in the Spanish army of Flanders 1572–1607', in *Past and Present*, lviii (Feb. 1973).

THE PRICE REVOLUTION

Since Earl J. Hamilton's pioneering study, *American Treasure and the Price Revolution in Spain 1501–1650* (cited by Professor Tapié p. 512) and his article, 'The decline of Spain', published in *The Economic History Review* in 1938,[1] the literature on this subject (which receives its full share of attention in *The New Cambridge Modern History*, vols. iii and iv, and *The Cambridge Economic History of Europe*, iv) has become enormous and there is no point in surveying it here. Hamilton himself contributed a paper on the history of prices before 1750 to the International Congress of Historians held in 1960 (see *Congrès International des Sciences Historiques: Rapports* vol. 1, Stockholm, 1960). The conclusions of the colossal work by H. and P. Chaunu, *Séville et l'Atlantique 1504–1650*, 12 vols. (Paris, 1955–9), are conveniently approached through the review by H. G. Koenigsberger in *English Historical Review*, lxxvi (1961), 675–81, and R. S. Smith, *Journal of Economic History*, xxii (1962), 253–9. The comments of F. Braudel, J. H. Elliott and J. Lynch in their various books and articles should also be noted, and the recent findings of F. C. Spooner—see, in particular, his monograph cited p. 534 above.

I have not read D. L. Gadiel and M. E. Falkus, 'A comment on the "price revolution"' (*Australian Economic History Review*, ix). 'Price revolution or price revision? The English and Spanish trade after 1604' by Harland Taylor in *Renaissance and Modern studies*, xii (1968) (Sisson and Parker, for the University of Nottingham), which is based on wide reading, is in fact concerned with a great deal more than Anglo-Spanish trade and makes some interesting points. Another article by this historian on Anglo-Spanish trade is listed under GREAT BRITAIN.

R. B. Outhwaite, *Inflation in Tudor and Early Stuart England* (London: Macmillan, 1969) gives a good brief survey and critique of present knowledge and of explanations so far put forward. Note also Peter H. Ramsey (ed): *The Price Revolution in Sixteenth-Century England* (London: Methuen, 1971).

---

[1] These are only two of a number of works by this historian on Spanish finances during the sixteenth and seventeenth centuries. Note, for instance, his article 'Spanish Banking Schemes before 1700' (*Journal of Political Economy*, lvii (1949), and *War and prices in Spain 1651–1800* (Cambridge, Mass.: Harvard University Press, 1947).

ITALY

Owing to the diversity of the topics dealt with in this sub-section, works have been cited under the names of authors given in alphabetical order. No general histories of Italy or of Venice, Florence or other cities are listed since particulars of these may easily be obtained elsewhere. Anyone interested in Venice should read James Morris's brilliant portrait of that wonderful city—*Venice* (London: Faber and Faber, 1960).

Alessandro Manzoni's famous historical novel *I promessi sposi* (which is set in the area of Lake Como and Milan during this period) can be read in a good up-to-date translation by Archibald Golquhoun under the title *The Betrothed* (London: J. M. Dent, 1952). It contains an excellent description of a bread riot.

In addition to works cited under GENERAL EUROPEAN RELIGIOUS HISTORY, HISTORY OF ART and MUSIC, BALLET AND THEATRE, note references to books and articles that relate to Italy on pp. 548, 560 above. Braudel's book is of course of fundamental importance. Koenigsberger's study of Spanish rule over Sicily in the reign of Philip II is likewise listed under SPAIN. For the importance of Italy in Spanish policy see Parker's book and article cited p. 577. For the powerful influence of Genoese bankers on Spanish finances see *inter alia* Braudel's and Spooner's works (pp. 574, 534).

A very useful short introduction by A. D. Wright to libraries and archives in Italy (including the Vatican) is published in *History*, lvi (1971). This cites a number of sources of bibliographical information that are available to English readers. It should be noted that *The Secret Archives of the Vatican* by Maria Luisa Ambrosini and M. Willis (London: Eyre and Spottiswoode, 1970) is not a guide but a highly readable though episodic history of archives which have long ceased to be secret.

Note the journal *Italian Studies*.

Berner, S., Article on 'The Florentine patriciate, 1530–1609', in *Studies in Medieval and Renaissance History, ix (1972).*

Bouwsma, W. J., *Venice and the Defense of Republican Liberty: Renaissance values in the age of the Counter-Reformation* (University of California Press, 1968). See Brian Pullan's complimentary but not uncritical review in *History*, lv (1970); *cf.* Bouwsma's essay in Cochrane below.

Brinton, S., *The Gonzaga—Lords of Mantua* (London: Methuen, 1927), although old-fashioned, is still of service for the background to the Mantuan crisis which forms the subject of the last two chapters.

Burke, Peter, 'Patrician culture: Venice and Amsterdam in the seventeenth century', in *Transactions of the Royal Historical Society*, 5th series xxiii (1973): this essay (cited p. 564 above) is a preparatory study for a wider survey of the ruling classes of these two cities which should be published by Maurice Temple Smith, London in 1974.

Carter, F. W., 'The commerce of the Dubrovnik Republic 1500–1700', in *Economic History Review*, xxiv (1971), points out that, once trade between North Europe and the Mediterranean had begun to follow the route by sea round the west European peninsula rather than the overland routes (from *c.* 1580 onwards), ports like Dubrovnik ceased to be a strategic transit point between long-distance land and sea routes and became termini of sea routes alone. As a result of shipping from northern Europe invading the Mediterranean in force and establishing a virtual monopoly of such traffic, Dubrovnik's merchant navy inevitably declined over the years.

Cipolla, C. M., Any book or article by this author is worth reading and some of these have already been cited; amongst others should be mentioned here 'The decline of

Italy: the case of a fully matured economy' in *The Economic History Review*, v, no. 2 (1952). This article which is concerned with northern and central Italy puts forward the view that a general economic decline set in early in the seventeenth century. It attributes Italy's failure to maintain exports (of woollen and silk goods in particular) both to the effects of British, French and Dutch competition at lower prices and to the partial loss of her traditional markets in Spain, Flanders and Germany, owing to economic decay and civil disturbance in those countries. The rise of the free port of Leghorn reflects the expansion not of Italian but of British trade in the Mediterranean. A revised and enlarged version of this article is included in Pullan's *Crisis and Change*, mentioned below.

    Money Prices and Civilisation in the Mediterranean World, Fifth to Seventeenth Centuries (Princeton University Press, 1956) consists of five lectures of which the third, 'The big problem of the petty coins' is perhaps the most particularly concerned with the seventeenth century.

    Cristofano and the plague: a study in the history of Public Health in the age of Galileo (London: Collins, 1973): refers to the outbreak of 1629–31.

Cochrane, Eric (ed.) *The late Italian Renaissance 1525–1630* (London: Macmillan, 1970). This collection of essays which has already been cited several times is not a comprehensive survey; for example, as the editor points out in his interesting introduction, Piedmont, Genoa, Modena and Sicily are virtually ignored: in addition several of the articles Cochrane has translated are primarily of interest to specialists. To say this, however, is not to decry the importance of this volume. Relevant essays which have not already been listed include the following: Benedetto Croce: 'The crisis of Italy in the *cinquecento* and the bond between the Renaissance and the Risorgimento'. (This essay was written in 1939.) E. Cochrane, 'The end of the Renaissance in Florence.'—scholarly and valuable. This short survey is a prelude to a full-scale work on post-Renaissance Florence. G. Spini, 'The art of history in the Italian Counter-Reformation': includes comments on Possevino, Biondi, Sarpi and Davila. P. Prodi, 'The application of the Tridentine decrees: the organisation of the diocese of Bologna during the episcopate of Cardinal Gabriele Paleotti'. This was a preparatory study for a two volume biography of Paleotti who died in 1597. J. Delumeau, 'Political and administrative centralisation in the Papal State in the sixteenth century.' ('By the end of the century the popes disposed of a state that administratively was the equal, if not the superior of any other state in Europe . . . what was lacking . . . was not an adequate administrative structure but a healthy society and a healthy economy'.) R. Villari, 'The insurrection of Naples of 1585'. This is a translation of the first part of the second chapter of his book *La rivolta antispagnola a Napoli: Le origini 1585–1647* (Bari: Laterza, 1967)—referred to later. D. Sella, 'The rise and fall of the Venetian wool industry', also included in Pullan; *Crisis and change* (referred to below): his valuable article dates the decline from 1602 onwards and attributes it partly to English competition in the Levant. W. J. Bouwsma, 'Venice, Spain and the Papacy: Paolo Sarpi and the Renaissance tradition.' A preparatory study for his book mentioned above. Most of these essays have been translated and extensively annotated by Cochrane himself,—a formidable undertaking. These notes give valuable bibliographical information and I take this opportunity of acknowledging my indebtedness to his scholarly editorial work. The index is also admirable.

Croce, Benedetto, *A History of the Kingdom of Naples*, trans. Frances Frenaye, ed., with introduction, by H. Stewart Hughes (University of Chicago Press, 1970) This classic first appeared in 1924; cf. the more recent work of Villari on this period, mentioned later.

Davis, J. C., *The decline of the Venetian nobility as a ruling class* (Baltimore; Johns Hopkins University Press, 1962). The same author's book on Venetian ambassadorial reports is cited under SPAIN.

Koenigsberger, H. G. 'The revolt of Palermo in 1647', in *The Cambridge Historical Journal*, viii, no. 3, reprinted in this author's *Estates and Revolutions* (cited p. 527 above), as is his long article 'The Parliament of Piedmont during the Renaissance 1460–1560.'

Lane, Frederic C., *Venice and History: The collected Papers of Frederic C. Lane* (Oxford University Press, 1966): contains 33 essays mainly concerned with maritime and commercial history.

Logan, Oliver, *Culture and Society in Venice 1470–1790* (London: Batsford, 1972), primarily concerned with sixteenth and eighteenth centuries, and given a devastating review by Cochrane in *The Catholic Historical Review*, lix, no. 3 (Oct. 1973).

Mack Smith, D., *Medieval Sicily 800–1713*, (London: Chatto and Windus, 1968). This is the second volume of a history of Sicily from ancient times. Mack Smith, a leading authority on nineteenth-century Italian history, has also written the third volume *Modern Sicily after 1713*. Both volumes have received high praise from a specialist in early modern Sicilian history: 'a fine scholarly book based on wide reading . . . by far the best general history of Sicily in any language' (H. G. Koenigsberger in *The English Historical Review*, July 1970)

McMullin, Ernan (ed.), *Galileo Man of Science* (New York: Basic Books, 1968), includes an essay by Cochrane entitled 'The Florentine Background of Galileo's Work'.

Parks G. B. (ed.), *Roma Sancta (1581)* (Rome: Edizione di Storia e Letteratura, 1969). This is a description of Rome by Gregory Martin (d. 1582) a former scholar of St John's College, Oxford, who subsequently fled abroad to join Allen at Douai and translated the Vulgate into English. It has been edited from the original manuscript.

Pullan B. S. (ed.), *Crisis and change in the Venetian economy during the sixteenth and seventeenth centuries* (London: Methuen, 1968). This volume which contains a useful introduction and bibliography consists of eight essays, all published previously, but some of them revised since or translated into English for the first time. Those by Cipolla and Sella have already been mentioned p. 580 above. The latter, and that by S. J. Woolf, 'Venice and the Terra Firma', which suggests that between 1570 and 1630 the Venetian aristocracy began to engage increasingly in investment in land rather that in commercial activity, are particularly important for the Venetian economy in the seventeenth century.

Pullan, B. S., *Rich and Poor in Renaissance Venice: The social implications of a Catholic state to 1620* (Oxford: Blackwells, 1971). An important book—see S. J. Woolf's review in *Italian Studies*, xxvii (1972). Earlier writings on Venetian history by Pullan include 'Poverty, charity and reason of state: some Venetian examples' in *Bolletino dell' Istituto per la Storia della Società e dello Stato Veneziano*, ii (1960), and 'Wage-earners and the Venetian economy 1550–1630' (*Economic History Review*, xvi (1963–64)) which studies the connection between economic decline and high wages.

Tenenti, A.: *Piracy and the decline of Venice 1580–1615*, (London: Longmans, 1967), trans. J. and B. Pullan, attributes the damage done to Venetian maritime trade not only to the effects of commercial competition but also to a sharp increase in piracy, both caused by the irruption into the Mediterranean of newcomers from northern Europe.

Usher, A. P., *The early history of deposit banking in Mediterranean Europe* (Cambridge Mass.: Harvard University Press, 1943).

Villari R. Although his book on the hostility of Naples towards Spanish rule has not yet been translated into English, it has been widely reviewed and highly praised, for instance, by John J. Renaldo in *The Journal of Modern History*, xli, no. 4 (Dec. 1969). Renaldo points out that Villari, who spent twenty years working on his book, has completely demolished the myth of Neapolitan torpor and decadence after the middle of the sixteenth century which Croce had accepted, and that, in particular, Villari has shown conclusively that the revolt of 1647 was not a flash in the pan limited to the town of Naples 'but the final fruition of a process that essentially began in the country-side and spread to the city . . . not a minor riot but a general and widespread break-down of bureaucratic society'. Note the reference to this book on p. 580.

Woolf, S. J., 'Economic problems of the nobility in the early modern period: the example of Piedmont' (*Economic History Review*, xvii (1964–5)). This article begins with a very useful short survey of the Piedmontese economy generally during the period, gives abundant references to recent Italian historical writings on Piedmontese economic history and concludes, 'the example of Piedmont cannot but create grave misgivings about current images of the economic ruin of the western continental nobility in the sixteenth and seventeenth centuries, a ruin generally attributed to the price rise and apparently only averted by the emergence of a more "business-like" mentality through large-scale ennoblements of merchants in the eighteenth century'. *Cf.* this historian's article 'The aristocracy in transition' cited p. 528 above.

THE HOLY ROMAN EMPIRE AND THE THIRTY YEARS WAR

INTRODUCTORY

Like the volumes in the same series devoted to France and Spain, *Germany: a companion to German studies*, ed. Malcom Pasley (London: Methuen, 1972) is a useful introduction. In addition to chapters on German literature and institutions, it includes two chapters on German history by Barrie Dobson and Agatha Ramm which span this period. Gustav Freytag, *Pictures of German Life in the fifteenth, sixteenth and seventeenth centuries*, trans. Georgiana Malcolm 2 vols. (London: Chapman and Hall, 1862), is also worth consulting. Bertolt Brecht's play, *Mother Courage and her Children*, is set in Germany during the Thirty Years War.

An excellent little guide to works in English on German history, which includes some books on literature and is remarkably full in view of its size, is *Medieval and Reformation Germany (to 1648): a select bibliography* by Laurence D. Stokes (London: Historical Association, 1972). I have already referred to this pamphlet above under the heading GENERAL EUROPEAN RELIGIOUS HISTORY where a number of works relating to German and Central European history have been mentioned; their titles are not repeated below since their subject matter has been clearly indicated.

Stokes mentions some but by no means all of the works listed below, much of this subsection having been drawn up before a copy of his bibliography had reached me. He also cites a number of books and articles which I have omitted because it seems unnecessary to refer to them for a second time. In compiling the list of works relating to the Thirty Years War I have restricted myself to the course of events in Germany, Austria and Bohemia. Wallenstein and Gustavus Adolphus have been treated separately.

THE EMPIRE—GENERAL SURVEYS

See Stokes, pp. 7–8 for a number of titles. I do not think it is necessary to list the classic account by Bryce written in the nineteenth century. A standard text book which has been generally well received is Hajo Holborn, *A History of Modern Germany*, of which vol. i, *The Reformation*, carries the story up to 1648 (New York: Knopf, 1959; London: Eyre and Spottiswoode, 1965). Friedrich Heer, *The Holy Roman Empire* (London: Weidenfeld and Nicolson, 1968), trans. Janet Sondheimer, is an abridgement of the German original published in 1967 and covers a thousand years of history in about 280 pages. The result is a book whose presentation of the sixteenth and seventeenth centuries at least is rambling and confused. R. W. Seton-Watson, *A History of the Czechs and Slovaks* (London: Hutchinson, 1943) is the only full-length survey of the history of the Bohemian part of the Empire in English. A recent work on another Slavonic people who also lived within the boundaries of the Empire is Gerald Stone's *The Smallest Slavonic Nation: The Sorbs of Lusatia* (London: Athlone Press, 1972). Lusatia formed part of the Kingdom of Bohemia till 1635. For the house of Habsburg, the history of Bohemia between 1600 and 1648 and the role of Wallenstein, see below pp. 586–8.

THE EMPIRE—SPECIALISED STUDIES

Different aspects of the internal history of the Holy Roman Empire during the seventeenth century are considered in the following: F. L. Carsten, *The Origins of Prussia* (Oxford University Press, 1954) and, by the same author, *Princes and Parliaments in Germany from the fifteenth to the eighteenth century* (Oxford University Press, 1959). (See the review by J. H. Elliott in *Past and Present*, April 1960.) Both these books are of great importance. Macartney's book on the Habsburgs and Hohenzollerns is listed on p. 586.

H. F. Schwarz, *The Imperial Privy Council in the seventeenth century* (Cambridge, Mass: Harvard University Press, 1943) is of value not only for the light it throws upon the Imperial and Habsburg administrative systems but also for the short biographies it gives of a large number of individual Privy Councillors. It must be remembered that the latter included at some time or other military careerists like Piccolomini and Collalto (not to mention drunks like Gallas) drawn from all over Western Europe.

See also P. Dollinger, *The German Hansa*, (London: Macmillan, 1970), trans. and ed. D. S. Ault and S. H. Steinberg, the last chapter of which gives a useful account of the decline and disintegration of this once powerful league during the seventeenth century. The book includes documents and statistical tables and is provided with a detailed bibliography. Note also J. Jorgenson, 'Denmark's relations with Lübeck and Hamburg in the seventeenth century', in *The Scandinavian Economic History Review*, xi. Claus-Peter Clasen, *The Palatinate in European History 1559–1660*, 2nd ed. (Oxford: Blackwell, 1966) is a short but useful essay. Good accounts of the cultural and political implications of the marriage between James I's daughter, Elizabeth, and the Elector Palatine in 1613 are given in the first chapter of Frances A. Yates, *The Rosicrucian Enlightenment* (cited p. 539) and in the biographies of Elizabeth by Oman and Green mentioned below.

Note that *The Age of Expansion: Europe and the World 1559–1660*, mentioned under the heading GENERAL EUROPEAN HISTORIES above, includes a chapter by Clasen on the Empire up to 1618 which is greatly to be preferred to the relevant chapter in Heer's book above; *cf.* G. D. Ramsay, 'The state of Germany (to 1618)', in *The New Cambridge Modern History*, vol. iv.

THIRTY YEARS WAR—GENERAL SURVEYS

There is no point in mentioning well-known nineteenth-century histories such as that by Gindely. On the other hand Parber's recent work (p. 577) should not be ignored.

A. W. Ward's two lectures *The House of Austria and the Thirty Years War* were published as long ago as 1869 but are still a useful outline. The same author was later responsible for the relevant chapters in *The Cambridge Modern History*. Note the chapter contributed by H. G. Koenigsberger to *The Age of Expansion* under the title 'The Thirty Years War: the European Civil War'. (This chapter, reprinted in the same author's *The Habsburgs and Europe 1516–1660* is referred to under SPAIN.) That contributed by E. A. Beller to *The New Cambridge Modern History*, vol. iv, is more traditional in its approach, being to a large extent confined to events in Germany.

Dame Veronica Wedgwood's *The Thirty Years War* (London: Jonathan Cape) is one of her earlier works and first appeared in 1938. As she has not hitherto attempted to rewrite it and only minor revisions appear to have been made for the latest edition (1964), it is important to bear this context in mind in considering a book which is now an historical classic. This is essentially a beautifully written and often moving narrative which concentrates excessively on events in Germany; for example, there is relatively little about Bohemia after the defenestration, and the course of the war in the Netherlands after 1621 is largely ignored. It is strong on the analysis of personal and political motives and combines masterly descriptions of battles with a compassion for human suffering that steers clear of sentimentality; but there are a number of questions that lie outside the limits that the author set herself when she wrote this book—some of which are dealt with by the writers listed below. The fact remains that, considered as the work of a young historian grappling with a vast subject of great complexity which necessitated the use of sources in a variety of European languages, this history of the Thirty Years War in a single volume deserves to be regarded as an outstanding achievement.

George Pagès, *The Thirty Years War* (recently translated into English which is sometimes too colloquial) is mentioned in Professor Tapié's bibliography. I have referred several times to both the English translation and the French original of this masterly work in my editorial notes.

S. H. Steinberg, *The 'Thirty Years War' and the conflict for European Hegemony 1600–1660* (London: Coward Arnold, 1966). This short book (favourably reviewed by Michael Roberts in *History*, liii (Feb. 1968), 110) argues that the term 'Thirty Years War' is misleading and fictitious for a number of reasons, one of them being that the contest between Bourbon and Habsburg of which it forms a part, neither began in 1618 nor ended in 1648 nor was confined to Germany. The economic and cultural effects of the war on Germany, which Steinberg maintains have been grossly exaggerated, are also examined. There is a good short bibliography of books and articles in a number of European languages. An article by the same writer, 'The Thirty Years War: a new interpretation', joining issue with C. V. Wedgwood's views as to its causes and results, was published in *History* as long ago as 1947 (xxxii, 89–102).

J. V. Polišenský's recent book on the Thirty Years War is cited under Bohemia below but two important articles by him that have appeared in *Past and Present* should be mentioned here: 'The Thirty Years War' (Nov. 1954) and 'The Thirty Years War and the Crises and Revolutions of Seventeenth Century Europe' (April 1968).

THIRTY YEARS WAR—SPECIALISED STUDIES

Theodore K. Rabb (ed.), *The Thirty Years War: problems of motive, extent and effect* (Boston, Mass., 1964) is a selection from the writings of a number of European and American historians which I have been unable to examine. The same applies to two other works: E. A. Beller, *Propaganda in Germany during the Thirty Years War* (Princeton University Press, 1940): mentioned in the bibliography to the latest edition of C. V. Wedgwood's book;[1] R. Ergang, *The myth of the all-destructive fury of the Thirty Years Ear* (Pocono Pines, Pa., 1956): see Steinberg's bibliography for a brief description.

Note the following by Fritz Redlich: *De praeda militari: looting and booty 1500–1815* (Wiesbaden, 1956); 'Contributions in the Thirty Years War' (*Economic History Review*, 2nd series, xii (1959–60). *The German Military Enterpriser and his Work Force*, 2 vols. (Wiesbaden, 1964): concerned with the evolution of systems of recruitment of mercenaries in Germany 1450–1650—see the review in *English Historical Review*, lxxxii (1967), 136–8.

On the economic situation in Germany, see also R. Ludloff, 'Industrial development in 16th–17th century Germany', in *Past and Present*, xii (November 1957); Helen P. Liebel, 'The bourgeoisie in South Western Germany 1500–1789: a rising class?' (*International Review of Social History*, x, 1969); F. L. Carsten, 'Was there an economic decline in Germany before the Thirty Years War?' in *English Historical Review*, lxxii (1956), 240–7; and Theodore K. Rabb, 'The effect of the Thirty Years War on the German economy', *Journal of Modern History*, xxxiv (1962), 40–51, which gives a valuable summary of the con-

---

[1] Beller has also been responsible for at least two other publications on this subject: *Caricatures of the 'Winter King' of Bohemia* (Oxford University Press, 1928) and 'Contemporary English printed sources for the Thirty Years War' in *American Historical Review*, xxxii (January 1927)—slight but useful.

troversy up to that date. Since then an important article by Henry Kamen, 'The economic and social consequences of the Thirty Years War', *Past and Present* (April 1968), while arguing that 'the economic experience of Germany during the Thirty Years War was part of a general European crisis' has re-emphasised that the devastation took place largely on German soil, even if the political aspects of the war were European, and that the damage to the German economy and loss of population were very considerable. Gerhard Benecke, 'The problem of death and destruction during the Thirty Years War: new evidence from the Middle Weser front' (*European Studies Review*, ii, no. 3 (July 1972)) is based on examination of archives in Detmold and Lemgo and refers to the former county of Lippe in E. Westphalia. This predominantly Calvinist area was from 1623 onwards mostly occupied by an Imperialist garrison; but for part of the time monthly war levies were paid to the Swedes as well who occasionally raided the county. The evidence suggests that Lippe got off pretty lightly and that internal dissensions mattered more than the horrors of war which tended to be exaggerated in the hope of securing large damages as compensation—for loss of property, however, not for loss of life. Finally it should be noted that Francis C. Springell's *Connoisseur and diplomat* (cited p. 592) contains, amongst other relevant material, the diary kept by William Crowne who accompanied the Earl of Arundel on his journey through Germany in 1636.

BOHEMIA AND THE HOUSE OF HABSBURG
Both Evans and Polišenský give information about archive collections in Czechoslovakia in the bibliographies to their works cited below. The journal *Historica* published by the Czechoslovak Academy of Sciences contains articles in English on Czech history, Literature, art, etc. The first number (1959) includes an article by Polišenský in the English language on archive material which was formerly in private hands but has been acquired by the State since 1945. In addition to works by Seton-Watson, Stone and Schwarz, cited above, note Professor Tapié's book, *The Rise and Fall of the Habsburg Monarchy*, (London: Pall Mall Press, 1971), trans. Stephen Hardman, chapters 3 and 4 of which cover the period 1516–1648, together with his chapter 'The Habsburg Lands 1618–57' in *The New Cambridge Modern History*, iv—both referred to in my editorial notes.

A. Wandruszka, *The House of Habsburg* (London: Sidgwick and Jackson, 1964), trans. C. and H. Epstein, also the work of an authority on this period, is a general account which emphasises the sense of dynastic continuity and awareness of a 'mission' felt by the Austrian Habsburgs as a family. C. A. Macartney, (ed.), *The Habsburg and Hohenzollern dynasties in the seventeenth and eighteenth centuries* (London: Macmillan, 1970) consists of documents accompanied by valuable commentaries. R. J. W. Evans, *Rudolf II and his World: a study in intellectual history 1576–1612* (Oxford: Clarendon Press, 1973), a fascinating study based on very wide knowledge, is only partly concerned with politics, but the first chapter at least, 'The Habsburgs, Bohemia and the Empire', should be compulsory reading for anyone who teaches this period of history. The same historian was responsible for the recent translation of J. V. Polišenský's *Thirty Years War* (London: Batsford, 1971) which, despite its title, is not an account of the war as a whole. Polišenský certainly considers its broad European aspect but otherwise it is events in Bohemia and Moravia rather than in Germany which claim his attention; in particular we are shown the changing fortunes of the small town of Zlín in southern Moravia between 1600 and 1648. Polišenský effectively refutes Steinberg's contention that the Thirty Years War was not appallingly destructive at least for the kingdom of Bohemia, and his book is extremely hostile to the Habsburgs, the Jesuits and their supporters. The rebellion of 1618 was in his eyes a national rising for constitutional and religious not economic reasons; but he writes with evident admiration and sympathy for Wallenstein about whose connections by birth or by marriage among the Bohemian aristocracy he gives valuable information. The book contains a thirty-page critical bibliography which discusses the work of Czech and west European scholars both past and present in considerable detail. Polišenský's work does not supersede that of other writers on the Thirty Years War, but his examination of its Bohemian aspects has revealed much that was virtually unknown to historians of other countries, and supplied a much needed corrective to the view that it was essentially a German war.

Two other important but more limited books by J. V. Polišenský should also be mentioned, for although they have yet to appear in an English translation a summary in English is in both cases included at the end of the book. Neither of them is superseded by his work on the Thirty Years War: *Anglie a Bílá Hora* (Prague, 1949)—the literal translation of this title is 'England and [the battle of] the White Mountain', but an apter title is 'The Bohemian War and British policy 1618–20'; *Nizozemská politika a Bílá hora*, i.e. 'The Bohemian War and Dutch Policy 1618–20' (Prague, 1958). The latter is a larger-scale work because the author establishes clearly that in one way or another Dutch assistance to the Bohemian rebels was on a considerable scale. A similar monograph on Spanish policy and the Bohemian question had still not been published in 1970.[1] An essay by Polišenský entitled 'Denmark–Norway and the Bohemian cause in the early part of the Thirty Years War' is included in *Festgabe für L. L. Hammerich* (Copenhagen, 1962). For the aftermath of the battle of the White Mountain in Bohemia, note, in addition to the general works cited above, R. J. W. Evans, 'The significance of the White Mountain for the culture of the Czech lands' (*Bulletin of the Institute of Historical Research*, xliv (May 1971)).

A good general account of the life of the 'Winter Queen' is given by Carola Oman in *Elizabeth of Bohemia* (London: Hodder and Stoughton, 1938) but no use is made of Czech articles or publications. The biography by M. A. E. Green, *Elizabeth, Electress Palatine and Queen of Bohemia* (the 1909 edition was revised by the author's niece, S. C. Lomas, who was also an editor for the Public Record Office) is less readable but perhaps more scholarly. *The Letters of Elizabeth, Queen of Bohemia*, compiled by L. M. Baker (London: Bodley Head, 1953) include a number that are taken from State Papers—Germany in the Public Record Office.

For the social importance but political ineffectiveness of Karel of Žerotín after 1618, see Polišenský's *Thirty Years War*, which offers valuable insights into the links between Bohemian and Moravian aristocratic families generally from 1600 onwards, as well as throwing light on their political and religious affiliations.

This is an appropriate place to mention Otakar Odložilík's article 'Karel of Žerotín (1564–1636) and the English Court' in the *Slavonic and East European Review*, xv (Jan. 1937).[2]

For Gabriel Bethlen (*alias* Bethlen Gábor), reference may be made to a rather slight study in the same journal (xvii, July 1938), entitled 'Gabriel Bethlen: Transylvania in the seventeenth century' by Dominic Kosary.

---

[1] Works that refer to Spain's policy towards the Empire are cited on p. 576 above.

[2] Žerotín's contacts with Duplessis-Mornay to which Professor Tapié refers in this book are also mentioned in Evans's book on Rudolf II. The latest contribution to this topic is František Hrubý, *Étudiants tchèques aux écoles protestantes de l'Europe occidentale à la fin du 16ème et au début du 17ème siècle* (Brno, 1970).

WALLENSTEIN

Francis Watson's biography *Wallenstein: soldier under Saturn* (London: Cape, 1938) is by present-day standards old-fashioned and uncritical. Fortunately there are two excellent short studies in the *Slavonic and East European Review* which have so far stood the test of time and serve to complement each other: Veit Valentin, 'Wallenstein after three centuries' (July 1935) and Josef Pekař, 'Wallenstein and the Habsburgs' (Jan. 1938). The second of these is a translation of the epilogue of the German edition of Pekař's book on Wallenstein, which was published in 1937, the year of the author's death: see the footnote at the end of Professor Tapié's bibliography. (There is a good obituary of Pekař by R. W. Seton-Watson in the *Slavonic and East European Review*, xvi (July 1937), 203–4.) Valentin is more sympathetic in his attitude than Pekař, pointing out that the mere fact that Wallenstein was a Germanised Slav placed him in an equivocal position; he was neither German nor Czech, neither Catholic nor Protestant but an unbeliever riddled with superstition. Pekař, who is strongly hostile, emphasises his greed, vindictiveness and passion for intrigue, comparing him with the *condottieri* of the Renaissance and calling him a true bird of prey by nature. Polišenský, who as already noted adopts a far more sympathetic attitude to Wallenstein in his book *The Thirty Years War*, has drawn attention to the availability of unused materials among archive collections in Czechoslovakia, and mentioned that a number of historians are engaged on new biographies of Wallenstein. He suggests that Pekař's explanation of his downfall is due for revision.[1]

GUSTAVUS ADOLPHUS

Michael Roberts, *Gustavus Adolphus: a History of Sweden 1611–1632*, 2 vols. (London: Longmans, 1953–8) is a masterly achievement; its account of the Thirty Years War between 1626 and 1632 is the best available in English. Note that the same author's *Essays in Swedish History* (London: Weidenfeld and Nicolson, 1967) include the following: 'Gustav Adolf and the Art of War' and 'The Political Objectives of Gustav Adolf in Germany 1630–32'. These two papers were published originally in 1958 (Cambridge: Bowes and Bowes, for the Irish Committee of Historical Sciences) and in 1957, in the *Transactions of the Royal Historical Society*, 5th. series, vii. In *Sweden as a Great Power 1611–97* (London: Edward Arnold, 1968) Roberts has assembled, translated and linked with a commentary a selection of documents several of which relate to Sweden's part in the Thirty Years War. He has since edited a volume of essays on Swedish history after the death of Gustavus Adolphus which also contains relevant material—*Sweden's Age of Greatness 1632–1718* (London: Macmillan, 1973).

---

[1] For details of the above, see Polišenský's article published in *Past and Present* (April 1968) and the bibliographical note to his book, pp. 283–6, which also cites works by non-Czech historians, but not those by Suvanto (mentioned in Professor Tapié's bibliography) or by G. Mann (published in Germany, 1971).

GREAT BRITAIN

For obvious reasons this section is to a large extent concerned with works that have some bearing on Anglo-French relations, more particularly between 1610 and 1643. It omits standard authorities such as S. R. Gardiner and C. V. Wedgwood, biographies of James I., Charles I or their ministers other than Buckingham, and also books and articles concerned with English colonisation, commercial policy and overseas trade, except in connection with Spain and the Mediterranean. I have not included works on the English Catholics whether at home or abroad or on relations between the Stuarts and the Papacy. On the other hand, I have included some books and articles on the 'popular' English attitude towards Spain and Italy. Generally speaking, I have refrained from citing works already mentioned in the bibliographies of Read and Davies.

BIBLIOGRAPHIES

Do not overlook C. H. Carter's *The Western European Powers* (cited p. 521) as a general guide to historical sources for this period especially diplomatic material.

Reference should be made to the full and admirably arranged bibliographies of British history during the Tudor and Stuart periods edited by Conyers Read and Godfrey Davies respectively, (already cited p. 577 above). The second edition of the latter prepared by Mary F. Keeler appeared in 1970; although far more comprehensive than the first edition, it includes few works published since the early 1960s. A series of bibliographical handbooks on British history under the general editorship of J. Jean Hecht is being published by Cambridge University Press; the consultant editor is G. R. Elton. *Tudor England 1485–1603*, ed. M. Levine, (1968) contains some 2400 entries as compared to more than 6000 in Read's bibliography of British History during the same period. The editor for the succeeding volume, which has not so far as I know yet been published, is David Berkowitz.

BRITAIN AND EUROPE—GENERAL

Britain and Europe in the Seventeenth Century by J. R. Jones (London: Edward Arnold, 1966) provides an introductory sketch which shows more understanding of James's pro-Spanish policies than most previous writers. It may be supplemented by the same author's 'English attitudes to Europe in the seventeenth century', in *Britain and the Netherlands in Europe and Asia*, ed. J. S. Bromley and E. H. Kossmann (London: Macmillan, 1968). See also J. P. Cooper, 'Differences between English and continental governments in the early seventeenth century', in *Britain and the Netherlands* (London: Chatto and Windus, 1960), also edited by these two historians.

Yet another aspect of the same broad theme is considered in J. W. Stoye's *English Travellers Abroad 1604–1667* (cited together with de Beer's edition of Evelyn's Diary pp. 533 above). In addition to the edition of Fynes Moryson's *Itinerary*, cited in chapter 7, note 17, note that published by C. Hughes under the title *Shakespeare's Europe*, 2nd ed. (New York: Benjamin Blom, 1967).

BRITISH ATTITUDES TO SPAIN AND ITALY

A few works that refer to Spanish and Italian literary influences on England during this period are incidentally cited under FRANCE, LITERARY HISTORY above and some examples of cultural relations between England and Italy are mentioned under HISTORY OF ART and under MUSIC.

The following works which refer for the most part to the English attitude towards Spain are mainly politico-religious in character: P. A. Jorgenson, 'Foreign sources for the Elizabethan notion of the Spaniard', printed in *Viator: Medieval and Renaissance Studies*, i (1972); C. V. Wedgwood's lecture, *Oliver Cromwell and the Elizabethan inheritance* (London: Cape, 1970); W. S. Maltby, *The Black Legend in England: the development of anti-Spanish sentiment 1558–1660* (Durham, North Carolina: Duke University Press, 1971)—, see De Lamar Jensen's review in *Renaissance Quarterly*, xxvi, no. 3 (autumn 1973); K. S. Van Eerde, 'The Spanish match through an English Protestant's eyes' (*Huntingdon Library Quarterly*, xxxii (1968)); Marvin Arthur Breslow, *A Mirror of England: English Puritan views of foreign nations 1618–40* (Cambridge, Mass: Harvard University Press, 1970)—based on Parliamentary debates as well as pamphlets, sermons etc.—see D. H. Pennington's review in *The English Historical Review*, lxxxvi (April 1971).

In this connection it should be mentioned that each of the Parliaments of James I's reign has now formed the subject of a scholarly monograph. For Parliament's attitude to James's foreign policy note, in particular, Robert Zaller, *The Parliament of 1621: a study in constitutional conflict* (University of California Press, 1971), important for the question of the Palatinate; Robert E. Ruigh, *The Parliament of 1624: politics and foreign policy* (Cambridge, Mass.: Harvard University Press, 1971) includes a detailed examination of the policy of James and Buckingham. See the reviews by G. E. Aylmer in *English Historical Review*, lxxxviii (Oct. 1973) and by G. R. Elton in *The Historical Journal* (Dec. 1972).

For the English attitude towards Italy, see *inter alia*: J. L. Lievsay, *The Elizabethan image of Italy* (Washington, D.C.: Folger Library, 1964); G. B. Parks, 'The decline and fall of the English Renaissance admiration of Italy' (*Huntingdon Library Quarterly*, xxi (1968)); and J. Arthos, *Milton and the Italian Cities* (Cambridge: Bowes and Bowes, 1968). Bertonasco's book on Crashaw has already been cited p. 542 above.

ANGLO–FRENCH RELATIONS

(i) *Guides to sources*

Lists of French ambassadors in England between 1509 and 1714, compiled by A. Baschet, are printed in the *37th Report of the Deputy Keeper of the Public Records* (1876). A valuable collection of transcripts from their dispatches made by this historian is preserved in the Public Record Office. A complete list of these dispatches is printed in the 39th Report (1878), pp. 573–826. See also the short list of transcripts given in 42nd to 47th reports inclusive. Note in addition the Public Record Office Descriptive List of State Papers Foreign, France (S.P. 78), prepared by A. B. Hinds, which gives brief particulars of manuscripts in this series from vol. xx (1589) to vol. cxiv (1659), the overwhelming majority of which have remained unpublished. C. H. Firth and S. C. Lomas *Notes on the Diplomatic Relations of England and France 1603–88* (Oxford University Press, 1906) gives lists of ambassadors from England to France as well as from France to England and contains references to printed dispatches.

F. G. Davenport's 'List of materials for English diplomatic history 1509–1783', printed in Appendix ii to the Eighteenth Report of the Historical Manuscripts Commission (1917), is intended to include references to all the important bodies of material for the diplomatic history of England from 1509 to 1783 referred to in the Reports of the Historical Manuscripts Commission and in the Catalogues of Manuscripts at the British Museum. The list is arranged chronologically and many of the entries refer to large groups of documents, those listed for the period 1610–43 occupying 5 closely printed pages.

Finally it should be noted that a volume concerned with British diplomatic representatives during the period 1509–1688 has been provisionally accepted for future publication in the Camden series by the Royal Historical Society; the editor is to be Professor C. H. Carter.

(ii) *Printed sources*

Five volumes which have appeared under the auspices of the Historical MSS Commission since F. G. Davenport's list was printed deserve particular attention. *Downshire MSS*, vols. ii, iii and iv; ed. A. B. Hinds (H.M.S.O., 1936–40) consist of the papers of William Trumbull the Elder between 1605 and 1614 and give a considerable amount of information about both French and European affairs. *De L'Isle and Dudley MSS*, vols. v, ed. W. A. Shaw and G. D. Owen, and vi, ed. G. D. Owen, were published in 1962 and 1966 and cover the period 1611 to 1698. Vol. v, like the earlier volumes, consists for the most part of correspondence to or from Sir Robert Sidney (to give him his original title) in his capacity as governor of Flushing. (Flushing was held by England as a cautionary town until 1616.) It is therefore only indirectly concerned with Anglo-French relations; vol. vi, however, prints the papers of his son Robert who succeeded him as 2nd Earl of Leicester in 1626 and was subsequently sent by Charles I on embassies to Denmark and France, the second of these lasting from 1636 to 1641. The introduction by the editor provides a scholarly short narrative and draws partly on the unpublished series of State Papers, France in the Public Record Office.

(iii) *Secondary authorities*

C. H. Carter's articles and his book on Habsburg diplomacy between 1598 and 1625 (referred to under the heading SPAIN) have some relevance to Anglo-French relations. J. B. Black, *Elizabeth and Henry IV* (Oxford University Press, 1914), described by Read as 'brief', is also good. An essay by J. D. Mackie on James and Henry IV is printed in D. R. Haggis (ed.), *The French Renaissance and its Heritage* (London: Methuen, 1968). More substantial than either is Maurice Lee's *James I and Henry IV* (Chicago: University of Illinois Press, 1970), which is justifiably censorious of James's dithering diplomacy but has met with some criticism for over-reliance on English sources and for exaggerating England's role in international affairs—see R. J. Knecht in *The English Historical Review* (Oct. 1972). A Soman's article, 'The theatre, diplomacy and censorship in the reign of Henri IV', in *Bibliothèque d'Humanisme et Renaissance*, xxxv, no. 2 is concerned with a French play on Mary Queen of Scots that was considered objectionable by the English ambassador whilst Elizabeth was alive but less so when she was not.

For Anglo-French relations towards the end of James's reign, see Zaller's and Ruigh's works on the Parliaments of 1621 and 1624 mentioned above. On the negotiations for and outcome of the marriage between Charles I and Henrietta Maria, see the biographies of Richelieu, A. F. Allison's article 'Richard Smith, Richelieu and the French Marriage' (cited pp. 555) and the relevant volume of Pastor's *History of the Popes*. I. A. Taylor, *The Life of Queen Henrietta Maria*, 2 vols. (London: Hutchinson, 1905) is long-winded and dull and has been superseded by Carola Oman's *Henrietta Maria* (London: Hodder and Stoughton, 1936)—a very readable biography. See also *Letters of Queen Henrietta Maria*, ed. M. A. E. Green (London, 1856). Of the various biographies of Buckingham, by far the best of a poor bunch is that by M. A. Gibb, *Buckingham 1592–1628* (London: Cape, 1935). The connections between England and the Huguenots are adequately outlined in J. A. Clarke, *Huguenot Warrior: the life and Times of Henri de Rohan (1579–1638)* (The

Hague: Nijhoff, 1966). A valuable contemporary narrative, *The Expedition to the Isle of Rhé*, written by Edward Herbert, Lord Cherbury, was published by the Philobiblon Society London in 1860.

Anglo-French relations at various stages are also touched upon in the two biographies of Elizabeth of Bohemia, mentioned above p. 587. For the end of Louis XIII's reign, P. Geyl's essay 'Frederick Henry and Charles I, 1641–47', in *History of the Low Countries; episodes and problems* (London: Macmillan, 1964) has also something to say about French policy towards these two rulers. See also D. A. Bigby, *Anglo-French Relations 1641 to 1649* (London: University of London Press, 1933), which makes use of Baschet's transcripts and State Papers France in the Public Record Office and has some interesting comments on Richelieu's attitude to the Scots.

ENGLISH DIPLOMACY IN WEST AND CENTRAL EUROPE
(i) *Guides to sources*
See the information given under Anglo-French relations. Hinds compiled descriptive lists of all the State Papers Foreign of this period. They are mostly arranged under the name of the country or state concerned—e.g. S. P. Spain, S. P. Venice, S. P. Germany —Empire and so on.

(ii) *Secondary authorities*
Maurice Lee Jnr., 'The Jacobean diplomatic service' (*American Historical Review*, lxxii (1967)). For works on Anglo-Spanish relations, see SPAIN. L. Pearsall Smith, *The life and letters of Sir Henry Wotton*, 2 vols. (Oxford University Press, 1907) is indispensable for English relations with Venice in particular and valuable for diplomatic and cultural history generally.

M. J. Brown, *Itinerant ambassador: the life of Sir Thomas Roe* (Lexington: University of Kentucky Press, 1970) is devoted to the career of another able diplomat who not only served in India, Turkey and Germany but by mediating between Sweden and Poland helped to facilitate the intervention of Gustavus Adolphus in the Thirty Years War. Nevertheless Brown concludes that Roe was ultimately a failure: 'he was an Elizabethan and the Elizabethan Age was dead'.

For English policy during the early years of the Thirty Years War in addition to those just mentioned and those cited under SPAIN, see the works by Polišenský and others cited pp. 587 above; E. MacCabe, 'England's foreign policy in 1619' (*Mitteilungen des Instituts für Oesterreichischer Geschichtsforschung*, lviii (Graz: 1950)) and the books by Zaller and Ruigh referred to above.

For Charles I's abortive attempt to mediate between the Emperor and his nephew the Elector Palatine in the 1630s, see F. C. Springell (ed.), *Connoisseur and diplomat: the Earl of Arundel's embassy to Germany in 1636 . . . . with a catalogue of the topographical drawings made on the journey by Wenceslaus Hollar* (London: Maggs, 1963). See also p. 564 above.

COMMERCIAL RELATIONS WITH SPAIN AND THE MEDITERRANEAN
Note Albion's bibliography, for which see NAVAL HISTORY and relevant works cited under GENERAL EUROPEAN ECONOMIC AND SOCIAL HISTORY, SPAIN, ITALY and TURKEY. R. Davis, *The rise of the English shipping industry in the seventeenth and eighteenth centuries* (London: Macmillan, 1963) is a very important general survey of the development of seaborne trade which shows how and why the English merchant fleet which had been smaller than that of Venice, Genoa or even Dubrovnik at the outset of Elisabeth's reign,

grew to outstrip all rivals. Note also the same author's pamphlet, 'A commercial revolution? English overseas trade in the seventeenth and eighteenth centuries' (published by the Historical Association, 1967) and his essay 'England and the Mediterranean 1570–1670' in *Essays in the economic and social history of Tudor and Stuart England in honour of R. H. Tawney*, (ed.) F. J. Fisher (Cambridge University Press, 1961). W. E. Minchinton (ed.), *The growth of English overseas trade in the seventeenth and eighteenth centuries* (London: Methuen, 1969) also reprints articles by other historians, as well as by Davis and adds to them a useful bibliographical essay. A. C. Wood, *The Levant Company* (Oxford University Press, 1935) is still valuable. In addition to 'Price revolution or price revision? The English and Spanish trade after 1604' (cited p. 578), note Harland Taylor's 'Trade, neutrality and the "English road" 1630–48' in *Economic History Review* (May 1972). This article points to the considerable commercial expansion that resulted from English neutrality in the Thirty Years War after the Anglo-Spanish peace treaty of 1630. Before 1609 and again after 1621, English shipowners had already been able to benefit from the valuable contraband traffic between the United Provinces and Spain. To this was added the fact that, when France entered the war in 1635, Spain became dependent on English shipping to supply the French raw materials and foodstuffs that she needed—in particular linen, canvas and grain. Taylor gives useful information on English trade with Spain generally and with Bilbao in particular. J. S. Kepler, 'Fiscal aspects of the English carrying trade during the Thirty Years War' in the same issue of the same review also stresses the commercial advantages of English neutrality after 1630—in the Mediterranean English ships were often hired by the Spanish government to carry troops to Italy and, after the French declaration of war on Spain, we find English shipping competing with that of German and Italian neutrals in the contraband traffic between Marseilles and Genoa. The extent of French (as well as Spanish) dependence upon English carriers after 1635 is shown by the relative speed with which the French government released English ships that had been impounded in retaliation for the activities of a privateer.

MILITARY AND NAVAL HISTORY

The following is a brief selection only, which does not include works on the English
Civil War.

MILITARY

The Encyclopaedia of Military History by R. E. and T. A. Dupuy (New York: Harper and
Row, 1970) is inadequate for this period. The authors seem to be unaware of the works of
Michael Roberts mentioned below.

See the chapter in *The New Cambridge Modern History*, vol. iv, on 'Military forces and
warfare' by J. W. Wijn.

The following are of value: Sir George Clark, *War and Society in the seventeenth century*
(Cambridge University Press, 1958). Michael Roberts, 'The Military Revolution
1560–1660' in *Essays in Swedish History* (London: Weidenfeld and Nicolson, 1967). The
same author's book on Gustavus Adolphus (cited p. 588), which also considers his revolutionary changes in tactics, etc., is of course invaluable for all Gustavus's campaigns, for
his armies and for his general qualities as a military commander. Roberts also has some
perceptive things to say about Wallenstein. Both these great soldiers feature in B. H. Lid-
dell Hart's *Great Captains Unveiled* (London, 1928. repr. 1971).

See also other works cited under the heading Thirty Years War, in particular those by
Redlich. For the Spanish army during this period see Parker's authoritative work (cited
p. 577). For French commanders reference should be made to E. Godley, *The Great
Condé: a life of Louis II de Bourbon* (London, 1915) and the late General Weygand's
Turenne: Marshal of France (Boston and New York, 1930), trans. George B. Ives. There is
a very evocative short article on the battle of Rocroi in C. V. Wedgwood's *Velvet studies*
(London: Cape, 1946). Finally note J. U. Nef's *War and human progress* (cited p. 528
above).

NAVAL

I have omitted works about Grotius, freedom of the seas, fisheries and colonial maritime
history (apart from one by Cipolla). Apart from bibliographical information, this sub-
section is largely concerned with the Mediterranean.

R. G. Albion, *Naval and maritime history: an annotated bibliography* (Mystic, Connecticut:
Maritime Historical Association, 4th edition, 1972). This bibliography does not include
articles in periodicals but does give details of many unpublished U.S. doctoral theses. It
was first issued privately in 1951; since the third edition in 1963 the number of entries has
increased from 3000 to over 5000. Nearly one-third of the volume is devoted to Commerce and Shipping: 'an essential reference book for all those interested in trade and shipping'—R. Davis. Note also *The National Maritime Museum: Catalogue of the Library*, part i,
'*Voyages and travel*', part 2, '*Biography*' (2 vols.) (H.M.S.O., 1968–69). The first volume of
the latter lists titles of biographies, both collective and individual, the second contains a
biographical reference index of more than 15,000 names of British, American and European persons associated with maritime history.

There are several periodicals devoted to naval history. A newcomer concerned with
the history of merchant shipping is *Maritime History*.

Note J. P. Cooper's chapter on Seapower in *The New Cambridge Modern History*, vol.
iv.

A number of books concerned with naval history during this period have been cited under the headings FRANCE, ECONOMIC AND SOCIAL HISTORY, ITALY, GREAT BRITAIN and TURKEY.

C. M. Cipolla's *Guns and Sails in the early phase of European expansion 1400–1700* (London: Collins, 1965) furnishes some of the material for the same author's *European culture and overseas expansion* (Harmondsworth: Penguin Books, 1970). For the Mediterranean, Braudel (cited p. 574) is of course of fundamental importance.

An essay by Ruggiero Romano in Pullan's *Crisis and change* (cited p. 581) deals with the construction and manning of Venetian warships. Note also the essays of F. C. Lane.

E. H. Jenkins, *A History of the French Navy* (London: Macdonald and Jane's, 1973) which is the first survey of this subject in English contains two chapters on the navy in the time of Richelieu.

D. J. Buisseret, 'The French Mediterranean Fleet under Henry IV', *The Mariners Mirror*, l (1964), in fact carries the survey up to 1622 and prints contemporary plans of the ports of Marseilles and Toulon. R. C. Anderson in nos. lv and lvi of the same periodical gives an account of the subsequent naval warfare in the Mediterranean. C. R. Boxer, 'M. H. Tromp 1598–1653', *The Mariners Mirror*, xl (1954), is useful on the strategic and political background to Tromp's destruction of the Spanish fleet in 1639, as well as on the actual Battle of the Downs, and also comments on Richelieu's attitude towards Dunkirk privateers. Carl J. Kulsrad, *Maritime neutrality to 1780: a history of the main principles governing neutrality and belligerency to 1780* (Boston, 1936) should be mentioned here; and, in conclusion, three books concerned with a later period of French maritime history should be listed since some of the subjects they discuss are in fact relevant to the first half of the seventeenth century; P. W. Bamford, *Forests and French Sea Power 1660–1789* (University of Toronto Press, 1956); the same author's *Fighting Ships and Prisons: the Mediterranean Galleys of France in the age of Louis XIV* (Minneapolis: University of Minnesota Press, 1973); Eugene Asher, *The resistance to the maritime classes: the survival of feudalism in the France of Colbert* (University of California Press, 1960).

TURKEY

Here again only a brief selection is given which does not include any general histories of Turkey.

The Encyclopaedia of Islam, 2nd. ed. in progress, vol. i (A–B) 1960; vol. ii (C–G) 1965; vol. iii (H–Iram) 1971; Leiden: Brill; London: Luzac), is an indispensable work of reference. Note *The Cambridge History of Islam*, ed. P. M. Holt, A. K. S. Lambton and B. Lewis, 2 vols. (Cambridge University Press, 1970) and *The Cambridge History of Iran* (planned to consist of eight volumes of which two, neither of them relevant to this period, have so far been published).

Among various journals mention should be made of the *International Journal of Middle East Studies* and *Journal of the Economic and Social History of the Orient*.

Bernard Lewis, *Islam in History* (London: Alcove Press, 1973) is a collection of twenty one essays by the Professor of History at the School of Oriental and African Studies of the University of London; one of them is on the Muslim discovery of Europe. See also the same author's *The Arabs in History* (London: Hutchinson, 1950) and his essay 'Some reflections on the decline of the Ottoman Empire', in *The Economic Decline of Empires* (cited p. 527).

V. J. Parry in *The New Cambridge Modern History*, vols. iii and iv, gives a good survey of the Ottoman Empire from 1566 to 1650 and an excellent synthesis of recent work on economic and social history; *cf.* H. Inalcik, 'Capital Formation in the Ottoman Empire', *Journal of Economic History*, xxix, no. 1 (1969). Note also this author's essay 'The Ottoman economic mind and aspects of the Ottoman economy' in M. A. Cook (ed.), *Studies in the economic history of the Middle East* (Oxford University Press, 1970) which also contains a contribution from R. Davis, 'English imports from the Middle East 1580–1780'.

An excellent book on diplomatic relations is D. M. Vaughan, *Europe and the Turk—a pattern of alliances 1350–1700* (2nd ed., Liverpool, 1967). P. H. Coles, *The Ottoman Impact on Europe* (London: Thames and Hudson, 1968) is short and disappointingly superficial.

W. H. McNeill, *Europe's Steppe Frontier 1500–1800* (University of Chicago Press, 1964) is stimulating but not always reliable.

L. S. Stavrianos, *A History of the Balkans since 1453* (New York: Rinehart, 1959) and P. M. Holt, *Egypt and the Fertile Crescent 1516–1922* (New York: Cornell University Press, 1966) give good sketches of Ottoman rule in Europe and the Arab lands.

C. M. Kortepeter, *Ottoman Imperialism during the Reformation: Europe and the Cancasus* (New York: New York University Press, 1972) is concerned with the northeastern and eastern frontiers, 1566–1608.

For the Ottoman Empire and the Mediterranean world during this period Braudel (cited p. 574) is again indispensable. Sir Godfrey Fisher's survey of war, trade and piracy in North Africa (for which see p. 534) also deserves to be mentioned here. A useful Venetian source of information is J. C. Davis's *Pursuit of power* (mentioned p. 576 above). Note also N. Steensgaard, 'Consuls and nations in the Levant 1570–1650', in *The Scandinavian Economic History Review*, xv (1967).

A. C. Wood, *The Levant Company* (Oxford University Press, 1935) has a good deal to say about trade in the Eastern Mediterranean generally which takes into account French commercial penetration. Clarence D. Rouillard, *The Turk in French history, thought and literature* (cited p. 560) is decidedly thin on commercial relations but illuminating on literary and cultural influences; the same may be said of S. C. Chew, *The Crescent and the Rose*, which deals with Turkish cultural influences on England during this period.

Index